CASE STUDIES

 SAMPLE CLIENT CARE PLANS

 CULTURAL ASPECTS BOXES

FOUNDATIONS
OF
MENTAL HEALTH NURSING

FOUNDATIONS
OF
MENTAL HEALTH NURSING

MICHELLE MORRISON, RN, BSN, MHS, FNP

Nurse Educator/Consultant
Health and Educational Consultants
Williams, Oregon

 Mosby

St. Louis Baltimore Boston Carlsbad Chicago Naples New York Philadelphia Portland
London Madrid Mexico City Singapore Sydney Tokyo Toronto Wiesbaden

Vice President and Publisher: Nancy L. Coon
Senior Editor: Susan R. Epstein
Associate Developmental Editor: Laurie K. Muench
Project Manager: Linda McKinley
Production Editor: Cathy Bricker
Editing and Production: Top Graphics
Designer: Lee Goldstein
Design Coordinator: Elizabeth Fett
Manufacturing Supervisor: Don Carlisle
Chapter Opener Art: Laura Eslinger, The Painted Page

Printed in the United States of America
Composition by Top Graphics
Printing/binding by Von Hoffmann Press

Mosby–Year Book, Inc.
11830 Westline Industrial Drive
St. Louis, Missouri 63146

Library of Congress Cataloging in Publication Data

Morrison, Michelle.
    Foundations of mental health nursing / Michelle Morrison.
        p.   cm.
    Includes bibliographical references and index.
    ISBN 0-8151-6964-7
    1. Psychiatric nursing.   2. Mental health services.   3. Mental
illness.
    [DNLM: 1. Mental Disorders—therapy.   2. Mental Health Services—
trends.   WM 400 M881f 1997]
    RC440.M68   1997
    616.89—dc20
    DNLM/DLC
    for Library of Congress   96-42058
                                                               CIP

97 98 99 00 01 / 9 8 7 6 5 4 3 2 1

REVIEWERS

Sharon Beasley, RN, MSN
Nursing Professor
Rend Lake College
Ina, Illinois

Cynthia Maxine Davis, RN, BA, BSN, MEd
Associate Professor of Nursing
Bainbridge College
Bainbridge, Georgia

Barbara Maniotis, RN, BSN
Nursing Instructor
Monroe County Area Vocational–Technical School
Bartonsville, Pennsylvania

PREFACE

This book is intended for students and practitioners of the health care professions. Both basic and advanced students of nursing will find the information in this text useful and easy to apply in a variety of clinical settings. Students in related fields such as social work, respiratory therapy, physical therapy, recreational therapy, occupational therapy, and rehabilitation will discover concise explanations of effective and maladaptive human behaviors as well as the most current therapeutic treatments and interventions. Practicing health care providers—anyone caring for clients in a therapeutic manner—will find this book a practical and useful guide in any health care setting.

The purpose of this book is threefold:
1. To help soften the social distinction between mental "health" and mental "illness." It is all a matter of how effectively one is coping.
2. To assist nurses and other health care providers in comfortably working with clients who exhibit a wide range of maladaptive behaviors.
3. To apply the concepts of holistic nursing and caring when assisting clients in developing more effective attitudes and behaviors.

Contents

Unit 1, "Mental Health Care: Past, Present, and Future," provides a framework for mental health care. The evolution of care for persons with mental health problems from primitive to current times is described. Selected ethical, legal, social, and cultural issues relating to mental health care are explored. Community mental health care is explained, followed by chapters pertaining to theories of mental illness, therapeutic modalities, and psychotherapeutic drug therapy.

Unit 2, "The Caregiver's Therapeutic Skills," focuses on the skills and conditions necessary for working with clients. Eight principles of mental health care are discussed and then applied to the therapeutic environment, the helping relationship, and effective com-

munications. A chapter devoted to self-awareness encourages the reader to develop introspection—a necessary component for working with people who have behavioral difficulties. Characteristics of basic human needs, personality development, stress, anxiety, crisis, and coping behaviors help the reader explore the behaviors common to us all. The section concludes with a description of basic mental health assessment skills needed by every health care provider who works directly with mental health clients.

The clients for whom we care are the subject of Unit 3. "Mental Health Problems Throughout the Life Cycle" focuses on the growth of "normal" (adaptive) mental health behaviors during each developmental stage. The most common mental health disorders associated with children, adolescents, adults, and older adults listed in the *Diagnostic and Statistical Manual of Mental Disorders (DSM-IV)* are discussed.

Unit 4, "Clients With Psychological Problems," explores common behavioral responses and therapeutic interventions for illness, hospitalization, loss, grief, and depression. Maladaptive behaviors and mental health disorders are described in chapters on somatoform, anxiety, eating, sleeping, mood, sexual, and dissociative disorders.

The chapters in Unit 5, "Clients With Psychosocial Problems," relate to the important social concerns of anger and its expressions, suicide, abuse and neglect, AIDS, and substance abuse. Sexual and personality disorders are also discussed. Chapters on schizophrenia and chronic mental illness focus on a multidisciplinary approach for treatment. A chapter titled "Challenges for the Future" concludes the section.

Features

Throughout the text, **cultural aspects** of various mental health principles are explored. Because the majority of mental health care takes place outside the institution, the importance of using therapeutic mental health interventions during every nurse-client interaction is emphasized. Numerous **case studies** with thought-provoking questions encourage readers to consider the psychosocial aspects of providing therapeutic care in both **community** and **hospital** settings. Descriptions of each mental health disorder are drawn from DSM-IV criteria. Nursing diagnoses are stated in terms approved by the North American Nursing Diagnosis Association (NANDA).

Each chapter includes **learning objectives** stated in specific terms, a list of **key terms,** and a brief review of **key concepts** following the text. **Suggestions for further reading** encourage further exploration of the topics presented in the chapter.

Unique to this text are the **review worksheets** for each chapter, which are located at the end of the book. Because the worksheet section is perforated, the sheets can be removed and submitted to the instructor on completion, eliminating the need for a separate student workbook. Throughout the text, the liberal use of **boxes, tables,** and **figures** simplifies important concepts and stresses essential information. Boxes relating to **critical thinking** and **cultural aspects** stimulate further thought and discussion. **Client care plans** demonstrate the application of the nursing process to the caring for individuals with various mental health disorders. The holistic approach to care offers readers in fields other than nursing a view of the "whole person" context of health care. A **glossary,** written in easy-to-understand terms, follows the text. The text concludes with **appendices** relating to standards of mental health care and a tool for assessing the side effects of antipsychotic medications.

About the Chapter Opener Illustrations

Throughout history, symbols have been used to communicate. Symbols for the chapter opener illustrations have been chosen from the numerous symbolic communications found in *Symbol Sourcebook* (New York, McGraw-Hill, 1972) by H. Dryfuss.

Many of the symbols are self-explanatory (book = knowledge; scales = balance; houses = community). Others require a short description.
From medical symbology:

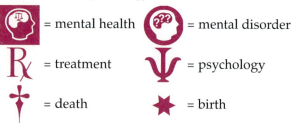

The folklore signs:

⚕⊘ = family   ⋈ = disordered intellect

The chapter opener illustration for Chapter 15, "Problems of Adolescence," was created by Crystal Masters, a 15-year-old with insight beyond her years. Last, the chapter opener illustration for Chapter 33, "Challenges for the Future," symbolizes the interconnectedness of all people. Illustrator Laura Eslinger is to be commended for her ability in using symbology in her artwork to present the complex concepts associated with the study of the human psyche.

Instructor's Resource Manual

The *Instructor's Resource Manual* was developed to assist health care educators, from the beginning novice to those with long-term teaching experience. Each chapter includes chapter outlines, key terms, learning objectives (which are referenced to the text by page numbers), case studies, guidelines for discussion, clinical activities for both hospital and community health care settings, a list of audiovisual resources, and answers to each chapter's review worksheets (text referenced). A special feature called "Guidelines for Integration" helps instructors merge and blend the important principles of mental health care into medical, surgical, pediatric, geriatric, maternity, and rehabilitative areas of nursing and client care.

Mosby's latest **video series on psychiatric care** offers 12 videotapes relating to the care of clients with specific mental health disorders. The series dovetails well with the text and provides stimulating audiovisual learning experiences. A set of **transparency masters** and a 500 multiple-choice question **test bank** complete the package.

Acknowledgments

No text is written alone. The continued support of my husband, loved ones, friends, and colleagues has provided the energy to complete this project when my own was low. The guidance, expertise, and encouragement from my editors, Suzi Epstein and Laurie Muench, are much appreciated. Finally, I would like to thank the nurses and other health care providers who so freely share their time and expertise with those who want to learn more about the dynamic nature of the complex creatures known as human beings.

MICHELLE MORRISON

BRIEF CONTENTS

DETAILED CONTENTS

UNIT 4 CLIENTS WITH PSYCHOLOGICAL PROBLEMS

UNIT 1

MENTAL HEALTH CARE: PAST, PRESENT, AND FUTURE

1

THE HISTORY OF MENTAL HEALTH CARE

LEARNING OBJECTIVES

1. Develop a working definition of mental health and mental illness.

2. List three major factors believed to influence the development of mental illness.

3. Describe the role of the Church in the care of the mentally ill during the Middle Ages.

4. Identify the contributions made by Philippe Pinel, Dorothea Dix, and Clifford Beers to the care of persons with mental disorders.

5. Discuss the impact of World Wars I and II on American attitudes toward the mentally ill.

6. State the major change in the care of the mentally ill resulting from the discovery of psychotherapeutic drugs.

7. Describe the development of community mental health care centers during the 1960s and 1970s.

8. Discuss the shift of mentally ill clients from institutional care to community-based care.

9. Explain how the Omnibus Budget Reconciliation Act of 1981 and the Omnibus Budget Reform Act (OBRA) have affected mental health care.

KEY TERMS

catchment area
deinstitutionalization
demonical exorcisms
electroconvulsive therapy

health-illness continuum
humoral theory of disease
lobotomy
lunacy

mental health
mentally ill
psychotherapeutic drugs
Reformation

2

Mental or emotional health is interwoven with physical health. Behaviors relating to health exist over a broad spectrum, often referred to as the **health-illness continuum** (Fig. 1-1). People who are exceptionally healthy are represented at the high-level wellness end of the continuum. Those who are severely ill fall at the continuum's opposite end. Most of us, however, function somewhere between these extremes. As we encounter the stresses of life, our abilities to cope are repeatedly challenged and we strive to adjust in effective or adaptive ways. When the stress is physical, the body calls forth its defense systems and wards off the signs and symptoms of physical illness. When the challenge is of an emotional or developmental nature, we respond by creating new (and hopefully effective) behaviors.

In its simplest terms, **mental health** is the ability to "cope with and adjust to the recurrent stresses of living in an acceptable way" (Anderson, 1994). Mentally healthy people are able to successfully carry out the activities of daily living, solve problems, set goals, adapt to change, and enjoy life. They are self-aware, directed, and responsible for their actions. In short, mentally healthy people cope well.

Mental health is influenced by three factors: inherited characteristics, childhood nurturing, and life circumstances. When a problem arises in any one of the three areas, the risk of developing ineffective coping behaviors increases. If ineffective or maladaptive behaviors interfere with daily activities, impair judgment, or alter reality, the person is said to be **mentally ill.** Simply put, a mental disorder (illness) is a disturbance of a person's ability to cope effectively, which results in maladaptive behaviors and impaired functioning. History is rich with examples of man's changing attitudes toward people with mental health problems.

Early Years

Illness, injury, and insanity have concerned mankind throughout history. However, illness and injury were easy to detect with the senses; insanity (mental illness) was something different—something that could not be seen or felt—and therefore a condition to be feared.

Primitive Societies

Although the historical record is vague, it can be assumed that some care was given to the sick. Illness, both mental and physical, was thought to be caused by the wrath of evil spirits. Early societies believed that everything in nature was alive with good or evil spirits. People with mental illnesses were therefore possessed by demons or evil forces.

Treatments for mental illness were designed by medicine men and shamans and focused on removing the evil spirits from the patient. Magical treatments made use of "frightening masks and noises, incantations, vile odors, charms, spells, sacrifices and fetishes" (Kelly, 1991). Physical treatments included bleeding, massage, blistering, inducing vomiting, and the practice of trephining—cutting holes in the skull to encourage the evil spirits to leave.

Mentally ill people were allowed to remain within the society as long as their behaviors were not disruptive. The more severely ill or violent members of the group were driven into the wilderness to fend for themselves.

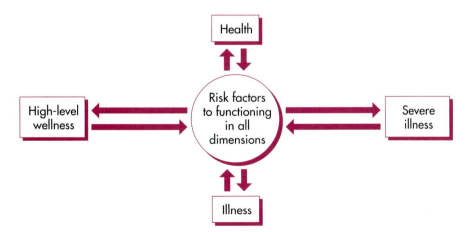

Fig. 1-1 The health-illness continuum, ranging from high-level wellness to severe illness, provides a method of identifying a client's level of health. Level of health is a reflection of the client's level of functioning in all dimensions. (Redrawn from Potter PA, Perry AG: *Basic nursing: theory and practice,* ed 3, St Louis, 1995, Mosby.)

Greece and Rome

Superstitions and magical beliefs dominated men's thinking about illness until the Greeks introduced the idea that mental illness could be rationally explained through observation. Explanations about the cause and effect of illnesses gradually replaced most superstitions.

The Greeks incorporated many concepts about illness from other civilizations of the day. By the sixth century BC, medical schools were well established. The greatest physician in Greek medicine, Hippocrates, was born in 460 BC. Hippocrates was the first physician to base treatment on the assumption that nature has a strong healing force. He believed that the role of the physician was to assist in, rather than direct, the healing process. Proper diet, exercise, and personal hygiene were his mainstays of treatment. Hippocrates viewed mental illness as a result of an imbalance of humors—the fundamental elements of air, fire, water, and earth. Each basic element had a related humor or part in the body: blood, yellow bile, phlegm, and black bile. An overabundance or lack of one or more humors resulted in illness. This view was called the **humoral theory of disease,** and it persisted for centuries.

Plato (427-347 BC), a Greek philosopher, recognized life as a dynamic balance maintained by the soul. According to Plato, the soul was further divided into a "rational soul," which resided in the head, and an "irrational soul," which was found in the heart and abdomen. He believed that if the rational soul was unable to control the more primal and undirected parts of the irrational soul, mental illness resulted. In theory, Plato anticipated Sigmund Freud by almost 2000 years.

The principles and practices of Greek medicine became established in Rome around 100 BC. Romans believed that mental disease originated in the body. Most physicians still thought that demons caused mental illness. The practice of frightening away evil spirits to cure mental illness was reintroduced about this time and was continued well into the Middle Ages.

The Romans showed little interest in learning about the body or mind, and most Roman physicians "wanted to make their patients comfortable by pleasant physical therapies" (Alexander and Selesnick, 1966), such as warm baths, massage, music, and peaceful surroundings.

Middle Ages

The era between AD 500 and AD 1400 is called the Medieval or Middle Ages. Reasons for the collapse of the Roman Empire remain unclear, but repeated invasions from barbaric tribes and plague were two important elements in its downfall. By AD 300, "six epidemics killed hundreds of thousands of people and desolated the land" (Alexander and Selesnick, 1966). Churches became sanctuaries for the sick, and soon hospitals were built to accommodate the sufferers. By AD 370, Saint Basil's Hospital in England offered services for the sick, orphaned, crippled, and mentally troubled.

Dark Ages.   From about AD 500 to AD 1100, care for the sick shifted from physicians to priests. Great plagues had ravaged Europe, and barbarians had warred their way into power. The Church developed into a highly organized and powerful institution. Early Christians believed that "disease was either punishment for sins, possession by the devil, or the result of witchcraft" (Ackerknecht, 1968).

To cure mental illness, priests performed **demonical exorcisms**—religious ceremonies in which the patients were physically punished to drive away the evil possessing spirit. However, these practices were tempered by the spirit of Christian charity because members of the community cared for the mentally ill with concern and sympathy.

As time passed, medieval society declined. Repeated attacks from barbaric tribes led to chaos and moral decay. Epidemics, natural disasters, and overwhelming taxes wiped out the middle class. Cities, industries, and commerce disappeared. "The population declined, crime waves occurred, poverty was abysmal, and torture and imprisonment became prominent as civilization seemed to slip back into semi-barbarianism" (Donahue, 1996). The monasteries remained the last refuge of knowledge.

Throughout the Middle Ages, medicine and religion were interwoven; however, by AD 1130, laws were passed forbidding monks to practice medicine because it was considered too disruptive to their way of life. As a result, the responsibility for the care of the sick once again fell to the community.

By the late 1100s, a strong Arabic influence was felt in Europe. Knowledge of the Greek legacy had been retained and improved on by the Arabs, who had an extensive knowledge of drugs, mathematics, astronomy, and chemistry, as well as an awareness of the relationship between emotions and disease. The Arabic influence resulted in the establishment of learning centers. Many of these universities were devoted to the study of medicine and surgery and the care of the sick.

Problems of the mind, however, did not receive medical but spiritual attention. Church doctrine still stated that man was the center of the universe and if a person was insane, it must be the result of some external force—a heavenly body such as the moon. Thus the term **lunacy** was coined and "literally means a disorder caused by a lunar body" (Alexander and Selesnick, 1966).

In time, large institutions were established, and the mentally ill were herded into these "lunatic asylums." Magic was still relied on to explain the torments of the mind. A few church scholars even suggested that witches might be the source of human distresses.

Superstitions, witches, and hunters. Several developments during the thirteenth and fourteenth centuries dramatically changed the status quo. The invention of the printing press allowed people to educate themselves. Gunpowder was discovered, and common people could arm themselves. These changes threatened the political system known as feudalism (many serfs working for one nobleman). Severe plagues wiped out more than half of Europe's population, and abuses within the most sacred of institutions, the Church, were being attacked.

The Church's doctrine of imposed celibacy had done little to curtail many of the clergy's sexual behaviors. As social institutions began to crumble, the Church began an antierotic movement that focused on women as the cause of men's lust. Obviously, according to this movement, women were carriers of the devil because they stirred men's passions. "Psychotic women with little control over voicing their sexual fantasies and sacrilegious feelings were the clearest examples of demoniacal possession" (Alexander and Selesnick, 1966). This movement in turn flamed the public's mounting fear of mentally troubled people.

Witch hunting was officially launched in 1487 with the publication of the book *The Witches' Hammer,* a textbook of both pornography and psychopathology. Soon after its publication, Pope Innocent VIII, the King of Rome, and the University of Cologne voiced support for this "textbook of the Inquisition."

As a result of this one publication, women of all stations of life, as well as children and the mentally ill, were tortured and burned at the stake by the thousands. There were few safe havens for individuals with mental illness during these times.

Bethlehem Royal Hospital. The first English institution for the mentally ill was initially a hospice founded in 1247 by the sheriff of London. By 1330, Bethlehem had become a hospital and then a lunatic asylum that eventually became infamous for its brutal treatments. Violently ill patients were chained to walls in small cells. These patients provided "entertainment" for the public; the hospital would charge fees for their "tourist attractions" and conduct tours

through the institution. Less violent patients were forced to wear identifying metal armbands and beg on the streets. The insane were harshly treated; however, Bethlehem Hospital, commonly known as Bedlam, was preferable to burning at the stake (Fig. 1-2).

Plagues. By the middle of the fourteenth century, the European continent and England had endured several devastating plagues and epidemics. Four outbreaks of the Black Death (bubonic plague) as well as a "sweating sickness" (believed to be a virulent form of influenza) invaded the European continent after sweeping through Asia and Africa. One quarter of the Earth's population, *over 60 million people,* perished from infectious diseases during this period in history.

The last centuries of the Middle Ages were times of tremendous change. The feudal system lost power and declined. Cities began to flourish and house a growing middle class. "Luxury and misery, learning and ignorance existed side by side" (Donahue, 1996). Society was at last beginning to demand reforms.

Yet, as the age of art, medicine, and science dawned, the hunting of "witches" became even more popular. It was a time of great contradictions. Society's spirit of revolution, mixed with the new quest for knowledge, brought about two great movements—the Renaissance and Reformation.

The Renaissance

The Renaissance began about 1400 in Italy and spread throughout the European continent within a century. Upheavals in economics, politics, education, and commerce brought the real world into focus. The power of the Church to regulate people's activities slowly declined as an intense interest in material gain and worldly affairs began to develop.

Man had been discovered as a real flesh-and-blood individual. The medieval view of a sinful, naked body was replaced by a celebration of the human form by such artists as da Vinci, Raphael, and Michelangelo. Thousand-year-old anatomy books were replaced by realistic anatomical drawings. Observation, rather than ancient theories, revolutionized many of the concepts of the day.

Sixteenth-century physicians, relying on observation, began to record what they saw. Mental illness was at last being recognized without bias. By the mid-1500s, behaviors were accurately recorded for melancholia (depression), mania, and psychopathic personalities. Precise observations led to classifications for different abnormal behaviors. Mental problems were now thought to be caused by some sort of brain disorder, except in the case of sexual fantasies, which were still considered to be caused by God's punish-

Fig. 1-2 Bethlehem Royal Hospital in London. (William Hogarth, "The Rake in Bedlam," c. 1735. From the series entitled *The Rake's Progress.* Copyright The British Museum, London.)

ment or possession by the devil. However, despite the great advances made in the study of human nature, the actual treatment of the mentally ill remained inhumane.

The Reformation

Another movement that influenced the care of the sick—the **Reformation**—occurred in 1517. People were displeased with the conduct of the clergy and the widespread abuses occurring within the Catholic Church. Martin Luther (1483-1546), a dissatisfied monk, and his followers broke away from the Catholic Church. This group of separatists became known as Protestants, meaning "those who pro-

tested." As a result of this separation, many hospitals operated by the Catholic Church began to close, and once again the poor, sick, and insane were turned out into the streets.

Seventeenth Century

During the seventeenth and eighteenth centuries, developments in science, literature, philosophy, and the arts laid the foundations for the modern world. Although reason was slowly beginning to replace magical thinking, a strong belief in the influences of demons persisted.

The 1600s produced many great thinkers. Man was beginning to discover the secrets of nature, and this knowledge brought with it a sense of self-reliance. However, many people were uncomfortable and insecure with these inquiries, so they once again moved toward the security of witch hunting as a means of protecting themselves from the unexplainable.

It was during the seventeenth century that conditions for the mentally ill were at their worst. While physicians and theorists were making observations and speculations about insanity, the mentally troubled were bled, starved, beaten, and purged into submission. Treatments for these people remained in this unhappy state of affairs until the late 1700s.

Eighteenth Century

During the latter part of the eighteenth century, psychiatry developed as a separate branch of medicine. The inhumane treatment and vicious practices of earlier years were now openly questioned. A few physicians actually protested that insanity was a medical problem and stated that mentally troubled patients needed humane, respectful treatment. In 1792, Philippe Pinel (1745-1826), the director of two Paris hospitals, liberated the mentally ill from their chains "and advocated acceptance of the mentally ill as human beings in need of medical assistance, nursing care, and social services" (Donahue, 1996). During this same period, the Quakers, a religious order, established asylums of humane care in England.

In the American colonies, the mentally troubled were also housed in lunatic asylums and almshouses. In 1731, the Philadelphia Almshouse was erected. It accepted sick, infirm, and insane patients as well as prisoners and orphans. In 1794, Bellevue Hospital in New York City was opened as a pesthouse for the victims of yellow fever. By 1816, the hospital had enlarged to contain an almshouse for the poor, wards for the sick and insane, staff quarters, and even a penitentiary.

Unfortunately, the care and treatment of people with mental illness remained as harsh and indifferent in the United States as it was in Europe. The practice of allowing the poor to care for the mentally ill continued well into the late 1800s and was only slowly abandoned. Actual care of mentally ill persons in the United States did not begin to improve until the arrival of Alice Fisher, a Florence Nightingale–trained nurse, in 1884.

By the close of the eighteenth century, treatments for people with mental illness still included the medieval practices of bloodletting, purging, and confinement. Newer therapies included the tranquilizing chair, whirling devices, and circulation swings (Figs. 1-3 and 1-4). The study of psychiatry was in its infancy, and those who actually cared for the insane still relied heavily on the methods of their ancestors.

Fig. 1-3 Tranquilizing chair. (Courtesy National Library of Medicine, Bethesda, Md.)

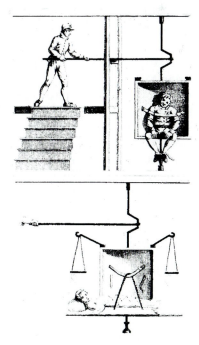

Fig. 1-4 Circulating swing and bed. (Courtesy National Library of Medicine, Bethesda, Md.)

Nineteenth-Century United States

By the early 1800s, the Revolutionary War had ended and the United States was a growing nation. Changes that occurred during this century had an enormous impact on the care of the mentally ill for years to come.

One of the most important figures in nineteenth-century psychiatry was Dr. Benjamin Rush, a crusader for the insane. Dr. Rush (1745-1813) graduated from Princeton University at age 15 and then studied at the University of Edinburgh in Scotland. By age 31, Rush had been a professor of chemistry and medicine, a chief surgeon in the Continental Army, and a signer of the Declaration of Independence. His book, titled *Diseases of the Mind,* was the first psychiatric text written in the United States. In his book, he advocated clean conditions; good air, lighting, and food; and kindness. As a result of Rush's efforts, the mentally troubled were no longer caged in the basements of general hospitals; however, only a few institutions for the insane were available in the United States at this time. The more mildly affected people were commonly sold to the highest bidder at slave auctions, whereas the more violent remained in asylums that were a combination of zoo and penitentiary.

Dorothea Dix

During the 1830s, attitudes toward mental illness slowly began to change. The "once insane always insane" concept was being replaced by the thought that cure may be possible. A few mental hospitals were built, but the actual living conditions for the patients remained deplorable.

It was not until 1841 that a frail 40-year-old schoolteacher exposed the sins of the system. Dorothea Dix was contracted to teach Sunday school at a jail in Massachusetts; while there, she observed both criminals and mentally ill prisoners living in squalid conditions. For the next 20 years, Dix surveyed asylums, jails, and almshouses (any institution that housed the mentally ill) throughout the United States, Canada, and Scotland. It was not uncommon for her to find mentally ill people "confined in cages, closets, cellars, stalls, and pens . . . chained, naked, beaten with rods and lashed into obedience" (Dolan, 1968).

Dorothea Dix's untiring crusade had results that shook the world. She presented her findings to anyone who would listen. Presidents, legislatures, civic groups, and concerned citizens became so aroused by Dix's efforts that millions of dollars were raised, more than 30 mental hospitals throughout the United States were constructed, and standards for the care of the insane were greatly improved.

Two-Class System

By the late 1800s, a two-class system of psychiatric care had emerged: private care for the wealthy and publicly provided care for the remainder of society. The newly constructed mental institutions quickly became filled, and soon chronic overcrowding began to strain the system. Cure rates fell dramatically. The public became disenchanted, and mental illness once again was viewed as incurable.

Only small, private facilities that catered to the wealthy had some degree of success, and those patients were well treated. State facilities evolved into large, remote institutions that became completely self-reliant and removed from society.

By the close of the nineteenth century, many of the gains in the care for the mentally ill had been lost. Overpopulated institutions could offer no more than minimal custodial care. Psychiatry was at a dead end. The dominant theories of the day gave no satisfactory explanations about the causes of mental problems, and current treatments were ineffective. It was a time of therapeutic despair for the mentally troubled and those who cared for them.

Twentieth Century

The 1900s were ushered in by reform movements. Political, economic, and social changes were beginning. The population became interested in dealing with major social issues. For the first time in history, disease prevention was emphasized. For the mentally ill, however, conditions remained intolerable until 1908, when a single individual began his crusade.

Clifford Beers

Clifford Beers was a young student at Yale University when he attempted suicide. Consequently, he spent 3 years as a patient in mental hospitals in Connecticut. On his release in 1908, Beers wrote a book that would set the wheels of the mental hygiene movement in motion. His book, *A Mind That Found Itself,* recounted the beatings, isolation, and confinement of a mentally ill person.

As a direct result of Beers' work, the Committee for Mental Hygiene was formed in 1909. In addition to prevention, the group focused on removing the stigma attached to mental illness. Under Beers' energetic guidance, the movement grew nationwide. The social consciousness of a nation had finally been awakened.

Psychoanalysis

In the early 1900s, a neurophysiologist named Sigmund Freud published the article that introduced the term *psychoanalysis* to the world's vocabulary. Freud believed that forces both within and outside the personality were responsible for mental illness. He developed an elaborate theoretical system around the central theme of repressed sexual energies. Although Freud's methods demanded intense, long-term contact between therapist and patient, his contributions to psychiatry cannot be overestimated. Freud was the first person who succeeded in "explaining human behavior in psychological terms and in demonstration that behavior can be changed under the proper circumstances" (Alexander and Selesnick, 1966). The first comprehensive theory of mental illness based on observation had emerged, and psychoanalysis began to gain a strong hold in American medical schools and institutions.

Influences of War

By 1917, the United States had entered World War I. The war was expected to last only a few short months, but as it continued to drag on, the material, medical, and personnel resources of the nation became severely strained. Men were drafted into service as rapidly as they could be processed, but many were considered too "mentally deficient" to fight. As a result, the federal government called on Beers' Committee for Mental Hygiene. The committee's task was to develop a master plan for screening and treating mentally ill soldiers. The completed plan included methods for early identification of problems, removal of mentally troubled personnel from combat duty, and early treatment close to the fighting front. The committee also recommended that psychiatrists be assigned to station hospitals to treat soldiers who returned from combat with acute behavioral problems and to provide ongoing psychiatric care after patients returned to their homes.

Because of the war, a renewed interest in mental hygiene evolved. During the 1930s, new therapies for treating insanity were developed. Insulin therapy for schizophrenia induced 50-hour comas via the administration of massive doses of insulin. Passing electricity through the patient's head (**electroconvulsive therapy**) helped to improve severe depression, and **lobotomy** (surgical procedure that severs the frontal lobes of the brain from the thalamus) almost eliminated violent behaviors. A new class of drugs that lifted the spirits of depressed people, amphetamines, was introduced. These therapies improved behaviors and made patients more receptive to Freud's psychotherapy. In terms of legislation, in 1937 the Hill-Burton Act, which allotted funds for the construction of psychiatric units throughout the country, was passed.

From 1941 to 1945, the United States was immersed in World War II. Despite the National Committee for Mental Hygiene's reports and sporadic government efforts, a high incidence of psychiatric disorders still existed in military personnel. Many draftees were rejected on enlistment because of mental health problems. A large number of soldiers received early discharges based on psychiatric disorders, and many active-duty personnel received treatment for neuropsychiatric problems.

In 1946, Congress passed the National Mental Health Act, which provided funding for programs in research, training of mental health professionals, and expansion of state mental health facilities (see box below). By 1949, the National Institute of Mental Health was organized to provide research and training related to mental illness. New approaches to the care of the mentally ill (e.g., therapeutic community movement, family care, halfway houses) began to spark the public's enthusiasm.

The Korean War of the 1950s and the Vietnam War of the 1960s and 1970s contributed significant knowledge to the understanding of stress-related problems. Posttraumatic stress disorders became recognized among soldiers fighting wars. Today, stress disorders are now recognized as the basis of many emotional problems encountered by mental health care providers.

Introduction of Psychotherapeutic Drugs

Psychotherapeutic drugs are chemicals that affect the mind. These drugs alter emotions, perceptions, and consciousness in several ways and are used in combination with various therapies for treating mental illness. Psychotherapeutic drugs are also called *psychopharmacologic agents, psychotropic drugs,* and *psychoactive drugs.*

"By the 1950s, more than half the hospital beds in the United States were in psychiatric wards" (Taylor, 1994). Patients were usually treated kindly, but effective therapies were still limited. Treatments consisted of psychoanalysis, insulin therapy, electroconvulsive (shock) therapy, and water/ice therapy. More violent patients were physically restrained in straitjackets or underwent lobotomy. Drug therapy of the 1940s con-

---

THE NATIONAL MENTAL HEALTH ACT (1946)

- Funded research for causes of mental illness
- Funded training of psychiatrists, psychologists, nurses, and social workers
- Expanded and improved state mental hospitals

sisted of the administration of sedatives (chloral hydrate and paraldehyde), barbiturates (phenobarbital), and amphetamines, which quieted patients but did little to treat their illnesses.

In 1949, an Australian physician, John Cade, discovered that lithium carbonate was effective in controlling the severe mood swings seen in bipolar (manic-depressive) illness. With lithium therapy, numerous chronically ill clients were again able to lead normal lives and many were released from mental institutions.

Sparked by the apparent success of lithium, researchers began to explore the possibility of controlling mental illness with the use of various antipsychotic drugs. Chlorpromazine (Thorazine) was introduced in 1956 and proved to control many of the bizarre behaviors observed in schizophrenia and other psychoses.

The decade of the 1950s was concluded with the introduction of imipramine, the first antidepressant drug. Within a 10-year span, three major drugs for the treatment of mental illness (lithium, chlorpromazine, and imipramine) had been developed. Soon other drugs, such as anxiety agents, became available for use in treatment.

As more patients were able to control their behaviors with drug therapy, the demand for hospitalization decreased. Many people with mental disorders could now live and function outside the institution. At this time, the federal government began the movement called **deinstitutionalization,** the release of large numbers of mentally ill persons into the community. To illustrate, in 1955, 560,000 patients were cared for in state hospitals. By 1986, the number of institutionalized patients had dropped to less than 120,000 people (Keltner and Folks, 1993). The introduction of psychotherapeutic drugs opened the doors of institutions and set the stage for a new delivery system—community mental health care.

From the Institution to the Community

The 1960s was a decade filled with social changes. With the introduction of psychotherapeutic drugs came the concept of the "least restrictive alternative." If patients could, with medication, control their behaviors and cooperate with treatment plans, then the restrictive environment of the institution was no longer necessary. It was believed that people with mental disorders could live within their communities and work with their therapists on an outpatient basis.

As a result of renewed public interest in mental illness, the Mental Health Study Act of 1955 created the Joint Commission on Mental Illness and Health, which in turn published a 338-page report titled *Action for Mental Health* in 1961. The report motivated President John Kennedy to appoint a special committee to study the problem of mental illness and recommend specific actions. The recommendations from the committee called for a bold new approach to mental health care, which included the development of an entirely new entity—the community mental health center.

Community Mental Health Centers Act

As the population of people with mental illnesses shifted from the institution to the community (deinstitutionalization), the demand for community mental health services expanded. To meet this demand, the federal government proposed to establish a nationwide network of community mental health centers. The Community Mental Health Centers Act (Public Law 88-164) was passed by Congress in October 1963.

This act was designed to support the construction of mental health centers in communities throughout the United States. There the needs of all people experiencing mental or emotional problems, as well as those of the acute and chronic mentally ill, would be met. Physicians (psychiatrists), nurses, and various therapists would develop therapeutic relationships with their clients and monitor their progress over time within the community setting. Each center was to provide comprehensive mental health services for all residents within a certain geographic region, called a **catchment area.**

It was believed that the community mental health centers would provide the link in helping mentally ill people make the transition from the institution to the community and thus meet the goal of humane care delivered in the least restrictive way. Passage of the Medicare/Medicaid Bill of 1965, combined with the Community Mental Health Centers Act, led to the release of more than 75% of institutionalized mentally ill persons into the community (Morrissey and Goldman, 1984). Unfortunately, most chronically mentally ill people were "dumped" into their communities before realistic strategies, programs, and facilities were in place.

Community mental health centers expanded throughout the 1970s, but their funding was inadequate and sporadic. Demands for services overwhelmed the system, and non–revenue-generating services relating to prevention and education were eliminated. Services for the general public dwindled as these centers began to close their doors. Finally, in

1975, Congress passed amendments to the Community Mental Health Centers Act that provided more federal funding for community centers based on a complex set of guidelines.

The President's Commission on Mental Health was established in 1978 by President Jimmy Carter. Its task was to assess the mental health needs of the nation and recommend possible courses of action to strengthen and improve existing community mental health efforts. The commission's final report resulted in 117 specific recommendations grouped into four broad areas: coordination of services, high-risk populations, flexibility in planning services, and least restrictive care alternatives.

By 1980, Congress passed one of the most progressive mental health bills in history. The Mental Health Systems Act addressed community mental health care and clients' rights and prioritized research and training goals. Mental health care had at last become a priority at all levels of government. However, before any of these recommendations could be nationally implemented, the country elected a new president, and mental health reform changed dramatically.

Omnibus Budget Reconciliation Act

Just as legislation that comprehensively dealt with mental health issues was about to be enacted, the political climate changed. In 1981, Ronald Reagan and his conservative administration drastically reduced federal funding for all mental health services (including research and training). The Omnibus Budget Reconciliation Act of 1981 essentially repealed the 1980 Mental Health Systems Act. Passage of this bill by the Congress resulted in "block grant" funding whereby each state received a "block" or designated amount of money. The state then determined where and how the money was spent. As a result of severe fiscal constraints, many of the hospitalized mentally ill (especially the elderly) were transferred to less appropriate nursing homes or other community facilities.

To stem the practice of inappropriate placement for the chronic mentally ill, the Omnibus Budget Reform Act (OBRA) was passed in 1987. People with chronic mental problems could no longer be "warehoused" in nursing homes or other long-term facilities, and many were discharged to the streets.

As concern for a rapidly expanding federal budget deficit grew, funding for mental health care dwindled. By the late 1980s, funding was curtailed for most institutional (inpatient) psychiatric care. Following the trend, most insurance companies withdrew their coverage for psychiatric care.

Today, many of our population's most severely mentally ill wander the streets in abject poverty and homelessness as a result of federal and state funding cuts. Many community mental health centers have closed their doors permanently or drastically reduced their services. Federal funding is limited to block grants (for all health care) to each state. Community mental health care limps along via an uncertain patchwork of decreased federal monies, state support, collected fees, and private funds. The original goals of comprehensive care, education, rehabilitation, prevention, training, and research became lost in the efforts to curtail costs.

Currently, lawmakers in the United States are struggling to define a new national health policy. Models for delivering effective, cost-effective health care are being investigated. Other countries, such as Canada and the United Kingdom, are faced with similar mental health care issues. It is in all of our best interests that we accept the challenge to address and provide for our societies' mental and physical health care needs. The box below offers food for thought.

THINK ABOUT

What do you consider to be the most important priorities for a national health care plan? Do you think that prevention and treatment of mental illness should be covered in the plan?

❖ KEY CONCEPTS

- Mental health is the ability to cope with and adapt to the stresses of everyday life.

- Mentally healthy people are self-aware, directed, and responsible for their own actions.

- Mental illness is an inability to cope, which results in impaired functioning.

- The history of mental illness and its treatment is based on superstition, magical beliefs, and demonic possession from primitive societies into the 1800s with an occasional dissenter.

- Priests cared for the sick and exorcised demons, but the mentally troubled were treated with care by the Christian community during the Middle Ages.

- By the late Middle Ages, large institutions (asylums) housed the insane and the belief that witches were the carriers of the devil led to the burning of thousands of women, children, and mentally ill people.

- By the 1500s, psychotic behaviors were being accurately observed and recorded, but the Reformation movement returned many of the insane to the streets as church sanctuaries closed.

- Conditions for the mentally ill were at their worst during the seventeenth century when patients were bled, beaten, starved, and purged into submission.

- During the 1800s, Americans Dr. Benjamin Rush and Dorothea Dix crusaded for the humane care of the mentally ill.

- Standards for the care of the insane improved during the mid-1800s until huge waves of people overwhelmed the mental health care system, causing the conditions for patients to deteriorate.

- A book written by Clifford Beers about his 3-year experience as a mental patient set the mental hygiene movement of the early 1900s into motion.

- During the 1920s, Sigmund Freud's psychoanalytical theories had become a popular method for treating emotional problems.

- The First and Second World Wars pointed out the need for comprehensive mental health care.

- With the introduction of psychotherapeutic drug treatment, many psychiatric institutions closed.

- Community mental health centers were built to accommodate the mentally ill during the 1970s, but a change in political climate left the project uncompleted.

- Today, many legislative changes once again challenge us to develop comprehensive, cost-efficient care for society's mentally ill.

❖ SUGGESTIONS FOR FURTHER READING

An excellent text that discusses psychiatric thoughts and practice through the ages is *The History of Psychiatry*, written by Franz Alexander and Sheldon Selesnick.

❖ REFERENCES

Ackerknecht, EW: *A short history of medicine,* New York, 1968, The Ronald Press.

Alexander FG, Selesnick ST: *The history of psychiatry,* New York, 1966, The New American Library.

Anderson KN, editor: *Mosby's medical, nursing, and allied health dictionary,* ed 4, St Louis, 1994, Mosby.

Dolan J: *History of nursing,* Philadelphia, 1968, WB Saunders.

Donahue MP: *Nursing: the finest art,* ed 2, St Louis, 1996, Mosby.

Kelly LY: *Dimensions of professional nursing,* ed 6, New York, 1991, Pergamon Press.

Keltner NL, Folks DG: *Psychotropic drugs,* ed 2, St Louis, 1997, Mosby.

Morrissey JP, Goldman HH: Cycles of reform in the care of the chronically mentally ill, *Hosp Comm Psychiatry* 35(89): 785, 1984.

Taylor CM: *Essentials of psychiatric nursing,* ed 14, St Louis, 1994, Mosby.

2

CURRENT
MENTAL HEALTH CARE
SYSTEMS

1. Describe the present system of mental health care delivery in Canada, the United Kingdom, Australia, and the United States.
2. State the differences between inpatient and outpatient psychiatric care.
3. Differentiate between voluntary and involuntary admission to mental health care facilities.
4. Explain the community support systems model of care, and list four settings for community mental health care delivery.
5. Identify five components of the case management method of mental health care.
6. Explain the purpose of the interdisciplinary mental health care team.
7. Name four high-risk populations served by community mental health centers.
8. List five community-based mental health services for people with HIV/AIDS.
9. Explain how the concept of holistic care can be applied to care of the mentally ill.

advocacy
case management
community mental health centers (CMHCs)
community support systems (CSS) model
consultation
crisis intervention
health maintenance organizations (HMOs)

holistic concept of care
homelessness
human dimensions
inpatient psychiatric care
involuntary admission
locus of control
multidisciplinary mental health care team
outpatient psychiatric care

preferred provider organizations (PPOs)
psychosocial rehabilitation
repeat offenders
resource linkage
stress
therapy
therapeutic environment
third-party payments
voluntary admission

The delivery of a population's health care varies with the culture. Because cultures, values, and beliefs differ, international comparisons of health care systems are difficult to make. The more developed nations of the world have complex systems for providing health care for their citizens. The health care systems of many developed countries "are undergoing financial strains due to the increasing cost of high technology, drugs, and the aging of the populations" (Foster, Siegel, and Landes, 1995).

Mental Health Care in Canada

By the late 1960s, "comprehensive, government-administered health insurance plans were established in all provinces of Canada" (Stanhope and Lancaster, 1996). Today a "single-payer arrangement" is used in the Canadian health care system, which is based on five guiding principles: universality, portability, accessibility, comprehensiveness, and public administration. Each guiding principle is explained in the box below.

Each province or territory organizes, administers, and monitors the health care delivery system of its citizens. Although benefits may vary, all Canadian citizens are eligible for medical, hospital, convalescent, and mental health services. Medications for people over age 65, diagnostic procedures, and emergency and outpatient services are also provided. Private insurance is available for those services not covered by standard health care benefits.

The official agency responsible for the health of Canadians is the Department of National Health and Welfare. It provides technical and financial support for each provincial health care program; enforces federal food and drug laws; promotes health, fitness, and amateur sports; and administers social welfare programs (Laschinger and McWilliams, 1992).

Canada's health care system is divided into curative and preventive operations. As with the United States health care system, the major focus is on cure and treatment. Preventive services, including mental health, are delivered through public health departments. Many persons with mental illness are treated within the community via private medical providers and clinics. Acute and chronic psychiatric clients are provided care through general and psychiatric hospitals.

Mental Health Care in Great Britain

All British citizens are provided health care through a government-managed national health care system. The Secretary for Social Services is responsible for setting fees for private physicians, budgets for hospitals, and salaries for hospital physicians. Parliament allocates funds for the health care system and regulates the rates at which general practitioners are paid. Tax revenues provide most of the financing for health care.

Mental health care is available for all British citizens as part of the standard benefit package. Physician services, preventive care, home care, and long-term care are all provided by the government. Emergency surgeries, hospital stays, and prescription drugs are also covered. Eye care is not included and dental care is limited, but all other basic health care needs are provided. Private insurance is also available.

Mental Health Care in Australia

Australians are provided an interesting mix of health care plans. The government provides a public health plan that covers all public hospitals and physician services. Also available is a national private plan, which supplements the basic public plan. In addition, numerous private insurance plans are available for eye care, rehabilitative services, and psychiatric treatment.

National health care is financed by a tax on all citizens who earn above a certain income. Two Ministers to the Portfolio of Community Services and Health are responsible for policy and budgetary decisions at the federal level. Individual states are responsible for the administration and delivery of health care services, which are available through local government agencies, semivoluntary agencies, and profit-oriented, nongovernmental organizations. Because mental health care is not provided in Australia's basic health plan, treatment for psychiatric disorders is more common for those with large incomes or private insurance plans.

FIVE PRINCIPLES OF THE CANADA HEALTH ACT

1. *Universality.* Everyone in the nation is covered.
2. *Portability.* People can move from province to province and from job to job or onto unemployment rolls and still retain their health coverage.
3. *Accessibility.* Everyone has access to the system's health care providers.
4. *Comprehensiveness.* Provincial plans cover all medically necessary treatment.
5. *Public administration.* The system is publicly run and publicly accountable.

From Edelman CL, Mandle CL: *Health promotion throughout the lifespan,* ed 3, St Louis, 1994, Mosby.

Mental Health Care in the United States

Health care in the United States is based on the private insurance model. Today, over 75% of the population is covered by private insurance and 14% is covered by public programs (Medicare and/or Medicaid). About 13% of U.S. citizens have no health care coverage at all, whereas 14% hold multiple health insurance coverage (Foster, Siegel, and Landes, 1995).

Health Insurance

During the 1960s, third-party payments became sporadically available. With **third-party payments**, medical costs were covered by a "third-party"—usually an insurance company or the state or federal government. By the late 1970s, many employers provided insurance, which included coverage for mental health care, for their employees. As a result, the number of psychiatric treatment centers increased. Mental health care was available but expensive during the 1980s. Today, private sector care is delivered by independent practitioners, preferred provider organizations, and health maintenance organizations.

Preferred provider organizations. During the 1980s, **preferred provider organizations (PPOs)** were established to help curtail the rapidly growing increases in health care costs. Commonly referred to as PPOs, they consist of a network of physicians, hospitals, and clinics that agree to provide care for different organizations at a discount. The client may see any health care provider within the network, and 80% to 100% of the costs to the client are covered.

Health maintenance organizations. Health maintenance organizations (HMOs) deliver health care to a certain group of enrolled clients who pay a fixed, prenegotiated price. Health care costs are covered as long as clients receive care within the system. The HMO retains responsibility for organizing, delivering, and financing the health care of its members. Physicians are salaried, and clients may or may not have a choice of care providers. Costs are contained by monitoring of the delivery of care as well as limiting access to specialists and/or expensive procedures.

Institutional Care

By the 1900s, the U.S. government established a state hospital system specifically designed for treating the mentally ill. Most state hospitals were large institutions of the same design. Once people were admitted to a state hospital, they usually stayed for months or years, regardless of their ability to function in the community.

Today, publicly financed mental health services are also available in community hospitals and clinics; but, because the "old state hospital system" is no longer in place, communities have been forced to provide increased emergency psychiatric services and short-term inpatient care for an expanding number of acutely ill, aggressive psychiatric clients. The distinction between public and private sector mental health care is beginning to blur as federal funds (Medicare) and state funds (Medicaid) are being used to cover health care costs in both the private and public sectors.

Types of Psychiatric Admissions

The decision to seek psychiatric care, whether made by the client, family, or community, is difficult. Many misconceptions about mental illness still exist, and the majority of people are not accustomed to seeking help for emotional or mental health problems.

Voluntary Admission

When the client originates the request for mental health services, the admission is considered a **voluntary admission.** Because they are commonly aware of their problems, most voluntarily admitted clients are active participants in their treatments and therapies.

Normally healthy people may seek admission to work through specific problems or to obtain support during a crisis situation. Some clients seek to withdraw from addictive substances, whereas others feel the need for mental health educational services. Clients who seek voluntary admission to mental health services are usually able to function adequately on a daily basis and have a low potential for violence.

Involuntary Admission

One of the characteristics of mental illness is a lack of insight into one's own problems. When individuals engage in behavior that is harmful to themselves or others, the involuntary admission process is undertaken.

The 1953 Act Governing Hospitalization defines an **involuntary admission** as a process for institutionalization initiated by someone other than the client. When disturbed people become suicidal, violent, or acutely psychotic, they are protected from harming themselves or others. Involuntary psychiatric admissions relate to inpatient care because a protected, therapeutic environment is usually necessary for the client's safety. Clients may stay for days to years.

Family members are often the first to notice abnormal responses or a deterioration of appropriate behaviors. They usually admit a loved one through private physicians, local hospitals, or community agencies to inpatient psychiatric care.

Physicians, police, and representatives of a county administrator may commit an individual for emergency treatment without a warrant, but a court order is usually required for long-term stays. Procedures for commitment in the United States vary from state to state. Each state has its own Mental Health Procedures Act that governs involuntary admissions.

Clients may also be committed to psychiatric care by way of the criminal justice system. The legal aspects of involuntary commitment are discussed in Chapter 3. Society will protect itself from its more dangerous members. The involuntary commitment process is one method by which this is accomplished.

Inpatient Care Settings

Admission rates to psychiatric inpatient facilities were at an all time low by 1983. However, by 1988, hospitalizations for mental illness had again increased. Emergency rooms in general hospitals saw huge increases in clients with psychiatric problems as many high-risk populations received little mental health care.

Individuals are admitted to inpatient psychiatric services on the basis of need. Several factors are considered when making the choice of an inpatient setting. The severity of the client's illness, the level of dysfunction, the suitability of the setting for treating the problem, the level of client cooperation, and the client's ability to pay for services all enter into the decision regarding **inpatient psychiatric care.**

Clients who receive care in inpatient settings remain at the institution for 24 hours a day. There, all aspects of the client's environment are focused on providing therapeutic assistance.

Inpatient psychiatric care settings provide clients with safe, stable, and therapeutic surroundings. This principle of the **therapeutic environment** is based on the concept that every interaction within the client's environment has therapeutic potential. Therefore the physical surroundings are pleasant but safe. Activities are structured, and clients are expected to participate in their treatment. Discharge from inpatient facilities occurs when client behavior has appropriately improved and treatment goals have been attained. Clients may be discharged into the community, to a group home or other structured setting, or to another institution for long-term psychiatric care.

The most important advantage of inpatient psychiatric care is that it provides a safe, secure environment that allows clients to take a "time out" from the world—a time to focus on and work with the problems that brought them there.

Outpatient Care Settings

As the emphasis shifts from institutional to community mental health care, the demand for outpatient psychiatric services grows. An outpatient mental health care setting is a facility that provides services to people with mental problems within their home environments. The consumers of **outpatient psychiatric care** are able to remain within their communities, associating with the real world.

Mental health services are available through a variety of community agencies and support groups. Services offered in these settings focus on prevention, maintenance, restoration (treatment), and rehabilitation of mental health. Some agencies or groups limit their focus to one area (e.g., Alcoholics Anonymous focuses on treatment of alcohol addiction).

Treatment Environment

Unlike the controlled, limited environment of inpatient treatment facilities, community-based mental health therapy occurs within the context of a dynamic society. Supervision of the client's environment is limited, and the responsibility for controlling behavior lies squarely with the client. Consumers of outpatient mental health care may include individuals, families, or groups. Clients are assessed in relation to relevant elements in the environment, and therapies are designed to assist clients in functioning appropriately within their communities. Mental illness is considered and treated from a broader social perspective. The therapeutic environment is the world in which the client must function.

Unfortunately, the number of outpatient psychiatric care facilities in the United States is rapidly being outpaced by the mental health needs of a nation undergoing many changes.

Community Mental Health Care

In 1990, 5205 mental health facilities existed in the United States to care for a population of over 250 million. About 3000 of these facilities offered inpatient psychiatric care. Of the 2200 community outpatient facilities, approximately 1400 centers provided only partial psychiatric care services. Only 34% of community hospitals offered emergency psychiatric services, and less than 21% provided outpatient treatment (U.S. Bureau of Census, 1993). In addition, the census of public mental hospitals dropped from 559,000 in 1959 to 150,000 by 1980 (Steering Committee on the Chronically Mentally Ill, 1981). One can see why community mental health care systems are overtaxed.

Mentally ill people make use of community services only sporadically. Many wait until a major problem occurs before seeking treatment. When community mental health services are used, a "Band-Aid" approach that treats only the presenting complaint without addressing the underlying problem is often used. Consequently, many of the mentally ill end up in the emergency rooms of general hospitals in need of inpatient psychiatric care.

Unable to cope in the community setting, people with chronic psychiatric problems often return to institutions or use community services on a revolving door basis. This behavior pattern is known as *recidivism* and means a relapse of a symptom, disease, or behavior pattern. Mental health clients with this behavior pattern are called **repeat offenders.** Recidivism is a major problem because it "implies negative treatment outcomes, inappropriate use of services, and increased frustration for staff" (Beebe, 1990). Fortunately, coordination and cooperation among community agencies and mental hospitals is beginning to result in a lower rate of recidivism (Worley and Lowery, 1991).

Psychiatry and mental health care policies are based on the medical treatment model: identify the symptom then treat it. This point of view worked well for institutionalized psychiatric clients, but it became woefully inadequate once clients were released into the community. A broader, community-oriented, more flexible outlook was needed.

Community Support Systems Model

For mentally ill people to function well within their communities, a wide range of support services is necessary. The **community support systems (CSS) model** views the client holistically—as a person with basic human needs, ambitions, and rights. The goal is to create a support system that fosters individual growth and movement toward independence through the use of coordinated social, medical, and psychiatric services.

Effective community support systems are consumer oriented, culturally appropriate, flexible enough to meet individual needs, accountable, and coordinated. A typical program may coordinate such services as health care, housing, food, income support, rehabilitation, advocacy, and crisis response (Fig. 2-1).

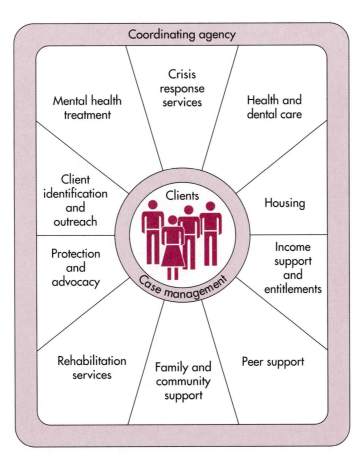

Fig. 2-1 Community support system. (Redrawn from Stroul BA: *Psychosoc Rehabil J* 12:14, 1989.)

The community mental health center was considered the most logical agency for administration of the CSS concept. The most successful community mental health centers have forged strong links with available community agencies, services, and government. Other centers have developed slowly, stifled by lack of funding and public interest, but the CSS model of mental health care is proving to be one of the most comprehensive and workable concepts for the future.

Delivery of Community Mental Health Services

Mental health services and support systems are available through several community and civic organizations. Individuals, families, and the community itself benefit from the activities of various groups. The box below lists several examples of commonly available community services.

Mental Health Care Settings

Community mental health services are based on the identified needs of specific populations. Also, mentally ill people must be treated in the least restrictive manner. Therefore a wide range of services are offered in various settings throughout the community.

Emergency psychiatric care is available through emergency psychiatric clinics in large cities and general emergency rooms at local community hospitals. The primary focus is to stabilize the client, assist with the crisis, and locate appropriate resources in the community for referral. Clinics usually operate evenings, nights, and weekends when other agencies are unavailable. Staff members include nurses, psychologists, counselors, therapists, and social workers. Many of the chronically mentally ill use psychiatric emergency settings as an entry into the mental health services network.

Residential programs are becoming more common in many communities. These programs offer the chronically mentally ill a protected, supervised environment within the larger community. Services provided include the provision of food, shelter, clothing, supervision of personal care, and counseling. Vocational training is frequently provided. Opportunities for leisure and socialization activities are included in most programs. Types of residential programs range from group homes to single-room occupancies, but all provide direct therapeutic support and treatment for the chronically mentally ill.

Psychiatric home care delivers mental health services to individuals and families in their homes. With short institutional stays and the release of people with

---

EXAMPLES OF COMMUNITY SERVICES

SERVING INDIVIDUALS
Rape crisis center
Churches and synagogues
Job training agencies
Art shows
Recreation clubs (e.g., chess clubs and automobile clubs)
Adult education programs
Literacy programs
Employment agencies
Mediation groups
Renewal centers
Meals on Wheels
Colleges and universities
Mental health agencies

SERVING FAMILIES
Women, Infants, and Children (WIC)
Nutritional Services
Community "Welcome Wagon"
Sex-counseling agencies

Family planning agencies
Recreation centers
Children's groups (e.g., Camp Fire Girls)
Church groups
Day care centers for children, the disabled, and the elderly
Family recreation centers and groups
Shelters for victims of domestic violence

SERVING THE COMMUNITY
Fresh Air Fund
Environmental groups
Education groups (e.g., American Lung Association and March of Dimes)
Utility companies
Community emergency shelters
Government agencies
Police department
Fire department
Fair housing bureau or agency
Prisons
Performing arts centers
Public forests and parks

From Haber J and others: *Comprehensive psychiatric nursing*, ed 4, St Louis, 1992, Mosby.

chronic mental illness into the community, the need for home psychiatric nurses to fill the gap between institution and community is rapidly growing. Some nurses receive advanced training in psychiatric home care. These clinical nurse specialists (CNSs) ease the transition from hospital to home for clients and families, assist clients in gaining entry into the mental health care system, provide psychosocial crisis interventions, and collaborate with clients, families, and other professionals to deliver the most appropriate, effective, and cost-accountable psychiatric care. CNSs act as case managers for their clients by assessing the need for and coordinating specific community services. The case history presented in the box below illustrates the role of the mental health CNS in the home care setting.

Partial hospitalization (day treatment) programs began in Canada following World War II. The goal of day treatment programs is to provide more structure and intensive therapy than outpatient or clinic services for clients who are not dysfunctional enough for full-time hospitalization but too ill to be independent within the community. Usually partial hospitalization or day treatment programs last from 30 to 90 days and require attendance for 6 to 8 hours a day for 5 days a week. Programs are staffed by psychologists, nurses, therapists, and counselors. Multidisciplinary assessments help to formulate individualized treatment (care) plans, which are reviewed by the staff at weekly intervals. Treatment methods include various therapies, education, and vocational training. Clients are gradually reintroduced into the community once support systems are in place and coping behaviors are appropriate.

Clients enrolled in these programs become more adept with work and social situations, have fewer psychiatric symptoms and return hospitalizations, and are able to function within the community. With the current emphasis on cost containment and limited health care resources, partial hospitalization programs are effective, viable methods for working with the mentally ill.

Community mental health centers (CMHC) provide several important services for the general public as well as for people with chronic mental illness. The goal of the CMHC is to "develop community programs for reducing psychological stress and aiding individuals and their families to adjust to life difficulties. They were also established to provide rehabilitation to those most seriously impaired; both mandates required that services be delivered in the least restrictive way." (Werner and Tyler, 1993).

Services offered by most CMHCs include crisis intervention, individual and family counseling, and mental health education. Clients with chronic mental illness also receive regular medication reviews, medical care, and vocational and social skills training. CMHCs are staffed by mental health professionals

---

CASE STUDY

Joanne is a 59-year-old woman who was treated for severe depression, anorexia, and suicidal ideation. The psychiatric home care referral was a last-ditch effort by the husband to prevent nursing home placement. Joanne presented with a 30-year history of scleroderma with numerous surgeries and hospitalizations and a 10-year psychiatric history with numerous suicide attempts. She also presented with severe anxiety and agoraphobia (fear of crowds and open spaces). Her anorexia was severe, with her weight at its lowest point being 77 pounds. Her medical problems were interwoven with the psychiatric problems, and she needed comprehensive intervention. The CNS served as case manager for the other home care nurses and for the occupational and physical therapists. Because Joanne could not leave home and needed psychotherapeutic medication management, a psychiatrist was enlisted to make home visits. Companion services were also needed so that someone would be with the client while the husband was at work. The husband was actively involved in the decision making regarding his wife's care, but he needed supportive mental health intervention.

Over a 4-month period, Joanne progressed from a severely withdrawn, suicidal person to someone who was dealing with her panic attacks, agoraphobia, and scleroderma. Her weight at discharge was 90 pounds. Although she would continue to cope with a chronic illness, the sense of hopelessness was gone, and her ability to function in her daily life had markedly improved. The alternative of nursing home placement was offset, and the client was able to continue living in her home and community with the help of community mental health services.

Clinical Decisions
1. What follow-up care would you plan for Joanne?
2. How could you help to prevent her feelings of hopelessness from returning?

From Mellon SK: *Issues Ment Health Nurs* 15:229, 1994.

(psychologists, nurses, social workers, and therapists and their assistants). Those CMHCs with firm funding also focus on prevention—identification and screening of high-risk populations—in addition to education and interventions aimed at reducing mental disorders.

Unfortunately, financing for many community mental health programs has been sporadic, resulting in fragmented services. As the country's policymakers struggle to define a national health policy, consumers and mental health professionals continue to grapple with the everyday problems of mental illness within their communities. The future holds many changes for mental health care in the United States as social, political, and economic forces shape health care policies.

Case Management Systems

Case management is defined as a holistic system of interventions designed to support the transition of mentally ill clients into the community. The major components of case management include psychosocial rehabilitation, consultation, resource linkage (referral), advocacy, therapy, and crisis intervention. Clients are involved with the assessment, planning, and evaluation of their care. Goals are stated as client outcomes. Success is measured in terms of client satisfaction, improved coping behaviors, and appropriate use of services. The overall goal of case management is a successfully functioning client who is able (with support) to avoid relapse and achieve productive patterns of living. A look at each component of case management may help clarify the process.

Psychosocial rehabilitation is the use of multidisciplinary services to help clients learn the skills needed to carry out the activities of daily living as actively and independently as possible. Clients are first assessed for physical, social, emotional, and intellectual levels of function. Then specific plans for teaching needed skills are developed. If clients are capable of work, vocational rehabilitation is offered.

Psychosocial rehabilitation (also called *psychiatric rehabilitation*) is unlike the traditional model of passive, custodial care for the mentally ill in which clients were considered "too sick" to make decisions. Psychosocial rehabilitation encourages decision making, thus empowering clients. This empowerment fosters a sense of self-esteem and mastery, which results in improved coping abilities. As clients feel the success of making their own decisions, they are encouraged to take control over other areas of their lives. Education is also a strong component of psychosocial rehabilitation because mastering daily living skills motivates

clients to more productive and independent levels of functioning within the community setting.

Consultation in mental health care is defined as a process in which the assistance of a specialist is sought to help to identify ways in which to cope effectively with client problems. The case management system relies on the expertise of psychiatrists, nurses, psychologists, social workers, counselors, and various therapists to find ways for clients to receive the services and support that help them to achieve their goals. For example, a nurse might work with a client on personal grooming skills while a social worker is locating supported housing and the vocational counselor seeks out an appropriate work setting. By covering all the bases, so to speak, care providers hope to maintain clients in the least restrictive setting (the community) and assist them with their needs.

Resource linkage is the process of matching clients' needs with the most appropriate community services. Health care providers, including nurses, have traditionally referred clients to other services, but resource linkage adds the component of periodic monitoring. The advantages of coordinating and linking services together are several: clients can be more easily moved into different programs because background information moves with clients; duplication of services is avoided; and as the clients' level of functioning improves, services can be tailored to support the new, more effective behaviors. With resource linkage, the focus for treatment of clients with chronic mental illness is on care instead of the more traditional emphasis on psychiatric symptoms and illness. Because the nursing profession is rooted in supporting clients with the activities of daily living, nurses are in an ideal position to act as resources for matching client needs with community services (see box below).

Advocacy is a critical concept of case management. As the nurse coordinates client care, so does the case manager. In the strict sense of the word, advocacy is providing the client with the information to make certain decisions, but advocacy for the mentally ill involves more. Advocates work to protect clients' rights,

> ### THINK ABOUT
> You are a nurse who has recently moved to this area. As a case manager in a CMHC, you are responsible for referring clients to various agencies. How would you go about locating the agencies in the community that provide services for the mentally ill?

help to clarify expectations, provide support, and act on behalf of clients' best interests. Every person involved in mental health care can act as an advocate by supporting community efforts and policies that encourage healthy living practices.

Therapy is provided for each client based on assessed needs, client cooperation, and available services. Medications may be included as part of the overall plan of treatment. Therapies may include the use of counseling, support groups, vocational rehabilitation programs, and techniques to assist clients with problem-solving and adaptive behaviors.

The last component of case management, **crisis intervention,** is crucial to the success of the client. People with chronic mental dysfunction have great difficulty in coping with stress. What may be bothersome or inconvenient to us could provoke a crisis in someone with mental illness. When problems, frustration, anxiety, or even loneliness become too intense, a crisis erupts; the client becomes unable to cope and retreats into the safety of his/her illness. Crisis intervention describes a short-term, active therapy that focuses on solving the immediate problem and restoring the client's previous level of functioning. Crisis services can help to stabilize the client, prevent further deterioration, and support the readjustment process for the client. The use of crisis services also results in better distribution of resources. Emergency room visits decrease, rehospitalization is prevented, and law enforcement agencies spend less time involved with "crisis cases."

For those clients with severe, treatment-resistant mental illness, a new approach known as *continuous intensive case management* is being used. One inner-city CMHC has established a continuous care team who accepts "full responsibility for patients at all times, whether they are in or out of the hospital" (Arana, Hastings, and Herron, 1991). The team consists of a nurse–social worker, psychiatrist, addictions counselor, and four clinicians (two social workers and two registered nurses). Clients are seen individually and in supportive therapy groups. They attend day treatment programs or pursue vocational training. Many clients live in supervised housing arrangements. A clinician is available to the client 24 hours a day via a beeper system routed through an answering service. Table 2-1 provides a summary of the continuous care team's treatment activities. In short, the care team effectively directs the client's treatment during all encounters with the mental health care system.

Continuous intensive case management programs have demonstrated that clients with chronic and severe mental illness could be effectively stabilized within the community with appropriate support systems. As the twin pressures of increased demand for services and cost restrictions force the system into trying new approaches, mental health care professionals must not lose sight of the most important element in the equation—that individual called "the client."

◆ **TABLE 2-1**
Continuous Care Team Treatment Strategies

Setting	Mental Health Care Team Interventions
Community	Meets with clients 2-4 times a week
	Accompanies client to appointments and other community activities
	Helps with daily living/social skill needs
	Monitors medications
	Nurtures relationships with persons interested in client's well-being
	Encourages client to call team instead of using ER
Emergency room	Prearranges for ER staff to notify clinician on arrival of continuous care client
	Conducts assessment of client and planning of care jointly with ER physician
	Avoids unnecessary hospitalizations
Hospital	Care team psychiatrist and primary therapist remain in charge of the client's case
	Makes decisions regarding admission, treatment, and discharge
	Coordinates treatment with inpatient staff

Modified from Arana JD, Hastings B, Herron E: *Hosp Comm Psych* 42(5):503, 1991.
ER, Emergency room.

Client Populations

Community mental health care was originally designed to provide prevention, education, and treatment services for all members of a community. Mental health services "play a large role in helping communities solve their social problems by working to create an interdependent service delivery system through consultation and education" (Werner and Tyler, 1993). Community mental health services for the general public include crisis interventions, working with businesses to decrease the costs of mental health programs while improving their effectiveness, and providing aid for individuals and families to adjust to life difficulties.

However, there are groups of people who are at a high risk for developing mental health problems in every community, large or small. They include the more obvious populations such as the homeless or seriously mentally ill, and more subtle high-risk groups, such as children, families, adolescents, the aged, and people who are HIV-positive. Clients living in rural areas present a challenge because of distances between services. Although the chronically mentally ill have received attention lately, there are those silent populations who need help just as much.

Many community mental health services offer services for homeless people. Currently, short-term strategies for working with the homeless include temporary shelters, assisted housing programs, and volunteer efforts such as Habitat for Humanity.

Clients with HIV infection or AIDS are using community mental health services in ever-growing numbers. To illustrate, between 1981 and 1984, 7354 cases of AIDS were reported in the United States. By 1985, 6682 people had died of the disease. By 1992, those figures had exploded to 45,472 AIDS cases with 22,675 deaths (U.S. Bureau of Census, 1993). With statistics like these, it becomes easy to understand that AIDS is likely to become a major mental health problem.

People with AIDS face overwhelming physical, emotional, and social consequences. Mental health problems associated with HIV disease include organic problems, such as impairments in memory, judgment, or concentration progressing to dementia. Psychosocial problems include anxiety, depression, adjustment disorders, increased substance abuse, panic disorders, and suicidal thoughts. In addition, many researchers believe that stress has a direct effect on the immune system. Fear of AIDS may hasten the onset of complications in HIV-positive persons. AIDS-related anxiety can increase everyday apprehensions in the lives of many people. Individuals with little education or poor adaptation skills often have difficulty coping with the thought of contracting this disease.

Comprehensive community mental health services for people with HIV/AIDS are not yet available in all communities. Those CMHCs that do offer comprehensive services focus on three groups: persons with AIDS, their families and friends, and the general public.

Clinicians at CMHCs accept referrals from other agencies, provide mental status and suicide risk assessments, offer crisis intervention services, and provide individual or group therapies for clients with HIV/AIDS. Family members and significant others are encouraged to join support groups. Some CMHCs train family members in techniques for keeping clients oriented or on task. Respite care (time off for the caregiver) services are sometimes coordinated through the CMHC. At the community level, CMHCs work with other interested groups to provide prevention strategies and education about AIDS for all citizens of the community.

Clients living in rural areas present a special challenge for community mental health care providers. Small villages, settlements, and farms dot the country landscape of the United States and Canada. In the United States, almost 25% of the elderly live in rural areas (U.S. Bureau of Census, 1993) where poverty and mental illness can go hand in hand. Recent research (Petti and others, 1986, 1987) has indicated that children and adolescents living in rural areas have less access to mental health services.

Mental health care providers (e.g., nurses, therapists) who work in rural areas cope with clients of all ages and with all types of problems. They are also expected to "make appropriate referrals to coordinate a comprehensive continuum of care in spite of sparse resources" (Bushy, 1994).

Other populations such as families, the elderly, children, and adolescents are vulnerable to mental health problems. Community mental health services are a vital link to the well-being of a population. Social and economic changes will continue to influence community mental health care, but as the system matures, the goal of individualized, holistic mental health care for all people should not be forgotten.

Multidisciplinary Mental Health Care Team

Professionals working within the mental health system have various educational backgrounds. In the past, each would work with clients from their particular point of view or specialty. This approach resulted in disjointed, fragmented client care. In some cases, care providers worked at cross-purposes, leaving clients unsure and confused. The need for coordinated assessment and treatment was filled by the **multidisciplinary mental health care team** concept.

The main purpose of the team approach to treating mental illness is to provide effective client care. The mental health care team "provides a forum where psychiatrists, social workers, psychologists, nurses, and others can democratically share their professional expertise and develop comprehensive therapeutic plans for clients" (Haber and others, 1992). The team approach can also be cost-effective by preventing duplication of services and fragmentation of care. Clients and their significant others contribute to the plan of care and remain actively involved throughout the course of treatment.

Multidisciplinary mental health care teams exist in both inpatient and outpatient settings. The number of team members may vary, but the "core" of the team is almost always composed of a psychiatrist, psychologist, nurse, and social worker. Other team members, known as *adjunct therapists,* join the team as needed.

Each team member holds a degree or certificate in a specialized area of mental health. This approach allows for clients to be assessed and treated from various points of view. As data are compiled, a broad, hopefully holistic picture of the client emerges and individualized therapeutic plans are developed. Table 2-2 identifies team members, their educational preparation, and their functions.

Client and Family

No discussion of the mental health team is complete without including the client. As the consumers of services and the focus of therapeutic interventions, clients contribute important information that may make the difference between the success or failure of therapeutic plans. Including clients and their families in the treatment process "reflects a fundamental change in attitude toward those who have a mental illness and their families" (Taylor, 1994). Mental illness no longer calls forth images of demonical possession. Today it is considered to be a manageable, even treatable, complex of disorders.

Trends Toward Holistic Care

Most current mental health care delivery systems are diagnosis and treatment oriented. Traditionally, most people received mental health care only after the onset of behavioral signs and symptoms. This resulted in more acute conditions that were more difficult and expensive to treat. Emphasis was rarely on prevention or early diagnosis.

During the 1970s and 1980s, researchers found that emotions caused chemical changes within the body that in turn affected the physical state. As health care models were developed to recognize the interrelatedness of mind, body, and environment, a new movement (known as "holism") began to emerge.

The word "holism" is derived from the Greek word *holos,* meaning "whole." Holism today is a philosophical concept in which a person is viewed as more than just the sum of his/her parts. People are dynamic. We live in a rapidly changing, dynamic world. To understand a fellow human being, all the factors that make up that person must be considered.

The concept of holism helps to blend many aspects of mental health care. The primary goal of nurses and other mental health care providers is to "help clients develop strategies to achieve harmony within themselves and with others, nature, and the world" (Rawlins, Williams, and Beck, 1993). This statement reflects the **holistic concept of care.** We are no longer content to treat the illness. We are learning to treat the whole person. The holistic approach to health care considers four general concepts when working with clients (Fig. 2-2).

Human Dimensions

Examination of the major areas of an individual allows one to begin to gain a view of that unique person's complex interactions of mind, body, and spirit—the **human dimensions.** Although each area or dimension is presented separately, they are all interwoven. In reality, each person is more than just a combination of dimensions or parts. Problems arising within one dimension can affect functioning in other areas of functioning. For example, if John has the flu, he is unable to attend church services.

Human dimensions focus on five areas: physical, emotional, intellectual, sociocultural, and spiritual. Table 2-3 explains each human dimension and offers several examples of functions within each area.

Self-Responsibility

One of the most important concepts of holistic care is that of responsibility for one's self. People are ultimately responsible for their own lives. They continually make decisions and choose their direction in life. Even when the choices are limited or the options unclear, people *will* select among alternatives.

Self-responsibility includes two components: self-awareness and locus of control. Self-awareness is the philosopher's task to "know thyself." As people explore their connections with themselves, other people, and their environment, they emerge with a sense of their own reality. "Only then can they identify their contributions to life events, acknowledge the choices they make, and fully assume responsibility for themselves" (Rawlins, Williams and Beck, 1993).

Locus of control refers to the power an individual holds. When individuals perceive they have power over the events that affect them, they are more apt to assume personal responsibility. If the locus or center of control is *internal,* people feel they have some influence within their environments. If the locus of control is *external,* people feel that their lives are the result of fate, the odds, or something beyond their control. Many long-term mentally ill clients feel powerless as a result of the passive roles they have assumed so often. Responsibility for self is a new ex-

---

◆ TABLE 2-2
Mental Health Team Members

Team Member	Educational Preparation	Responsibilities and Functions
Psychiatrist	M.D. with residency in psychiatry	Physician; leader of the team; responsible for administration and planning; diagnostic and medical functions are main tasks
Clinical psychologist	Ph.D. in clinical psychology	Specializes in study of mental processes and treatment of mental disorders; performs diagnostic testing; treats clients
Psychiatric social worker	Master's degree in social work (M.S.W.)	Evaluates families; studies environmental and social causes of illness; conducts family therapy; admits new clients
Psychiatric nurse	Master's degree; advanced level preparation; baccalaureate degree; diploma nurse; associate degree nurse; licensed practical nurse	Responsible for client's daily living activities/environment management and individual, family, and group psychotherapy; coordinates care team activities; supervises technicians and psychiatric assistants; active in various community roles
Psychiatric assistant or technician	High school education; special on-job training in setting of employment	Supervised by professional nurse; assists in providing basic needs of clients; carries out nursing functions; maintains the therapeutic environment; supervises leisure-time activity; assists with individual/group therapy
Occupational therapist	Advanced degree in occupational therapy (O.T.)	Assesses potential for rehabilitation; provides socialization therapy and vocational retraining
Expressive therapist	Advanced degree and specialized training in art therapy	Helps make use of spontaneous creative work of the client; works with groups; encourages members to analyze artwork; adjunct to care team in diagnosis and treatment of children
Recreational therapist	Advanced degree and specialized training in recreational therapy	Provides leisure-time activities for clients; teaches hospitalized clients useful pastimes; uses pet therapy, psychodrama, poetry, and music therapy
Dietitian	Advanced degree and special training in dietetics (R.D.)	Provides attractive, nourishing meals; helps treat food-related illnesses
Auxiliary personnel (housekeepers, volunteers, clerks, secretaries)	Various backgrounds and on-job training	Assists clients with activities of daily living and other practical jobs; can be invaluable in helping clients
Chaplain	Seminary pastoral counselor or rabbinical education	Attends to the spiritual needs of clients and families; pastoral, marital counseling

Modified from Haber J and others: *Comprehensive psychiatric nursing,* ed 4, St Louis, 1992, Mosby.

pectation for health care consumers, but the transition from receiver of care to participant in care, although not always easy, is well worth the effort for both clients and providers.

Adaptation to Stress

Another major component of holistic health care is one's adaptation to stress. Human beings continually strive to maintain a balance in their lives. Stress results when a circumstance or event alters that balance. **Stress** is defined as any factor that brings about a response or change within a person. Stress is neither inherently good or bad. It is only when the individual perceives or labels the stress as positive or negative that it is assigned an emotional value. To cope with stress, people develop behaviors that may be adaptive or maladaptive. Stress is discussed more thoroughly in later chapters, but what one must recognize here is that stress affects every human area of function as well as an individual's ability to adapt to changing circumstances. Nurses and other mental health care providers must always take into account the stress factor when working holistically with clients.

Environment

People are intricately interwoven with their environment. The world is dynamic—people, places, events, interactions continually change. Each person relates to his/her surroundings individually. Nurses who take into consideration the influences of the client's environment are better able to provide holistic interventions.

Viewing people holistically leads to a fuller understanding of clients—who they are and how they function within their worlds. When working with clients, one must keep in mind the concepts of human di-

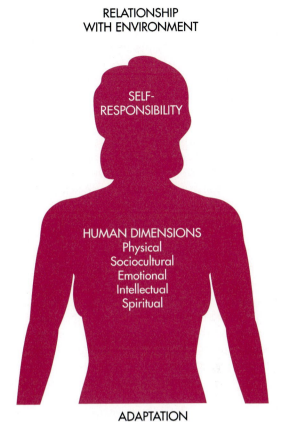

RELATIONSHIP WITH ENVIRONMENT

SELF-RESPONSIBILITY

HUMAN DIMENSIONS
Physical
Sociocultural
Emotional
Intellectual
Spiritual

ADAPTATION TO STRESS

Fig. 2-2 Holistic health care concepts: human dimensions, self-responsibility, adaptation to stress, and environment.

◆ TABLE 2-3 Human Dimensions		
Dimension	**Description**	**Examples of Functions**
Physical	Aspects associated with body	Nutrition, sleep, body image, physical activity, energy, movement, autoimmune functions, healing capacity
Emotional	Aspects related to feelings, moods, affect	Affect—observable behavior that reflects emotion, awareness of emotions; fight or flight response; motivation of behavior
Intellectual	Aspects related to receiving, processing, storing, and using information	Perception, learning, memory, thinking processes, speaking, writing, expressions, communication, problem solving, abstracting
Sociocultural	Aspects that enable one to function in society	Interactions, relationships, roles, status, personal identity, culture, self-concept, sexuality, communication
Spiritual	One's life principles, philosophy, belief systems	Values, morals, ethics; relatedness to a supreme being or life force, people, and nature; self-actualization

mensions, self-responsibility, stress, and environment. These concepts will help you remember that each person is a dynamic, changing individual.

Impact of Mental Illness

Mental illness affects everyone directly or indirectly. Many people know of someone (or of many individuals) with behavioral problems. Indirectly, mental illness costs taxpayers millions of dollars as the costs of health care escalate. Today, health care reform is part of an overall strategy to distribute scarce resources and control an ever-growing national debt while the number of mentally ill in society continues to expand.

Incidence of Mental Illness

Although exact statistics are unavailable, it is estimated that at any given time there are 30 to 40 million Americans living with a diagnosable psychiatric disorder; this number appears to be growing. Chronic severe mental disorders, such as schizophrenia and depression, have emerged as major challenges to treatment. Substance abuse has become a national problem. Recent research shows that 11 to 14 million children and adolescents have diagnosable mental disorders while almost 7 million other children have maladjustment problems (Stuart and Sundeen, 1995). Two million divorces a year place families in crisis situations (U.S. Bureau of Census, 1993). The incidence of Alzheimer's disease and other dementias is currently estimated at 3 million; that number is expected to increase threefold in the next 15 years (Hamdy and others, 1994). Social problems such as AIDS, homelessness, violence, and abuse may be related to mental problems. It is easy to see why there is a growing number of mentally troubled people in today's society.

Economic Issues

The nationwide movement to treat people with mental illness in the least restrictive environment is part of a plan to reduce mental health care costs while still providing ongoing client care. This movement has resulted in the shift of federal funds from the institution (long-term care) to acute care treatment centers. Unfortunately, the funding has not kept pace with the need for services. Because insurers have "capped" or limited the amount of money they will pay for psychiatric care, strict limits have been set on mental health care. Inpatient stays for acute problems are usually funded for a maximum of 14 days. Clients who require longer periods of treatment can be funded for up to 60 days. Long-term stays are becoming less common as clients are discharged rapidly into the community.

In another effort to control costs, Congress established the Health Care Financing Administration in 1983. This administration developed a cost containment method whereby health care providers are paid at predetermined rates. A group of 467 diagnostic-related groups (DRGs) classifies each illness. Medicare, the currently funded health plan for the elderly and disabled, adopted these groups. Constructed payment guidelines, based on clients' average lengths of inpatient stay, determine each DRG. If clients are not discharged from hospitals within the specified time, funding is stopped and the facility or client becomes responsible for payment. DRG coverage for mental illness remains limited.

Today, over 5200 mental health facilities provide services for more than 30 million mentally troubled people in the United States. Clearly a need for mental health care exists at all levels of society, but present levels of service cost taxpayers over $28 million in 1991 (U.S. Bureau of Census, 1993).

Mental illness also influences economics in less direct ways. Unemployed, homeless, and troubled families cost society in many ways more than mere dollars. Loss of productivity and unfulfilled potential are difficult to appraise financially. It is clear that economic issues have and will continue to play a major role in the availability and delivery of mental health care.

Social Issues

Many social problems are related to mental illness. Changing lifestyles, work patterns, family structures, and health are a few of the many changes that are influencing society. Many of the mentally ill, however, are apt to be coping with the more basic issues such as poverty, homelessness, and substance abuse.

By 1991, "nearly thirteen percent of U.S. citizens lived below the poverty line" (U.S. Bureau of Census, 1993). Of those, a significant number are incapable of making a living as a result of mental problems. These individuals exist along the fringes of society, attempting to meet the most basic needs of food, shelter, and clothing. Within this environment of poverty grows hopelessness, and it becomes easier to retreat into one's mental illness than face the grim reality of poverty.

After a time, homelessness becomes poverty's companion. It is estimated that over 3 million of our nation's citizens are homeless on any given day (U.S. Bureau of Census, 1993). Many are families who have had no control over the social forces that determined their situation, but many of the homeless are the deinstitutionalized or chronically mentally ill. Estimates vary as to the number of homeless mentally ill people. Most experts, however, agree that "25% to 50% of adult homeless have a psychosis and that 33% to 50% are alcoholics" (Keltner, Schwecke, and Bostrom, 1995).

Homelessness is a condition that was historically limited to a very small part of the population, but in recent years the numbers have begun to grow. The National Academy of Sciences defines homelessness as the lack of a regular and adequate nighttime residence. The actual number of homeless people is difficult to count because with no regular residence they tend to melt into society and disappear into the world of soup kitchens and temporary shelters.

In the past, most homeless people were single men, usually with alcohol problems. However, today's statistics present a different picture. Women, children, and families now account for as many as one third of the homeless. "Persons age 60 and over are estimated to constitute at least 10 percent of the homeless population" (Cohen, Onserud, and Monaco, 1993), and up to one third of homeless people have diagnosable mental disorders.

Several factors contribute to homelessness. Social conditions such as a lack of low-income housing, tight public assistance eligibility requirements, and the movement of chronically mentally ill people into communities that lack adequate support systems have all had a strong impact on homelessness. Community factors relating to available housing, steady employment, and welfare services affect homeless people. Family dysfunction, poverty, and health status all relate to the homeless problem.

Numerous families live "from paycheck to paycheck," with little savings and just enough money to scrape by until the next check. Because their resources are so marginal, a small event can trigger a crisis. An increase in the rent, for example, may drive a family out of their home.

Society's use of mind-altering chemicals has resulted in many of the mentally ill becoming addicted to "recreational drugs" such as crack, cocaine, lysergic acid diethylamide (LSD), and heroin. When used in combination with prescribed psychotherapeutic drugs, overdoses, permanent psychotic states, and death occur. Street drugs also cost money. It is not uncommon for people with mental problems to spend money on drugs before they buy food. Addicted clients with mental disorders suffer from two separate disorders, with each compounding the severity of the other. Illicit drugs and mental illness become a vicious circle.

The current mental health care system in the United States is undergoing major changes as budgets decline, social issues emerge, and needs for treatment grow. Organization and technology may address some of the system's problems, but the provider-client contact is and will remain the core of mental health treatment.

❖ KEY CONCEPTS

- The health care systems of many developed countries are undergoing financial strains as the result of the increasing cost of high technology, drugs, and aging of the populations.
- Canada's health care system is administrated by each province under the guidance of the Department of National Health and Welfare and includes coverage for most medical, hospital, convalescent, and mental health services.
- All British citizens are provided health care through a government-managed national health care system.
- Australians are provided a mix of health care plans, including a public health plan, which covers all public hospitals and physician services; a supplemental national private plan; and private insurance plans for eye care, rehabilitative services, and psychiatric treatment.
- Funds for health care in the United States are provided through federal (Medicare) and state (Medicaid) programs, private insurance coverage, and direct client payments.
- Admissions to inpatient mental health care settings are usually on a voluntary basis, but people with acute illness can be admitted involuntarily if they pose a threat to themselves or others.
- The community support systems (CSS) model for mental health care is defined as an organized network of people committed to assisting people with long-term mental illness to develop their potential without undue isolation from the community.
- Community mental health care settings include emergency psychiatric clinics, general hospitals, residential care programs, day treatment facilities, and psychiatric home care.
- The case management system is a holistic system of interventions designed to support the integration of mentally ill clients into the community.
- Psychosocial rehabilitation is the use of multidisciplinary services to help clients learn or reestablish the skills and supports needed to carry out the activities of daily living as actively and independently as possible.
- Psychosocial rehabilitation, consultation, resource linkage, advocacy, crisis intervention, and therapy are the basic components of the case management system.
- Intensive case management may use continuous care teams who assume responsibility for the client in and out of the hospital.
- Community mental health services serve several high-risk (or vulnerable) populations such as the general public in crisis situations, the homeless, clients with

HIV/AIDS, clients living in rural areas, the elderly, and children.

- Mental health services are commonly delivered by the multidisciplinary care team—a group of physicians, nurses, psychologists, and therapists who each contribute to the client's plan of care and treatment.

- In an effort to develop a more comprehensive understanding of people, the concept of "holism" evolved. Holistic health care focuses on assisting clients to achieve harmony and balance within their lives.

- The holistic approach includes the five human dimensions (physical, emotional, intellectual, social, and spir-

itual), self-responsibility, adaptation to stress, and the environment.

- Social and economic issues must be considered when discussing the prevalence of mentally troubled persons.

❖ SUGGESTIONS FOR FURTHER READING

Chapters 1, 2, and 3 in *Health Promotion Throughout the Life Span*, ed. 3 by C.L. Edelman and C.L. Mandle (St. Louis, 1994, Mosby) offer a thorough discussion of our current health policies and health care delivery system.

❖ REFERENCES

Arana JD, Hastings B, Herron E: Continuous care teams in intensive outpatient treatment of chronic mentally ill patients, *Hosp Comm Psych* 42(5):503, 1991.

Beebe LH: Reframe your outlook on recidivism, *J Psychosoc Nurs* 28(9):31, 1990.

Bushy A: When your client lives in a rural area—part II: rural professional practice—considerations for nurses providing mental health care, *Iss Ment Health Nurs* 15:267, 1994.

Cohen C, Onserud H, Monaco C: Outcomes for the mentally ill in a program for older homeless persons, *Hosp Comm Psych* 44(7):650, 1993.

Foster CD, Siegel MA, Landes A, editors: *Information plus: health: a concern for every American,* ed 7, Wylie, TX, 1995, Information Plus.

Haber J and others: *Comprehensive psychiatric nursing,* ed 5, St Louis, 1997, Mosby.

Hamdy RC and others: *Alzheimer's disease: a handbook for caregivers,* ed 2, St Louis, 1994, Mosby.

Keltner NL, Schwecke LH, Bostrom CE: *Psychiatric nursing,* ed 2, St Louis, 1995, Mosby.

Laschinger HKS, McWilliams CL: Health care in Canada: the presumption of care, *Nurs Health Care* 13(4):204, 1992.

Petti TA, Benswager EG, Fialkov MJ: The rural child and child psychiatry. In *The Basic Handbook of Child Psychiatry,* New York, 1987, Basic Books.

Petti TA, Leviton L: Re-thinking rural mental health services for children and adolescents, *J Public Health Policy* 7:58, 1986.

Rawlins RP, Williams SR, Beck CK: *Mental health-psychiatric nursing: a holistic life-cycle approach,* ed 3, St Louis, 1993, Mosby.

Stanhope M, Lancaster J: *Community health nursing: promoting health of aggregates, families, and individuals,* ed 4, St Louis, 1996, Mosby.

Steering Committee on the Chronically Mentally Ill. *Toward a national plan for the chronically mentally ill: A report to the secretary* (DHHS Publication No. 81-1077). Washington, DC: U.S. Government Printing Office, 1981.

Stuart GW, Sundeen SJ: *Principles and practices of psychiatric nursing,* ed 5, St Louis, 1995, Mosby.

Taylor CM: *Essentials of psychiatric nursing,* ed 14, St Louis, 1994, Mosby.

U.S. Bureau of Census: *Statistical abstract of the U.S.: 1993,* ed 113, Washington, DC, 1993.

Werner JL, Tyler M: Community-based interventions: a return to community mental health centers' origins, *J Counsel Dev* 71(7):689, 1993.

Worley NK, Lowery BJ: Linkages between community mental health centers and public mental hospitals, *Nurs Res* 40(5):298, 1991.

3

ETHICAL AND LEGAL ISSUES

1. State the differences between values, rights, and ethics.
2. Explain the purpose of the Patient's Bill of Rights.
3. List five steps for making ethical decisions.
4. Identify the legal importance of nurse practice acts.
5. Describe the process of involuntary psychiatric commitment.

6. Name four areas of potential legal liability for nurses and other mental health care providers.
7. Know the difference between the legal terms *negligence* and *malpractice*.
8. Explain three legal responsibilities that relate to nursing practice.

KEY TERMS

assault
battery
belief
civil law
codes of ethics
confidentiality
contract law
controlled substances
criminal law
defamation
duty to warn
elopement

ethical dilemma
ethics
false imprisonment
felonies
fraud
informed consent
invasion of privacy
involuntary commitments
laws
libel
malpractice
misdemeanors

morals
negligence
nurse practice act
Patient's Bill of Rights
reasonable and prudent nurse
right
slander
standards of practice
tort law
value
values clarification

Nursing, like other professions, is defined by certain beliefs, rights, and principles. Ethical and legal concepts offer a framework for delivering effective therapeutic interventions. This chapter presents a brief discussion of ethical and legal issues that affect the care of clients with mental disorders and their care providers.

Values and Morals

Attitudes, beliefs, values, and morals influence who we are. As we develop, we internalize our concepts of right and wrong, good and bad. To be effective nurses (especially when working with mentally ill clients), we must understand the connections of these concepts within ourselves as well as within our clients and their support persons.

A **value** is something that is held dear, a feeling about the worth of an item, idea, or behavior. Values are formed in childhood and shape our reactions to other individuals. They influence our behaviors, reflect the society in which we live, and are often used as a basis for making decisions. Values are individual—they vary from person to person—and they may change as an individual matures (Edelman and Mandle, 1994).

Morals consist of one's attitudes, beliefs, and values. One's morals define the basis for right or wrong behavior. People who are morally responsible act according to society's accepted standards of goodness or rightness. Once established, morals become deeply ingrained and are not easily changed. Attitudes and beliefs help to form the basis for moral behavior.

How Values Are Acquired

Newborns enter this world with a clean slate. As they grow, they observe and then adopt the reactions of others in their environment. These adopted reactions become our earliest attitudes.

Preschool children begin to learn the difference between "right" and "wrong" behavior. They also begin to adopt the family's beliefs as their intellectual and abstraction abilities begin to grow. A **belief** is a conviction that is intellectually accepted as true, whether or not it is based in fact. Family traditions are examples of beliefs. As attitudes and beliefs develop, children begin to form values (see box below).

<table>
<tr><td>

♦ **THINK ABOUT**

Does the statement, "We've always done it this way," reflect a belief?

What are the values associated with this statement?

</td></tr>
</table>

Children are exposed to a variety of values at school. It is during this time that they develop work habits, learn to solve problems, and make decisions. They continue to model parental values because the family remains the major source of values until adulthood.

During the teen years, adolescents begin to identify their own significant values. By early adulthood, an individual value system (which may differ from the family's) is established. Adults may feel secure with their values or discard them for new ones. Older adults may feel threatened by the changing values of society, but they tend to hold onto their own value systems.

How Values Are Transmitted

Culture, society, personality, and experiences all help to shape our values. How values are shared depends to a large extent on the sociocultural environment, but most societies use a combination of modeling, laissez faire, moralizing, reward/punishment, and responsible choice (Potter and Perry, 1993).

Modeling is copying an example. One person behaves in the ideal or preferred manner while the other imitates or copies the behavior. Counting a pulse, for example, is much easier after one has seen someone take a pulse.

Moralizing sets standards for right and wrong. Values are transmitted with no room for questions or alternatives, and people must conform to what is defined as "right" or "wrong." Independent choice is not allowed. Children raised by moralizing parents commonly have problems making independent decisions.

The *laissez-faire mode of value transmission* involves unrestricted choices. No direction is given, so people are free to explore and learn from their experiences. With children and adults who are learning new roles, the laissez-faire method may result in confusion or frustration because no guidance is provided.

The *reward/punishment system* offers rewards for valued behaviors and punishes undesirable acts. Preferred behaviors are strengthened by positive payoffs, whereas punishments are thought to decrease or eliminate unacceptable actions. Because reward/punishment is an authoritarian mode of value transmission, children tend to learn that might (strength, authority) is right. Punishment may also inadvertently send the message that violence is acceptable.

Last, *responsible choice* transmits values through a balance of freedom and restriction. Individuals are given limited choices as well as the freedom to choose among the stated options. As choices are made, new behaviors and their consequences are explored. "Children who can freely discuss their behavior and its effects will learn to understand their own values" (Potter and Perry, 1993).

People who choose to work in the health care profession usually arrive with a strong set of personal values. They value life, and they work to improve its quality. They value human dignity, and they show concern for people. They treat others fairly and equally. Human values that enhance the giving of care include a concern for the welfare of others (altruism), respect for the uniqueness and worth of people (human dignity), equality, justice, truth, freedom, and acceptance. Nurses care about their clients. This single value—caring—is the foundation for the practice of nursing for if we are unable to care for our clients, we will be unable to effectively treat, teach, or collaborate with them.

Values Clarification

Every society has a value system. "In more traditional societies, values are embedded in habit, customs, and traditions. In societies in which rapid change occurs, values can become a source of controversy and conflict" (Davis and Aroskar, 1991). Modern societies are rapidly changing, and we are not always aware of our values. Like breathing, we simply accept and do not think about our values until something goes wrong. It is when we are experiencing difficulties that we become more aware of our values.

Values clarification is a step-by-step process that encourages one to identify his/her significant values. Nurses routinely make decisions about client care. Each decision, although based on subjective/objective data, is colored by the nurse's values. It is important to make the correct decisions about client care. Therefore every nurse must be aware of his/her values and how they affect interactions with clients.

The values clarification process involves three steps: choose, prize, and act (Table 3-1). The process works equally well for clients and health care providers. The first step, choosing, involves looking at all possible alternatives and consequences and then freely selecting the best option. Once a choice is made, the value must be prized or cherished. That is, the value is important to the individual, who feels good about the choice. Many times the value is acted on by sharing it with others. This sharing reaffirms the importance of the choice for the individual. Last, the value is internalized, that is, made a part of the individual's behavioral patterns. The value is then reflected repeatedly and consistently in the individual's behaviors.

To illustrate the process, let us assume that you are a nurse who works at the local drop-in clinic. You see yourself as a caring person and have no problems interacting with clients, but today a large, scruffy man

◆ **TABLE 3-1**
Values Clarification Process

Step	Process
Choosing	Consider all possible alternatives.
	Consider all possible consequences.
	Choose freely without pressure or coercion from others.
Prizing	Cherish or prize the choice.
	Share choice with others.
	Reaffirm importance of value.
Acting	Make value a part of behaviors (internalize value).
	Generalize value to all situations.
	Repeatedly act with consistent behavioral pattern.

who has not bathed in weeks presents himself for care. There is a wild look in his eye, and he is arguing with himself as he approaches you. What you really want to do is run away, but you are the nurse who must cope with this client. How does your value of caring apply here?

First, you have freely chosen to care about people; otherwise you would have selected another line of work. Second, you prize the value of caring because you work well with your clients. They see you as compassionate and concerned for their welfare. Third, you act on your values by accepting the unkempt, scruffy man as a person worthy of care. You ask him what you can do to help him feel better. He begins to cry and tells you that since the death of his wife and children in a house fire, no one has cared if he lives or dies. By acting on your value (caring), you have touched this person and paved the way for him to improve his situation. You have *chosen* to care. You *cherish* the value of caring enough to *act*, even when that value is threatened. Be clear about your values. Be aware of your client's values because these are the guides for one's lifestyle, conduct, and interpersonal relationships.

Rights

Most modern theories of government believe strongly in the rights of people. The rights to privacy, freedom of movement, and the pursuit of happiness are written into the United States Bill of Rights. But what exactly is a right? How do rights apply to me, and how do they affect my mental health care clients?

A **right** is described as a power, privilege, or existence to which one has a just claim. Rights have several roles in our society; they can be used as an expression of power, to justify actions, and to settle disputes. Rights help to define the parameters of social interactions because they contain the principle of justice; they equally, impartially, and fairly apply to all citizens. For example, we all have the right to be respected as human beings and treated with dignity. Rights carry with them obligations. The fact that you have a right to drive down the road but also have the obligation to obey traffic laws illustrates this point.

Client Rights

During the late 1960s, the Welfare Rights Organization began to campaign for the rights of the disadvantaged people. From that campaign arose the Patients' Rights Movement, which focused on health care and its providers. Issues such as consent, telling the truth, and the imbalance of power within provider-patient relationships were addressed. People wanted a cooperative partnership with their health care providers, not a relationship based on paternalism (i.e., father knows best). Issues of confidentiality, informed consent, and the right to refuse treatment became aspects of client rights.

By 1972, the American Hospital Association (AHA) addressed these concerns by issuing the **Patient's Bill of Rights.** Although unenforceable by law, the statement "is important because it not only reminds people that they have rights, it also encourages them to assert them and to make further demands" (Annas, 1989).

Basically, the bill states that all clients have the rights to respectful care, privacy, confidentiality, continuity of care, and relevant information. Also addressed are clients' rights to examine their bills, refuse treatment, and participate in research. The Patient's Bill of Rights also serves as a model for the development of specific bills of rights for many health care organizations.

Since the publication of the AHA Patient's Bill of Rights, many specialized rights statements have evolved. Statements of rights now exist for the old, young, disabled, pregnant, dying, retarded, and mentally ill—the most vulnerable people in society.

People with mental illness tend to lose their rights in two ways. First, the problems with which they are coping require energy, so much energy that sometimes reality eludes them. Second, the organization of the mental health delivery system can impose limits on clients' abilities to exercise their rights. In addition, many mental health clients are not able to recognize their rights, much less exercise them. To protect the rights of these vulnerable people, the Mental Health Systems Act Bill of Rights was passed by the U.S. Congress in 1980. This bill served as a pattern from which state bills of rights for the mentally ill were developed (see box below).

> ### MENTAL HEALTH PATIENT'S BILL OF RIGHTS
>
> 1. The right to appropriate treatment in the least restrictive setting
> 2. The right to treatment based on a current, accurate, individualized, written treatment plan that includes a description of mental health services that may be needed after discharge
> 3. The right to ongoing participation in the planning of treatment, along with appropriate explanations of its objectives, potential adverse effects, and alternatives
> 4. The right to refuse treatment, except in an emergency or as provided by law
> 5. The right not to participate in experimentation. When consent is given, the client has the right to have a full explanation of the procedure, its anticipated benefits, potential discomforts and risks, and alternative treatments, along with the right to revoke such consent at any time
> 6. The right to freedom from restraint or seclusion, except in an emergency or when these are prescribed as a part of treatment
> 7. The right to a humane treatment environment
> 8. The right to confidentiality of the client's mental health care records
> 9. The right to access of the client's own mental health care records, except to that information provided by third parties and that information deemed by a mental health professional to be detrimental to the client's health
> 10. The right to converse with others privately, to have convenient and reasonable access to the telephone and mails, and to see visitors during regularly scheduled hours, except when denied access to a particular visitor as part of the written treatment plan
> 11. The right to be informed promptly about these rights
> 12. The right to assert grievances regarding infringement of these rights, including the right to have such grievances heard in a fair, timely, and impartial manner
> 13. The right to obtain assistance from designated or otherwise qualified advocates
> 14. The right to exercise these rights without reprisal, including the denial of any appropriate, available treatment
> 15. The right to referral to other providers of mental health services on discharge
>
> From Taylor CM: *Essentials of psychiatric nursing,* ed 14, St Louis, 1994, Mosby.

It must be remembered that the basis for the development of these statements was a basic dissatisfaction with the treatment of health care clients. It is up to nurses and other care providers to make certain that each person's rights are ensured and protected and to act as advocates for their clients.

Care Provider Rights

Nursing is becoming self-governing, with all the rights and responsibilities of a profession. As nurses achieve and exercise their own rights, they are better able to advocate the rights of their clients, improve services, and engage in ethically sound nursing practices. Essentially, the rights of nurses and other care providers can be grouped into four categories: respect, safety, competent assistance, and compensation.

Nurses have the right to be respected as individuals. The human rights of dignity, choice, and equality apply to all people. Nurses have the right to fulfill their responsibilities as professionals, and they have the right to full and equal participation as members of the health care team. They also possess the right to set standards for quality in practice and help to develop policies that affect nurses and client care.

All health care providers have the right to function within a safe environment. This right applies to both the physical environment (i.e., properly maintained equipment) and the affective or feeling environment. Nurses, technicians, and other care providers who work to minimize the physical and emotional stresses of the working environment are exercising their right to function safely.

The right to competent assistance includes the right to receive assistance with nursing care by people who are actually capable of performing at the stated level. For example, the CNA who is assigned to work with you is able to function adequately and safely as a nursing assistant.

Because nursing has always been a giving or helping profession, most nurses find it difficult to discuss compensation. On employment, nurses as well as other providers enter into a relationship with the employer that implies that the nurse (worker) will fulfill the responsibilities of the job. In turn, the nurse has a right to be compensated or paid for those services rendered.

Health care providers, especially nurses, need to exercise their rights. The health care delivery system is large and impersonal. Nursing care is considered a commodity, and it is through the exercising of rights that we remind the system of the therapeutic values inherent in the nurse-client relationship.

Ethics

Throughout civilization, men have attempted to answer the great questions of life. The body of knowledge that arose from this process is called *philosophy.* A branch of philosophy, called *moral philosophy* or **ethics** "deals with the questions of human conduct that have great relevance to us as individuals and as health professionals" (Davis and Aroskar, 1991). In short, ethics is a set of rules or values that govern right behavior.

Ethics reflects values, codes of morality, and principles of right and wrong. The purpose of ethical behavior is to protect the rights of people. Health care ethics focuses on the moral aspects of health care availability, delivery, and policy. It is also called *biomedical ethics, bioethics,* or *medical ethics.*

Ethical principles are guidelines by which a profession governs itself. They are the behaviors that define what is good or right conduct. These principles form the basis for professional **codes of ethics.** Ethical codes serve two purposes: (1) they act as guidelines for standards of practice and (2) they let the public know what behaviors they can expect from their health care providers.

Primary Ethical Principles

The concepts of autonomy, beneficence, nonmaleficence, and justice are the main ethical principles on which nursing codes of ethics are established. Remember these principles because they will serve you well as you encounter the many ethical situations inherent in the nursing profession.

Autonomy refers to the right of people to act for themselves. It includes the right to make personal choices, including refusal of treatment. Nurses who practice the principle of autonomy encourage clients to participate in informed decision making. The procedure, known as **informed consent,** promotes client autonomy by providing relevant information and choice for the client.

Beneficence means to actively do good. Actions that promote client health and levels of function are beneficent. Nurses assess their clients and then weigh the benefits and risks of any nursing action. Choosing the nursing action that is the most therapeutic for the client is an example of beneficence.

The principle of *nonmaleficence* can be stated in three simple, but profound words: *do no harm.* Perhaps it is the most important ethical principle of the caregiving professions. Although nurses must sometimes carry out procedures that result in pain, the harm of the pain must be considered in light of the benefits gained. Nursing interventions are delivered only after client safety and comfort are considered. Nonmaleficence ensures that clients will not be harmed during nursing care.

Justice implies that all clients are treated equally, fairly, and respectfully. Because most health care resources are limited and not all people are equal in every way, the application of justice can be difficult. Severely ill clients require more attention. Finances may not be readily available. However, all clients deserve respect and a share of the available resources.

Secondary Ethical Principles

The concepts of confidentiality, fidelity, and veracity are interwoven into the four primary ethical principles. The client's rights to privacy, truth, and duty are protected by these ethical principles. **Confidentiality** is the duty to respect privileged or private information. It is a legal as well as an ethical duty of health care providers to keep all information about clients limited to only those directly involved with client care. Sharing private information is not only unethical but also may be grounds for legal action.

Fidelity is the obligation to keep promises. Telling the client that you will return in 10 minutes is a promise. The client expects you back within the stated time. Keep that appointment because your client relies on you, and your credibility grows or diminishes depending on how well you keep your promises. Do what you say you will do or do not say it.

The final principle, *veracity,* is the duty to tell the truth. Be careful here. Answer client's questions honestly but remember to stay within your standards and limitations of practice. It is not within your realm, for example, to discuss the disease prognosis or lead the client in any manner toward a certain decision.

Nursing Codes of Ethics

Codes of ethics for practical (vocational) and registered nurses have been developed by the International Council of Nurses, the American Nurses Association, the National Federation of Licensed Practical Nurses, and the Canadian Nurses Association (Table 3-2). Codes of ethics may differ as the result of the educational preparation of the nurse, but all codes of ethics are based on the same ethical principles.

Provide information to clients, be truthful, and support your clients, but consult your supervisor if there is any question of appropriateness. Practice your profession with ethical principles in mind. These principles are the foundation of quality holistic health care.

Ethical Conflict

In today's world of advanced technologies and complex situations, no clear-cut answers exist for the complicated questions that arise. **Ethical dilemmas** (conflicts) exist when there is uncertainty or disagreement about the moral principles that endorse different courses of action (behaviors) (McDonald, 1994).

In the health care profession, ethical dilemmas arise when problems cannot easily be solved by decision making, logic, or use of scientific data. Answers to ethical dilemmas usually have a broad impact. Because of this situation, many health care institutions have established bioethics committees to study, educate, and assist staff members in coping with ethical dilemmas.

Most of the time no clear-cut right or wrong solutions exist for ethical dilemmas. Answers are not black or white; they are all shades of gray. Although each ethical dilemma is unique, the method for making ethical decisions can be applied to all situations. Potter and Perry (1993) offer guidelines for dealing with such dilemmas (see box below). "Making ethical decisions in an orderly systematic manner increases one's ability to deal with the dynamic and sometimes complex issues relating to ethics. The quality of one's nursing care depends on the skills and ethical integrity of the practitioner" (Morrison, 1993).

GUIDELINES FOR MAKING ETHICAL DECISIONS

1. *Identify all elements of the situation.* Gather as much data as possible. Identify every person who is involved in the decision-making process.
2. *Assume good will.* All care providers want a satisfactory resolution to the problem. When working with emotionally charged issues, remember that we are all on the same side. There is no need for competition in these situations.
3. *Gather relevant information.* Thoroughly assess lifestyle, preferences, wishes, and support systems. Try to form an "ideal picture" of the resolution for the dilemma.
4. *List and order values.* Using the ethical principles of autonomy, nonmaleficence, beneficence, justice, confidentiality, fidelity, and veracity, decide which principles are most important in the situation. List them in order of importance, then determine a plan or course of action.
5. *Take action.* Implement the plan. Monitor any changes.
6. *Evaluate* the effectiveness or success of the plan.

From Potter PA, Perry AG: *Fundamentals of nursing: concepts, process, and practice,* ed 3, St Louis, 1993, Mosby.

◆ **TABLE 3-2**
Codes of Ethics for Nurses

Registered Nurse	Practical/Vocational Nurse
Participates in activities that contribute to ongoing development of profession's body of knowledge	Knows scope of maximum utilization of the LPN/LVN and functions within that scope
Participates in profession's efforts to implement and improve standards of nursing	Recognizes and appreciates cultural backgrounds and spiritual needs
Participates in profession's efforts to establish and maintain conditions of employment that encourage high-quality care	Respects religious beliefs of individual patients
Participates in profession's effort to protect the public from misinformation and to maintain integrity of nursing	Safeguards confidential information acquired from any source about clients
Collaborates with health professionals and other citizens in promoting community and national efforts to meet health needs of public	Refuses to give endorsement to sales and promotions of commercial products or services
Provides services with respect for human dignity and uniqueness of the client unrestricted by considerations of social or economic status, personal attributes, or nature of health problems	Upholds high standards of personal appearance, language, dress, and demeanor
Safeguards client's right to privacy by judiciously protecting confidential information	Accepts responsibility for membership in NFLPN and participates in its efforts to maintain established standards of nursing practice and employment policies that encourage quality client care
Acts to safeguard client and public when health care and safety are affected by the incompetent, unethical, or illegal practice of any person	Safeguards client's right to privacy by judiciously protecting confidential information
Maintains competence in nursing	Safeguards client and public when health care and safety are affected by incompetent, unethical, or illegal practice of any person
Exercises informed judgment and uses individual competence and qualifications as criteria in accepting responsibilities, delegating nursing activities, and seeking consultation	Maintains competence in nursing
	Exercises informed judgment and uses individual competence and qualifications as criteria in accepting responsibilities and seeking guidance

NFLPN, National Federation of Licensed Practical Nurses.
From American Nurses Association: *Codes for nurses with interpretive statements,* Kansas City, Mo, 1985, The Association; and The National Federation of Licensed Practical Nurses: *Code for licensed practical/vocational nurses,* 1979.

Laws and the Legal System

Nurses, like every health care provider, must be familiar with the basic concepts of the legal system that governs their society. Without laws and the system that creates and enforces them, life would be chaotic. **Laws** are the controls by which a society governs itself. They are derived from rules, regulations, and moral and ethical principles, and they pertain to all members of the society.

General Concepts

Laws exist at every level of government. In the United States, federal law "defines or establishes the very organization of the government" (Creighton, 1986). Federal law is based on the U.S. Constitution.

Laws at the state level are derived from the state's constitution and apply to the citizens living within its boundaries. Local and city laws evolve from state law. They are usually limited to the areas of authority defined by the state.

Laws change as society changes, but they are all based on four fundamental principles: justice (fairness), change, standards, and individual rights and responsibilities.

Laws have several functions in our society. They define and redefine relationships, describe which behaviors are or are not acceptable, and explain what kind of force is applied to maintain rules. Laws also help to provide solutions for many social and legal problems.

In general, laws serve to protect the rights of people and define the limits of acceptable behaviors. Laws of both the United States and Canada are derived from English common law. Sources of laws are the nation's constitution, legislative statutes, and court decisions.

Basically two types of law govern relationships: public law and private law. Public law focuses on the relationship between the government and its citizens. The division of public law that is of importance to nurses is known as **criminal law,** the main function of which is to protect the members of society. Serious crimes, known as **felonies,** are punishable by death or imprisonment. Less serious crimes are called **misdemeanors,** with punishments ranging from fines to prison terms of less than 1 year.

Private law is commonly called **civil law.** Its function is to deal with relationships between individuals. Two important types of civil law for nurses are contract law and tort law. **Contract law** deals with agreements between individuals or institutions. These agreements or contracts may be written or implied. To illustrate, on employment, nurses enter into either implied or written contracts with the employing institution.

"A tort is a legal wrong that is committed against the person or the property of another individual" (Morrison, 1993). **Tort law** relates to individuals' rights and includes the need to compensate a person for a wrong. Tort law is of special importance to nurses because many potential liabilities exist in all health care settings. Fig. 3-1 lists the areas of law that are most significant for nurses.

Legal Concepts of Nursing

The practice of the nursing profession is defined and regulated by several legal mechanisms. Criminal and civil laws that protect the public also protect the client. State boards of nursing define the practice of nursing through nurse practice acts and regulate nursing via mandatory licensing procedures and disciplinary actions (Trudeau, 1994).

Each state's board of nursing defines the limits and scope of nursing practice via a series of regulations known as that state's **nurse practice act.** Nurses need to be familiar with their state's nurse practice act because it is the legal framework for nursing practice in that state.

Nurses are legally responsible for their actions. They are expected to know the parameters of their practice. Guidelines for sound nursing practice can be found in each state's nurse practice act, professional standards of practice, and the employing institution's policies.

Institutional policies also help to define nursing. The policies, procedures, job descriptions, and contracts of an employing agency all influence nursing practice. Policies are statements that define a course of action. What is to be done is stated in policies. How a task or skill is to be performed is defined in the institution's procedure manual. Job descriptions define

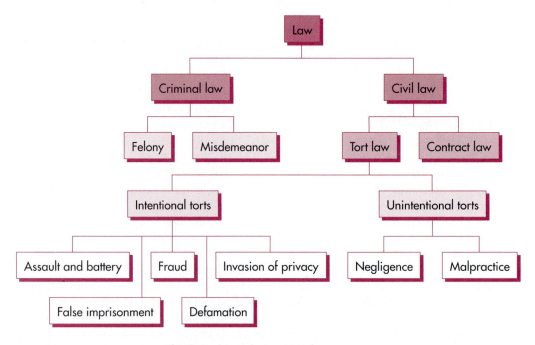

Fig. 3-1 Laws important for nurses.

the job, its functions, its qualifications, and to whom the nurse reports (Calfee, 1994).

On employment, nurses enter into a contract with their employers, which may be written, verbal, or implied. Frequently, an agency's application for employment will include a contractual agreement. It is wise to understand your contractual obligations because you are legally liable for meeting the contract's terms once you have accepted employment.

Standards of Practice

A standard is a measurement for comparison. It serves as a yardstick by which one evaluates an action. Every health care provider practices with certain standards, called **standards of practice.** They are usually developed by each specific discipline.

Standards of nursing practice, for example, are a set of guidelines for providing, monitoring, and evaluating nursing care. The purpose for standards of nursing practice is to provide measurable criteria for nurses, clients, and others to evaluate the quality and effectiveness of nursing care. Psychiatric mental health standards for nursing practice were first developed in 1973 by the American Nurses Association and then later revised in 1982 (see Appendix A).

Remember, guidelines for the parameters of nursing practice may be found in your state's nurse practice act, practice standards, or institutional policies. The nurse who functions with these guidelines in mind is assured of legally sound, ethical practice.

Law and Mental Health Care

Historically, people with mental illnesses were afforded few legal rights. Only since the 1960s have mental health clients been able to exercise their claims to fair and adequate treatment in settings helpful to their care. Nurses and their colleagues need to be aware of their clients' legal rights to freedom, privacy, and choice. Laws relating to mental health issues "attempt to balance the basic rights of the individual against society's interest in being protected from persons who, because of mental disorder, present a threat of harm" (Keltner, Schwecke, and Bostrom, 1995).

Client-Nurse Relationship

Nurses enter into contractual agreements when they consent to work with clients. An awareness of the obligations relating to the nurse-client relationship ensures safe, legal practice. From a legal point of view, the nurse and client enter into an implied contract on acceptance of service. The nurse gives professional services that are accepted by the client. The concept of contractual obligations is one legal aspect of the nurse-client relationship. Two other important aspects are liability and standards of care.

The concept of liability states that nurses are legally responsible for their professional obligations and behaviors. This concept includes the obligation to remain competent, maintain a current knowledge base, practice at a level appropriate to one's education, and practice unimpaired by drugs, disability, or illness (Moore, 1993).

Standards of care (practice) are defined by nurse practice acts and professional organizations. They help to define the legal parameters of nursing by stating how a "**reasonable and prudent nurse**" would guide nursing actions. Keep the concepts of contractual obligations, liability, and standards of care in mind when working with clients. These concepts will assist you in providing the respectful, holistic mental health care so needed by clients.

On entry into the mental health care system, clients still retain their legal rights. The 1980 Mental Health Systems Act protects the rights of clients with mental illness. The resultant bill stated that the mentally ill have rights to obtain information and treatment within a supportive, humane environment. Rights relating to access to records, telephone use, mail, visitors, grievance procedures, confidentiality, participation in treatment, and referral on discharge are also addressed. Individuals who are admitted to psychiatric facilities retain the right to vote, to buy and sell property, and to possess a driver's license.

People with mental illness may be unaware of their legal rights or unable to exercise them. Clients' judgments may be limited as the result of their illness. It is important therefore that nurses and their colleagues recognize and safeguard their clients' legal rights. Behind every mental disorder lives a real person.

Adult Psychiatric Admissions

According to the U.S. Bureau of Census (1993), over 230,000 people received psychiatric inpatient care in 1990. Admission to these facilities is usually voluntary; the client recognizes the need for help and seeks out treatment. A small number of admissions, however, occur against a client's will.

A voluntary admission is initiated by the client, who applies in writing for admission (admission process) and agrees to receive treatment and abide by the rules. Voluntarily admitted clients may legally discharge themselves at any time. Admissions that occur against a client's will are known as involuntary admissions or **involuntary commitments.**

During the 1940s, "almost 90% of admissions to state mental hospitals in the United States were involuntary" (Stuart and Sundeen, 1995). That number has dropped to less than 50% in the 1990s. Involuntary commitment has endured intense scrutiny because it is based on the legal premises of police power (protection of the people from dangerous actions) and the power of the state to care for those people who are unable to care for themselves. Each state establishes its own standards for commitment, but most laws allow involuntary admission (commitment) only if the person is dangerous to self or others or cannot function in a reasonable manner without treatment. Most states have similar procedures for admitting individuals for psychiatric care against their wishes.

The commitment process begins when a formal petition is filed by a family member, friend, or concerned citizen. The client is assessed and examined by one or two physicians. Then a determination to either release the person or hospitalize him/her is made. If hospitalized, the length of stay may be on an emergency, temporary, or indefinite basis.

Emergency hospitalization for severe, acute illness is usually limited to 30 days. If no improvement is noted, the client is temporarily committed for an additional 2 to 6 months.

Indefinite commitments are reserved for people with chronic, severe mental disorders. The client must be gravely disabled and unable to provide for himself/herself as a result of mental illness. Usually the court provides a guardian or conservator to protect the client's rights. Indefinite commitments are most often an action of the courts. They are subject to yearly review; clients retain the right to consult a lawyer and petition the court for discharge.

Commitment proceedings may be based on medical, judicial, or administrative decisions. Medical commitment decisions are made by a specified number of physicians, including one or more psychiatrists. Judicial (court) commitments are made by courts of law, whereas special hearings are required for administrative commitment decisions (Parry, 1994). Because clients have a right to due process of the law, medical commitment decisions are most commonly used only in emergency situations. Fig. 3-2 illustrates the process of involuntary commitment.

Areas of Potential Liability

Mental health care providers are placed in the unique position of balancing their clients' rights with the need to protect society. Many legal issues relate to the care of the mentally ill. An awareness of the potential liabilities of psychiatric nursing will help to safeguard the nurse's practice as well as clients' rights.

The most common crimes in the health care settings are homicide, controlled substance violations, and

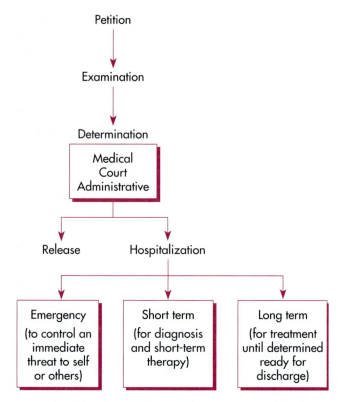

Fig. 3-2   The involuntary commitment process. (Redrawn from Stuart GW, Sundeen SJ: *Principles and practice of psychiatric nursing,* ed 5, St Louis, 1995, Mosby.)

theft. Legally, *homicide* is the killing of a human being, whereas murder is killing with intent to do harm. For example, a nurse who unknowingly gives a client the wrong drug and he dies as a result may have committed homicide, but a nurse who knowingly administers a lethal drug may be guilty of murder.

The Controlled Substances Act of 1970 was passed by Congress to regulate the supply and distribution of certain powerful drugs. **Controlled substances** currently include narcotics, stimulants, depressants, hallucinogens, and some tranquilizers. As agents of the physician, nurses administer controlled drugs and are responsible for adhering to their institution's policies and procedures regarding storage, distribution, and documentation of controlled substances.

Robbery, theft, and *larceny* all describe the taking of another person's personal property. Each involves the intent to deprive someone of ownership. Clients who lose valuable items can hold the agency liable for theft. So ensuring that a valuables disposition list is completed for every client is an important protection against theft.

Fraud is the giving of false information with the knowledge that it will be acted on. For example, a nurse documents on a chart that a medication was administered when actually it was not. The physician then bases a treatment decision on the client's lack of response. The nurse is guilty of fraud. Practicing your profession with the utmost honesty is the best protection against fraud.

Defamation is defined as a false communication that results in harm. It is subdivided into two categories: written defamation, or **libel**, and verbal defamation, referred to as **slander**. Psychiatric care providers, especially nurses, should base their communications on objective data and clinical observations, not on judgments or opinions.

Assault is any act that threatens a client. No physical contact needs to occur, just a threatening action. Telling a client that he/she will be physically forced to take medication if he/she does not cooperate is an example of assault. **Battery** is when touching occurs without the client's permission. The best preventative for assault or battery is clear communication. Make sure clients understand what you intend to do *before* you begin a nursing action.

An important area of potential liability relates to **invasion of privacy.** In our society, individuals have the right to protect themselves from public scrutiny. "The right to privacy includes privacy related to the body, confidential information, and the right to be left alone" (Morrison, 1993). An invasion of privacy occurs when a client's space, body, or belongings are violated. Although nurses must be continually vigilant to protect a client's privacy, those rights may occasionally be outweighed by the need to ensure the client's safety. For example, a client who behaves in a suicidal manner may have his/her belongings searched for potentially dangerous objects.

The client's right to privacy also includes **confidentiality,** which is the sharing of information about the client only with those persons who are directly involved in care. Discussing any client with noninvolved people constitutes a breach of confidentiality (see box below).

All mental health care providers can protect the client's privacy by treating each person with dignity

and respect. Nurses who work in inpatient treatment settings need to orient clients to their environment and inform them of their privacy rights as well as how those rights may be restricted. Clients trust their care providers. It is up to all of us to maintain, nurture, and safeguard that trust.

Detaining a competent person against his/her will constitutes **false imprisonment.** Any time a client's freedom of movement is restrained (against his/her will), the potential for liability exists. The criteria for false imprisonment are (1) the client is aware of the confinement, (2) the intent to confine exists, and (3) the confinement takes place against the client's will. Both physical force and verbal intimidation are included in the concept of false imprisonment. For example, threatening a client with confinement to obtain cooperation constitutes grounds for false imprisonment.

Involuntarily committed clients may make false imprisonment claims in some states, but usually the public's right to safety takes precedence over a client's claim of false imprisonment. Health care providers can confine mentally ill persons only to protect safety and prevent injury; medical or legal authority must be obtained as soon as possible.

The application of protective devices and restraints may constitute false imprisonment. Nurses must be very careful to know when and how to employ restraints correctly. Restraints must be used only to protect the *client,* not for the staff's convenience. The least restrictive measures should first be attempted and documented. A written medical order for restraints must be on file in the client's chart. Once restraints have been applied, the nurse has an increased obligation to observe, assess, and monitor the client every 15 minutes. The restraints must be removed, one limb at a time, and range of motion exercises provided every 2 hours. All observations and nursing actions must be documented. Restraints are removed as soon as the client's behavior is controlled (Leger-Krall, 1994).

The concepts of both negligence and malpractice are rooted in the "reasonable and prudent person" theory. **Negligence** is defined as the omission (or commission) of an act that a reasonable and prudent person would (or would not) do. For example, a public swimming pool owner who did not repair a slide that then caused a child's injury could be guilty of negligence.

The concept of **malpractice** applies to professionals and is defined as a failure to exercise an accepted degree of professional skill that results in injury, loss, or damage. Mental health nurses are most commonly involved with negligent acts that relate to medication administration; client injuries (e.g., falls, burns), record keeping, and abandonment (NSO Risk Advi-

---

◆ THINK ABOUT

You overhear two psychiatric aides discussing Mrs. Samson while making the bed in Mrs. Jones' room.

How would you handle this situation?

Are there any ethical principles being violated by the aides' behaviors?

sor, 1992). No matter what the cause, to be considered negligent, the professional misconduct must meet four requirements:

1. The nurse owed a *duty* to the patient.
2. The nurse did not carry out the duty *(breach)*.
3. The patient was injured as a result of the nurse's action or inaction *(proximate cause)*.
4. Actual loss or *damage* resulted from the nurse's actions.

To illustrate, a suicidal client is to be continuously observed (duty). The nurse goes to lunch, leaving the client alone (breach of duty). During this time, the client commits suicide (proximate cause) and dies (damage). The nurse in this case is guilty of malpractice because no reasonable and prudent nurse would leave a client unattended in a similar situation.

Care Providers' Responsibilities

The main responsibilities of nurses and other mental health care providers are to assist clients in coping with their mental and emotional problems. Dignified, humane treatment of the mentally ill includes the protection of their rights as human beings, citizens, and clients. Nurses and their colleagues are responsible for protecting these rights within the treatment setting.

Relating to Clients

Mental health clients have specific rights to treatment, refusal of treatment, informed consent, examination by the physician of their choice, confidentiality, and freedom from restraints. Other legal issues that relate to psychiatric care include elopement and the duty to warn.

Informed consent is an agreement between the client and providers of care that documents the client's knowledge of and agreement to treatment. The client must be aware, informed, and capable of consenting. Mental health clients are "presumed competent and therefore able to consent to treatment while hospitalized" (Northrop and Kelly, 1991).

Obtaining consent for treatment is the physician's responsibility, but nurses are frequently called on to act as witnesses. Be sure the client has no undiscussed questions or concerns before signing a consent. Be sure to document whether the discussion relating to the consent or only the signature was witnessed (Brent, 1993).

The importance of confidentiality for mental health nurses cannot be overemphasized. Nurses have a duty to keep all verbal and written information relating to clients protected. Keep clients' records secure, and consider the implications of discussing confidential information *before* you speak. Good communication among treatment team members is important but so is the client's right to privacy.

A special situation, known as **elopement,** sometimes arises during hospitalization when clients run away or elope from the institution. Nurses who fail to prevent client elopement may be held liable if the client is injured as a result of the elopement. Keeping clients under supervision plus accurate documentation of client behaviors and nursing actions can prevent elopement from occurring.

All nurses have the **duty to warn.** The right to confidentiality is not absolute. In situations in which serious harm or death may occur, mental health professionals have a duty to protect potential victims from possible harm by a client. For example, if your client states that he intends to kill his barber, you have a duty to warn the barber. Contact the client's physician and your supervisor, and document the action.

In some states, nurses and their colleagues have a duty to report certain information. Examples of reportable data include suspected incidents of abuse, gunshot wounds, and certain communicable diseases. The rights of the client must sometimes be balanced by the right of the public to be protected.

Relating to Nursing Practice

Nurses have the overall responsibility to practice in a competent, safe manner. This involves an active pursuit of new knowledge as well as a willingness to conduct oneself according to ethical and legal standards. Even so, areas of potential liability exist in many situations. Awareness of any foreseeable problems will help you to practice effectively.

Documentation in client records is used in court to prove or disprove a claim (Mandell, 1992). All client records should be completed in ink, dated and timed, and be legible and complete. Data should be objective, with client statements in quotation marks. Documentation should reflect the nursing process, standards of care, and client responses. Accurate, objective documentation is an excellent defense against potential legal problems.

In 1970, the Controlled Substance Act was enacted in an attempt to regulate the manufacture, distribution, and dispensing of certain classes of drugs (Table 3-3). Nurses act as agents of the physician when they administer drugs. They have the responsibility to keep all controlled drugs under double lock, to complete all records pertaining to the administration of and response to drugs, and to question an order for medication that appears unreasonable (Gillis, 1994).

◆ **TABLE 3-3**
Controlled Substances

Classification	Drugs
Schedule I	No accepted medical use in the United States
Schedule II	Narcotics, amphetamines, amobarbital, pentobarbital, secobarbital
Schedule III	Nonnarcotic depressants, short-acting barbiturates
Schedule IV	Long-acting barbiturates, tranquilizers, depressants
Schedule V	Exempt narcotics (e.g., cough syrups that contain codeine)

AVOIDING LEGAL PROBLEMS

1. Remember the reasonable and prudent nurse principle. What would a good nurse of equal training do in the same situation?
2. Know and follow your state's nurse practice act.
3. Use professional standards of nursing practice.
4. Follow the agency's policies, procedures, and job descriptions.

The Reasonable and Prudent Nurse Principle

The law judges a nurse's professional actions by asking the question, "What would a reasonable and prudent nurse do under similar circumstances in a similar situation?" Then a comparison between behaviors is made. Nurses who consult with others and seek out new information before acting are following the reasonable and prudent nurse principle.

Nurses can practice "reasonable and prudent" nursing by following the state's nurse practice act; the profession's standards of practice; and the employing agency's policies, procedures, job descriptions, and contracts (see box above). Safe, legal nursing practice is based on your knowledge of the parameters that define nursing in your practice setting.

❖ KEY CONCEPTS

- Many aspects of society are defined by common values, morals, and rights, which influence behaviors and serve as foundations for making decisions.
- Values, morals, and beliefs are acquired in childhood.
- Values clarification is a three-step process to identify one's significant values.
- Rights are described as powers or privileges to which one has a just claim.
- Clients' rights are addressed in each state's Patient's Bill of Rights and the federal Mental Health Systems Act Bill of Rights.
- Nurses and their colleagues have the rights to practice their professions in safety and with competent assistance, respect, and compensation.
- Ethics are a shared set of codes, rules, or laws that govern right behavior.
- Ethical principles for nurses have been organized into codes of ethics by several nurses' organizations based on primary and secondary ethical principles.
- A five-step process assists nurses and other health care providers in resolving ethical dilemmas.
- Laws are the controls by which a society governs itself.
- Laws function to define relationships, describe acceptable behaviors, maintain rules, and protect the public.
- Legal concepts that govern nursing practice are found in each state's nurse practice act; standards of nursing practice; and institutional policies, procedures, and job descriptions.
- Nurses are obligated to protect their clients' rights and provide competent care at the appropriate level of education and according to standards of care (practice).
- Because detaining a person against his/her wishes violates rights, most states have a formal commitment process that limits and monitors inpatient stays in psychiatric facilities.
- Nurses who care for people with mental illnesses need to be aware of the potential liabilities inherent in many client care situations.

❖ SUGGESTIONS FOR FURTHER READING

The Nurse's Liability for Malpractice, ed. 6, by E.P. Bernzweig (St. Louis, 1994, Mosby) is an excellent programmed text for legal principles and concepts that relate to nursing.

❖ REFERENCES

Annas G: *The rights of patients: the basic ACLU guide to patient rights,* ed 2, Carbondale, Ill, 1989, Southern Illinois University Press.

Brent NJ: How informed are you about consents? *NSO Risk Advisor* 7:3, 1993.

Calfee BE: Steering clear of trouble: litigation lessons, *Nursing 94* 24(1):46, 1994.

Creighton H: *Law every nurse should know,* ed 5, Philadelphia, 1986, WB Saunders.

Davis AJ, Aroskar MA: *Ethical dilemmas and nursing practice,* ed 3, Norwalk, Conn, 1991, Appleton & Lange.

Edelman CL, Mandle CL: *Health promotion throughout the lifespan,* ed 3, St Louis, 1994, Mosby.

Gillis LK: Concealing a med error, *Am J Nurs* 94(2):55, 1994.

Keltner NL, Schwecke LH, Bostrom CE: *Psychiatric nursing,* ed 2, St Louis, 1995, Mosby.

Leger-Krall S: When restraints become abusive, *Nursing 94* 24(3):54, 1994.

Mandell M: Practical ways to survive a lawsuit, *Nursing 92* 22(8):56, 1992.

McDonald S: An ethical dilemma: risk versus responsibility, *J Psychosoc Nurs Ment Health Serv* 32(1):19, 1994.

Moore GM: Surviving a malpractice lawsuit: one nurse's story, *Nursing 93* 23(10):55, 1993.

Morrison MW: *Professional skills for leadership: foundations of a successful career,* St Louis, 1993, Mosby.

Northrop CE, Kelly ME: *Legal issues in nursing,* St Louis, 1991, Mosby.

NSO Risk Advisor: Legal tips and tidbits, *NSO Risk Advisor* 1(7):1, 1992.

Parry J: Involuntary civil commitment in the 90s: a constitutional perspective, *Caps Comm Psychiatr Nurs* 1(4):69, 1994.

Potter PA, Perry AG: *Fundamentals of nursing: concepts, process, and practice,* ed 4, St Louis, 1997, Mosby.

Stuart GW, Sundeen SJ: *Principles and practices of psychiatric nursing,* ed 5, St Louis, 1995, Mosby.

Trudeau S: The law adds force to your voice, *RN* 57(1):65, 1994.

U.S. Bureau of Census: *Statistical abstract of the US: 1993,* ed 113, Washington, DC, 1993.

SOCIOCULTURAL ISSUES

1. Compare the concepts of culture, ethnicity, and religion.
2. Describe the consequences of stereotyping mental health clients.
3. List seven characteristics of culture.
4. Identify three ways in which cultural orientation influences health and illness behaviors.
5. List six components of cultural assessment.
6. Explain the importance of recognizing clients' spiritual or religious practices.
7. Identify four specific topics included in the assessment of a client who is a refugee.
8. Integrate cultural factors into a holistic plan of nursing care.

KEY TERMS

culture	illness	religion
disease	norms	role
environmental control	nuclear family	spirituality
ethnicity	nursing process	stereotype
extended family	prejudice	territoriality
gender roles	race	transcultural nursing

Culture has a profound influence on mental illness and its treatment. In fact, mental illness is defined within a cultural context. To illustrate, in some cultures male offspring are preferred, so it is not uncommon to allow newborn girls to die of neglect. Other societies value the lives of all children to the point that great energies and resources are spent to ensure a single newborn's survival. If a mother in our society neglected her child, we may question her state of mind. The lesson is that what may be appropriate behavior in one culture might be considered insanity in another. This point is most important to remember because awareness of each client's cultural background will help us to understand the client as a whole person who deserves respect and dignity.

Nature of Culture

Concepts are thoughts that, when grouped together, form a "picture" of something. The "picture" of a person is incomplete without consideration of the cultural, ethnic, and religious concepts that help to define and guide an individual's life.

Simply put, **culture** is a total way of life. It is the learned pattern of behavior that shapes an individual's thinking and serves as the basis for one's social, religious, and family structure. Culture is a shared system of values that helps to provide the framework for who we are.

Race is a biological term that describes a group of individuals who share physical characteristics that are distinct. Race is described by such properties as skin color, facial features, and hair texture. **Ethnicity** is more of a social term associated with the socialization patterns, customs, and cultural habits of a particular group.

When many people with a regional identity migrate to a new country, they become identified as *ethnics.* Life in the new land slowly becomes a combination of old customs mixed with new behaviors. The ethnic group then begins to function as a subsociety within a larger society.

Ethnic groups play important roles in preserving cultures. The values, traditions, expectations, and customs of a society are passed from one generation to another within ethnic groups. They help people to form relationships with others of similar backgrounds, and they provide established guidelines for living. In addition, ethnic groups function as focal points for evaluating the value systems of other groups. In short, ethnicity helps establish one's point of view.

Spirituality and religion play important roles in the concept of culture. The term **spirituality** refers to a be-

lief in a power greater than man. **Religion** relates to a defined, organized, and practiced system of worship. Religious groups may have values that range from allowing for individual variation to requiring a commitment to place the religion before family, work, and friends. Many times, mental health clients have religious components to their illnesses. "Delusions of religiosity" may be strongly ingrained in the illness. "The challenge to the nurse is to balance pathological behavior with appropriate cultural expression of religion" (Taylor, 1994).

Components of Culture

Culture is an abstract concept. We can touch the symbols or observe certain customs that represent a cultural orientation, but until we understand what makes up a culture, its importance will escape us. Culture is comprised of the values, beliefs, roles, and norms of a group. Large multicultural societies such as our own have many cultural variations and subgroups.

Nurses and their colleagues have varied cultural backgrounds themselves. The need to understand how the components of one's own culture relate to clients' cultural backgrounds is a key to establishing effective nursing care.

Although they may seem vague to an outsider, cultural values form a complex pattern that strongly influences the thinking and actions of a culture's members. People of different cultures respond in various ways to time, activity, relationships, the supernatural, and nature. Learning about the client's cultural values is important for considering the whole person (Rosella, Regan-Kubinski, and Albrecht, 1994).

Conflicts in cultural value systems can lead to mental illness when individuals can find no adequate resolutions. People may also express one value and then act out another. Observing behaviors, rather than merely listening, will allow nurses to gain a more accurate picture of the client's values.

A culture's belief system develops over generations. It arises from the feelings and convictions that are believed to be true within the society. Belief systems can be found in a culture's political, social, and religious practices.

Beliefs about mental health have a strong impact on the outcome of treatment in most cultures. When people with illnesses believe in the treatment and their care providers, successful outcomes are much more frequent. Know and respect the client's beliefs. Some things that you find strange may be of great cultural importance to the client.

Values and beliefs help define **norms,** which are a culture's behavioral standards. Norms are the established rules of conduct that define which behaviors are encouraged, accepted, tolerated, and forbidden within the culture. Simply put, norms are the rules for behavior.

A **role** is an expected pattern of behaviors associated with a certain position, status, or gender. For example, the expected role of a policeman is to protect the public. Cultures commonly describe roles on the basis of age, sex, marital status, and occupation. Individuals within the culture are expected to fulfill their roles and conform their behaviors to meet the expectations defined by the role. Some cultures have clearly defined role expectations, whereas others may be vague and ambiguous.

"A **stereotype** is an oversimplified mental picture of a cultural group" (Haber and others, 1992). Some beliefs about certain groups are passed on through generations, and they tend to color the perceptions and influence the behaviors of persons who hold them.

Stereotyping may take negative, positive, or traditional forms. The extreme form of negative stereotyping is called **prejudice.** People who are prejudiced use stereotyping to "scapegoat" other groups; that is, they displace unacceptable impulses and behaviors onto a culturally different group. Positive stereotyping describes a favorable oversimplified picture of a cultural group, but this act can be just as harmful as prejudice. To illustrate, the stereotyping of the American working mother as "being able to handle it all" has overlooked the problem of providing safe, enriching daycare facilities for children. Traditional stereotyping occurs when one assumes that all members of a culture behave in the traditional manner.

Stereotypes develop unconsciously in many people, especially those who have had little exposure to culturally diverse groups. Nurses and other health care providers need to know and understand their own racial, ethnic, religious, and social stereotypes. Clients, especially those with mental problems, are very sensitive to discrimination. If they sense such treatment, they will resist interventions and not cooperate with their care. Removing stereotypes allows each person to be treated as an individual, with the respect and dignity that is his/her right (Gaut, 1993).

Characteristics of Culture

To understand others, we must view people within the context of their culture. Each individual is the product of a unique cultural experience. Nurses who assess the behaviors of culturally different clients without personal biases are better able to distinguish adaptive behaviors from dysfunctional ones (see box below).

Cultures vary greatly in values, beliefs, and behaviors, but they all share several characteristics (Table 4-1). Culture is a social phenomenon. It is not genetically inherited or based on individual behaviors. It is the passing on of shared systems to others.

The main characteristics of culture relate to the passing on of cultural information. First, culture is learned through life experiences as a part of the society. Second, culture is also transmitted or passed from one generation to another through language, symbols, and practices. Without these transmissions, children remain unaware of their heritage.

Third, culture is shared. Values, beliefs, and standards of behavior that are known to all members allow children to learn right from wrong and adjust their behaviors according to the cultural norms.

Fourth, culture is integrated. Shared values of a culture provide the framework for political, social, religious, and health practices. Although we tend to look

---

CASE STUDY

Hauni is a 22-year-old woman who recently arrived from Sumatra. She has been ill for 3 days and arrives at the clinic with a friend. Although Hauni speaks English, the nurse who is obtaining her history must frequently repeat her questions. With patience, Hauni responds to nurse Sally's questions, but she immediately freezes when Dr. Dan enters the examination room. She refuses to be examined by Dr. Dan despite her feeling very ill. Sensing the patient's uneasiness, Sally confers with Dr. Dan, who recommended that the case be turned over to Dr. Linda. Much to Sally's relief, Hauni cooperated fully with Dr. Linda, even to the point where she became talkative.

Clinical Decisions

1. What difference did the recognition of the client's cultural background make in the delivery of her care?

2. What do you think would have happened if the nurse failed to take the client's culture into consideration?

◆ **TABLE 4-1**
Characteristics of Culture

Characteristics	Description	Example
Culture is learned.	Culture is a learned set of shared values, beliefs, and behaviors and is not genetically inherited.	Cuban family members learn that humor is a way of making fun of people, situations, or things called *chateo*. Humor also includes modifying situations through exaggeration, jokes, and satirical expressions or gestures.
Culture is transmitted.	Culture is passed from one generation to another.	In the Asian culture, the concept of family extends both backward and forward. The individual is seen as a product of all generations of the family from the beginning of time. This concept is reinforced by rituals, such as ancestor worship and family record books. Personal actions reflect on not only the individual, but also all generations.
Culture is shared.	Culture is a shared set of assumptions, values, beliefs, attitudes, and behaviors of a group. Members predict one another's actions and react accordingly.	In the Arab culture, a woman will not make eye contact with a man other than her husband. All decisions are made by her husband. Because a woman may not be touched by another man, health care may be provided only by another woman.
Culture is integrated.	Universal aspects of culture include religion, politics, economics, art, kinship, diet, health, and patterns of communication. All categories of culture are interrelated.	In Ireland and the United States, the primary cultural force and national unifier of Irish culture has been the Catholic Church. The parish, rather than the neighborhood, has traditionally defined the family's social context.
Culture contains ideal and real components.	Ideal cultural patterns are called norms, which prescribe what people ought to do and may be legally or socially reinforced. Real behavior may diverge from ideal behavior and still be acceptable.	The American mainstream culture condemns the drinking of alcohol on a daily basis. However, those who do so but "hold their liquor well," are regarded with only minimal disapproval.
Culture is dynamic and continuously evolving.	Cultural change is an ongoing process. All aspects do not change at the same time. Cultural habits and newer behaviors are easier to alter than deep-rooted values and beliefs.	Although Italian-Americans have become an integral part of American society, values regarding the family roles of men and women are often more traditional than values regarding the roles of men and women in the workplace.
Individual behavior is not necessarily representative of the culture.	Although culture defines the dominant patterns of values, beliefs, and behaviors, it does not determine all the behaviors in any group. Variation from the major pattern of behavior is called *eccentric behavior*. The meaning of this behavior within the culture will determine whether it is regarded as normal, eccentric, or deviant.	Male and female roles are strictly defined in traditional Greek culture. Women are secondary; the man is the head of the family. Men work and provide for their families; it is a dishonor if the wife works outside the home. Within this cultural context, a Greek woman who is a proponent of the feminist movement might be viewed as eccentric or deviant.

Modified from Haber J and others: *Comprehensive psychiatric nursing,* ed 4, St Louis, 1992, Mosby.

at a single facet or area, all aspects of a culture are interwoven.

Fifth, because a culture reflects its members, it is dynamic, changing, and adaptive. Sixth, cultural habits are also satisfying. They fill a need within the society and result in gratification.

Seventh, people within a culture usually follow the approved behavioral patterns (norms) of their peers. Norms arise from shared ideas of what constitutes appropriate actions. These ideas form group habits that become culturally ingrained over time. Individual behaviors may differ from the major behavioral patterns and still be tolerated, but only to a certain extent. When a person's actions go beyond a culturally acceptable point, they are considered eccentric, maladaptive, or deviant. Cultures without ideation (shared ideas) are unable to set standards of conduct.

Each of these seven characteristics helps to explain the framework of a culture. To deliver holistic, effective mental health care, nurses must assess the impact and meaning that each cultural characteristic has for the client.

Influences of Culture

In the United States and Canada today, people base many health decisions on both scientific and cultural values. As a result of mixed points of view, many people seek health care from folk healers as well as medical practitioners.

Health Beliefs

"The practice of Western medicine is viewed as professional care" (Boyle and Andrews, 1989). It is based on objective cause and effect (scientifically proven treatment methods) and tends to discredit anything that cannot be explained by scientific research. Providers of health care are specifically licensed and trained in one area of expertise. Health care is offered in institutions and is often delivered in an impersonal, assembly-line manner.

Folk medicine, "on the other hand, embodies the beliefs, values and treatment approaches of a particular cultural group" (Edelman and Mandle, 1994). Its foundation is based on empirical knowledge—observation and experience without an understanding of cause or effect. Folk practitioners explain disease culturally as an imbalance of energies. Providers of care may receive training through an older, experienced practitioner, religious groups, or self-study. Care is provided in the home or community in a personal, individualized manner (Table 4-2). Nurses and providers of care within the Western system of medicine need to know about clients' folk medical practices because many people seek out professional care only after folk healing proves ineffective.

Traditional health beliefs may vary from culture to culture, but most beliefs involve an explanation of the fundamental cause of health and disease. For example, Navajo and traditional black cultures view health as a state of harmony with nature. The mind and body

---

◆ **TABLE 4-2**
Comparison Between Folk and Western Health Care Systems

Criteria	Western	Folk
Philosophy of care	Curative	Curative
Approach to care	Fragmented specialization Often impersonal	Personalized
Setting for services	Institutions	Homes, community, other social places
Treatments	Technology Approved pharmacological agents	Herbs, charms, amulets, massage, meditation
Providers	Licensed professionals	Healers, shamans, spiritualists, priests, other lay unlicensed therapists
Support for care	Other ancillary personnel and agencies	Family, relatives, friends
Payment for services	Third-party insurers Personal funds	Negotiable
Philosophy of health	Influenced by the professional's definition and dealt with in terms of illness and treatment	Reflected as a quest for harmony with nature
Definition of disease	Result of cause-effect phenomena; cure is achieved by scientifically proven methods	Imbalance between person and physical, social, and spiritual worlds

From Edelman CL, Mandle CL: *Health promotion throughout the lifespan*, ed 3, St Louis, 1994, Mosby.

are unified and function harmoniously with the earth and the supernatural (Tshotsho, 1993). Disease is a disharmony caused by evil spirits or the breaking of a taboo. Chinese cultures consider health to be a balance of positive and negative energy forces (yin and yang). An imbalance of yin or yang results in disease. Hispanics feel that good health is a gift from God, sprinkled with good luck. Illness is an imbalance of the hot and cold body properties and is considered God's punishment (Geissler, 1994). Low-income families define health as the ability to work. Because they deal with many daily problems, an attitude toward illness as being unpreventable develops.

Throughout the years, millions of people have sought health care from alternative (folk) sources. Understanding and respecting the client's cultural health beliefs and practices promotes effective treatment for those who seek the Western system of health care.

Illness Behaviors

Disease is a condition in which a physical dysfunction exists, whereas **illness** is a state of social, emotional, intellectual, as well as physical dysfunction. Culture has no impact on disease, but illness, and its attendant behaviors, is strongly influenced by one's culture.

When the signs and symptoms of illness appear, an individual may take any one of four courses of action: (1) do something to relieve the symptoms, (2) do nothing, (3) vacillate without taking any real action, or (4) deny the existence of the problem.

Several studies have compared the illness behaviors of men from various cultural backgrounds. Results found that Italian-Americans sought medical help when social or personal relationships were affected by the illness, "whereas Irish-Americans would seek help for their symptoms only after receiving approval of others. Americans of Anglo-Saxon origin would seek medical assistance only when their symptoms interfered with specific vocational or physical activities" (Wu, 1973).

Illness behaviors are also affected by ideological beliefs (e.g., Christian Scientists do not seek medical help for illness) and the norms of the culture. For example, if headaches are considered a sign of weakness, to seek treatment would be to deny group expectations and act counter to the cultural heritage. To be effective, nurses must assess each client's attitudes and behaviors relating to illness.

On Mental Illness

Mental health clients and their care providers may have very different belief systems about how mental disorders are caused, defined, and treated. Members within a cultural group may define normal and abnormal behaviors differently than those outside the culture. To illustrate, in several cultures the practice of altered states of consciousness or trances is considered acceptable, whereas in modern Western society a participant's sanity would be questioned. When working with clients from diverse cultural backgrounds, the nurse must ascertain *their* cultural definitions of mental health and illness.

Cultural descriptions of mental dysfunction are classified as arising from two points of view: naturalistic illness or personalistic illness. According to Haber and others (1992), "naturalistic illnesses are caused by impersonal factors without regard for the individual." Illness or disease is the result of an imbalance of energy forces. The Chinese, Hispanic, and Navajo cultures all share this belief. Mental illness is the result of an excess or deficiency of forces caused by such external variables as diet, exercise, sexuality, or changes in climate. In short, forces that exist *outside* the individual cause mental illness.

Illnesses that are categorized as personalistic illnesses are seen as aggression or punishment that is directed toward a specific person. Examples include voodoo, witchcraft, and the evil eye.

Beliefs in witchcraft are widespread in Haitian, Puerto Rican, and African-American cultures. Spells, hexes, and incantations are used to cause a person injury, illness, or even death. Mental illness is considered the result of witchcraft, magic, or evil spells.

The practice of voodoo calls forth the spirits of the dead back to the world of the living to bless or curse specific people. People with mental disorders are thought to be cursed by spirits. Although the causative forces exist outside the body, the chosen individual "takes on" or internalizes the behaviors associated with the hex.

Stress and Coping

All cultures classify their members by sex and age. Inherent in these age and sex roles are certain norms, status, and expectations. Stress may result for the person who is trying to fulfill the role requirements. Some cultures, for example, value the elderly and respect their acquired wisdom, whereas others consider their elders as nonproductive burdens. It is clear that the role of elders in the latter example is associated with more stress.

Adolescence in many cultures can be a stressful time. Societies that clearly define adolescence and its roles tend to be less stress inducing than cultures who lack a clear definition of adolescence and offer a variety of cultural choices.

Women are often placed in stressful roles as a result of their culture. Traditional Greek culture, for example, sees the man as the breadwinner for the family. A Greek wife who works brings embarrassment to the entire family group. A great deal of stress would result for a working woman of this particular culture.

Stress is associated with various culturally defined roles. Ways or mechanisms for coping with role-induced stress are also culturally determined. Crying, screaming, and other displays of emotion are viewed as healthy outlets for stress in one culture, whereas others expect quiet, unemotional responses to stress. Nurses who are aware of clients' cultural stresses and their associated behaviors are better able to assist them in developing effective coping skills.

Cultural Assessment

If mental illness is defined within a cultural context, then how are we to know whether clients' problems are the result of cultural conflict or mental dysfunction? "Rather than impose personal cultural values on others, the professional nurse is an active listener and analyst who develops appropriate care plans based on the insights, knowledge, and beliefs of other cultures" (Deloughery, 1995). Nurses and all care providers who work with culturally different clients must guard against the tendency to transfer their own cultural expectations onto clients or to make generalizations about clients based on their own cultural attitudes. Each client is uniquely molded by his/her culture.

It is the responsibility of all care providers to learn how clients perceive and cope within their worlds. Cultural assessments are the tools that allow us to do that. Several models and data collection tools have been developed, but all have in common six areas of assessment: communication, environmental control, space and territory, time, social orientation, and biological factors (Fig. 4-1) (Giger and Davidhizar, 1995).

Communication

People of all cultures communicate with one another. The process of communication, however, involves more than just the use of language. Communication is a complex, interwoven tapestry of voice, gesture, and touch. Both verbal and nonverbal com-

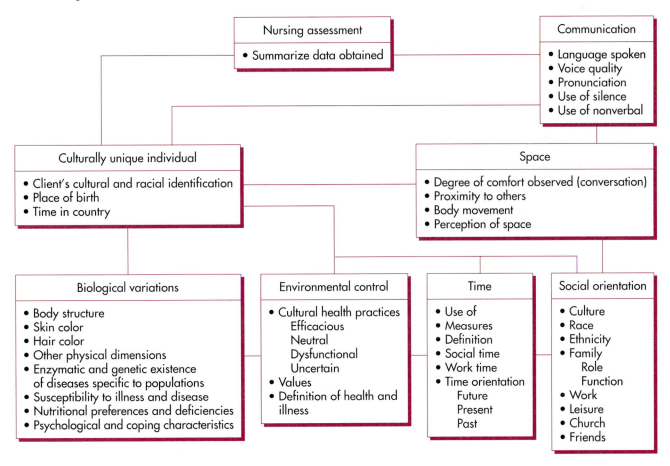

Fig. 4-1 Cultural assessment. (Redrawn from Giger JN, Davidhizar RE: *Transcultural nursing: assessment and intervention,* ed 2, St Louis, 1995, Mosby.)

ponents of communication have cultural meaning (Table 4-3).

Clients communicate their emotional states based on their cultural backgrounds. In some cultures, verbal expressions of emotion are approved, whereas members of other cultures value communicating indirectly and may resent the frankness of mental health care providers. Clients require sensitivity if nurses are to be therapeutically effective. We all communicate; some of us are just louder than others.

Cultural traditions, practices, and kinship systems all communicate. A society's religious practices communicate its basic beliefs. Attitudes toward children, family health care, and dying are all communicated through cultural customs. It is wise to learn the important customs of a culture if one is caring for many of its members (see box below).

Environmental Control

Environmental control focuses on the individual's ability to perceive and control the environment. Does the client feel that the power to effect change lies within, or is everything the result of fate, chance, or luck? What are the client's values relating to the nature of man, the supernatural, health, and illness? How are the causes and treatments for mental illnesses viewed?

In addition, environmental control includes an assessment of clients' cultural health practices. (A note of caution is necessary here. Maintain objectivity. Do not pass judgments. The goal is to provide effective care in a manner that is acceptable to the client. Do not filter their information through your values.) Have any alternative practitioners been consulted? What were the treatments? Were they effective? What is their definition of "good health" and what is done to maintain health? When alternative (folk) practices are considered in treatment, both clients and their care providers increase the potential for success.

Space and Territory

Also included in the cultural assessment are the concepts of space and territory. Space is the area that surrounds the client. It is an invisible "bubble" that travels with the person. The physical distance that a person maintains between himself/herself and others is influenced by one's culture. People consciously maintain a "comfortable" distance from each other. These space comfort areas are divided into four distances: public, social, personal, and intimate (Fig. 4-2). Observe and respect your client's degree of comfort at each distance and use of their surrounding space.

Some clients, such as the majority of people from the United States, have a need to establish territory. **Territoriality** is the need to gain control over an area

CULTURAL ASPECTS

Your client is a Xhosa from Southeastern Africa. His people believe that displeasing the ancestors results in illness. Explain how this information will affect the client (nursing) care plan.

◆ **TABLE 4-3**
Cultural Communication Assessment

Verbal Communications	Nonverbal Communications
Language	Touch
Dialect	Use of touch
Pronunciation	How touch is perceived and received
Voice quality	Space
Rate of speech	Interpersonal distance
Style of speech	Use of silence, eye contact, facial gestures (e.g., smiles, frowns)
Volume of speech	Communicates emotions nonverbally
Use of small talk, laughter	More behaviorally oriented
Music	
Written language	
Formal usage	
Regional usage	
Communicates emotions verbally	
More verbally oriented	

of space and claim it for oneself. For many people, a territory helps to provide a sense of identity, security, autonomy, and control over the environment. People will protect their territory even if it has shrunk to the size of a hospital bed and a nightstand, and health care providers can be casually careless about invading these precious spaces. Nurses need to know and respect the client's territorial space if culturally appropriate holistic care is to be given.

Time

The concept of time is rooted in a culture's basic orientation. Cultures oriented to the past (e.g., the Chinese, Amish) strive to maintain the customs and traditions of previous generations. Present-oriented cultures are focused on the current daily events of life but may not necessarily adhere to a schedule. Many Native Americans are present-oriented but not to time. Cultures with future time orientations use today as a tool for meeting future goals. Schedules are established and people are oriented to the time of day. An example of a future-oriented culture is the middle class of the United States and Canada. Western society's concept of time is linear. For cultures who feel one with nature (e.g., Native Americans), this linear concept of time is difficult to understand.

Clients with mental dysfunctions frequently have misperceptions about time. Time may pass too slowly or quickly. An inability to tell the difference between day and night can exist, and the inability to adhere to time schedules is commonplace. For mental health clients, problems with time may be based in the client's cultural orientation or the psychiatric illness. Until the nurse can discover the difference, the delivery of effective care is difficult.

Social Orientation

To assess a client's social orientation, nurses must consider the family unit as a dynamic force operating within the culture. The family unit and its importance in the society are culturally defined. It is the family unit that imparts the culture's important traditions, beliefs, values, and customs. Social orientation also includes a consideration of the meaning of work, gender roles, friends, and religion to the client.

Although the functions of the family unit (e.g., caring for the young, providing identity, security) remain similar among most cultures, the size and composi-

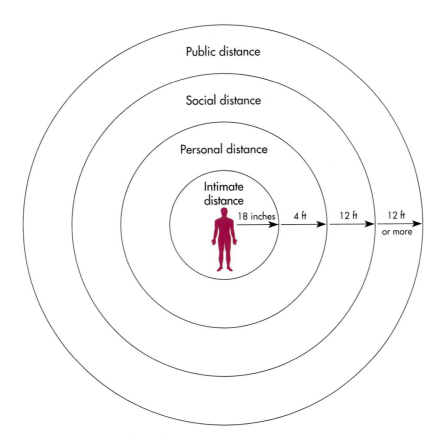

Fig. 4-2 Space and distance zones.

tion differ. Middle-class Americans live within a **nuclear family** unit consisting of a father, mother, and one or more children. However, in many cultures, aunts, uncles, grandparents, cousins, and/or godparents are included as part of the family unit. This family unit is called an **extended family**, and its importance to the client may be significant. Many groups—such as traditional Chinese, Mexicans, and Puerto Ricans—believe the family to be the supreme social organization. Family causes take priority over personal or national causes in these cultures. When nurses fail to consider the significance of the whole family, culturally sensitive nursing goals cannot be achieved.

Gender roles must also be considered when a client's culture is assessed. The traditional roles for men and women in one society may collide with the expectations of another. Women who have been enculturated to fill a serving, passive gender role may have great difficulties assuming the assertive and outspoken role of the modern Western woman. Be sensitive to this area of assessment. Few women will identify themselves as having a culturally based gender role conflict. Mental health problems more frequently seen in women include eating disorders, phobias, and depression. Men, on the other hand, tend to demonstrate more violent and abusive behaviors. Perhaps the cultural norms that identify gender roles encourage the expression of conflict in different ways.

Assessment of social orientation also includes an assessment of the client's religious beliefs and practices. Religious practices serve many functions in a culture. They bind people together in a common belief system. Religion helps to explain the unexplainable, such as unexpected deaths or natural catastrophes, and it helps to provide meaning and guidance for living.

Religious beliefs and practices vary widely. Attitudes toward health, illness, death, burials, procreation, food, and stress all have religious components. Although it is impossible to discover the inner workings of every religion, it is necessary to be aware of the religious practices of those clients with whom nurses frequently interact. Only then will you be able to differentiate between those behaviors that are appropriate cultural expressions of religious beliefs and those behaviors that indicate a pathological disorder.

Biological Factors

The final area of the cultural assessment focuses on the biological or physical differences that exist among different cultural groups. When assessing for biological factors, the nurse considers physical, enzymatic, and genetic variations; reactions to medications; sus-

ceptibility to disease; and psychological characteristics of the client's cultural group.

Physical variations include differences in body structure, eyes, ears, noses, teeth, muscle mass, and skin color. People of some races are taller than others. For example, African-Americans are usually taller than Asian-Americans. The shape of the eyelids and nose vary from one racial group to another. Even teeth vary in size and shape: "Australian aborigines have the largest teeth in the world, as well as four extra molars" (Giger and Davidhizar, 1995). In contrast, white Americans tend to have small teeth. Certain muscles of the wrist and foot are absent in some racial groups. Differences in skin color range from pale white to black, and other visible physical characteristics may be seen in certain groups. Mongolian spots, for example, are bluish discolorations of the skin that may be found in black, Asian, Mexican, and Native American newborns. In this case, knowing the client's cultural background may prevent possible misdiagnosis because Mongolian spots can be mistaken for bruises resulting from child abuse.

A person's genetic makeup is largely determined by racial group. Physical appearance, metabolic activities, and susceptibility to disease are all influenced by racial factors. To illustrate, sickle cell anemia is commonly found in the African-Americans but rarely in white Americans. Lactose (milk) intolerance is very common in black, Native American, and Asian groups yet is rare in northern European whites. Tuberculosis is common in Native Americans, whereas diabetes is rare in Eskimos.

The relationships between race and physical health have been well documented, but the relationship between race and mental health remains much hazier. Most research, however, suggests that factors other than race or ethnicity influence the development of mental illness.

Certain psychological characteristics may be related to different cultural groups. The low socioeconomic status of some groups can affect mental health when housing, education, and health care are substandard. Feelings of insecurity can result when a client's views of health care are threatened. The Hmong people of Laos, for example, believe that "losing blood saps strength and may result in the soul leaving the body, causing death" (Rairdan and Higgs, 1992). Therefore great anxiety is produced in a Hmong client when blood is drawn.

Cultural factors do affect mental health. Nurses and their colleagues must become aware of group differences if they are to consistently deliver culturally appropriate mental health care.

Culture and Mental Health Nursing

Although no society is immune to mental disorders, researchers have yet to study mental illness from a worldwide perspective. The definition and treatments of mental illness vary among cultures.

To understand and treat clients from diverse backgrounds, the practice of **transcultural nursing** has evolved. As the name implies, transcultural nursing seeks to deliver the culturally diverse nursing approaches needed for appropriate client care (Stuart, 1993). To accomplish this, the nursing process is applied within a cultural context.

It is important here to understand the unique status of refugees. By definition, a *refugee* is a person who, because of war or persecution, flees from his/her home or country and seeks refuge elsewhere. Many refugees have seen or experienced imprisonment, torture, and harrowing escapes. Some have lost family members, and all must learn to cope within a new reality.

When assessing a person who is a refugee, be extra sensitive to the possibility of stress-related problems. In addition to the routine cultural assessment, tactfully obtain the following information: immigration history, length of time in the new country, a history of the flight and arrival in the new country, and who or what was lost (Lipson, 1993). Because of a usually traumatic history, higher incidences of depression, anxiety, and stress disorders occur in refugee groups. Nurses who work with the whole person are sensitive to the special circumstances of refugees.

Nursing Process and Culture

The **nursing process** serves as an organizational framework for the practice of nursing and consists of five steps: assessment, nursing diagnosis, planning, implementation, and evaluation. Use of the nursing process encourages us to consider the client's cultural characteristics and develop appropriate, as well as effective, care measures.

The nursing assessment is the data-collection step of the nursing process. Information or data relating to the client are collected from every possible source. Medical records are reviewed. A nursing history is obtained, and observations are made. Discussions with family members or friends take place. Soon a picture of the client begins to emerge. Using this mass of information or database, the nurse plans care based on the needs, abilities, preferences, and concerns of the client. Because we understand that a person does not exist in a vacuum, an assessment of the client's sociocultural background is an important area of focus.

When conducting a cultural assessment, the nurse must remember to focus on six areas common to all cultural groups: (1) communication, (2) environmental control, (3) space and territory, (4) time, (5) social orientation, and (6) biological factors (see Fig. 4-1).

Next, data are sorted into related areas, and problems or concerns are identified. Each problem is then examined, and a nursing diagnosis is developed. Examples of nursing diagnoses that may have a strong cultural component include altered health maintenance, ineffective management of therapeutic regimen, impaired thought processes, fear, anxiety, powerlessness, self-esteem disturbance, impaired coping, and social isolation (Gordon, 1995). The importance of culture must be remembered when a nursing diagnosis is being developed.

During the planning phase, the nurse projects the outcome of each client's diagnosed problem by identifying the behaviors that indicate that the problem is solved. These "expected outcomes" are then used to monitor the client's progress. Specific goals are developed, and nursing actions (interventions) are planned.

Once nursing actions are formulated, they are communicated via a written care plan and implemented. The implementation phase includes the actual delivery of the planned nursing actions. Client responses to care are monitored. It must be remembered that many nursing actions are culturally significant to the client. To illustrate, "some Hindus believe that bathing after a meal is injurious" (Giger and Davidhizar, 1995). Knowing this, only the culturally insensitive nurse would schedule a Hindu client's bath immediately after breakfast. The nurse must work to keep an open mind when observing the client's responses to care and remember that many reactions are culturally determined.

The final phase of the nursing process, evaluation, determines the effectiveness of nursing care. By comparing expected outcomes with actual results, the nurse is able to note which nursing actions met the goal and which did not. Those actions that did not result in improvement are reassessed, and the process of planning nursing care is begun again.

Clients from other cultures, however, may evaluate their care differently (Phillips, deHernandez, and deArdon, 1994). Haitian-Americans, for example, may feel that improvement in health was not the result of good nursing care but the mystical healing power of the tree leaves kept close to the body. There exist many such customs and beliefs (see box on p. 54). If nurses, as culturally sensitive health care providers, are able to consistently view clients as unique, dynamically functioning individuals, then effective, culturally appropriate health care will be one step closer to becoming a reality.

> ◆ **THINK ABOUT**
>
> You are on vacation in Bali when you suddenly become ill with a high fever, vomiting, and diarrhea. After a long search, you finally locate a hospital. You enter the building and find that everything is strange and uncomfortable. You can't even speak the language, but you know you must be treated.
>   How do you feel about this situation?
>   What would you do to cope?

❖ KEY CONCEPTS

- Culture is a learned pattern of behaviors, values, beliefs, and customs shared by a group of people.

- Stereotyping is basing one's behavior on an oversimplified mental picture of a cultural group and may arise from positive, negative, or traditional points of view.

- Culture has several characteristics: it is learned, transmitted, shared, integrated, dynamic, and satisfying.

- Culture influences people's health beliefs and practices.

- Illness behaviors are influenced by one's perceptions and cultural outlook.

- When caring for clients from diverse cultural backgrounds, the nurse must assess each client's definition of health and illness.

- The cultural assessment focuses on six areas: communication, environmental control, space and territory, time, social orientation, and biological factors.

- Working with refugees requires added assessments and great tact because of their frequently traumatic experiences and losses.

- Because no universal descriptions of mental health and illness exist, the definition and treatment of mental illness varies among cultures.

- Transcultural nursing seeks to deliver the culturally diverse nursing actions necessary for appropriate, effective client care.

- The nursing process is an organizational framework for nursing practice. The five steps of the nursing process are assessment, nursing diagnosis, planning, implementation, and evaluation.

- When nurses are able to consistently view each client as a unique dynamic individual functioning within a sociocultural context, then culturally appropriate health care will become a reality.

❖ SUGGESTIONS FOR FURTHER READING

Transcultural nursing: assessment and intervention, ed 2, by J.N. Giger and R.E. Davidhizar (St. Louis, 1995, Mosby) is interesting reading as well as an excellent source of information for 14 cultural groups.

❖ REFERENCES

Boyle JS, Andrews MM: *Transcultural concepts in nursing care,* Glenview, Ill, 1989, Scott Foresman/Little, Brown.

Deloughery GL: *Issues and trends in nursing,* ed 2, St Louis, 1995, Mosby.

Edelman CL, Mandle CL: *Health promotion throughout the lifespan,* ed 3, St Louis, 1994, Mosby.

Gaut DA, editor: *A global agenda for caring,* New York, 1993, National League for Nursing Press.

Geissler EM: *Pocket guide to cultural assessment,* St Louis, 1994, Mosby.

Giger JN, Davidhizar RE: *Transcultural nursing: assessment and intervention,* ed 2, St Louis, 1995, Mosby.

Gordon M: *Manual of nursing diagnosis: 1997-1998,* St Louis, 1997, Mosby.

Haber J, and others: *Comprehensive psychiatric nursing,* ed 5, St Louis, 1997, Mosby.

Lipson JG: Afghan refugees in California: mental health issues, *Issues Ment Health Nurs* 14:411, 1993.

Phillips LR, deHernandez IL, deArdon ET: Strategies for achieving cultural equivalence, *Res Nurs Health* 17:149, 1994.

Rairdan B, Higgs ZR: When your patient is a Hmong refugee, *Am J Nurs* 92(3):52, 1992.

Rosella JD, Regan-Kubinski MJ, Albrecht SA: The need for multicultural diversity among health professionals, *Nurs Health Care* 15(5):242, 1994.

Stuart DL: Social and cultural perspectives: community intervention and mental health, *Health Educ Q* (suppl)1:S99, 1993.

Taylor CM: *Essentials of psychiatric nursing,* ed 14, St Louis, 1994, Mosby.

Tshotsho N: Creating a therapeutic milieu for black patients, *Nurs ASA Verpleging* 11(8):28, 1993.

Wu R: *Behavior and illness,* Englewood Cliffs, NJ, 1973, Prentice-Hall.

5

EARLY THEORIES
AND THERAPIES

1. Explain how theories can be applied to mental health care.
2. Identify the theory of human behavior that was popular from 350 BC to AD 1400.
3. Describe how Darwin's theory of evolution changed the popular attitudes of the day toward mental illness.
4. List three parts of Freud's psychoanalytic theory of human behavior.
5. Name four therapeutic techniques used in psychotherapy.
6. Identify how humanistic and behavioral theories differ in their viewpoints.
7. Discuss how Maslow's human needs theory can be used in the nursing care of people with emotional problems.
8. Explain why it is important for nurses and other health care providers to be familiar with different theories of human nature and their explanations of mental illness.

KEY TERMS

affective
anxiety
cognitive
defense mechanisms
dynamic
ego
id

inferiority
libidinal energy
model
natural selection
personifications
psyche
psychoanalysis

psychotherapy
soma
superego
theory
the unconscious

Human beings exist within an orderly but **dynamic** (ever-changing) universe; this world has sparked people's curiosity for millennia. As our ancestors evolved, they began to observe the world about them and develop ideas to explain nature and its cycles. Eventually their ideas became related to each other. When these related ideas were combined, they began to provide a framework or point of view that helped provide possible explanations for the workings of their world. The concept of theory had arrived. Today, a **theory** is defined as a statement that predicts, explains, or describes a relationship among events, concepts, or ideas. Modern theories are developed through observation and then tested through research. Although ancient people did not conduct scientific research as we know it, they did rely on their keen powers of observation and deduction. Later, theorists (people who devise theories) used models to help explain their ideas more simply. A **model** is an example or pattern that helps to explain a theory. For example, a model of an airplane can be used to present the theory of flight.

Models and theories that relate to human behavior and development have been devised to help explain the complicated creature known as the human being. Today there are theories that attempt to explain the physical, psychological, social, and cultural aspects of people. Nurses, physicians, therapists, and others in the helping professions use theories as frameworks for describing the relationships between people and various aspects of their environments. Theories are also used to help to describe the psychodynamics of people: the basic needs, drives, conflicts, perceptions, values, attitudes, belief systems, and cultural influences that shape every individual.

Historical Theories

Some of the earliest questions about the nature of man began with the alert observations of a Greek physician, Hippocrates (460-377 BC) (see Chapter 1). His humoral theory of disease linked personality types (temperaments) to each basic element or humor of the body. The humoral theory influenced the fields of medicine and philosophy for almost fifteen centuries. It was not until the dawn of the Renaissance, around AD 1400, that the humoral theory began to lose its popularity as an explanation for mental health and illness.

People during the Middle Ages perceived or thought of the world symbolically. Today we think in terms of "cause and effect": we say we understand something when we have discovered the cause or reason that brought it about. Medieval people, however, thought in terms of the *meaning* of the event, not the *cause*. "For the Middle Ages there was a perfect spiritual world just beyond the imperfect world of physical suffering and decay; one could attempt contact with the perfect reality through visions, religious ecstasy, or sorcery, and by deciphering the spiritual meaning behind everyday events" (Corsini, 1994). Medieval thinking was symbolic and magical and was used to explain how the world worked.

Paracelsus (1493-1541) revolutionized the study of mental health and illness by distinguishing between natural (physical) illnesses and spiritual (psychological) illnesses. He is credited with being the first to recognize the role of unconscious forces in illness. Apparently, he was also the first person to develop the notion of individual personality, a concept that was not readily accepted until the middle of the nineteenth century.

Darwin's Theory

Charles Darwin (1809-1882) was a naturalist, but his theory of evolution was to have a strong and lasting impact on the emerging field of psychiatry. Basically, Darwin's theory explained why some animal species became extinct while other species flourished. His theory stated that only the fittest organisms would adapt and survive and that, through the process of **natural selection,** increasingly superior creatures would evolve. In this way, nature culls the weak and preserves the strong. Darwin also published the first comprehensive work on the expression of emotion in both man and animals.

During the latter half of the nineteenth century, Darwin's theory led to the persistent belief that "mental illness was a reflection of the degeneracy of the affected individual" (Maher and Maher, 1994). It was believed that people who were impaired or unsuccessful in life were by nature lower on the evolutionary scale than their more flourishing counterparts. Poverty, disease, alcoholism, and mental illness were all claimed to be the product of a fundamentally inferior genetic makeup. High incidences of tuberculosis, rickets, infant mortality, and low adult life expectancies all "indicated that Nature was at work trying to eliminate the sufferers and prevent them from reproducing" (Maher and Maher, 1994). This popular theory of man's nature may have continued for many years had it not been for the work of new theorists who were willing to challenge the commonly held beliefs of the time.

Functional Psychology

William James (1842-1910), an American psychologist and philosopher, was a man of the world. Educated in Europe, England, and the United States, he taught the first psychology course in an American university (Harvard) in 1875 and published the first textbook on psychology in 1890. However, he is best remembered for his view of the human mind as "functional, adaptive mental processes" (Corsini, 1994).

James built on Darwin's theory of natural selection by viewing behaviors as adjustments and adaptations to the environment. His theory of emotions stated that the general causes of emotions were internal, physical, and nervous processes, not just mental or psychological events. This innovative approach to the study of man's mental processes or functions laid the groundwork for a new system of thinking in psychology known as *functionalism.* The functionalists believed that psychology should have practical applications and deal with commonsense issues. They believed that mental functions were part of a whole complex world of functioning, which included both physical and mental adaptive processes. Although functionalism no longer exists as a separate theory, it has contributed to our understanding of man by including studies relating to adaptation, experience, intelligence testing, learning, child behavior, and abnormal behavior. Today, many of the principles of functionalism have been incorporated into the mainstream of American psychology.

Psychoanalytical Theories

By the middle of the nineteenth century, various theories of mental health and illness had circulated throughout the scientific world. Physicians everywhere were exploring new curative treatments for mental illness. Dr. Joseph Breuer (1842-1905) employed the technique of hypnosis along with a new method of "talking out" symptoms. A brilliant young neurosurgeon, Sigmund Freud, heard of this "talking cure" and sought to work with the distinguished physician. By 1895, Breuer and Freud had published *Studies in Hysteria,* a collection of successful case histories in which the therapeutic use of hypnosis and the "talking cure" were used. Freud's association with Breuer faded as disagreements over the use of hypnosis as a therapy grew, and Freud began to delve further into the use of talking as a therapy for emotionally disturbed people.

After years of observation and documentation, Freud came to believe that unconscious thoughts and emotions can have a strong impact on mental functioning and behavior. By 1902, Freud had become convinced of the value of the talking cure. He called his approach to therapy **psychoanalysis,** which means to explore the unconscious. Weekly discussion groups about this new form of therapy evolved at Freud's home in Vienna. These early discussions, attended by a small number of Freud's colleagues (e.g., Alfred Adler, Otto Rank, and Carl Jung), later provided the framework for various new and different theoretical beliefs.

The nucleus of Freud's theories was that feelings of which the patient was unaware could affect behavior, usually through the expression of hysterical symptoms. His study of the unconscious processes of the mind evolved into theories about the development of the personality in psychosexual stages, the structure of the personality, and the dynamics of the personality as an energy system. These ideas, together with Freud's ability to apply his concepts to such varied topics as dream content, hysterical paralysis, and the biological nature of man, made psychoanalysis the most influential set of theories in the early twentieth century (Freud, 1964, 1966).

Over a period of the next 30 years, Freud worked to develop and test his theories of personality. By the 1920s, the one definition of psychoanalysis had broadened into three: Freud's theories of personality, a therapy for certain emotional disorders, and a method for investigating the workings of the mind. Today, the term **psychotherapy** is used to describe any therapy relating to mental health or illness. Freud's theories that are of importance to nurses and other health care providers relate to the development, dynamics, and defenses of the personality.

Theory of Personality Structure

Freud believed that the human mind was made up of three interacting structures, which he labeled **id, ego,** and **superego.** Simply stated, the id is the storage site for all the basic drives and early childhood experiences. It contains the instinctual drives for self-preservation, reproduction, and association with others. Drives arising from hunger, cold, physical discomfort, and isolation are centered in the id. The demand, "I want what I want *now,*" is characteristic of id behavior. The id is responsible for the infant's survival; the id demands satisfaction immediately and motivates all the infant's behavior until the ego begins to emerge and gain some control. Freud stated that the id is governed by the "pleasure principle" and seeks out immediate gratification (pleasure or avoidance of pain) for any and all impulses without regard to the outcome. Infants disregard all other parts of their environment as they demand immediate attention. In fact, infants have been called "bundles of id."

The word *ego* is derived from the Latin word meaning "I" and is the part of the mind that is in active awareness; in other words, the ego is the conscious mind. When people discuss one's personality, character, or intellect, they are referring to the ego. A person's character is often described by the activities of his/her ego. For example, when someone says that Mary is very intelligent or Sam has a jolly disposition, they are describing ego traits.

The ego develops as soon as the child becomes aware of "self," usually around 2 years of age. As the child grows and develops, the ego gradually gains control over the more primitive id. As the child learns about the outside world, the pleasure principle is slowly overtaken by the reality-based ego. The ego becomes the part of the personality that must cope with the external world (reality).

The superego is the last component of the personality to develop. All the attitudes, values, role expectations, taboos, rules, ideals, and standards to which the child is exposed help to form the superego.

There are two parts of the superego: the conscience, which punishes the individual through guilt and anxiety when behaviors move away from its strict, rigid standards, and the ego ideal, which rewards the individual with feelings of satisfaction and well-being for behaviors that are in keeping with the superego's expectations. The superego does not base rewards or punishments on reality. It uses internal standards of good/bad and right/wrong, which were learned early in life. These standards, according to Freud, are primarily stored in the unconscious, where they remain unavailable to awareness but still influence the ego. The superego is as demanding as the id. It is the controller of the id due to its strict, rigid, moralistic rules. The statement, "I want what I know is the right thing," is characteristic of the superego.

According to Freud, the id and the superego are not bound by the rules of the outside world. Their demands go straight to the ego, unhampered by values or external world rules. Therefore the ego must maintain the delicate balancing act of meeting id and superego needs within the limitations of the real world.

People with strong egos are considered to have a great degree of control, but too much control can be just as harmful as not enough. Behavior that is ruled by the superego can result in repressed, guilt-ridden, inhibited people. Id-dominated behavior may result in antisocial, lawless people with little control. It is the continual task of the ego to successfully balance the rigid superego with the impulses of the id, all the while interacting with the environment and realities of the world. The mentally healthy adult is said to be one who has achieved a dynamic balance among all the elements of the personality.

Theory of Personality Development

Freud's theory of personality development has the central theme of sexual instinct growth through four stages from newborn to adult. He believed that the most powerful primitive motivation was the drive to reproduce. He called this drive **libidinal energy** and originally described it as the need to seek pleasure. However, the term gradually evolved to refer to sexual energy. Thus Freud's stages of personality development came to be known as the *psychosexual theory of development*.

Freud placed great emphasis on early childhood experiences and their impact on personality development. He believed that what happens to the child during each particular stage becomes part of the adult character. Furthermore, he characterized each stage with a primary erogenous zone (an area of the body that serves as focus for excitation and pleasure) and named them the oral stage, anal stage, phallic stage, latency stage, and genital stage. Mental health results when the individual successfully moves through each stage and, as an adult, can maintain a mature sexual relationship. On the other hand, mental difficulties arise when the individual becomes fixated or stuck in a particular stage; either too much or too little satisfaction results in energy demands for the concerns of a certain stage that last throughout adulthood.

To illustrate, followers of Freud state that such activities as smoking or overeating are the remnants of unresolved oral stage demands.

Theory of Personality Dynamics

According to Freud, emotional disturbances and behavioral dysfunctions arise from five sources: (1) instinctual-biological drives, (2) early childhood experiences, (3) deeply buried unconscious experiences and attitudes, (4) fixations left over from earlier psychosexual stages of development, and (5) defensive maneuvers that help to prevent the person from changing. Freud believed that all individuals have some conflict embedded within themselves and that all individuals (sick or well) make use of psychological tools to help to lessen negative feelings. He called these psychological tools **defense mechanisms** and defined them as "psychological strategies by which persons reduce or avoid negative states such as conflict, frustration, anxiety, and stress" (Corsini, 1994) (Table 5-1). Although defense mechanisms are used to avoid negative emotional states, individuals are not consciously aware when they are being used. Furthermore, most defense mechanisms contain some inaccurate pictures of reality. For example, individuals may ignore environmental clues (denial) or express feelings toward one person that really should be ex-

◆ **TABLE 5-1**
Common Defense Mechanisms

Mechanism	Definition	Example
Compensation	Attempt to overcome feelings of inferiority or make up for deficiency	A girl who thinks she cannot sing studies to become an expert pianist.
Conversion	Channeling of unbearable anxieties into body signs and symptoms	A boy who injured an animal by kicking it develops a painful limp.
Denial	Refusal to acknowledge conflict and thus escapes reality of situation	A child covered with chocolate refuses to admit eating candy.
Displacement	Redirecting of energies to another person or object	A husband shouts at his wife, the wife then berates her child, who then scolds the dog.
Dissociation	Separation of emotions from situation; isolation of painful anxieties	A soldier casually describes the battle in which he lost his legs.
Fantasy	Distortion of unacceptable wishes, behaviors	A teenager doing poorly in school daydreams about owning a private jet airplane.
Identification	Taking on of personal characteristics of admired person to conceal own feelings of inadequacy	Teen-aged adolescents dress and behave like the members of a popular singing group.
Intellectualization	Focusing of attention on technical or logical aspects of threatening situation	A wife describes the details of nurses' unsuccessful attempts to prevent the death of her husband.
Isolation	Separation of feelings from content to cope unemotionally with topics that would normally be overwhelming	A soldier humorously describes how he was seriously wounded in combat.
Projection	Putting of one's own unacceptable thoughts, wishes, emotions onto others	A woman is afraid to leave her house because she knows people will ridicule her.
Rationalization	Use of a "good" (but not real) reason to explain behavior to make unacceptable motivation more acceptable	A student justifies failing an examination by saying that there was too much material to cover.
Reaction formation	Prevention of expression of threatening material by engaging in behaviors that are directly opposite to repressed material	A young man with homosexual feelings, which he finds to be threatening, engages in excessive heterosexual activities.
Regression	Coping with present conflict, stress by returning to earlier, more secure stage of life	A 4-year-old boy whose parents are going through a divorce starts to suck his thumb and wet his pants.
Restitution	Giving back to resolve guilt feelings	A man argues with his wife and then buys her roses.
Sublimation	Unconscious channeling of unacceptable behaviors into constructive, more socially approved areas	A hostile young man who enjoys fighting becomes a football player.
Substitution	Disguising of motivations by replacing inappropriate behavior with one that is more acceptable	A man who is attracted to pornography campaigns to ban adult book stores in his community.
Suppression	Removal of conflict by removing anxiety from consciousness	A woman with a family history of breast cancer "forgets" her appointment for a mammogram.
Symbolization	Use of an unrelated object to represent hidden idea	A girl who feels insignificant draws a picture of her family in which she is the smallest character.
Undoing	Inappropriate behavior that is followed by acts to take away or reverse action and decrease guilt and anxiety	A man physically abuses his wife and then cleans her wounds and nurses her back to health.

pressed toward another (displacement). No matter which mechanism is used, the goal remains the same—to reduce uncomfortable negative emotions.

Psychoanalytical Therapies

Early therapies based on Freud's theories were designed to assist the patient in discovering the causes of unconscious, repressed conflicts and working through the serious fixations (anxieties) that resulted from those conflicts. Freud first used dream analysis to delve into the origins of the patient's symptoms. He believed that, during sleep, the individual's censor (superego) is less active; therefore **the unconscious** (id) could express itself in dreams. Therapy centered around interpreting the dream's symbols to discover the unconscious wishes that were causing the conflicts.

The technique of free association soon followed dream analysis. With free association, the patient was presented with a series of words or phrases and then asked to state the first words that came to mind. The therapist would then "interpret" each response and give the patient the "real" meaning behind each association. This process, Freud thought, would eventually lead to the discovery of the patient's problems.

Psychoanalysis was the main form of therapy for Freud and many of his followers. Because behavioral problems were considered the result of several different factors, the process of psychoanalysis lasted for many sessions, sometimes for 2 or more years. The therapist and the patient would develop and work through an intense transference relationship, in which the patient not only remembered past experiences but also actually transferred emotions associated with significant persons (mainly parents) in the past to the therapist. Reliving the original maladaptive responses allowed the patient to use adult strengths to solve emotional difficulties that were overwhelming as a child. To achieve a cure in psychoanalysis, the patient must first recall past events and then develop insight into the meaning of each event.

Many of Sigmund Freud's theories have been challenged in today's era of scientific inquiry. Psychoanalysis is a long and usually expensive form of therapy. There has been frequent criticism for his strong focus on sexual drives as the primary motivation for all behavior, and it appears that Freud himself suffered from some of the very anxieties he described. However, his contributions have influenced the fields of psychiatry, psychology, the humanities, education, history, and the social sciences. Sigmund Freud's revolutionary theories "brought about a new level of awareness and, for better or worse, a permanently altered image of humankind" (Corsini, 1994).

New Theories Emerge

The early 1900s was a time for several new but related theories about the nature of man. By this time it was generally agreed that man was more than just a physical body. The term **psyche** was borrowed from Plato and used to define the mental or spiritual part of the person (as compared to the term **soma**, which relates to the body). Interest in this new area of study attracted such people as Carl Jung, a noted German physician; Alfred Adler, a Viennese ophthalmologist (eye specialist) and neurologist; and other far-thinking people. Here we consider a few of the more important contributions to the understanding man's nature.

Analytical Psychotherapy

Carl Jung, the founder of analytical psychotherapy, was a colleague of Freud. Jung was a physician and university lecturer whose theories differed from Freud's in two basic respects: (1) the energy that Freud labeled sexually-based libido was, according to Jung, actually a more generalized life energy, and (2) Freud stated that the personality is determined in childhood, whereas Jung believed that the personality could be changed during adulthood and is actually influenced by future plans, goals, and dreams (Jung, 1968).

Jung built on Freud's theory of personality by dividing the psyche (mind/spirit) into three levels: the conscious ego, the personal unconscious, and the deeper collective unconscious, which stores all the experiences of man's ancestral past. The components, or parts, of the collective unconscious he called *archetypes*. He identified these archetypes as the persona, the anima and animu, and the shadow (Fig. 5-1). He also coined the terms *extroversion* and *introversion* to describe outward-going and inward-focused personalities.

Jung's concept of the self focused on the importance of balance and wholeness. His theory goes beyond Freud's concepts by recognizing the spiritual realm and creative power of the individual as well as the potential for psychological growth in every person.

Jung's ideas became known as the analytical theory or school of thought. Although Jung used traditional psychoanalytical techniques, he believed that the primary effort in life was to gain more awareness. Therefore he developed therapeutic techniques in which patients learned that suffering was caused by a loss of meaning and that discovering one's archetypes could have healing powers. He helped patients understand their problems and conflicts by uncovering the symbolic meanings of their disorders. Jung and his followers also encouraged patients to experience rather

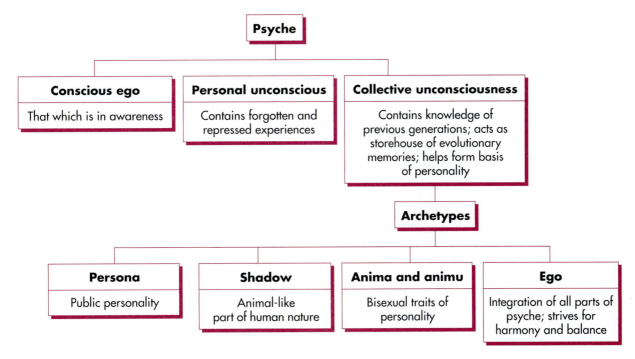

Fig. 5-1   Jung's personality system.

than just intellectually understand something, and they routinely encouraged individuals to contact and value their own inner worlds.

The analytical view of psychotherapy (therapy for the mind) did not survive as a separate discipline, but many of its concepts remain in the mainstream of psychological thought. Jung himself wrote many books and articles, but translations of his works did not reach the United States until the 1950s. He died in 1961 while working on the draft for his twenty-ninth book titled *Man and His Symbols.*

Individual Psychotherapy

Alfred Adler graduated from the Vienna School of Medicine as an ophthalmologist (eye specialist) in 1895. As a result of his interests in public health issues, Adler was invited to attend Freud's weekly discussion sessions on neurosis. These meetings eventually evolved into the Vienna Psychoanalytic Society with Adler as its president. In 1911, Adler resigned from the organization to pursue his own theories, and, by 1918, he had developed his own theory of personality and a new way of thinking that became known as individual psychology (also called Adlerian psychology).

Adler's personality theory states that the human infant, because of dependency and helplessness, starts out in this world in a position of **inferiority** (of being inadequate or less than others). The child must learn to master his/her environment by sizing up (assessing) the environment and then making certain con-

clusions about it. Each person wants to belong, to be considered as significant, and to be treated as an individual. Thus as the child grows, he/she finds where he/she fits within the family. Adler believed that it is the perceptions of the child's position within the family that help to create one's evaluations of self and other people. These evaluations in turn become incorporated into the adult lifestyle, which influences the person's movement through life.

As human beings, Adler believed that the general goals of life are to gain mastery over the environment. To do this, the adult must cope with three tasks. First is work, which includes schooling, vocational choices and preparation, use of leisure time, satisfaction with work, and retirement. Second is the social task, subdivided into the tasks of belonging and social interactions. Third is the task of coping with members of the other sex. (Adler disliked the term "the opposite sex" and thought it encouraged conflict between the sexes.) Later analysis of Adler's writings uncovered two additional life tasks, those of self and spirit. The task of self states that people must find out who they are (define themselves) and find meaning in their lives. Tasks of the spirit include the consideration of religious, philosophical, and spiritual questions.

Adlerian or individual therapy uses the fundamental techniques of psychoanalysis, but it has several of its own basic assumptions. For one, man is viewed as a total organism, functioning within the environment. This was to become the first holistic point of view.

Adlerians believed that people have the ability to make choices. They are not the victims of heredity, the environment, or their past, but individuals who are responsible for their own behavior.

Because all behavior is goal directed, people are capable of perceiving and assessing events to arrive at conclusions. However, each individual perceives the world subjectively from an individual, unique point of view. To understand a person "we must be able to see with his eyes and listen with his ears" (Adler, 1964).

All behavior is best understood within a social context. People move about in groups of other people. Therefore behavior becomes meaningful only when viewed within the social setting. Because of this viewpoint, Adlerian psychology is often called *social psychology.*

The concept of a value system was introduced by Adler. The highest value is thought to be the value for people (social interest). The concepts of choice, individual responsibility, and finding the meaning in life evolved and later became the foundation for the humanistic school of psychology.

Adlerian psychologists dislike the use of labels and do not categorize people into groups. People with mental dysfunctions are not considered psychopathic or mentally ill. They are referred to as "discouraged." Therapy is designed to encourage them to assume responsibility for directing their lives in more positive ways. To summarize, the Adlerian point of view sees people holistically as creative, evolving, responsible individuals who are moving toward goals within a social world.

Other Therapies

Other therapists during the early twentieth century also broke with the Freudian tradition. Karen Horney (1855-1952), an early follower of Freud, stressed the importance of social and environmental conditions on personality development. Her concept of "basic anxiety" stated that a child's isolation is not inherited but the result of culture and social upbringing.

Erich Fromm (1900-1980) stressed human loneliness as the motivation for social interaction (Fromm and Xirau, 1968). His general theme of productive love is seen in many of his writings. Fromm also developed several personality or character types (Table 5-2).

Interpersonal Psychology

Harry Stack Sullivan (1892-1949) considered the personality as a study of interpersonal relations. His comprehensive theory of interpersonal relationships emphasizes the social nature of people and the critical role of anxiety in the formation of the personality (Sullivan, 1968). Sullivan also believed that social interactions serve as the process for the development and treatment of mental disturbances. He viewed the personality as a pattern of interpersonal relationships. Mental health problems were considered to be the result of the patient's distorted images of certain relationships. Sullivan called these distorted images **personifications** and believed that the behavioral patterns arising from the personifications of one relationship spill over or transfer into other relationships. According to Sullivan, therapy becomes a matter of assisting the patient in discovering which personifications are unhealthy and then substituting more effective behavioral patterns.

A central theme of Sullivan's theory is the concept of **anxiety,** which he defined as a vague feeling of uneasiness felt in response to stress. Threats to one's security bring about anxiety, and the helpless infant soon learns to decrease its anxiety by communicating its discomfort. To decrease anxiety, the infant discovers which behaviors are most desired by other people. Behaviors bringing approval are strengthened, and conversely, behaviors bringing disapproval are inhibited. If the infant has not had its needs consistently met, it experiences much anxiety. As a result, avoiding anxiety becomes a central goal in later years. Sullivan described six stages of psychological interpersonal development, beginning with infancy and ending with late adolescence (Table 5-3). One of Sullivan's greatest contributions was his great sensitivity

◆ **TABLE 5-2**
Fromm's Personality Types

Personality Type	Description
Exploitative character	Satisfies needs through use of behaviors such as force and cunning
Hoarding character	Sees outside world as threat; keeps all he/she has to self and does not share
Marketing character	Considers self as commodity that can be bought, sold, or traded
Receptive character	Demands all that he/she can get; willing to take, but resists giving
Productive character	The most desirable; realizes own potentials; devotes self to welfare and well-being of all people

to the isolation and anxiety experienced by disturbed persons. Many forms of therapy have benefitted from his theories.

Psychoanalytical therapies have expanded to include several different techniques, but the foundation of treatment still lies in the use of "talking therapies." Psychoanalytical theories and therapies have had an enormous impact on the treatment of mental disorders. This view of mental illness takes into account the importance of humane, dignified care for mentally ill people. As new information about the complexities of human functioning arises, many old ideas will be challenged. Psychotherapeutic techniques will evolve as well, but the striving for a deeper understanding of ourselves never changes.

Developmental Theories and Therapies

As Freud and his followers were studying psychoanalysis, other theorists were looking at the nature of humans from the moment of arrival to the time of departure. Using Freud's theory of personality as a foundation for their inquiries, many theorists offered their views of human psychological development. Whereas Freud thought that the personality evolved through certain stages of psychosexual growth, theorists such as Sullivan believed the personality to be a collection of interpersonal experiences. Jean Piaget and Erik Erikson attempted to understand the relationships among the body, mind, and society throughout the life cycle. One of the most commonly used theories in nursing is Erikson's eight stages of psychosocial development, which represents the first attempt to explain human behavior throughout the entire life cycle.

Psychosocial Development

Erik Erikson (1902-) was trained in traditional psychoanalysis by Freud's daughter, Anna. By 1933, he had moved to the United States and accepted a position as the city of Boston's first child psychoanalyst. In 1939, he opened a private practice in Berkeley, California, where he specialized in treating disturbed youths. His academic career included teaching positions at the University of California, Yale University, and Harvard University, but he is best known for his work in developmental psychology.

Erikson described the human life cycle as composed of eight stages (Table 5-4). According to Erikson, each stage is marked by a developmental or core task, a normal crisis that must be confronted and resolved. As each crisis is resolved, it leaves its impression on the developing person, and it is these impressions that form one's total personality. The building and uniting of the personality occur as each developmental psychosocial task/crisis is mastered. Erikson believed that each developmental stage is interwoven

◆ TABLE 5-3
Sullivan's Stages of Interpersonal Development

Developmental Stage	Age	Description
Infancy	Birth–18 mo	Uses crying to communicate; needs human contact; organizes patterns of sensation and emotional responses *Task:* to develop security by learning to rely on others to meet needs
Childhood	19 mo–6 yr	Identifies self; masters space, objects, language; needs interaction with peers and adults; shows anxiety, guilt, shame, and anger *Task:* to learn to accept outside control and interference with own wishes
Juvenile	7-9 yr	Uses competition, cooperation, compromise to cope; needs to be accepted; develops self-esteem *Task:* to develop satisfying relationships with peers
Preadolescence	10-12 yr	Uses cooperation, group agreement as tools; needs a chum, friend or loved one; develops compassion and capacity to love *Task:* to learn to relate to same-sexed friend
Early adolescence	13-14 yr	Needs intimacy; experiences lust and anxiety; develops capacity for love and empathy *Task:* to develop satisfactory relationships with members of opposite sex and become independent
Late adolescence	15-21 yr	Masters social conventions; develops capacity for happiness *Task:* to become interdependent and establish intimate and durable sexual relationships

◆ **TABLE 5-4**
Erikson's Stages of Psychosocial Development

Developmental Stage	Age	Core Task and Associated Quality	Description
Oral-sensory (infancy)	Birth–1 yr	Trust/mistrust Associated quality: hope	Dominated by biological drives and needs; learns to trust that needs will or will not be met; learns to trust or mistrust others and world in general
Anal-muscular (early childhood)	1-3 yr	Autonomy/shame and doubt Associated quality: will (to do the expected)	Demands for self-control influence feelings of self-confidence vs. shame and doubt in own abilities; ego is developing; parallel play
Genital-locomotor (preschool years)	3-6 yr	Initiative/guilt Associated quality: purpose	Actively explores environment; activities are directed with purpose; conscience develops; cooperative play; uses fantasy; imitates adults; beginning to evaluate own behavior
Latency (school age)	6-12 yr	Industry/inferiority Associated quality: competence (learning skills of adult)	Site of learning moves from home to school; masters skills and tasks valued by teachers and society; learns to behave according to rules; develops confidence and perseverance; practices self-restriction
Puberty (adolescence)	12-18 yr	Identity/diffusion Associated quality: fidelity (commitment to value system)	Combines experiences to form sense of personal identity; forms sexual relationships; plans for future; feels confused and indecisive; if successful with prior crises, will develop strong sense of identity; peer groups important
Young adulthood	18-25 yr	Intimacy/isolation Associated quality: love	If has strong sense of identity, is willing and able to unite own identity with another; develops devotion; commits to relationships, career If weak sense of identity, has impersonal, short-term relationships; shows prejudice; becomes socially isolated
Middle adulthood	25-65 yr	Generativity/stagnation Associated quality: caring	Strives to actualize identity that was formed in earlier stages; generates or produces children, ideas, products, services; is creative, productive, concerned for others; demonstrates caring through parenting, teaching, guiding others; adults who do not care become stagnant, self-indulgent, absorbed in themselves
Maturity	65 yr–death	Integrity/despair Associated quality: wisdom (to accept one's life and value contribution that one has made)	Adjusts to changes; senses flow of time, past, present, and future; accepts worth and uniqueness of own life as it was and is; finds order and meaning in own life; despairs when life is viewed as waste; adults who focus on what "might have been" blame others, feel a sense of loss and contempt for others

with the next and that success with the crises of one developmental stage prepares individuals to move into the next stage. Poorly resolved developmental (core) tasks continue to haunt the person throughout successive stages until they are dealt with and mastered. The box below presents a case study of a person with an inadequately resolved developmental task. Erikson's theory is commonly used by nurses as a framework for assessing and planning individualized client care.

Cognitive Development

Jean Piaget (1896-1980) devised a theory of intellectual (cognitive) development. His first scientific paper was published at the age of 10; by 21, he had earned his doctorate degree. In 1952, he became a professor of child psychology at the Sorbonne in Paris. There he continued to develop and revise his theories of intellectual growth during childhood.

Basically, Piaget believed that the personality is the result of interrelated intellectual (**cognitive**) and emotional (**affective**) functions (Piaget and Inhelder, 1969). Growth is an increasing intellectual ability to organize and integrate (combine) experiences. Piaget observed that certain organizational patterns (behaviors) occurred in steps at certain age groups, so he divided these patterns into four main stages of intellectual growth: the sensorimotor stage, the preoperational stage, the stage of concrete operations, and the stage of formal operations (Table 5-5).

CASE STUDY

Susan is an attractive 42-year-old housewife and mother of four teenaged children. She has been married to Jeff, a long-haul truck driver and her high school sweetheart, for 22 years. The family is well respected in the community because Susan frequently volunteers for charitable projects. All the children are considered well behaved and polite. In all respects, Susan is a model wife, mother, and community member. Last week, however, Susan announced her unhappiness, left everything behind, and ran away with a 25-year-old traveling salesman.

Clinical Decision

1. How would Erikson's theory of psychosocial development explain Susan's behavior?

◆ TABLE 5-5
Piaget's Stages of Intellectual (Cognitive) Development

Developmental Stage	Age	Developmental Task	Description
Sensorimotor	Birth–2 yr	To recognize permanence of objects	Unable to do things or distinguish self from environment; reflexes evolve into repeated actions that become coordinated movements; learns that objects in environment are still present even when they are not seen, touched, tasted; begins goal-directed and imitative behavior
Preoperational	2-7 yr	To develop symbolic mental abilities	Thinking limited; centered on self; learns to use language as tool; establishes routines; thought is focused on only one part of situation; cannot understand more than one dimension of object; justifies own behavior at all costs
Concrete operations	8-11 yr	To develop logical, objective thinking	Understands numbers, length, mass, area, weight, time, and volume; can see interrelations; able to reflect and discover relationships in environment
Formal operations	12-15 yr	To learn to think abstractly	Able to consider all possibilities of situation; can think in terms of probability and proportions; uses problem-solving approach to conflicts

Piaget believed that as children grow, they struggle to find a balance (equilibrium) between themselves and their environments. Piaget believed that they seek this balance through assimilation and accommodation. *Assimilation* is the process of developing abilities to handle new situations using existing coping mechanisms. The process of *accommodation* occurs when children must handle new situations or experiences that go beyond their previous coping abilities. The equilibration process (as Piaget called it) is the integrating or weaving of new knowledge into one's existing structure. Although no specific therapies are based on Piaget's work, his theories have become essential components of our understanding a uniquely human characteristic—intellectual growth and development.

Theories of psychological and personality development are important for nurses and other health care providers. By understanding where a client is in relation to the developmental tasks that challenge us all, nurses are better able to provide effective health care and individually tailored emotional support. Time spent by the nurse in supporting clients through their developmental phases may help to provide the energy that moves them toward success.

Behavioral Theories and Therapies

The foundation for the behavioral theories and their therapies lies in the assumption that all behavior is learned. The behavioral school of thought stated that human behavior is the outcome of past learning, current motivation, and biological differences (Corsini and Wedding, 1989). Learning is a behavioral change that results when individual actions repeatedly prove successful and are thus reinforced. Dysfunctional behaviors are the result of learned maladaptive behavioral habits. Behavioral theories take a mechanical approach to human behavior by focusing only on objective, observable, and measurable behaviors. The influence of the environment on both human and animal subjects is stressed, but all behaviors are seen as responses to stimuli. Four important figures were instrumental in establishing the behavioral movement: Pavlov, Watson, Skinner, and Wolpe.

Cornerstone of Behaviorism

Ivan Pavlov (1849-1936) studied animal physiology in Russia and medicine in Germany. By 1897, he had become director of the physiology department at the Institute of Experimental Medicine in Saint Petersburg, Russia. There he pioneered his experiments and devised his theories on conditioning for which he was awarded the Nobel Prize in 1904 (Pavlov, 1941).

Basically, Pavlov's precise and objective research methods allowed him to evaluate the responses of dogs to various stimuli. By studying the animal behaviors, Pavlov discovered that a given behavior was the response to a given stimulus. His famous experiment of conditioning dogs to salivate when they heard a bell demonstrated the mechanical aspects of behavior. Pavlov then went on to discover that behaviors were more likely to be repeated when they were rewarded or reinforced and faded or became extinct when ignored or not rewarded. Behaviors that were successful in the past tended to become generalized over time and were applied to current situations. Although Pavlov was fundamentally a physiologist, his work on conditioning laid the foundation for the development of the American behavioral movement led by John B. Watson.

American Behaviorism

The behavioral school of thought was established in the United States during the 1920s by John B. Watson (1878-1958), an animal psychologist who only gradually developed an interest in human subjects. Watson was the first graduate of the University of Chicago with a degree in psychology in 1903. After completing his doctorate on animal education, he left Chicago for a professorship at Johns Hopkins University. There he devised the basic viewpoint for behaviorism: psychology is an objective science, the science of behavior. He published two books on behaviorism, and by the 1920s, Watson's theories gained popularity. However, in 1920, Watson's career took a drastic turn when he was abruptly dismissed from Johns Hopkins. Although he continued to publish a few papers on human conditioning, he never regained his enthusiasm for behaviorism. However, when he died in 1958, his views on behaviorism were a strong force in American psychology.

B.F. Skinner

Burhus Fredrick Skinner (1904-1990) was one of the most influential minds of the twentieth century. As a continual promoter of objective psychology, Skinner stated that only observed behaviors in current situations were open to analysis. Using this point of view, he developed the concepts of operant conditioning, positive and negative reinforcement, and shaping (Skinner, 1963).

Skinner's first research efforts were focused on developing a set of learning principles. White rats and pigeons were taught to press a certain lever in their cages to receive a pellet of food, which Skinner labeled a *reinforcer*. Positive reinforcers served as rewards for specific behaviors, as demonstrated by the results of his experiments with animals. He also found that negative reinforcers produced anxiety when the organism engaged in specific unacceptable behaviors. (Punishment is an example of a negative reinforcer.) Skinner believed that all organisms moved toward pleasure and away from pain. Therefore his theory proposed that the continual rewards of positive conditioning strongly enforce the desired behaviors, whereas negative reinforcements weaken and fade out undesirable behaviors. The process of guiding the individual to replace unacceptable responses with more desirable behaviors was called *shaping,* and the overall approach to changing observable behavior became known as *operant conditioning.*

By 1953, Skinner was applying his theories of behavior and learning to human subjects. His results were published in his book titled *Science and Human Behavior.* Throughout the 1960s, Skinner crusaded for improvements in the educational system in the United States. He developed the concept of programmed learning, a process whereby new knowledge is broken down to small bits of information and presented at the learner's own pace. Today, programmed learning techniques are commonly used in business and industrial training courses. Many of his ideas remain controversial, but his contributions to the objective study of human behavior had a strong influence on the science of psychology.

Other Behavioral Therapies

Others researchers built on the foundations laid down by these early theorists. During the 1960s, Joseph Wolpe explained neuroses and anxiety as conditioned responses. Dollard and Miller developed their stimulus-response theory, which emphasized reward as the most essential element in forming new behavioral responses. Today's behavioral therapists believe that emotional problems stem from poor learning, conditioning, dysfunctional self-thinking, lack of skills, avoiding anxious situations, and misconceptions about reality. Therapeutic techniques focus on understanding the client's current behavior. Past history is important only to the extent to which it affects present actions.

Behavioral therapists actively teach clients how to change dysfunctional thought and behavioral patterns through the use of *behavior modification techniques.* They also provide social skills training if needed and assist clients in learning to control the stimuli that cause them problems. Assertiveness training is used to teach clients to express themselves in constructive, nonaggressive ways. Behavior modification therapies are used to replace undesirable behaviors with more appropriate actions. The behavioral school of thought is rooted in the use of research as a tool for the continual refinement and improvement of treatment strategies.

Humanistic Theories and Therapies

By the middle of the 1950s, the two main schools of thought in the study of human behavior were the psychoanalytical and the behavioral. One stressed the powers of the unconscious, whereas the other defined behavior in terms of stimulus and response. Much of the data for both theories was collected through experimental research, and most of the work was conducted within the academic setting. Critics began to believe that something was missing in the theories of the day, and several of them began to look at human nature from a different point of view. As a new humanistic outlook was considered and adopted, a "third force" in American psychology evolved into the field of humanistic psychology.

Humanistic theories are an important part of many of today's therapies. The humanists view a person as a whole and emphasize the totality of an individual. All realms of the human condition are considered important. The physical, emotional, spiritual, intellectual, and social aspects of one's life influence the journey toward reaching one's greatest potential. Humanists also believe in the innate goodness of human nature, and they focus on the positive aspects of humanity. In short, humanistic psychology views the nature of man as holistic and as a multidimensional (many-sided) individual who adapts to stress within a dynamic environment. These ideas serve as the foundation for the concept of holism and the model of comprehensive health care delivery. As the values of personal freedom, equal opportunity, and individual responsibility gain popularity, so will the humanistic theories that embrace these concepts.

Perls and Gestalt Therapy

The first contribution to the humanistic movement was made by Fredrick Perls (1893-1970), a German-born physician who worked with brain-injured soldiers after World War I. Although he studied psychoanalysis, it was his years of work with his injured patients that sparked the idea of the gestalt, which means "whole." From this concept, Perls developed his own psychotherapy, which he termed *Gestalt therapy.*

Perl's therapy accepted the notion of unresolved conflicts in the past, but he also stressed the present, freedom, responsibility, and attempts to become whole (or "actualized," as it was later called). Clients were encouraged to "act out" their emotions, frustrations, and conflicts to work through their difficulties.

The therapist assumed an authoritarian role, which emphasized candor and frank emotional expression. Critics of Gestalt consider this approach to be too strict to foster personal growth, but the contributions of Perls' Gestalt therapy paved the way for further exploration into the human side of man's nature.

Maslow's Influence

Abraham Maslow (1908-1970) and his theories have had a strong impact on the practice of nursing and health care delivery. Maslow's background was in Gestalt therapy, which served as the fuel for his ideas about a holistic psychology. He received his Ph.D. from the University of Wisconsin in 1934 and published his first paper on human motivation in 1943. Maslow published extensively on such subjects as personality, motivation, self-actualization, and human nature. Along with Carl Rogers and other holistic thinkers, he founded the American Association of Humanistic Psychology. Maslow died in 1970, leaving behind a rich legacy for the appreciation of the more positive aspects of humanity.

The core concept of Maslow's theories is that human nature is essentially good and contains the inherent potential for self-fulfillment (Maslow, 1968, 1971). From this basic viewpoint, Maslow explored how people cope with and adapt to their situations. His investigations of people who function at highly successful levels led to his theory of motivation, which has become widely adopted throughout the health care professions.

Basically, Maslow grouped human needs into a hierarchy (ranking). He then categorized two basic realms of human needs: those that allow us to function adequately as people and those "that enable us to be optimally functioning human beings" (Epting and Suchman, 1994) (Fig. 5-2). The lower order needs include the physical and social requirements of the human organism. Without the fulfillment of these fundamental needs, the individual will perish. The physical (physiological) needs for air, water, food, elimination, and reproduction take first priority. For example, when the relief worker asked the starving child who he was, he replied "I'm hungry." The child's need for

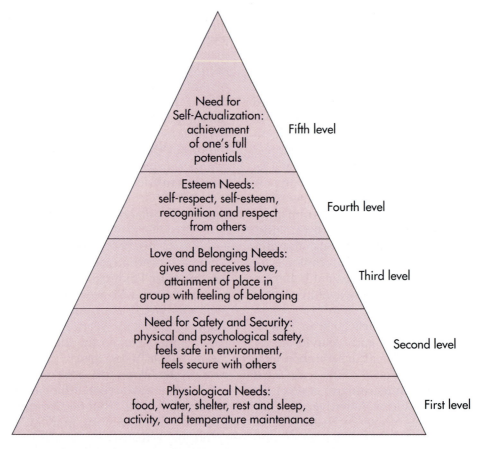

Fig. 5-2   Maslow's hierarchy of needs. (Data from Maslow A: *Motivation and personality,* ed 2, New York, 1970, Harper & Row.)

self-respect was not as great as his need for food. Second-priority needs relate to safety and the need to feel secure and protected. Intellectual and social growth are difficult when a person must be constantly vigilant or protective. Love and belonging needs come next. Every individual needs to feel accepted as part of a group or family. People who are lonely or isolated have unfulfilled belonging needs. Last are the needs for esteem and respect. These needs include the need for self-respect and esteem and the need for the respect of others.

The higher order needs for optimal functioning include aesthetic and self-actualization needs. Aesthetic needs relate to the values of beauty, goodness, order, justice, and simplicity, whereas self-actualization needs encourage individuals to develop to their highest potential—in other words, to be the best one can be. Maslow believed that when these needs go unmet, the individual can actually develop physical and psychological illnesses. For example, if one's need for order is unfulfilled, then anxiety may result. Unmet needs for truth may result in suspiciousness and a distrust of others, whereas the lack of beauty can result in a vulgar, negative outlook.

To understand the nature of self-actualized people, Maslow believed it was important to study the characteristics of individuals who were highly successful. He found that they all had several similar characteristics (see box below).

Today, Maslow's hierarchy of needs is the basis for much of the planning done for client care. His theories also serve nurses as a method for prioritizing care. For example, maintaining a client's airway (a physical need) takes priority over his/her need for belonging, and the need to be loved and accepted must be met before one can achieve full potential. Many clients encountered in today's health care environments are suffering from unmet basic needs. To deliver effective health care, nurses and other providers must be able to accurately assess and plan therapeutic interventions according to the client's most critical unmet needs. Teaching a client to correctly self-administer insulin, for example, will be ineffective if the client has

no home or way of obtaining regular meals. Maslow was instrumental in the development of humanism, but he also gave health care providers the tools for designing effective health care.

Rogers' Client-Centered Therapy

Another founding member of the humanistic school was Carl Rogers (1902-1987), the developer of a new approach to psychotherapy. Rogers studied Freud's teachings and received his Ph.D. from Columbia University in 1931. After 6 years of working as a child guidance therapist, he became influenced by the theories of Otto Rank, a psychoanalyst who stated that people have a self-directing ability that emerges during therapy. Rank broke from the traditional, mechanical techniques of therapy and stated that the client should direct the therapeutic relationship using the therapist as a guide to self-understanding and acceptance. Planted with these seeds of Rank's ideas, Rogers moved to Ohio State University and began work on a new system of psychotherapy.

Rogers built on Maslow's work by stressing the goal of self-actualization (Rogers, 1961). He believed that the goal of therapy is to assist clients to become increasingly more aware of their own experiences and emotions. From Otto Rank's ideas, he built on the concept of the therapeutic relationship between client and therapist. Contrary to the controlled and focused psychoanalytical therapies, Rogers thought that the therapeutic relationship should be warm and accepting, with an open, trusting climate in which clients can safely and freely express themselves. He believed that the therapist's task is to reflect clients' feelings and support their work toward healthy functioning and self-actualization.

With further research, Rogers refined his theories and spent the last 15 years of his life applying his methods to areas outside psychology (Rogers, 1980). Such disciplines as nursing, pastoral counseling, and education have benefitted from his efforts. He also worked with many leaders, policy-makers, and groups experiencing conflict, but his greatest legacy was his focus on the positive, achieving side of man's

CHARACTERISTICS OF HIGHLY SELF-ACTUALIZED PEOPLE

Comfortable with reality	Accepts self and others
Expresses self spontaneously	Able to solve problems
Independent, self-directing	Needs privacy and detachment
Has emotional depth	Identifies with humanity
Has a high social interest	Appreciates life
Expresses creativity	Has gentle sense of humor
Shows democratic values	Knows difference between "means" and "ends"

nature, which gave many people the permission they needed to accept themselves.

Current Humanistic Therapies

Many humanistic theories are with us today. The concept of "holism" has led to the development of a holistic health care model in which every client is viewed as a unique person functioning within a dynamic, changing environment. The concept of basic needs is used today to plan and prioritize nursing care, to allocate scarce resources, and to assist others as we all travel the path of self-development.

Mental illness, from the humanistic point of view, results when individuals refuse to risk living fully, are unwilling to control their own lives, overconform, or refuse to experiment with their desires and emotions. Therapy is designed to promote change by helping clients to find a sense of inner truth, release emotions, and take charge of their lives.

Several new therapies have evolved from the humanistic movement. Everett Shostrom developed a system of therapy based on the goal of self-actualization rather than cure or symptom relief. His actualizing therapy assists clients in learning to trust their inner or "core" selves despite life's negative influences.

Viktor Frankl's psychotherapy was based on a person's need to search for meaning and values in life. He called his system of treatment *logotherapy,* based on the Greek word *logos,* which is defined as "meaning." His ideas of human worth and dignity grew out of his 3-year experience in a concentration camp (after having lost his entire family) during World War II.

Even the traditional psychoanalytical school of Freud was influenced by humanism. I.H. Paul blended traditional analysis with Roger's client-centered therapy and developed nondirective psychoanalysis, a 2- to 4-year system of therapy that involves introspection, reflection, and a willingness to look into oneself. As time passes, newer therapies will evolve, but each will be grounded in the basic premise of humanism: people are complex, dynamic, multidimensional beings who strive for personal fulfillment.

Early theories about the nature of man sparked inquiries that further encouraged investigations and experiments of new thoughts as well as refinements of old ideas. Because of these efforts, our concepts of human behavior are entirely different than those of Freud's time. As new knowledge is discovered, our understanding of human nature will expand and encourage us to explore the most complex of all worlds, the one inside the self.

❖ KEY CONCEPTS

- Theories and models help to explain human development and behavior.
- The humoral theory began with Hippocrates around 400 BC and remained unquestioned until the 1400s.
- Charles Darwin's theories led to the belief that mental illness was the result of inferior genetic makeup and a lower place on the evolutionary scale.
- Sigmund Freud's study of the unconscious processes of the mind evolved into theories about the development, structure, defenses, and dynamics of the personality.
- Analytical psychology was founded by Carl Jung, who built on Freud's theories and recognized the spiritual and creative powers of people as well as their potential for growth.
- Alfred Adler's individual therapy focuses on the concepts of choice, individual responsibility, and finding the meaning in life.
- Harry Stack Sullivan described six stages of interpersonal (social) development and believed that the therapist's role was to sensitively assist clients in understanding how distorted images contribute to the anxiety and isolation in their lives.
- Current psychoanalytical therapies include talking and behavioral therapies.
- Erik Erikson's theory of the stages of psychosocial development states that as each developmental (core) task is mastered, the individual builds and unites his/her personality.
- Jean Piaget's theory of cognitive (intellectual) development describes four stages of intellectual and emotional growth.
- The foundation for behavioral theories and their therapies lies in the assumption that all behavior is learned and is seen as responses to stimuli.
- Ivan Pavlov developed the concept of conditioning, and John B. Watson stated that psychology was the objective science of behavior and began the movement known as behaviorism.
- B.F. Skinner's experiments found that positive reinforcement enforced behaviors, whereas negative reinforcement weakened behaviors.
- Behavioral therapies today focus on teaching clients how to change their dysfunctional thoughts and behavioral patterns.
- Examples of behavioral therapies include behavior modification techniques, assertiveness training, and training in the social skills.
- Humanistic theories view the individual as a whole and as a multidimensional person who adapts to stress within a dynamic environment while striving for self-fulfillment.

- The concept of gestalt (whole) led Fredrick Perls to develop a system of therapy that stressed the present, personal freedom, and attempts to become a whole person.
- Maslow's hierarchy of needs theory categorizes physical and psychological requirements for optimal functioning and describes the characteristics of successful, highly self-actualized people.
- Carl Rogers built on Maslow's work by stressing the goals of self-actualization and awareness.
- Current humanistic theories have led to the concepts of holistic health care, planning based on priorities of human needs, and therapies designed to assist clients in taking charge of their lives.

❖ SUGGESTIONS FOR FURTHER READING

Creative coping: a cognitive behavioral group for borderline personality disorders, by Miller, Eisner, and Allport in *Archives of Psychiatric Nursing* (8:280-285, 1994) describes the application of two theories (behavioral and cognitive) as part of a treatment group for clients with diagnoses of borderline personality disorders.

❖ REFERENCES

Adler A: *The individual psychology of Alfred Adler: a systematic presentation in selections from his writings,* ed 2, New York, 1964, Harper & Row.

Corsini RJ, editor: *Encyclopedia of psychology,* ed 2, New York, 1994, John Wiley.

Corsini RJ, Wedding D, editors: *Current psychotherapies,* Itasca, Ill, 1989, F.E. Peacock.

Epting FR, Suchman DI: Optimal functioning. In Corsini RJ, editor: *Encyclopedia of psychology,* ed 2, New York, 1994, John Wiley.

Freud S: The history of the psychoanalytic movement. In *The standard edition of the complete psychological works of Sigmund Freud,* vol 14, London, 1964/1914, Hogarth Press.

Freud S: *The complete introductory lectures on psychoanalysis,* ed 2, New York, 1966/1933, Norton.

Fromm E, Xirau R: *The nature of man,* New York, 1968, Macmillian.

Jung CG: *Analytical psychology: its theory and practice,* New York, 1968, Random House.

Lowry RJ: *Abraham Maslow: an intellectual portrait,* Monterey, Calif, 1973, Brooks/Cole.

Maher BA, Maher WB: Personality and psychopathology: a historical perspective, *J Abnorm Psychol* 103(1):72, 1994.

Maslow AH: *Toward a psychology of being,* ed 2, New York, 1968, vanNostrand Reinhold.

Maslow AH: *The farthest reaches of human nature,* New York, 1971, Viking Press.

Pavlov IP: *Conditioned reflexes and psychiatry,* New York, 1941, International Publishers.

Piaget J, Inhelder B: *The psychology of the child,* New York, 1969, Basic Books.

Rogers CR: *On becoming a person,* Boston, 1961, Houghton Mifflin.

Rogers CR: *A way of being,* Boston, 1980, Houghton Mifflin.

Skinner BF: Behaviorism at fifty, *Science* 140:951, 1963.

Sullivan HS: *The interpersonal theory of psychiatry,* ed 2, New York, 1968, Norton.

6

CONTEMPORARY THEORIES AND THERAPIES

LEARNING OBJECTIVES

1. Explain the main concept underlying systems theories.
2. Discuss how Glasser's reality therapy differs from Ellis' rational-emotive-behavioral therapy.
3. Describe the concept of homeostasis.
4. Explain how Selye's theories of stress and adaptation influence the delivery of nursing and other health care.
5. State the primary purpose of crisis intervention.
6. Identify how theories of nursing can be applied to the care of people with mental-emotional problems.
7. Discuss why psychobiology is being called the "fourth revolution" in mental health care.
8. Describe three kinds of psychotherapy used in the treatment of mental disorders.
9. List three somatic therapies for treating mental illness.

KEY TERMS

acupuncture
closed system
cognition
coping mechanisms
covert modeling
crisis
crisis intervention

equilibrium
homeostasis
life space
neuropeptides
neurotransmitters
open system
phototherapy

psychobiology
psychoneuroimmunology (PNI)
psychosurgery
psychotherapy
somatic therapies
stressor

By the 1950s, four schools of thought (psychoanalytical, behavioral, Gestalt, and humanistic) existed in American psychiatry. Behaviorism was popular until the 1960s when the "cognitive revolution" emerged as an attempt to expand the narrow "stimulus-response" viewpoint of pure behaviorism. Since then, theories about human systems, communications, sociocultural natures, and biobehavioral responses have been developed. Separate fields of study have combined their efforts and developed into interdisciplinary sciences as explorations of human nature spilled over into the disciplines of anthropology, sociology, medicine, nursing, and economics. Many innovative therapies have been introduced as the results of new research become available. This is an exciting time for mental health care providers.

Systems Theories

Systems theorists view human beings as functioning within a set of related units (called systems), which interact continually with the individual. Historically, the origins of systems theories lie in Gestalt psychology. Royce and Powell (1983) built on earlier theorists' work by developing the "open and closed systems" concept. They defined an **open system** as having boundaries that are permeable, passable, and accessible. Matter-energy and information pass easily among open systems; thus the organism grows and flourishes. A **closed system**, however, has rigid, impermeable boundaries that shut out information and energy. If the system remains closed, the organism no longer grows and eventually will die.

Field Theory

Kurt Lewin (1890-1947), who was trained in Gestalt psychology, developed his field theory from the belief that to understand any behavior, the total situation must be considered. Lewin rejected any notions of the past, the future, or cause and effect. The immediate present was the only focus of attention. He thought of people as systems, interacting with other systems across boundaries. His concept of **equilibrium** states that each system attempts to maintain a balance or steady state within itself and among other systems.

Lewin also developed the concept of **life space:** the psychological field or space in which one moves. Life space includes oneself, other people, and objects as they are perceived by the individual. Behavior is thus viewed as a function of life space. Lewin also posed the concept of *psychological tension,* which he believed results from the interaction of opposing forces or systems. Although his work is involved and difficult to understand, Lewin's theories have influenced the development of several therapies.

Cybernetics

The idea of systems with feedback or regulating mechanisms that controlled, or at least influenced, behavior sparked further studies of the self-regulating systems of the body. Maxwell Maltz published a popular book in 1960 titled *Psycho-cybernetics,* which explained how "positive thinking" works by programming one's behavior to automatically achieve the self-image that has been adopted (thought about). Maltz defined psychocybernetics as the study of the automatic control system formed by the brain and nervous systems. He believed that thoughts influence this system, so positive thoughts and images would therefore encourage the system to replace unwanted behaviors with new actions (Maltz, 1960).

Systems theory psychology has provided a point of view that differs from other theoretical approaches. Systems theorists believe that behavior does not occur in response to an external stimulus but originates within the organism. All living creatures are open systems with input, output, and regulating feedback mechanisms. People are open systems in a state of continual exchange, interacting with other people, with their environment, and within themselves. The systems theorists developed the concept of people as dynamic and evolving.

Cognitive Theories and Therapies

The word **cognition** is a general term that means "to know." It includes the mental activities of attention, language, imagery, memory, perception, and problem solving. The development of modern cognitive psychology began around the turn of the century with the work of Paul DuBois, a Swiss psychologist who believed that mental illness resulted from incorrect ideas. His *rational psychotherapy* changed the incorrect ideas through the use of reason and logic. Somewhat later, Alfred Adler's *individual therapy* replaced maladaptive behaviors, thereby increasing social interest and cooperation. Jean Piaget contributed to cognitive psychology by demonstrating the importance of intellectual factors in human development.

Even the behaviorists, who believed that all behavior was the result of stimuli, began to recognize the importance of the intellect in governing human behavior. Albert Bandura's *social learning theory* established a relationship between cognition and behavior. His work focused on the importance of learning through imitation, the use of symbols, and one's capacity for self-regulation through reflection and control. According to Bandura, people learn by observing the outcomes of various situations (Bandura, 1986). These observations then develop into related expectations and emotions. As a result, people compare themselves to others and make judgments based on their own expectations. Thus our decisions determine our behaviors.

Today's cognitive therapies differ from traditional psychotherapies in several areas. The importance of intellect is stressed more than emotions and behaviors. From the cognitive theorists' point of view, it is the understanding of an event that triggers emotions and thus causes behavior. The main goal of all cognitive therapies is to replace dysfunctional assumptions, beliefs, and thoughts to bring about a change in the client's personal, private views. By attacking dysfunctional behaviors head on and then teaching specific coping skills, cognitive therapists assist their clients to develop successful self-control strategies. Current cognitive therapeutic techniques are grouped into three categories: cognitive restructuring, coping skills, and problem-solving skills.

Cognitive Restructuring Therapies

The best examples of these techniques can be seen in Ellis' rational-emotive-behavioral therapy, Beck's cognitive therapy, and Meichenbaum's self-instructional therapy. The focus of the first two approaches is to change or restructure faulty beliefs and assumptions. Self-instructional therapy has the goal of changing one's self-verbalizations or "self-talk."

During the 1950s, Alfred Ellis developed a theory of personality and system of treatment based on the irrational beliefs and unrealistic expectations people hold of themselves. He saw emotions as arising not from the event but from the cognition (perception) of the event. In short, it is not the event or situation but the belief or value placed on the event that determines behavior. Based on this premise, Ellis developed treatment approaches that became known as *rational-emotive-behavioral therapy (REBT)*.

The goals of REBT are to help clients gain insight into the irrational beliefs that cause their disturbed behaviors, cease actively reinforcing the disturbed behaviors, monitor the effects of their thoughts, and adopt more appropriate outlooks by practicing (modeling) more effective thoughts.

Aaron Beck described how distorted thinking could lead to depression (Beck and others, 1979). Focusing on one's failures tended to generalize a failure into other areas, which resulted in a tendency to see nothing but negative outcomes. His *cognitive therapy* helped clients to recognize their self-defeating tendencies and replace them with more adaptive thinking.

Donald Meichenbaum's *self-instructional training* took a different approach to therapy. He believed that undesirable behaviors were the result of faulty instructions given in childhood (Meichenbaum, 1989). Patterns of behavior that may have been useful in the past (e.g., fighting) may now be considered maladaptive. Therapy, according to Meichenbaum, consists of learning a pattern of new self-instructions. The techniques of imagery, modeling, and anxiety control are used to help the client adopt the new self-instructional (self-talk) pattern.

Coping Skills Therapies

Several models have recently been designed to teach clients how to develop more successful daily living skills. During the 1970s, Joseph Cautela described the process of **covert modeling,** the act of mentally rehearsing a difficult performance or event before actually doing the activity. This "mental practice" has been used by sport psychologists to improve the performance of their players.

Coping skills training is similar to covert modeling except that anxiety is first induced and then the client is trained to "relax the images away." In addition to anxiety management, other coping skills taught by cognitive therapists include training in assertiveness, progressive relaxation, and techniques to reduce the physical responses to stress.

Problem-Solving Therapies

Some cognitive therapists believe that the cause of dysfunctional emotions is an inability to successfully solve problems. "Failure to solve significant problems in life, they (cognitive therapists) maintain, leads to these unhappy states" (Matheny and Kern, 1994). Problem-solving therapy teaches clients to solve their problems in more constructive and satisfying ways. The box on p. 75 lists the steps in the problem-solving process. Note the similarities between this and the nursing process.

Reality Therapy

William Glasser (1925-) received his M.D. from Case Western Reserve University in 1953. After moving to California, he founded the Institute for Reality Therapy and began to educate people about his therapeutic techniques.

Glasser's theory, like Maslow's, states that people are born with certain basic needs. The following are among the most important needs:

1. The need to be loved and belong
2. The need to gain self-worth, respect, and recognition

Unlike Freud, Glasser believed that the problems of mental illness are rooted in the failure in the social realms (areas) of human functioning. His "three Rs"

PROBLEM-SOLVING PROCESS

1. State the problem.
2. Collect information about the problem.
3. Identify the causes or patterns of the problem.
4. Examine all possible options.
5. Choose the best option and apply it to the problem.
6. Examine the outcomes of the options application.
7. Evaluate and revise actions based on outcomes.

of therapy encourage clients to do what is "realistic, responsible, and right" (Glasser, 1965).

Reality therapists help clients to examine and evaluate the effectiveness of their behaviors. Many mentally troubled persons deny the world about them. Reality therapists help clients to face their situations and then develop more effective and appropriate ways to meet their needs. Therapists and clients plan the behavioral changes that will best fulfill the client's most basic needs first.

Glasser defined responsibility as the ability to meet one's needs in a way "that does not deprive others of the ability to fulfill their needs" (Glasser, 1965). He described people with mental illness as irresponsible and believed that values, ethics, and morals provide the basis for right behaviors. Beside being used as a therapy for mentally troubled individuals, Glasser's methods have been taught to thousands of educators, who follow the principles of his book *Schools Without Failure.*

Sociocultural Theories

Theories that focused on the social nature of people were introduced in the early twentieth century with the inquiries of George Mead, who believed that the social setting is extremely important in the development of self-consciousness and that the concept of self is developed through interactions with significant others (Mead, 1934). Mead believed that as children learn the rules and norms of their society, they take on or assimilate the behaviors associated with those controls. Breaking the rules results in social rejection. An individual becomes labeled if behaviors do not fall within acceptable social limits. Mead's concepts encouraged theorists to consider the social aspects of behavior.

Mental Illness as Myth

Thomas Szasz was born in Budapest in 1920 and received his education as a psychiatrist in the United States. During the mid-1950s, he began to publish a series of books and articles attacking the concepts of mental illness. His main argument was that deviant (different or unusual) behavior was culturally defined. Szasz stated that all societies have individuals whose behaviors are considered abnormal, but what may be viewed as normal in one society may be seen as unusual, threatening, or psychotic in another society. Szasz believed that societies must have a way of controlling their more undesirable members. Many societies do this by labeling these people as "mentally ill" and removing them to institutions where they are taught to conform to society's approved behaviors (Szasz, 1974).

According to Szasz, people are responsible for their own behavior. Even those labeled mentally ill have the choice to take part in the labeling process by allowing it to occur. He also strongly objected to describing maladaptive behaviors as illnesses. Illness lies in the body only. Mental illness is not an illness at all but a socially defined condition. Szasz believed that the purpose of institutionalization is to remove the labeled individual from the community and exert some control over the person's behaviors.

Regarding treatment, Szasz believed that psychiatric clients should be able to freely choose their own therapist and treatment plans based on the premise that clients can be helped only if they ask for it. Clients initiated therapy, defined the problems they wanted to solve, and worked with the therapist to change their behaviors. The role of the therapist was to make suggestions, point out possible ways to change, and act as the client's advocate, but the therapist never directed or pushed the client. Therapy was completed when the client felt satisfied with the behavioral changes. Szasz's social perspective of deviant behavior has sparked many a debate and the reexamination of the moral, legal, and political aspects of modern psychiatry.

Multicultural Outlooks

The sociocultural aspects of human behavior continue to be a strong topic of research and discussion. From the research of many cultures comes the realization that any unusual behavior must be considered within the context (environment) within which it occurs. Culture is the framework for behavior, and mental health care providers throughout the world are considering the need for a multicultural viewpoint for the care of those people who do not adapt well to their particular society.

The field of *community psychology* has evolved from the social changes of the 1960s and focuses on promoting changes in society at the community level.

Community therapists work with local groups and organizations to correct or improve any number of social conditions such as hunger, homelessness, teen pregnancies, and social conflict.

The failure to consider a client's background can lead to difficult interpersonal situations and ineffective nursing care. Understanding sociocultural aspects of a client's behaviors allows nurses to plan and deliver individualized, effective health care with respect for each unique person.

Biobehavioral Theories

Biological and biobehavioral theories follow the medical model, which states that disease (mental and physical) is the result of abnormalities in the structure, function, or chemistry of the body. Mental health practitioners using the medical model focus on the physical or biological aspects of the problem. First, a thorough medical history and physical examination are performed. Next, laboratory tests, certain imaging techniques, and electroencephalograms (brain wave recordings) are used to assist in diagnosis. The problem-solving approach is then applied to the data, and treatment plans are developed. Therapy is considered effective when the cause of the problem has been eliminated. Today, the fields of behavioral medicine and psychophysiology are dedicated to uncovering new knowledge about man's inner chemical and biological workings.

Homeostasis

Walter Cannon, in the 1920s, was the first theorist to consider the physical or biological aspects of mental illness. His research on the changes in the body's physiology during emotion led to the observation that the body always attempts to stabilize itself. Cannon believed that an emotion is a reaction that causes the body to use its resources. He described an "emergency syndrome," which consists of a total body response that results in flight, fright, or fight behaviors when the individual is challenged or threatened. He also identified the roles of the hypothalamus and adrenal glands in the stress response. These and other discoveries about the autonomic nervous system led Cannon to formulate the concept of **homeostasis**, which he defined as the tendency of the body to achieve and maintain a steady internal state. Disease, in his view, was the fight to maintain the body's homeostasis (balance) within an open system.

Cannon's concept of homeostasis served as the foundation for many later developments. The concept of homeostasis has also been applied to family systems (Jackson, 1968), holistic health, and world ecology.

Stress Adaptation Theory

Hans Selye (1907-1982) was educated in Paris, Rome, Germany, and Canada. During his many years of study, he repeatedly observed students who were "just feeling sick." This undefinable syndrome led him to study Cannon's emergency syndrome, which launched Selye toward years of research into the physical and biochemical changes associated with stress. The results of his studies led Selye to believe that many physical problems (e.g., hypertension, arthritis, coronary artery disease) are related to an individual's inability to control stress (Selye, 1976).

Selye described the physical response of the body to stress. He defined a **stressor** as a nonspecific response of the body to any demand placed on it. Stressors may be physical, chemical, or emotional in origin and positive or negative in quality. Marriage or graduation from college are examples of positive stressors, whereas illness or financial troubles illustrate negative stressors. Selye thought that every person coped with many stressors on a daily basis. This daily dose of stressors made up what Selye called the "wear and tear" on the body. His objective measurements demonstrated that most people respond to stress in the same physical manner regardless of the stressor.

Selye's stress adaptation theory (also called the *general adaptation syndrome*) is used to describe the body's physical responses to stress and the process by which people adapt. The general adaptation syndrome states that the body reacts to stress through three stages of adaptation: alarm, resistance, and exhaustion (Fig. 6-1).

When stress is first perceived, Selye noted that the brain triggers an alarm reaction that releases hormones (epinephrine, norepinephrine) and prepares the body to stand and defend itself or run away from the threat, the fight-flight response (Fig. 6-2). If the individual successfully adapts by coping with the stress, the body's heightened level of functioning returns to its usual, prestress state. However, if the stress cannot be resolved, the body continues to function at a high metabolic rate and progresses toward the next stage of adaptation.

The stage of resistance is the body's optimal attempt to cope with the stress. All the individual's coping skills and defense mechanisms are mobilized. Hormone levels and other physical measurements may return to normal, but problem solving becomes difficult. The individual becomes more susceptible to other, unrelated stresses. During the stage of resistance, one either adapts to the stress or progresses to the body's final attempt at homeostasis, the stage of exhaustion.

When stressors have been overwhelming or unrelenting (lasting too long), the individual's resources

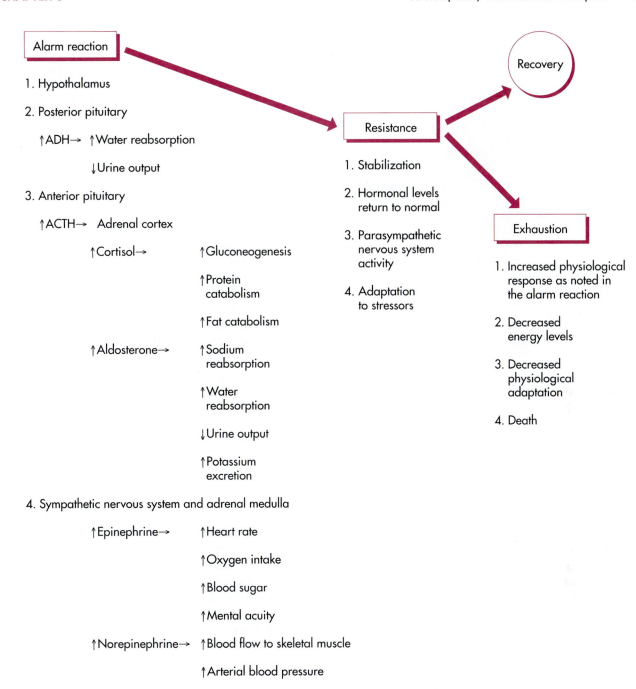

Alarm reaction

1. Hypothalamus

2. Posterior pituitary

   ↑ADH→ ↑Water reabsorption

   ↓Urine output

3. Anterior pituitary

   ↑ACTH→ Adrenal cortex

   ↑Cortisol→ ↑Gluconeogenesis

   ↑Protein catabolism

   ↑Fat catabolism

   ↑Aldosterone→ ↑Sodium reabsorption

   ↑Water reabsorption

   ↓Urine output

   ↑Potassium excretion

4. Sympathetic nervous system and adrenal medulla

   ↑Epinephrine→ ↑Heart rate

   ↑Oxygen intake

   ↑Blood sugar

   ↑Mental acuity

   ↑Norepinephrine→ ↑Blood flow to skeletal muscle

   ↑Arterial blood pressure

5. "Fight-flight"

Resistance

1. Stabilization

2. Hormonal levels return to normal

3. Parasympathetic nervous system activity

4. Adaptation to stressors

Recovery

Exhaustion

1. Increased physiological response as noted in the alarm reaction

2. Decreased energy levels

3. Decreased physiological adaptation

4. Death

Fig. 6-1   General adaptation system. *ADH,* Antidiuretic hormone; *ACTH,* adrenocorticotropic hormone. (Redrawn from Potter PA, Perry AG: *Basic nursing: theory and practice,* ed 3, St Louis, 1995, Mosby.)

become depleted (used up) and the organism begins to exhaust itself. Body processes begin to break down as glands cannot continue to produce the elevated levels of hormones required to meet the threat. Thinking becomes illogical and distorted. Problem solving and sometimes communication are ineffective. Unless the prolonged stress is removed or adapted to, the individual continues to use all physical and emotional resources until death from exhaustion results. Chilling examples of Selye's general adaptation syndrome can be observed in the accounts of prisoners of war and concentration camp survivors of the World War II.

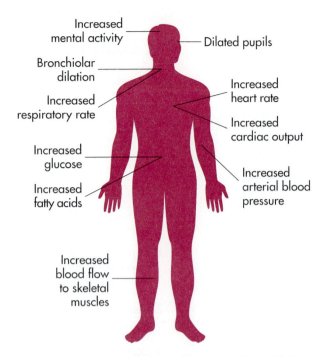

Increased
mental activity

Dilated pupils

Bronchiolar
dilation

Increased
heart rate

Increased
respiratory rate

Increased
cardiac output

Increased
glucose

Increased
fatty acids

Increased
arterial blood
pressure

Increased
blood flow
to skeletal
muscles

Fig. 6-2 Physical assessment findings of fight-flight response. (Redrawn from Potter PA, Perry AG: *Basic nursing: theory and practice,* ed 3, St Louis, 1995, Mosby.)

Selye's research on the effects of stress have strong implications for caregivers. Nurses must take into account the stress levels of each client. The effectiveness of many treatment plans has been diminished by overlooking a client's stresses. Selye's work also illustrated the tremendous impact that stress has on the body systems. This finding reminds us that effective health care can neither be given nor received if stress levels are ignored.

Crisis Intervention

Each person copes with stress in his/her own way. When experiencing stress, people call on or use their resources to direct their efforts toward decreasing their discomfort. These efforts are known as **coping mechanisms,** and they are defined as any thought or action aimed at reducing stress. All of us use coping mechanisms throughout our lives. Coping mechanisms are the tools that help us cope with the ups and downs of daily living.

All aspects of the personality are involved with coping mechanisms, and for the sake of discussion these aspects are divided into three main types: psychomotor (physical), cognitive (intellectual), and affective (emotional). Table 6-1 describes each type of coping mechanism. When coping mechanisms are successfully used, an individual is able to solve the problem and reduce the anxiety or stress. These are considered adaptive or constructive coping mechanisms. However, when the efforts to decrease stress are used without resolving the conflict, then the coping mechanism is labeled as maladaptive or destructive.

Crisis is an upset in the homeostasis or steady state of an individual. A crisis has several characteristics that separate it from other stressful situations. First, the definition of crisis is a very individual matter. Whether an event or situation is defined as a crisis depends on the individual's perception of the event, the severity of the threat, and the available coping strategies and resources. The crisis can be viewed as a threat to basic needs, a loss, or a challenge. "If the problem is viewed as a challenge, it is more likely to be met with a mobilization of energy and purposeful problem-solving activities" (Parad, 1965).

Second, a crisis occurs when an individual's usual coping mechanisms are ineffective. The crisis demands a new solution outside the person's previous life experiences. The individual must now strive to develop new coping strategies.

Third, crisis is self-limiting. Because human organisms cannot endure high levels of continued stress, crises are usually resolved (successfully or otherwise) within approximately 6 weeks. The solution to the crisis may result in a return to the precrisis state, a higher level of functioning, or maladaptive behaviors that foster a lower level of functioning.

Fourth, a crisis usually affects more than one person. Every significant other within the person's social support system is affected by the crisis. It is important to remember that clients function within social systems. No nursing or other therapeutic intervention is successful until clients are assessed within the context of their total situation and appropriate social systems are considered.

As people experience a crisis, they travel through similar stages. The components or parts of the crisis state are perception, crisis, denial, disorganization, recovery, and reorganization (Fig. 6-3).

Once an event or situation is defined as a crisis, an overwhelming feeling of denial is experienced. This emotion may last for several hours, and it serves to protect the individual or family from a sudden onslaught of intense stress. As the reality of the situation begins to sink in, an increase in tension is felt as attempts are made to eliminate the problem. All efforts to cope are ineffective, and the individual or family enters a stage in which everything seems to "fall apart."

During the disorganization phase, activities of daily living are no longer continued. Individuals become obsessed and preoccupied with the crisis situation.

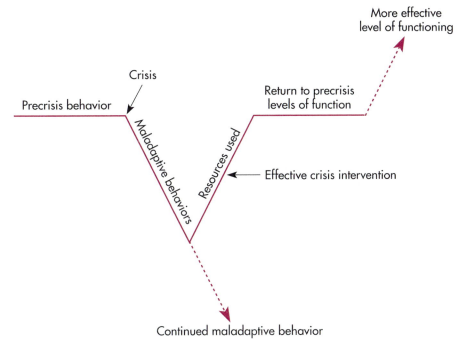

Fig. 6-3 Stages of crisis.

◆ TABLE 6-1		
Types of Coping Mechanisms		
Mechanism	**Description**	**Example**
Psychomotor (physical)	Efforts to cope directly with problem	Confrontation, fighting, running away, negotiating
Cognitive (intellectual)	Efforts to neutralize threat by changing meaning of problem	Making comparisons, substituting rewards, ignoring, changing values, using problem-solving methods
Affective (emotional)	Actions taken to reduce emotional distress; no efforts are made to solve problem	Ego defense mechanisms such as denial and suppression; see Chapter 5 for other ego defense mechanisms

Past experiences may be symbolically linked to the present situation, and the person or family becomes "flooded" with anxiety. Attempts are made to reorganize or escape the situation. Individuals may blame others or consciously pretend the situation does not exist, but neither behavior defuses the crisis. This is the stage at which most people seek help. Once all attempts to deny, solve, escape, or ignore the problem have failed, the individual or group will slowly move toward the last stage—reorganization.

Reorganization occurs when the first attempt to cope with the problem results in a success. This one successful situation encourages the person or family to try something else. Soon one success builds on another, and the normal activities of daily living are resumed. When the crisis is successfully resolved, the in-

dividual or family is able to function at a higher level than before. Growth, however difficult, has taken place, and the individual or group becomes stronger and more capable of coping with the next crisis.

Crises can also result in unsuccessful resolutions or pseudoresolutions (Taylor, 1994). Unresolved crises result when maladaptive behaviors are used to obscure (hide) the problem. An example is the husband who sends his wife to counseling for depression while he continues to abuse her when he drinks. The problem of his pattern of alcohol consumption and abusive behavior is hidden by the focus on her depression. Crises with unsuccessful resolutions usually result in a return to homeostasis but at a lower level of functioning.

Pseudoresolution occurs when nothing is learned from the crisis experience. As a result, there is no change in the level of functioning because the opportunity for growth was missed. Mechanisms such as repression or denial help to stuff the crisis into the background, where it will not demand energy. However, the appearance of any new stressors may trigger the buried conflicts of the unresolved crisis. The inability to solve future crises may be compounded by these old conflicts.

Crisis intervention is the emotional first aid provided for victims of physical or psychological trauma. The main goal of every crisis intervention procedure is to help individuals and families to manage their immediate crisis situations by offering immediate emotional support. People are then assisted to develop new or more effective coping mechanisms, which in turn allow time to reorganize their resources and support systems.

Crisis intervention procedures do not follow hard and fast rules. Because crisis is an immediate situation, the individual or family often demonstrates confused, disorganized, or even dangerous behaviors. Many times, people are not even aware that they are in a state of crisis. Their anxiety is revealed through vague complaints or symptoms, sometimes accompanied by feelings of dread or doom. Sensitive and skillful intervention is needed to prevent further disorganization and to return the client to homeostasis.

Victims of crisis are treated in such settings as emergency rooms, clinics, jails, places of worship, homes, and even over the telephone. Crisis hotlines are 24-hour telephone lines that are staffed by volunteers trained in crisis intervention techniques. Emotional support and referral to various community resources are offered to any caller.

Guidelines relating to crisis intervention have been developed and refined by the National Institute for Training in Crisis Intervention and other organizations. These guidelines have been taught to health care providers, educators, police officers, attorneys, ministers, and volunteers. Because crisis situations are high-stress encounters for all parties, the following guidelines can assist in providing safe effective crisis interventions:

First, *care is needed immediately.* As soon as the client is encountered, actions must be taken to reduce anxiety levels. Sometimes this may require only reassurance. In other instances, actions must be taken to ensure safety and prevent harm. Therapeutic interventions that require only minutes can have a lasting effect on the client.

Second is *the issue of control.* Persons who are experiencing a crisis are often unable to exercise control over themselves or their situation. Safety for both client and care providers must be considered. The therapist or intervener must quickly assume control over the client's behavior and the situation but only until the client is able to recover self-control. Again, the level of control is determined by the individual situation. Some people are relieved that someone else is in control, whereas others resort to physical aggression during a crisis. Control is important in a crisis situation because without it, the client cannot be helped to work with the problems that triggered the crisis.

Third is *assessment.* Although assessments usually are the first step in the care process, the issues of immediacy, safety, and control must be considered first in cases of crisis. During this phase, the situation is assessed thoroughly. Ask direct questions such as "What happened? What led up to the crisis? Who is involved? What attempts have been made to reduce the stressful situation?" Have the client explain the crisis situation and review the events of the past 2 weeks. A quick, accurate assessment of the total situation helps to determine the most appropriate therapeutic interventions.

Fourth, the client's *disposition* is determined. A treatment plan is developed that assists the client with working on the problems triggering the crisis. The "game plan" encourages clients to work things out themselves. The focus of crisis intervention therapy is not to resolve clients' problems but to help them manage their problems more effectively.

Fifth is *referral,* an often overlooked part of crisis intervention. Once emotionally stabilized and in control, clients may be referred to professional, community, or support group resources. The most successful referrals are the result of matching the client's needs with the most appropriate service. Know which resources are available within your community before interacting with the client. Corsini (1994) reminds us that "looking through the yellow pages during an intervention generates lack of confidence and invites problems for all concerned."

Sixth is *follow-up,* the last guideline of crisis intervention. Care providers must see if the referrals were actually contacted. Often a follow-up telephone call to a person seen in a crisis will reveal new problems that prevent the client from receiving needed care.

All people experience crisis. When new coping mechanisms are needed but are unavailable because of immaturity, an individual experiences a developmental or maturational crisis. Severe stresses within one's environment may bring about a situational crisis. Any trauma, physical or emotional, can result in a crisis. Assisting people in crisis to mobilize their resources is an important goal for any provider of health care.

Psychobiology

With the great advances in technology, scientists have been able to objectively document the inner workings of the brain and its relation to behavior. To accomplish this requires the efforts of researchers from varied disciplines. The fields of psychology, sociology, epidemiology, and anthropology are melding their knowledge with the biomedical sciences of physiology, biochemistry, immunology, and endocrinology. This uniting of knowledge and technology is introducing a new movement known as the "psychobiological revolution."

"**Psychobiology** is the study of the biochemical foundations of thought, mood, emotion, affect, and behavior" (Wilson, 1994). By applying the latest developments in imaging technology and biochemistry, researchers are beginning to explore human mental experiences and emotional states. Such techniques as positron emission tomography (PET) and magnetic resonance imaging (MRI) are linked to powerful computers that are now able to actually "see" thought processes. The techniques "show how specific regions of the brain 'light up' when activities such as reading are performed and how neurons and their elaborate cast of supporting cells organize and coordinate their tasks" (Raichle, 1994). Researchers are now using these technologies to learn about mood disorders, schizophrenia, language problems, and many other conditions. Biochemists are exploring the role of **neurotransmitters** and other messenger systems in behavior, while immunologists are attempting to unravel the secrets of the body's defense systems, especially when exposed to stress.

This area of research is spawning new theories, fields of study, and therapies. Psychobiological theories about the causes of mental illness relate to genetics, neurotransmitter activity, viruses, fetal development, and immune system dysfunction. The developing field of *neuropsychology* is devoted to the study and treatment of behaviors related to brain functioning. The interdisciplinary field of *cognitive psychophysiology* blends the disciplines of psychology and physiology to study mental processes by monitoring selective body systems, and the new science of *neurobehavioral toxicology* is exploring the behavioral changes that result from exposure to toxins in the environment. It is truly an exciting time for the discovery of new knowledge about the inner workings of the human being.

Psychoneuroimmunology

The division of man into parts was made by Plato. Based on this theory, philosophers stated that one set of laws governed physical events, whereas another, separate set of laws governed mental events. This view dominated philosophical and psychological thought for centuries. Recently, however, researchers concluded that the mind/body division was a "socially constructed" concept and have begun to favor models that illustrate the united mind and body into one wholly functional unit. Simply stated, researchers are beginning to see the human being as holistic, that is, more than just the sum of many parts (systems).

Jonas Salk (1961) developed a model of disease that encompassed the genetic, neurological, immune, and behavioral systems. Ader (1981) later built on this model by reframing the traditional ideas of the mind and body. His studies on the effects of stress on the immune system led him to coin the term *psychoneuroimmunology,* abbreviated as PNI. **Psychoneuroimmunology (PNI)** is the study of the *interactions* between the body's central nervous system, its immune system, and aspects of the personality.

Ader's studies demonstrated that anxiety and depression can decrease immune system functions. Other researchers (Wickramasekera, 1988) found that opiate (pain-relieving) mechanisms in the brain could be activated by the body's own neuropeptides (endorphins) and by electrical stimulation of certain sites in the brain. Pain control by activating the opiate pathways of the brain has been seen in athletes, yogis, and women during labor. Some nurses are using this knowledge to help their clients cope with severe pain by teaching them to turn on the body's own pain-relieving mechanisms.

Research into neurotransmitters (the body's messenger system) uncovered the existence of **neuropeptides,** a type of neurotransmitter composed of amino acid strings. Further research found that amino acid strings of neuropeptides actually connect the endocrine, immune, and nervous systems. Other studies have demonstrated the two-way neuropeptide communication network that links the brain and immune system with other systems. It is believed this neurobiochemical system provides the pathway for emotional reactions, which the body uses to defend itself. As research continues to expand our knowledge, there is mounting evidence that emotions, stress, and attitudes have an impact on the body's immune response.

Just as stress can decrease immune functioning, studies are beginning to demonstrate that various interventions can have a positive impact on the immune system. Research conducted by Gruber, Hersh, and DuBois (1988) found that relaxation exercises increased the production of antibodies. Positive emotional states, with humor and laughter, have been shown to increase an immune component in saliva (Dillon, Minchoff, and Baker, 1985-1986). As the results of new research become known, our concepts of mental health and illness will change. What we know now *will* change during the upcoming psychobiological revolution.

Nursing Theories

It is important for nurses to understand human behaviors from a helping point of view. Theories of nursing apply to the care of people's emotional problems as well as their physical problems. Theories of nursing began in the 1860s with Florence Nightingale, who saw illness as the body's attempt to repair itself. By the 1960s, several models of nursing attempted to explain the health and illness behaviors of people.

Today, most theories and models of nursing consider people as biopsychosocial entities who respond to stress in highly individualized ways. Some nursing theorists view people as dynamic open systems who continually interact within physical and social environments. A disruption in one system affects the whole person, with each individual displaying a continuum (range) of behavioral responses to stress.

The focus of the therapeutic process for nursing is on assisting clients to use appropriate resources and abilities to cope with their problems. Nurses collaborate with the client and other caregivers to develop a specific plan of care that addresses each area of difficulty. Long-term and short-term goals are identified, and clients participate in the evaluations and revisions of their care plans. Nurses may work with many therapeutic techniques, but all therapy is designed to assist clients in achieving their highest possible level of wellness. (See Table 6-2 for a brief explanation of several nursing theories.)

As the results of research studies become available, new therapies will be introduced and our understanding of "mental illness" will broaden. Current therapies for mental health problems are grouped into two basic categories: psychotherapy and somatic therapy.

Psychotherapies

Psychotherapy is a broad term that includes a number of distinct therapeutic approaches. It is defined as the treating of mental and emotional disorders by psychological rather than physical means. Psychotherapies began with Freud's talking cure (psychoanalysis) and now include behavior therapies, cognitive therapies, crisis intervention, and hypnosis. Psychotherapeutic sessions may be on a client-therapist basis (individual therapy) or may take place in a group setting. Therapists now tend to use several therapies rather than identifying with a single orientation.

Individual Therapies

Clients who are involved on a one-to-one basis with a therapist are involved in individual therapy. *Psychoanalysis* is a type of individual therapy that sees deviant behavior as the result of poorly resolved conflicts, inadequate ego defenses, and anxiety. Clients analyze the meaning of certain behaviors and symbols and learn to cope with their problems by understanding the meaning or significance of their behaviors.

Another commonly used Freudian-based therapy is *client-centered psychotherapy*, which is based on the premise that "each person has within themselves the resources for constructive change" (Smoyak, 1993). Although client-centered therapy uses the same theory base as psychoanalysis, the role of the therapist differs considerably. In psychoanalysis, the therapist remains aloof; in client-centered therapy, he/she expresses empathy to encourage growth and healthy change. Mobilizing the client's inner resources via the therapeutic relationship is the goal of client-centered therapy.

Cognitive therapy is designed to help clients intellectually identify and correct their distorted thinking and dysfunctional beliefs. The therapist's role is active and structured to focus on solving the problem within a limited time.

Recently, a form of this type of therapy, called *brief-term therapy*, has been introduced in the United States. Studies at St. Louis University (Librach, 1994) have demonstrated that brief-term therapy (6 to 12 sessions) can be as effective as long-term psychotherapy. The focus of brief-term therapy is to attend to the problem that faces the client at the moment. Brief-term therapy has been effective for managing depression, marriage and family problems, and stress (Cade and O'Hanlon, 1993). Further research is needed to determine the impact on clients with more severe problems.

Behavioral therapy is a type of individual therapy that is tailored to each person's needs, behavior, and environment. Behavior modification techniques are used by therapists and clients to define positive behaviors and develop programs with specific reinforcements to change behaviors. This type of therapy has proven effective with mentally retarded persons and persons with severe forms of mental illness.

Hypnosis and *meditation*, although not distinct therapies, are often used in combination with individual psychotherapies. The traditional definition of hypnosis is the induction of a relaxed, trancelike state in

◆ **TABLE 6-2**
Summary of Nursing Theories

Theorist	Goal of Nursing	Framework for Practice
Hildegard Peplau	To develop interpersonal interaction between client and nurse	Interpersonal theoretical model emphasizing relationship between client and nurse
Faye Abdellah	To delivery nursing care for whole individual	Problem solving based on 21 nursing problems
Ida Orlando	To respond to client's behavior in terms of immediate needs	Three elements, including client behavior, nurse reaction, and nurse action, composing a nursing situation
Virginia Henderson	To help client gain independence as rapidly as possible	Henderson's 14 basic needs
Dorothy Johnson	To reduce stress so that client can recover as quickly as possible	Adaptation model based on seven behavioral subsystems
Martha Rogers	To help client achieve maximal level of wellness	"Unitary man" evolving along life process
Imogene King	To use communication to help client to reestablish positive adaptation to environment	Nursing process as dynamic interpersonal state between nurse and client
Dorothea Orem	To care for and help client to attain self-care	Self-care deficit theory
Betty Neuman	To assist individuals, families, and groups to attain and maintain maximal level of total wellness by purposeful interventions	Systems model of nursing practice having stress reduction as its goal; nursing actions in one of three levels: primary, secondary, or tertiary
Myra Levine	To use conservation activities aimed at optimal use of client's resources	Adaptation model of human as integrated whole based on "four conservation principles of nursing"
Sister Callista Roy	To identify types of demands placed on client and client's adaptation to them	Adaptation model based on four adaptive modes: physiological, psychological, sociological, and independence
Madeleine Leininger	To care for individuals and groups in a culturally specific method meeting their health conditions	Cultural sensitivity with attention to the social structure through ethnonursing care
Jean Watson	To promote health, restore clients to health, and prevent illness	Philosophy and science of caring: caring is an interpersonal process comprising interventions that result in meeting human needs

From Potter PA, Perry AG: *Basic nursing: theory and practice,* ed 3, St Louis, 1995, Mosby.

which the individual is receptive to appropriate suggestions. However, Bierman (a full-time emergency room physician) offers the idea that "hypnosis is simply ideas evoking responses" (Bierman, 1995). He focuses on the concepts of human patterns and consciousness, and his work with acutely traumatized clients demonstrates the power of the health care providers' words and actions.

Bierman believes that the therapeutic hypnotic situation consists of three patterns: (1) rapport between therapist and client, which is used to build (2) linkage (or patterns of momentum, rhythm) with the client.

Once this interaction is established, the therapist can move to the therapeutic suggestion, using (3) the pattern of authority.

Bierman states that, as a result of the need to be instructed when we are young, we are all linked to a pattern of authority, which most health care providers fail to recognize. He believes that authority patterns influence the care provider–client relationship and that ideas communicated by care providers bring forth certain client responses. These responses may be beneficial or harmful for the client, whose attention or consciousness becomes "linked" to the words of the care provider. No special state or trance is needed. No special relationship or process is required. Hypnosis is just ideas and responses.

This viewpoint has profound implications for all care providers. We must be aware of the power and importance of our communications. Carefully expressed ideas, using well-crafted phrases, will produce more positive client response and avoid the harm of negative patterning. The box below illustrates the use of Bierman's response-evoking hypnosis.

Meditation has been used as a part of Eastern religions for more than 2500 years. It has recently gained popularity in the West as a tool for combating stress. Many therapists who recommend meditation for their clients practice meditation daily themselves (Goleman, 1992).

Although there are many techniques and systems for meditation, each has four common elements: concentration, retraining the attention to one item while excluding all other thoughts, mindfulness, and an altered state of consciousness (Goleman, 1992). The physical effects of twice daily meditation sessions include "slower heart rate, decreased blood pressure, lower oxygen consumption, and increased alpha brain wave production" (Moore, 1994). Meditation techniques have been used successfully in the fields of education, business, medicine, and mental health care. As the objective evidence for the stress-reducing effects of meditation becomes known, more people will engage in this form of self-improvement.

Other psychotherapies will continue to be introduced as our knowledge of the human creature broadens. Cultural differences are beginning to influence how therapies are designed and applied. Various therapeutic approaches will be developed, but all are founded in the most important concept of therapy: that of one human being caring for another.

Group Therapies

A group is two or more people who come together for a specific cause. The use of groups to help people in distress has been recorded throughout history, but systematic group psychotherapy developed only after World War II. Because of a shortage of psychiatrists, the idea of treating clients in groups was attempted. The success of those first group therapies suggested that some psychological difficulties might be related to relationship problems with other people.

Groups whose purpose is therapeutic are called healing groups or *change induction groups.* Today, over 15 million Americans have participated in some form of self-help healing or change group (Lieberman and Boreman, 1979). The central task of any therapeutic (healing) group is twofold: (1) to relieve emotional discomfort and human misery and (2) to bring about psychological and behavioral changes. The four major types of therapeutic groups are discussed in the following paragraphs.

Group therapy gatherings follow the medical model. Membership in the group is limited by the therapist. Group members are called "patients" who consider themselves "ill" and consequently exhibit "sick" behaviors. The goal of a professional therapist is to bring about mental health or "cure" patients of their problems.

Self-help groups are not led by professional therapists, although they may be recommended or required as part of a treatment program. Membership in the group is limited to those people who share a common problem, symptom, or life situation. Examples include Alcoholics Anonymous (alcohol use problems), Synanon (drug use problems), Reach for Recovery (for postmastectomy women), and many support groups for families of persons with mental illness.

CASE STUDY

Larry, an alert six-year-old, arrived at the clinic just knowing that he would be on the receiving end of a "shot." He dreads the sight of the approaching nurse and begins to whimper. The nurse says, "I would like you to—*Larry,* hold still now and look very closely at that orange circle-square over there.

Tell me whether it is getting bigger or smaller, and really *look!* Just *look* there and tell me . . ." By this time the injection has been given. "But I don't see it," says Larry. "That's right," says the nurse, "and you didn't feel it either!" Soon Larry, his mother, and the nurse are all laughing.

Clinical Decision

Modified from Bierman SF: *Adv J Mind-Body Health* 11(1):65, 1995.

1. What do you think made the outcome of this situation so positive?

T-groups evolved with Kurt Lewin's systems theories. During the 1950s, basic skills training (BST) groups were formed by the National Education Association and the Research Center for Group Dynamics at M.I.T. to study the development, membership, leadership, and dynamics of group behavior. The name of the study groups was later changed to T-groups. Professionals from different disciplines began to adapt the T-group concept to their own fields. Therapists with a client-centered clinical focus developed the *encounter group,* which uses a professional trainer to encourage intense group interaction. Other practitioners focused on small work groups and productivity. This area of interest eventually led to the "quality circle groups" and "total quality management" concepts.

Last, *consciousness-raising groups* offer the support of self-help groups with a broad membership base. The goal of consciousness-raising groups is to use the interactions among its members as a vehicle for achieving behavioral changes. The group is supportive of change, allowing individuals to analyze their interactions and perceptions and then "try out" new behaviors with people from varied backgrounds.

Some therapeutic (healing) groups follow certain theories of behavior. Groups with humanistic models, such as Ellis' rational-emotive-behavioral therapy, stress the developing person and self-actualization, whereas behavioral theorists use groups to change behaviors through modeling or desensitization techniques. Psychoanalytical groups rely on the internal conflict model of Freud, whereas the sociocultural theories emphasize the social framework of the group.

Group therapy brings about changes in behavior through one or more change mechanisms (Table 6-3). The evidence compiled over 35 years demonstrates that many groups do provide benefits for their members. Whether group therapy is prescribed by a professional or sought out by a person in distress, it appears that the emotional support of one person for another is an effective therapeutic tool.

Somatic Therapies

The word *somatic* refers to the body. Historically, therapies for people with psychological distresses have been divided into those that work primarily with the mind (psychotherapies) and those that affect the body (**somatic therapies**). However, this division will soon fade as our knowledge of the effects of emotion on the dynamics of human physiology evolves.

Today, the somatic treatment of mental illness is growing with the introduction of new therapies based on biochemical and physiological research. Drug treatment therapy (pharmacotherapy) and electroconvulsive therapy were established years ago and are still in use today. Psychosurgery and phototherapy are relatively recent developments. The use of acupuncture as a therapy for addictions is the application of an ancient treatment method to modern problems.

Pharmacotherapy

The use of drugs to change behavior dates back centuries, but it was not until the 1950s that effective

◆ **TABLE 6-3**
Group Change Mechanisms

Therapeutic Mechanism	Description
Expressiveness	Group members share emotional expression of positive and negative emotions.
Experience of intense emotion	Generating intense group emotion activates individual issues.
Altruism	The experience of helping others improves low self-esteem and poor self-concept.
Self-disclosure	The sharing of deeply personal material involves risk and develops trust.
Cognitive factors	Intellectual knowledge leads to a deeper understanding of self.
Communion	Groups foster a sense of oneness and belonging.
Discovering similarities	Relief is experienced when individuals discover that their problems are not unique.
Experimentation	Working with new behaviors within the low-risk group setting encourages change.
Feedback	Receiving information about how one is perceived by others is unique to groups.
Feelings of hope	Groups help individuals feel and believe that they can change with the group's help.

medications for the control of mental illness were widely available. Currently, there are several groups of medicines that affect the mind. See Chapter 7 for a more detailed discussion of psychotherapeutic medications.

Psychosurgery

A few medical centers in the United States and Canada have successfully used a specialized surgical technique called **psychosurgery.** This technique is helpful for persons with temporal lobe epilepsy, who have seizures that result in bizarre physical behaviors such as undressing in the middle of a shopping mall or walking into traffic unaware of their surroundings. If these "behavioral seizures" can be localized to a single discharge point within the brain, then neurosurgeons can open the skull and interrupt the electrical pathway for the seizures with laser techniques. Psychosurgery also benefits those people whose acute behavioral changes can be traced to tumors or space-occupying lesions within the brain.

Phototherapy

A relatively new development in somatic therapy is the use of bright lights for the treatment of depression. **Phototherapy,** also known as light therapy, has been used with success in the treatment of seasonal affective disorder (SAD). During the winter months when the available daylight hours are lessened, many people become irritable, unable to concentrate, and even depressed. Researchers found that exposure to full-spectrum light for at least 20 minutes per day resulted in an improvement of depressive symptoms (Rosenthal, 1993). Phototherapy appears to be a promising form of treatment for some disorders, but further studies and research are needed to determine its long-term effectiveness.

Acupuncture

For over 2000 years, acupuncture, a treatment in Oriental medicine, has cured disease and alleviated suffering. The practice of **acupuncture** is defined as the inserting of fine needles into the skin along specific sites on the body. These sites, known as acupuncture points, travel along energy channels called *meridians.* Stimulating these points is thought to restore the energy or *chi* balance within the body. More Western explanations of acupuncture relate to the release and movement of neurotransmitters, neuropeptides, and hormones (Bennett, 1995).

Whatever the explanation, acupuncture has been successfully used in combination with other therapies for the treatment of certain drug addictions. Nurses working with crack-cocaine–addicted pregnant women found that daily acupuncture treatments allowed these mothers to remain drug-free during their pregnancies. "In recent years over 10,000 cocaine/crack abusers have been treated with acupuncture at Lincoln Hospital in the Bronx, a borough of New York City" (Bennett, 1995). Acupuncture is proving to be a cost-effective, safe form of therapy. The melding of acupuncture into basic nursing practice may some day be a reality as nurses move to bridge the gaps between scientific knowledge and the art of caring for others.

Future Developments

As we move into a new millennium, scientific knowledge will grow faster than our ability to make sense of it all. Evolving theories and their research activities now flow across many fields of study. Interdisciplinary researchers are investigating many aspects of human consciousness and describing their effects on the body's physical systems. Investigations are being made into the area of extrasensory perception (ESP) and other phenomena outside our current realm of understanding.

Several innovative therapies have recently been introduced. Feminist and women's therapy grew from the feminist movement of the 1970s; creative aggression therapy arrived in the 1970s and taught clients to redirect their aggression and "fight fairly"; and movement therapy attempts to bring the body in tune with itself and restore balance.

Theories about the nature of human beings and their environments will continue to evolve as will advances in therapies and treatments. We each must face the challenge of being open to new learning during and beyond "the decade of the brain."

❖ KEY CONCEPTS

- Systems theories view humans as functioning within a set of interacting and related units known as open or closed systems.

- Cognitive theories focus on the importance of intellectual factors in human development and function.

- Glasser's reality therapy, based on Maslow's needs theory, attempts to teach people how to fill their needs in an effective, satisfying, and appropriate way.

- Sociocultural theories focus on the impact of a society on its people's behaviors and view mental illness as the result of social conditions.

- Szasz believed that mental illness is a culturally and socially defined concept with which people cooperate.

- The concept of homeostasis was developed during the 1920s by Cannon, who found that the body has a tendency to achieve and maintain a steady internal state.

- The general adaptation syndrome, described by Seyle, consists of the alarm stage, the resistance stage, and the stage of exhaustion.
- If nurses and other health care providers are to be effective, they must consider each client's stress and anxiety levels.
- Guidelines for crisis intervention procedures focus on the concepts of immediacy, control, assessment, disposition, referral, and follow-up.
- Psychobiology is the study of the biochemical foundations of thought, mood, emotion, affect, and behavior.
- Psychoneuroimmunology is the study of the interactions among an individual's central nervous system, immune system, and personality.
- Research has demonstrated that anxiety, stress, and depression can decrease immune functions, whereas relaxation exercises and other positive emotional states increase the production of antibodies and stimulate immune system functions.
- Most theories of nursing view people as biopsychosocial beings who respond to stress in highly individualized ways.
- Current treatments for mental health problems include both psychotherapies and somatic therapies.

❖ SUGGESTIONS FOR FURTHER READING

The article titled "American Psychiatric Nursing: History and Roles," by Dr. Shirley Smoyak in the *AAOHN Journal* (41[7]:316, 1993), presents a broad view of the work of American psychiatric nurses for the past 100 years with some exciting thoughts about the future.

❖ REFERENCES

Ader R: *Psychoneuroimmunology,* New York, 1981, Academic Press.

Bandura A: *Social foundations of thought and action: a social cognitive theory,* Englewood Cliffs, NJ, 1986, Prentice-Hall.

Beck A and others: *Cognitive therapy of depression,* New York, 1979, Guilford Press.

Bennett C: The tao, acupuncture, and crack cocaine, *Capsules Comm Psychiatr Nurs* 1(4):2, 1995.

Bierman SF: Medical hypnosis, *Adv J Mind-Body Health* 11(1):65, 1995.

Cade B, O'Hanlon WH: *A brief guide to brief therapy,* New York, 1993, WW Norton.

Corsini RJ, editor: *Encyclopedia of psychology,* ed 2, New York, 1994, John Wiley.

Dillon KM, Minchoff B, Baker KH: Positive emotional states and enhancement of the immune system, *Int J Psychiatr Med* 15:13, 1985-1986.

Glasser W: *Reality therapy: a new approach to psychiatry,* New York, 1965, Harper & Row.

Glasser W: *Schools without failure,* New York, 1987, Harper & Row.

Goleman D: *The varieties of the meditative experience,* New York, 1992, Dutton.

Gruber BL, Hersh SP, DuBois P: Immune system and psychological changes in metastatic cancer patients using ritualized relaxation and guided imagery: a pilot study, *Scand J Behav Ther* 17:25, 1988.

Jackson DD, editor: *Communication, family, and marriage,* vols 1 and 2, Palo Alto, CA, 1968, Science & Behavior Books.

Librach PD: Briefly, new therapy approach helps patients, *St Louis Post-Dispatch,* July 12, 1994.

Lieberman MA, Boreman LD: *Self-help groups for coping with crisis: origins, members, processes, and impact,* San Francisco, 1979, Jossey-Bass.

Maltz M: *Psycho-cybernetics: a new way to get more living out of life,* Englewood Cliffs, NJ, 1960, Prentice-Hall.

Matheny KB, Kern RM: Cognitive therapies. In Corsini RJ, editor: *Encyclopedia of psychology,* ed 2, New York, 1994, John Wiley.

Mead GH: *Mind, self, and society: from the standpoint of a social behaviorist,* Chicago, 1934, University of Chicago Press.

Meichenbaum D: *Cognitive behavior modification: an integrative approach,* ed 2, New York, 1989, Plenum.

Moore S: Meditation. In Corsini RJ, editor: *Encyclopedia of psychology,* ed 2, New York, 1994, John Wiley.

Parad HJ, editor: *Crisis intervention: selected readings,* New York, 1965, Family Service Association of America.

Raichle ME: Visualizing the mind, *Sci Am* 270(4):58, 1994.

Rosenthal N: *Winter blues: SAD—what it is and how to overcome it,* New York, 1993, Guilford Press.

Royce JR, Powell AD: *A theory of personality and individual differences,* Englewood Cliffs, NJ, 1983, Prentice-Hall.

Salk J: Biological basis of disease and behavior, *Perspect Biol Med* 5:198, 1961.

Selye H: *Stress in health and disease,* Toronto, 1976, Butterworth Press.

Smoyak S: American psychiatric nursing: history and roles, *AAOHN J* 41(7):316, 1993.

Szasz TS: *The myth of mental illness: foundations of a theory of personal conduct,* ed 2, New York, 1974, Harper & Row.

Taylor CM: *Essentials of psychiatric nursing,* ed 14, St Louis, 1994, Mosby.

Wickramasekera IE: *Clinical behavioral medicine: some concepts and procedures,* New York, 1988, Plenum.

Wilson HS: The 1990s as the decade of the brain, *Capsules Comm Psychiatr Nurs* 1(1):1, 1994.

7

PSYCHOTHERAPEUTIC DRUG THERAPY

1. Briefly explain how psychotherapeutic medications affect humans.

2. Name four classifications of psychotherapeutic medications.

3. List three classes of antianxiety agents and name the side effects associated with each.

4. Describe the nursing implications for clients who are receiving both antidepressant and antimanic medications at the same time.

5. List the client care guidelines for monitoring antipsychotic (neuroleptic) drug therapy.

6. List five care guidelines for clients receiving psychotherapeutic drug therapy.

7. Discuss the nursing responsibilities for teaching clients about their medications.

8. Describe how informed consent and noncompliance relate to psychotherapeutic medications.

KEY TERMS

affective disorder
akathisia
akinesia
antipsychotics
autonomic nervous system (ANS)
central nervous system (CNS)
drug-induced parkinsonism
dyskinesia

dystonia
extrapyramidal side effects (EPSEs)
hypertensive crisis
informed consent
lithium
mania
monoamine oxidase inhibitors
  (MOAIs)

mood disorders
neuroleptic malignant syndrome
neurotransmitter
noncompliance
peripheral nervous system (PNS)
psychotherapeutic medications

Psychotherapeutic medications are powerful chemical substances that produce profound effects on the mind, emotions, and body (Keltner and Folks, 1993). Their history is relatively young. The first psychotherapeutics were discovered as a result of exploring the side effects of other drugs, such as antihistamines for allergies. In 1949, lithium was found to be effective in treating the mania of bipolar illness, and the early 1950s brought the use of chlorpromazine (Thorazine) into the therapeutic regimen. The tranquilizer meprobamate (Miltown) became so popular in 1955 that drugstores were "required to place signs in the window when they sell out" (Keltner, Schwecke, and Bostrom, 1995). By the early 1960s, tricyclic antidepressants, monoamine oxidase inhibitors (MAOIs), and haloperidol (Haldol) had been placed on the market. The antianxiety drug diazepam (Valium) became extremely popular, and soon it was the most often prescribed medication in the world. Since the late 1980s, many new psychotherapeutic drugs have been introduced; even more of these medications will be available in the 1990s and beyond. Ongoing research will result in the introduction of new psychotherapeutic drugs. Health care professionals who work with these drugs must remember that psychotherapeutic medications are powerful chemicals with many, sometimes severe, side effects.

How Psychotherapeutic Drug Therapy Works

Medications that are used to treat people with mental health problems act mainly on the body's nervous system by altering the delicate chemical balance that continually exists within that system. Most psychotherapeutic medications produce their effects by interrupting the chemical messenger (neurotransmitter) pathways within the brain. Major nerve pathways that connect the deeper brain to the frontal lobes and limbic system are suppressed by psychotherapeutic medications.

The frontal lobes of the brain are the source of the higher human functions, such as love, creativity, insight, planning, judgment, and abstract reasoning. The limbic system is responsible for emotions, motivation, memory, and the fight-flight response. When these areas of the brain have been affected by medications, profound changes in behavior result. People usually become less agitated and demonstrate more stable moods, but many higher brain functions are impaired (Breggin, 1991). As with *all* medications, there is a trade-off between therapeutic effects and un-

wanted reactions. One of the nurses' primary responsibilities is to recognize this difference.

The human nervous system consists of an "intensive, intricate network of structures that activates, coordinates, and controls all the functions of the body" (Anderson, Anderson, and Glanze, 1994). All parts of the nervous system work together. It is important to remember that if a drug has an effect on one part of the nervous system, it will, without a doubt, have an impact on the other activities of that system.

The **central nervous system (CNS)** is composed of the brain and spinal cord, which together control all the motor and sensory functions of the body. Information about movement travels from the brain down through the spinal cord, reaches the appropriate muscle group, and results in the movement of a body part. Sensory information (e.g., touch, temperature, position) is relayed in the opposite direction: from the muscles and other body areas, up through the spinal cord, and into the brain. Throughout the process, the CNS combines all incoming (sensory) and outgoing (motor) data.

The **peripheral nervous system (PNS)** is composed of the 31 spinal cord nerves plus the 12 pairs of cranial nerves. The peripheral nervous system is further divided into a "motor" system and an "autonomic" (automatic) system. Fig. 7-1 illustrates the divisions of the nervous system.

Each spinal nerve contains motor and sensory neurons (nerve cells). The motor portion of the spinal nerve activates cardiac, smooth, and skeletal muscles, as well as glandular secretions. The sensations of touch, temperature, pain, and spatial perception are transmitted by the sensory portion of the spinal nerves. The cranial nerves carry a mixture of information. Some cranial nerves are mainly motor, whereas others carry mainly sensory information. A few cranial nerves perform both motor and sensory functions.

The **autonomic nervous system (ANS)** is responsible for regulating the vital functions of the body. The activities of the cardiac muscle, smooth muscles, and glandular secretions are all controlled "automatically" (without awareness) by this remarkable system. Two branches of the autonomic nervous system work together to monitor and govern "automatic" body responses.

The sympathetic nervous system prepares the body for immediate adaptation through the fight-flight mechanism. The heart rate increases its output and moves blood into the muscles. Vessels to the stomach and other nonvital organs constrict and detour blood to the skeletal muscles. The pupils of the eyes dilate

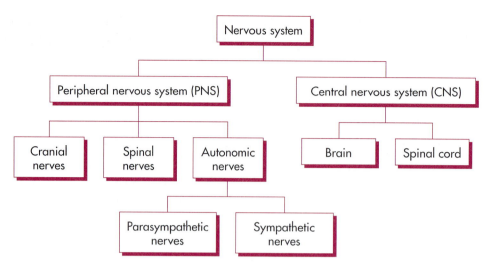

Fig. 7-1 Divisions of the nervous system.

to improve visual acuity, and the bronchioles of the lungs expand to allow for greater exchange of air flow. Increases in blood sugar and fatty acid levels provide glucose for fuel, and all digestive and excretory processes are slowed. This results in greater cellular energy production and increased mental activity. Physically, the organism is preparing to protect itself. People who are highly stressed demonstrate many sympathetic nervous system responses.

On the other hand, the parasympathetic nervous system is designed to conserve energy and provide the balance for the sympathetic system's excitability. The main functions of this system are to monitor and maintain control over the "regulatory" processes of the body, which it accomplishes by governing smooth muscle tone and glandular secretions. Parasympathetic stimulation slows the heart rate, decreases circulating blood volume, relaxes sphincters, and increases intestinal and glandular activity. Respiratory, circulatory, digestive, excretory, and reproductive functions respond to parasympathetic messages. The parasympathetic nervous system uses the neurotransmitter acetylcholine to do its work and is often referred to as the cholinergic nervous system.

As you can see, the sympathetic and parasympathetic divisions of the autonomic nervous system act oppositely to each other. Fortunately, this excite/calm interaction provides a balance. Organs within the body are rich in both adrenergic (sympathetic) and cholinergic (parasympathetic) receptor sites, and this allows the organism to maintain itself in a state of balance or homeostasis (Clark, Queener, and Karb, 1993). Table 7-1 lists the physical responses to parasympathetic and sympathetic nervous system stimulation. It is wise to be familiar with these responses because

many clients receiving psychotherapeutic medications demonstrate side effects related to autonomic nervous system functions.

The basic unit of the nervous system is the neuron or nerve cell. The function of the neuron is to transmit electrical information to other neurons. To accomplish this, the electrical information traveling through a neuron generates a chemical messenger called a **neurotransmitter** to inform other neurons of its arrival. Neurotransmitters are divided into four groups: monoamines, cholinergic group, amino acids, and neuropeptides.

Although nerve cells are found in great abundance throughout the body, they are not physically connected to one another. Each neuron is separated by a small space or gap called a *synapse.* Neurotransmitters travel across this gap, open a channel for the electrical information to pass, and then quickly become inactivated once the message has been sent. Many psychotherapeutic drugs act in or around the synapse by altering the flow of message exchanges.

The study of the neurochemistry of behavior is young, but it has already changed the way in which mental-emotional problems are considered. Future discoveries are waiting as we attempt to unlock other mysteries of the human brain.

Classifications of Psychotherapeutic Drugs

Basically, there are four classes of psychotherapeutic medications: (1) antianxiety agents, which exert a calming influence; (2) antidepressants and (3) antimanics, which are used to treat major mood or emo-

◆ **TABLE 7-1**
Autonomic Nervous System Actions

Tissue	Parasympathetic (Cholinergic or Muscarinic) Response	Sympathetic (Adrenergic) Response
Eye	Constriction (miosis)	Dilation (mydriasis)
	Accommodation (focus on near objects)	
Glands	Increased salivation (copious, watery)	Increased sweating*
	Increased tears and secretions of respiratory and gastrointestinal tract	Increased salivation (thick, contains proteins)
Heart	Decreased rate	Increased rate
	Decreased strength of contraction	Increased strength of contraction (increased contractility)
	Decreased conduction velocity through the atrioventricular node	Increased conduction velocity through the atrioventricular node
Bronchioles	Smooth muscle constriction (restricts airways)	Smooth muscle relaxation (opens airways)
Blood vessels	Constriction of vessels in heart (not a prominent effect in humans)	Dilation of vessels in heart and skeletal muscle
	Dilation of vessels in salivary gland and erectile tissues	Constriction of vessels in skin, viscera, salivary gland, erectile tissues, kidney
Gastrointestinal tract		
Smooth muscle	Contraction	Relaxation
Sphincters	Relaxation	Contraction
Urinary bladder		
Fundus	Contraction	Relaxation
Trigone and sphincter	Relaxation	Contraction
Uterus		Contraction
Liver		Glycogenolysis

Modified from Clark JF, Queener SF, Karb VB: *The pharmacologic basis of nursing practice,* ed 4, St Louis, 1993, Mosby.
*Acetylcholine is the neurotransmitter for this sympathetic response. This is the exception to the rule that norepinephrine is the postganglionic neurotransmitter.

tional disorders; and (4) antipsychotics, which help to curb the hallucinations and loss of reality suffered by those individuals with psychotic disorders.

It is estimated that over 15 million people are currently being treated with psychotherapeutic drugs (Breggin, 1991). People receiving psychotherapeutic medications must be routinely monitored for effectiveness, side effects, and potentially life-threatening adverse reactions. Because of this need for close monitoring, nurses in all practice settings must be knowledgeable about the roles these powerful chemicals play in treating mental illness.

Antianxiety Medications

Anxiety is common to us all; however, when it interferes with one's ability to function, it becomes an *anxiety disorder.* In today's world, anxiety disorders are a common mental health problem. "The National Institute of Mental Health (NIMH) estimates that 6% to 10% of the general population currently suffers from an anxiety disorder" (Blair and Ramones, 1994). A thorough discussion of anxiety and its treatments can be found in Chapter 20. Here we consider the antianxiety medications that are a usual part of the therapeutic treatment plan.

Clients with severe anxiety are treated with a variety of psychotherapeutic medications. Antianxiety agents are drugs that reduce the psychic tension of stress. They are also referred to as anxiolytics. Older practitioners sometimes refer to this group as the "minor tranquilizers." Medications in the antianxiety group are divided by chemical formulas into nonben-

◆ **TABLE 7-2**
Benzodiazepine Antianxiety Drugs

Generic Name (Trade Name)	Adult Dosage and Route
Alprazolam (Xanax)	Anxiety: 0.25-0.5 mg t.i.d., PO Dosage: not to exceed 4 mg/day
Chlordiazepoxide (Librium)	Anxiety: 5-25 mg t.i.d., PO Alcohol withdrawal: 50-100 mg t.i.d., PO/IM/IV Dosage: not to exceed 300 mg/day
Clonazepam (Klonopin)	To prevent seizures: 1.5 mg/day/divided doses
Diazepam (Valium)	Anxiety: 2-10 mg t.i.d.-q.i.d., PO Seizures: 5-20 mg IV bolus Dosage: not to exceed 40 mg/day
Flurazepam (Dalmane)	For sedation Dosage: 15-30 mg h.s., PO
Halazepam (Paxipam)	For anxiety Dosage: 20-40 mg q.d.-q.i.d., PO
Lorazepam (Activan)	Anxiety: 2-6 mg/day/divided doses Preoperatively: 2-4 mg IM/IV Insomnia: 2-4 mg h.s., PO for 2 wk or less
Midazolam (Versed)	Used preoperatively Dosage: 0.07-0.08 mg/kg, 30 min to 1 hr before anesthesia
Oxazepam (Serax)	For anxiety Dosage: 10-30 mg t.i.d.-q.i.d., PO
Quazepam (Doral)	Used as sedative-hypnotic Dosage: 7.5 mg h.s., PO
Temazepam (Restoril)	Used as sedative-hypnotic Dosage: 15-30 mg h.s., PO
Triazolam (Halcion)	Used as sedative-hypnotic Dosage: 0.125-0.5 mg h.s., PO

h.s., Nightly or at bedtime; *IM,* intramuscularly; *IV,* intravenously; *PO,* by mouth or orally; *q.d.,* once daily; *q.i.d.,* four times daily; *t.i.d.,* three times daily.

zodiazepines and benzodiazepines (Table 7-2). Today, the drugs of choice for the treatment of anxiety are the benzodiazepines.

The *benzodiazepines* have almost completely replaced other medications in the treatment of anxiety disorders. They are effective, are generally well tolerated, and do not adversely affect sleeping patterns (a common problem with many psychotherapeutic drugs). Benzodiazepines are prescribed to provide sedation, to induce sleep (called a hypnotic), to prevent seizures, and to prepare clients for general anesthesia, but they are mainly used to decrease anxiety.

Benzodiazepines act by decreasing the transmission of nerve impulses, which results in decreased anxiety. The rate of absorption is rapid, with the onset of action occurring within 1 hour. Peak action is 1 to 2 hours, and the drug exerts its action (duration) for about 4 to 6 hours. Because of this rapid action, clients experience relief from symptoms within hours.

Benzodiazepines are metabolized by the liver and excreted by the kidneys. People with impaired liver or kidney function must be carefully monitored if this drug class is prescribed. Pregnant and nursing women are usually not treated with benzodiazepines because these medications cross the placenta and enter the breast milk. Caution must also be used when administering antianxiety agents to older or debilitated adults because of their slower metabolism.

Antianxiety drugs have several drug interactions, including CNS depression when the benzodiazepines are combined with other CNS depressants such as alcohol and some types of street drugs. Alcohol combined with antianxiety agents can produce serious, even fatal, reactions. Health care providers should caution all clients who are receiving antianxiety medications about the possibility of serious problems if they drink alcohol while taking these drugs. Concentrations of the cardiac drug digoxin may be increased during treatment with antianxiety medications, so clients taking this cardiac medication must be routinely assessed for signs or symptoms of digoxin toxicity. Antacids should not be taken because they interfere with absorption of the antianxiety agent into the bloodstream.

The side effects of benzodiazepines are usually minimal but they include fatigue, sedation, dizziness, and orthostatic hypotension (a drop in blood pressure on standing). Long-term use of antianxiety drugs can result in physical and psychological dependence. These medications have a potential for abuse. For this reason, antianxiety drugs are not recommended for people with a history of drug or alcohol abuse. Therapy for all clients is usually limited to a few months.

A new antianxiety drug, called *buspirone* (BuSpar), was recently introduced. This drug differs from benzodiazepines in several ways. First, it belongs to a different chemical class, the azapirones, and does not cause the sedation, sleepiness, or muscle relaxation as do other antianxiety drugs. Second, the therapeutic effects are not seen for 3 to 6 weeks after beginning treatment. Buspirone has less potential for abuse because it does not significantly interact with other chemicals (except MAOIs and haloperidol); however, clients are still cautioned to avoid alcohol. Third, the potential for overdose with buspirone is lessened because the drug has a wide dosage range. Side effects are few: lightheadedness, dizziness, headache, and nausea (Keltner and Folks, 1993).

Nursing care for clients receiving antianxiety agents include frequent assessments of the therapeutic actions and side effects experienced by the client. Nurses need a thorough knowledge of antianxiety agents because many of the drugs are prescribed on an "as needed" (p.r.n.) basis. Medications used on this basis require accurate nursing assessments, good judgment, repeated evaluations of the medication's effects, and objective documentation.

Antidepressant Medications

Feelings of great joy and deep sadness are common human experiences. We are all familiar with these emotional extremes and tend to think of them as the natural highs and lows of everyday life, but when one's mood begins to interfere with the ability to perform the routine activities of daily living, intervention is needed. **Mood disorders** are ineffective emotional states, ranging from deep depression to excited elation. They are also called **affective disorders** because the word "affect" means emotions. The major mood disorders are discussed in detail later. Here, we focus on the medications used to treat depression and other emotional problems.

Basically, antidepressant medications exert their action in the body by increasing certain neurotransmitter activities (Kramer, 1993). Based on their chemical formula, antidepressants are divided into five cate-

gories: tricyclics, nontricyclics, **monoamine oxidase inhibitors (MOAIs),** selective serotonin reuptake inhibitors (SSRIs), and nonselective serotonin reuptake inhibitors (NSSRIs).

Antidepressants are usually the physician's first choice for the treatment of depression. They are also indicated for bipolar disorders, panic disorders, obsessive-compulsive disorders, enuresis (bed wetting), bulimia, and neuropathic pain. Antidepressants have been used with some success in posttraumatic stress disorder, organic mood disorders, attention deficit-hyperactivity disorder, and conduct disorders in children (FDA, 1994). Many people take antidepressant drugs, and nurses must be aware of the effects of these powerful agents if they are to be effective in helping people successfully cope with their life circumstances.

Antidepressants interact with a variety of other substances. Because they block the destruction of specific major neurotransmitters (dopamine, norepinephrine, and serotonin), higher levels of these chemicals circulate throughout the body. Ingesting foods or drugs that contain certain chemicals produces more neurotransmitters, which can result in overstimulation of the nervous system. Antidepressant drug interactions can also produce serious cardiovascular and hypertensive reactions, as well as CNS depression, when combined with several other chemicals. Table 7-3 gives a description of the more serious drug interactions encountered with the MOAI antidepressants. If you are unsure about combining any medications, check with the pharmacist, physician, or supervisor *before* administering them to the client. Safety is always a primary consideration for nurses.

Antidepressant medications require 1 to 2 weeks before symptom relief is noticed. However, many of the side effects make themselves known soon after beginning therapy. Some side effects are a nuisance, like a dry mouth. Others, such as a **hypertensive crisis,** can be life threatening. Nurses need to be able to ascertain the difference between a minor problem and a serious undesired effect. Clients should be routinely monitored for physical and behavioral changes. Those experiencing orthostatic hypotension should be protected from falls, and basic nursing comfort measures should be implemented. Kidney and liver function should be monitored monthly. Signs of toxicity (e.g., headache, stiff neck, palpitations) should be reported to the physician immediately.

Clients should also be assessed for changes in attitudes and any suicidal gestures. Frequently, depressed people attempt suicide when taking antidepressants because antidepressants increase energy levels, which can lead to a renewed interest in plan-

◆ **TABLE 7-3**
Drug Interactions With Monoamine Oxidase Inhibitors

Type of Interaction	Signs/Symptoms
Anticholinergic reactions	Dry mouth, decreased tearing, blurred vision, constipation, urinary hesitancy or retention, excessive sweating
Hypertensive crisis	Throbbing, radiating headache, stiff neck, palpitations, tightness in chest, sweating, dilated pupils, very high blood pressure and pulse rate
CNS depression	Changes in level of consciousness; sedation, increasing lethargy, disorientation, confusion, agitation, hallucinations, lower seizure threshold

CNS, Central nervous system.

ning a suicide attempt and acting on those plans. Changes in a client's behavior may indicate a therapeutic improvement, a drug side effect, a drug/food interaction, or an emerging psychosis. Good communication with clients helps to assess the subtle changes that may indicate problems. Take precautions to protect clients if you believe they may be suicidal. Spend time with them and offer emotional support because there are few people lonelier than a depressed suicidal person.

Although millions of people are currently taking antidepressant medications, it must remembered that only the symptoms or feelings of depression are affected. The cause of the emotional distress is not cured by medications. The underlying problems still remain, and nurses should plan their care with this fact in mind.

Clients, no matter which medications they are taking, must be taught about their drug therapy. This instruction includes information about dosages, actions, and wanted and unwanted effects. Clients who are just beginning drug therapy tend to feel tired or sedated. If instructions must be given at this time, the nurse must be sure to *write them down* so the client can refer to them later. Clients who are taking MAOIs must understand their dietary and drug restrictions. (See the box at right for a list of the foods and medications that must be avoided while taking MAOIs.)

Antimanic Medications

Depression lies on one side of the "mood continuum," whereas mania lies on the other. **Mania** is an extreme emotional state characterized by excitement, great elation, overtalkativeness, increased motor activity, fleeting grandiose ideas, and agitated behaviors. Some therapists refer to mania as "agitated depression" because it frequently occurs with severe depression. Antidepressant drug therapy helps clients cope with their depression, but it has little effect dur-

---

DIETARY AND DRUG INTERACTIONS WITH MONOAMINE OXIDASE INHIBITORS

MEDICATIONS TO AVOID
Prescription and Over-the-Counter Drugs
Nasal and sinus decongestants; cold, allergy, and hayfever remedies; inhalants for asthma; weight-loss pills, pep pills, stimulants; narcotics (especially meperidine [Demerol]); local anesthetics (Any medication should be approved by the physician before taking.)

Illicit Drugs
Cocaine, any amphetamine (uppers)

FOODS TO AVOID
Alcoholic Drinks
Beer, ale, red wines (Chianti), sherry wines, liqueurs, cognac
Dairy Products
Avocados, bananas, fava and broad beans, canned figs, any overripe fruit
Meats
Pickled or smoked proteins, bologna, chicken or beef liver, dried fish, meat tenderizer, salami, sausage
Other Foods
Large amounts of caffeinated coffee, tea, or cola; chocolate; licorice; soy sauce; yeast

---

ing the manic stage of behavior. For that, lithium is prescribed.

Lithium is a naturally occurring salt not unlike sodium. The word *lithium* is derived from the Greek word for stone. Its calming effects on people suffering from mania were first observed during the early 1800s, and it soon became a popular remedy for the treatment of gout, epilepsy, and other conditions. During the 1940s, people with heart problems used lithium in place of salt. When several died from lithium toxicity, the practice was abandoned. In 1949,

◆ **TABLE 7-4**
Antimanic Drugs and Their Actions

Drug Class	Generic/Trade Names	Mechanism of Action
Alkali ion salt	Lithium carbonate (Carbolith, Duralith, Eskalith CR, Lithane, Lithotabs)	Mechanism unknown; replaces sodium ions and changes neuron response to neurotransmitters
Anticonvulsant	Carbamazepine (Tegretol)	Mechanism unknown; used to treat rapid-cycling manic depression
Anticonvulsant	Valproic acid (Depakene)	Mechanism unknown; used in combination with other neuroleptics and anticonvulsants
Benzodiazepine, anticonvulsant	Clonazepam (Klonopin)	Inhibits certain electrical activity in brain

lithium was found to be effective in the treatment of mania, but because of the reports of fatal side effects, the drug was not available in the United States until 1970. Today, lithium is the mainstay for the treatment of the excitement phase of bipolar depression. Newer products are currently under investigation for the treatment of those clients who do not respond or cannot tolerate lithium therapy. Table 7-4 lists the major antimanic medications and their mechanisms of action.

Lithium is currently used in the United States only for the treatment of manic episodes. In other countries, lithium is used as a therapy for various psychiatric problems, but this practice remains controversial. Because lithium stabilizes mood, it is indicated for the treatment of acute mania and as a prophylaxis (preventative) for clients with bipolar disorders. Lithium has also been investigated for the treatment of drug abuse, alcoholism, phobias, and eating disorders (Harris, 1989). Therapy is contraindicated (not prescribed) for pregnant women and people with acute renal failure. Caution is exercised when monitoring therapeutic responses in clients with cardiovascular, cerebral, or electrolyte disorders; diabetes mellitus; Parkinson's disease; ulcerative colitis; acne; and osteoporosis. Lithium is well absorbed into the bloodstream and excreted faster than sodium by the kidneys. For this reason, clients who are taking lithium must be cautioned about salt intake, fluid intake, and activity. Lithium interacts with a variety of other drugs ranging from alcohol to valproic acid. For a list of significant drug interactions associated with antimanic drugs, consult a drug reference.

The difference between therapeutic and toxic levels of lithium is minimal. The drug is usually well tolerated by most clients, but how efficiently the drug is excreted varies from client to client. The "narrow therapeutic index" of lithium requires close observation of client responses. If the blood levels are too low,

manic behavior returns; however, if levels are too high, an uncomfortable and possibly life-threatening toxicity may result. Lithium levels above 1.5 mEq/L are considered toxic.

Clinical improvement commonly takes from 5 to 14 days and may take as long as 3 weeks. Clients in the acute manic stage usually require the addition of antipsychotic or sedative medications until the effects of lithium take hold. Clients are monitored monthly for thyroid and kidney function because long-term use of lithium can cause altered thyroid function (hypothyroidism) and loss of the kidney's ability to concentrate urine. Great care must be taken to frequently assess and monitor each client's responses to each medication. Undesirable effects are present with *every* medication the client receives.

The major nursing guidelines for safe and effective client care relate to three areas: performing the prelithium workup, educating the client to maintain stable blood levels of the drug, and monitoring for side effects and possible toxic reactions.

The prelithium workup consists of a complete physical, history, electrocardiogram (ECG), and numerous blood studies. The physician orders a complete blood count (CBC), fasting blood sugar, renal function studies (blood urea nitrogen [BUN], creatinine, electrolytes, 24-hour creatinine clearance), and thyroid function studies (thyroid-stimulating hormone [TSH], thyroxine [T_4], triiodothyronine resin uptake [T_3RU], free thyroxine index [T_4I]). Nurses are responsible for obtaining a complete nursing history, a functional assessment that describes the client's habits and activities of daily living, and a review of the results of all diagnostic tests. The data from these assessments allow the nurse to plan appropriate care and prepare for any potential problems.

Stabilizing lithium levels involves teaching the client and family about expected side effects without causing undue anxiety, assisting them in identifying the difference between common side effects and those requiring immediate notification of the physician, and teaching them how to cope with the lifestyle changes required by this medication. The box at right lists the most important guidelines for clients who are receiving lithium. Nurses must be sure that the client and family understand each bit of information. Have them repeat what they have learned, apply it to several "what if" situations, and describe the appropriate actions for each side effect to ensure understanding. If any doubts exist, write down the information and instruct the client to carry it with him/her as a readily available resource. The informed client is a more willing participant in treatment.

Antipsychotic (Neuroleptic) Medications

People with major psychiatric disorders received little drug treatment until the 1950s when the drug chlorpromazine (Thorazine) was found to exert a strong calming effect on seriously disturbed people. Since that time, many antipsychotic drugs (antipsychotics) have been marketed, the populations of most mental institutions have been released, and many inpatient treatment facilities for the mentally troubled have disappeared.

Antipsychotic medications are also referred to as *major tranquilizers, ataractics* (serenity-producing drugs), or *neuroleptics* because of their effect on the nervous system. Most antipsychotic medications are available in tablet, liquid, and parenteral forms. Each class of antipsychotics has profound effects on the most complex of all the body's systems—the brain and nervous system.

Most antipsychotic drugs are used to treat the symptoms of major mental disorders. These medications are indicated for clients suffering from schizophrenia, acute mania, and organic mental illnesses. They are also used to treat some resistant bipolar disorders, paranoid disorders, Huntington's disease, and other disorders of movement. A few antipsychotics are used to treat nausea, vomiting, and intractable hiccups and as preanesthetic agents.

The psychosis called schizophrenia is associated with two kinds of symptoms: Type 1, positive schizophrenic symptoms, and Type 2, negative schizophrenic symptoms (Table 7-5). According to the biochemical theory, positive symptoms are the result of too much dopamine in the brain, which activates delusions, illusions, and hallucinations. Negative schizophrenic symptoms relate to a lack normal behavioral responses. These "negative" symptoms, such as emotional dampening, are the result of too little dopamine caused by structural or organic changes in the brain (Breier and others, 1994). An-

CLIENT GUIDELINES FOR TAKING LITHIUM

To achieve a therapeutic effect and prevent lithium toxicity, clients taking lithium should be advised of the following:

1. Lithium must be taken on a regular basis, preferably at the same time daily. For example, a client taking lithium on a three-times-daily schedule who forgets a dose should wait until the next scheduled time to take the lithium but should not take twice the amount at that time because lithium toxicity could occur.
2. When lithium treatment is initiated, mild side effects, such as fine hand tremor, increased thirst and urination, nausea, anorexia, and diarrhea or constipation, may develop. Most of the mild side effects are transient and do not represent lithium toxicity. Also in some clients taking lithium, some foods such as celery and butter fat will have an unappealing taste.
3. Serious side effects of lithium that necessitate its discontinuance include vomiting, extreme hand tremor, sedation, muscle weakness, and vertigo. The prescribing physician should be notified immediately if any of these effects occur.
4. Lithium and sodium compete for elimination from the body through the kidneys. An increase in salt intake increases lithium elimination, and a decrease in salt intake decreases lithium elimination. Thus it is important that the client maintain a balanced diet, liquid, and salt intake. The client should consult with the prescribing physician before making any dietary alterations.
5. Various situations can require an adjustment in the amount of lithium administered to a client; for example, the addition of a new medication to the client's drug regimen, a new diet, or an illness with fever or excessive sweating.
6. Blood for determination of lithium levels should be drawn in the morning approximately 8 to 14 hours after the last dose was taken.

Modified from Keltner NL, Folks DG: *Psychotropic drugs*, St Louis, 1993, Mosby.

tipsychotic medications appear to be much more effective in controlling the positive symptoms of acute schizophrenia. Their use for clients with chronic brain disorders remains controversial because these drugs block already depleted dopamine pathways.

Antipsychotic medications interact with many other chemicals. For example, antacids hinder the absorption of antipsychotic drugs, so they must be administered 2 hours after the oral antipsychotic. Most

◆ **TABLE 7-5**
Positive and Negative Types of Schizophrenia

	Type 1: Positive Schizophrenia	Type 2: Negative Schizophrenia
Signs and symptoms	Delusions, illusions, hallucinations	Anergia (lack of energy); anhedonia (inability to feel happiness or pleasure); apathy (does not care about anything); avolution (unable to choose or exert own will); flat affect (no emotional responses); will not speak unless spoken to
Anatomy and physiology	Hyperdopaminergic reactions (too much dopamine)	Nondopaminergic reactions (too little dopamine)
	Brain size and structure normal	Brain has structural changes: decreased blood flow, increased size of ventricles, decrease in size of brain
Response to antipsychotic medications	Usually good	Usually poor

CNS depressants such as alcohol, antianxiety medications, antihistamines, antidepressants, barbiturates, meperidine (Demerol), and morphine produce severe CNS depression when mixed with antipsychotics.

As a nurse (or other health care provider who administers medications), you are responsible for the safety of your clients (O'Donnell, 1994). Therefore you are obligated to research every medication that may possibly interact with the prescribed antipsychotic and to monitor your clients' responses to each drug. If drug references do not contain enough information, consult the pharmacist or physician.

The side effects and adverse reactions of antipsychotic medications are numerous and troublesome for the client. Both the central and peripheral nervous systems are affected by antipsychotics. **Extrapyramidal side effects (EPSEs)** are CNS side effects described as abnormal movements produced by an imbalance of neurotransmitters in the brain. They include the following:

akathisia, the inability to sit still
akinesia, absence of physical and mental movement
dyskinesia, the inability to execute voluntary movements
dystonia, impaired muscle tone (rigidity in the muscles that control gait, posture, and eye movements)
drug-induced parkinsonism, a term used to describe a group of symptoms that mimic Parkinson's disease

Tardive dyskinesia is a serious, irreversible side effect of long-term treatment (Dave, 1994). The word *tardive* means "appearing later," and many clients will exhibit the signs of tardive dyskinesia after several months of drug treatment. This condition is discussed in detail in Chapter 31.

Peripheral nervous system side effects include dry mouth, blurred vision, and photophobia (sensitivity to bright light), tachycardia, and hypotension. Nurses must protect clients from falls during the first few weeks of therapy because the hypotensive response is greatest when clients stand or change positions suddenly. These hypotensive episodes cause tachycardia as the body attempts to adapt to a lower blood pressure. Antipsychotic drugs affect each person uniquely. Antipsychotic medications are powerful; they must be administered with great care.

Client Care Guidelines

Nurses and those who administer psychotherapeutic drugs have five basic responsibilities relating to these medications: (1) assess clients, (2) coordinate care, (3) administer medications, (4) monitor and evaluate client responses, and (5) teach clients about their medications. Each area of responsibility involves careful observation and an understanding of each drug's therapeutic and adverse actions (Blair, 1990).

Assessment

The first step of the nursing process is the most important because an accurate and complete database enhances the quality and effectiveness of client care. Many nurses are very skilled with the psychosocial and mental status assessments necessary for the care of clients with mental-emotional problems. However, it is important to remember that physical difficulties are common companions of psychic problems. (See the box on p. 98 for a vivid example of this principle.)

CASE STUDY

Gary T., a 36-year-old man, was admitted to the mental health unit of the community hospital with a diagnosis of paranoid schizophrenia. He is considered a danger to others because of his aggressive and uncooperative behaviors during last evening's admission process. After a major tranquilizer, he spent a relatively quiet night but cried out frequently. Today, Mary S. has been assigned to care for him.

After reviewing the change-of-shift report and Gary's record, Mary decided that he needed a thorough nursing assessment so she gathered together her equipment and went in search of her client. On entering Gary's room, she was surprised to find a rather burly, bearded man lying curled on his side and whimpering quietly to himself. While knocking on the door, she introduced herself and requested a few minutes of his time. "Hardly matters," he grumbled softly.

Mary approached his bed carefully, remembering his tendency for physical aggression. As she seated herself near his bedside, she thought she caught an expression of pain. Acting on this nonverbal message, Mary gently questioned, "Where are you hurting?"

Gary, who had averted her gaze, looked straight into her eyes and said through clenched teeth, "I think it's my back or legs or something. Ever since this pain started, I've been unable to control myself. All I want to do now is make everybody who is messin' with me hurt as much as I do."

This was the clue that sent Mary on the path of assessing Gary's pain. She discovered in his past medical history that Gary had fallen off a roof about 3 months ago. The injuries had not resolved, and attempts at treatment were resulting in ever-increasing discomfort. Pain medications, even when combined with alcohol, had little effect on the pain. Mary's physical assessment revealed difficulties with walking, sitting, and changing positions. He was not able to lift his leg off the bed.

Mary was not a physician, but she knew something was physically wrong. Her first priority of care was to help Gary find some relief from his pain. After sharing her findings with her supervisor, Mary consulted the physician in charge of Gary's case who ordered several diagnostic tests. The results of the tests revealed a large herniated disc in his back. Gary was immediately transferred and prepared for surgery.

Weeks later, a large, burly man approached Mary in the hallway. He reminded her of someone familiar, but she couldn't quite place him. As he drew closer, she recognized Gary, who had come to thank her for listening to him. "I told the others that I was hurtin', but they didn't listen, so I got upset. I guess I can be pretty rowdy when I'm hurtin'. But you listened to me and I had surgery and the pain is gone. I can be a nice guy again. If you hadn't listened to me, I'd really be crazy by now. Thanks for saving me from becoming a psych case."

Mary felt great, but she reminded herself to carefully and thoroughly (physically, emotionally, socioculturally, and spiritually) assess each client as a unique individual. The answer to a complex problem may lie in a simple solution, but one must be alert enough to recognize the clues.

Clinical Decision

1. What do you think may have happened if Mary had not assessed a physical problem with this mental health client?

A *nursing history* should be completed for every client whether the presenting problems are of physical or mental origin. A complete nursing history includes a profile of the client's current living situation, family structure, and daily activities. Attention should also be paid to his/her past medical, family, and social histories. An investigation of the client's chief complaint (presenting problem) rounds out the basic database. Laboratory and other diagnostic studies may be ordered by the physician or nurse practitioner, and special medication assessments must be conducted for clients receiving psychotherapeutic medications (Stewart, 1995). Table 7-6 offers an example of a medication history assessment tool.

Assessing clients is a continual process. Good physical and psychosocial assessments add an important dimension to the client's overall plan of holistic care.

Coordination

Physicians prescribe treatments, psychologists recommend therapies, and social workers propose plans, but it is the nurse who coordinates and ensures that each component of the treatment plan is appropriately carried out. Nurses juggle scheduling for diagnostic tests, treatments, and therapies; teach clients and their significant others about medications, treatments, and other aspects of therapy; and encourage clients to become actively engaged in treatment.

◆ TABLE 7-6
Medication History Assessment Tool

Psychotherapeutic Medications	Other Prescriptions	Over-the-Counter Drugs	Substance Use
			Alcohol, caffeine, street drugs
Each drug ever taken	**Each drug in past 6 mo**	**Each drug in past 6 mo**	
Drug name?	Drug name?	Drug name?	Substance(s)?
Reason for prescription?	Reason for prescription?	Reason for taking?	When used?
When started?	When started?	When started?	
Length of time taking drug?	Length of time taking drug?	Frequency of use?	Frequency of use?
Highest daily dose?	Highest daily dose?	Highest dose?	
Effectiveness?	Effectiveness?	Effectiveness?	Effects?
Side effects, adverse reactions?	Side effects, adverse reactions?	Side effects, adverse reactions?	Side effects, adverse reactions?
Any physical changes since starting medication?	Any physical changes since starting medication?		Any problems associated with use?
Was drug taken as prescribed (compliance)?	Was drug taken as prescribed (compliance)?		

Modified from Laraia MT, Stuart GW: *Quick psychopharmacology reference,* ed 2, St Louis, 1995, Mosby.

Nurses coordinate clients' schedules, act as advocates, consult with other members of the treatment team throughout the client's stay, and provide the care that encourages clients toward wellness. Clients who are receiving psychotherapeutic medications are continually monitored for side effects because the nurse coordinates the prescribed drug therapy and investigates for possible drug interactions. In short, it is the nurse who coordinates all daily aspects of the client's care and treatment.

Drug Administration

One traditional role of nurses is the administration of medications to clients. Today, in some facilities, this task has fallen to the certified medication aide (CMA). CMAs are usually nursing assistants with specialized training in the administration of certain oral medications. However, it still remains a primary responsibility of nurses to monitor the clients in their charge for drug effectiveness and adverse reactions.

It is not uncommon to treat clients with two or more psychotherapeutic medications at a time. Here the nurse must be especially vigilant for side effects and signs of drug interactions. Nurses are also responsible for making sure that clients actually ingest or take their medications. Hiding medications in the cheeks (cheeking) or pretending to swallow the pills then spitting them out is not an uncommon occurrence. Liquid medications are usually available and are recommended in these instances. Although nurses may not actually administer medications to their clients, they are responsible for ensuring they receive them.

Many psychotherapeutic medications are listed as controlled substances. Usually, only licensed nurses administer medications that are controlled substances. Their responsibilities include keeping all controlled medications under double lock and key, accounting for each dose by documenting when each dose is received on the unit and administered to the client, and observing the client for therapeutic and unwanted effects.

Monitoring and Evaluating

Physicians evaluate client responses and adjust medical therapies, but it is the nurse who is in the best position to observe the physical and behavioral changes that accompany the administration of psychotherapeutic medications. Nurses must be familiar with the major side effects and adverse reactions for each class of psychotherapeutic drugs used in their practice settings.

Interactions with other medications and substances can become life threatening. For example, when alcohol is combined with antidepressant drugs, severe CNS depression occurs, which results in lethargy, progressing to respiratory depression, coma, and even death.

Certain groups of people are at an increased risk for developing drug interactions. These include older adults, the debilitated, people with immunosuppressed or compromised organ systems (especially liver and kidneys), and clients who have physical illnesses. Monitoring clients' responses to their medications is an important, potentially life-saving nursing intervention. Do not take this responsibility casually because your clients depend on you and your knowledge of their medications.

Client Teaching

Every individual has a right to be informed about his/her diagnosis and treatment plan, and each nurse has the obligation to keep clients informed. Client education is a major role of nurses. In regard to psychotherapeutic medications, each client must be prepared to safely take each medication, monitor daily for side effects, and know what to do when side effects occur.

Nurses must be able to reach clients "on their own level" of understanding. It is ineffective to teach about adverse reactions when the learner cannot even define the words used. To prevent miscommunication, the nurse must speak in terms that the client can understand and proceed at a pace that allows for understanding and the formulation of questions. Most psychotherapeutic medications slow the client's ability to follow and comprehend a line of thought. Therefore it is important to repeat the essential points. Make sure the client understands by having him/her repeat the most important information. As extra insurance, *write the important information.* Having a written explanation gives the client something tangible and real that can be reviewed and referred to when memory fails. Clients taking psychotherapeutic medications are like highly anxious people; they easily forget what has been taught them. Preprinted drug information is helpful, but there is no substitute for individualized client teaching. If possible, such teaching should include the family or significant others. They can be very helpful in assisting the client to follow the medication regimen (Table 7-7).

Helping clients and their significant others to adapt to change is a primary nursing responsibility. Psychotherapeutic medications are designed to produce

---

◆ **TABLE 7-7**
Teaching Clients About Psychotherapeutic Medications

Nursing Process	Examples of Actions

Assessment	Assess client for the following:
	    Level of understanding
	    Ability to self-administer medications
	    Willingness to take medications on a daily basis
	    Level of cooperation
	    Ability to obtain and purchase medications
	    Support of family
	    Past medication history including side effects of any drug taken

Planning	Nursing diagnoses:
	    Knowledge deficit: psychotherapeutic medications
	    Risk for noncompliance
	    Plan to teach use of *(specify)* medications

Interventions	For each drug, teach client to recognize the following:
	    Generic and brand names
	    Purpose and action
	    Therapeutic effects
	    Dosage, route, schedule of drug
	    Administration, what to do if a dose is missed
	    Specific precautions (driving, operation of power equipment)
	    Side effects and actions to take if they occur
	    Possible drug/food interactions
	    Signs of overdosage or underdosage
	    Drug storage, expiration dates
	Provide information in written form.
	Develop written medication schedule.
	Reinforce other data given by care team.

Evaluation	Observe client to evaluate effectiveness of teaching. Reassess if any areas of instruction were not understood by client or family.

behavioral changes, and these changes affect the client and other people within the client's environment. A well-taught client and family are aware of and able to cope more effectively with the life changes that result from psychotherapeutic drug therapy.

Special Considerations

Because most psychotherapeutic medications discussed in this chapter affect the body's nervous system, they are potentially harmful chemicals. Professionals with prescriptive authority must weigh the benefits of therapy with the possible harm that may result from taking a medication.

Adverse Reactions

Nurses must constantly remain vigilant for the effects on clients receiving psychotherapeutic medications. Clients who are taking psychotherapeutic drugs (especially antipsychotics) are at risk for developing the serious problems of **neuroleptic malignant syndrome** (a serious extrapyramidal side effect) and tardive dyskinesia (Blair and Dauner, 1993). Accurate identification of the signs and symptoms of each may prevent many complications. Detailed descriptions of both are found in Chapters 31 and 32.

Noncompliance

Noncompliance is defined as an informed decision, made by a client, not to follow a prescribed treatment program. Many psychiatric clients choose to discontinue or reduce their medications because of the distressing side effects. Others have difficulty following treatment programs because of the very nature of their problems. For example, paranoid or delusional persons seldom cooperate with medication regimens or schedules. Recent research has demonstrated that as many as 65% of outpatient clients do not take their medications as prescribed (Kelly and Scott, 1990). Even clients within inpatient settings do not take their medications consistently. It is not uncommon for people to hide their drugs in the cheek, pretending to swallow, and then discarding or hoarding them. Inspecting the inside of the mouth after administering a client's medication decreases the incidence of cheeking. If the practice continues, the physician should be notified and permission to use a liquid form of the medication should be requested.

Informed Consent

Another special consideration relating to psychotherapeutic medications is the issue of **informed consent.** The concept of informed consent is to present clients with the information about the benefits, risks, and side effects of specific treatments, thus enabling them to make voluntary and competent decisions about their care.

With the treatment of physical disorders, the process is straightforward: treatments are described and the client makes the decision to accept or reject the plan. However, with the situation of mental disorders, the picture is not so clear. In the past, psychiatric clients who were considered a danger to themselves or others were routinely medicated without their permission.

In 1986, the New York Court of Appeals held that "in nonemergency situations, involuntary patients cannot be forced to take psychotic medications" (Keltner, Schwecke, and Bostrom, 1995). This ruling has led to an uncomfortable compromise between client rights and people's needs to feel safe.

When a client becomes noncompliant with medications, the care guidelines center around ensuring safety and assessing for the return of symptoms. When caring for the client within an inpatient setting, the nurse should observe for any changes in behavior, be prepared for the client to become aggressive or act out, and protect the client and others from harm. If the setting is the clinic, the nurse should instruct the client's family or significant others about the return of psychiatric symptoms, the signs and symptoms of side effects and adverse reactions, and the available community resources. Although nurses cannot manipulate or force a client into taking medications, they can use their rapport with clients to assist them in making decisions based on complete information and sound judgment.

❖ KEY CONCEPTS

- Psychotherapeutic medications are powerful chemical substances that produce profound effects on the mind, emotions, and body.
- Most psychotherapeutic medications produce their effects by interrupting the chemical messenger (neurotransmitter) pathways within the brain.
- The drugs of choice for the treatment of anxiety are benzodiazepines, which are known as antianxiety agents.
- Antidepressant medications treat depression and other mood disorders by increasing certain neurotransmitter activity within the brain and CNS.
- Mania and bipolar depressive illnesses are treated with lithium, a naturally occurring mood stabilizer.
- Antipsychotic (neuroleptic) drugs are indicated for clients suffering from schizophrenia, acute mania, organic mental illnesses, some resistant bipolar disorders, paranoid disorders, some disorders of movement, nausea and vomiting, and intractable hiccups. Antipsychotic drugs are also used as preanesthetic agents.

- Extrapyramidal side effects are CNS alterations that produce abnormal involuntary movement disorders, including akathisia, akinesia, dyskinesia, dystonia, and drug-induced parkinsonism.
- Clients who are receiving psychotherapeutic drugs (especially antipsychotics) are at risk for developing the serious problems of neuroleptic malignant syndrome and tardive dyskinesia.
- Nurses who work with clients who are receiving psychotherapeutic drugs have five basic responsibilities: assess, coordinate, administer, monitor and evaluate, and teach.
- A special medication assessment (drug history) must be conducted for clients receiving psychotherapeutic medications.
- A primary responsibility of nurses is to monitor the clients for drug effectiveness and adverse reactions.

- Client education is a major role of nurses.
- Noncompliance is defined as an informed decision, made by a client, not to follow a prescribed treatment program.
- Informed consent is presenting clients with the information about the benefits, risks, and side effects of specific treatments, thus enabling them to make voluntary and competent decisions about their care.

❖ SUGGESTIONS FOR FURTHER READING

The article titled "What's Wrong With This Patient?" by Kay Stewart in *RN* (February 1995, pp. 45-48) offers an excellent clinical example of a client experiencing neuroleptic malignant syndrome.

❖ REFERENCES

Anderson KN, Anderson LE, Glanze WD: *Mosby's medical, nursing, and allied health dictionary,* ed 4, St Louis, 1994, Mosby.

Blair DT: Risk management for extrapyramidal symptoms, *Qual Assur Rev Bull* 17:116, 1990.

Blair DT, Dauner A: Neuroleptic syndrome: liability in nursing practice, *J Psychosoc Nurs* 31(2):5, 1993.

Blair DT, Ramones VA: Psychopharmacologic treatment of anxiety, *J Psychosoc Nurs* 32(7):49, 1994.

Breggin PR: *Toxic psychiatry,* New York, 1991, St Martin's Press.

Breier A and others: Effects of clozapine on positive and negative symptoms in outpatients with schizophrenia, *Am J Psychiatry* 151:20, 1994.

Clark JF, Queener SF, Karb VB: *Pharmacologic basis of nursing practice,* ed 5, St Louis, 1997, Mosby.

Dave M: Clozapine-related tardive dyskinesia, *Biol Psychiatry* 35:886, 1994.

FDA-approved drug bulletin: Venlafaxine hydrochloride (Effexor), *RN* 57(10):51, 1994.

Harris E: Lithium: in a class by itself, *Am J Nurs* 89(2):190, 1989.

Kelly GR, Scott JE: Medication compliance and health education among outpatients with chronic mental disorders, *Med Care* 28:1181, 1990.

Keltner NL, Folks DG: *Psychotropic drugs,* ed 2, St Louis, 1997, Mosby.

Keltner NL, Schwecke LH, Bostrom CE: *Psychiatric nursing,* ed 2, St Louis, 1995, Mosby.

Kramer P: The transformation of personality, *Psychol Today* 26(4):44, 1993.

O'Donnell J: Drug therapy: 20 ways your role will change, *Nurs 94* 24(3):47, 1994.

Skidmore-Roth L: *Mosby's 1997 nursing drug reference,* St Louis, 1997, Mosby.

Stewart KB: What's wrong with this patient? *RN* 58(2):45, 1995.

UNIT 2

THE CAREGIVER'S THERAPEUTIC SKILLS

8

PRINCIPLES OF MENTAL HEALTH CARE

LEARNING OBJECTIVES

1. Describe three characteristics of a mentally healthy adult.

2. Explain how the phrase "do no harm" applies to mental health nursing.

3. List five components of the art of nursing.

4. Discuss the importance of mutual trust in the mental health caregiver–client relationship.

5. Identify the four components of any behavior.

6. Predict the outcome for a mental health client who develops more effective adaptive (coping) skills.

7. Describe the concept of consistency and its use in providing effective mental health care.

8. Explain the advantages of setting and enforcing limits when working with clients who are experiencing mental health problems.

KEY TERMS

adaptation
advocacy
behavior
caring

consistency
empathy
holistic health care
mentally healthy adult

principle
responsibility
standards of care

A **principle** is a code or standard that helps people to govern their conduct. Principles guide the decisions and actions of the persons who choose to follow them. Professional principles were developed to provide guidelines for those people who practice within a certain profession. Helping professions, such as medicine, nursing, psychology, and social work, all have established sets of principles. The profession of nursing is guided by **standards of care,** state practice acts, and principles. In addition, each specialty within the nursing profession is guided by a set of principles specific to the special area of practice. This chapter examines seven basic principles for nurses who work with mentally and emotionally troubled clients.

The Mentally Healthy Adult

The concepts of mental health and mental illness are not so easily defined. Health, by its very nature, is a dynamic and changing state that is influenced by an individual's patterns of behavior and interactions with the environment (Haber and others, 1992). Mental health is just as dynamic and fluid, changing as the stresses of life are encountered.

Most people manage to cope with and adapt to the changes in their lives. They remain contributing members of their group, community, and society. Although problems may exist, these people are basically content with who and where they are in life. They are able to love and express love freely without the fear of losing their independence. Flexibility and a willingness to try something new or different lead to an eagerness for learning. Life is considered important, and its special moments are cherished. Adversity is seen as a challenge or opportunity for growth. To simplify, a **mentally healthy adult** is a person who can cope with and adjust to the recurrent stresses of daily living in an acceptable way. Although mentally healthy adults experience unhappiness, anxiety, or other psychic distresses, they manage to pool their resources, rise above the negativity, and continue with their lives.

In our culture, mental illness results when the problems associated with an individual's life become so overwhelming that the person is unable to cope *and* develops maladaptive behaviors or impaired functioning. Although millions of people function with various levels of anxiety, they are not considered mentally ill because they can carry out the activities of daily living and function independently. Citizens of the industrialized cultures label a person as mentally ill only after the ability to function independently in society is impaired for a period of time (Zwerding, 1994). Other cultures have different definitions of mental illness (see the box at right for an example of another culture's viewpoint).

Mental Health Nursing Practice

The practice of the principles of mental health nursing is the responsibility of all nurses, but advanced education and training is required for nurses to become psychiatric specialists. The American Nurses Association describes two levels of mental health practitioners: (1) the generalist nurse who has completed a basic nursing program and (2) the specialist who has a master's degree in psychiatric nursing, has undergone supervised clinical experience at the graduate level, and has demonstrated a depth of theoretical and therapeutic knowledge. As practitioners of this specialty, psychiatric nurses focus on caring for the more severely or chronically mentally ill members of society in both inpatient and community settings. Generalist nurses are called mental health or psychiatric nurses, whereas those with graduate-level training are referred to as mental health or psychiatric nurse specialists (Table 8-1).

However, *every* nurse addresses the mental health needs of each person who becomes a client. One of the foundations of the nursing profession is based on the care of the whole person. No matter which nursing specialty practiced or where the setting is located, every nurse helps people cope with their problems. To do this effectively, nurses must consider clients' mental-emotional status, how they view their problems, and which resources and supports are available for resolving the difficulties (Starck and McGovern, 1992). This holds true for the client undergoing surgery or medical treatment as well as for the person with a psychiatric diagnosis.

It must be remembered that the world of health care becomes familiar and comfortable for those who practice within its realm. The sights, sounds, and smells of the health care environment are known and familiar. Daily routines are established, and the facility's employees all understand what behaviors are expected of them.

However, to a person who is ill (disabled, stressed) in some way, visiting a medical facility can be a terrifying experience. When illness or disability affects an

 CULTURAL ASPECTS

Laos is a country in southeast Asia. Its inhabitants, the Lao, believe that 32 spirits live within the body and govern its functions. Illnesses, including mental disturbances, are thought to be the result of an imbalance of the spirits, unhealthy air currents, or bad winds. Pinching or scratching parts of the body to produce red marks helps to let the bad winds out of the body and restore health. Strings are worn around the wrists, neck, ankles, or waist to prevent soul loss.

◆ **TABLE 8-1**
Levels of Practice for Psychiatric Nurses in Ambulatory Settings

	Level 1	Level 2	Level 3
Educational requirements	No formal education is necessary other than current state licensure	Baccalaureate degree in nursing	Master's degree in psychiatric nursing
Experience requirements	Minimum of 1 yr of experience in acute psychiatric nursing care	Minimum of 2 yr of experience in acute psychiatric care settings	Advanced knowledge and expertise in psychiatric care and principles of supervision and consultation
Nature of practice	Supportive treatment	Supportive treatment	Insight treatment
Therapeutic functions	Communicating with other professionals and agencies relative to patient care Assisting in assessment and data collection Assisting patient to use environmental resources Assisting in community primary prevention programs	Primary responsibility for supportive therapy Assessment of patient functioning Initiation and attendance at all conferences regarding patients Assignment to interdisciplinary teams responsible for delivery of primary mental health care in ambulatory units	Primary responsibility for insight-oriented psychotherapy Responsibility for patients cared for by nurses in levels 1 and 2 of practice Assessment of patient pathology Supervision of other health team members Participation in primary community prevention programs Responsibility for obtaining supervision consultation Responsible for assumption of nursing leadership

Modified from Gardner K: *J Psychiatr Nurs* 15:26, 1977.

individual, the result is almost always anxiety. No matter how casual a client may appear to be, one can be sure that a heightened stress level is present every time interactions with health care providers take place. Some people are so intimidated by the thought of visiting a health care provider that they wait until their problems become severe and not easily treated. Nurses who remember that clients are "out of their element" when seeking health care are able to provide much needed emotional support and more effective nursing care (Sorrell, 1994).

The skills developed when working with the mental and emotional needs of people will be used throughout your career, for yours is the profession of caring. May these seven principles of mental health nursing help to guide you in that care:

1. Do no harm.
2. Accept each client as a whole person.
3. Develop mutual trust.
4. Explore behaviors and emotions.
5. Encourage responsibility.
6. Encourage effective adaptation.
7. Provide consistency.

Do No Harm

The first rule of medicine, nursing, and other helping professions states that if you cannot do something right, at least do not do something wrong. No matter what the circumstances, avoid any action that may result in harm to the client. The "do no harm" principle also relates to the "reasonable and prudent nurse" concept found in U.S. law. It is taken from the ancient writings of Hippocrates, who believed in the natural ability of the body to heal itself. Hippocrates appreciated the value of supportive care. His principle of "do no harm" proves to be as true and valid today as it was in his era. It offers nurses a valuable guideline for making decisions and planning cares.

Nurses' Tools

Every occupation has its tools. The carpenter finds the saw, drill, and level indispensable. The accountant cannot function without the computer, calculator, or calendar. The surgeon uses specialized instruments, and the cook is lost without pots and pastry cutters. Nurses, however, are a bit different.

CASE STUDY

Mike S. was the charge nurse for the medical unit on the evening shift at the community hospital. The shift began uneventfully, and nothing amiss was noted during Mike's assessments of his clients. However, Mike was stuck with an uncomfortable feeling about Mr. B., a 60-year-old motor vehicle accident victim with a fractured left femur. Although Mr. B.'s vital signs and physical assessments were within normal parameters, he was becoming increasingly anxious and restless as the evening progressed. He even admitted to Mike that he felt that "something was going to happen."

Nurse Mike had no physical data but decided to act based on his observations of Mr. B.'s increasing anxiety. He called the physician, who listened politely and then ordered tests for blood gas levels. As the respiratory therapist was entering the room, Mr. B. suddenly became cyanotic and unresponsive. Because of Mike's uneasy perception and his ability to grasp the meaning of the interactions with his client, Mr. B. received prompt, life-saving treatment for the pulmonary embolism he sustained that evening.

Clinical Decision

1. What information do you think led Mike to act on his perceptions or feelings?

Nurses use several tools to practice their profession. We all can identify the more obvious tools, such as a stethoscope, blood pressure cuff, and intravenous line; but beneath the visible tools lie the skills of the nurse herself/himself. Nurses, no matter where they practice, use skills of the "self." The ways in which nurses communicate, interact, and behave all require the use of therapeutic tools (techniques), which require study and practice to learn. Some of these therapeutic tools include the use of eye contact, facial expressions, body movement, and other nonverbal behaviors. Other tools are developed when therapeutic communication skills are practiced. Interactions with people from various cultures and backgrounds help to refine the nurse's tools.

The point is that *you, the nurse, are the therapeutic tool* that guides clients toward wellness. Learn to "see" yourself working with clients. Analyze your behaviors and try new approaches. Work to improve your ability to become a "therapeutic tool," and clients will respond because they want to feel better even more than you want them to (Renz, 1995).

For nurses, the "do no harm" principle serves as a guide for nursing actions. Nurses in every client care setting have the responsibility to protect clients, but sometimes a well-intended action can actually result in a harmful situation. To illustrate, teaching a client about the side effects of chemotherapy before the physician has spoken with the client could alter the client's decision about chemotherapy treatment. The nurse had good intentions—to help the client cope— but the outcome could result in the client refusing chemotherapy because of a fear of side effects.

For nurses working with mental health clients, this principle is especially important because the main therapeutic tool of the mental health nurse is the "self." The therapeutic use of the self can result in great improvements in clients' behaviors when the "do no harm" principle is applied. When the principle is overlooked or forgotten, the one who loses is the client, the very person we are obligated to protect.

Nursing Arts

The therapeutic use of the self, combined with the skills of the nurse, result in a practitioner of the nursing arts. The art component of nursing has always been vaguely defined, but recent research has attempted to explore the nature of the art of nursing. The results of a study done at the University of British Columbia (Johnson, 1994) identified five concepts (nursing abilities) as nursing arts.

First is the nurse's ability to *grasp the full meaning in client interactions.* This involves combining the observations of the senses with the emotions, gestures, objects, sounds, and other energies of the interaction. The nurse perceives the meaning of the interaction with the client and forms an understanding. It is often called "the nurse's sixth sense" because these perceptions include more than the area of objective data.

Learn to grasp, pick up, and perceive the meaning of clients' verbal and nonverbal messages. This ability can save lives and defuse potentially harmful situations. Experience will teach that your "sixth sense" is correct many more times than it is wrong. (See the box above for a vivid example of this concept.)

Second, the artful nurse has the ability to *establish a connection with the client that bridges the technology gap.* Through the nurse's behaviors and communications, an expressive capacity emerges. The nurse connects with the client as one human being to another, and it is this connection, this relationship, that helps clients cope with the impersonal, technologically oriented world of modern medicine. Establishing this connection requires genuine caring from the nurse, care that is expressed in both verbal and behavioral actions. It does not matter if the medical diagnosis is physically or psychologically based—every client needs to know that his/her nurse really cares (Brady, 1995).

Third, the ability to *perform nursing activities with skill and proficiency* is the next concept of the nursing arts. Because most nursing activities consist of a combination of verbal and manual skills, the artful nurse is able to effectively implement nursing actions while gaining client cooperation at the same time. This principle also states that nurses can learn and grow through practice, repetition, and experience.

Fourth is the ability to *rationally choose an appropriate course of nursing action.* The nursing process serves as a tool for defining and solving client problems, but the use of the tool is only as effective as its practitioner. Use of the nursing process becomes an art when the nurse is able to analyze the data collected to arrive at the best course of action for the situation. The art of choosing the best course of action must be practiced carefully. Let the "do no harm" principle guide you as you grow.

Fifth is the ability to *practice the profession of nursing morally.* The nursing profession is directed and focused toward the good of the client. Nurses must possess the personal beliefs, attitudes, and moral principles that support caring for others (Gaut, 1993). Without this framework, the practice of nursing will fade into the category of caretaker. Moral nursing practice also includes the duty to stay competent and up-to-date with new nursing knowledge.

Accept Each Client as a Whole Person

People present themselves for health care "as is." This means that the whole person, not just the complaint, must be considered. People are complex beings with many aspects to their personalities. The influences of culture, society, and one's personal group all have an impact on the person called "the client." Add to that the inner dialogue (self-talk) that we all carry on with ourselves, and one can begin to understand the complexity of the human creature.

The principle of acceptance is important in nursing because you will care for many people who are different. Those differences do not have to be understood, but they *must be accepted.* You may even disapprove of clients' attitudes and actions, but you must accept the person because it is the person who is the focus of your nursing activities. This section discusses two points of view that encourage us to practice the principle of acceptance.

Holistic Framework

Remember the definition of holistic care: a concept designed to help clients achieve harmony within themselves (and with others, nature, and the world). **Holistic health care** is based on the concept of "whole." Understanding clients in relation to their work, family, and social environments encourages nurses to consider their many interwoven needs. Interventions that are tailored to the individual can then be planned and implemented.

Nurses who practice holistically realize that each person must also be accepted for who and what he/she is, no more no less. Even the nastiest client is anxious and scared inside. Our culture does not encourage the expression of emotion, especially negative feelings. Men are expected to suffer in silence, whereas women can express only a few socially acceptable emotions. Admitting to being anxious leaves one vulnerable, open, and unprotected. To maintain some control over their environments, clients may become uncooperative or disruptive.

Accept the person, uncomfortable behaviors and all. Search for the meaning of their behaviors because actions are attempts to fill needs. Your acceptance will be communicated to the clients, and your nursing actions will eventually result in success. However, if you pass judgment on clients' behaviors, the clients will sense your disapproval. Nursing actions in these cases usually fall on fallow ground.

Viewing clients holistically also involves an acceptance of their lifestyles, attitudes, and living conditions. Sometimes this can be difficult, especially when their environment or lifestyle is harmful. For example, a nurse once cared for a beautiful young woman who was addicted to heroin. Once the nurse accepted her, heroin addiction and all, she was able to meet the goal of providing the client with good prenatal care. At first, it was not easy to accept her destructive lifestyle, but as the nurse became more accepting and less judgmental, an intelligent, witty, and caring woman emerged.

Persons with mental or emotional difficulties may display some odd behaviors or verbalize unusual beliefs. Nurses must identify their own reactions to clients who engage in actions that are considered unusual or bizarre (Freeman, 1994). These people need to be accepted just as much as, may be more than, clients with physical maladies. Their behaviors also have meaning, but *our* reactions can sometimes cloud their messages. Work to develop an acceptance of each client by considering the whole individual. A holistic point of view helps us to accept all persons, regardless of how different from ourselves they are.

Health-Oriented Attitude

The traditional medical model views illness or dysfunction as a pathological condition: something is *wrong* with the client, and a repair or return to function constitutes a "cure." A health-oriented model, however, focuses on clients' *abilities*—what they *can* do—instead of on their *dis*ability or *dis*ease. Clients are assessed in terms of their strengths and abilities. Goals of care are mutually developed. Interventions are designed for the individual, and clients receive the services most important and relevant to them. Responsibility for success is shared among clients and care providers.

Distress of the human spirit can be far more damaging than a medical diagnosis. Different emotional states have been found to trigger the release of specific neurotransmitters (McCain and Smith, 1994). Therefore it seems only reasonable that a focus on the positive aspects of a situation stands a greater chance of success. A positive health-oriented attitude alone may make a difference in functioning. Learn to approach problems with an attitude that focuses on the client's strengths, assets, and resources.

When working with clients who are experiencing mental health problems, the nurse may find that progress comes slowly. A health-oriented point of view encourages both care providers and clients to strive for success. It also allows psychiatric clients the respect and dignity that are not readily available to them within the medical model.

When it is assumed that the mental health client will succeed, he/she will usually live up to expectations and do just that—succeed. One small success fosters and breeds other triumphs. When enough small successes are experienced, dignity begins to return. Keep your focus on the "can do." It can have surprising results. Know that an intervention in one area of the client's life has an impact on all other daily activities, so keep the focus on the positive.

Develop Mutual Trust

Individuals who are unable to trust cannot rely on others for help. The word *trust* means assured hope and reliance on another. Words used to describe trust include "hope," "have faith in," and "depend." Trust is an important concept for human beings, who are by nature social and group oriented. It implies cooperation, support, and a willingness to work together.

Trust occurs on many levels. For example, the moment you drive your motor vehicle onto a road, you are engaging in an act of trust: you have the trust that oncoming drivers will stay on their side of the small, painted yellow line that divides the road. When you purchase an item from a reputable manufacturer, you trust that it will be repaired or replaced if it is defective. Numerous other small acts of trust occur throughout the day. We are just too busy to notice many of them. Yet to nurses the concept of trust holds much importance.

Trust is the foundation of the therapeutic relationship. It forms the basis for the success or failure of all nursing actions. People who become your clients, no matter what their diagnoses, need to trust that they will be cared for in a safe and supportive manner. Only then can they release their energy for healing.

The development of trust between a client and the nurse involves three concepts: caring, empathy, and advocacy (Keltner, Schwecke, and Bostrom, 1995). When the client feels that his/her nurse cares, understands, and acts with his/her best interests in mind, then trust is established. The development of the therapeutic relationship is more fully discussed in Chapter 10.

Caring and Empathy

Illness or disability restricts a person's ability to perform daily work and social activities. Mental illness has the additional impact of negative cultural and social attitudes.

Researchers have found that people with mental disorders experience significantly higher levels of disability than those with physical disorders (Ormel and others, 1994). People seem to readily accept the physically infirmed, but for those with mental-emotional difficulties, the road can be rocky and lonely. Plus, coping with mental illness is difficult and takes courage. Some people have written about their experiences of mental illness in an attempt to help others understand and accept their conditions. Several such authors have identified that the acceptance, caring, and support of their friends and care providers played a major role in their recovery.

Caring is the thread that connects people and moves them toward their own levels of recovery. On occasion, when the client ceases to care, nurses have been known to care enough for both; that caring has pulled more than one client from despair. "The demonstrations of caring brought forth physical and mental changes, positive outcomes that resulted in a trusting relationship" (Sherwood, 1993).

For persons with mental illness, caring plays an especially important role. Most have felt the stigma of the "mentally ill" label, the unacceptance of being different, and the suspiciousness of misunderstanding. They know, subconsciously, whether you actually care or regard them as just another client. Before trust can be developed, clients must truly believe that their nurses care.

Empathy is the ability to recognize and share the emotions of another person. It includes an understanding of the meaning and significance of that person's behavior. In short, empathy is the willingness to walk a mile in another's shoes, to see the world as he/she does. Although we may have never experienced the anxiety of having no home or being harassed by insulting voices inside our heads, we have all felt discomfort, pain, and insecurity (Kelly, 1995). Clients with mental illnesses frequently live in a lonely world of personal suffering, detached from mainstream society. Empathy in these cases becomes a powerful therapeutic tool, one that can reestablish a person's self-worth and dignity. If clients believe that their nurses are willing to share in their discomforts, they become more interested in learning to help themselves.

Many people with mental-emotional problems struggle with the problem of trusting others. Sometimes the person's internal conflicts result in suspicion, paranoia, and fear of the unknown. Nurses who work with these clients must routinely demonstrate that they can be trusted. To communicate the messages of trust, remember one important thing: *do what you say you will do.* If you tell a client that you will return in 10 minutes, be back in 10 minutes (better yet, be there in nine). Clients soon learn which nurses follow their words with actions, which nurses care enough to keep their words. Trust begins to grow when clients know they can depend on their nurse.

Client Advocacy

Advocacy is the process of providing a client with the information, support, and feedback needed to make a decision (Keltner, Schwecke, and Bostrom, 1995). Client advocacy frequently goes a step further by adding the obligation to act in the client's best interest. Persons with mental-emotional difficulties are not always capable of making informed decisions. In cases like these, the nurse intervenes to ensure that the client's basic needs are being met (Geller, 1993). For example, if a client decides not to eat, the nurse may act in the client's best interests by making the food easily available. The client cannot be forced to eat, but he/she can be encouraged to make more healthful choices.

Client advocacy involves the concept of empowerment. As changes in the health care system continue, a move toward mutual participation is replacing the traditional sick-role model in which clients are passive receivers of health care. For mental health clients, this remains difficult because of the longstanding cultural and social stigma attached to people with psychiatric problems. Many mentally ill persons are quite capable of taking part in their care and treatment. Some are not, but all deserve the opportunity to make the decisions they are capable of making.

Nurses act as advocates by assisting clients through the decision-making process. Providing information and education assists clients in making appropriate decisions about their care. "There is no doubt that an educated patient can more successfully comply with the prescribed medical regimen, achieve more positive medical outcomes, and decrease readmission rates" (Weaver and Wilson, 1994). When people know that their nurses care enough to help them make the best decisions they can, trust has been established.

Explore Behaviors and Emotions

All **behavior** has meaning. An individual's actions are the result of attempts to fill personal needs and goals. Behaviors can be better understood when one considers the person's internal frame of reference and the context in which the behaviors occur.

Each of us lives within a private world of our own. Most people's private worlds (internal frames of reference) are agreeable with others. However, people with mental-emotional difficulties have private worlds that may be difficult for the average person to understand.

"Behavior consists of perceptions, thoughts, feelings, and actions" (Stuart and Sundeen, 1995) (Fig. 8-1). A disruption in any one of these areas may result in behavioral problems. Distorted perceptions, impaired thought processes, and alterations of emotional expression lead to maladaptive actions.

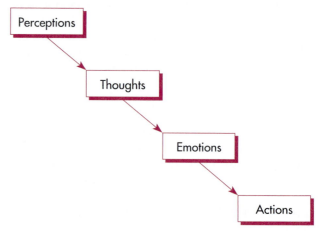

Fig. 8-1 Components of a behavior.

Behaviors also must be understood in terms of the context or setting in which they occur. Most people are more comfortable in certain environments than they are in others. Sometimes a particular environment is threatening because of uncomfortable past experiences in similar settings. A nurse who cared for wounded soldiers in a war zone and experiences anxiety when she cares for trauma clients in the emergency room is an example of how the context or setting can influence behaviors.

Meanings to the Client

All behavior serves a purpose, and all behavior has meaning. However, it is sometimes difficult to accurately interpret or receive the message that a client's behavior is sending. Actions may be clouded with symbols, such as the client who is sure that the government has planted a microphone in his brain to read his thoughts. In this case, the individual feels so powerless that he knows he is being controlled by others with authority, such as the government.

Actions may also be influenced by chemical substances. Alcohol and other drugs affect perceptions, emotional expression, judgment, and behavior. People may behave in bizarre ways while under the influence of a chemical and then feel very remorseful and apologetic after the substance has been cleared from the body. The same can hold true for the chemicals that are called medications and prescribed as medical therapies.

Remember, most psychotherapeutic medications cause definite changes in clients' behaviors and emotional states. Nurses are challenged with assessing which behaviors indicate that the desired therapeutic effects are being achieved and which behaviors may be the result of unwanted or unexpected reactions to medications.

Meanings to Others

An often overlooked method of understanding the meaning of a client's behaviors is to simply ask the individual. Many clients are willing to share the emotions attached to their behaviors when (1) they have trust in you and (2) you are willing to take the time to listen. When people with mental health problems can discuss their behaviors or share their emotions, they are not looking for approval or reproach. Acceptance and a gentle exploration of what the behaviors mean to them will help clients to develop and practice insight (Brady, 1994). Once individuals can look at their own actions and realize how they affect other people, they can begin the process of learning to control or manage their own behaviors. Recognizing ineffective behaviors and replacing them with more appropriate and effective actions is

the first step toward gaining some control over one's situation.

Explaining how you view the client's behaviors allows for perception checks. Is the client sending the same message that you are receiving? Do each of you see the same communication in the client's symbols? If the client says he feels like a duck, do you know what he is really trying to portray? Sharing your perceptions helps clients to see how their behavioral messages are being received by other people. It also allows nurses the opportunity to gain insight into their clients' worlds.

Some clients are so caught up in their own worlds that they are unable to verbally share the meanings of their behaviors. They speak with their actions only. With these individuals, nurses must develop acute observational skills. Some repeated behaviors are attempts to undo or fix something. The classical example of this is Shakespeare's Lady Macbeth and her ritualized hand washing. Other actions can be cries for help or forms of self-punishment for wrongful deeds. The meaning of a client's actions may be shrouded in mystery, but time, trust, and persistent observations will assist in discovering the real meanings that lie behind the messages.

Encourage Responsibility

The fourth basic principle of mental health care relates to the concept of **responsibility.** Responsible people are capable of making and fulfilling obligations. They are answerable and accountable for their decisions or actions. Responsibility implies that a person is able to exercise capability and accountability. Individuals who are unable to make or keep an obligation are usually not considered to be responsible. People vary in their abilities to cope with the stresses of life, thus some persons live more responsibly than others.

Nurses work with clients who exhibit a wide variety of coping styles and behaviors. Encouraging responsibility is a primary intervention for clients with mental-emotional difficulties because it helps to build self-worth, dignity, and confidence and assists clients in learning more successful coping behaviors. Responsibility is a cornerstone of modern societies and a goal of mental health care (Wichowski and Kubsh, 1995).

Responsibility for Self

As children grow and develop the necessary skills for living within a society, so do their responsibilities. Infants are not required to be responsible, but as soon as the child begins to explore and manipulate the environment, responsibilities are shouldered. To illustrate, learning to play with other children involves the responsibility of being cooperative, and understanding the concept of truth brings with it the responsibility not to lie, even if the results are negative.

Responsibility is learned early. The primary instructor is the family, but the social group and culture exert strong influences. As children learn about "right behaviors" (the culturally defined actions that are labeled right and wrong), they develop the responsibility to engage in them. There is a saying that states:

> If the family does not teach responsibility, the school will. If the school does not teach responsibility, then the group will. If the group does not teach responsibility, then society will; and society sends its irresponsible people to jail.

Many people with mental-emotional problems have difficulty acting in responsible ways. Some have never been taught about obligations and the duty to fulfill them because of their dysfunctional family or childhood experiences. Others cannot remember or hold onto a logical picture long enough to discharge their responsibilities. However, *every person has the capacity for growth* and therefore some degree of responsibility. Nurses and other professionals who work with the mentally ill plan and implement specific interventions designed to help clients achieve their highest level of responsibility.

The first step in developing self-responsibility relates to care of the self. The basic physical needs of life (Maslow's lower order needs) must be met, no matter what the circumstances. Every adult and sadly many children must procure food, clothing, and shelter for themselves daily. People with mental-emotional problems commonly have difficulty in meeting these basic needs, so the lessons of self-responsibility usually begin with something as fundamental as caring for one's daily personal hygiene needs.

Nurses should assess their clients' abilities to perform the skills that make up the activities of daily living. For example, sometimes the reason for poor hygiene is a lack of knowledge. A person may never have been taught to bathe frequently or brush his/her teeth after every meal. In such cases, the responsibility is for the nurse to teach and the client to learn the basic skills of personal cleanliness.

Assuming responsibility for something even as simple as personal hygiene leads people to improved feelings of self-worth. When one looks good, one feels better. Small successes become positive steps that help equip clients with the skills necessary for functioning at their highest possible levels.

The next step in assuming self-responsibility is to be accountable for one's own emotions. "I'm sorry. I

lost my temper," does not excuse the action. Losing one's temper is not a rationale that describes a responsible person. Mental health clients *frequently* have poor control over their emotions (called *poor impulse control*). They feel the emotion and then immediately act without considering the consequences of their behaviors. Becoming responsible for one's emotions involves the willingness to identify and then "own" the problems and emotions. It also requires a willingness and determination to try new, more effective behaviors when coping with emotional reactions.

Replacing an unacceptable behavior with a more effective action helps clients to achieve a degree of control over their lives. As individuals become responsible, they begin to succeed. Those small successes help them to remove themselves from the role of victim and realize the value of taking self-responsibility.

Responsibility to Others

People who seek treatment for mental or emotional problems must assume the responsibility for cooperating with and following their therapeutic plan of care. This involves a personal commitment to become actively involved with a group of mental health care providers by sharing personal information, being open to new ideas, and being willing to try new ways of doing things. Nurses have the obligation to help clients adapt and succeed, whereas clients are responsible for working toward self-improvement.

Clients are also responsible for the effects of their actions on others. The enjoyment of social interactions is accompanied by the responsibility of behaving appropriately. People who have problems with emotional (impulse) control can become a threat to the safety of others when their behaviors are inappropriate. It is important for nurses to assist clients in controlling their behaviors because people who act in irresponsible ways are soon removed from social settings. The loneliness of mental illness is great, but the loneliness of a socially isolated mentally ill person is immense.

Responsibility is a fundamental concept in mental health care. It is a key to developing more effective behaviors and building self-worth. We do our clients no favors when we relieve them of the duty to be responsible. Some psychiatric therapies are designed around the concept of responsibility. William Glasser's reality therapy uses responsibility as a therapeutic tool (see box on p. 113).

Encourage Effective Adaptation

Clients may be labeled with one or more psychiatric diagnoses, but all mental health clients have one thing in common: unsuccessful (maladaptive) coping behaviors. The very nature of mental illness is characterized by actions that are not in keeping with society's definitions of appropriate behaviors. Mental health nurses provide clients with education about and opportunities to engage in more effective behaviors. Encouraging effective adaptation is the sixth principle of mental health nursing. Clients who can change or adapt their behaviors will cope more effectively with life's realities.

Cure vs. Care

With some mental-emotional difficulties we can speak of cures. Situational depression, for example, is frequently cured when the client is removed from or changes the situation that brought on the distress. Many cases of confusion or delirium are cured when a physical pathological condition is discovered. However, some mental problems are chronic and force clients and their significant others to make permanent changes in how they live their lives.

Despite this reality, many persons with chronic illnesses (physical and mental) adapt and progress to leading full, satisfying, and meaningful lives. **Adaptation** (recovery) "in this context is not the same as the 'cure' of a medical illness. Instead, it means sufficient improvement to carry on everyday activities" (*Menninger Letter,* 1995). The importance of this viewpoint for nurses lies in the fact that if we can teach clients to replace maladaptive behaviors with more effective actions, they will improve their abilities to live more successfully.

Nurses are in an important position to take advantage of many informal teaching opportunities because clients often share personal attitudes, opinions, and emotions with nurses during the course of their interactions. Nurses are able to provide constructive feedback for clients who are seeking more satisfying behaviors.

Many mentally ill persons find it difficult to cope with even minor changes. They require support and education to learn the skills that allow them to adapt. Clients who are able to adapt eventually become willing to take some risks and engage in new behaviors. Self-worth is enhanced, followed by an improvement in abilities. Slowly, the focus is changed from what cannot be done to what has been accomplished.

Encourage clients to problem-solve and consider new solutions. Offer praise for attempts at learning new actions and attitudes. The person with mental illness must fulfill the needs of life just as we all do.

One Step at a Time

There is an old saying, "The longest journey begins with a single step." This was never so true as it is in mental health care. To people with mental-emotional problems, everything seems overwhelming. Even the simplest decisions, such as what to wear that day, are monumental to a person suffering from depression. People diagnosed with schizophrenia may not be able to differentiate one world from another long enough to follow a train of thought to a logical conclusion. Therefore it is important for nurses to give instructions simply and repeat them often.

When planning therapeutic interventions, remember the importance of mastering the first item before proceeding onto other or more complex steps. This process involves breaking down a task or concept into smaller, simpler units. For example, the goal is for the client to arrive on time for appointments. This may involve wearing a watch, being able to tell time, remembering the appointment, and transporting oneself to the building where the appointment takes place. The first step in meeting the goal may be the purchase of a watch.

There are two points to be made here. The first is "do *not* assume, assess." Using the example above,

---

REALITY THERAPY

William Glasser's reality therapy is based on the concept of responsibility. Reality therapists do not accept the concept of mental illness. They believe that when people are unable to fulfill their needs, they behave unrealistically. Calling people "irresponsible" rather than "mentally ill" and describing *how* they are irresponsible help clients to develop the responsibility to meet their needs satisfactorily.

Reality therapy differs from psychoanalysis in six ways:

1. Because reality therapy does not accept the notion of mental illness, clients cannot become involved in therapy as mentally ill persons who have no responsibility.
2. Reality therapy works in the present with an eye on the future. It does not accept the limitations of the past.
3. Reality therapists relate to clients as themselves, not as aloof professionals or transference objects.
4. Reality therapists do not look for unconscious conflicts. Clients cannot excuse their behaviors on the basis of unconscious motivations.
5. Reality therapy emphasizes the morality of behavior. Issues of right and wrong are defined and enforced.
6. The goal of reality therapy is to help clients help themselves fulfill their needs right now.

one assumes that every adult can tell time, but the results of this assessment revealed that the client could not tell time because of blurred vision. Unless the nurse helps the client deal with the visual problems, he/she will not be successful in meeting the goal of routinely keeping all appointments.

Second, remember that success is built on many small steps. Every person needs to feel successful when attempting something new or different. By breaking each learning experience down into smaller units, the chances of mastering the skill or knowledge is enhanced. Make sure that the client will succeed within the first few steps if at all possible. The taste of success is especially sweet in the early stages, and it encourages people to continue trying. One small, successful step soon becomes two, and those small triumphs can become symbolic of the client's potential for growth and change.

Provide Consistency

The last principle for mental health care providers relates to the concept of **consistency.** Persons with mental illness often lack the security of someone who is always there when they are needed, someone who nurtures them. Without consistent parental guidance, children find their own ways to cope with the world, and some of these ways become maladaptive, ineffectual behaviors. In some cases in which individuals were not routinely guided as children, the consistency and the reliability of mental health care providers is sometimes their only stability. The link that serves as a bridge between the client's world and the world of reality is frequently the reliability of the therapeutic relationship (McConnell, 1995).

The concept of consistency is usually addressed in the client's plan of care, but each therapeutic intervention must be routinely used by every member of the care team. Clients often test staff members by "playing one against the other" or attempting to manipulate the situation and gain control. However, when each care provider responds by giving the same message, clients learn that members of the care team can be relied on to do what they say they will do. Two general guidelines for providing consistency are to set limits and focus on the positive changes that clients are making.

Set and Enforce Limits

Every culture has its definitions of "right" and "wrong" behaviors. Children are taught from an early age which actions are acceptable in their society and which are not. Through systems of trial and error, behavioral modeling, and reward and punishment, children learn about the behaviors of other people in their environment. When the behavioral messages are mixed or inconsistent, children become confused and attempt to discover which actions best meet their needs in various settings. They learn that different rules apply to different situations. A good example of this is the mother who teaches her children to always tell the truth and then instructs them to tell the salesman on the telephone that she is not at home. In this case, the children have received the message that it is permissible to tell a lie under certain conditions. When enough of these double messages are received, children begin to devise their own rules for living which may or may not be in keeping with society's notions of right behavior.

Setting limits involves clients, staff members, and institutional policies (Chenevert, 1994). As the plan of care is developed by the care team and the client, each rule or limitation is established. Facility policies must be followed by everyone, so the facility policies themselves define some limitations. The remainder of the "rules" relate to therapeutic activities, social interactions, and personal behaviors. Whatever the limitations, the client must be informed and willing to cooperate with the plan of care.

Each member of the care team has the responsibility to understand the purpose of each limitation and the methods for enforcing them. To illustrate, the facility's policy is for all clients to remain out of bed during the day. To accomplish this the staff informs each client every morning that the doors to the rooms will be locked by 9 AM. Then the aide makes 9 AM rounds and locks the door to each room. The clients were informed and then reminded of the rule. Last came the enforcement or actual action that demonstrated the limitation would be followed. Something as simple as providing a routine can teach clients about the value of reliability, consistency, and stability.

This brings us to an important and valuable point: Do not commit yourself unless you are able to fill the commitment. Nurses play an essential role in the care of people with mental-emotional problems. If your actions are not reliable, if you do not behaviorally demonstrate stability and consistency, then the therapeutic relationship will be established only with great difficulty. Clients are people, and people need to know if someone truly cares and is willing to make the connection that helps them to heal.

These seven principles are offered as guidelines for working with people who are suffering (see the box on p. 115). Although the focus has been on the person labeled "mentally ill," every client in the health care system needs to be offered acceptance, trust, and emotional support. The whole person, not the pathological condition, is the focus of the nursing profession.

PRINCIPLES OF MENTAL HEALTH CARE

1. Do no harm.
2. Accept each client as a whole person.
3. Develop mutual trust.
4. Explore behaviors and emotions.
5. Encourage responsibility.
6. Encourage effective adaptation.
7. Provide consistency.

❖ KEY CONCEPTS

- A mentally healthy adult is a person who can cope with and adjust to the stresses of daily living in a socially acceptable way.

- One of the foundations of the nursing profession is the care of the whole person, which includes the emotional dimension.

- The principle of "do no harm" provides a valuable guide for nursing actions.

- The therapeutic tools of the self, combined with the skills of the nurse, result in a practitioner of the nursing arts.

- Understanding clients in relation to their work, family, and social environments encourages nurses to practice holistic health care.

- Trust is the foundation of the therapeutic relationship and forms the basis for the success or failure of nursing actions.

- Behaviors can be better understood when nurses consider the person's internal frame of reference (private world), the context in which the behaviors occur, and the meaning of the action.

- Encouraging responsibility is a primary nursing intervention because it helps to build self-worth, dignity, and confidence; offers opportunities for learning to problem solve; and assists clients in learning more successful coping behaviors.

- In mental health terms, adaptation means sufficient improvement to carry out everyday activities.

- When therapeutic nursing interventions are planned, the importance of mastering the first item before proceeding onto more complex steps must be kept in mind.

- The link that serves as a bridge between the client's world and the world of reality is frequently the consistency and reliability of the therapeutic relationship.

- Nurses and other health care providers must be willing to set and reinforce clients' behavioral limits with gentle firmness and consistency.

❖ SUGGESTIONS FOR FURTHER READING

Diane Kelly's article, "Three Tips for Closer Caring in *Nursing 95* (25[5]:72, 1995), offers three suggestions for bridging the distance between nurses and their clients.

❖ REFERENCES

Brady J: All in a day's leisure, *Am J Nurs* 95(2):45, 1995.

Brady J: Being there, *Am J Nurs* 94(5):54, 1994.

Chenevert M: *STAT: special techniques in assertiveness training,* ed 4, St Louis, 1994, Mosby.

Coping with mental illness requires courage, *Menninger Lett* 3(4):3, 1995.

Freeman DL: Quantum consciousness, *Discover* (6):89, 1994.

Gaut DA, editor: *A global agenda for caring,* New York, 1993, National League for Nursing Press.

Geller JL: Treating revolving-door patients who have "hospitalphilia": compassion, coercion, and common sense, *Hosp Comm Psychiatry* 44(2):141, 1993.

Haber J and others: *Comprehensive psychiatric nursing,* ed 5, St Louis, 1997, Mosby.

Johnson JL: A dialectical examination of nursing art, *Adv Nurs Sci* 17:1, 1994.

Kelly D: Three tips for closer caring, *Nurs 95* 25(5):72, 1995.

Keltner NL, Schwecke LH, Bostrom CE: *Psychiatric nursing,* ed 2, St Louis, 1995, Mosby.

McCain NL, Smith JC: Stress and coping in the context of psychoneuroimmunology: a holistic framework for nursing practice and research, *Arch Psychiatr Nurs* (8):221, 1994.

McConnell EA: Making the invisible visible, *Nurs 95* 25(4):53, 1995.

Ormel J and others: Common mental disorders and disability across cultures: results from the WHO collaborative study on psychological problems in general health care, *JAMA* 272(22):1471, 1994.

Renz MC: All the wrong reasons, *Nurs 95* 25(5):47, 1995.

Sherwood G: A qualitative analysis of patient response to caring: a moral and economic imperative. In Gaut DA, editor: *A global agenda for caring,* New York, 1993, National League for Nursing Press.

Sorrell J: Simple gestures of caring, *Am J Nurs* 94(8):33, 1994.

Starck PL, McGovern JP, editors: *The hidden dimension of human suffering,* New York, 1992, National League for Nursing Press.

Stuart GW, Sundeen SJ: *Principles and practice of psychiatric nursing,* ed 5, St Louis, 1995, Mosby.

Weaver SK, Wilson JF: Moving toward patient empowerment, *Nurs Health Care* 15(9):480, 1994.

Wichowski HC, Kubsh S: Improving your patient's compliance, *Nurs 95* 25(1):67, 1995.

Zwerding M: Nursing care for the societal client, *Nurs Health Care* 15(8): 422, 1994.

9

THE THERAPEUTIC ENVIRONMENT

LEARNING OBJECTIVES

1. List two situations that indicate a need for hospitalization.
2. Describe three types of clients treated in the inpatient therapeutic environment.
3. State two goals of the therapeutic environment.
4. Discuss five environmental factors that must be assessed daily.
5. Explain the importance of setting limits on clients' behaviors.
6. Identify three ways in which the therapeutic environment helps clients meet their needs for love and belonging.
7. Examine how nurses' expectations influence clients' behaviors.
8. List three techniques to improve client compliance.

KEY TERMS

acceptance
chronicity
communication
compliance
crisis stabilization

expectations
involvement
limit setting
nurse-client relationship
physical properties

recidivism
self-actualization
social relationships
therapeutic milieu

The history of the treatment of mentally troubled people has not been kind. In the United States, most of the mentally ill were housed in large, custodial care institutions until after World War II. With the introduction of psychotherapeutic drugs during the 1950s, a new interest in caring for the mentally ill developed, and researchers began to look at the environment in which people were treated.

In 1953, a small book by Maxwell Jones was published in England. In it, he described the value of the environment as a therapeutic tool. When his book was published in the United States, it bore the title *The Therapeutic Community.* Soon it became a main factor in the development of treatment settings that fostered personal worth and dignity. Today, the therapeutic environment is an important part of clients' treatment plans.

The term **therapeutic milieu** is used to describe certain settings or environments designed to help clients replace inappropriate behaviors with more effective personal and psychosocial skills (Stuart and Sundeen, 1995). Therapeutic milieus can exist within hospital, home, or community settings, but each environment helps clients meet their needs and assists them with their problems.

Because most therapeutic environments require certain limits and controls, they are usually established in inpatient settings, as part of a community hospital, for example. Standards describing the therapeutic milieu are set forth by the Joint Commission on Accreditation of Hospitals, and several tools for assessing the therapeutic environment have been developed.

Most people with mental-emotional problems manage within the communities in which they live. However, there are times when a more secure and stable environment is needed. Admission to a psychiatric inpatient facility occurs after one of the following:

1. A person becomes a threat to the safety of himself/herself or others.
2. People within the environment are not able or willing to continue supporting the mentally troubled person.
3. The person perceives himself/herself as unable to cope or maintain behavioral control.

Admission to an inpatient facility can be on a voluntary or involuntary basis, but every treatment plan is designed to return clients to their communities as soon as possible.

Nurses who work in therapeutic inpatient settings provide the framework for the quality of the environment. "Without a nursing staff with insight, understanding, personal warmth, and skill in directing groups, the concept of a therapeutic community could not have developed into a reality" (Taylor, 1994).

Psychiatric nursing practice has moved from custodial care to the management of complex therapeutic environments. Nurses now require the knowledge and expertise necessary to manage clients' environments, implement therapeutic interventions, coordinate and integrate multidisciplinary care delivery, and evaluate the outcomes of treatment for each client with whom they work.

Use of the Inpatient Setting

Before the 1960s, stays in psychiatric units often lasted months or even years. When clients were actually discharged, little support was found in the community. In contrast, today's psychiatric facilities offer shorter stays, more intensive therapies, and support during the transition from institution to community. Services are provided for three main groups of people: those experiencing crises, those with acute mental or emotional problems, and those with chronic mental illness.

Crisis Stabilization

One of the most often provided mental health services is crisis intervention. People experiencing a crisis are unable to cope with their problems. Many seek help when their discomfort becomes greater than their need to privately solve their problems. In many cases, therapeutic interventions are provided by placing clients in 1- or 2-day treatment settings where balance (homeostasis) can be reestablished. Clients undergo intensive counseling designed to solve their immediate problems. Psychotherapeutic medications, such as antidepressants or sedatives, may be prescribed. Stress management techniques are also taught to help to modify stressful behaviors. Cognitive, relaxation, and behavioral therapies are often used to assist clients in coping with the crisis situation. The goal of inpatient crisis therapy is **crisis stabilization.** After clients are discharged from the crisis stabilization unit, they may be referred for assertiveness training; time, anger, or conflict management training; or problem-solving education.

Acute Care and Treatment

The inpatient environment is also needed when people become so unable to function that they cannot meet their basic needs. By the time people seek voluntary admission to a treatment facility, they usually feel weakened and hopeless (Cohen, 1994). Frequently clients are impaired or intoxicated, but all are unable to engage in the activities of daily living. Some have recently experienced a severe stressor such as a job layoff, illness, or loss of support systems.

People who are hospitalized involuntarily experience an intense discomfort during their first hospital experience and a great sense of failure on subsequent admissions (Joseph-Kinzelman and others, 1994). Admission to an inpatient psychiatric unit is a highly emotional experience for most people. It can "dehumanize" an individual: personal items are taken away, and staff members sometimes remember the diagnosis before the name. Nurses should try to "humanize" the hospital experience because the foundation of the client's success or failure lies with the first experiences in the therapeutic environment. Most people with acute psychiatric problems can be successfully treated if interventions are vigorous and well coordinated. However, some individuals, even with the best of therapies, progress to chronic maladaptive responses and a cycle of repeated admissions.

The Chronically Mentally Ill

In the United States today, 72% of every mental health insurance dollar is spent on inpatient psychiatric care (Mental Health Policy Resource Center, 1992). Many mental health problems are associated with a degree of **chronicity**, which means that the problems tend to persist for a long period of time. People with chronic mental disorders may have periods of relative comfort and ease of functioning and then fall rapidly into acute psychiatric states. For these people, life grows into a see-saw existence between two worlds.

Many persons with chronic mental health problems are able to figure out when they are beginning to decompensate (or "lose it" as some clients say) and will voluntarily admit themselves to an inpatient facility. Many more, however, do not have the insight or judgment to know when they are acting in maladaptive ways. Others are paranoid (suspicious, afraid of others) and do not seek help or refuse treatment when it is offered. Last, there is the growing number of mentally troubled individuals who have never sought assistance or received treatment. They live with their distresses the best they can.

The inpatient therapeutic environment fills many needs for troubled individuals. It provides the physical necessities of clean water, wholesome food, clean clothing, and a comfortable bed (see box above, at right). Plus, an inpatient facility provides protection, safety, and security from a harsh world and a staff of mental health care providers who offer more individual attention and emotional support than most people on "the outside." From the chronically troubled person's point of view, life in the inpatient facility may actually be better than the lonely existence they face in the community.

> ### THINK ABOUT
> Many clients with chronic mental problems will admit themselves to an inpatient unit because they are looking for "three hots and a cot."
>   What is the meaning of the statement?
>   How does this statement relate to Maslow's hierarchy of needs theory? (Hint: see Chapter 6).
>   Do you think it affects the client's attitude toward the therapeutic treatment plan?

Recidivism (repeated inpatient admissions) has become a way of life for many of the chronically mentally troubled. This is especially true for clients with cycles of assaultive behaviors. Aggressive clients also had longer inpatient stays than suicidal or depressed people.

Recidivism, also called the "revolving-door syndrome," continues to be a problem for clients and their care providers (Geller, 1993). With the focus on the "least restrictive environment," many chronically mentally ill clients now live in small, homelike, sheltered group settings within the community, but there are others are who are continually involved in the revolving-door syndrome of admission and discharge.

Goals of a Therapeutic Environment

A therapeutic environment is possible in every health care delivery setting to some degree (Murray and Baier, 1993). However, some people with mental-emotional problems need the protective environments that are offered by inpatient psychiatric settings. Dr. Peter Breggin, author of *Toxic Psychiatry* (1991), defines mental illness as "overwhelm" and believes that people should be offered mental health care in small, local "sanctuaries" (rather than in psychiatric institutions) until they were able to cope with the demands of everyday life once again. The concept of providing sanctuary for the mentally troubled helps to release people from the label of being admitted to a "psychiatric hospital" or "mental institution."

Effective therapeutic environments provide the safety, security, and time to cope with difficulties (Moos, 1974). Members of the health care team offer therapeutic human contact designed to assist clients in learning about themselves and how they relate to others.

The goals of a therapeutic environment (milieu) are as follows:

1. Protect the client and others during periods of maladaptive behaviors.
2. Help individuals develop self-worth and confidence.

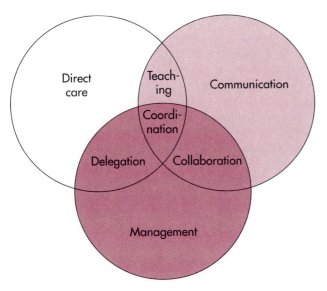

Fig. 9-1   Mental health nursing practice. (Redrawn from Stuart GW, Sundeen SJ: *Principles and practice of psychiatric nursing,* ed 5, St Louis, 1995, Mosby.)

3. Teach more effective adaptive (coping) skills for meeting their needs.

A treatment team, composed of several mental health specialists, is assigned to work with each client. On admission, a thorough assessment is done, and a therapeutic plan of care is developed. Fig. 9-1 illustrates the nurse's role as a member of the mental health treatment team.

Help Clients Meet Needs

People are frequently admitted to inpatient psychiatric settings because they are unable to maintain their activities of daily living or their pain (mental or physical) has become unbearable. Individuals with depression, for example, may stop interacting with friends, refuse to go to work, or even stop eating. Teens who suffer from anorexia nervosa and other eating disorders often have a long history of dieting, uncontrolled eating, and vomiting.

Many people with mental-emotional problems manage to meet their basic needs while living within the community as long as their lifestyles are stable and routine. If that stability is disrupted or someone important is removed from the client's world, a crisis results, and the individual becomes overwhelmed and unable to effectively function. Sometimes individuals can be assisted with their problems and stay within the community by receiving treatment through partial or day hospitalization programs. Others benefit from the security of the more controlled and limited setting of the inpatient environment where they can focus on meeting their needs in more appropriate ways.

Teach Psychosocial (Adaptive) Skills

People use behaviors that tend to work. When actions result in success, the behavior that made that success possible is more likely to be repeated, whether it is socially acceptable or not. Similarly, admission to an inpatient therapeutic treatment environment allows persons with maladaptive behaviors the opportunity to learn more acceptable ways of behaving. With the help of the treatment team members, clients can learn to replace their usual ways of behaving with more effective and adaptive actions.

The Therapeutic Environment and Client Needs

Maslow's theory of a hierarchy of needs states that if a basic physical need goes unmet, it will be fulfilled before other, higher level needs. Simply put, this means that a person must be able to breathe easily and obtain water, food, shelter, and rest (basic physical needs) before he/she will be able to pursue other needs. People who are suffering from mental and emotional troubles frequently are unable to procure even the most basic of life's requirements.

We all feel hunger and thirst, but the person with a mental illness may not be able to recognize or act on the body's signals. Sometimes their reality makes no provisions for the care of the body. Some persons may believe that it is inappropriate to eat or practice good hygiene, whereas others just do not care about the condition of the body. The therapeutic environment offers a constructive setting for people to learn how to meet their own needs as well as the support and encouragement to practice new and more effective behaviors.

Remember that people are holistic beings. A change in one area of functioning brings about a response within the whole person. Therefore assisting clients in meeting their more basic needs prepares the way for changes in other areas of life. Using Maslow's hierarchy of needs as a guide, consider how the therapeutic environment relates to meeting human needs.

Physical Needs

All people need to breathe. This is the first and most basic need. Without air or the ability to exchange it, a person will not survive for more than a few minutes. For most people, breathing is not a problem, but for those with lung disease, for example, the simple act of exchanging air can be their first and major priority throughout each day.

Nourishment is another area that is commonly taken for granted—until one is unable to obtain food. Many clients who are experiencing hallucinations or paranoid (suspicious) thoughts will refuse to eat or drink for fear of being poisoned, drugged, or controlled by the use of food. Other persons have eaten poorly before admission and welcome the opportunity to receive wholesome food and clean drinking water. Some clients may require special diets because of their medical conditions or medications. The box below is a reminder of the importance of monitoring diets.

The act of eating and sharing food is a social event in many cultures. Numerous customs have evolved around the obtaining, preparation, and consuming of food and drink. Learn about clients' perceptions associated with food. How does the cultural background of your clients influence the foods they consume? What are their food preferences? Do any of their mental health problems involve food? Assessing client behaviors associated with food allows nurses to

intervene at a basic level, prevent further problems, and evaluate the effectiveness of nursing actions. Table 9-1 lists client problems and the nursing actions related to food.

Hygiene needs are important in the therapeutic environment. Clients are frequently admitted in various states of cleanliness ranging from obsessively tidy to slovenly. People who are experiencing acute episodes of schizophrenia, for example, seldom relate to their physical appearance or state of hygiene. Some individuals will dress inappropriately, putting on several shirts at one time or wearing undergarments over their coats.

Encourage good hygiene habits. Discover if the client has a preference or ritual for bathing or dressing. Encourage good daily hygiene but do not become forceful. Compliment clients on their appearance when efforts have been made. Appropriate hygiene practices help to fill more than one basic physical need; they also communicate a willingness for social contact.

The physical surroundings of the therapeutic environment are important. The institutions of the past were designed with small rooms, locked doors, and long corridors that allowed the staff to control clients' movements and monitor each activity. Today, the architecture of the old asylum has been replaced by a more normalized environment, which includes provisions for personal space and privacy.

The **physical properties** of the environment have an effect on each other and the people who live within that space. Nurses are responsible for monitoring how each aspect of the physical environment affects clients. The physical properties of a therapeutic environment include temperature, lighting, sound, cleanliness, and aesthetics.

The temperature, air circulation, and humidity of the unit all have an effect on clients. People respond to

---

 DRUG ALERT

Remember that clients who are taking monoamine oxidase inhibitors (MAOIs) are not allowed to eat certain meats (bologna, liver), dairy products (aged cheeses, sour cream, yogurt), vegetables (fava beans, avocados), fruits (bananas, figs), and alcoholic beverages (beer, ale, red wines, sherry). Such clients should eat no chocolate and avoid caffeine in large amounts.

Monitor clients' food and fluid intake daily. Also routinely monitor vital signs, especially the pulse and blood pressure. Report any complaints of chest tightness, stiff neck, or throbbing headache to the physician immediately because these symptoms may herald the onset of hypertensive crisis.

◆ **TABLE 9-1**
Mental Health Problems and Nursing Interventions Associated With Food

Problem	Nursing Intervention
Client believes food is poisoned or tainted.	Serve each food in single-serving, disposable containers. Allow client to casually observe other people eating same food items.
Client has no interest in food or eating.	Serve meals at regular intervals. Leave food within easy reach of client. Offer frequent snacks. Use odors of certain foods to encourage client to eat.
Client uses food as emotional substitute.	Provide opportunities for interactions with other people that do not relate to eating. Work with client to discover which needs are being met through use of food.

these factors in highly individual ways. For example, an agitated or hyperactive individual may find the environmental temperature too high and react by becoming even more distressed. Hot days and high humidity can increase aggressiveness or make clients lethargic. People who are depressed and hypoactive may be more affected by cooler temperatures. Nurses must be aware that the environmental temperatures and humidity levels have an impact on behavior. Therefore the daily assessment of the therapeutic environment should include temperature and humidity.

Next the environment's lighting should be assessed. Lighting includes the "amount of light, its diffusion, and the reflection of light waves off environmental surfaces combined with the impact of surface colors" (Haber and others, 1992). It is important that lighting be constant and of the right intensity. Flickering lights can trigger delusions or hallucinations, whereas lighting that is too bright can result in overstimulation and aggressive behaviors. Lighting that is too low in intensity can present inadequate or inaccurate stimuli, resulting in misperceptions of actual objects. For example, it becomes easier to perceive an animal where the chair usually is located when the lighting distorts environmental cues.

Sunlight has an effect on clients who are receiving psychotherapeutic medications. When outdoors, these people must wear protective clothing, sunscreen lotion, and a large-brimmed hat. They also require extra fluids.

Some clients experience hypersensitivity to color, especially if they are confused, agitated, or hyperactive. Colors are very symbolic for human beings. Bright colors are stimulating, whereas dark colors are depressing. Neutral colors tend to calm emotions and behaviors. Certain colors hold meaning for some clients who associate a particular color with a specific person, event, or situation. The nurse should try to assess the impact of color and lighting for each client and observe client behaviors in various lighting and color settings.

The acoustical or sound environment is composed of noises generated by people and equipment. Walls, floors, and objects within the environment have sound-absorbing or acoustical qualities. Floors with carpeting, for example, absorb sound waves and quiet the environment, whereas hard tile floors tend to magnify sounds. Upholstered furniture absorbs more sound than wooden or plastic furniture.

Environmental noise can have a calming or agitating effect on clients. Calm music, the sound of ocean waves, or a light rain can produce relaxation. High noise levels can lead to distorted perceptions, altered analytical thinking, and sensory overload. People experiencing mental illness are commonly hypersensitive to sounds. When noise levels become too intense, clients tend to become distracted, agitated, and possibly assaultive. This does not imply, however, that each staff member must walk around in silence, but it does alert you to the fact that sound plays an important role in the therapeutic environment (Table 9-2).

The hygiene associated with the environment refers to the state of cleanliness of the physical space and the objects within it. Because many clients live closely to one another, the likelihood of infection is increased. The stresses of mental illness can decrease clients' resistance to infection. In addition, the potential for nuisances such as mice, cockroaches, and other vermin is increased if the physical surroundings are not kept clean.

People with mental or emotional difficulties can have little regard for the cleanliness of their surroundings. Sometimes persons with lice, scabies, or crabs are admitted to the therapeutic environment, and if allowed to continue unchecked, every client within the immediate environment will require treatment. Nurses must include an assessment of the state of the unit's cleanliness on a daily basis. This small assessment today may prevent large problems from developing tomorrow.

Last is the issue of aesthetics. Is the environment pleasing to the eye? Does the environment make one

◆ TABLE 9-2
A "Sound" Exercise

Action	Evaluation
Listen to a short composition of classical music. Listen to a hard rock musical selection.	Record how you felt as soon as the piece was finished. Record your feelings as soon as the song is finished.
Compare your immediate feelings associated with both musical selections.	Did one composition make you feel more excited, calmer? How do you think different types of music affect your mental health clients?

want to stay and relax or leave quickly? The condition of the furniture and other objects within a setting leaves people with a certain impression. An environment that is tidy and in good condition sends a message of caring and pride in appearance. The careful use of color and texture can also produce an environment that communicates a sense of hospitality and belonging.

It is important for other health care providers to remember that we go home every night to our own homes. Clients who are living within the therapeutic setting do not. They are there 24 hours of every day. If you were in this situation, you would appreciate the efforts of others to make the physical environment as pleasant as possible.

Safety and Security Needs

The safety and security offered by the therapeutic environment is one of the most important factors in mental health care. Safety and security needs within the therapeutic environment include the feeling of physical safety, the security of a limited setting, and the ability to feel secure with others. For clients who are depressed or suicidal, the therapeutic environment offers special protection from self-harm. Clients with aggressive behaviors are offered protection from themselves and assurance that limits will be placed on their actions.

Safety also includes a freedom from hazards. Most psychiatric environments are open and allow for observation of clients' activities. Objects that have the potential for harm are removed, and the design of electrical fixtures, doors, and other equipment helps to promote safety. Paging systems with identification codes allow help to be summoned when needed. Not infrequently, a client will act out or behave impulsively. When this occurs, members of the treatment team set limits on the maladaptive actions and then attempt to identify the feelings that motivated the inappropriate response.

People also need to feel secure within their environments. The inpatient therapeutic environment provides the comfort of order and organization in the form of a daily routine, a set of rules, schedules, and activities. For many psychiatric clients, knowing what is going to happen tomorrow adds to their sense of security today.

The use of space is important in maintaining a therapeutic environment. The design of the physical setting has an influence on how space is used for daily activities. Such factors as the location of the recreation room, medication area, and clients' sleeping areas define how physical space is used, but nurses are more concerned with the concepts of space that relate directly to client care: territory and distance.

Chapter 4 discusses distance and territory in detail, but the importance of these two concepts to the therapeutic environment is emphasized here. Each person needs personal space with defined boundaries and control (Goren and Orion, 1994). Mental health clients in an inpatient setting establish a territory that "belongs to them." Usually clients claim their rooms, dressers, and sleeping areas as their own. Nurses and every person who works with clients or their environments (e.g., housekeepers) must be aware of invading clients' territories. Behaviors such as knocking or announcing oneself *before* entering clients' spaces fosters self-worth and demonstrates respect for clients' personal space.

The distance between people affects clients. People with suspicious feelings usually feel more comfortable when the nurse is outside their intimate space. Depressed persons may need the touch and physical contact of the nurse. Aggressive clients may interpret the close presence of a nurse as a threatening act. Each client must be observed carefully; it is usually possible to tell which distances are most comfortable for interacting with each client.

Limit setting allows the therapeutic environment to be consistent and predictable. Every human being must function within certain limits. These limits are established by one's culture, social group, and laws that govern one's society. Many clients with mental problems have difficulty behaving within these limits. Clients know that nurses will enforce the external controls that keep them and others within the environment safe. This knowledge fosters a sense of safety and the security of knowing that aggressive actions will be contained.

Two important nursing interventions for setting limits are:

1. Reinforce the established structure (rules, routine) of the therapeutic setting.
2. Be consistent.

When the environment is controlled, clients have an opportunity to safely explore their feelings and learn new, more effective behaviors.

The concept of time is impaired for many psychiatric clients, which causes various degrees of disorientation and insecurity about the environment. The perception of the flow of time may be altered, and time may pass very quickly or too slowly. Recognizing the divisions of time (seconds, minutes, hours) may be a problem, and the client may not pay attention to time. As a result of these impairments, clients have problems with appointments, scheduled events, and tasks—anything that involves the concept of time (Table 9-3).

◆ **TABLE 9-3**
Examples of Impaired Time Concepts

Disorder	Change in Concept of Time
Organic mental disorders (Alzheimer's disease, and others)	Difficulty understanding passage of time *Example:* Clients ask frequently about date, day, schedules. Clients think they were just admitted when they have been there for several days. Clients are poor historians.
Substance abuse Hallucinogenics	Time passes quickly, space is smaller. *Example:* Clients arrive early, write larger than usual.
Tranquilizers	Time passes slowly, space is larger. *Example:* Clients arrive late, writing is small, cramped. All ignore past, focus on present, and are unrealistic about future.
Depression	Time passes slowly. Clients tend to focus on past, ignore present, and show little interest in future.

Modified from Haber J and others: *Comprehensive psychiatric nursing,* ed 4, St Louis, 1992, Mosby.

Nursing interventions for clients with a distorted sense of time focus on routinely orienting clients to time through the use of clocks, written schedules, and diaries kept by clients.

Love and Belonging Needs

The fact that a person is struggling with a mental health problem does not dismiss the need to be accepted and find one's place within a group. Life in the community can be a lonely existence, with no friends, few acquaintances, and fewer resources. The isolation of mental illness is intense. Sometimes, the lack of human contact, combined with the existing psychiatric problem and the roadblocks created by stigmas, overwhelms the individual and results in more intense or frequent psychotic episodes and ultimately admission to an inpatient setting.

The therapeutic environment offers clients many opportunities to appropriately fulfill their needs for companionship and group identification. Clients' love and belonging needs are fulfilled within the therapeutic setting through the use of communication, social interactions, and nurse (care provider)–client relationships.

Communication is the method by which one person interacts with another. It takes place on several levels, and not all aspects of every communication are obvious. It is important to understand that when nurses communicate with their clients, they are usually sending more than one message. In the inpatient setting, clients are respected as individuals who have the right to express themselves as long as their behaviors are appropriate. Nurses communicate respect by encouraging clients to interact with each other and staff members. Through their caring, sensitive communications and interest in each person, nurses help their clients fill their needs for human companionship (Kelly, 1995).

Love and belonging needs for people in the therapeutic environment are also fulfilled through the social group to which one chooses to belong. Whenever people are together, they tend to form groups. Clients with mental health problems are no different in this respect. If their illness is not too severe, clients will attempt to form relationships with others. An activity as simple as walking together to an appointment helps clients meet their belonging needs.

Social relationships can contribute greatly to meeting clients' needs for belonging, but the potential for abuse does exist. Nurses must be alert to the social relationships that are forming within the therapeutic environment. They must observe, monitor, and evaluate the appropriateness of certain relationships and discuss their concerns with the treatment team. Social relationships within the therapeutic environment have the same potential for positive growth or negative adaptation as any other relationship. Therefore nurses must protect the more vulnerable and easily led clients from becoming dependent on more aggressive or manipulative persons.

The **nurse-client relationship** is another major tool for meeting clients' love and belonging needs. All members of the treatment team interact therapeutically with clients, but it is the nurse who assists clients with the activities of daily living (and coping). Thus nurses are in the special position of always being there, demonstrating consistency, reliability, and acceptance. It is the energy exchange of the therapeutic relationship that helps clients move from the overwhelming aspect of their illness, to the dependency of the therapeutic environment, and then to the independence of autonomy. Chapter 10 explores the therapeutic relationship in greater detail.

Self-Esteem Needs

Respect, esteem, and recognition must be given by the self first, then by others. Self-respect, self-esteem, and self-recognition must be internalized or realized first. To state it simply: You must love and respect yourself before others can love and respect you. In the therapeutic setting, nurses assist clients in building self-esteem needs through acceptance, expectations, and involvement.

Acceptance, in the mental health context, means that the nurse acknowledges the client as a human being who is worthy of respect and dignity. Although clients may behave in maladaptive or unacceptable ways, they are still worthy of respect. It is very important to *separate the behavior from the person.* You may not approve of the client's actions, behaviors, or attitudes, but you do accept the person. If a client must be corrected or reminded, focus on the *behavior* rather than on the *person.* For example, the statement "I have trouble following your thoughts when you speak so loudly" communicates more acceptance than "Stop yelling. You are so loud that I can't follow what you are saying." Correcting or refocusing the *behavior* spares the self-esteem of the person.

Expectations play a role in the development of clients' abilities to meet self-esteem needs. The inpatient therapeutic setting provides established rules of conduct, consistent routines, and a stable environment. The expectations of this world and its consequences are known.

Nurses' expectations also have an impact on clients' behaviors. When nurses communicate what is expected, clients commonly live up to those expectations. This can work both ways, however. If the nurse expects a client to behave in an inappropriate way, he/she usually does. If the nurse places high but realistic expectations on the individual, many times the client will strive to meet those expectations. There is a valuable lesson here: do not limit clients with your own expectations. Assume that they will succeed, but keep observations and assessments based in reality.

You may be surprised at what clients are capable of achieving.

Clients also need **involvement** to meet their self-esteem needs. Involvement is the process of actively interacting with the environment and those persons within it. When clients are involved, they are actively sharing activities. These experiences foster ego strength and feelings of worth and importance. Involvement also offers opportunities to modify ineffective behaviors and try out new ones. Therapeutic treatment settings that focus on involvement use cooperation, compromise, and confrontation to foster behavioral control, effective social interactions, and a sense of self-worth in clients.

Self-Actualization Needs

The need to achieve one's full potential lies within us all. However, not all people will become self-actualized. Remember Maslow's basic point: Lower order needs must be met before the person can take steps to meet higher order needs. Consequently, people who cannot meet their basic physical necessities will have little success in addressing their self-esteem or self-actualization needs. As clients in the inpatient psychiatric setting begin to stabilize, they become more able to cope. With the treatment team's assistance, new ways of coping are developed and tried. The process of trying and of becoming actively engaged helps to lead clients in the direction of **self-actualization.** Living up to one's full potential means being the best one can be. People with mental-emotional problems deserve the opportunity to strive for this goal no less than the rest of us.

Nursing Care in the Therapeutic Environment

Psychiatric hospitalization is a traumatic experience. Before being admitted to the inpatient environment, people often experience intense discomfort with the activities or details of their lives. Individuals who are admitted for the first time to an inpatient treatment setting report a sense of panic and lack of control over their situation. Those clients who are facing readmission most often express a sense of failure and worthlessness (Joseph-Kinzelman and others, 1994).

Nurses who work in the inpatient setting can do much to relieve the discomforts faced by clients. The mental health treatment team develops the therapeutic treatment plan, and each specialist plays a role in caring for the client. However, it is the nurse who assists clients with the activities of daily living and monitors each step made toward the goals of treatment.

Admission

The process of admitting a client to a health care facility is usually detailed but fairly straightforward. However, when clients are admitted to a psychiatric setting, their emotional state plays a large role in the actual process of admission. During admission, nurses commonly try to explain the rules, routines, and rituals of the unit. Clients, however, are almost always too anxious to understand or remember anything in detail. They are then expected to follow the rules and engage in the appropriate activities even though the memory of the first few days at the facility is absent or blurred.

Nurses need to remember that people with high anxiety levels seldom remember what was said, especially when they are in unfamiliar settings. Approach clients in a calm and respectful manner. Give simple but clear explanations and repeat them as necessary. Answer any questions the client may have. Make sure that the client is more important than the admission form you must complete. Take the time to behaviorally communicate that you are concerned for the welfare of this person. Remember the feelings of helplessness felt by mental health clients and make efforts to support the client in adapting to the therapeutic environment.

Most inpatient facilities have an established procedure for admitting clients and standard forms for data collection (see box on p. 126, top). During the admission process, a person may be interviewed by several members of the treatment team, all of them asking the same questions. This situation causes unnecessary anxiety for clients and is a poor use of therapist time. Having one person perform the initial admission interview prevents confusion and added stress for the person being admitted. Once the client is emotionally stabilized, the information necessary to complete the database can be easily obtained.

The experience of being admitted to an inpatient setting establishes the tone for the client's entire stay. It is the first component of the person's experience with the therapeutic environment, and as we all know, the first impression is usually a lasting one.

Discharge

The process of preparing for discharge begins on admission. The length of stay for mental health clients has decreased dramatically in the recent past. The goal of inpatient treatment has shifted from custodial care to actively returning people to their communities (Haddock, 1994). Because of this, discharge planning has assumed an important role in treatment. It is the bridge from the sheltered therapeutic environment to the reality of life in the community.

Little research has been done to discover how well ex-psychiatric clients reintegrate themselves into their communities; however, one study demonstrated that "transitional care services for mentally ill patients who are discharged from the hospital are inconsistent and not very adequate" (Dorwart and Hoover, 1994). Nurses who work with mental health clients are in an excellent position to assist clients in applying the new, more effective behaviors learned within the therapeutic setting to the less predictable world of the community.

By the time most clients are ready for discharge, they are actively participating in their treatment program. Decisions about housing, employment, treatment, and management of their mental health problems are made with the treatment team's assistance. A multidisciplinary discharge care plan is developed. Appropriate referrals to various agencies are initiated, and follow-up care in the community is planned. A case manager is assigned to work with the client after discharge from the inpatient therapeutic environment.

Returning to the community is a hopeful but demanding time for mental health clients (Vellenga and Christenson, 1994). The support of the treatment team, as well as family and friends, is needed to ease the transition. As one researcher stated, the mentally ill "have no formal ceremonies to transform them back to 'normal' status" (Herman, 1993). The activities of the treatment team, especially nurses, serve to reinforce and strengthen clients' adaptive abilities throughout the discharge process.

Compliance

Clients who follow prescribed treatments are said to be in **compliance.** The term *noncompliance* refers to not cooperating with the treatment plan. Assisting clients to comply can be a nurse's biggest challenge, especially when working with mentally/emotionally troubled people. It is estimated that "40% to 80% of patients don't comply with their prescribed therapeutic course" (Wichowski and Kubsch, 1995). Although all members of the treatment team are involved in helping clients to comply (cooperate and become involved with their treatment), it remains the responsibility of the nursing staff to educate and encourage each client to play an active and responsible role in his/her own care.

To improve clients' compliance, nurses must understand the reasons for clients' unwillingness to follow the treatment plan (see box on p. 126, bottom). A

ADMISSION ASSESSMENT

Demographic data: full name, sex, age, date of birth, address, marital status, family members' names and ages, and (sometimes) religious preference.

Admission data: date and time of admission, type of admission (voluntary or committed).

Reason for admission: current problems as perceived by the patient. These include stressors, difficulty with coping, and "emergency behaviors" (suicidal or homicidal ideas/attempts, aggression, destructive behaviors, risk of escape).

Previous psychiatric history: dates, inpatient/outpatient, reasons for and types of treatment, and their effectiveness.

Drug and alcohol use/abuse: amount, frequency, duration of past and present use of legal/illegal substances, date and time of last use.

Disturbances in patterns of daily living: sleep, intake, elimination, sexual activity, work, leisure, self-care, and hygiene.

Support systems: amount of contact, nature/quality of relationships, and availability of support.

General appearance: type and condition of clothing, cleanliness, physical condition, and posture.

Behaviors during the interview:

Expression of anger: covert, overt, verbal, or physical.

Degree of cooperation, resistance, or evasiveness.

Social skills: positive/unpleasant habits, shyness, withdrawal.

From Keltner NL, Schwecke LH, Bostrom CE: *Psychiatric nursing,* ed 2, St Louis, 1995, Mosby.

Amount/type of motor activity: psychomotor retardation, agitation, restlessness, tics, tremors, hypervigilance, lack of activity.

Speech patterns: amount, rate, volume, pressure, mutism, slurring, or stuttering.

Degree of concentration and attention span.

Orientation: to time, place, and person; level of consciousness.

Memory: recent/remote, amnesia, blackouts, confabulation.

Thought processes reflected in speech: blocking, circumstantiality, loose associations, flight of ideas, perseveration, tangential ideas, ambivalence, neologisms, or "word salad."

Thought content: helplessness, hopelessness, worthlessness, guilt, suicidal ideas/plans, homicidal ideas/plans, suspiciousness, phobias, obsessions, compulsions, preoccupations, antisocial attitudes, blaming of others, poverty of content, or denial.

Hallucinations: visual, auditory, or other.

Delusions: of reference, influence, persecution, grandeur, religious, or somatic.

Intellectual functioning: use of language and knowledge, abstract vs. concrete thinking (proverbs), or calculations.

Affect/mood: anxiety level; elevated or depressed mood; labile, blunted, or flat affect; or inappropriate affect.

Insight: degree of awareness of problems and their causes.

Judgment: soundness of problem solving and decisions.

Motivation: degree of motivation for treatment.

REASONS FOR NONCOMPLIANCE

- Lack of one or more of the following:
  Understanding
  Finances to pay for treatment
  Access to treatment services
  Support from family and significant others
- Adverse effects of treatment:
  Physical side effects
  Emotional-mental side effects
- Inability to understand or follow treatment plan

complete assessment of clients, their daily activities, their attitudes toward treatment, and their coping resources will help identify the overt (outward) causes of noncompliance. However, many times the reasoning for not complying with the therapeutic regimen lies within clients' negative attitudes toward their treatments and recovery. Alert nurses can help their clients to change many of the self-defeating attitudes that bind them to their problems.

Challenging client's expectations is one technique for increasing compliance. Too many times people limit themselves by believing that it is impossible to change. Helping clients to remove these self-imposed boundaries offers them the hope that improvement is possible, even attainable.

Other techniques involve offering a positive outlook and redirecting negative behaviors or attitudes into more constructive ones. A genuine concern is a powerful tool for establishing trust and cooperation. Each of these techniques is designed to help your clients improve their outlooks on life. When one believes that success is attainable, it becomes easier to comply with the therapies and medications prescribed in the plan of care.

Remember, no matter how therapeutic and safe an inpatient treatment environment may be, its primary goal is to return clients to their communities as soon as possible. Your sensitivity, compassion, and consistency help to provide clients with the energy to make the needed changes in their lives.

❖ KEY CONCEPTS

- The term *therapeutic milieu* is used to describe an environment that is structured to assist clients in controlling inappropriate behaviors and learning more effective adaptive (coping) personal and psychosocial skills.

- The inpatient psychiatric settings of today provide services to three main groups of people: those experiencing crises, those with acute mental or emotional problems, and those people with chronic mental illness.

- The basic goals of a therapeutic environment (milieu) are to protect the client and others during periods of maladaptive behaviors, help individuals develop self-worth and confidence, and teach more effective adaptive (coping) skills for meeting their needs.

- The therapeutic environment helps clients to meet the physical needs associated with nourishment, personal hygiene, and clean surroundings.

- The physical properties of a therapeutic environment include temperature, lighting, sound, cleanliness, and aesthetics.

- Limit setting allows the therapeutic environment to be consistent and predictable because clients know that external controls will be enforced.

- In the therapeutic setting, nurses assist clients in building their self-esteem needs through acceptance, expectations, and involvement.

- The process of being admitted to an inpatient setting establishes the tone for the remainder of a client's stay.

- Discharge planning is the bridge from the sheltered therapeutic environment to the reality of life in the community.

- An important responsibility of the nursing staff is to educate and encourage clients to play an active and responsible role in their own care.

❖ SUGGESTIONS FOR FURTHER READING

"Three Tips for Closer Caring," written by Diane Kelly and published in *Nursing 95* (25[5]:72, 1995), describes some excellent tips for decreasing the emotional distances between nurses and their clients.

❖ REFERENCES

Breggin PR: *Toxic psychiatry,* New York, 1991, St Martins Press.

Chafetz L: Comment on Newman SJ: The housing and neighborhood conditions of persons with severe mental illness, *Hosp Community Psychiatry* (45):338, 1994.

Cohen LJ: Psychiatric hospitalization as experience of trauma, *Arch Psychiatr Nurs* 8(2):78, 1994.

Dorwart RA, Hoover CW: A national study of transitional hospital services with mental health, *Am J Public Health* 84:1229, 1994.

Geller JL: Treating revolving-door patients who have "hospitalphilia": compassion, coercion, and common sense, *Hosp Community Psychiatry* 44(2):141, 1993.

Goren S, Orion R: Space and sanity, *Arch Psychiatr Nurs* 8:237, 1994.

Haber J and others: *Comprehensive psychiatric nursing,* ed 5, St Louis, 1997, Mosby.

Haddock KS: Collaborative discharge planning: nursing and social services, *Clin Nurse Spec* 8:248, 1994.

Herman NJ: Return to sender: reintegrative stigma-management strategies of ex-psychiatric patients, *J Contemp Ethnography* 22:295, 1993.

Jones M: *The therapeutic community,* New York, 1953, Basic Books.

Joseph-Kinzelman A and others: Clients' perceptions of involuntary hospitalization, *J Psychosoc Nurs Ment Health Serv* 32:11, 1994.

Kelly D: Three tips for closer caring, *Nurs 95* 25(5):72, 1995.

Mental Health Policy Resource Center: *Fact or fiction: interpretations of mental health expenditures data,* Washington, DC, 1992, The Center.

Moos RH: Evaluating treatment environments: a social-ecological approach, London, 1974, John Wiley.

Murray RB, Baier M: Use of therapeutic milieu in a community setting, *J Psychosoc Nurs Ment Health Serv* 24(10):33, 1993.

National Advisory Mental Health Council: Health care reform for Americans with severe mental illness: report of the National Advisory Mental Health Council, *Am J Psychiatry* 6(150):1447, 1993.

Stuart GW, Sundeen SJ: *Principles and practice of psychiatric nursing,* ed 5, St Louis, 1995, Mosby.

Taylor CM: *Essentials of psychiatric nursing,* ed 14, St Louis, 1994, Mosby.

Vellenga BA, Christenson J: Persistent and severely mentally ill clients' perceptions of their mental illness, *Iss Ment Health Nurs* 15:359, 1994.

Wichowski HC, Kubsch S: Improving your patient's compliance, *Nurs 95* 25(1):67, 1995.

10

THE THERAPEUTIC RELATIONSHIP

The therapeutic relationship is a directed energy exchange between two people, a flow that moves clients toward more effective behaviors. A poem from the Strong Spirit Path of a Native American tradition (Spencer, 1991) sums up the essence of a therapeutic relationship:

> UNIVERSE
> is Space
> which contains Energy
> Energy
> of its nature moves
> as it moves
> it produces Change
> Change is
> it was <> it is <> it will be
> sometimes we call this past, present, future
> and we say it is Time
> it is not Time
> it is Change
> you see how it is
> how everything in Universe
> is Energy
> flowing from one place to another
> what we call Matter
> is merely a relatively stable form
> of Energy
> which is also changing
> also moving
> only more slowly
> like Earth and Ocean
> each at its own pace
> all things that contain Energy
> are alive
> as all things are formed of Energy
> all things are alive
> and all things are *related*
> each to the other
> *always*

The energies of nurses are used to direct clients toward more constructive ways of thinking and more effective ways of coping with their problems. Nurses use their abundance of health-directed energies to first balance or stabilize clients. Then they assist clients to mobilize and direct their own energies into more life-fulfilling directions.

The art of nursing involves an energy exchange that takes place every time nurses interact with their clients. This chapter focuses on how nurses and other health care providers use their energies to establish and direct the therapeutic relationship.

Dynamics of the Therapeutic Relationship

Dynamics refers to the interactions that occur among various forces. The dynamics of a therapeutic relationship are different from the dynamics of other types of relationships. For example, a social relationship includes such dynamics as having fun together, supporting each other through difficult times, and enjoying one another's company. A social relationship is a two-way energy exchange based on the sharing of personal opinions, attitudes, and tastes.

A work relationship has the purpose of achieving certain goals. It includes the dynamics of motivation, performance, and evaluation. People within a work relationship are there to achieve a goal, produce a product, make a profit, or deliver a service.

The **therapeutic relationship** differs from other relationships in several ways. First, the focus of energies is primarily on the client. This was an often-forgotten idea until Hildegard Peplau (1952), a nurse, introduced the concept of therapeutic interaction as a tool to assist in clients' recoveries. Carl Rogers (1966) later described the helping relationship as one that has the intent of improving the life of another. Imogene King (1971), a nursing theorist, saw the nursing process as a changing interpersonal relationship that helps clients adapt positively to their environments.

Second, the therapeutic relationship is consciously directed. Friendships and other social relationships happen mostly by chance. In therapeutic relationships, however, nurses consciously establish a connection with clients to help them cope with their particular life demands.

The dynamic components or parts of the therapeutic relationship include the concepts of trust, empathy, autonomy, caring, and hope. Using these concepts as a framework encourages nurses to develop the skills and sensitivity necessary to direct their energies into effective helping relationships.

Trust

Trust is defined as "a risk-taking process whereby an individual's situation depends on the future behavior of another person" (Anderson, Anderson, and Glanze, 1994). Without trust, people become isolated and incapable of relying on other people. Attitudes regarding trust are based on past experiences, but they have the power to influence the client's present and future.

Within the therapeutic relationship, trust is "the assured belief that other individuals are capable of assisting in times of distress and will probably do so"

(Travelbee, 1971). Trust is an important part of any therapeutic relationship. Each and every person for whom we care needs to be able to trust that their nurses will act in their best interests.

Illness or dysfunction of any kind requires much energy. When clients arrive for care, their energies are usually at very low levels. The role of "receiver of care" fosters a dependency on caregivers and feelings of vulnerability. Nurses who recognize this situation work to establish a sense of trust with each client.

There are several ways in which nurses direct their energies toward establishing trust with clients. They first assess the client's ability to trust others. Each nursing behavior is then designed to promote success. For example, a nurse who says she will be back in 10 minutes returns at the appointed time. This one simple action reassures clients that nurses will follow through on their verbal statements. The likelihood that clients will trust their nurses increases with each nursing action that sends this nonverbal message.

Second, nurses must be honest with their clients. To tell a child, for example, that the injection will not hurt makes him/her less likely to believe the next health care provider's explanations or instructions. If these experiences are repeated often enough, people develop a mistrust of the entire medical care system (see box below).

The third focus in the establishment of trust is clear communications. Give information to clients slowly using terms that can be understood by the average person. Clients cannot learn to trust if they cannot understand. Offer clients the time to share their feelings and apprehensions. "Without the establishment of trust, the helping relationship will not progress beyond the level of mechanical provision for tending to superficial needs" (Sundeen and others, 1994).

Empathy

Empathy is the ability to walk a mile in another person's shoes. It enables nurses to enter into the life of a person, to share his/her emotions, meanings, and attitudes. Empathy is communicated verbally, nonverbally, and behaviorally. It is the interconnectedness between nurse and client that improves the effectiveness of the therapeutic relationship. In short, empathy is the ability to share in the client's world.

Unfortunately, there are no specific directions for the development of empathy. However, you can become more empathetic by focusing your attention (energies) on what clients are trying to communicate. Learn to listen with more than just your ears. Concentrate on the speaker and listen objectively, without passing judgment. Accept what is being said. You do not have to agree with anything the client says, but you do have to communicate acceptance of the person who said it.

The development of empathy can also be nurtured by becoming secure in your nursing actions. When nurses are confident with their abilities, their energies can be devoted to clients and their situations instead of being wasted on worrying about how well they performed a certain skill or task. The nurse's confidence sends a message that encourages clients to share more of themselves.

Last, learn to consciously focus on your client. Enter each client's room expecting to learn something new. Become aware of the entire message the client is sending. Observe body motions, gestures, eye movement, facial expressions, and vocal tones. Together, these small cues send powerful messages. The nurse who can receive these communications is in the position to develop the empathy that distinguishes a caregiver relationship from a truly therapeutic one.

Autonomy

The concept of **autonomy** relates to the ability to direct and control one's own activities, one's destiny. When people seek health care, they risk losing their autonomy because health care is a specialized, complex world, full of the unknown.

Frequently, health care providers think that clients are incapable of making good health care decisions. They assume an attitude of paternalism in which care providers become the judge of what is best for the client. This attitude limits the client's ability to make decisions and increases the client's dependency on

---

THINK ABOUT

Mary J. is a 42-year-old woman who has been receiving treatment for severe depression for 21 years. She has received several electroconvulsive therapy treatments, which she was told would relieve her depression; they did not. She has also been treated with various psychotropic medications on several occasions with little success. Currently, you, as the community mental health center's nurse, have been following Mary's care.

Although Mary is required to return to the clinic weekly for medication monitoring, she keeps her appointments only when she wants more medication. When questioned about her refusal to keep her appointments, she tells you that no one really cares about her so why go through the motions. "Just fill the prescription, keep your mouth shut, and let me go," she replies to your statement of concern.

Has Mary lost her ability to trust?

How would you handle this situation?

others. People with mental health difficulties have problems with autonomy because the nature of their illness sometimes results in their making inappropriate decisions. However, autonomy is just as important for these individuals. Autonomy is encouraged by the nurse through the use of the concept of mutuality.

The concept of **mutuality** relates to the process of sharing with another person. Williamson (1981) defines mutuality as "the process through which the client assumes an appropriate level of autonomy without blocking the provision of necessary health care services." When a therapeutic relationship has mutuality, both the client and the nurse focus their unique strengths on meeting health care needs. The nurse has the theoretical knowledge that can assist the client in identifying specific problems and possible solutions. The client has the knowledge of self and needs that are important to him/her. Both contribute to the plan of care.

Because clients are unique individuals, nursing interventions are modified to meet each person's needs. For example, clients who are unable to remember their appointments are reminded by the nurse. The interventions are based on the nurse's knowledge of the unique needs of the individual. Mutuality also helps both clients and care providers meet goals. When goals are based on the client's needs, they are more apt to be achieved because clients have a role in establishing them.

Caring

Every person has the universal human need for love. Maslow's hierarchy of needs lists the need for love and belonging as the first nonphysical requirement after safety. Infants who do not receive enough loving touch fail to grow and thrive. Adults who do not meet their needs for love become isolated, lonely, and depressed. Human beings are gregarious creatures. They are meant to live with others. They need to belong and to identify with a certain group. Although physical appearances, behavioral patterns, and communication styles may differ, each person carries with him/her the need to belong and be loved.

Caring is a vital part of the therapeutic relationship; its thread is interwoven through every aspect, every interaction. Caring is the energy that allows nurses to unconditionally accept each person, even when they are most unlovable. That is one of the reasons why nursing is called "a caring profession."

Clients will often question nurses about their ability to truly care. Statements such as "You are just doing this because it's your job" or "You don't really care—you're getting paid to be nice to me" express the need to be accepted and cared for, to be loved. People who have had negative experiences with the health care delivery system can become cautious and suspicious of the intentions of their care providers. They "can tell" when someone is sincere or merely concerned with the diagnosis, test, or function instead of the person. Some clients are able to unconsciously read the energies (the messages) that their health care providers are actually sending (see box below).

Nurses who demonstrate a high degree of caring are able to enjoy the rich uniqueness of each individual without the anxieties related to other peoples' opinions of them. They are able to give of themselves without losing their own identity. To develop and nurture your caring abilities, practice these four steps:

1. Become aware of the client as an individual.
2. Learn to respect the uniqueness and individuality of each person for whom you care.

CASE STUDY

Sarah was working at a large mental health facility for veterans located 90 miles away from her home. During her work week, she stayed in a small apartment not far from the facility. On her days off, she would commute to her home to be with her family.

On one particular day, she and her husband argued about some trivial item. During the drive back to the facility, Sarah fussed and fumed about men and their silly behaviors. By the time she arrived for duty, she was feeling downright hostile; but she took a deep breath and tried to focus her energies on her clients.

One of her long-term clients, Randy, approached her later in the evening. She smiled and said, "What can I do for you, Randy?" He looked straight into her eyes and, holding her gaze, blurted out, "You don't like sex!" He then turned abruptly and walked out of the room.

Clinical Decisions

1. What message was Randy receiving?
2. What do you think motivated him to tell Sarah this?
3. Was the topic really about sex?
4. Do you find a lesson in this incident?
5. If so, what is it, and how could it be applied to your own nursing practice?

3. Increase your knowledge of the client's needs.
4. Develop mutual sharing.

The art of caring is demonstrated through every behavior, every touch, and every interaction with clients. Caring is an energy that communicates concern, sensitivity, and compassion. Cherish and nurture your ability to care because it is the key to the connectedness that enhances the therapeutic relationship.

Hope

The concept of hope involves the future. For many people, especially those who are ill or distressed, the future can appear bleak. Hope is not easily defined; however, from a nursing point of view, we can say that **hope** is "a multidimensional dynamic life force characterized by a confident yet uncertain expectation of achieving a future good" (Dufault and Martocchio, 1985). For a hope to be achievable, it must be realistic, possible, and personally significant. It is a highly personal concept, and for people with chronic problems (physical or mental), hope can be the energy that motivates them toward their optimal state of health. The reverse is also true. An unwillingness to face the future and to have hope can slow any progress toward a goal.

For nurses, hope is a therapeutic energy tool that can have a powerful effect on client care outcomes. The emotions and behaviors relating to hope are many, ranging from feelings of despair to inspiration and determination. They can be illustrated on a continuum or range (Fig. 10-1), with the behaviors of despair on one end and the behaviors of great hope on the other.

Dufault and Martocchio (1985) have described six dimensions related to the concept of hope. The first is known as the affective or emotional dimension. It includes all the feelings that one has about hope such as anticipation, the desirability attached to the outcome, and dread. It is the emotional aspect of hope.

The second area, the affiliative dimension, addresses how hope is related or interwoven. It includes spirituality—how one relates to life and other people. Behaviors in this dimension include the seeking or receiving of help, using others as a source of hope, and seeking support and encouragement.

Third is the behavioral dimension. This area consists of the actions or behaviors that may make the hoped-for situation come true. For example, people who begin an exercise program in the hope that they will prevent heart problems are operating in the behavioral dimension.

The fourth dimension is the cognitive dimension of hope or the thinking area. It is the process of thinking through and analyzing the hope. Some people operate within this dimension by defining what their hopes are. Others explore all the factors that relate to the hoped-for situation, whereas some compile facts to encourage a successful outcome. The acts associated with problem solving are in the cognitive dimension.

Fifth is the temporal dimension of hope. It is the experience of time as it relates to hope. Although some persons' hopes depend on a specific time frame, others are more indefinite. Because hope is accompanied by time, one's past, present, and future interact. One may hope to repeat the pleasant experiences of the past and use them as a frame of reference to avoid problems in the future.

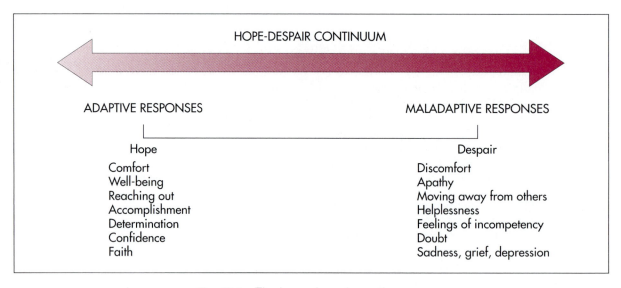

Fig. 10-1   The hope-despair continuum.

Last is the contextual dimension of hope, which includes one's personal life situation as it relates to hope. It becomes much easier to have hope if one's environment or living situation is stable. Inadequate resources (physical, financial, emotional) provide a context in which hope may be difficult to muster. Hope is modified based on an individual's point of view.

There are several effective nursing interventions relating to hope. Table 10-1 lists an intervention for each dimension of hope. The concept of hope is a basic component of the therapeutic relationship because without it, no movement or progress toward a goal is real.

The dynamics of the therapeutic relationship are not overt. They lie quietly, waiting to be energized by the nurse or other therapeutic agent. Trust, empathy, autonomy, caring, and hope are the techniques with which nurses build the foundation of the therapeutic relationship. Look closely. Notice that the first letters of each word, when taken together, spell the word *TEACH*. With these tools, nurses can guide the therapeutic relationship and "teach" (move) their clients toward their highest levels of wellness.

Characteristics of the Therapeutic Relationship

The therapeutic relationship varies in importance to clients. When a person is having blood drawn, for example, he/she is more interested in how well the technician uses the needle to enter the vein. In this case, a therapeutic interaction, although nice, is not a requirement. For clients who are hospitalized or institutionalized, the therapeutic relationship assumes a greater importance. People with chronic conditions usually place a high degree of importance on their relationships with caregivers. Persons with emotional or mental problems may need the therapeutic relationship to serve as the bridge between mere existence and success. To successfully establish a therapeutic relationship, the qualities of acceptance, genuineness, and rapport must be communicated to the client.

Acceptance

The verb *accept* means to receive or take what is being offered. People entering the health care system arrive as complex individuals with past histories, internal needs, and external realities. Each person must be accepted exactly as they are. Nurses and others in the helping professions relate to all sorts of people. Most are cooperative and interested in working toward relieving the problems for which they have sought health care. However, some persons are more difficult to accept, especially when their behaviors are not socially appropriate or unusual. "It is difficult to fully understand the overwhelming experience of having to live with mental illness" (Vellenga and Christenson, 1994), but the importance of accepting these individuals cannot be stressed enough in the therapeutic relationship.

Whereas therapists and other care providers may be concerned with the long-term aspects of a client's mental illness, distressed individuals are more concerned with their present pain and the need for relief. Not only must they cope with the discomforts of their illness, but they must also deal with the emotional and physical alienation forced on them by others. The stigma of being mentally ill follows them into the home and workplace and results in the loss of emo-

◆ **TABLE 10-1**
Nursing Interventions Related to the Dimensions of Hope

Dimension	Nursing Intervention
Affective	Provide an opportunity for expression of feelings
	Respond empathically
	Assist in coping with feelings
Affiliative	Support helpful relationships
Behavioral	Encourage appropriate dependent, independent, and interdependent actions
	Enhance self-esteem to decrease feelings of helplessness
Cognitive	Clarification
	Provide information
Temporal	Help to see the relationship between past experiences and hope
Contextual	Help to create a supportive, hopeful environment

Modified from Dufault K, Martocchio BC: *Nurs Clin North Am* 20:379, 1985.

tional relationships and vocational opportunities. The distress felt by many of these individuals is described as feelings of hopelessness, fright, and an inability to function. "Clients believed that acceptance lent them a sense of strength and value and made them feel more normal" (Vellenga and Christenson, 1994). For people with mental-emotional problems, acceptance is of prime importance.

Nurses can develop acceptance by remembering that it is the person—the individual—who must be accepted, not the behaviors or the attitudes. The very purpose of mental health care is to replace inappropriate behaviors with more effective actions. However, if the client feels accepted for who he/she is, then treatment strategies will be far more effective (Baker, 1995).

Rapport

The second ingredient that nurses need for an effective therapeutic relationship is **rapport,** the ability to establish a meaningful connection with clients. Rapport is a dynamic process, an energy exchange between nurse and client that provides the background for all other nursing actions.

It is much easier to establish rapport with some clients than others. Nurses, just like everyone else, are attracted toward some people and repelled by others. Nurses who have suffered themselves in some way often demonstrate a greater compassion for the suffering of others. In short, rapport is an individual, personal concept. It is the person of the nurse therapeutically interacting with the person of the client.

Rapport is characterized by a concern for others and an active interest in the well-being of one's clients. Essential to forming rapport is the belief in the worth and dignity of each individual along with an accepting attitude. Every nurse has a certain degree of skill in establishing rapport with clients, but every person is different, and nurses themselves continue to grow and change. Actively work to improve your abilities to establish meaningful connections with clients. Rapport is not a scientific tool but an application of our willingness to care.

Genuineness

Something that is genuine is real. **Genuineness,** in the therapeutic relationship, "implies that the nurse is an open, honest, sincere person who is actively involved in the relationship" (Stuart and Sundeen, 1995). It means that nurses are not saying one thing while feeling another. The quality of honesty is a part of being genuine. However, the goal of the therapeutic relationship is to move the client toward wellness, not the nurse (Wolfe, 1994). Sharing yourself must be

done while remembering that the client is the primary focus. In this way, nurses are able to be genuinely involved without using the therapeutic relationship to meet their own needs.

Therapeutic Use of Self

The most therapeutic tool of any nurse is the self: the ways in which we interact, attend to, and encourage clients. Nurses are role models for health and coping, especially with people who are mentally or emotionally troubled. Nurses' behaviors set examples for successful actions.

Nurses direct themselves therapeutically by focusing energies on the client. Sometimes nurses share small bits of personal information, but that sharing always has a purpose that benefits the client. For example, a client asks how many children the nurse has. The nurse answers the question and then puts the focus on the client by asking him how many children he has. This technique allows nurses to maintain the focus on the client while sharing information about themselves.

To improve your skills in using "self" therapeutically, remember two important thoughts. First, feel good about yourself. You cannot be therapeutically effective when your personal life is in turmoil. Clients can sense a nurse's emotional discomfort. Work to become aware of your own feelings and attitudes and how they affect the therapeutic relationships with clients.

Second, work to develop an awareness of how your actions, gestures, and expressions affect other people. During each interaction, "step out" of the situation and consider how the client is reacting. With experience and effort, the majority of your nursing actions will be therapeutic, no matter what the practice setting or type of client you encounter.

Phases of the Therapeutic Relationship

The therapeutic relationship, like plants and people, needs time to grow even though it is a time-limited, purposeful series of interactions. Every therapeutic relationship moves through four phases. Each stage has identifiable tasks and goals (Table 10-2). As these tasks are accomplished, a readiness to move onto the next phase is experienced. Nursing interventions are guided by the therapeutic goals of the client's treatment plan throughout the relationship. The four stages or phases of the therapeutic relationship are called the preparation, orientation, working, and termination phases.

◆ TABLE 10-2
Goals of and Nurse Behaviors in Each Phase of the Nurse-Client Relationship

Phase of Nurse-Client Relationship	Goal	Nurse Behaviors
Orientation	Develop mutual trust Establish nurse as significant other to client	Establishes mutually acceptable contract Responds to testing behavior of client by adhering strictly to terms of contract
Maintenance	Identify and address client's problems	Highly individualized to nature of client's problems Empathic, nonpunishing limit setting
Termination	Assist client to review what was learned and to transfer this learning to interactions with others	Understands client's sense of loss Helps client express and cope with feelings Encourages client to channel feelings into constructive activity such as farewell party Recognizes own feelings of loss

Modified from Taylor CM: *Essentials of psychiatric nursing,* ed 14, St Louis, 1994, Mosby.

Preparation Phase

This is the data-gathering stage in which the nurse prepares for the relationship. Although complete information about the client is usually unavailable, it is very important to learn as much as possible about the client before meeting him/her. This is also the time for you to look at your own possible reactions. The nursing goals for this phase are to establish a client database and assess your own feelings relating to the client.

To establish a client database, review all possible information relating to the client. Past medical records, current records, and interactions with significant others in the client's life are excellent sources of information. Once the information is gathered, look for the recurring patterns of behavior to develop a picture of the client. Armed with this knowledge, the nurse can now begin to form ideas about the relationship and hopefully forecast possible problems. A word of caution: do not accept labels as fact. Keep an open mind. Because a client is labeled psychotic, do not expect him/her to behave in the same way that other people with the same label do. People are individuals with their own unique behaviors.

The second part of the preparation phase is to look inward to your own reactions. Nurses are also unique individuals, and their attitudes and behaviors affect the therapeutic relationship. First identify your initial reactions to the client. Is there anything that may block your ability to help? For example, the fact that a nurse is attending an Alanon support group for the spouses of alcoholics may have an effect on his/her ability to help a client who is being treated for alcoholism.

Next, assess for stereotyping: Do you think that, because the client is a member of a particular group or culture, he/she will behave in a certain way? The belief that people with mental illness cannot behave responsibly is an example of a stereotype that has an impact on the therapeutic relationship. For this reason, it is important to be aware of any preconceived ideas or attitudes about the client.

Finally, recognize the anxiety that is generally present in the nurse during this phase. Mild anxiety is common and sharpens the senses. High anxiety levels can affect a nurse's judgment, so seeking assistance from one's supervisor is advised when anxiety may affect the therapeutic relationship.

The last step in the preparatory phase is to make plans for the first interaction with the client. Find a quiet setting, free from interruptions. Plan for sufficient time, and identify what information must be covered during the first interaction. Make a mental outline, and your preparations are complete.

Orientation Phase

During the orientation phase, nurse and client become acquainted, agree to work with each other, and establish the purpose for the relationship. The first meeting establishes the tone and forms the impressions that both people will carry with them throughout the entire relationship. The basic goals for this phase are to build trust and establish the nurse as a significant other in the life of the client.

The first and most important step at this time is to identify each other by name. Introduce yourself by name and position. When the client responds, an exchange begins.

Next, explain your role, particularly as it relates to the client. This gives the client an idea of what may be expected in the relationship. Once client and nurse are comfortable, an agreement to work with each other is established.

Establishing a working agreement or nurse-client contract is the next step in the orientation phase of the therapeutic relationship. The nurse-client contract is simply an agreement that describes the nature of the relationship. Both client and nurse discuss their expectations and then agree on the goals they want to meet. The contract, which includes a description of each person's roles and responsibilities, is then written or verbally established. The word *contract* may provoke anxiety in some persons, so it is not often used when interacting with clients. The term is less important than actually gaining the client's agreement. Once arrangements have been made, it is extremely important for the nurse to keep his/her end of the bargain or, as Taylor (1994) states, "to respond to the client's behavior with meticulous consistency."

During the orientation phase both the client and the nurse carry out assessments or "size up" each other. It is the time when the nurse becomes aware of the client as a real person, unique and individual. The label of "client" falls by the wayside, and a genuine person-to-person energy exchange begins to evolve into a therapeutic relationship.

Many times clients will test the reliability of their nurses. Testing is an important step in establishing trust in the therapeutic relationship. Although clients may not appear for scheduled appointments, may use profane language, or may resist sharing their feelings, the nurse must demonstrate a willingness to continue the therapeutic relationship by doing what was promised in the nurse-client contract. This reliability is important because many troubled people have never had a reliable or consistent relationship. When the nurse has established reliability and the client has gained enough trust to no longer test the nurse, the therapeutic relationship is ready for the next stage.

Working Phase

The focus of the working phase of the therapeutic relationship is to achieve the goals that were agreed on in the nurse-client contract. This is the time for work: for solving problems and trying out new behaviors. During this phase, nurses are guided by their knowledge of human behavior, the client's plan of care, and the agreed-on goals in the nurse-client contract.

The working phase consists of periods of growth and resistance. If the relationship is moving toward its goals, the client's behavior changes. At this time it is important to explore the meaning of the change with the client and mutually decide if the behavioral change is meeting the agreed-on goals.

Periods of growth are accompanied by episodes of resistance. Changing one's behavior is very hard work. It requires energy and self-disclosure. Clients often feel self-conscious, shameful, and vulnerable during this time. The nurse's gentle acceptance and reliability help clients move through their periods of resistance.

An important technique for nurses is knowing when to set limits. Limit setting is a nursing intervention designed to prevent clients from harming themselves or others. The necessity for setting limits often occurs during the working phase because the client may be experiencing many painful emotions. When setting limits, do so in a calm, nonthreatening manner. The client is not being punished, just protected until self-control can be regained. Clients often feel a sense of relief and trust when they know that someone cares enough to protect them, even if the threat is from themselves.

Client and nurse continue to work on meeting the goals of the relationship. Other members of the treatment team may also be involved in specific areas of the client's therapy. Therefore it is important to understand how each member of the team functions and shares responsibility in relation to the client.

During the working stage, nurses frequently assess for behaviors that indicate the goals are being met. Preparations for ending or terminating the relationship are made. The time arrives when the goals are accomplished or one of the persons is no longer able to maintain the relationship. It is the signal for the final phase—termination.

Termination Phase

When the goals of the therapeutic relationship are achieved, both the client and nurse share a sense of accomplishment, which is balanced by the loss of a meaningful person in the client's life. When the mutual goals have not been met, termination can be even more difficult. This is a major reason why it is important to set realistic goals at the beginning and frequently monitor the client's progress toward those goals.

Steps toward termination should begin *before* the last meeting. Both the client and nurse need time to prepare the client for independence. During this phase, the nurse reviews the steps taken toward meeting the goals. Clients feel a sense of pride and accomplishment when they can review their progress. This time is also an opportunity to teach and encourage clients to expand and apply their new, more effective behaviors to other situations.

People respond to the loss of a therapeutic relationship as they would any loss. Some may show signs of regression or withdrawal or engage in behaviors to continue or intensify the relationship (Table 10-3). The feelings behind these behaviors should be identified and shared. Looking toward the future and reminding clients of their progress help to ease the transition to independence. Saying goodbye is never easy, but a client who is able to function more effectively as a result of your nursing interventions is the reward of a successful therapeutic relationship.

Roles of the Nurse

Throughout the course of the therapeutic relationship, the nurse plays several roles. Each role is designed to assist clients in meeting specific therapeutic goals. Nurses who work with mental health clients assume the roles of therapeutic change agents, teachers, technicians, and therapists. Each role of the nurse is designed to assist clients in developing more successful and adaptive coping behaviors.

Change Agent

The therapeutic environment is more than a physical space. The psychological atmosphere created by the nurses who care for clients is one of the major contributions toward successful recovery. Nurses provide a warm, accepting atmosphere that values the contributions of every individual. Nurses accept the fact that some client behaviors may not be appropriate, but they never discredit the person. Individuals are supported and encouraged to exchange their unsuccessful actions for more effective behaviors. Nurses' attitudes foster a climate that anticipates, expects, and promotes positive change. Hopefully, each staff member acts as a role model for successful living, thus demonstrating to clients that there are other ways of behaving. When the atmosphere promotes change and then provides the security to practice those changes, clients are more likely to improve.

Nurses also function as socializing agents. They assist clients to participate in group activities and various social interactions. They introduce clients to each other, encourage conversations, and help clients focus on the healthy aspects of their lives. Interactions with others are seen as opportunities for nurses to encourage successful social experiences for their clients.

Teacher

Nurses are constantly alert for opportunities to teach. In the mental health care setting, teaching opportunities range from instructions about daily living activities to major lifestyle changes (see box below). All clients must be instructed about areas such as their medications and diet, but equally important areas of instruction exist with every client interaction. Here, nurses are able to assess and monitor existing prob-

---

TEACHING OPPORTUNITIES FOR MENTAL HEALTH NURSES

Activities of daily living
Mental illness and its treatments
Effects, side effects, adverse reactions of medications
Early signs and symptoms of return to maladaptive functioning
How to cope with stressors of daily living
What to say to others about the mental illness
Teaching the public about mental health and illness

◆ **TABLE 10-3**
Behavioral Responses to Termination

Regression	Withdrawal	Continuation
Return to previous maladaptive behavior	Denial of nurse's help	Tries to continue relationship
Increased anxiety	Demand to stop relationship now	Brings up new problems
Tardiness or absence from appointments	Absence from appointments	Becomes helpless
Expresses doubts about value of relationship	Superficially interacts with nurse	Wants nurse to solve his/her problems

Modified from Sundeen SJ and others: *Nurse-client interaction: implementing the nursing process,* ed 5, St Louis, 1994, Mosby.

lems, plan for corrective learning opportunities, and forecast possible difficulties (Trygstad, 1994). Clients and their families trust nurses, and they often confide in them. These times of sharing become great teaching opportunities for the alert nurse. Teaching is an important part of nursing because it provides a solid bridge for the passage from existence to effective adaptation.

Technician

The technical role of the mental health nurse is focused on the whole client. Mental health nurses must be informed about the physical conditions of their clients and their mental status. Too many times, providers involved with the client's care focus on the mental-emotional status of the client and exclude the physical realm. For this reason, nurses must remain alert to the physical problems that may be present with mental health clients. Remember Maslow's hierarchy of needs—physical needs are met first. Nurses apply their knowledge of physical and psychological functioning to every client. Many mental health clients suffer from physical problems, just as many medical clients suffer from psychological problems. The technical nursing role in the mental health setting includes administering, monitoring, and evaluating medications; managing medical problems within the mental health environment; assessing the difference between physical and psychiatric conditions; maintaining safety; and managing environmental factors.

Therapist

Nurses who practice as therapists are usually educated at the master's level in the principles of psychotherapy. They are instrumental in developing the client's plan of care and serve as members of the multidisciplinary treatment team. Although all nurses who work with mental health clients use every opportunity to assist their clients in developing more effective behaviors, nurses who function as therapists are more formally involved in routine and regular sessions with their clients.

Nurses who formally engage in the therapist role routinely consult with a more experienced, skilled professional therapist who acts as a resource and provides guidance. These interactions help to increase the nurse's therapeutic effectiveness, knowledge, and skills.

• • •

Nurses function in many roles when working with mental health clients. Through "practiced awareness," they are able to use a variety of roles to assist clients toward their goals. The therapeutic use of self is ap-

plied each time nurses interact with their clients, and every interaction is seen as a learning opportunity for both clients and nurses.

Problems Encountered in the Therapeutic Relationship

Throughout the therapeutic relationship, nurses are continually assisting their clients toward more effective functioning. However, problems or barriers arise and challenge nurses to devise creative solutions. The most common problems can be grouped into three broad areas: the environment, the nurse, and the client. By remaining alert for these potential areas of difficulty, nurses are able to prevent larger problems and increase their effectiveness when interacting with clients.

Environmental Problems

Problems with the environment include such things as a lack of privacy, an inappropriate meeting place, or uncomfortable furniture, lighting, or temperature. Noise and frequent interruptions disrupt nurse-client interactions and become troublesome, especially if clients are attempting to share personal information.

To minimize environmental problems, nurses should make appropriate arrangements for each session with the client. Find an area within the environment where interruptions and distractions will be minimal. Spend the allotted time focusing on the client. Being interrupted stops the communication flow between nurse and client and does little to foster the relationship. Be alert to how the environment affects the therapeutic relationship, and problems will be easier to prevent.

Problems With the Nurse

The barriers relating to the nurse in the therapeutic relationship include difficulties with attitude, setting helping boundaries, and countertransference.

Nurses are human beings with attitudes, opinions, and problems of their own. Working within a therapeutic relationship requires energy, time, and persistence. If the nurse is expending his/her energies in coping with personal difficulties, there is little left for the client. Historically, nurses were taught to leave their personal lives at the door and to ignore them during work hours. Now we know that it is not possible to separate the nurse from the person. They are one, and it is the person part of the nurse that is so effective in helping clients. Personal health is a primary ingredient of effective nursing care.

Attitude is also important in how the nurse views the client. Nurses who are skeptical about the client's willingness or ability to change are already dooming the relationship to failure. Discomfort with the feelings expressed by the client can also slow the relationship. To be an effective mental health nurse, one must know thyself.

Compassion is a key quality in a good nurse; however, when that compassion leads one to "rescue" clients, the nurse is becoming too involved. "Owning" client problems wears the nurse out and does nothing to promote the client's abilities to solve problems. To prevent this situation, establish your own professional boundaries. "For the nurse, professional boundaries define the needs of the nurse as distinctly different from the needs of the patient: what is too helpful and what is not; and what fosters independence vs. unhealthy dependence" (Pilette, Berck, and Achber, 1995). The major focus in the therapeutic relationship is the client. A delicate balance exists between being helpful and taking on the client and his/her problems. Clients must be allowed to own their problems or the therapeutic relationship loses its effectiveness. The involvement of the nurse must always be designed to move the client toward the goals of therapy (see box below).

SELF-ASSESSMENT OF HELPING BOUNDARIES

1. Have you ever felt too involved with a client?
2. Have you ever received feedback that you are overly intrusive or overly involved with clients and/or their families?
3. Do you have difficulty setting and enforcing limits?
4. Do you spend more than the allotted time with the client, arrive early or stay late for appointments?
5. Do you relate to clients or peers as you do family members?
6. Do you feel that you are the only one who "really understands" the client?
7. Do you feel that other staff members are too critical of "your" client or jealous of the relationship you have with the client?
8. Do you find it difficult to handle the client's unreasonable requests or behaviors?
9. Do you look forward to the client's praise, appreciation, or affection?

A "yes" answer to any question indicates a need to identify the behaviors that are blurring the boundaries of the therapeutic relationship.

Modified from Pilette PC, Berck CB, Achber LC: *J Psychosoc Nurs Ment Health Serv* 33:40, 1995.

Countertransference is a barrier in the therapeutic relationship based on the nurse's emotional responses to the client. It is an inappropriate emotional response on the part of the nurse. Although it is natural to be emotionally affected by clients with countertransference, "the nurse's responses are not justified by reality" (Stuart and Sundeen, 1995). The nurse identifies with someone from the past, and personal needs begin to inhibit the effectiveness of the therapeutic relationship. Common reactions usually include intense feelings of caring, involvement, disgust, hostility, or anxiety. To prevent countertransference, remember that the focus of the relationship is the client's needs. Recognizing when one's personal needs are beginning to overshadow the client's needs is a good way to prevent countertransference.

Problems With the Client

The progress of the therapeutic relationship can also be slowed or blocked by the client. Not infrequently, clients engage in various behaviors to stall or block the effectiveness of nursing actions. Client activities that block the progress of the therapeutic relationship fall into three basic categories: resistance, transference, and compliance.

Resistance was first defined by Freud as a client's attempts to avoid recognizing or exploring anxiety-provoking material. These attempts are further classified into primary and secondary types of resistance. Clients who demonstrate behaviors associated with primary resistance are unwilling to change even when they are aware of the need for change. Behaviors include attempts to thwart the therapeutic process, a refusal to work toward the therapeutic goals, and attempts to manipulate the situation. Clients may also resist in reaction to the nurse's interventions. If the nurse is not an appropriate role model for therapeutic behavior, primary resistance may occur.

Secondary resistance is seen when the client is motivated by drives other than the need to regain mental health. Many times the payoff for remaining ill outweighs the advantages of recovery. Some clients actually profit or avoid unpleasant situations by remaining ill. This situation is known as **secondary gain.** For example, the client who is facing legal problems on discharge attempts to remain in the therapeutic environment because he does not want to go to jail. Secondary gain can be a powerful motivation for resisting the treatment team's therapeutic efforts.

Transference is a client's emotional response to the nurse that is based on earlier relationships with significant others. The most outstanding characteristic of transference is the inappropriateness of the client's response. Because the client is generalizing the emo-

SAMPLE CLIENT CARE PLAN

THERAPEUTIC RELATIONSHIP

Assessment

History: Heather is a 14-year-old girl who is being treated for an eating disorder. She and the members of the treatment team have set a goal for a weight gain of 2 pounds a month. Sue, the treatment team's nurse, has assumed responsibility for seeing Heather weekly and monitoring her weight gain.

Current Findings: Heather keeps her appointments but tends to display negative reactions to every suggestion offered by the treatment team. Discussions with other care providers are superficial with little meaning. When interacting, Heather assumes a challenging attitude. Her weight has remained stable for the past 3 weeks.

Nursing Diagnosis

Ineffective individual coping related to a disturbance in self-concept.

Planning/Expected Outcomes

Heather will establish a trusting relationship with a member of the treatment team by September 23.

Nursing Interventions

Interventions

1. Prepare for first meeting by researching data about Heather, her family, and her past history.
2. Plan time, setting, and outline of goals for each meeting.
3. Establish an atmosphere of warmth and acceptance during first meeting.
4. Help Heather define her problems.

5. Develop a contract (working agreement) for self-motivated weight gain of 6 pounds per month.
6. Assist Heather to learn positive thinking techniques.

Rationale

1. Helps to define the client as an individual with particular strengths and problems.
2. Helps to define and focus on goals of the relationship.
3. Communicates respect and a willingness to become involved with Heather.
4. Helps reduce emotional reactions and break problems into small, more manageable units.
5. Defines limits, expectations of goals; helps to plan steps for meeting goals.

6. Helps replace self-defeating thoughts and actions with more effective ways of coping.

Evaluation

Heather remained silent during the first two interactions with Sue. By September 10, she was willing to talk to Sue. By September 19, Heather began the interaction and stated that she would be willing to work on gaining weight and discussing her problems.

---

tions associated with one person to another (the nurse), little opportunity for self-awareness exists. Clients may become hostile and express their feelings by demanding an end to the relationship or showing no interest in the nurse's interventions. Other clients can become dependent, submissive, and passive; with transference cases, clients overvalue the nurse's characteristics and place unreachable expectations on the relationship.

To prevent or cope with transference, first listen. Hear what the client is trying to communicate. Recognize areas of resistance and then clarify them with the client. Explore behaviors and try to identify possible reasons for their use. With time and experience, you will become adept when working with the uniquely human behavior of transference.

Noncompliance is the behavior of not following the prescribed treatment regimen. For individuals with mental-emotional problems, noncompliance is very high. According to Forman (1993), the main reasons for noncompliance are a lack of knowledge, medication side effects, and the nurse-client relationship.

Throughout the therapeutic relationship, nurses are continually assessing and monitoring the progress of their clients. Identifying and sharing problems of compliance with the client helps to remove another barrier from his/her recovery.

When clients are prescribed medications for the control of their symptoms, nurses must remain especially alert for side effects. Many clients stop taking their psychotropic medications because of distressing side effects. Other clients simply feel that they do not need their medications. Whatever the reasons, nurses are in excellent positions to improve their clients' compliance. "Through a working relationship, the nurse and the patient share the responsibility for complying with medication regimens" (Forman, 1993).

The therapeutic relationship provides nurses with a powerful tool for client care. Interventions are designed to promote the client's growth and movement toward self-awareness and independent functioning. Throughout each phase of the relationship, nurses encourage their clients in focusing their energies toward more effective and adaptive ways of living. The sample client care plan in the box on p. 140 describes several nursing interventions for establishing a therapeutic relationship.

❖ KEY CONCEPTS

- The therapeutic relationship is a directed energy exchange between two people that guides clients toward more effective behaviors.
- The dynamic components of the therapeutic relationship include the concepts of trust, empathy, autonomy, caring, and hope.
- The four stages or phases of the therapeutic relationship are the preparation, orientation, working, and termination phases.
- To successfully establish a therapeutic relationship, the nurse communicates the qualities of acceptance, genuineness, and rapport to the client.
- Nurses who work with mental health clients function as therapeutic change agents, teachers, technicians, and therapists.
- The most common problems in the therapeutic relationship relate to the environment, the nurse, and the client.

❖ SUGGESTIONS FOR FURTHER READING

Christine Heifner, author of "Positive Connectedness in the Psychiatric Nurse-Patient Relationship" in the *Archives of Psychiatric Nursing* (7[1]:11, 1993), explores the factors that contribute to the development of a positive connectedness with mental health clients and enhance the effectiveness of the therapeutic relationship.

❖ REFERENCES

Anderson KN, Anderson LE, Glanze WD: *Mosby's medical, nursing, and allied health dictionary,* ed 4, St Louis, 1994, Mosby.

Baker W: Making the extra effort, *Nurs 95* 25(5):65, 1995.

Dufault K, Martocchio BC: Hope, its spheres and dimensions, *Nurs Clin North Am* (2):379, 1985.

Forman L: Medication: reasons and interventions for noncompliance, *J Psychosoc Nurs Ment Health Serv* 31(10):23, 1993.

King I: *Toward a theory for nursing,* New York, 1971, John Wiley.

Peplau HE: *Interpersonal relations in nursing,* New York, 1952, GP Putnam.

Pilette PC, Berck CB, Achber LC: Therapeutic management of helping boundaries, *J Psychosoc Nurs Ment Health Serv* 33:40, 1995.

Rogers CR: *On becoming a person,* Boston, 1966, Houghton Mifflin.

Spencer PU: A native American worldview, In McNeill B, editor: *Noetic Sciences Collection 1980-1990,* Sausalito, CA, 1991, The Institute of Noetic Sciences.

Stuart GW, Sundeen SJ: *Principles and practice of psychiatric nursing,* ed 5, St Louis, 1995, Mosby.

Sundeen SJ and others: *Nurse-client interaction,* ed 5, St Louis, 1994, Mosby.

Taylor CM: *Essentials of psychiatric nursing,* ed 14, St Louis, 1994, Mosby.

Travelbee J: *Interpersonal aspects of nursing,* Philadelphia, 1971, FA Davis.

Trygstad LN: The need to know: biological learning needs identified by practicing psychiatric nurses, *J Psychosoc Nurs Ment Health Serv* 32(2):13, 1994.

Vellenga BA, Christenson J: Persistent and severely mentally ill clients' perceptions of their mental illness, *Iss Ment Health Nurs* 15:359, 1994.

Williamson JA: Mutual interaction: a model of nursing practice, *Nurs Outlook* (20):104, 1981.

Wolfe PL: Risk taking: nursing's comfort zone, *Holistic Nurs Pract* 8(2):43, 1994.

11

THERAPEUTIC COMMUNICATION

LEARNING OBJECTIVES

1. Describe two theories of communication.
2. Identify two types of communication.
3. List the five components or parts of any communication.
4. Compare the characteristics of verbal and nonverbal communications.
5. Identify three interventions for communicating with persons who do not speak English.
6. List eight principles of therapeutic communication.
7. Describe eight therapeutic communication skills.
8. Name three techniques for communicating with clients who have mental-emotional problems.

KEY TERMS

aphasia
communication
communication style
disturbed communications
dyslexia
evaluation

feedback
incongruent communications
interpersonal communications
intrapersonal communications
nontherapeutic communications
nonverbal communication

perception
responding strategies
speech cluttering
therapeutic communications
transmission
verbal communication

Communication is an essential component of survival for all creatures. Even plants communicate. Research has demonstrated that when a tree is attacked by insects, it sends a chemical message to other trees in the area. Animals communicate in subtle and complex ways using both sound and movement; but the master communicator, the user of language, is the human being. Infants are born communicating with their first squall, and the elderly die listening to the last communications in a world they are about to leave. The fulfillment of man's basic needs requires interactions with others. Fulfilling even the most basic needs for food and water requires the cooperative efforts of people, and cooperation is not possible without communication and understanding. "**Communication** refers to the reciprocal exchange of information, ideas, beliefs, feelings, and attitudes between two persons or among a group of persons" (Taylor, 1994). All people communicate, but members of the health care professions modify ordinary communications to promote the health of their clients. Nurses and other health care providers practice therapeutic communications based on certain principles. Those who work with the mentally and emotionally troubled refine their therapeutic communication skills to become highly skilled listeners "who can plan and carry out interactions specifically designed to achieve client outcomes" (Rawlins, Williams, and Beck, 1993). In this chapter we explore the elements and skills of therapeutically designed communication techniques.

History

The study of interactions between human beings has been a source of interest for centuries. Paintings on the walls of caves attest to prehistoric man's desire for communication. The Roman alphabet was introduced around 2000 BC. Chinese, Egyptian, and Mesopotamian cultures used writing as a major means of communication for centuries before Christ.

With the introduction of the printing press during the fifteenth century, the mass production of the written word was now possible. As people slowly learned to read and write, education evolved from an oral form of learning about the world to a visual one. Communications became more complex and a step removed from face-to-face interpersonal contact.

The inventions of the telegraph, telephone, radio, and television made more information available to everyone. Today, satellite communications, interactive computers, and "the Internet" are moving communications and information exchanges into new and unknown realms. Tomorrow's technological developments will move us further, but the need for effective verbal and nonverbal communication abilities will never be replaced by technology.

Theories of Communication

Probably one of the earliest theorists on therapeutic communications was Florence Nightingale, whose book *Notes on Nursing* emphasized the need to effectively understand and communicate with patients. However, the rest of the medical world placed little focus on the value of interacting therapeutically until the 1950s, when the publication of several theories sparked an interest in client-caregiver communications.

Ruesch's Theory

A theory of communication that considers communications as the social matrix (framework) for health care was developed by J. Ruesch in the late 1950s. He believed that communication included a broad range of activities that were designed to affect another person. Communications were viewed as a circular process, whereby messages traveled from within one person to another person and back again (Fig. 11-1).

Events within the sender prompt the sending of a message. The message is then transmitted to another who receives it, processes it internally, and responds. Successful communications occur when agreement about the meaning of the message has been reached. Communications are unsuccessful when there is a lack of agreement or understanding about the message. Ruesch (1961) coined the term **disturbed communications** to describe unsuccessful interactions that he believed resulted from an interference in the sending or receiving of messages, inadequate mastery of the language being used, insufficient information, or little or no opportunity for feedback.

Therapeutic communications are distinguished from ordinary communications by the intent of one of the participants to bring about a positive change. According to Ruesch's point of view, a therapist is one who directs the exchanges to bring about more satisfying social relations. Therapists seek to find the nature of clients' distresses and develop an understanding of their problems. Then, with the use of therapeutic communication techniques, both the client and the therapist agree on the nature of the problem and what should be done about it. Many of Ruesch's theoretical ideas are used by nurses when interacting with clients.

Transactional Analysis

In 1961, Dr. Eric Berne, a physician with training in psychoanalysis, published *Transactional Analysis in*

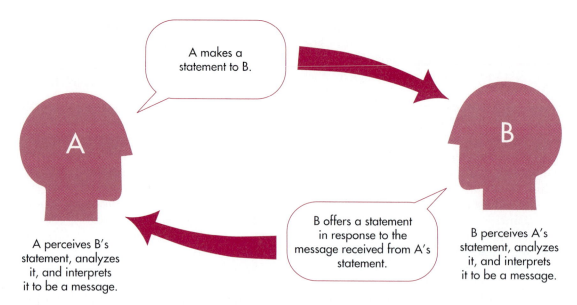

Fig. 11-1 Ruesch's feedback loop of communication. (Redrawn from Rawlins RP and others: *Mental health-psychiatric nursing,* ed 3, St Louis, 1993, Mosby.)

Psychotherapy. Three years later, his book titled *Games People Play* became a best-seller even though it was intended for a professional audience rather than the general public. In each book Berne described his system of group therapy and therapeutic communications. He coined the term *transactional analysis* to refer to the process of investigating what people say and do to each other. Berne also believed that three ego states exist within all of us: the parent (P) who focuses on rules and values, the child (C) who focuses on emotions and desires, and the adult (A) who bases his/her approach to the world on previous observations. These ego states make up one's individual personality, and Berne coined the term *structural analysis* to refer to the study of the personality.

Many of the interactions in which people engage, Berne noticed, have ulterior or hidden motives used to manipulate others. He labeled these manipulations psychological games and rackets and offered his *game analysis* to refer to the hidden interactions that lead to a payoff.

The main goal of transactional analysis, according to Berne, is to "establish the most open and authentic communication possible between the affective (feeling) and intellectual components of the personality" (Berne, 1964b). Analyzing one's structure, transactions, and games encourages people to gain insight and determine what changes are most desirable. Because Berne (like Maslow) believed that every person needs positive feedback or "strokes" to thrive, he encouraged communications that are positive in nature. This approach is valuable for nurses and other health care professionals. The focus on one's abilities (instead of disabilities) fosters more effective and satisfying communications for everyone involved with the client (James and Jongeward, 1977).

Neurolinguistic Programming

Much of the basis for neurolinguistic programming lies in the work of Milton H. Erickson who, until his death in 1980, was considered the greatest medical hypnotist of his time. To find the keys to his success, Richard Bandler and John Grinder spent several years doing careful and systematic analyses of Erickson's work and extensive writings. Using their observations as a framework, they developed a method for analyzing an individual's system of communication based on the theory that any effective communication is a state of hypnosis. Effective communications alter a person's state of consciousness (see the box on p. 145 for an exercise that demonstrates this point). By learning the patterns of an individual's communications, one is able to achieve more effective and fulfilling interactions. Patterns include eye-accessing clues (ways in which people move their eyes while thinking), different language patterns, and the pace and rhythm of speech.

Nurses, therapists, and other professionals are finding the principles of neurolinguistic programming a valuable asset for communications. Because neurolinguistic programming is a powerful tool for communicating, specialized training is recommended. The Society for Neurolinguistic Programming offers approved seminars, workshops, and training programs throughout the United States.

THINK ABOUT

Picture yourself in the forest, surrounded by tall, stately trees. You look up to see the sun filtering through the dense canopy of tree branches. Below you the forest floor is dappled with sunlight and shade patterns dance slowly across your shoes. The air is cool and musty, damp from the mist left over from the night. The world is silent except for the chirping of a lone songbird.

What did you experience when you were reading the above paragraph?

Did you actually experience a moment in the forest?

Do you wish that you could go there yourself? If your answer is "yes" to any of these questions, then the communication was successful. The pattern of communication in the paragraph altered your state of consciousness, which allowed you to share an experience. This is the "hypnosis" of neurolinguistic programming.

Other theories of communication focus on the use of body language (kinesics), how people use their space (proxemics), and channels of communication. Becoming familiar with several theories allows nurses to expand and improve their communication skills and abilities.

Characteristics of Communication

Communication is the act of sending and receiving information. When this definition is applied to a computer or some other mechanical mover of data, the interaction is simple. One machine contacts the other, data are exchanged, and the interaction is over. With people, however, the information exchange is much more complex. Human behaviors influence communications. Communication is a tool people use for establishing relationships with others. When human beings communicate, their interactions are rich with messages, but the goal of every communication is to understand and be understood.

Types of Communication

People engage in two types of communications: intrapersonal and interpersonal. Each may occur singly or in combination, and each may be used in effective or maladaptive ways.

Intrapersonal communications take place within oneself. They are commonly referred to as our "self-talk" or "self-dialogue." They consist of the conversations that we have with ourselves when solving problems, making plans, and emotionally reacting. The prefix *intra* means within, so intrapersonal communications are those messages that we send to ourselves.

Intrapersonal communications are adaptive when they help people to cope with stress or focus their energies in specific directions. When intrapersonal communications are dysfunctional, clients experience altered states of functioning. Hallucinations are an example of dysfunctional intrapersonal communications (Table 11-1).

Intrapersonal messages can also be communicated nonverbally to others. Nurses who are aware of this are careful to use their nonverbal behaviors therapeutically. For example, notice the position of your body when you are interacting with someone who you find unpleasant. Are your arms crossed? Is your body position open and inviting communication or closed with crossed legs or an angled stance?

Our intrapersonal communications affect our communications with others because the energy that makes up our self-talk is the same energy that we expend on clients. If your intrapersonal communications are upbeat and optimistic, then your interactions with clients will be too. If your self-talk is negative and glum, your communications will reflect this.

Interpersonal communications are those interactions that occur between two or more persons. They are the verbal and nonverbal messages that are sent and received during every interaction. Symbols, language, culture, and behaviors have an impact on communications among people. As a result, interpersonal communications are complex and sophisticated. No matter what the communication, the importance of each message lies in its clarity. Clear communications offer a greater chance of success in every interaction.

Process of Communication

For a successful communication to occur, five elements must be in place (Fig. 11-2). There must be a *sender* who forms the message and transmits it. A *message* is also needed because most persons do not communicate unless they have something to convey. A *receiver* is necessary to accept the message and respond in return. **Feedback** refers to the responses and self-talk of each person when messages are being sent and received. Last, though not an actual part of the message, the *context* or setting in which the communication takes place must be considered (Smith, 1992).

When a message is sent, a whole chain of events is triggered. First, **perception** is needed to recognize the presence of a message. Perception refers to the use of the senses to gain information. During communication, visual, auditory, and tactile senses are used to perceive or sense the meaning of the communication. A person's perceptions can be affected by many fac-

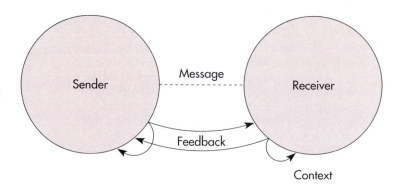

Fig. 11-2 Components of the communication process. (Redrawn from Sundeen SJ and others: *Nurse-client interactions: implementing the nursing process,* ed 5, St Louis, 1994, Mosby.)

◆ **TABLE 11-1**
Examples of Intrapersonal Communications

Adaptive Intrapersonal Communication	Dysfunctional Intrapersonal Communication
While receiving the change-of-shift report, a nurse says to herself, "I feel very rushed today. I wish that Ms. Jones would wait to be admitted until tomorrow, but we told her to return to the hospital at the first sign of trouble. So I'll just take a deep breath and plan my day to include some time for Ms. Jones. It'll be a good day."	While receiving the change-of-shift report, a nurse says to herself, "I feel very rushed today. I wish that Ms. Jones would wait until tomorrow to be admitted. She is such a demanding old witch, always crying for something. I just know that my blood pressure will be sky high by the end of this day and I'll probably get another headache. What a day this is going to be!"

---

tors, including past experiences, emotional states, and physical problems.

The second step in the process of communicating is **evaluation,** the internal assessment of the message. All the overt, as well as the hidden, messages of the communication are considered and then compared to past experiences. The result is an emotional reaction to the message and preparation to return a message to the sender.

Transmission (a response) is the last step in the communication process. It includes the conscious and unconscious response to the message received. As the receiver of the message responds with a message of his/her own, the cycle begins again and is repeated with every interaction. If a person has difficulty with any one step of the communication process—perceiving, evaluating, or transmitting messages—a communication problem may exist. Alert nurses are aware of each client's process of communication and are prepared to intervene when clients are having communication difficulties.

Factors That Influence Communication

The process of interacting with others is influenced by many factors, but among the most important are culture, social class, values, relationships, perceptions, and parts of the message.

The *social class* to which one belongs has a profound influence on communications. People of various social classes interact using their own terminology, slang, cliches, rate of speech, gestures, and appearances. This variation in communication patterns can create problems for health care providers who interact with clients from different social classes than their own. The tendency to stereotype is influenced by how one communicates. Nurses must be careful not to label clients based on their communications.

Communicating with clients from different social classes requires effort and patience. Both the nurse and client will feel misunderstood and attempt to withdraw unless steps are taken to establish effective communication exchanges. The box on p. 147 lists several nursing interventions for interacting with people from different social classes.

Relationships affect communications because of the level of relatedness of each person involved in the interaction. Levels of relatedness refer to the degree of intimacy, authority, and role status of the communicators. People communicate differently with strangers than they do with family members.

The *emotional climate* of a relationship can affect communications. If hidden feelings or agendas are present, the flow of communications tends to become stifled. Mixed messages are often sent because the

COMMUNICATING WITH CLIENTS FROM DIFFERENT SOCIAL CLASSES

- Show acceptance and respect for the person.
- Consider the environment with which clients must cope, especially those from social classes of poverty.
- Assess the client's patterns of communication, verbal and nonverbal.
- Use terms the client can understand.
- Do not talk "up" or "down" to clients.
- Ask clients to clarify any terms that are not understood.
- Invite the client to take an active part in the treatment plan and its activities.

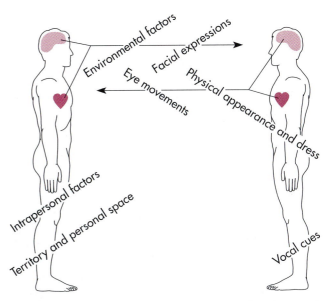

Sender-receiver   Receiver-sender

Fig. 11-3 Factors influencing communication. (Redrawn from Smith S: *Communications in nursing: communicating assertively and responsibly in nursing—a guidebook,* ed 2, St Louis, 1992, Mosby.)

emotional tone of the relationship is different than the communications being sent. A good course of action is to recognize the emotional climate, openly discuss the underlying emotions, and clarify the true intent of the communications.

Perceptions and *values* color one's communications. Perceptions are one's internal experiences, an individual's point of view of the world. When combined with the personal rules by which one lives (values), the result is a unique frame of reference for communicating. It is important for nurses to remember this point because it may be *your perceptions* that are impeding effective communication.

The content and context of a message have a strong impact on communications. The *content* of a message is the information being sent. The receiver of the message is affected by the content of the communications and must choose an appropriate reaction. The receiver can recognize the communications, ignore everything, or change the subject. For example, during the preparation for a routine physical examination, the client hints that she was recently raped by her cousin. The content of this message arouses emotions within the nurse that will affect the communication. The nurse may choose to ignore the hint, ask only yes/no questions in an attempt to avoid this area of communication, or convey interest in exploring the message sent by the client. An awareness of the emotional impact related to the content of messages helps nurses to communicate more effectively with clients, especially those with mental-emotional difficulties.

Communications are also affected by the *context,* or environment, in which they take place. Nurses who expect clients to share personal information about themselves must provide an environment that fosters privacy and prevents interruptions. The day room or lounge is not a place for self-disclosure. Becoming

aware of the context of communications helps nurses to send and receive messages with greater success.

Many other factors have an impact on communications. Even total strangers are affected by the messages sent by another's appearance, expressions, and body movements. The act of communicating is filled with overt and subtle elements (Fig. 11-3).

Levels of Communication

The act of communicating is an energy exchange that takes place on several levels. Each person involved in the sending and receiving of messages is a complete and unique personality who interacts on several levels at one time. For the sake of discussion, these levels are divided into verbal and nonverbal. Communications at each of these levels occurs with every person-to-person interaction.

Verbal Communication

Verbal communication relates to anything associated with the spoken word. Verbal communications include speaking and writing, the use of language and symbols, and the arrangement of words or phrases.

Using verbal communications requires the ability to perceive, understand, and transmit verbal or written messages. For many clients with mental-emotional problems, communicating with others can be difficult. Certain clients have difficulties in perceiving.

The person who is experiencing hallucinations, for example, may be unable to understand a message is being sent because the communications within his/her inner world are drowning out the messages from the reality outside.

Understanding verbal messages involves the ability to form abstract ideas and concepts. Persons with schizophrenia often have great difficulty with abstraction and using words that are reality oriented. Transmitting messages is a problem for many depressed clients; identifying and verbalizing how they feel is commonly stated in one or two words. Nurses must take these things into consideration when interacting with such clients.

Music is a form of communication that is gaining attention as a possible therapy for some kinds of mental illness. A recent study by a nurse working in a center for the homeless (Peden, 1993) demonstrated that music tended to promote a sense of relaxation and increased interactions with others. It also decreased the sense of loneliness experienced by the homeless people in the study. For the nurse, music provided her with an opportunity to interact with persons who did not ordinarily communicate. This interaction opened the door to the possibility of therapeutic relationships and allowed the nurse to provide screening and intervention services for clients who would have otherwise refused her offers. An avenue for communication was opened through the use of music.

Although verbal communication is the most overt or obvious form of interaction, it actually represents only a small part of an entire communication. Words are only symbols; they do not have the same meaning to all people. To illustrate, the word *dog* can mean a small, furry, living animal to one person. For another, the word may denote a large, growling, ferocious beast; for a third individual, the word *dog* may mean an ugly person. Using the word *dog* when communicating with these people results in a different message being received by each person.

To make matters more complicated, the problem intensifies as the words become more abstract. Emotions are an excellent example of abstractions that cannot be easily communicated on the verbal level (Dean, 1993). This is an important point for nurses to remember. If communications are to be effective, you must understand the client's meaning of the word.

Nonverbal Communication

Messages sent and received without the use of words define **nonverbal communication.** The nonverbal level includes one's intrapersonal communications—the messages created through the body's motions and use of touch, space, and sight. It also refers to the unspoken interpersonal communications and includes such behaviors as eye movement, gestures, movement of the body, expressions, posture, and eye contact.

Nonverbal communications are recognized through observation, touch, smell, taste, and even hearing. Messages sent at the nonverbal level are expressed in at least one of four ways: appearance, body motions, use of space, and nonlanguage sounds. One's appearance can convey strong nonverbal messages. The state of hygiene and personal grooming habits and choice of clothing and accessories, hairstyle, and jewelry send messages. Facial expressions, gestures, posture, and use of the body can communicate one's emotions more easily than words. The use of space and distance (see the discussion on territoriality in Chapter 4) communicates concepts such as authority and intimacy. Nonlanguage sounds are verbalizations without words. The scream of a woman in danger and the grunt of someone lifting a heavy load do not rely on words to convey their messages. In short, the nonverbal level of communications includes everything outside the realm of speaking, writing, or singing. It is a subtle world, rich in variation. The more nurses are able to recognize and use the nonverbal level of communication, the more effective their nursing interventions (actions) will become.

Each level of communication—verbal and nonverbal—sends and receives messages during every interaction. If the messages are being successfully sent and received, the results are communications rich in variety and complexity.

Intercultural Communication

When communicating with people from other cultures, nurses must take special considerations to ensure understanding. How people communicate is based on their cultural backgrounds, language systems, and social patterns. Cultures are transmitted through communication, and cultures define how emotions are expressed and shared. The use of touch and other nonverbal forms of communication varies considerably with different cultures (see box on p. 149).

Cultures, and the social groups within them, have variations in the use of verbal and nonverbal communications. The expression of warmth and humor varies among cultures. For nurses who work with clients from culturally different backgrounds, it is important to resist the tendency to stereotype people and to learn the most important, culturally appropriate methods for communication.

CULTURAL ASPECTS

In 1971, Sidney Jourard studied the cultural differences relating to the use of touch by observing the behaviors of pairs of people in coffee shops throughout the world. The results of his observations revealed that more touch occurred in certain cities.

City	Couples Touched Each Other (times/hr)
San Juan, Puerto Rico	180
Paris, France	110
Gainesville, Florida	2
London, England	0

The use of touch can be a powerful therapeutic tool, but only when it is culturally appropriate.

Intercultural Differences

Every person works to fulfill his/her basic needs. To do this, people must interact and communicate with each other. For persons of differing cultures, this interacting with others can be a difficult process. Communication styles, nonverbal behaviors, and values, as well as the use of the language, are areas in which cultural communications basically differ (Lynch, 1993).

Communication style refers to the rituals connected with greeting and departure, the lines of conversation, and the directness of communication (Giger and Davidizar, 1995). Greeting rituals should be assessed by considering the process of the greeting interaction, including the use of compliments and physical behaviors such as touching, handshaking, or kissing.

Are the lines of communication linear or circular? *Linear communication styles* come directly to the point. The message is sent in a straight line toward a specific point. To illustrate, most Anglo-American men favor an open, frank, even blunt conversation style, whereas Thai Americans practice *kreng jai,* a consideration for the feelings and needs of others.

Circular communication styles direct the conversation in circles around the main point. Often, the main point is left unstated. Once the important information has been communicated, it is assumed that the receiver got the point. "There's a fire in the wastebasket" is an example of a linear message, whereas "I saw someone drop a match in the wastebasket earlier; now it appears to be smoking" illustrates a circular style of communication, which is often found in Oriental and far Eastern cultures.

The directness and openness with which people solve their problems influence communications. Are problems communicated directly, communicated in a circular manner, or denied and ignored? How appropriate is it to state an opinion or offer help?

Differences in cultural behaviors, especially nonverbal ones, have an impact on communication (Grossman and Taylor, 1995). Cultural differences affect the nonverbal tone of the receiver. Body language, such as eye contact, gestures, and distance, are culturally determined. Much of the message is lost when one does not understand the communications of the body.

Values guide many communications within cultures. They help determine whether the individual or the group is more important and how persons of various statuses should be treated. How individuals from various cultures use time is an example of cultural value that affects communications.

Cultures that place a high value on nonverbal communications practice "high-context" communications. Here, nonverbal cues and sensitivity play a larger role than the actual verbal message. Actions speak louder than words. Cultures that practice "low context" communications tend to focus more on the words of the message rather than the feeling tone. Words speak louder than actions in these cases.

The last major cultural communication difference is the use of the society's language. Language use considers a culture's use of names and titles; the structure of grammar; the use of vocabulary, jargon, and slang; and vocal qualities such as tones, pronunciation, rhythm, and speed of communications. The meaning of silence varies from culture to culture (Pore, 1995).

Nurses must be aware of the possible meanings of culturally different communications. The effectiveness of the therapeutic relationship depends on it.

Interventions to Improve Communication

Nurses who work with people from different societies must pay particular attention to possible cultural differences. Communications are improved by the following (Bennett, 1994):

1. Recognize what is different from your own cultural style.
2. Adapt your behavior to accommodate the difference.
3. Call attention to the difference to explain the confusion in communication.

The most important nursing intervention for communicating with culturally different clients is an acceptance of the client as a person and a willingness to work toward the therapeutic goals of care.

Therapeutic Communication Skills

The goal of any communication is to send and receive messages. However, the goals of therapeutic communications are to focus on the client and foster the therapeutic relationship. Therapeutic communication techniques are skills that assist the nurse in effectively interacting with clients.

Principles of Therapeutic Communication

Each therapeutic communication skill or technique is based on the eight principles of therapeutic communication: acceptance, interest, respect, honesty, concreteness, assistance, permission, and protection (Table 11-2). The principles of therapeutic communication serve as guidelines for effective interactions with clients. Refer to them often. They will help you cope with the complexities of human communication.

Therapeutic communication techniques are divided into two equally important areas: listening skills and interacting skills. Each is vital if communications are to be clearly understood and nursing actions are to be successful.

Listening Skills

In our fast-paced, time-oriented modern world, people are so intent on sending their messages that they seldom take the time to listen, to truly hear what the other person is trying to communicate. The art of listening is a necessary ingredient for every health care provider, not just those who work in "psychiatry." Effective listening improves nurses' abilities to meet their clients' needs. In addition, effective listening can help to spot hidden messages and agendas, minimize misunderstandings, and clarify messages. "Good listeners are perceived as intelligent, perceptive, and sensitive—exactly the image professional nursing strives to project" (Paternostro, 1993). Although it may require time and practice to perfect your therapeutic listening skills, the rewards are worth the efforts (see box on p. 152).

To polish your listening skills, first concentrate on the speaker. Next, try to listen objectively. Many words call forth emotional responses that can color communications. Learn which words trigger your emotional responses. This awareness helps you to remain tuned in and attentive to the speaker even when an emotional "button" has been pushed.

Use appropriate eye contact and body language. Remember the speaker's cultural background. Body language communicates a wealth of information, even about the listener. Maintaining a relaxed body position at eye level with the speaker communicates acceptance of and interest in the speaker. Make sure that your nonverbal messages match the verbal messages.

If at all possible, do not interrupt. Let the speaker be fully expressive. Jot down notes for clarification later, but let the speaker finish. If time becomes a problem and you must interrupt, explain that the conversation is important but your time is limited. Follow up with telling the speaker when you will return to finish the conversation.

The last and most important guideline for becoming an effective listener is to clarify what the speaker said. If you are uncertain about what was communicated, ask for clarification. "Never assume you've understood another's thoughts" (Paternostro, 1993). Clarification is a main therapeutic communication technique that, when used in combination with good listening skills, enhances every nurse's abilities to successfully interact with clients.

Interacting Skills

Therapeutic techniques that relate to the nurse's actions while communicating are called responding strategies or interaction skills. These are the verbal and nonverbal responses that encourage clients to communicate in a way that will encourage their growth. When using therapeutic interactions, the nurse uses words that have meaning to the client. Communications are direct and pertinent (related to the situation). Messages have a clear meaning, are easily understood, and allow enough time for a response. Questions should not contain the word *why* because it requires a response justifying one's actions or opinions.

There are twelve commonly used therapeutic communication techniques (Stuart and Sundeen, 1995). They are often referred to as **responding strategies** because their use by the nurse encourages clients to continue communicating. Carefully study the information in the box on p. 153. Practice these techniques with clients, peers, and even people outside the health care environment, and note the results. With patience and practice, these techniques become important tools for effectively interacting with all types of clients.

Nontherapeutic Communication

Messages that hinder effective communication are referred to as **nontherapeutic communications.** They are interactions that slow or halt the development of the helping relationship, which is a vital ingredient of client care. Nontherapeutic communications include barriers that arise within the environment, the nurse, or the client, plus the responses that block further communications.

◆ TABLE 11-2
Principles of Therapeutic Communication

Principle	Illustration	Example
Acceptance	Accepting nurses communicate a favorable reception of another person by implying, "You have a right to exist, to live your life, to have somebody care about you." One does not have to approve of another's behavior to be accepting. It is only when people feel accepted for what they are that they will consider changing.	*Client:* I know it's been destructive for me to live with my parents, and I get irresponsible living there, but I feel like that's where I need to go after I leave the hospital. *Nurse:* I may not agree with your decision about where to live, but I accept your choice to do that and will work with you to evaluate how it works out for you.
Interest	Nurses communicate interest when they are genuinely curious and express a desire to know another person. Interest is conveyed by asking about those aspects of a person's life that others often reject. Nurses communicate by their attitude that "everything can be talked about here." This suggests to the client that "I want to know all about you, both the good and the bad."	*Client:* I'm so ashamed of what I've done, I can't tell you about it. You won't ever talk to me again! *Nurse:* Sandy, I'm interested in everything about you, the good, the bad, the sad, the happy. This is not just a "good times only" relationship. You and I have committed to working on a number of issues of importance, and I have a feeling that this is one of them. So why not go ahead and begin?
Respect	Nurses show consideration for another by communicating their willingness to work with the client and accept the client's ideas, feelings, and rights. It is communicated by listening attentively, expressing belief in the client's ability to solve personal problems with assistance and assume responsibility for his/her own life, collaborating on shared goals, calling the client by name, arriving and leaving on time, and keeping one's word. False reassurance and critical judgment are to be avoided; both are forms of disrespect that convey the message "your feelings are unfounded or unimportant."	*Client:* I know it's silly for me to feel so frightened about living alone, but I'm terrified. *Nurse:* I could tell you that you have nothing to worry about, that you'll do just fine. But, I hear your terror, your voice is shaking, and you're all perspired. It must be hard to imagine being able to survive on your own after being married for 30 years.
Honesty	Nurses are honest when they are consistent, open, and frank. Nurses do not take refuge behind a professional mask but instead communicate with the client as an authentic person. They use tact and timing in judging the use of honesty so that clients are not burdened with information or feedback they are not ready to hear. Nurses are honest and nondefensive about their thoughts and feelings that they discover through self-assessment. Honest nurses are willing to take the risk of selectively using self-disclosure with clients.	*Client:* I hate the way he treats me; he takes me for granted, leaving on business trips and not telling me where he's staying, when he's coming home. If one of us got sick, how would I know where to reach him? It will never change. *Nurse:* Carol, we've discussed this pattern before, and it remains the same, despite the alternative ways we've discussed for dealing with the situation. Quite honestly, I think a major reason for Lou's not changing his behavior is that you allow him to continue it. *Client:* What do you mean? *Nurse:* I mean that unless or until you let him know that his behavior is unacceptable, why should he change? This way he doesn't have to be accountable to anyone, even his wife.

From Haber J and others: *Comprehensive psychiatric nursing*, ed 4, St Louis, 1992, Mosby.

Continued

◆ **TABLE 11-2**
Principles of Therapeutic Communication—cont'd

Principle	Illustration	Example
Concreteness	Concrete nurses are specific, to the point, and clear when they communicate. They use understandable language and avoid the use of jargon. Clients who speak in vague, general, unfocused ways are helped to be more specific and focused.	*Client:* I feel sort of uneasy, I get a feeling like . . . that every so often . . . (perspiring, wringing hands, tapping feet, shifting in chair) *Nurse:* Describe the feeling for me in detail.
Assistance	Nurses assist clients by committing time and energy to therapeutic relationships. They convey that they are present and available and have tangible aid to offer that will help the client choose and develop more functional ways of living.	*Nurse:* While you're in the hospital, you and I will be meeting every day at 2 PM for 45 minutes. I am available to you to help you work out the problems that are bothering you. I'll also see you lots of other times, since I work on the unit. I hope you'll feel free to approach me if you need something.
Permission	Nurses communicate permission by conveying the message that it is acceptable to try new ways of behaving. Often clients are afraid to choose freely and act autonomously. They are bound by misconceived archaic rules and magical thinking and need to be given permission and encouragement to see and do things in new ways.	*Client:* How can I suddenly trust people when I've been hurt so badly in the past? *Nurse:* Clarify for me who hurt you? *Client:* Well, my brother, you know how he hurt me. *Nurse:* Yes, I do know that. What about other people. Can you tell me about them? *Client:* Well, I can't tell you any others specifically. It's just the way I feel about people. *Nurse:* I think you may be looking at other people and seeing your brother in them. You might be bringing the past into the present. *Client:* What should I do? *Nurse:* Well, what about trying to look at a few people in a different way and giving them just a little bit of a chance?
Protection	Nurses protect clients by ensuring clients' safety. Nurses assume responsibility of working with clients to anticipate trouble spots with new behavior and develop effective ways of dealing with anticipated or actual problems, thus maximizing the possibility of success.	*Client:* I'm really scared to go home on my pass this weekend. What will people say? How will they expect me to behave? *Nurse:* I hear that you're scared, and that's very natural for you to feel. Let's work together to try to anticipate what will happen over the weekend and see if, together, you and I can come up with some strategies for dealing with those "hot spots."

THERAPEUTIC LISTENING SKILLS

- Concentrate on the speaker and the message.
- Keep distractions and interruptions to a minimum.
- Change the setting (environment) if necessary.
- Assess nonverbal communications and metacommunications.
- Listen objectively.
- Discover which words trigger emotional responses in you.
- Use eye contact and body language that is culturally appropriate.
- Do not interrupt. Let the speaker finish delivering the message.
- Jot down notes if needed.
- Do not assume that you have understood another person's thoughts.
- Clarify any message about which you are unsure.

THERAPEUTIC COMMUNICATION TECHNIQUES

LISTENING

Definition: Active process of receiving information and examining reaction to messages received

Example: Maintaining eye contact and receptive nonverbal communication

Therapeutic value: Nonverbally communicates to client nurse's interest and acceptance

Nontherapeutic threat: Failure to listen

BROAD OPENINGS

Definition: Encouraging client to select topics for discussion

Example: "What are you thinking about?"

Therapeutic value: Indicates acceptance by nurse and value of client's initiative

Nontherapeutic threat: Domination of interaction by nurse; rejecting responses

RESTATING

Definition: Repeating main thought the client expressed

Example: "You say that your mother left you when you were 5 years old."

Therapeutic value: Indicates that nurse is listening and validates, reinforces, or calls attention to something important that has been said

Nontherapeutic threat: Lack of validation of nurse's interpretation of message; being judgmental; reassuring; defending

CLARIFICATION

Definition: Attempting to put into words vague ideas or unclear thoughts of client to enhance nurse's understanding or asking client to explain what he/she means

Example: "I'm not sure what you mean. Could you tell me about that again?"

Therapeutic value: Helps to clarify feelings, ideas, and perceptions of patient and provide explicit correlation between them and client's actions

Nontherapeutic threat: Failure to probe; assumed understanding

REFLECTION

Definition: Directing back client's ideas, feelings, questions, and content

Example: "You're feeling tense and anxious and it's related to a conversation you had with your husband last night?"

Therapeutic value: Validates nurse's understanding of what client is saying and signifies empathy, interest, and respect for client

Nontherapeutic threat: Stereotyping client's responses. Inappropriate timing of reflections; inappropriate depth of feeling of reflections; inappropriate to cultural experience and educational level of client

HUMOR

Definition: Discharge of energy through comic enjoyment of imperfect

Example: "That gives a whole new meaning to the word *nervous*," said with shared kidding between nurse and client

Therapeutic value: Can promote insight by making conscious repressed material, resolving paradoxes, tempering aggression, and revealing new options, and is socially acceptable form of sublimation

Nontherapeutic threat: Indiscriminate use; belittling client; screen to avoid therapeutic intimacy

INFORMING

Definition: Skill of information giving

Example: "I think you need to know more about how your medication works."

Therapeutic value: Helpful in health teaching or client education about relevant aspects of client's well-being and self-care

Nontherapeutic threat: Giving advice

FOCUSING

Definition: Questions or statements that help client expand on topic of importance

Example: "I think that we should talk more about your relationship with your father."

Therapeutic value: Allows client to discuss central issues and keeps communication process goal-directed

Nontherapeutic threat: Allowing abstractions and generalizations; changing topics

SHARING PERCEPTIONS

Definition: Asking client to verify nurse's understanding of what client is thinking or feeling

Example: "You're smiling but I sense that you are really very angry with me."

Therapeutic value: Conveys nurse's understanding to client and has potential for clearing up confusing communication

Nontherapeutic threat: Challenging client; accepting literal responses; reassuring; testing; defending

THEME IDENTIFICATION

Definition: Underlying issues or problems experienced by client that emerge repeatedly during course of nurse-client relationship

Example: "I've noticed that in all of the relationships that you have described, you've been hurt or rejected by the man. Do you think this is an underlying issue?"

Therapeutic value: Allows nurse to best promote client's exploration and understanding of important problems

Modified from Stuart GW, Sundeen SJ: *Principles and practice of psychiatric nursing,* ed 5, St Louis, 1995, Mosby.

Continued

THERAPEUTIC COMMUNICATION TECHNIQUES—cont'd

Nontherapeutic threat: Giving advice; reassuring; disapproving

SILENCE
Definition: Lack of verbal communication for therapeutic reason
Example: Sitting with client and nonverbally communicating interest and involvement
Therapeutic value: Allows client time to think and gain insights, slows pace of interaction and encourages client to initiate conversation, while conveying nurse's support, understanding, and acceptance
Nontherapeutic threat: Questioning client; asking for

"why" responses; failure to break nontherapeutic silence

SUGGESTING
Definition: Presentation of alternative ideas for client's consideration relative to problem solving
Example: "Have you thought about responding to your boss in a different way when he raises that issue with you? For example, you could ask him if a specific problem has occurred."
Therapeutic value: Increases client's perceived options or choices
Nontherapeutic threat: Giving advice; inappropriate timing; being judgmental

Barriers to Communication

Barriers to effective interactions can arise during each step of the communication process. They are erected during the interaction as protective behaviors when one feels threatened. The problem with their use is that they are likely to increase the client's "self-exposure, insecurity, and helplessness" (Haber and others, 1992). If allowed to go unchecked, the use of barriers will smother the therapeutic relationship and prevent the client from reaching the treatment goals.

Because the setting or environment is difficult to control, it can often have a negative effect on communications. Factors within the environment may make it too noisy or crowded for the sharing of personal information. Sometimes the client will attempt to send an important message in an inappropriate setting. For example, while waiting in line at the lunchroom, your client announces that he is leaving his wife. In this instance, the environment acts as a barrier to further exploration of an emotionally charged topic because of the noise level and lack of privacy.

Problems with the individuals involved in the communication can arise. The nurse may be physically tired or would actually prefer not to interact with the client. Such feelings may lead to **incongruent communications,** in which the verbal messages being sent do not match one's nonverbal communications. Incongruent communications can be sent by either the client or the nurse, but it is the nurse's responsibility to match each level of his/her communication with the message.

On occasion, a client will refuse to communicate or cooperate. This lack of cooperation erects a large barrier and prevents other people from attempting to

interact. Such a client requires extra patience and repeated messages of acceptance. With time and persistence, clients usually become more willing to interact because no person likes to be lonely and cut off from their fellow human beings.

The following are methods for coping with the barriers to communications:

1. Recognize that a problem exists.
2. Identify what purpose or need the problem is filling.
3. Explore appropriate alternative behaviors.
4. Implement the alternative behaviors when interacting.
5. Evaluate whether therapeutic communications have improved. If they have not, reassess and try another approach.

Being aware of communication barriers allows nurses to intervene early and effectively.

Nontherapeutic Communication Techniques

According to Sundeen and others (1994), nontherapeutic communications fall into two areas: nontherapeutic techniques that relate to omission and nontherapeutic techniques of commission.

Nontherapeutic communication techniques of *omission* relate to the nurse's failure to do something (act, to use a therapeutic technique) when the moment is right. Communication acts of omission include such behaviors as failure to listen, probe, elicit descriptions, or explore the client's point of view. Giving vague descriptions and inadequate answers, parroting, and following the standard forms too closely also are considered in this category (Table 11-3).

◆ **TABLE 11-3**
Nontherapeutic Communications of Omission

Nontherapeutic Technique	Description	Example
Failure to listen	Placing own thoughts above client, not being involved in communication	Yawning when client is speaking, looking at watch frequently, missing client's messages
Failure to explore client's point of view	Does not ask client to describe abstract words such as *pain*, *angry*, *sick*	*Client:* "My head hurts." *Nurse:* "You're just getting used to your new medication."
Failure to probe	Does not seek clarification or validation from client	*Client:* "I've had bad experiences with doctors." *Nurse:* "That's too bad."
Eliciting vague descriptions	Does not encourage client to explain or expand on message	*Client:* "I keep hearing voices." *Nurse:* "O.K."
Giving inadequate answers	Does not collect enough data to answer client's question accurately	Instructs client about medication then finds out he is allergic to it
Parroting	Continuous repeating of client's words	*Client:* "I feel terrible." *Nurse:* "You feel terrible." *Client:* "I haven't slept in two nights." *Nurse:* "You haven't slept in two nights."
Following standard forms too closely	Using a question-and-answer format to elicit specific information	*Nurse:* "Do you have any problems chewing?" *Client:* "No, but I have this pain in my jaw at night." *Nurse:* "Do you have any problems with indigestion or constipation?"

Modified from Sundeen SJ and others: *Nurse-client interactions: implementing the nursing process,* ed 5, St Louis, 1994, Mosby.

Those nontherapeutic techniques in which the nurse performs or communicates in an undesirable manner fall into the category of nontherapeutic communications of *commission.* This area includes giving advice or disapproval, being defensive, making judgments, patronizing, making stereotyped responses, reassuring, or rejecting clients' messages (Table 11-4).

Become an observer of your own communications. See if your verbal and nonverbal communications give the same message. Evaluate your use of communication techniques and enhance your ability to effectively communicate.

Problems With Communication

For many people in our society, communicating with others can be a difficult process. Clients with communication problems challenge the nurse's skill and ingenuity.

Sensory-impaired clients have difficulty receiving or sending messages because of problems with sight, hearing, or understanding. The first step in interacting with sensory-deprived persons is to achieve a successful introduction. If the client knows your name and purpose, cooperation is more likely. Next, encourage the client to become actively involved in the communication process. If possible, learn how the client communicates (signing, writing, touch). Maintain good eye contact and attentive nonverbal behaviors. Speak directly to the client, not the person who may be with him/her. Do not try to finish the client's sentence or fill in words. Allow extra time for the client to think and form responses. Last, do not forget the importance of the use of touch. For people who have diminished sight or hearing, touch is a powerful way of communicating.

Some people may have problems with sending messages. Persons with **aphasia** (inability to speak), **dyslexia** (impaired ability to read sometimes accompanied by a mixing of letters or syllables in a word when speaking), and **speech cluttering** (rapid, confused delivery of unrhythmic speech patterns) cannot focus on verbal communications as their main form of human interaction. Therefore it is important for the nurse to tune into the client's nonverbal behaviors and become extra alert for the messages being sent. For clients with communication problems, the speech therapist can be a valuable member of the multidisciplinary treatment team.

Communicating With Mentally Troubled Clients

Problems with communication are a common feature in many forms of mental illness. People with mental-emotional difficulties find it difficult to develop trust in other people. Loneliness is the companion of mental illness and only the sincere, respectful caring of another person can remove the barrier that isolates the mentally ill from the world (Pfeifer, 1995).

To communicate effectively with mentally and emotionally troubled clients, the nurse must learn that every interaction and every conversation is a part of the total therapeutic process. The nurse must establish a climate of trust and respect before clients feel safe enough to honestly share themselves. Establishing this trusting climate requires patience, persistence, and, most important, consistency. Mental health clients need routine, the security of a dependable en-

vironment, and nurses with calm, reliable temperaments. This consistency meets clients' basic needs and allows them to focus on communicating.

As with every other client, nurses begin their interactions with mental health clients by introducing themselves and explaining their purpose. The nurse then starts the conversation by introducing a neutral subject, such as weather, sports, or entertainment events. The sensitive nurse then waits quietly for the client to comment, using the opportunity to assess for any nonverbal behaviors or barriers to communication.

Once the client is communicating, the nurse must avoid a verbal assault of questions. Data may have to be obtained but not at the expense of threatening the fragile communication line so recently established. As long as the client is interacting, necessary data will eventually be revealed and recorded.

One of the most important tools for communicating with mentally ill clients is therapeutic listening. Attentive listening alone communicates acceptance and respect, which are messages not often received by mental health clients. Once the client believes that you sincerely care about him/her as a person, not just a diag-

---

◆ **TABLE 11-4**
Nontherapeutic Communications of Commission

Nontherapeutic Technique	Description	Example
Being judgmental: giving approval, agreeing or disagreeing	Many responses that tell clients that they must think as you do	*Client:* "I saw my wife today." *Nurse:* "You should be nicer to her."
Giving advice	Telling clients what to do; gives message that they are inferior and not able to make good decisions	*Client:* "I'm nervous about meeting Dr. Dow." *Nurse:* "You just march in there and say what you want, but don't raise your voice."
Being defensive	An attempt to protect something or someone; prevents clients from communicating	*Client:* "That last nurse is a dope." *Nurse:* "All of our nurses here are highly trained."
Challenging	Inviting or daring client to explain, act, or compete	*Client:* "I'm really dead, you know." *Nurse:* "If you are really dead then why is your heart still beating?"
Giving reassurance	Messages that negate feelings of client and offer false hope	*Client:* "I'll never get out of here." *Nurse:* "Everything will turn out for the best."
Rejecting	Refusal to discuss feelings or areas of concern	*Client:* "You know that I raped my sister." *Nurse:* "Let's not talk about that."
Using stereotyped responses	Using cliches, popular sayings, or trite expressions	*Client:* "I feel so depressed today." *Nurse:* "Everyone gets the blues now and then."

Modified from Sundeen SJ and others: *Nurse-client interactions: implementing the nursing process,* ed 5, St Louis, 1994, Mosby.

nosis, a flow of communications will come easily. The box below presents a client care plan based on the use of therapeutic communication principles.

Assessing Communication

Because the flow of information between people occurs naturally, we seldom take the time to assess a client's abilities to communicate. However, a communication assessment is an important part of the mental health workup.

First, assess the client's ability to hear and speak. Second, note the content, quality, and pace of the client's speech. Is it coherent, logical, easy to follow? Is the pace fast or slow? Is the volume loud, too soft, or whispered? Are there any physical speech problems, like stuttering? Are the number of words used exces-

---

SAMPLE CLIENT CARE PLAN

COMMUNICATION

Assessment

History: Amy, a 30-year-old married woman, is suffering from depression. Currently, she refuses to speak or acknowledge anyone, including her husband and children. Today she is being admitted for evaluation and treatment of her depression.

Current Findings: An untidy woman who stares at the floor and does not respond to staff members' questions. Sighs frequently. Sits immobile in chair for long periods.

Nursing Diagnosis

Impaired verbal communications related to emotional state.

Planning/Expected Outcomes

Amy will communicate her wishes and feelings with at least one staff member by April 22.

Nursing Interventions

Intervention

1. Present a calm, patient attitude rather than attempting to make Amy speak.
2. Actively listen, observe for verbal and nonverbal cues and behaviors during interactions.
3. Encourage alternative ways of communicating, such as drawing or writing.
4. Anticipate needs until Amy can communicate them.
5. Spend time (at least 15 minutes q.i.d.) with Amy.
6. Praise any attempt to communicate.

Rationale

1. Helps to decrease fears and anxieties and demonstrates respect and acceptance.
2. Helps to piece together communication methods in an effort to understand Amy's messages.
3. Demonstrates empathy, helps to develop trust, and encourages Amy to comunicate.
4. Provides safety, comfort, and support and develops trust.
5. Promotes trust and interest and helps self-esteem.
6. Encourages communication and demonstrates interest.

Evaluation

The second day after admission, Amy began to draw. By the fourth day of hospitalization, she answered "yes" or "no" questions. On April 17, Amy was able to discuss her feelings with one nurse.

q.i.d., Four times daily.

◆ **TABLE 11-5**
Speech Patterns Associated With Psychiatric Problems

Speech Pattern	Description	Example
Blocking	Loses train of thought, stops speaking because of unconscious block	"Then my father . . . what was I saying?"
Circumstantiality	Describes in too much detail, cannot be selective	When asked "How are you?" replies "My left hand aches a bit, my nose has been leaking, may hair won't stay in place. . . ."
Echolalia	Repeats last word heard	"Please wait here" is responded to with "Here, here, here. . . ."
Flight of ideas	Shifts rapidly between unrelated topics	"My cat is grey. The food here is good."
Loose associations	Speaks constantly, shifting between loosely related topics	"Martha married Jim who is a cook. I can cook. Cows are something that we can cook."
Mutism	Able to speak but remains silent	
Neologism	Coins new words and definitions	"Zargleves are good to eat" referring to any candy snack
Perseveration	Repeats single activity, cannot shift from one topic to another	Answers new question with previous question's answer
Pressured speech	Speech becomes fast, loud, rushed, and emphatic	Persons with mania often move and speak very rapidly with great urgency
Verbigeration	Repeats words, phrases, sentences several times over	*Nurse:* "It's time to take your pill." *Client:* "Take your pill, take your pill, take your pill. . . ."

sive or few? How much time lapses before the client responds to your message? Can the client read or write? Is a cultural communication assessment necessary? The answers to these questions provide the nurse with a solid database and offer valuable information that is used by the multidisciplinary treatment team to establish appropriate therapeutic goals. Table 11-5 describes some of the more common abnormal speech patterns demonstrated by clients with psychiatric problems.

The ability to effectively communicate is perhaps the most important therapeutic skill of nurses. Good communication skills are not learned like bed making. They must be practiced and evaluated frequently.

To evaluate the effectiveness of your communications, assess each interaction. Ask yourself, "Was the interaction appropriate to the goals of care? Was there enough communication and feedback to meet the goals? Was the interaction flexible enough to allow for a balance between spontaneity and control? Was the communication effective?" Practice, patience, and a continual willingness to evaluate your interactions are the keys to developing effective communication skills. Work hard to become a good communicator. Your clients' well-being depends on it, no matter what the diagnosis.

❖ **KEY CONCEPTS**

- Communication is the reciprocal exchange of information between two persons or among a group of persons.
- In the 1960s, Dr. Eric Berne coined the term *transactional analysis* to describe the process of investigating what people do and say to each other.
- Neurolinguistic programming focuses on learning the patterns of an individual's communications, which include eye accessing clues, different language patterns, and the pace and rhythm of speech.
- For a communication to occur, there must be a sender, a message, a receiver, feedback, and context.
- The process of communicating involves perception, evaluation, and transmission.
- Communications occur on verbal and nonverbal levels.
- Health care providers who work with clients from culturally different backgrounds must resist the tendency to stereotype people and learn the most important, culturally appropriate methods for communication.
- Therapeutic communication techniques are skills that assist the nurse in effectively interacting with clients.
- The goals of therapeutic communications are to focus on the client and foster the therapeutic relationship.
- The art of listening is a necessary ingredient for every health care provider.
- Responding strategies are the verbal and nonverbal re-

sponses that encourage clients to communicate in ways that help them to grow.

- Messages that hinder effective communications are referred to as nontherapeutic communications.
- Sensory-impaired clients have difficulty receiving or sending messages.
- Problems with communication are a common feature of many forms of mental illness.
- To communicate effectively with psychiatric clients, the nurse must learn that every interaction is a part of the total therapeutic process.

- Practice, patience, and a continual willingness to evaluate your interactions are the keys to developing effective communication skills.

❖ SUGGESTIONS FOR FURTHER READING

"What To Do When The Patient Does Not Speak English" by M.E. Lynch, in *The Journal of Practical Nursing* (6:38, 1993) is an excellent article, chockful of practical tips, for communicating with people from different cultural backgrounds.

❖ REFERENCES

Bennett MJ: *Checklist for intercultural communications,* Portland, Oreg, 1994, The Intercultural Communication Institute.

Berne E: *Transactional analysis in psychotherapy: a systematic individual and social psychiatry,* New York, 1961, Grove Press.

Berne E: *Games people play: the psychology of human relationships,* New York, 1964a, Grove Press.

Berne E: *Principles of group treatment,* New York, 1964b, Oxford University Press.

Dean M: Effective communication with patients, *Lancet* 342(8885):1477, 1993.

Giger JN, Davidizar RE: *Transcultural nursing: assessment and intervention,* ed 2, St Louis, 1995, Mosby.

Grossman D, Taylor R: Cultural diversity on the unit, *Am J Nurs* 95(2):64, 1995.

Haber J and others: *Comprehensive psychiatric nursing,* ed 5, St Louis, 1997, Mosby.

James M, Jongeward D: *Born to win: transactional analysis with gestalt experiments,* Reading, MA, 1977, Addison-Wesley.

Jourard S: *The transparent self,* New York, 1971, Van Nostrand.

Lynch ME: What to do when . . . the patient does not speak English, *J Pract Nurs* 6:38, 1993.

Paternostro JM: Improving your listening skills, *Nurs 93* 23(11):84, 1993.

Peden AR: Music: making the connection with persons who are homeless, *J Psychosoc Nurs Ment Health Serv* (31)7:17, 1993.

Pfeifer GM: A soul in pain, *Am J Nurs* 95(7):59, 1995.

Pore S: I can't understand what my patient is saying, *Adv Nurse Pract* 3(7):47, 1995.

Rawlins RP, Williams SR, Beck CK: *Mental health-psychiatric nursing: a holistic life-cycle approach,* ed 3, St Louis, 1993, Mosby.

Ruesch J: *Therapeutic communications,* New York, 1961, WW Norton.

Smith S: *Communications in nursing,* ed 2, St Louis, 1992, Mosby.

Stuart GW, Sundeen SJ: *Principles and practice of psychiatric nursing,* ed 5, St Louis, 1995, Mosby.

Sundeen SJ and others: *Nurse-client interactions: implementing the nursing process,* ed 5, St Louis, 1994, Mosby.

Taylor CM: *Essentials of psychiatric nursing,* ed 14, St Louis, 1994, Mosby.

12

THE MOST IMPORTANT SKILL: SELF-AWARENESS

1. List three characteristics of caring.

2. Describe how failure contributes to the development of insight.

3. Explain the concept of helping boundaries.

4. Identify three ways to prevent overinvolvement.

5. Discuss the importance of personal and professional commitments.

6. Describe three techniques for developing a positive mental attitude.

7. List six principles for nurturing yourself and other caregivers.

8. Identify four practices that help develop self-awareness.

KEY TERMS

acceptance
commitment
compassion
confidence
conscience

courage
failure
insight
introspection
nurture

risk taking
self-awareness
value

The profession of nursing is seen by the public as composed of knowledgeable, gentle, and giving people. Nurses are still described as "angels of mercy" because of the compassion and sensitivity they display. Notice that most descriptions of nurses focus on the behavioral qualities of the nurse, not the skills. The actions that connect us as people are what clients remember about their nurses. The nurse who sat with the grieving parent or comforted the anxious preoperative client is remembered long after the nurse who monitored the IV or administered a medication.

For people with mental-emotional problems, the interactions of a nurse may serve as a vehicle toward improved functioning and more satisfying relationships. Nurses serve as therapeutic instruments, with each interaction designed to move clients toward the goals of care. Nurses also serve as role models for good mental and physical health. They are expected to handle problems successfully and graciously cope with the varied personalities of many individuals. Nurses work to instill confidence in their clients and encourage them to change, trying new behaviors within the security of the therapeutic relationship.

To practice nursing effectively, a nurse's approach to clients must continually be monitored and adjusted. Thought and consideration must be given to each nursing action. Nurses routinely evaluate how well they perform a skill. For example, while administering a medication, a nurse will review if each of the "five rights" is being followed. The process of reviewing a skill is straightforward. One compares the nursing action to an established procedure. However, the evaluation given to therapeutic interactions, especially those with mentally and emotionally troubled persons, require much more energy. Making a positive, therapeutic use of your personality requires "a consistent, thoughtful effort directed toward developing an awareness of self and others" (Taylor, 1994).

Definition of Self-Awareness

Simply defined, **self-awareness** is a consciousness of one's own individuality and personality. It is the act of looking at oneself: considering one's abilities, characteristics, aspirations, and concepts of self in relation to others. It is an alertness to one's personal and social behaviors and their impact on others (Morrison, 1993). In short, self-awareness is the ability to objectively look at oneself.

The development of self-awareness does not occur overnight. It requires time, patience, and a willingness to routinely consider behaviors, attitudes, and values. The rewards, however, are worth the efforts because both clients and nurses benefit when therapeutic goals are achieved. Personally, self-awareness allows individuals to direct and mold the pattern of their lives, to be in charge of their own growth and development. Nurses encourage the development of self-awareness in their clients. Now they must be ready to practice it themselves.

To improve self-awareness requires insight, caring, a consideration of values, acceptance, a positive outlook, and the willingness to nurture yourself. If you are willing to put effort into these areas, then you will evolve into a person who is able to use your personality to achieve therapeutic change and personal fulfillment.

Caring

The profession of nursing is established around the concept of caring for one's fellow human beings (Kelly, 1995). Without it, nursing would be relegated to an automated service of technical skills. *Caring* is the energy on which nursing is built. It is defined as a concern for the well-being of another person and includes such behaviors as accepting, comforting, honesty, attentive listening, and sensitivity. "Caring is encouraging growth of the other . . . having mutual connectedness. Our purpose as caregivers is to improve the human condition, to produce positive changes, to encourage growth, to enable others to live life to its fullest, to alleviate suffering" (Sherwood, 1992).

Caring is a fundamental human imperative; it must be done if we are to grow as a civilization. People's ability to care for others has preserved cultures, saved lives, and produced nations. When a society loses the ability to care, its citizens decline into violent and self-serving activities. Caring is the glue that binds each individual to the other. It is the energy of the soul, freely given in hopes of helping another human being; and it is the component of self-awareness that drives all the others. Caring cannot be taught as a procedure or skill. It must be developed and encouraged, and it must be molded into the therapeutic behaviors that make up the personality of the nurse.

Characteristics

Theorists have tried to explain the concept of caring, but its elusive nature defies description. In 1987, the theorist M. Roach identified attributes of caring and labeled them the five Cs. They are commitment, compassion, competence, confidence, and conscience. The attributes of commitment and competence are discussed later in the chapter. Here we focus on the qualities of compassion, confidence, and conscience.

The quality of **compassion** relates to feeling the sorrows, sufferings, or troubles of another. It includes *empathy,* the willingness to try to understand how another person is feeling. Tolerance for the many differences of individuals is also a component of compassion. Compassion enables us to share in the emotional state of another person. When used therapeutically, it helps nurses to understand and guide clients toward more effective and satisfying lives. Become aware of your feelings of compassion. They are powerful motivators for nurses.

Confidence is "the quality which fosters trusting relationships" (Roach, 1987). It is a belief in the nurse's ability to assist clients cope with the difficulties and implications of their health problems. Confidence is also trust and belief in your own abilities. Self-awareness grows as long as one has the confidence to investigate his/her own thoughts and actions.

The word **conscience** describes a knowledge or feeling of what is right and wrong. It is often accompanied by a strong desire to do the right thing. People with well-developed consciences act based on firm values and beliefs. They are aware of their definitions of right and wrong. They do not hesitate to follow their moral principles and attempt to correct what they recognize as wrong.

To the five attributes of caring, one more can be added: the quality of courage. **Courage** is the response that allows us to face and cope with the dangerous, difficult, or painful aspects of life. Courage is the quiet companion of caring that enables nurses to take the first step in establishing a connection with each client. It is also a part of the energy-engine that supplies us with the motivation to learn and grow each day.

The Caring Connection

An old Persian poem sums up the connection among people:

> Human beings are like parts of a body, created from the same essence,
> when one part is hurt and in pain, the others cannot remain in peace and quiet;
> if the misery of others leaves you indifferent and with no feelings of sorrow,
> you cannot be called a human being.

Caring is an international attribute. It occurs on a daily basis in every social group in the world. Agnes Aamodt, a contributing author of the book, *A Global Agenda for Caring,* describes a Maori term that literally means "the sneeze of life." It is often used to begin speeches and it means "I salute the breath of life in you." For the people of the Maori culture, this saying acknowledges the interconnectedness of all things and celebrates the relationship of life to nature. Many societies believe that all things in life are related and connected to each other.

The interconnectedness of people is demonstrated through the act of caring, which can be as personal as an embrace or as removed as stopping your car for someone to cross the street on a busy day. For nurses, caring serves as the vehicle for interacting with people and peers, for making the connection with clients that communicates respect and dignity. The box below lists several nursing actions that demonstrate caring. When the nurse and client experience connectedness, "the intensity of the work accomplished seems to be enhanced, benefiting both" (Heifner, 1993). Caring acts as the connection that binds each human being to the other. The quality of caring, when combined with insight, acceptance, and a positive outlook on life, helps nurses to develop the self-awareness that leads to becoming an effective therapeutic personality.

Insight

Nurses are responsible for their own growth and development, both professionally and personally. They, like most people, gain insight and wisdom through experience. **Insight** is the ability to clearly see and understand the nature of things. For nurses, it includes a sensitivity to people, the ability to make keen observations, and the willingness to seek out new knowledge.

Insight also relies on the skills of common sense, good judgment, and prudence. Self-awareness is expanded when one strives to learn and to become knowledgeable and competent. Although not always comfortable, our insights provide us with new op-

---

NURSING ACTIONS: CARING

- Address client by *Mr.* or *Ms.* (last name) until otherwise instructed.
- Respect the client's unique personality.
- Do not judge the client's behaviors or attitudes.
- Share often with the client that every person has the potential for change.
- Show interest in the whole person, not just the diagnosis.
- Customize information to the client's level of understanding.
- Watch for nonverbal messages.
- Promote self-esteem by recognizing and communicating that the client is a worthwhile and valuable individual.
- Assess your own interactions, nonverbal actions, and communications.

portunities to take risks, to explore our own potentials, and to fail as well as succeed.

Insight also refers to two types of knowledge: the wisdom to know oneself and the clear-sightedness to learn about others. For nurses, insight is especially important because it serves as a valuable tool for developing self-awareness and thus therapeutic effectiveness.

Know Thyself

The first duty of a health care provider is to know thyself. The very success of one's professional practice depends on it. If nurses or other health care providers are unable to assess their learning needs or communications skills, they will remain stagnant and refuse to grow or evolve. The same holds true for all persons.

Self-awareness is developed through the practice of **introspection,** which is the process of looking into one's own mind. Simply, introspection is an analysis of self, including one's feelings, reactions, attitudes, opinions, values, and behaviors. It is also a process for observing and analyzing one's behavior in various situations. Introspection allows us to "step out" of the interaction and watch our own behaviors. This process is assisted when nurses can view themselves interacting with various clients on videotape or television.

Introspection allows nurses to identify both personal and professional learning needs. The process of seeking new knowledge is a fundamental requirement of the profession of nursing. Practicing nurses are responsible for remaining knowledgeable. Only the comfort and confidence of a strong knowledge base can ease the anxiety of the "What shall I do now?" syndrome.

Practice professional introspection by keeping a small notebook with you. Throughout the day, jot down any questions or subjects that relate to the diagnoses or nursing care of your clients—anything about which you feel you need to know more. After work, make it a point to research at least one question or topic everyday. This practice will serve as a valuable aid for routinely gaining new knowledge. Professional knowledge breeds competence, and from competence grows the confidence to provide the best possible nursing care.

Personal introspection is the process of learning who you are: your likes, dislikes, habits, and behavior patterns. This type of introspection is not always painless because it may be accompanied by the emotional discomfort of an unexpected discovery about yourself. If you know, for example, that you do not especially like a certain behavior or habit but have been too preoccupied to deal with it, the process of intro-

spection can bring it to the surface (accompanied by its emotional storehouse) and compel you to at least consider coping with it. However, for those individuals who can overcome their own emotional defenses, introspection serves as a valuable tool for developing self-awareness.

Risk Taking and Failure

Developing self-awareness is also based on enlarging one's experiences. Purposefully engaging in unfamiliar activities and observing your responses allow you to expand your knowledge, examine your reactions, and reconsider your beliefs (Wolfe, 1994).

The process of developing self-awareness includes the elements of risk and failure. If one is to grow, then one must take risks. Without a willingness to take chances and possibly fail, a person remains tied to the same pattern of life. Taking risks exposes oneself to the possibility of failure, loss, or even injury. One engages in risk-taking behaviors when the rewards of success are at least as large as the consequences of failure.

More than ever before, today's nurses will be called on, to take risks and function much more independently than their predecessors. The profession of nursing needs its members to take the risks necessary to provide adequate health care services for every person. Several hints for taking risks are presented in the box below.

Risk taking implies the possibility of **failure.** For most of us, the word *failure* has a negative meaning. It implies defeat, a "you lose" attitude, and a lack of success. However, failure can be filled with positive, growth-promoting experiences. Failure provides the opportunity for change. It encourages creativity, stimulates learning, and sharpens one's judgments. Fail-

DEVELOPING RISK-TAKING SKILLS

- Plan the risk-taking activity only after thorough assessment of the situation and consideration of all possible outcomes.
- Eliminate fear and other roadblocks to risk taking.
- Give yourself permission to fail, to make mistakes, and to learn from them.
- Reward yourself for trying something new regardless of the outcome.
- Review your history of both personal and professional successes. This process helps to build the self-confidence essential for taking risks.
- Find a mentor who is a successful risk taker and learns from previous mistakes.
- Support other nurses who are engaging in risk-taking behaviors.

ure is a price that must be paid for improvement. When used as a learning tool, the experiences of failure can provide the foundations for the next step toward success. The nurse who never makes a mistake or never fails cannot savor the rewards of success.

How do we grow from our failures? The first and most important step is to "realize that failure is a necessary part of change" (Vestal, 1991). Biologist Lewis Thomas (1979) maintains "that humankind is set apart from the rest of creation by our unique ability to make mistakes. If we were not provided with the knack of being wrong, we could never get anything useful done." Failure is a part of the growth experience and thus self-awareness.

The second step is to be sure to give yourself permission to fail. The guilt associated with failure can generate feelings of inadequacy that can paralyze you into denying yourself valuable opportunities for learning. The odds of a person living a lifetime without a failure are about zero. Failure, learning, and growth are all partners in the development of self-awareness.

The third step is to consider your failure a learning experience. Examine the elements of the failure: the "what, how, when, who, where, and why" aspects. Discover what could have been done differently and what improvements could be made. This examination is an important part of one's self-education because more effective actions avoid the failures of the past.

The fourth and last step in using failure as a tool for developing self-awareness is to discover the opportunities that are created by failure. Many times a failure opens new doors or presents a problem in an entirely different light. To illustrate, the gold miners in the hills of Virginia City, Nevada, used to throw "that blue stuff" into piles outside their poorly producing gold mines. It was only after a young miner began to think about the blue material in a different way (and had it chemically analyzed) that the miners realized that "the cursed blue stuff" was actually high-grade silver ore, worth millions of dollars. Examining and learning from failure can create new options and opportunities. The box below lists several suggestions

for using failure as a positive experience. Remember, one really fails only when one refuses to grow from the experience.

Values and Beliefs

To briefly review, a **value** is something that is held dear or a belief about the worth of an item, idea, or behavior (Stuart and Sundeen, 1995). Individuals who choose nursing and related health care professions usually arrive with a strong set of personal values and beliefs, many of which are shared with other members of the profession. To illustrate, nurses place a high value on quality of life. They value human dignity and the right of clients to make their own decisions.

People's belief systems strongly affect their behaviors. People govern their day-to-day existences based on their beliefs. For many people, belief systems provide the comfort of stability and knowing what to expect. However, a static, unquestioning attitude is not enough for those health care professionals who truly want to be effective. We, as nurses, must routinely assess our value and belief systems if we are to improve our therapeutic effectiveness.

Because one's values and beliefs can influence behavior and color judgments, nurses must strive to develop a level of self-awareness that encourages an exploration of their values. Exploring one's values is not always easy because, by their very nature, values are cherished and difficult to change. Using the values clarification process of choosing, prizing, and acting (see Chapter 3) allows nurses to evaluate their own values and beliefs.

Guidelines for Nursing Actions

Every nurse and health care provider has a right to his/her own values and beliefs. The only time adhering to these values and beliefs is inappropriate is when they impede the therapeutic progress of the client. The value the nurse places on the client's behaviors has an influence on the relationship. If the nurse values the client as an individual and expresses faith in his/her abilities to change, then the client will strive for even greater achievements. Do not limit clients with the force of your values. Set expectations high and provide frequent encouragement. Clients have the right to achieve and to fail, just as we do. Limiting your clients' abilities by placing expectations on them based on your values and beliefs deprives them of opportunities for growth and achievement. Remember, nurses have the power to shape their clients' successes or failures based on their own personal values and beliefs.

THINK ABOUT

To use failure positively:
1. Realize that failure is a necessary part of growth.
2. Give yourself permission to fail.
3. Consider failure as a learning experience.
4. Discover new options and opportunities created by the failure.
5. Expect to succeed with the next attempt.

Guidelines for many nursing values can be found in the philosophical beliefs statement of psychiatric nursing practice (see box below). These beliefs can serve as a guide for discovering your own values. Examine your own value and belief systems. Their exploration is an essential step toward achieving the self-awareness that makes nurses the therapeutic instruments of healing.

Acceptance

Several philosophical beliefs of psychiatric nurses relate to acceptance of the person we call "the client." Although people may engage in behaviors that are considered inappropriate, each individual has worth and some degree of dignity. Each client must be given respect and the opportunity to participate in care if treatment is to be successful. To accomplish this, nurses practice **acceptance,** the receiving or taking of what is being offered or given. In the case of nursing, what is being offered is the client, his/her person, who is commonly in a state of distress. Acceptance in this context means the receiving of the entire person and the world in which he/she functions.

The value and belief systems of certain social groups differ strongly from other groups. Health practices and attitudes toward health care vary greatly. These differences and more must be accepted and respected if there is to be any therapeutic effectiveness. Clients *do* receive the nonverbal messages of acceptance or rejection transmitted by their care providers.

Accepting clients does not include approving of their behaviors. This is an important distinction; you must accept the person but not the behavior. Many nurses who work with mentally and emotionally troubled clients will not hesitate to tell a client when his/her behavior is inappropriate, but no mental health nurse should ever directly attack or correct the person. Table 12-1 presents examples of communications that focus on the difference between correcting the behavior and correcting the person. The very reason clients with mental-emotional problems have sought help is to correct their ineffective or unfulfill-

---

PHILOSOPHICAL BELIEFS OF PSYCHIATRIC NURSING PRACTICE

- The individual has intrinsic worth and dignity. Each person is worthy of respect solely because of each person's nature and presence.
- The goal of the individual is one of growth, health, autonomy, and self-actualization.
- Every individual has the potential to change and the desire to pursue personal goals.
- The person functions as a holistic being who acts on, interacts with, and reacts to the environment as a whole person. Each part affects the total response, which is greater than the sum of each separate component.
- All people have common, basic, and necessary human needs. These include physical needs, safety needs, love and belonging needs, esteem needs, and self-actualization needs.
- All behavior of the individual is meaningful. It arises from personal needs and goals and can be understood only from the person's internal frame of reference and within the context in which it occurs.
- Behavior consists of perceptions, thoughts, feelings, and actions. From one's perceptions thoughts arise, emotions are felt, and actions are conceived. Disruptions may occur in any of these areas.

- Individuals vary in their coping capacities, which depend on genetic endowment, environmental influences, nature and degree of stress, and available resources. All individuals have the potential for both health and illness.
- Illness can be a growth-producing experience for the individual. The goal of nursing care is to maximize positive interactions with the individual's environment, promote wellness, and enhance self-actualization.
- All people have a right to an equal opportunity for adequate health care regardless of gender, race, religion, ethics, sexual orientation, or cultural background. Nursing care is based on the needs of individuals, families, and communities and mutually defined goals and expectations.
- Mental health is a critical and necessary component of comprehensive health care services.
- The individual has the right to participate in decision making regarding physical and mental health. The person has the right to self-determination. It is the decision of the individual to pursue health or illness.
- An interpersonal relationship has the potential for producing change and growth within the individual. It is the vehicle for the application of the nursing process and the attainment of the goal of nursing care.

From Stuart GW, Sundeen SJ: *Principles and practice of psychiatric nursing,* ed 5, St Louis, 1995, Mosby.

◆ TABLE 12-1 **Focus on Correcting Behavior vs. Person**	
Focus on Behavior	**Focus on Person**
"Sam, undressing in the dayroom is inappropriate."	"Sam, I''ve told you not to undress in the dayroom."
"Mary, stop! No slapping is allowed here."	"Mary, stop that! Why are you slapping him?"
"I find it difficult to be here when you . . . ."	"You're disgusting when you do that."

ing behaviors. We, as their care providers, work with them to replace these behaviors with more successful and satisfying ways of functioning; but to do this, we must accept the entire person as a complete package, regardless of our own reactions. This acceptance then becomes the foundation on which other therapeutic actions are based.

Helping Boundaries

Nurses are expected to give of themselves in the care of others. Our history is full of examples of nurses who have sacrificed and even died for their clients. Today, however, we are realizing that nurses must care for themselves, recharge their batteries, if they are to maintain the necessary energy to therapeutically work with clients. One of the ways in which nurses maintain their energy levels is to define their helping boundaries (Heinrich, 1992).

We all have limits or boundaries over which we will not cross. Personal boundaries provide us with order and security as they help to establish the limits of one's behavior. To illustrate, you would not consider visiting friends and then stealing their household goods. Theft is an example of a personal boundary. You would not think of stealing from your friends because a personal boundary limits you from doing so.

Professional boundaries "define the needs of the nurse as distinctly different from the needs of the patient: what is too helpful and what is not; and what fosters independence vs. unhealthy dependence" (Pillette, Berck, and Achber, 1995). Once clients are stabilized, they are expected and encouraged to begin functioning independently with guidance and encouragement from the members of the health care team. When nurses become overhelpful or controlling, professional (helping) boundaries have been crossed. We all want our clients to succeed and to adapt and function happily, but sometimes that drive motivates us to exclude or ignore our clients' needs. In the end, the nurse may feel good but do the clients function any better as a result of his/her interventions?

The need for professional (helping) boundaries must be continually balanced with one's needs to be caring. To do this, nurses establish their own set of professional (helping) boundaries. Are you willing to see your clients socially? Do you allow clients access to your home phone number or address? Are you willing to spend your own time and money on clients? Most nurses are not. They have established the limits of both their personal and professional lives, and usually the two remain quite separate. The focus of the professional aspect of the nurse's life is the client, but the focus of the nurse's personal life is himself/herself. The boundaries of each remain distinct because one cannot focus on the client and the self at the same time.

To maintain their professional boundaries, nurses assess relationships with their clients often. If they find themselves having difficulty in setting limits or feel that they are the only one who "really understands" a certain client, then cause for concern exists and help should be sought from a supervisor or other members of the health care team. Discussing the situation with appropriate persons helps to provide perspective and increases the nurse's therapeutic effectiveness. The nurse-client relationship is anchored in the effective management of professional (helping) boundaries. When the focus of interaction is the client and progress is being made toward the therapeutic goals, the relationship is effective and satisfying for both client and nurse.

Detecting boundary violations is often difficult because "a person's own needs stimulate and maintain the violation" (Pillette, Berck, and Achber, 1995). However, early detection helps to prevent larger problems in the future. Frequent self-assessments assist in monitoring for problems.

A delicate balance exists between knowing when to help and when not to help clients. Nurses who are aware of this balance are less likely to be manipulated or coerced by clients. By keeping the client the major concern of focus, nurses are able to maintain the professional boundaries that help individuals progress toward achieving their therapeutic goals.

Overinvolvement

We have all had (or will have) special clients, those who have touched us so deeply that we have become too emotionally involved. Becoming overinvolved is not difficult to do because caring provides clients with the energy and support to work for change. However, to thrive and grow ourselves, nurses must learn to walk the fine line between compassion and overinvolvement.

Years ago, nurses were taught to always maintain a "professional distance" from clients. The rules clearly defined the nurse's role as that of caregiver and assistant to the physician. Today, however, we recognize the power of the therapeutic relationship and its effect on clients. We realize that nurses are people too, complete with their own set of attributes and problems.

Because nurses are individuals, it is easier to form a rapport with some clients than others. Sometimes that rapport leads to an overinvolvement because the client touches the nurse in some special way. Perhaps the client reminds the nurse of a family member. Possibly the client displays a trait or characteristic that attracts the nurse. It may be that the client and the nurse share the same concerns or problems. This initial attraction can soon result in conflict because the nurse begins to find it difficult to separate the professional relationship from the newly formed friendship with the client. Soon the relationship loses its therapeutic effectiveness, and the nurse or client withdraws, left with a mixture of unresolved feelings and unmet goals (Yates and McDaniel, 1994).

To protect yourself from becoming overinvolved with certain clients, remember this one rule of thumb: if you show a significantly greater level of concern for one client than for others, then you are running the risk of becoming overinvolved. If you recognize this risk early and discuss it with your supervisor, you will prevent overinvolvement. Exploring your feelings in relation to the client helps to regain the balance between professionalism and compassion. Often just the personal awareness of the potential of becoming overinvolved is enough to prevent it from occurring. Compassion, empathy, and acceptance are vital elements of nursing, but they must be balanced by professionalism, judgment, and therapeutic interactions that meet the needs of clients.

Many of the traits that make a good nurse—commitment, self-sacrifice, responsibility—can be self-defeating if they are taken to extremes. Nurses certainly must commit themselves to providing high-quality nursing care in a responsible manner but not to the exclusion of everything else in life. To be an effective nurse, one must be willing to accept and nurture a most important person, the self. We are better able to care for others when we accept and care for ourselves.

Commitment

A **commitment** is a personal bond to some course of action. The health care professions, including nursing, are undergoing radical changes. Many of these changes are influenced by sources outside the helping professions. If provision of high-quality care for every person is to remain a primary goal of our society, then a strong commitment from each health care provider will be needed to maintain the focus on our clients. We cannot sit idly by and allow others to decide the fates of those who need our care.

Nurses must be committed to providing competent health care, no matter what the setting or circumstances. If we settle for less, the well-being of our clients may be jeopardized. For the sake of discussion, the concept of commitment is divided into two areas: personal commitments and commitments to others.

Personal Commitments

The first and most important commitment is to yourself, the commitment to consciously take charge of your own personal and professional growth. A refusal to grow within the self cannot encourage growth or self-awareness in others. Self-commitment involves a promise to do the best you can in every situation and to be the best that you can be.

Each person has a unique set of talents, an individual personality, and areas of their lives that need improvement. People who are committed to improving themselves are able to consider both the positive and negative characteristics of their personalities without guilt or remorse. They realize their mistakes and attempt to profit from them by extracting the lessons hidden in each error. They then commit themselves to applying those hard-earned lessons to new situations, thus enhancing self-awareness and expanding their ability to cope with new experiences.

Commit to your personal growth. Consider who you are. What attitudes or behaviors would you like to change? Accept who you are and love who you are, but commit to strive for greater learning.

Commitments to Others

Nurses have strong commitments to other people. As with most people, nurses are committed to the members of their family units, social circles, and communities. However, nurses have a commitment larger than that of the community—the commitment to caring about the welfare of humankind.

Nurses demonstrate dedication to their clients by continually seeking out new knowledge, keeping up-to-date with the latest professional developments, and striving to improve their therapeutic effectiveness. They realize that nursing is an art as well as a science, and they put much effort into becoming skilled practitioners, both physically and psychosocially (Trygstad, 1994).

The importance of one's commitment to others cannot be overestimated; without the promise to improve the welfare of others, nursing would not be the profession it is today. Those individuals who choose nursing as their career must commit to several long years of study and many more years of hard but rewarding work. They are committed, promising to spending their energies on improving the lives of others.

You are committed, otherwise you would not be reading these words. Take the time to discover what you feel is most important in life. Then look behind the topic and you will find yourself committed to a certain course of action. The exercise of describing one's commitments helps to expand self-awareness and remind us of the interconnectedness of all human beings.

Positive Outlook

One of the most effective and important tools for developing self-awareness is a positive or optimistic attitude. One's outlook on life affects every perception, every thought, and every emotion. A person with a positive outlook radiates energy and well-being and cheers up everyone in the vicinity. People are attracted to individuals with positive attitudes. They hope that a bit of that radiant energy will be somehow passed on to them.

On the other hand, persons with negative attitudes tend to discourage other people from interacting with them. They tend to see only the negative or down side of life. Their attitude of doom and gloom actually fosters the development of many physical and mental problems.

Researchers have already found that "negative thoughts about self and future have been found to predict future depression" (Lightsey, 1994). Currently science is attempting to discover the role of positive thinking on health. This new knowledge is significant, especially for nurses and other providers of health care.

Positive attitudes and thoughts can act as buffers against stress and conflict. They can prevent nursing "burnout," the syndrome that results when nurses give too much of themselves without renewing their energies. In addition, the nurse who practices positive thinking can act as a role model for those clients who have not learned to cope effectively within their worlds.

A positive outlook does not require the nurse to be continually upbeat and to exclude everything un-

pleasant or objectionable. The reality of each situation must be considered objectively, but there is no reason to harbor a negative attitude when a positive one is much more fulfilling.

Achieving and maintaining a positive outlook is especially important for nurses who work with the mentally and emotionally troubled persons of society. Much unhappiness and misfortune plagues these people, and remaining upbeat in the face of continuing adversity can be a challenge for any nurse. A positive attitude is the secret weapon for coping with the adversity of life. It is the key to maintaining physical and emotional health, especially for those who share their energies therapeutically. To develop a positive outlook on life, one needs only to become aware: to become aware of existing attitudes, to become aware of the need to add positive thinking to one's point of view, and to become aware of the level of therapeutic effectiveness that results from a positive outlook.

Daily Awareness

A positive attitude can be developed by replacing unwanted, negative feelings that stand in the way of self-awareness and growth (Heinrich and Killeen, 1993). Note that developing a positive attitude is a process that requires persistent and patient efforts because our current attitudes and habits are deeply ingrained. However, the process can be assisted by following these five tips:

First, listen to your self-talk. Pay attention to the words you use. Each word has an emotional connotation or attachment to it. The word *never,* for example, implies that at no time will something occur. Using it in relation to a client can have an impact on the outcome and well-being of that person. Statements such as "it will never work" or "that's impossible" are only self-defeating.

The human brain is programmed by thought patterns. Thoughts can become feelings, which, in turn, evolve into words and actions. Many people complain of being under too much stress or pressure. No one denies that modern life contains its share of stressors. However, it is how each stressor is perceived or defined that determines your point of view. If you do not define the event as stressful, then it is not. Practice listening to yourself. You may be surprised at what you discover.

Second, change recurrent negative themes. Any thought, emotion, word, or action that is self-defeating needs to be replaced with a positive, empowering one (see box on p. 169, top left). Releasing and replacing one's negative attitudes lead to greater self-esteem, awareness, confidence, and happiness, not to mention the added benefits of a highly effective im-

DEVELOPING A POSITIVE ATTITUDE
1. Recognize the negative thoughts, emotions, and attitudes and turn them away. Reject them and throw them out of your personality.
2. Replace each negative attitude by frequently repeating positive statements.
3. Repeat upbeat and enthusiastic words that help to build a feeling of success.

PRINCIPLES FOR NURTURING CAREGIVERS
1. Be knowledgeable.
2. Value each individual as a human presence.
3. Be responsible and accountable for your actions.
4. Be open to new ideas.
5. Connect with others. Support your colleagues.
6. Take pride in yourself.
7. Like what you do.
8. Recognize the moments of joy in the struggles of living. Stop to smell the roses.
9. Recognize and accept your own limitations but strive to improve.
10. Rest each day and begin anew.

From Sherwood G: The responses of caregivers to the experience of suffering. In Starck PL, McGovern JP, editors: *The hidden dimension of illness: human suffering,* New York, 1992, National League for Nursing Press.

mune system. Practice changing your negative themes because one's outlook determines the success or failure of an action.

Third, be your own cheerleader. Give yourself a pep talk every morning and whenever you are coping with the stresses of the day. Present yourself with positive, inspiring thoughts. Your brain does not question your thoughts. It only stores information for future use. Those stored thoughts, positive or negative, then become the basis for actions. Positive statements uplift the spirits and help to convince you of your value.

Fourth, visualize future successes. Take a few moments during each day to picture yourself achieving a goal. Fantasize about the feelings associated with achieving the goal, and think about the steps that lead to the goal. Picture yourself as a dynamic person and capable nurse. It will help to provide the blueprint for future growth; besides it is fun to do.

Fifth, act the part. Visualize yourself as a person with confidence and ability. You will find that your actual level of confidence grows each time you project an image of self-assurance.

Developing a positive outlook will serve you well. Positive mental attitudes help to develop self-esteem. Self-esteem in turn helps to build self-awareness, self-respect, and emotional acceptance of yourself.

Nurturing Yourself

A critical first step in the development of self-awareness is to recognize and tend to your own needs. People rely on the energies of nurses for comfort, guidance, and instruction. Nurses expend much personal time and energies outside the work environment to maintain and improve their levels of competence, and they are expected to work hard for the welfare of their clients. Nurses are capable of all this—but not without first caring and nourishing themselves because energy cannot be continually spent without being renewed.

Clients rely on their nurses for the energy to heal and change ineffective behaviors. Therefore nurses must function at a high level of wellness to provide the energy required by their clients. You have chosen to care for others. Part of the responsibility you accepted when making this decision was to care for yourself. If you are unable to **nurture** yourself, then you will never be able to nurture your clients.

Principles for Caregivers

In the practice of the nursing, "we seek to instill hope, empower others, encourage independence, and help improve the other's condition. When we are unable to achieve that, unable to alleviate suffering, we often experience a sense of frustration and failure" (Sherwood, 1992). When this frustration occurs over and over, we become emotionally worn out or "burned out" as many nurses call it. Somehow each nurse must find the balance between the moral duty to care amidst the stress of constant suffering and the concern for one's own well-being.

Gwen Sherwood (1992) offers us 10 basic principles essential for maintaining self in caring for others. Using these principles as guidelines will assist you in finding the balance between giving and renewing (see box above, at right). Remember these principles because they are guidelines for replenishing the energies that you so freely share with others.

Practices for Caregivers

To nurture yourself requires more than the ingestion of food and water or the needs for sleep and activity. To nourish the part of the self from which one's therapeutic energies are drawn requires special renewal. Nurses nurture themselves in different ways.

Some turn to a special source of comfort, whereas others find renewal in the adventure of trying new things. Spending time alone, removed from the stimuli of the day, recharges some nurses. Others need the challenge of physical activities, travel, or new relationships.

Recently, research has pointed out the many benefits of daily meditation for stress reduction, relaxation, and renewal (Fig. 12-1) (Kabot-Zinn, 1994). Basically, meditation, termed the *relaxation response* by Western medicine, is the practice of becoming still and quiet. First, one assumes a comfortable body position within a quiet environment. Then one concentrates on just breathing. As the mind begins to wander elsewhere, it is gently escorted back to the breath. This focus allows one's energies to become calm and concentrated instead of wandering through scattered bits of self-talk. Soon an inner stillness and peace are experienced, stress is relieved, and energies are renewed. Health care professionals who practice meditation for as little as 15 minutes a day find it a valuable source for self-renewal and stress reduction.

Fig. 12-1 Meditation can assume many forms. (From Taylor CM: *Essentials of psychiatric nursing,* ed 14, St Louis, 1994, Mosby.)

In this busy world it is easy to lose sight of one simple fact: your ability to care for your clients depends on how well you care for yourself. How you choose to nurture and renew yourself is a matter of personal preference. The important thing is that you do it regularly and without guilt. A good diet, adequate exercise, and restful sleep must not be ignored, but the essence of nursing, which is caring, must also be applied to the self.

The development of self-awareness is a necessary requirement for effective nursing. Work with varieties of people provides continual challenges. Nurses must consider their own abilities, values, and behaviors. They should be willing to assess the need for change, seek out new learning, and focus their own growth. In addition, nurses need to be willing to accept, love, and nourish themselves as much as they do their clients.

❖ KEY CONCEPTS

- Self-awareness is a consciousness of one's own individuality and personality.
- Caring is a concern for the well-being of another person; it includes behaviors such as accepting, comforting, honesty, attentive listening, and sensitivity.
- The characteristics of caring are commitment, compassion, competence, confidence, conscience, and courage.
- Nurses are responsible for their own growth and development, both professionally and personally.
- Insight is the ability to clearly see and understand the nature of things.
- Introspection is an analysis of self, including one's feelings, reactions, attitudes, opinions, values, and behaviors.
- To successfully cope with failure, one must realize that failures are a necessary part of change.
- Nurses have the power to shape their clients' successes or failures, based on their own personal values and beliefs.
- The exploration of one's own values and beliefs is an essential step toward achieving the self-awareness that makes nurses the therapeutic instruments of healing.
- Professional boundaries define what is too helpful and what is not.
- A commitment is an intellectual or an emotional bond that impels the individual to some sort of action.
- One of the most effective and important tools for developing self-awareness is a positive or optimistic attitude.
- A critical first step in the development of self-awareness is to recognize and tend to your own needs.
- Meditation, termed the relaxation response by Western medicine, is the practice of becoming still and quiet.
- Your ability to care for your clients depends on how well you care for yourself.

❖ SUGGESTIONS FOR FURTHER READING

"The Gentle Art of Nurturing Yourself," written by Kathleen Heinrich and Mary Ellen Killeen, in *The American Journal of Nursing* (93[10]:41, 1993), presents a fable that is written especially for nurses. The insights presented in this article will help nurses to give back to themselves the thoughtfulness and concern that is shown to others every day.

❖ REFERENCES

Aamodt AM: Experiencing the mystery in cross-cultural research on care. In Starck PL, McGovern JP, editors: *The hidden dimension of illness: human suffering,* New York, 1992, National League for Nursing Press.

Heifner C: Positive connectedness in the psychiatric nurse-patient relationship, *Arch Psychiatr Nurs* 7(1):11, 1993.

Heinrich KT: What to do when a patient becomes too special, *Nurs 92* 22(11):63, 1992.

Heinrich K, Killeen ME: The gentle art of nurturing yourself, *Am J Nurs* 93(10):41, 1993.

Kabot-Zinn J: Meditate! . . . for stress reduction, inner peace . . . or whatever, *Psychol Today* 26(4):36, 1994.

Kelly D: Three tips for closer caring, *Nurs 95* 25(5):72, 1995.

Lightsey OR: "Thinking positive" as a stress buffer: the role of positive automatic cognitions in depression and happiness, *J Counsel Psychol* 41:325, 1994.

Morrison M: *Professional skills for leadership: foundations of a successful career,* St Louis, 1993, Mosby.

Pillette PC, Berck CB, Achber LC: Therapeutic management of helping boundaries, *J Psychosoc Nurs Ment Health Serv* 33:40, 1995.

Roach M: *The human act of caring,* Ottawa, 1987, Canadian Hospital Association.

Sherwood G: The responses of caregivers to the experience of suffering. In Starck PL, McGovern JP, editors: *The hidden dimension of illness: human suffering,* New York, 1992, National League for Nursing Press.

Stuart GW, Sundeen SJ: *Principles and practice of psychiatric nursing,* ed 5, St Louis, 1995, Mosby.

Taylor CM: *Essentials of psychiatric nursing,* ed 14, St Louis, 1994, Mosby.

Thomas L: *The medusa and the snail: more notes of a biology watcher,* New York, 1979, Viking Press.

Trygstad LN: The need to know: biological learning needs identified by practicing psychiatric nurses, *J Psychosoc Nurs Ment Health Serv* 32(2):13, 1994.

Vestal K: Making failure a positive experience, *Nurs 91* 21(9):111, 1991.

Wolfe PL: Risk taking: nursing's comfort zone, *Holistic Nurs Pract* 8(2):43, 1994.

Yates G, McDaniel JL: Are you losing yourself in codependency? *Am J Nurs* 94(4):32, 1994.

13

MENTAL HEALTH ASSESSMENT SKILLS

LEARNING OBJECTIVES

1. Identify two purposes of the mental health treatment plan.
2. List and define each step of the nursing process.
3. Describe three methods of data collection.
4. Explain the importance of performing physical assessments on clients with psychiatric diagnoses.
5. List five parts of a holistic nursing assessment.
6. Identify four guidelines for conducting effective psychiatric interviews.
7. Explain the purpose of the mental status examination.
8. List the five general categories of the mental status examination.
9. Describe the process for conducting a mental status examination.

KEY TERMS

affect
assessment
calculation
data collection
insight
intelligence

interview
judgment
memory
mood
nursing process
perceptions

risk factor assessment
sensorium
thought content
thought processes

The ability to obtain and effectively use information about clients is the foundation of the nursing process and a vital part of the multidisciplinary treatment plan. Learning about clients' problems requires special abilities. Physical examination skills provide information regarding clients' physiological state. Special communication and interaction skills are needed for learning about the cultural, psychosocial, and spiritual aspects of individuals. All these skills go into assessing each client. This chapter provides the starting point for the practice of making thorough mental health assessments. It also describes the use of the mental status examination.

Good assessment skills are critical to quality nursing. This applies equally to nurses who care for clients with medical, surgical, or psychological problems. It is the individual who is treated, but nurses must first learn about the person before they can provide effective care or judge the effectiveness of any nursing action.

Mental Health Treatment Plan

People enter the health care system because they are distressed, disabled, or suffering. When problems are basically physical, a diagnosis is made, the client is treated, and the disorder is either resolved or becomes chronic. The diagnosis and treatment of people with mental-emotional problems become more of a challenge because problems cannot be as easily identified and defined. According to the American Psychiatric Association's *Diagnostic and Statistical Manual of Mental Disorders* (DSM-IV), "no definition adequately specifies precise boundaries for the concept of mental disorder" because the relationship between the physical and psychological self is difficult to separate (American Psychiatric Association, 1994). However, treatment that focuses primarily on assisting clients with behavioral or emotional problems falls into the area of psychiatric or mental health care. It is important to remember, though, that every psychological illness has physical effects and every physical illness is accompanied by psychological effects. The wise nurse is aware of both.

General Treatment Approaches

When individuals first enter the mental health care system, a comprehensive assessment is usually performed. Clients may be interviewed by several members of the multidisciplinary health care team. Physical and psychological diagnostic testing is done, and data are gathered from as many sources as possible.

Once the information is gathered, team members meet to compare data, identify problems, and develop treatment approaches. The team then meets with the client; as much as possible, the treatment goals are agreed on by the team and the client, and a course of action is planned. Usually a combination of medical approaches (medications) are combined with psychotherapies, behavioral therapies, and various social approaches. The overall health care treatment plan is then developed especially for the individual client. Therapeutic actions are implemented, and the client's progress toward each goal is routinely evaluated.

The mental health treatment plan serves several purposes. First, it is a guide for planning and implementing client care. Nurses are guided by the treatment plan when they develop specific nursing care plans. Psychologists, social workers, and other therapists use the mental health treatment plan as a framework for implementing their specialized therapeutic actions.

Second, the plan serves as a vehicle for monitoring the client's progress and assessing the effectiveness of the therapeutic interventions. Clients meet often with treatment team members to discuss problems or difficulties that may be hampering attempts to meet their goals. Therapeutic interventions are evaluated, and the treatment plan is revised to include new information.

Third, the mental health treatment plan serves as a vehicle for communicating and coordinating client care. It prevents costly duplication of services and provides a focus for all therapeutic activities, regardless of specialty, which increases the effectiveness of each member of the treatment team. Developing the mental health treatment plan is not a complex process, but it is a dynamic (changing) one that allows both clients and care providers the opportunity to work together.

DSM-IV Diagnosis

Most therapists who work with mental or emotionally troubled individuals use the DSM-IV to aid in diagnosis and help guide clinical practice. Clients are assessed and then classified according to five categories or axes (Table 13-1). Using a multiaxial (many category) system helps to gain a more complete understanding of clients: their mental and medical conditions, social and environmental problems, and levels of functioning. Using the DSM-IV categories helps nurses to appreciate the complexity of each person and promotes therapeutic interventions based on individual clients. The diagnosis of mental health problems remains the responsibility of the physician, but nurses should at least be knowledgeable of the multiaxial system of psychiatric assessment.

Nursing Process

Each step of the **nursing process** is designed to support goal-directed care for clients (Stuart and Sun-

◆ **TABLE 13-1**
DSM-IV Multiaxial Assessment Tool

Axis	Example
Axis I: Clinical disorders	Schizophrenia, mood disorder, anxiety disorder, substance-related disorder
Axis II: Personality disorders and mental retardation	Paranoid, antisocial, obsessive-compulsive personality disorders; mental retardation
Axis III: General medical conditions	Infections, parasitic diseases; metabolic, nutritional, endocrine, immunity disorders; disorders of each body system
Axis IV: Psychosocial and environmental problems	Educational, occupational, housing, economic, legal problems; social and environmental problems
Axis V: Global assessment of functioning	Clinician's judgment of client's overall level of functioning

Modified from American Psychiatric Association: *Diagnostic and statistical manual of mental disorders,* ed 4, Washington, DC, 1994, American Psychiatric Association.

deen, 1995b). Nurses perform holistic assessments, develop nursing diagnoses, and work with mentally troubled clients to set and achieve realistic treatment goals. Because the nursing profession is concerned with the impact of illness and dysfunction on clients' activities of daily living, many nursing diagnoses fit well with the multiaxial diagnoses of the DSM-IV. Nursing interventions guide clients toward their goals. Evaluations of both client and nursing actions allow for adjustments to be made in the dynamic process that is known as "treatment."

Because the nursing process respects the client's autonomy and freedom to make decisions, clients are involved as partners in care. Although some individuals with mental-emotional problems are unable or too discouraged to make decisions, most clients are capable of participating in some part of their care. Nurses help clients problem-solve by involving them in the care planning process. Clients do not have to cope with their problems in isolation.

Use of the nursing process allows health care providers to share information important for the client's care and treatment. Client responses to various treatments and therapies are assessed and documented throughout the nursing process. Medical and nursing care is adjusted and adapted as goals are reached and clients improve.

The nursing process requires knowledge, experience, and the use of good judgment. A knowledge of behavioral functioning is as important as learning about physical functions. Experience grows with the application and use of the nursing process, whereas sound judgments are learned by looking at every possible side of a problem before arriving at a decision.

Perhaps most important, the nursing process gives nurses a point of view from which client problems may be addressed. Nurses continually assess clients' behaviors and responses to treatment. They may gather much seemingly unrelated information in a short period of time and may observe behaviors that have meanings known only to the client. Here, the nursing process serves as a guide for sorting and understanding the challenging problems of mental illness. Each step of the nursing process—from assessment to evaluation—is designed to assist clients to meet the goals of care and solve (or at least learn to cope with) the problems that caused them to seek mental health care and assistance.

About Assessment

Assessment includes the "gathering, verifying and communicating of information relative to the client" (Anderson, Anderson, and Glanze, 1994). For nurses who use the holistic approach, assessment is the process of gathering information about the whole person, not just the "needs" or "dysfunctions" that are presented for treatment. Clients are viewed as dynamic (changing) individuals affected by more factors than an illness or disorder. For this reason, the holistic assessment includes the gathering of information about the physical, intellectual, social, cultural, and spiritual sides of each person. The more complete the picture of the client, the more effective the treatment approaches will be (Stuart and Sundeen, 1995a).

Data Collection

The words **data collection** refer to a variety of activities designed to elicit, gather, or discover information about a certain subject. Data (information) relating to clients are grouped into two types: objective and subjective data. The term *objective data* refers to information that can be measured and shared. This kind of information is gathered through the senses of sight, smell, touch, and hearing, and it can readily be shared with others. Blood pressure readings, pulse rates, and temperatures that are compared to "normal" illustrate the use of objective data. When working with mental health clients, the nurse obtains objective data through the use of physical examinations, daily nursing assessments, diagnostic testing results, and repeated observations of behaviors.

Subjective data relate to clients' perceptions. They include information that is abstract and difficult to measure or share. The experiences of pain, nausea, and anxiety, for example, cannot be measured by anyone but the individual experiencing them. Nurses may be able to understand and sympathize with a client in pain, but they cannot count, measure, or share the pain experience. Feelings, emotions, and mental states are all subjective and difficult to measure. Because of this, it is extremely important for all health care providers to document subjective information as descriptively and accurately as possible. Do not include interpretative statements (judgments). To document that the client is angry (unless he states that he is angry) is an interpretative statement or judgment. It is better to state that the client was pacing about the room while slamming his fist into the wall and swearing.

When documenting subjective data, quote the client as much as possible (Smith, 1995). Using the exact words spoken by the client is valuable for understanding. Subjective information is collected during the initial health history interview and during every interaction with clients. The simple question "How do you feel?" usually elicits much subjective information.

In nursing, the methods of collecting information are the same as those used in science. "Three principal data collecting methods are available: (a) interview, (b) observational techniques, and (c) rating scales/inventories" (Savage, 1991). Each method overlaps the other. For instance, during the health history interview with the client, the nurse uses observational techniques and interviewing skills.

The interview method of data collection is familiar to nurses. An **interview** is a meeting (usually face to face) of people with the purpose of obtaining or exchanging information (Keltner, Schwecke, and Bostrom, 1995). Interviews can be formal and highly structured or informal and casual. Information gathered from formal interviews is usually documented on a standardized form. Nurses have a professional responsibility to formally assess each client on admission. The interview is an excellent method for accomplishing this assessment. It also serves as the starting point for building the therapeutic relationship.

Informal interviews usually occur casually or by chance, but they provide great opportunities to learn more about clients and their families. Nurses use informal interview techniques when they investigate client problems or explore certain topics.

Data gathering through the use of observational techniques is commonly used. Observation is defined as the process of purposeful looking (Fortinash, Holoday-Worret, 1995). When using observation as a data-gathering technique, nurses must be careful to be objective. Personal bias or attitudes can alter the nurses' perceptions and affect the objectivity of the observations. The use of observation is an excellent method for gathering information but only when the nurse can remain impartial and does not pass judgment.

Physical examination skills are important to the data-gathering process. They include specialized methods for obtaining information about the body's level of physiological functioning. The technique of observation is called inspection, which in this case means a purposeful examination of the body. The skills of auscultation and percussion use the nurse's sense of hearing to detect sounds within the body. Last, the technique of palpation uses the sense of touch to draw out information about temperature, texture, and pulsations of the body. Physical examination skills are used by nurses to gather data during the initial assessment of the client, to investigate client complaints whenever a change in a client's physical condition is noted, and to evaluate the effectiveness of a nursing intervention.

Rating scales and inventories are frequently used by social workers, psychologists, and other therapists. They are data-gathering tools specifically designed to bring out certain kinds of information. The results are then compared to standardized measurements. For example, the Primary Care Evaluation of Mental Disorders (PRIME-MD), a questionnaire designed for physicians and nurses in general practice, screens clients for information about the four groups of mental disorders most commonly encountered in family practice (anxiety, alcohol, mood, and somatoform disorders) (Spitzer and others, 1994) (Fig. 13-1). Rating scales and inventories can be very useful for focusing on certain aspects of client problems, but like the other data-gathering tools, they must be used without passing judgment.

Assessment Process

To gain an understanding of clients, nurses learn to purposefully be observant and alert for information that may have an impact on clients' care. The process

PATIENT QUESTIONNAIRE

NAME: _____   TODAY'S DATE: _____

INSTRUCTIONS: This questionnaire will help your doctor better understand problems that you may have. Your doctor may ask you more questions about some of these items. Please make sure to check a box for *every* item.

During the PAST MONTH, have you OFTEN been bothered by...						During the PAST MONTH...		
	Yes	No		Yes	No		Yes	No
1. Stomach pain	☐	☐	12. Constipation, loose bowels, or diarrhea	☐	☐	22. Have you had an anxiety attack (suddenly feeling fear or panic)	☐	☐
2. Back pain	☐	☐	13. Nausea, gas, or indigestion	☐	☐			
3. Pain in your arms, legs, or joints (knees, hips, etc.)	☐	☐	14. Feeling tired or having low energy	☐	☐	23. Have you thought you should cut down on your drinking of alcohol	☐	☐
4. Menstrual pain or problems	☐	☐	15. Trouble sleeping	☐	☐	24. Has anyone complained about your drinking	☐	☐
5. Pain or problems during sexual intercourse	☐	☐	16. The thought that you have a serious undiagnosed disease	☐	☐	25. Have you felt guilty or upset about your drinking	☐	☐
6. Headaches	☐	☐	17. Your eating being out of control	☐	☐	26. Was there ever a single day in which you had five or more drinks of beer, wine, or liquor	☐	☐
7. Chest pain	☐	☐						
8. Dizziness	☐	☐	18. Little interest or pleasure in doing things	☐	☐			
9. Fainting spells	☐	☐				Overall, would you say your health is:		
10. Feeling your heart pound or race	☐	☐	19. Feeling down, depressed, or hopeless	☐	☐	Excellent ☐		
11. Shortness of breath	☐	☐	20. "Nerves" or feeling anxious or on edge	☐	☐	Very good ☐ Good ☐ Fair ☐ Poor ☐		
			21. Worrying about a lot of different things	☐	☐			

Fig. 13-1 Primary Care Evaluation of Mental Disorders (PRIME-MD). One-page patient questionnaire that is completed before seeing the physician. (Copyright Pfizer, Inc.)

of assessing clients is ongoing. It begins with the clients' admission to the facility or service and ends only after the clients' relationship with the health care system has ended. Good assessment skills require effective communication and active listening skills, as well as the ability to establish rapport with people.

Holistic Nursing Assessment

Physical function is only one small part of an individual, but it is deeply interwoven with all other aspects of the person. A person's cultural, social, intellectual, emotional, and spiritual areas have an impact on the physical body and its functions. Without a

◆ **TABLE 13-2**
Summary: Psychiatric Nursing Assessment Tool

Area of Assessment	Example
Appraisal of health/illness	Events leading to problem, definition of problem, client's goal, regular health care received
Previous psychiatric treatment	Diagnosis, type of treatment, medications, compliance, psychiatric history in family
Coping responses, physical status	Review of function in each body system, physical assessment, diet history, sleep patterns, exposure to toxic substances, activities of daily living
Coping responses, mental status	Appearance, speech, motor activity, mood, affect, interactions, perceptions, thought content and process, memory, concentration, calculations, intelligence, insight, judgment
Coping responses, discharge planning, needs	Client's ability to provide for food, clothing, housing, safety, transportation, supportive relationships, work needs, financial needs
Coping mechanisms	Adaptive mechanisms, maladaptive mechanisms
Psychosocial and environmental problems	Educational, occupational, economic, housing problems; difficulties with support group, culture, access to health care services
Knowledge deficits	Understanding of psychiatric problem, coping skills, medications, stressors

Modified from Stuart GW, Sundeen SJ: *Principles and practice of psychiatric nursing,* ed 5, St Louis, 1995, Mosby.

knowledge of these five aspects of a client, health care providers (nurses) become narrowed and limited in their effectiveness (Parker, 1992). The holistic assessment for nurses who work with mentally and emotionally troubled clients is the same as that used by nurses who care for medical/surgical clients. The difference is that, in psychiatric treatment situations, the emphasis is on mental-emotional functioning rather than physical functioning. The psychiatric nursing assessment tool is focused on obtaining data about the problems, coping behaviors, and resources of clients (Table 13-2).

The information collected from assessment activities serves as part of the database from which medical, nursing, and other treatment decisions are made. For clients suspected of being capable of violence toward themselves or others, a risk factor assessment should be done first.

Risk Factor Assessment

The purpose of a **risk factor assessment** is to "formulate a nursing diagnosis based on the identification of risk factors that potentially present an immediate threat to the patient" (Stuart and Sundeen, 1995b). With this assessment tool, eight areas of potential risk are identified (Fig. 13-2). Positive findings direct the nurse to begin more specific assessments or begin ap-

propriate safety precautions. Nursing diagnoses are identified and then incorporated into the client care plan. Although the risk factor assessment is usually completed by a registered nurse, health care providers (e.g., LPNs, LVNs, and psychiatric technicians) assist by gathering important information and making objective observations.

Nursing History

Each client should be interviewed on admission to the health care service. Within the health care framework, an interview is defined as "an organized conversation with a client" (Potter and Perry, 1995) that has the purpose of bringing forth certain information about the client's health status. The purpose of the nursing history interview is to obtain data about the unique individual who is the client. It offers nurses an opportunity to introduce themselves and serves as a starting point for establishing the therapeutic relationship. During the interview, nurses can gain insight into client concerns, worries, and expectations, and the interview offers the opportunity to obtain clues that may require further investigation during the physical assessment. When used appropriately, the interview is a powerful method for gathering important information about clients.

RISK FACTOR ASSESSMENT

DIRECTIONS

The purpose of this assessment is to formulate a nursing diagnosis based on the identification of risk factors that potentially present an immediate threat to the patient. A registered nurse must complete this assessment within the **FIRST HOUR** of the patient's encounter with the health care system.

The space labeled "Informants" should identify by name any source of information used to assess the patient. Examples are the patient, family member, an accompanying individual, or the referral source. The "Reason for This Encounter" should quote the patient when possible.

The tool comprises eight (8) areas of potential risk. Positive findings in any area direct the nurse to initiate a more specific assessment or to initiate appropriate precautions. At the end of the risk factor assessment, the nurse must list the nursing diagnoses and total number of risk factors identified. A nursing care plan must be initiated immediately to address any nursing diagnosis that reflects an identified risk factor.

RISK FACTOR ASSESSMENT TOOL

Date: _____

INFORMANTS: _____

REASON FOR THIS ENCOUNTER: _____

_____

_____

RISK FACTORS:

1. Potential for Suicide/Self-Harm:

☐ yes ☐ no   Is there evidence of active or recent suicidal or self-harm ideation or attempt?
☐ yes ☐ no   Is there a history of suicidal or self-harm ideation or attempt?

•If yes to either question, initiate a Suicide/Self-Harm Assessment.

2. Potential for Assault/Violence:

☐ yes ☐ no   Is there a history of assaultive, destructive, or violent behavior?
☐ yes ☐ no   Does the patient express feelings of anger or aggression?

•If yes to either question, initiate an Assault/Violence Assessment.

3. Potential for Substance Abuse Withdrawal (alcohol, illicit drugs, prescription drugs, or inhalants):

☐ yes ☐ no   Have you ever felt the need to cut down on your drinking or drug use?
☐ yes ☐ no   Have people annoyed you by criticizing your drinking or drug use?
☐ yes ☐ no   Have you ever felt bad or guilty about your drinking or drug use?
☐ yes ☐ no   Have you ever had a drink first thing in the morning (eye opener)?

•If yes to any question, initiate a Substance Withdrawal Assessment.

4. Potential for Allergic Reaction/Adverse Drug Reaction:

☐ yes ☐ no   Food
☐ yes ☐ no   Medication
☐ yes ☐ no   Other

•If yes to any item, initiate an Allergy Assessment.

Fig. 13-2   Risk factor assessment. (Courtesy of Division of Psychiatric Nursing, Medical University of South Carolina.)

5. Potential for Seizure.

☐ yes　　☐ no　　Is there a history of seizures?

•If yes to this question, initiate a Seizure Assessment.

6. Potential for Falls/Accidents:

☐ yes　　☐ no　　Ages 70 or older/5 or under
☐ yes　　☐ no　　History of confusion
☐ yes　　☐ no　　History of falls/accidents
☐ yes　　☐ no　　Sensory deficits
☐ yes　　☐ no　　Impaired mobility/balance
☐ yes　　☐ no　　Medications (check as many as apply)
　　　　　　　　　　　☐ yes　☐ no　　Sedatives/tranquilizers/narcotics
　　　　　　　　　　　☐ yes　☐ no　　Anesthetics
　　　　　　　　　　　☐ yes　☐ no　　Diuretics/antihypertensives
　　　　　　　　　　　☐ yes　☐ no　　Laxatives
　　　　　　　　　　　☐ yes　☐ no　　Substance abuse
　　　　　　　　　　　☐ yes　☐ no　　Psychotherapeutics

•If yes to two or more items, initiate Fall Precautions.

7. Potential for Elopement:

☐ yes　　☐ no　　Does the patient wish or intend to leave?
☐ yes　　☐ no　　Does the patient have a history of elopement?

•If yes to either question, initiate Elopement Precautions.

8. Potential for Physiological Instability:

☐ yes　　☐ no　　Existing unstable physical problem?

Vital signs:　T _____　P _____　R _____

BP Stand _____　BP Sit _____　Weight _____　Height _____

•If yes to unstable problem or data out of normal range, initiate Physical Assessment.

Total number of risk factors identified (1-8) _____

IDENTIFIED NURSING DIAGNOSES:

☐ yes　　☐ no　　Potential for violence (self-directed)
☐ yes　　☐ no　　Potential for violence (other-directed)
☐ yes　　☐ no　　Risk for self-mutilation
☐ yes　　☐ no　　Potential for injury, related to _____

RN Signature _____　Date: _____　Time: _____

Fig. 13-2, cont'd　For legend see opposite page.

Effective Interviews

The success of any client interview rests on the nurse's ability to listen objectively and respond appropriately. To enhance your interviewing skills, follow these guidelines.

Remember that personal values must not cloud professional judgments. Reacting to a client's personal appearance or behaviors can stereotype him/her and result in a negative impact on the effectiveness of the therapeutic relationship.

Do not make assumptions about how you think the client must feel. Discover what each event means to the client and how he/she views the situation. The experience of losing a loved one, for example, can be perceived with grief and sadness or relief and joy. It all depends on how an individual interprets or perceives an event.

Always take into account the client's cultural values and beliefs. With mental health clients, this point cannot be emphasized enough. Nurses must learn about their clients' cultures if they are to understand clients' points of view. With clients from unfamiliar cultures, it is wise to research information about the culture *before* conducting the interview.

Pay particular attention to nonverbal communications. Much can be learned if the nurse is observant. Note which subjects are avoided or quickly passed over during the interview. These behaviors can be clues that indicate a need for further investigation. Observing methods of self-expression helps the nurse to focus on the client's unspoken signals and the messages they communicate.

Have clearly set goals. Know the purpose of the interview. Is this an initial assessment interview or the investigation of a specific condition? The assessment interview is not a random discussion, but it is a purposefully planned interaction with the client.

Last, monitor your own reactions during the interview. Use self-awareness to signal when you are becoming too emotionally involved. A nurse may identify with certain clients with similar interests or situations, but self-awareness allows him/her to understand and cope with the emotional responses generated by certain clients.

Interviewing skills are used throughout the nursing process. Interviews may be focused on obtaining information about the whole client, as with the nursing history interview, or focus narrowly on one aspect of care, such as a client's sleeping patterns. Work to develop and refine your interviewing skills because they are an important tool of effective nursing practice.

Sociocultural Assessment

The health history includes obtaining information about both the physical and psychological functions of an individual. Sociocultural assessment focuses on the cultural, social, and spiritual aspects of an individual. During the nursing history interview, the nurse obtains information about a client's background. This time also offers an opportunity to observe the client's appearance, behaviors, and attitudes (areas also included in the mental status examination).

The sociocultural assessment includes six areas. Clients are asked questions about their age, ethnicity (culture), gender, education, income, and belief system. The client's risk factors and stressors are defined during the sociocultural assessment (National Depressive and Manic-Depressive Association, 1995). This information helps the nurse to develop accurate and appropriate plans of care.

Review of Systems

The holistic nursing assessment also includes a review of each body system and its functioning. Clients are first questioned about their general health care, past illnesses and hospitalizations, and family health history. Questions then are focused on the function of each body system. Last, the lifestyle and activities of daily living are assessed. The box on p. 181 lists the topics covered by the health history for physical functioning. When the results of the nursing history interview are added to the database, a clear picture of the individual begins to emerge. Data obtained from the physical assessment and various diagnostic examinations add even more important information and help to complete the picture of the individual client.

Physical Assessment

Each client usually receives a physical examination on admission to a psychiatric service. The purpose of the examination is to discover any physical problems that can be treated medically. Many alterations in behavior can often be traced to a physical cause. For example, low blood sugar levels can result in confused and uncooperative behavior. Hormone imbalances, exposure to toxic substances, and severe pain can also affect behavior.

A complete physical examination is most often performed by a physician or nurse practitioner. The client's current health status is explored, and then each system is examined. Nurses have an obligation to assess each client's health status on a routine basis. A complete physical assessment is not needed everyday, but nurses must be alert to changes in their clients' conditions. To do this, many nurses use a quick head-to-toe assessment (Table 13-3). The head-to-toe assessment takes less than 5 minutes. It can be performed any time information about physical functions is needed. "It will help you . . . prioritize your

NURSING HEALTH HISTORY FOR THE MENTAL HEALTH CLIENT

HEALTH CARE HISTORY

General Health Care
Regular health care provider
Frequency of health care visits
Last medical examination and test results
Any unusual circumstances of birth, including mother's preterm habits and condition

Hospitalizations and Surgeries
When
Why indicated
Treatments
Outcome

Brain Impairment
Diagnosed brain problem
Head trauma
Details of any accidents or periods of unconsciousness for any reason—blows to the head, electrical shocks, high fevers, seizures, fainting, dizziness, headaches, falls

Diabetes
Stability of glucose levels

Endocrine Disturbances
Thyroid and adrenal function particularly

LIFESTYLE

Eating
Details of unusual or unsupervised diets, appetite, weight changes, cravings, and caffeine intake

Medications
Full history of current and past psychiatric medications in self and first-degree relatives

Substance Use
Alcohol and drug use

Toxins
Overcome by automobile exhaust or natural gas
Exposure to lead, mercury, insecticides, herbicides, solvents, cleaning agents, lawn chemicals

Occupation (Current and Past)
Chemicals in workplace (farming, painting)

Cancer
Full history, particularly consider metastases (lung, breast, melanoma, gastrointestinal tract, and kidney are most likely to metastasize)
Results of treatment (chemotherapy and surgeries)

Lung Problems
Details of any condition or event that restricts flow of air to lungs for more than 2 minutes or adversely affects oxygen absorption (brain uses 20% of oxygen in body) such as with chronic obstructive pulmonary disease, near drowning, near strangulation, high-altitude oxygen deprivation, resuscitation events

Cardiac Problems
Childhood illnesses such as scarlet or rheumatic fever
History of heart attacks, strokes, or hypertension

Blood Diseases
Anemia resulting in hypoxia
Arteriosclerotic conditions
HIV
Work-related accidents (construction, mining)
Military experiences

Injury
Safe sex practices
Contact sports and sports-related injuries
Exposure to violence or abuse

PRESENTING SYMPTOMS AND COPING RESPONSES

Description—nature, frequency, and intensity
Threats to safety of self or others
Functional status
Quality of life

From Stuart GW, Sundeen SJ: *Pocket guide to psychiatric nursing*, ed 3, St Louis, 1995, Mosby.

nursing care. It can also help you uncover specific findings to follow up on later" (Poncar, 1995).

Diagnostic studies for clients with mental-emotional problems include standard blood and urine tests, evaluation of electrolytes, and hormone function examinations. Many clients are screened for tuberculosis (TB), HIV, and sexually transmitted diseases. Noninvasive studies, such as x-ray examinations, ECGs, and EEGs may also be ordered. Brain imaging studies (CT, MRI, positron emission tomography [PET] scans) are helpful in finding lesions or other abnormal conditions in the brain.

The physical assessment, along with the nursing health history and diagnostic test results, helps to form a picture of the individual. However, for the mental health client, the mental status examination offers important additional information about the client's current mental and emotional state (Goleman, 1994).

Mental Status Assessment

The mental status examination allows nurses to observe and describe a client's behavior in an objective,

◆ **TABLE 13-3**
Head-to-Toe Assessment

Steps	Procedures
Perform general overview of whole client	Observe the way the client walks, moves, and talks; assess level of consciousness, orientation, and response to questions; note skin temperature and circulation when shaking hands
Examine head and neck	Observe for eye contact; assess condition of eyes, skin, hair, facial expression, mouth, and teeth; palpate strength of carotid pulses
Examine arms and hands	Note temperature, texture, edema, and condition of skin; check capillary refill; do hand grips to determine strength and sensation
Examine chest and abdomen	Inspect and palpate chest wall; auscultate heart, lung, and bowel sounds
Examine legs and feet	Note length, position, and condition of legs and feet; assess temperature, texture, presence of edema, capillary refill, and sensation of lower extremities; palpate pedal pulses bilaterally

Modified from Poncar PJ: *Nurs 95* 25(3):59, 1995.

nonjudgmental way. It is a tool for assessing mental health dysfunctions and identifying the causes of clients' problems (Jess, 1988). Understanding each part of the examination enables nurses to plan and deliver the most appropriate care for each of their clients.

The mental status examination explores the following areas: general appearance, level of consciousness, behavior, speech, mood, affect, thought content, intellectual performance, insight, judgment, and perception (see box at right).

General Description

Under the category of general description, the nurse assesses the client's general appearance, speech, motor activity, and behavior during the interaction.

The general appearance category includes everything that can be readily observed about a client, such as physical characteristics, dress, facial expressions, motor activity, speech, and reactions. To assess a client's physical characteristics, observe each part of the client's body, noting anything unusual. Describe the person's body build, skin coloring, cleanliness, and manner of dress. Does the person appear neat and tidy or careless and unkempt? Note any body odors. If cosmetics are used, are they appropriately applied? Does the client's appearance match his/her sex, age, and situation? People with depression, for example, may look unkempt and neglected. It is not uncommon for manic clients to dress in colorful but bizarre clothing and wear many cosmetics and jewelry. Document *all* findings. For example, if the client is missing a finger or has tattoos, this information should also be charted.

CATEGORIES OF THE MENTAL STATUS EXAMINATION

GENERAL DESCRIPTION
Appearance
Speech
Motor activity
Interaction during interview

EMOTIONAL STATE
Mood
Affect

EXPERIENCES
Perceptions

THINKING
Thought content
Thought process

SENSORIUM AND COGNITION
Level of consciousness
Memory
Level of concentration and calculation
Information and intelligence
Judgment
Insight

From Stuart GW, Sundeen SJ: *Pocket guide to psychiatric nursing*, ed 3, St Louis, 1995, Mosby.

Facial expressions, eye contact, and pupil size should be noted. Do the client's facial expressions match his/her emotions and actions? Is eye contact avoided or held for long periods of time? Are there any tics or grimaces present? Note the size of the

◆ **TABLE 13-4**
Common Emotional Responses (Affects)

Name of Affect	Description
Inappropriate response	
Labile	Rapid, dramatic changes in emotions
Inconsistent	Affect and mood do not agree
Flat	Unresponsive emotions
Pleasurable response	
Euphoria	Excessive feelings of well-being (feeling too good)
Exaltation	Intense happiness, often with feelings of grandeur
Unpleasurable (dysphoric) response	
Aggression	Anger, hostility, or rage that is out of keeping with situation
Agitation	Motor restlessness, often seen with anxiety
Ambivalence	Having both positive and negative feelings
Anxiety	Vague, uneasy feeling, often from unknown cause
Depression	Sadness, hopelessness, loss that is present over time
Fear	Reaction to recognized danger

client's pupils. Large, dilated pupils are seen in persons with drug intoxication, whereas small pupils are associated with narcotic use.

The client's speech is then assessed. Speech is described by its rate, its volume, and its characteristics. Note any abnormal speech patterns (see Chapter 11).

Next, turn your attention to the client's motor activity, gestures, and posture. Observe the client's physical movements for the level of activity, the type of activity, and any unusual movements or mannerisms. Is the client agitated, tense, restless, lethargic, or relaxed? Are there any tics, grimaces, repeated facial expressions, or tremors present? Excessive body movements are seen in persons with anxiety or mania. They can also result from the use of stimulants or other drugs. Repeated movements or behaviors are seen in clients with obsessive-compulsive disorders, and picking at one's clothing is often seen in clients with delirium or toxic reactions.

To complete the general description, assess the client's behavior during the interaction. How did the client relate to you? Was he/she cooperative, hostile, or overly friendly? Did the client appear to trust you? Note if the client's verbal messages matched the behavior. Clients who use unconnected gestures may be having hallucinations.

Emotional State

To assess the client's emotional state, the nurse considers the client's mood and affect.

Mood is defined as the individual's overall feelings. Mood is a subjective factor that can be explained only by the person who is feeling it. Usually, people will have a basic mood, although it may change sometime during the day. To illustrate, a basically relaxed and happy person may feel disappointed by an incident during the day but soon forgets and returns to his/her commonly happy mood.

Affect is the client's emotional display of the mood being experienced. Table 13-4 explains several kinds of affect. A person's mood can range from overwhelming sadness to great elation and joy. These variations are referred to as one's range of emotion. Affect can be categorized as appropriate, inappropriate, pleasurable, or unpleasurable. To assess a client's mood, ask what he/she is feeling and then observe the reactions. Do the responses to your questions match with the subjects being discussed? Is the client overreacting, not reacting at all, or responding inappropriately? Document objective descriptions of the client's behaviors. Descriptions communicate much more information than a single medical term does.

Experiences

This category explores the client's **perceptions,** the ways in which he/she experiences the world. An individual's perceptions are often referred to as one's frame of reference. In short, a person's perceptions help determine his/her sense of reality.

People who are having mental health problems may have difficulty in perceiving the same reality as the rest of society. *Hallucinations* are perceptions that have no external stimulus. The client may hear voices or see things that are not perceived by other people.

Hallucinations involving taste, touch, or smell may indicate a physical problem. Visual and auditory hallucinations are associated with schizophrenia, the acute stage of alcohol or drug withdrawal, and organic brain disorders.

Alterations in perceptions that have a basis in reality are called *illusions*. External stimuli are present, but they are perceived differently by the client. For example, a client perceives the nurse walking down the hall as a wolf.

To assess clients' perceptions, ask them if they can hear voices or see things when other people are not present. If the answer is "yes," ask them to describe the experience. Questions that may be asked include the following:

How many different voices (images) do you hear (see)?
What do the voices say (images do)?
Do you recognize any of the voices (images)?
When did the voices (images) first begin? What was happening in your life at the time?
How do you feel about the voices (images)?

Remember that hallucinations or illusions are very real to the person experiencing them. Nurses cannot "talk them out of it" nor tell them to ignore what they are perceiving. However, because they are so real, clients usually are willing to describe them when asked.

Thinking

The "thinking" section of the mental status examination focuses on the client's thought content and process. Problems with **thought content** relate to *what* an individual is thinking. Clients may be experiencing delusions, obsessions, phobias, preoccupation, amnesia, or confabulations.

Disturbances in **thought processes** relate to *how* a person thinks—how he/she analyzes the world and connects and organizes information. Disorders of thought process include blocking, flight of ideas, loose associations, and perseveration (Table 13-5).

Another problem of thinking is *depersonalization*, which is defined as a feeling of unreality or detachment from oneself or environment. The unreal feelings produce a dreamlike atmosphere that overtakes the individual's consciousness. One's body does not feel like one's own. Events that are dramatic or important are perceived with a detached calmness, as if the person were watching instead of participating in reality. With functional people, feelings of depersonalization can occur when one is anxious, stressed, or

◆ **TABLE 13-5**
Disorders of Thinking

Disorder	Description
Thought processes (how one thinks)	
Blocking	Thoughts stop suddenly for no reason
Flight of ideas	Rapid changes from one thought to another related thought
Loose associations	Poorly organized or connected thoughts
Perseveration	Repeating same word in response to different questions
Thought content (what one thinks)	
Delusions	False beliefs that cannot be corrected by reasoning or explanation
Obsession	Thought, action, or emotion that is unwelcome and difficult to resist
Phobias	Strong fears of certain things, places, or situations
Preoccupations	All experiences and actions are connected to central thought that is usually emotional in nature
Others	
Amnesia	Inability to remember past events
Confabulation	Using untrue statements to fill in gaps of memory loss

very tired. Depersonalization disorders are commonly seen in clients with severe depression and in some forms of schizophrenia.

Assessment of the client's thought content and process is carried out throughout the entire mental status examination. Are the client's thoughts based in reality? Are ideas communicated clearly? Do the client's thoughts follow a logical order? Are there any unusual thoughts, preoccupations, or beliefs present? Does the client have any suicidal, violent, or destructive thoughts? (Forster, 1994). Are there any persistent dreams? Does the client believe that someone is intent on harming him/her (feelings of persecution)? Observe the client closely and listen intently. Much of this information will be revealed during the course of the interaction.

Sensorium and Cognition

The **sensorium** is that part of the consciousness that perceives, sorts, and integrates (combines) information. People with a clear sensorium are able to orient to time, place, and person. They are also able to use their memories to recall recent and remote information. Levels of consciousness and memory recall help to assess a person's sensorium.

The level of consciousness can be determined by observing the amount of stimuli it takes to arouse the client (see box below). If the client cannot be awakened by verbal stimuli, notify your supervisor immediately. If the client is awake, note his/her responses to your questions, the degree of interaction, and the amount of eye contact that is being made.

Memory is the ability to recall past events, experience, and perceptions. For the purpose of testing, memory is divided into three categories: immediate,

recent, and remote memory. Immediate memory is sometimes referred to as *recall.* To assess immediate memory (recall), ask the client to remember three things (e.g., a color, an address, and an object). Later in the conversation (at least 15 minutes), ask the client to repeat the three items. Recall can also be tested by having the client repeat a series of numbers within a 10-second period.

Recent memory includes those events within the past 2 weeks. Nurses test recent memory by asking the client to recall the events of the past 24 hours. Loss of recent memory is often seen in persons with Alzheimer's disease, anxiety, and depression.

Assessing *remote memory* involves asking the client questions about his/her place of birth, schools attended, ages of family members, and other questions about the person's background. This part of the mental status examination can easily be done during the nursing health history interview. Remember, it is sometimes difficult to tell if the client has accurate memories. The nurse may need to speak with family members or research past records to verify the information given by the client. Long-term memory loss is seen in clients with organic (physical) problems, conversion disorders, and dissociative disorders.

The level of concentration focuses on the client's ability to pay attention during the conversation. **Calculation** tests the ability to do simple math problems. Have the person count rapidly from 1 to 20; perform simple addition, multiplication, and division problems; and subtract 7 from 100, then 7 from 93, and so on. Then ask practical questions such as the number of dimes in $1.90. Note how easily the client becomes distracted during the tasks. People with mental-emotional problems commonly have difficulty with concentration and calculations. These difficulties are also seen in persons with physical disorders, such as brain tumors, so it is important to assess the client's ability to concentrate and do simple calculations.

Information and **intelligence** are areas of assessment that require special attention. It is very easy for the nurse to make an inaccurate judgment because of his/her own sociocultural background. To prevent this, document observations of the client's behaviors rather than your opinions of the client's behaviors.

During this phase of the mental status examination, the nurse assesses the client's education level, general knowledge, ability to read, use of vocabulary, and ability to think abstractly. General knowledge can be tested by asking the person to name the past five presidents, five large cities, or the occupations of well-known people in the community. Ask the client about the last grade completed in school.

LEVELS OF CONSCIOUSNESS

Comatose/unconscious: unresponsive to any verbal or painful stimuli

Stuporous: responds only to strong physical stimuli; falls asleep if not stimulated

Drowsy/somnolent: wakens with strong verbal stimuli; falls asleep if left undisturbed

Lethargic: can be verbally aroused; shows decreased wakefulness; may have periods of excitability alternating with periods of drowsiness

Alert: awake and responsive; oriented to time, place, and person

Hyperalertness: increased state of alertness or watchfulness (hypervigilance)

Mania: state of extreme excitement, elation, and activity

To determine reading ability, print a command, such as "Close your eyes," on a piece of paper. Ask the client to read it and follow the directions. During the conversation, note the client's choice of words and their use.

Assess the client's ability to think abstractly by having him/her explain the meaning of several well-known proverbs, such as the following:

A stitch in time saves nine.
A rolling stone gathers no moss.
When it rains, it pours.

Many people with mental health problems give concrete answers like "Moss only grows on the north sides of stones" or "People who live in glass houses should not throw stones because it will break the glass."

Judgment refers to the ability to evaluate choices and make appropriate decisions. During the health history interview, observe how the client explains personal relationships, his/her job, and economic responsibilities. Assess the client's judgment by asking such questions as: "What would you do if you . . .

- found an addressed envelope on the ground?"
- ran out of medication before the next appointment?"
- won $25,000?"

Judgment is often impaired in persons with chemical dependence, intoxication, schizophrenia, mental retardation, and organic mental disorders. Document the client's responses using the client's own words whenever possible.

Insight refers to the client's understanding of his/her situation. What is the client's understanding of the disorder? Questions that help the nurse assess insight include "Have you noticed a change in yourself recently?" and "What do you think is the cause of your anxiety (discomfort)?" Expect clients to have different degrees of insight. For example, a person with an alcohol problem may realize that he/she drinks too much but does not think that it is interfering with his/her job or family life. Again, be sure to document the client's statements rather than your opinions.

Although the mental status examination may appear to be a lengthy process, much of it can be performed during the nursing history interview. Checklists are available to make sure that the nurse addresses each area of the examination (Jess, 1988) (see box at right). Nurses who work with mentally troubled clients often use parts of the mental status examination to assess clients whose mental state changes frequently. For example, the nurse assesses the hallucinating client for thought content and process at intervals throughout the day.

MENTAL STATUS ASSESSMENT AT A GLANCE

1. Appearance
   _____ manner of dress
   _____ personal grooming
   _____ facial expressions
   _____ posture and gait
2. Speech
   _____ manner of response (frank, evading)
   _____ choice of words (to assess general intelligence, education, levels of function, thought)
   _____ speech disorder
3. Level of consciousness
   _____ level of alertness
   _____ orientation (time, place, person)
4. Attention span
   _____ ability to keep thoughts focused on one topic
   _____ repeat a series of numbers
   _____ serial 7s (ask client to subtract 7 from 100, 7 from 93, etc.)
5. Memory
   _____ immediate memory (ask client to repeat words after 15 minutes)
   _____ recent memory (ask client about yesterday's activities)
   _____ remote memory (ask client about dates of birth, marriage, schooling)
6. Understanding abstract relationships
   _____ understanding of proverbs (concrete or abstract)
   _____ ability to understand similarities (e.g., "How are a bicycle and an automobile alike?")
7. Arithmetic and reading ability
   _____ simple addition, subtraction, multiplication, and division (ask client to make change)
   _____ ability to read newspaper, magazine
8. General information knowledge
   _____ discuss newspaper or magazine article
   _____ general information questions (e.g., "How many days in a year? Where does the sun set?")
9. Judgment
   _____ responses to family, work, financial problems
   _____ responses to "What would you do if . . ." questions
10. Emotional status
    _____ ask "How do you feel today?" or "How do you feel about . . ." questions
    _____ affect
    _____ current situation and coping behaviors

Modified from Jess LW: *Nurs 88* 18(6):42, 1988.

Work to develop your powers of observation. Do not pass judgment or let your own opinions interfere with data gathering. Remember, the results of the mental status examination can be affected by attitudes and beliefs. Learn to use assessment skills. They will serve you well in all practice settings.

❖ KEY CONCEPTS

- The ability to effectively obtain and use information about clients is the foundation of the nursing process and a vital part of the multidisciplinary treatment plan.

- Every psychological illness has physical effects, and every physical illness is accompanied by psychological effects.

- Therapists who work with mentally and emotionally troubled individuals use the DSM-IV to aid in diagnosis and help guide clinical practice.

- The nursing process is a purposeful and organized approach to solving client problems that requires knowledge, experience, and the use of good judgment.

- For nurses who use the holistic approach, assessment is the process of gathering information about the whole person.

- Data collection refers to a variety of activities that are designed to elicit, gather, or discover information about a certain subject.

- The process of assessing a client is ongoing. It begins with the client's admission and ends only after the client's relationship with the health care system has ended.

- The psychiatric nursing assessment tool includes an appraisal of the client's health, previous psychiatric treatment, physical and mental coping responses, discharge planning needs, psychosocial and environmental problems, and needs for knowledge.

- The purpose of a risk factor assessment is to formulate a nursing diagnosis based on the identification of risk factors that may present an immediate threat to the client or others.

- The nursing history interview is an organized conversation with a client that has the purpose of bringing out certain information about the client's health status.

- The sociocultural assessment focuses on the cultural, social, and spiritual aspects of an individual.

- Head-to-toe assessments are a quick way to gather data about a client's current condition.

- The mental status examination explores general appearance, level of consciousness, behavior, speech, mood, affect, thought content, intellectual performance, insight, judgment, and perception.

- Nurses often use various parts of the mental status examination to assess clients whose mental state changes frequently.

❖ SUGGESTIONS FOR FURTHER READING

"Asking Questions Effectively" (*Nursing 95* 25[3]:83, 1995) written by Susan Smith offers some excellent hints for improving your interviewing skills.

❖ REFERENCES

Anderson KN, Anderson LE, Glanze WD: *Mosby's medical, nursing, and allied health dictionary,* ed 4, St Louis, 1994, Mosby.

American Psychiatric Association: *Diagnostic and statistical manual of mental disorders,* ed 4, Washington DC, 1994, American Psychiatric Association.

Forster P: Accurate assessment of short term suicide risk in a crisis, *Psychiatr Ann* 24:571, 1994.

Fortinash KM, Holoday-Worret PA: *Psychiatric nursing care plans,* ed 2, St Louis, 1995, Mosby.

Goleman D: Helping family doctors spot psychiatric problems, *The New York Times* 144(Dec 14):88, 1994.

Jess LW: Investigating impaired mental status: an assessment guide you can use, *Nurs 88* 18(6):42, 1988.

Keltner NL, Schwecke, Bostrom CE: *Psychiatric nursing,* ed 2, St Louis, 1995, Mosby.

National Depressive and Manic-Depressive Association: Patient's cultural background important in diagnosis and treatment, *DMDA Newslett* 7(3):3, 1995.

Parker BA: When your medical/surgical patient is also mentally ill, *Nurs 92* 22(5):66, 1992.

Poncar PJ: Who has time for a head-to-toe assessment? *Nurs 95* 25(3):59, 1995.

Potter PA, Perry AG: *Basic nursing: theory and practice,* ed 3, St Louis, 1995, Mosby.

Savage P: Patient assessment in psychiatric nursing, *J Adv Nurs* 16(3):311, 1991.

Smith S: Asking questions effectively, *Nurs 95* 25(3):83, 1995.

Spitzer RL and others: Utility of a new procedure for diagnosing mental disorders in primary care, *JAMA* 272(22):1749, 1994.

Stuart GW, Sundeen SJ: *Pocket guide to psychiatric nursing,* ed 3, St Louis, 1995a, Mosby.

Stuart GW, Sundeen SJ: *Principles and practice of psychiatric nursing,* ed 5, St Louis, 1995b, Mosby.

UNIT 3

MENTAL HEALTH PROBLEMS THROUGHOUT THE LIFE CYCLE

14

PROBLEMS OF CHILDHOOD

1. List two nursing interventions for each of the three common problems of childhood.

2. Describe the impact of homelessness and violence on children.

3. Identify two nursing interventions for the child with anxiety.

4. Name four behaviors that are seen in children with attention-deficit hyperactivity disorder.

5. Explain the importance of early diagnosis of disruptive behavioral (conduct) disorders.

6. State three nursing actions for children with mental retardation.

7. Identify three types of learning disorders.

8. Describe the behaviors seen in children with pervasive developmental disorders.

9. List three general nursing interventions for children with mental health problems.

KEY TERMS

abuse
anxiety
attention-deficit hyperactivity
  disorder (ADHD)
autism
communication disorders
conduct disorders
development

dyslexia
encopresis
enuresis
growth
homelessness
learning disorder
mental retardation
neglect

pervasive developmental disorders
pica
posttraumatic stress disorder
  (PTSD)
schizophrenia
somatoform disorder
stuttering
victimization

Growth and development are a vital part of life. Each individual is involved in a lifelong process of learning and mastering life's developmental and situational tasks. Children develop with great speed and constantly changing mental, social, and emotional abilities.

Children develop at individual rates and may master the skills in one area of development while lagging in another. Behaviors considered normal in one age group become worrisome when they are seen at another age. Nurses who work with children must have an understanding of normal development and an awareness of the child's individual pace of growth and development.

This chapter presents an overview of normal growth and development patterns for children, the mental health problems that can arise during childhood, and nursing actions for the care of mentally, emotionally, and developmentally troubled children.

Many theories about the growth and development of children have been composed. Freud's theory of psychosexual development states that individuals grow and develop by taming their primitive libidinal (sexual, pleasurable) energies as they move through the stages of childhood. Piaget's theory of intellectual (cognitive) development states that growth is the ability to organize and integrate (put together) experiences. Erikson's theory explains the stages of an individual's psychosocial development. As a person moves through each stage of development, a core task or problem needs to be resolved before the person can successfully move on to the next stage. Each theory describes an aspect of a child's development.

Children are presented with the awesome task of developing their mental, physical, social, and emotional abilities at the same time. They must master skills that move them from complete dependence to full independent functioning in only a few short years. It is the responsibility of every nurse to nurture and foster the growth of their youngest clients—the children.

Normal Childhood Development

Growth is the increase in physical size. It can be measured in pounds, inches, kilograms, or centimeters. **Development** refers to the increasing ability in skills or functions. To illustrate, a child must first grow the muscles of the legs before he/she develops the ability to walk. Although each child grows and develops at an individual pace, each follows an organized and orderly pattern throughout the growth process.

Growth is a continuing process, and what happens during one stage of a person's life has an impact on that person in other stages of life. Recognizing the general patterns and principles of growth and development allows nurses to more accurately assess, assist, and guide young clients (see box on p. 191).

Development is the result of growth, learning, and maturation (the ability to combine growth and learning). Children with growth or learning problems may mature later than other children.

Development proceeds from simple to complex, from gross to fine, or from large to small. Physically, children learn to control the large muscles of their bodies first (walking, running), then move on to develop the finer movements (writing, reading). A child's reasoning is simple and uncomplicated until the nervous system develops the more complex organization required for abstract thinking. Social and emotional development also moves from simple to complex. The younger the child, the more simple the emotions and the ability to communicate.

The emotional development of children is an ongoing process. During each stage, the child must learn to solve a central problem. If the child solves the problem successfully, the basis is laid for the next stage of development. If the child is unable to cope with the central developmental problem (task), then mental health difficulties may arise.

The process of growth includes sensitive periods. During the growth process, children have certain times at which they are more affected by influences (positive or negative) in the environment. For example, during the first year, according to Erikson, the task of the infant is to find security in a primary caretaker and to begin socializing with others. Without a consistent adult caregiver during this period, the child is especially vulnerable to developing problems with trusting other people. Without nurturing, a child is ripe for developing mental health problems that may last a lifetime. The growth and development of children are assessed by specially designed screening tests and by comparing the child's activities and behaviors to various developmental charts.

Common Behavioral Problems of Childhood

All children have problems during each developmental stage. Some of the most common behavioral difficulties during the early years of childhood are colic, problems with feeding and sleeping, temper tantrums, and breath-holding spells.

Colic is a set of behaviors most commonly seen in middle-class infants. Severe and unrelenting periods of late-afternoon crying are first noticed when the infant is about 2 weeks old. The infant cries with

DEVELOPMENTAL AGE PERIODS

PRENATAL PERIOD: CONCEPTION TO BIRTH
Germinal: Conception to Approximately 2 Weeks
Embryonic: 2 to 8 Weeks
Fetal: 8 to 40 Weeks (Birth)
A rapid growth rate and total dependency make this one of the most crucial periods in the developmental process. The relationship between maternal health and certain manifestations in the newborn emphasizes the importance of adequate prenatal care to the health and well-being of the infant.

INFANCY PERIOD: BIRTH TO 12 OR 18 MONTHS
Neonatal: Birth to 28 Days
Infancy: 1 to Approximately 12 Months
The infancy period is one of rapid motor, cognitive, and social development. Through mutuality with the caregiver (parent), the infant establishes a basic trust in the world and the foundation for future interpersonal relationships. The critical first month of life, although part of the infancy period, is often differentiated from the remainder because of the major physical adjustments to extrauterine existence and the psychological adjustment of the parent.

EARLY CHILDHOOD: 1 TO 6 YEARS
Toddler: 1 to 3 Years
Preschool: 3 to 6 years
This period, which extends from the time the child attains upright locomotion until he/she enters school, is characterized by intense activity and discovery. it is a time of marked physical and person-
ality development. Motor development advances steadily. Children at this age acquire language and wider social relationships, learn role standards, gain self-control and mastery, develop increasing awareness of dependence and independence, and begin to develop a self-concept.

MIDDLE CHILDHOOD: 6 TO 11 OR 12 YEARS
Frequently referred to as the "school age," this period of development is one in which the child is directed away from the family group and is centered around the wider world of peer relationships. There is steady advancement in physical, mental, and social development with emphasis on developing skill competencies. Social cooperation and early moral development take on more importance with relevance for later life stages. This is a critical period in the development of a self-concept.

LATER CHILDHOOD: 11 TO 19 YEARS
Prepubertal: 10 to 13 Years
Adolescence: 13 to Approximately 18 Years
The tumultuous period of rapid maturation and change known as adolescence is considered to be a transitional period that begins at the onset of puberty and extends to the point of entry into the adult world—usually high school graduation. Biological and personality maturation are accompanied by physical and emotional turmoil, and there is redefining of the self-concept. In the late adolescent period the child begins to internalize all previously learned values and to focus on an individual, rather than a group, identity.

From Wong DL: *Whaley and Wong's nursing care of infants and children,* ed 5, St Louis, 1995, Mosby.

---

clenched fists and pained looks and refuses attempts by adults to soothe him/her. Behaviors usually peak around 2 to 3 months, but they can persist until the infant is 4 or 5 months old. A colicky infant is defined as a healthy and well-fed child who cries for more than 3 hours every day for more than 3 weeks (Wong, 1995). Interventions designed to calm both parents and child appear to help. Nurses can help parents manage colic by educating them about the normal characteristics of crying and helping them to recognize their infant's cues. Changing the feeding procedure and allowing adequate time for burping and cuddling helps to control symptoms.

Creating a quiet, restful environment and avoiding overhandling of the infant can be effective measures. Most children outgrow their colicky behavior by 5 months, but parents need a great deal of emotional support and encouragement during this stressful time.

Feeding disorders occur in two forms: overeating, which leads to obesity, and undereating, which leads to malnutrition. Infants may refuse to eat if the feeding experience is not pleasant. Young children who have had an unpleasant experience with food (being forced to eat or choking) may refuse to eat, or children may be engaged in a conflict (power play) with caregivers by refusing to eat. Children suffering from depression often refuse to eat, and adolescents may engage in destructive eating behaviors.

To effectively treat children with eating problems, a comprehensive history and physical examination are performed. The feeding interaction between caregiver and child is observed. When all organic (physical) causes are ruled out, a plan for altering the actions that lead to the difficulty is developed. Nurses assist in the therapeutic effort by educating and supporting family members and monitoring the child's progress with routine assessments of height, weight, and eating patterns.

Problems with *sleep* are common to many children and include night terrors, problems falling asleep, and nighttime awakenings. In the past, the usual course of action was for the parents to let children "cry it out" until they fell asleep.

Today, each child's sleeping characteristics are considered. The parents' expectations and fears are addressed, and treatment is designed to assist both parents and child in establishing a restful pattern of sleep.

Temper tantrums are a common expression of anger and frustration for children between 1 and 4 years of age. In fact, temper tantrums are seen in 50% to 80% of children in this age group (Hagerman, 1995). Typically, children will throw themselves to the floor, kicking and screaming. Sometimes they will hit, throw things, or hold their breath.

In the young child, temper tantrums are considered normal behavior. Children are attempting to master their environments and become frustrated when they are unable to achieve control. Tantrums become a problem when children use them to express more emotions than just frustration or when the tantrums occur so frequently that they disturb family functioning.

Remember, temper tantrums are the result of a loss of control. Most children feel a blow to their self-image, and some children are quite upset about the experience. Adults in the environment should remain calm during the tantrum. Nursing interventions for children who are having temper tantrums are listed in the box at right.

Mental Health Problems of Childhood

Each stage of life flows into the other. In reality, there are no clear divisions of time or development. Many of the mental-emotional problems diagnosed in adulthood find their roots in the experiences of childhood. In today's societies, "large numbers of children and adolescents with serious emotional or behavioral disorders receive either no mental health treatment or treatment inappropriate to their needs" (Collins and Collins, 1994). Nurses play an important role in the recognition and treatment of children's mental health problems because without the love and assistance of every one of us many children are doomed to failure.

The major mental health problems of childhood are grouped into seven categories (Table 14-1). People do not easily fit into categories. Individuals may be labeled with one diagnosis yet engage in behaviors that belong to another diagnostic category. Remember, each person is an individual. The diagnoses are less important than the persons themselves. The success of any treatment is measured by the improvements in

---

NURSING ACTIONS FOR CHILDREN WITH TEMPER TANTRUMS

PREVENT TANTRUMS
1. Childproof the environment: remove anything that the child is not allowed to touch. Fewer restrictions lessen the chances for conflict.
2. Present choices and options: allow the child to choose (within acceptable limits). Offer the opportunity to practice autonomy and mastery skills.

CONTROL TANTRUMS
1. When frustration increases, use distraction. Focus the child's attention on calmer activities and reward positive behaviors.
2. Protect the child during the tantrum. Do not allow a child to hurt himself/herself or others.
3. Do not abandon the child during the tantrum. Stay close, but do not intrude on his/her space.
4. Point out to the child that he/she is out of control. Do not react negatively or try to discipline the child. Praise him/her when he/she regains control.
5. Fight only those battles that must be won. The conflicts that serve no important purpose should be avoided. However, do not give into the demands that led to the tantrum.

AFTER THE TANTRUM
1. Do not hold a grudge or hold on to negative emotions. Recognize that the child probably feels worse than you do.
2. Keep reinforcing desired behaviors. Do not overreact to undesirable actions.

---

clients' behaviors. Treat each mental health client as a person. Respect them for who and what they are. Your efforts will be handsomely rewarded, especially with your younger clients.

Every child has a "mental health problem" sometime during the journey from infant to adult. Emotional difficulties arise during periods of change in one's life. The birth of a sibling or a move to a new city can disrupt a routine, create new demands, or make children more vulnerable. Stresses can push children to behave in worrisome ways, and peers can have influences that are not always desirable. How do parents know when the problems of their children are a part of the normal (and sometimes uncomfortable) process of growing up and when they are serious enough to require professional assistance? When a child demonstrates an absence of growth, a failure to change, or a retreat from the developmental tasks of his/her age group, then help should be sought.

Fig. 14-1 Many of the homeless are young mothers with young children. (Copyright © Cathy Lander-Goldberg, Lander Photographics.)

◆ TABLE 14-1 Categories of Mental Health Problems in Childhood	
Category	**Examples**
Environmental problems	Poverty, homelessness, child abuse, child neglect, violence
Problems with parent-child interactions	Primary caregiver dysfunction, parent-child conflict
Emotional problems	Anxiety, depression, somatoform disorders (physical signs/symptoms with psychological causes), posttraumatic stress disorder
Behavioral problems	Attention-deficit hyperactivity disorder, disruptive behavior (conduct) disorder, antisocial disorder
Eating or elimination problems	Anorexia, bulimia, enuresis, encopresis
Developmental problems	Mental retardation, learning disorders, communication disorders
Pervasive developmental disorders	Autism, childhood disintegrative disorder, schizophrenia

Environmental Problems

Many children must cope with more than just developmental tasks. For children who are poor, homeless, abused, or neglected, growing up can be difficult. Problems associated with environment can have a strong impact on mental health. Poverty, for example, influences the growth and development of children more than one would expect. In 1991, the U.S. Census Bureau reported that more than 20% of the nation's children—about 14.3 million—lived in poverty-stricken families (Bower, 1994). The rate of poverty for children in the United States is two to four times greater than those rates of Canada and Western Europe.

Poverty and mental health problems go hand in hand. By age 5, poor children scored much lower on IQ tests, and demonstrated higher rates of anxiety, unhappiness, and fearfulness (Rafferty and Shinn, 1991).

Programs like Head Start help prepare children for school and attempt to improve thinking, communication, and social skills, but more remains to be done if we are to prevent the many mental health problems that accompany the lack of an adequate income. Poverty is also a factor in other problems, such as homelessness, abuse, and neglect.

Homelessness

The lack of a permanent residence (**homelessness**) affects children in many ways (Fig. 14-1). Studies of homeless children (Rafferty and Shinn, 1991) revealed that homeless children had the following:

Very high infant mortality rates
Twice the normal incidence of illness and disease
Elevated lead levels in the blood
Hunger or routinely did not have enough to eat

Carol had come to us a very lost, exhausted, and spent young girl, dressed in tattered jeans and with sad, red eyes that seemed to cry every time she opened her mouth to talk to us.

For her first few weeks at Covenant House, we could not really get her to talk about herself . . . who she was, why she was here, where she came from, how we could help her. The only words she spoke were cried out unconsciously in her nightmares, which crept up on her while she was vulnerable and alone at night, unable to run away.

"You don't want to know about me," she would say. "It hurts too much," she would say. "I . . . I can't talk about it."

Finally though, one night after another nightmare, her lonely pain got to be too much, and she began to open up. She came from South Carolina, but she had to run away because both her parents beat her. "They were on drugs," she shrugged

while she told us. "I guess they couldn't help it," she said.

Frightened for her life, unable to stand the abuse any longer, she had run away to the city. Penniless and alone, she soon began to sell the only worldly possession she had that anyone cared about—her body.

Then one night she met "him." He was 70, like a grandfather. "He said he would take care of me. I was so alone. And those first few days were great. He gave me everything—money, clothes. He made me feel great. And then he started crawling in bed with me at night . . . and doing terrible things. He began to give me cocaine and stuff to make it easier. He . . . I . . . he used me . . . I had no place to go. And then he started to beat me too. . . ."

Carol was lucky. She found the people at Covenant House, a community of volunteers who are dedicated to working with homeless and runaway children.

Modified from McGeady MR: *"Does God still love me?": letters from the street,* New York, 1995, Sr Mary Rose McGeady.

Clinical Decision

1. In which behaviors did Carol engage to fulfill her basic needs?

Behavioral problems, developmental delays, speech delays, sleep disorders, and immature motor actions

Short attention spans, withdrawal, aggression, return to toddler behaviors

Inappropriate social interactions with adults and immature peer interactions

Homeless children are also more likely to have clinically significant levels of anxiety, depression, and behavioral disorders (Milburn and D'Ercole, 1991). The case study described in the box above is unfortunately all too common. For these reasons, nurses must learn about the lifestyles of their clients and families, use good communication skills, and remain nonjudgmental. Table 14-2 offers a few special guidelines for nurses who work with homeless clients of all ages.

Abuse and Neglect

A victim is defined as someone who has been caused harm. **Victimization** is the process of causing harm. **Abuse** is defined as causing harm to or maltreating another. **Neglect** is not meeting a child's basic needs for food, clothing, shelter, love,

and belonging. In our modern societies today, "children suffer more victimizations than do adults, including more conventional crime, more family violence, and some forms unique to children, such as family abduction" (Finkelhor and Dziuba-Leatherman, 1994).

Child abuse and neglect are hitting crisis levels. The problems of abuse and neglect are becoming "one of the biggest threats to the lives of infants and small children in America" (U.S. Advisory Board on Child Abuse and Neglect, 1995). The actual statistics are grim:

1. Five children die each day at the hand of their parents.
2. Deaths caused by abuse or neglect in children ages 4 and younger outnumber those from falls, car accidents, suffocation, drowning, or choking on food.
3. 18,000 children a year are permanently disabled by abusive caregivers.
4. 142,000 children suffer serious physical injuries at the hands of their parents or other caretakers.

The victimization of children comes in many forms. Physical abuse commonly presents with burns,

◆ **TABLE 14-2**
Special Nursing Actions for Homeless Clients

Topic	Nursing Actions
Psychological	Know your own feelings about homeless people.
	Approach clients with a positive attitude.
	Greet clients and communicate that they will be treated as people worthy of care and respect.
Client interview	Delay asking questions about occupation, address, next of kin, educational level until later in the interview.
	Promise that information is confidential.
	Ask simple, concrete questions:
	Where do you get your money?
	When did you have your last drink?
	Relate to homelessness in matter-of-fact way.
Health assessment	Educate as you assess.
	Assess children for signs of malnutrition, abuse, or neglect.
Discharge planning	Ask these questions:
	Do you understand what your problem is?
	How will you get your prescriptions filled?
	Where will you sleep tonight?
	Help client to keep follow-up appointments.
	Write down all instructions.

Modified from Hunter JK: *RN* 55(12):48, 1992.

bruises, fractures, or head and abdominal injuries. Sexually abused children have been violated through inappropriate contact or activities. Emotional or psychological abuse erodes children's self-esteem through rejection, criticism, isolation, or terrorism. Children also suffer from physical, emotional, and medical *neglect*—the failure to provide for these necessities.

Childhood abuse and neglect also has long-term effects. A recent study (Mukerjee, 1995) demonstrated that survivors of child abuse may have a smaller than normal hippocampus. (The hippocampus is a region of the brain that may be important in dealing with recent memory and possibly long-term memory.) Other research has found that the neurochemicals of the fight-flight mechanism are altered in children who are victimized (Glod, 1993). Today, a wide variety of behavioral disorders seen in adulthood is thought to be associated with childhood abuse.

Preventing and treating child abuse and neglect is the responsibility of every single health care provider, no matter what training or title. Education is a powerful first step. Programs such as Don't Shake the Baby (Showers, 1992) and Feeling Yes, Feeling No (Hazzard and others, 1991) have resulted in greater awareness of child abuse.

Helping the victims of child abuse requires nurses to look at their own feelings about abuse. Being ob-

jective and supportive can be difficult in some situations, but it is important. Many children are fortunate enough to have families that love, nurture, and guide them. For those who do not, life becomes a daily struggle for survival. Nurses are in positions to recognize abuse and help provide early intervention because the problems of our children are the problems of us all.

Problems With Parent-Child Interactions

A healthy family is one that is able to cope with most of its emotional problems and knows when to seek help. Every child faces emotional difficulties throughout childhood. Change creates many new demands for children and their parents. One of the most common parent-child problems is conflict. The other—primary care dysfunction—occurs less frequently but has profound effects.

Parent-Child Conflicts

Children require consistent guidance and unconditional acceptance. Relationships with their caregivers serve as a testing ground for figuring out right from wrong and for learning which behaviors result in reward and which result in punishment. Problems between children and parents are inevitable—they will occur. Conflicts can take the form of verbal arguments or silent power struggles. No child or parent will escape childhood without conflict; but when the conflicts are constant and worsen over time, mental health assistance should be sought.

Primary Caregiver Dysfunction

When a parent is unable to meet the caretaking or developmental needs of a child, a disturbance in the parent-child interaction exists. The parent in this situation is commonly a person who has had difficult times in the past with personal relationships, psychiatric disorders, or behavioral difficulties. Perhaps the pregnancy was unwanted or the child seems unresponsive. The child is frequently described by the caretaker as difficult, defective, or disappointing.

The signs/symptoms that suggest the possibility of primary caregiver dysfunction include feeding and sleeping problems, delays in development, failure to thrive, signs of inadequate physical care or abuse, frequent visits to the physician, and excessive parental worry. If they go unrecognized, the child may suffer from problems later in life. Treatment is focused on supporting and educating the parents. Nurses are in excellent positions to help parents develop more effective and appropriate child care skills. With aggressive intervention, the long-term outlook for the children of these parents improves.

Emotional Problems

Emotional problems occur in children when they cannot successfully cope with their situations. Emotional problems can range from anxiety to severe depression and suicide. Fortunately, most children are able to cope successfully with life's anxieties when they are emotionally nurtured and supported. This section focuses on the emotional problems of children that are most likely to be encountered by the practicing nurse in everyday treatment settings: anxiety, depression, somatoform disorders, and posttraumatic stress disorders.

Anxiety

Anxiety, the vague, uneasy feeling that occurs in response to a threat, is frequently seen in children. Most children experience fear and anxiety as a part of growing up. One of the most frequent anxieties of children is a fear of being separated from their parents. This fear is referred to as *separation anxiety,* and it is common in infants and toddlers. Eventually, the fear decreases as children broaden their worlds to include others. However, if a child is older than 4 years and

separation anxieties last for more than a few weeks, a serious problem may exist.

Anxiety-based school refusal or school avoidance is a behavioral pattern in which the child refuses to attend school because of symptoms of anxiety:

Fear of leaving home (separation anxiety)
Fear of being ridiculed or embarrassed at school (social phobia)
Fear of some aspect of school (school phobia)

The main goal of treatment for children with school-related anxiety is to help the child confront and overcome the anxiety by returning to school. Many times, health care providers work with school personnel and parents to develop a plan for returning the child to school in a supportive manner. Tricyclic antidepressants are sometimes prescribed for severe symptoms of anxiety or depression.

Most children's bouts of anxiety are relieved when they receive reassurance and emotional support. If a child's anxiety does not interfere with family, friends, or school, the child is handling it effectively. However, when the anxiety is so pronounced that it is impossible for the child to function, then help should be sought.

Depression

Mood disorders, such as depression, are increasing in children. The term *depression* is used to describe a symptom, an emotional state, and a clinical syndrome. It is now known that depression can occur in children and adolescents. Children who have one or more depressed parents are more likely to be depressed themselves. Depression is seen more frequently as children grow older, and it occurs equally in boys and girls.

The clinical findings, or signs/symptoms, of depression arise from "an intense, persistent state of unhappiness and misery that interferes with pleasure or productivity" (Clark, 1995). Behaviors associated with depression vary little with age. The clinical signs/symptoms of depression are discussed in Chapter 21.

Careful, gentle questioning of the child often reveals a child who is aware of his/her moods and emotions. Treatment is designed to relieve the child's discomforting symptoms and help those in the environment to respond to the child's needs. Nursing interventions focus on reducing the problems that are causing the depression and providing the child with the emotional support to cope effectively.

Somatoform Disorders

A **somatoform disorder** is one in which the child (or adult) has the signs/symptoms of illness or disease without a traceable physical cause. The person does not consciously take on the signs/symptoms; he/she truly feels ill. Signs/symptoms actually suggest a physical disorder, but no known physical cause can be found.

Children often complain of headaches, stomachaches, or pain. Somatic symptoms are not unusual in school-aged children. They are thought to be expressions of stress or underlying conflict. Sometimes the child's signs/symptoms resemble those seen in another family member. In most cases, when the stress is relieved, the child returns to a healthy level of functioning. Somatoform disorders are covered in greater depth in Chapter 22. Here it is important to remember that children with somatoform disorders need understanding and reassurance.

Posttraumatic Stress Disorder

When children are repeatedly exposed to or participate in acts of violence, their psyches take steps to emotionally protect them. **Posttraumatic stress disorder (PTSD)** usually develops following an extreme traumatic event that involves injury or threat to the child. The child feels intense helplessness, fear, or horror. In younger children, behaviors become agitated and disorganized. Traumatic events are repeatedly relived, and the child goes to great lengths to avoid anything associated with the trauma. The traumatic event is generalized into nightmares of monsters or threats to the self. The past is relived through playing out of events related to the trauma. Somatic complaints, such as stomachaches and other discomforts, may occur. Treatment and nursing care for PTSD is focused on early recognition and emotionally supportive care.

Behavioral Problems

Children experiment with a variety of behaviors to test the limits of their environments and the people within them. Every child goes through periods of misconduct: refusing to do as told, lying, cheating, stealing, bullying others. Most often, these behaviors decrease with time and consistent parental guidance. For some children, however, undesired behaviors become more difficult to manage. These children clash with friends and classmates. They may develop a reputation for being unruly bullies or, worse yet, dangerous. When a child's conduct becomes inappropriate over a period of time, a disruptive behavioral disorder is usually diagnosed. The two disruptive behavioral disorders most commonly encountered by general nurses are attention-deficit hyperactivity disorders and conduct disorders.

Attention-Deficit Hyperactivity Disorder

During the 1850s, a German nursery rhyme told the story of "Phillip," a bad boy who could not sit down. A century later, the children who exhibit Phillip's behaviors are diagnosed as having **attention-deficit hyperactivity disorder,** commonly called ADHD. ADHD is now the most commonly diagnosed mental health problem in childhood. It affects about 3% of American children, and its symptoms can persist into adulthood (Grinspoon, 1995). ADHD is seen more frequently in boys, with a ratio of about seven boys to one girl. Although ADHD was thought to be a problem of childhood, "research in the last 20 years has shown that it is also a disorder of adolescents and adults" (Grinspoon, 1995).

ADHDs are not a single, distinct pathological condition. They are actually a syndrome, a cluster of behaviors relating to inattention and impulsive actions. The box on p. 198, at left, lists the diagnostic criteria for ADHD.

Within the ADHD category, a variety of subgroups exist: ADHD with learning disabilities, ADHD without hyperactivity, ADHD with speech disorders, ADHD with other psychiatric disorders, and ADHD with disorders of brain function. However, the importance does not lie in the diagnostic label placed on the child but in the love and guidance of the adults in his/her life.

There are two common clinical histories for children with ADHD. The first is the child who has been "fussy" or "a difficult child" from birth. As infants, they were difficult to soothe, and they have behaved impulsively as far back as family members can recollect. They are remembered as being "a handful." The second type of child is referred to as an "immature child" who displays silliness, distractibility (short attention span), restlessness, and clumsiness. Both types of children have problems with behavioral self-control, hyperactivity, relating to others, and focusing their attention. On entry into school, children with ADHD have difficulty in completing their schoolwork because they are so easily distracted. They are almost always academic underachievers. Research into the intellectual performance of children with ADHD (Farone and others, 1993) revealed that ADHD children are more likely to have learning disabilities, repeat a grade in school, or be placed in a special class for remedial tutoring. They may also have problems making friends because of their excitable and impulsive behaviors. Almost half the children with ADHD show symptoms of anxiety, aggression, depression, and resistance to any authority.

Treatment for children with ADHD requires a multidisciplinary approach (Murphy and Hagerman,

DIAGNOSTIC CRITERIA FOR ATTENTION-DEFICIT HYPERACTIVITY DISORDER

NOTE: Consider a criterion met only if the behavior is considerably more frequent than that of most people of the same mental age.

A. A disturbance of at least 6 months during which at least eight of the following are present:

1. Often fidgets with hands or feet or squirms in seat (in adolescents, may be limited to subjective feelings of restlessness)
2. Has difficulty remaining seated when required to do so
3. Is easily distracted by extraneous stimuli
4. Has difficulty awaiting turn in games or group situations
5. Often blurts out answers to questions before they have been completed
6. Has difficulty following through on instructions from others (not due to oppositional behavior or failure of comprehension) (e.g., fails to finish chores)
7. Has difficulty sustaining attention in tasks or play activities
8. Often shifts from one uncompleted activity to another
9. Has difficulty playing quietly
10. Often talks excessively
11. Often interrupts or intrudes on others (e.g., butts into other children's games)
12. Often does not seem to listen to what is being said to him/her
13. Often loses things necessary for tasks or activities at school or at home (e.g., toys, pencils, books, assignments)
14. Often engages in physically dangerous activities without considering possible consequences (not for the purpose of thrill-seeking) (e.g., runs into street without looking)

B. Onset before the age of 7 years
C. Does not meet the criteria for a pervasive developmental disorder

Modified from Wong DL: *Whaley and Wong's nursing care of infants and children*, ed 5, St Louis, 1995, Mosby.

DRUG ALERT

Psychotherapeutic medications are powerful chemicals. When prescribed for children, parents must be taught to routinely monitor for side effects, adverse reactions, or any unwanted effect. Nurses have an important responsibility to make sure that parents are aware of each unwanted reaction and willing to monitor the child throughout the period he/she is receiving psychotherapeutic drugs.

and reward the child for appropriate behaviors. In cases in which the child is receiving drug therapy (e.g., stimulants, antidepressants, and clonidine), nurses must carefully monitor each child's response to the medications (see box above).

Disruptive Behavioral (Conduct) Disorder

Misconduct is common in every child, but when a persistent pattern of unacceptable behaviors is present, a conduct or disruptive behavioral disorder is established. Children with **conduct disorders** are defiant of authority. They engage in aggressive actions toward other people, refuse to follow society's rules and norms, and violate the rights of others. Many come from broken homes and backgrounds of violence, drug abuse, alcoholism, poverty, and lack of consistent caregivers.

The typical picture (signs/symptoms) of a child with a conduct disorder is described as a boy with social and academic problems, truancy, and failure in school. He is defiant of authority and often engages in temper tantrums, running away, and fighting. Treatment focuses on providing a stable environment and consistent, enforced limits. Associated neurological, educational, or psychiatric problems are also treated. The long-term outlook for children with conduct disorders is poor if the problems are present before the child is 10 years old or antisocial behavior is displayed by the adults in the environment. Nearly half these children grow up to have antisocial or conduct disorders in adulthood. This makes early diagnosis and treatment very important if these children are to become productive members of society.

Problems With Eating and Elimination

The most common mental health problems seen in children that relate to eating are feeding disorders, pica, anorexia nervosa, and bulimia. Disorders of elimination include encopresis and enuresis. Anorexia

1992). Families are educated about the problem, and many children receive special education. Positive reinforcement programs help children choose more socially appropriate behaviors and reduce impulsive actions. Nursing interventions for children with ADHD focus on providing a consistent, structured therapeutic approach. Nurses must be prepared to set limits on clients' behaviors and then be consistently willing to enforce them. They should also strive to acknowledge nervosa and bulimia are most often encountered in adolescents and are discussed in the next chapter.

Eating Disorders

Children with eating disorders either do not eat enough or they eat the wrong things. The diagnostic category of *feeding and eating disorders of infancy or early childhood* describes children who routinely fail to eat adequately. Weight loss or a failure to gain weight for at least 1 month in a child with no gastrointestinal tract problems is the most significant sign. Food is available, but the child does not eat. Most feeding disorders occur in children under 1 year, but they are seen in some 2- and 3-year-olds. The long-term complications are malnutrition and delays in development.

Feeding disorders can result from repeated unsuccessful attempts to feed an irritable infant. Infants may be difficult to console, apathetic, or withdrawn during feedings. In some cases, faulty parent-child interactions, anxiety, or poor feeding techniques add to the problem. Some infants may have difficulty regulating their nervous systems, resulting in altered periods of alertness. Other factors associated with feeding disorders are parental mental health problems, abuse, and neglect.

Treatment focuses on ruling out any physical cause, teaching parents appropriate feeding techniques, and monitoring the child's weight and developmental gains. In some cases, family therapy is helpful.

Pica is the term used to describe persistent eating of nonfood items for a period of more than 1 month. The nonfood items chosen seem to vary with age. Infants and younger children will typically eat paint, hair, string, plaster, or cloth. Older children may eat sand, pebbles, insects, animal droppings, or leaves; adults may consume clay, soil, or laundry starch. Pica is often seen in children with mental retardation and pervasive developmental disorders (e.g., autism). Treatment includes ruling out any physical problems, such as vitamin or mineral deficiencies; removing the item from the child; and helping the child to replace the unacceptable items with more acceptable foods.

Elimination Disorders

The two most common elimination problems of childhood are enuresis and encopresis.

Enuresis is the involuntary urinary incontinence of a child 5 years or older. Enuresis is divided into three categories: primary nocturnal enuresis (wetting the bed at night), diurnal enuresis (daytime wetting), and secondary enuresis (develops after child has achieved bladder control for a period of time).

Primary nocturnal enuresis is common in children. It occurs three times more frequently in boys and of-

ten disappears without intervention. The actual cause of nighttime wetting is not known, but it is believed that a developmental delay in the sleep-wake mechanism or bladder capacity of the child may be a factor.

Daytime (diurnal) wetting is less common. It is usually seen in shy, timid children or those with ADHDs. Daytime wetting occurs equally between boys and girls. An estimated 60% to 80% also wet the bed at night.

Secondary enuresis develops when a bladder-trained child becomes incontinent. Usually it follows a stressful event, such as the birth of a sibling or a divorce. Both diurnal and secondary enuresis are associated with high levels of emotional stress, anxiety, and mental health problems.

Treatment for children with enuresis ranges from simple reassurance to various mental health therapies. Nurses can help parents cope by obtaining an accurate history of the child's problems, helping parents to establish a bedtime routine for the child, and providing emotional support. When mental health therapy is required, the focus is helping the child verbally express the feelings associated with the symptoms.

Encopresis is fecal incontinence in a child over 4 years of age with no physical abnormalities. It is defined as "the repeated, usually voluntary, passage of feces in inappropriate places" (Clark, 1995). It affects boys four times more than girls and is rarely seen in adolescence. After any physical digestive problems are ruled out, treatment focuses on establishing a routine bowel care program. Praising the child for continent periods and having him/her assume the responsibility for rinsing the soiled clothing is often effective. Children who show little concern or distress about their incontinence are more difficult to treat.

Developmental Problems

Children develop by mastering increasingly more difficult and complex tasks. Because each child is unique, some lags in certain areas of development are common and to be expected. However, if the child persistently falls behind in a developmental area, a disorder of intellectual functioning, learning, or communication is suspected. The developmental problems most often seen by nurses include mental retardation, various learning disorders, and several types of communication disorders.

Mental Retardation

Children who function significantly below the average intellectual level for their age group and are limited in their abilities to function are said to be mentally retarded. The diagnosis of **mental retardation** is a powerful label, too often applied in haste. For a child to be considered retarded, he/she must have problems functioning in two areas: general intellectual functioning and adaptive functioning.

The degree of intellectual functioning is established by having the child complete one or more standard intelligence (IQ) tests. Children who repeatedly score lower than 70 are defined as retarded. The more important measure is the child's adaptive functioning: how well the child copes with the demands of life. It includes the skill areas relating to self-care, home living, communication, social skills, use of community resources, academic skills, self-direction, and the child's work, leisure, safety, and health activities (Table 14-3).

Children with mental retardation problems are first assessed to find any possible causes. For 30% to 40% of all children, no clear cause can be found. Heredity, fetal development, problems of pregnancy or infancy, and environmental influences are thought to be related factors. Treatment is individually developed and focuses on encouraging the child to function at the highest levels possible. Nursing interventions (actions) focus on meeting the child's basic needs, providing a safe environment, and encouraging the development of life skills.

Learning Disorders

Formally called academic skills disorders, the category for problems with learning is broad. A **learning disorder** is diagnosed when a child's achievement on standard reading, mathematics, or written tests routinely falls below the results of other children in the same age and grade groups. Learning disorders can affect the child's thinking, reading, writing, calculation, spelling, and listening abilities.

Approximately 5% of children in the U.S. public school system have learning disabilities (American Psychiatric Association, 1994). Children with learning disabilities often feel low self-esteem and lack the social skills of other children. Many become discouraged and drop out of school early. Although no specific cause has been found for learning disorders, they have been associated with conditions such as fetal alcohol syndrome, lead poisoning, and fragile X syndrome (a genetic problem). Learning disorders are diagnosed only after the child has been assessed for hearing, speech, and visual problems. Cultural influences are also considered. A child is said to have a learning disorder only if the specific problem interferes with academic achievement or the activities of daily living.

Reading disorders are commonly diagnosed in boys, but the actual incidence is about the same for girls. Children with a reading disorder may have problems reading, understanding the written word, or reading out loud. Children and adults who have **dyslexia** have problems with reading because although they can see and recognize letters, they have difficulty integrating visual information and thus they tend to twist, substitute, distort, or omit many words. Reading is slow and sometimes difficult to under-

---

◆ TABLE 14-3
Classification of Mental Retardation Levels

Mild (85% Incidence)	Moderate (10% Incidence)	Severe (3%-4% Incidence)	Profound (2% Incidence)
Develops social and communication skills; has academic skills to sixth-grade level; has skills adequate for self-support; may need supervision and guidance but is able to successfully live in community	Develops communication skills; has academic skills to second-grade level; profits from vocational training; can attend to personal care with supervision; can work in sheltered setting or do semiskilled work in community under supervision; adapts well to community life in supervised environments	May learn to talk and do basic self-care skills; can learn key "survival" words (e.g., stop, bus, police); performs simple tasks with close supervision; adapts well to life with families or group homes	Exhibits associated neurological conditions, delays in development; has impaired sensorimotor function; is unable to care for self independently; may improve in highly structured environment; will always require sheltered environment with close supervision

Modified from American Psychiatric Association: *Diagnostic and statistical manual of mental disorders,* ed 4, Washington, DC, 1994, The Association.

stand for children with reading disorders. Children are seldom diagnosed before they have received several years of reading instruction in school. Early intervention is important. Special education often results in great improvement. Reading disorders may follow the child into adult life.

Many learning disorders are seen in children with ADHD. Other children with learning disabilities are quiet and hypoactive. They are frequently overlooked because of their quiet manners or are mistaken for being retarded. Most children with learning disabilities respond well to special education classes and encouragement.

Communication Disorders

In children, the most common **communication disorders** relate to problems with expression, receiving messages, the pronunciation of words, and stuttering. Communication disorders may be the result of neurological or other medical conditions, but most often the cause is unknown.

Problems with language are usually seen in children around age 3. The child may fail to use expected speech sounds for his/her age group (phonological disorder); speak at a rapid or slow rate, with strange rhythms and word use (expressive language disorder); or have a disturbance in the pattern of speech in which sounds are frequently repeated (**stuttering**). Each is considered a disorder only if the problem interferes with the child's activities of daily living or ability to academically achieve.

Children with developmental problems must struggle more than other children. They need love, patience, and encouragement on a daily basis. Too often, adults in their environments (including nurses) fall into the "label trap" and condemn these children to performing at levels far below their actual abilities. Nurses must remember that working with developmentally different children comes with a commitment to help them become the best that they can be.

Pervasive Developmental Disorders

The word *pervasive* is defined as a tendency to spread throughout. When applied to mental health, the word means that a problem is severe enough to affect several areas of functioning. Children who are suffering from **pervasive developmental disorders** have difficulty with social interaction skills, communication skills, and learning. Their behavior is definitely different from that of other children of the same age and developmental level. Actual causes for these disorders remain unknown, but they are often seen in combination with mental retardation, congenital in-

fections, and abnormal central nervous system functions.

Pervasive developmental disorders include the following:

Autism, a disorder of communication, social interactions, and behavior

Rett syndrome, the development of motor, language, and social problems and loss of previous skills that occurs between 5 months and 2 years of age

Asperger's syndrome, severe and long-lasting impairments in social interactions with repeated patterns of behavior

Childhood disintegrative disorder, which is defined as a period of severe regression in many areas following 2 years of normal development

Rett syndrome and childhood disintegrative disorder appear after a period of normal functioning, whereas autism and Asperger's syndrome are present in infancy. Autism is the most often encountered pervasive developmental disorder of childhood. It shares many of the same characteristics with the other listed disorders and serves as an example for learning about the behaviors of children with pervasive developmental disorders.

Autism

Autism is not a disease but a syndrome of associated behaviors. It results from some condition that affects the development of the nervous system, and it remains with the individual throughout life (Mays and Gillon, 1993). Autism is diagnosed when the child has serious problems with social interactions, verbal and nonverbal communication, and use of imagination and demonstrates a markedly restricted scope of activities and interests.

The onset of autistic signs and symptoms begins in infancy or early childhood. Autistic disorders affect children from all classes and groups. Typically, autism is seen four times more frequently in boys. The majority of autistic children measure low on IQ tests, with 60% measuring below an IQ of 50. Motor skill development may be good, but the child's use of motor skills is inappropriate. Many autistic children become functioning adults, whereas others are totally dependent for care. Children who are able to develop language skills before the age of 5 years have better outcomes. If the child has seizures around puberty, the outlook for improvement is generally poorer.

No single behavior or symptom is diagnostic of autism. Behaviors must be considered in relation to the whole child and his/her functioning. Monitoring children's early social responses, communication skills, and behaviors allows health care providers to intervene early when a problem is suspected.

The outstanding feature of autism is its deviance and its different behaviors. Autistic children's behaviors are not normal or average. They tend to use persons in the environment like objects; they are unable to imitate others or make social contact. Play is frequently inappropriate, with throwing of toys or ritual lining up of objects. Other characteristics of autistic disorder include abnormal speech and communications, abnormal play activities, preoccupation with certain objects and routines, restricted body movements, and a very narrow range of interests.

Nurses who work with children must become keen observers and careful history takers. Parents should be questioned about the child's birth, developmental history, social responses, and communications. The picture of an autistic child begins to emerge when it is learned that the child does not act appropriately for his/her mental age, even with family members and other familiar persons.

Once the disorder is suspected, the child receives a complete physical examination to rule out any condition that may be affecting the central nervous system. The child is then referred to a treatment team that specializes in treating children with autistic problems. Parents are encouraged to work with physicians, nurses, several types of therapists, and special educators. A program is then designed to meet the individual child's unique needs. Then parents, child, and treatment team work together for each small gain in functioning.

Schizophrenia

Schizophrenia is a condition associated with disturbing thought patterns and a distorted reality. Considerable disagreement exists about the onset of schizophrenia in childhood. Schizophrenia usually develops during late adolescence or early adulthood, but it has been seen in children. Recent research has demonstrated that schizophrenic children may have attention and memory problems that interfere with their ability to carry information into the short-term or working memory. As a result, many are unable to monitor the responses of other people. They interact and respond with illogical or disconnected statements.

The signs, symptoms, and behaviors of children with schizophrenia vary widely, but the core disturbance lies in a lack of contact with reality and the child's retreat into his/her own world. The more common behaviors seen in children with schizophrenia include bizarre movements; alternating periods of hypoactivity and hyperactivity; inappropriate affect, language, and use of body; distorted sense of time; treating self and others as nonhuman; compulsions; phobias; and temper tantrums.

Nursing Actions

Nursing interventions for children with mental health problems are first directed toward early identification and treatment. Nurses fill a valuable role by performing health screening and routine examinations for healthy children in a variety of settings (Table 14-4).

Once a disorder is diagnosed, special treatment programs and specific goals are developed for each child. Nurses are responsible for routinely assessing and monitoring the child's progress toward meeting each goal. In addition, they provide the emotional support and encouragement that is much needed by the parents and other family members.

The nursing care for each child is special and is

◆ **TABLE 14-4**
Pediatric Mental Health Screening Tool

Assessment	Subject
Childhood history	Ambulation, behavior problems, bowel and bladder training/habits, communication (problems in speech or learning), discipline, eating habits, playmates (social interactions), psychiatric history (treatments, medications, suicide potential), school (reactions, experiences), sleep habits, unusual illnesses or injuries, current problem (with description of events that led to current situation)
Family history	Current household (members, relationship to child), mother and father, type of family (birth, blended, adopted, foster), mental health history of family (e.g., drug, alcohol use, arguments, violence, suicide attempts)
Mental status examination	General appearance, communication, emotion (mood, affect), intellectual level, orientation, thought processes

based on individual needs. Nursing diagnoses for children with mental health problems are listed in the box below. Nursing actions for children with mental health problems are basically focused on providing holistic care within an environment that fosters growth and development. The box on p. 204 offers an example of a client care plan for a child with mental retardation. General nursing interventions are focused on meeting basic needs, providing opportunities, and encouraging self-care activities.

Meet Basic Needs

Meeting the child's basic physical needs can range from a gentle reminder to providing total personal care. Nurses are responsible for making sure the child adequately eats, sleeps, and eliminates. They must also ensure that the child's level of personal cleanliness is appropriate. Helping a child to meet his/her basic needs includes the provision of love and acceptance, no matter how unusual or odd the behaviors. Many children with mental health problems have a special need to be nurtured, and sometimes nurses are the only persons in the child's environment who provide that energy.

Provide Opportunities

Even the most profoundly retarded or mentally troubled child will achieve if given the opportunity, instruction, and support. Do not allow yourself to be limited by a label or a diagnostic category. Each mentally troubled child *is* capable of something. Encourage young clients to grow and to reach for higher levels of function. Provide opportunities for small successes, which encourage everyone (especially the child) to strive for more.

Encourage Self-Care and Independence

Mentally troubled children grow and develop just as ordinary children do. Despite their problems, many become productive adults, able to live successfully within their communities.

Nurses who work with these children help them learn the important skills of daily living. Daily hygiene skills, such as how to dress, bathe, brush teeth, and comb hair are taught and reinforced by nurses. Nurses coordinate with teachers, occupational therapists, and physical therapists to help teach the more complex skills of living, such as how to take a bus, spend money, or pay bills. Many of these children will not be able to engage in the more complicated activities of daily life, but each child deserves the encouragement to function as independently as possible.

Caring for children with mental health problems is challenging work, but the rewards are many and worth the efforts. Our children are our priceless gifts to the future, and even the most troubled deserve our best efforts.

MENTAL HEALTH NURSING DIAGNOSES FOR CHILDREN

Adjustment, impaired
Anxiety
Body image disturbance
Communication, impaired verbal
Coping, defensive
Coping, ineffective family
Coping, ineffective individual
Denial
Environment, impaired
Family process, altered
Fear
Growth and development, altered
Health maintenance, altered
Hopelessness
Infant behavior, disorganized
Infant feeding pattern, ineffective
Injury, risk for
Knowledge deficit
Loneliness, risk for
Nutrition, altered
Parent/infant/child attachment, altered
Parental role conflict
Parenting, altered, risk for
Personal identity disturbance
Posttrauma response
Powerlessness
Protection, altered
Rape-trauma syndrome
Self-care deficit

❖ KEY CONCEPTS

- Nurses and other health care providers who work with children must have an understanding of normal development and an awareness of the child's individual pace of growth and development.

- Common behavioral difficulties during the early years of childhood are colic, problems with feeding and sleeping, temper tantrums, and breath-holding spells.

- Many children must cope with the mental health problems that are a result of poverty, homelessness, abuse, or neglect.

- Primary caregiver dysfunction is diagnosed when a parent is unable to meet the caretaking or developmental needs of a child.

- The most common emotional problems of children include anxiety, depression, somatoform disorders, and posttraumatic stress disorders.

SAMPLE CLIENT CARE PLAN

MENTAL RETARDATION

Assessment

History: BJ is a 6-year-old boy with moderate mental retardation. His birth and the first 6 months of life were uneventful. At 7 months, BJ contracted "a virus" and since then has shown little developmental progress.

Current Findings: A slightly overweight 6-year-old boy who is screaming uncontrollably at the time of interview. Mother reports that BJ is able to speak but prefers to communicate by pointing at the desired object and grunting. When needs are not immediately met, BJ begins to scream in shrill voice. He feeds himself finger foods but refuses to use a spoon. He is not bowel or bladder trained and follows no daily routine at home. Eating and sleeping routines are nonexistent.

Nursing Diagnosis

Altered growth and development related to physical dysfunctions as evidenced by impaired developmental abilities

Planning/Expected Outcomes

BJ will develop a daily routine for eating, sleeping, and activities by October 2.

Nursing Interventions

Intervention

1. Supervise closely for first 7 days on unit.

2. Approach BJ in a calm, peaceful manner.
3. Introduce no more than two new people into the environment per week.
4. Establish a daily routine for food, naps, activity.

5. Name each object that BJ points to and encourage him to repeat the name.
6. Assist with personal care as needed; praise for any attempt at self-care.

Rationale

1. Helps assess strengths, capabilities, areas for intervention.
2. Promotes self-esteem, decreases anxieties.
3. Decreases anxiety, provides security, keeps pace at BJ's tolerance level.
4. Prevents anxiety, provides security. BJ performs better when he knows what to expect.
5. Encourages the use of speech and control over environment.
6. Promotes comfort, acceptance. Praise encourages further attempts at self-care.

Evaluation

By the tenth day in the unit, BJ was able to follow a simple daily routine with frequent coaching. Sleep at night progressed from 3-hour periods to 9-hour periods.

- The two disruptive behavioral disorders most commonly encountered by general nurses are attention-deficit hyperactivity disorders and conduct disorders.
- The most common pediatric mental health problems that relate to eating are feeding disorders, pica, anorexia nervosa, and bulimia.
- Disorders of elimination include encopresis and enuresis.

- The developmental problems most often seen by nurses include mental retardation, various learning disorders, and several types of communication disorders.
- Children who are suffering from pervasive developmental disorders have serious problems with social interaction skills, communication skills, and learning.
- Autism is diagnosed when the child has serious prob-

lems with social interactions, verbal and nonverbal communication, the use of imagination, and a markedly restricted scope of activities and interests.

- The signs, symptoms, and behaviors of children with schizophrenia vary widely, but the core disturbance lies in a lack of contact with reality and the child's retreat into his/her own world.

- Nursing actions for children with mental health problems are basically focused on providing holistic care within an environment that fosters each child's growth and development.

- General nursing interventions include meeting basic physical and emotional needs, providing opportunities for each child to grow and develop, and encouraging self-care activities.

❖ SUGGESTIONS FOR FURTHER READING

Read your local newspaper for 1 week. Note the articles relating to children. What picture do you get of children in your community?

❖ REFERENCES

American Psychiatric Association: *Diagnostic and statistical manual of mental disorders*, ed 4, Washington, DC, 1994, The Association.

Bower B: Schizophrenic kids' memory muddle, *Sci News* 141(21):351, 1994.

Clark RB: Psychosocial aspects of pediatrics and psychiatric disorders. In Hay WH and others, editors: *Current pediatric diagnosis and treatment*, ed 12, Norwalk, CT, 1995, Appleton & Lange.

Collins BG, Collins TM: Child and adolescent mental health: building a system of care, *J Counsel Dev* 72(3):239, 1994.

Farone SV and others: Intellectual performance and school failure in children with attention deficit hyperactivity disorder and their siblings, *J Abnorm Psychol* 102(4):616, 1993.

Finkelhor D, Dziuba-Leatherman J: Victimization of children, *Am Psychol* 49(3):173, 1994.

Glod CA: Long-term consequences of childhood physical and sexual abuse, *Arch Psychiatr Nurs* 7(3):163, 1993.

Grinspoon L: Attention deficit disorder—part 1, *Harvard Ment Health Lett* 11(10):1, 1995.

Hagerman RJ: Growth and development. In Hay WH and others, *Current pediatric diagnosis and treatment*, ed 12, Norwalk, CT, 1995, Appleton & Lange.

Hazzard A and others: Child sexual abuse prevention: evaluation and one-year follow-up, *Child Abuse Negl* 15:123, 1991.

Mays RM, Gillon JE: Autism in young children: an update, *J Pediatr Health Care* 17(1):17, 1993.

McGeady MR: *"Does God still love me?": letters from the street*, New York, 1995, Sr Mary Rose McGeady.

Milburn N, D'Ercole A: Homeless women, children, and families, *Am Psychol* 46(11),1159, 1991.

Mukerjee M: Hidden scars: sexual and other abuse may alter a brain region, *Sci Am* 273(4):14, 1995.

Murphy MA, Hagerman RJ: Attention deficit hyperactivity disorder in children: diagnosis, treatment, and follow-up, *J Pediatr Health Care* 16(1):2, 1992.

Rafferty Y, Shinn M: The impact of homelessness on children, *Am Psychol* 46(11):1170, 1991.

Showers J: "Don't shake the baby": the effectiveness of a prevention program, *Child Abuse Negl* (16):11, 1992.

U.S. Advisory Board on Child Abuse and Neglect, April 26, 1995.

Wong DL: *Whaley and Wong's nursing care of infants and children*, ed 5, St Louis, 1995, Mosby.

15

PROBLEMS OF ADOLESCENCE

1. Describe three common problems of adolescence.

2. Discuss three problems faced by adolescents with troubled family lives.

3. Identify the diagnostic criteria for behavioral disorders.

4. Explain how the signs/symptoms of adolescent depression differ from those seen in adult depression.

5. Define two eating disorders and describe the signs/symptoms and behaviors associated with each.

6. Describe the stages of chemical dependency in adolescence.

7. List four signs/symptoms indicating a teen may be thinking about suicide.

8. Identify four nursing interventions designed specifically for adolescent clients.

9. Explain how nurses and other health care providers help adolescents develop effective skills.

KEY TERMS

adolescence
adolescent suicide
anorexia nervosa
bulimia
chemical dependency
gang

introspection
maturation
obesity
peer group
personality disorder
puberty

schizophrenia
sexual disorders
substance abuse
surveillance

The period in one's life known as **adolescence** is a time of great change. "Generally, adolescence begins at age 11-12 years and ends between 18 and 21" (Kaplan and Mammel, 1994). Physical and sexual growth are usually complete by 16 to 18 years of age, but in Western societies "the adolescence period is prolonged to allow for further psychosocial development before the young person assumes adult responsibilities" (Kaplan and Mammel, 1994). Because the adolescent period includes the time between 13 and 19 years of age, adolescents are also called teenagers or teens.

All adolescents share the same growth and developmental processes, but each person's society and culture strongly influence that process of "growing up" (see box at right).

Adolescents and young adults make up almost 15% of the population in the United States. Data from the 1990 census revealed 17.9 million adolescents (15 to 19 years of age) and 19.1 million young adults (20 to 24 years of age) live in the United States today (Kaplan and Mammel, 1994).

Adolescent Growth and Development

The journey from childhood to adult is a time of physical and psychosocial growth. Adolescents undergo great changes in the physical, intellectual, emotional, social, and spiritual areas of their lives. Nurses, as well as other adults, must understand how adolescents grow and change if they are to assist them through this important developmental stage because many adult problems find their roots in adolescence.

Physical Development

Growth in the physical domain during adolescence occurs in two general areas: (1) physical maturation and (2) sexual development.

Maturation is the process of attaining complete development (Wong, 1995). Physical maturation is the process of developing an adult body. Many physical changes occur during adolescence. Weight and height increase. Muscles grow. The major organs of the body double in size. The voice changes.

Adolescence is also a time for sexual development. As changing bodies begin to secrete certain hormones known as gonadotropins, the process of puberty is begun. **Puberty** is defined as the stage during which an individual becomes physically capable of reproduction. It begins with a 24- to 36-month growth spurt around 9 years and ends at approximately 18 years.

With girls, puberty begins between 8 and 14 years of age. Today, the average girl in the United States ex-

CULTURAL ASPECTS

Researchers at the University of Michigan assessed the frequency of stressed and anxious feelings in over 4000 U.S., Taiwanese, and Japanese teenagers and found some interesting results. Japanese adolescents were found to have the fewest reports of physical problems and depressed moods, whereas Taiwanese teens displayed the opposite (more physical complaints and depressed moods). Students in the United States and Taiwan thought of school as a source of stress, but only U.S. teens mentioned out-of-school activities and sports as sources of stress. Japanese teens felt that their peers served as a greater source of stress.

Parents in the United States expected lower academic performances of their teens than the parents of Japanese and Taiwanese adolescents. Doing well in school was more supported and encouraged by the families and peers of Asian teenagers. High achievers in the United States reported that they were frequently torn between their desires to put extra time into their studies and to follow other, nonacademic activities, such as dating, working, playing sports, and socializing.

periences the puberty growth spurt around 9 years of age and begins to menstruate (menarche) at about 12 years and 9 months, although menarche may begin as early as 10 or as late as 16 years of age. Breast development, body fat distribution, and the other physical changes that prepare the teen's body for adulthood are usually complete by ages 16 to 18 years.

Boys develop more slowly. The first signs of puberty are seen in boys around ages 10 to 12 years. The testicles enlarge, pubic hair develops, and the penis increases in length and width. The male growth spurt begins at age 11 and continues until about 14. Puberty lasts until about 18 years of age for most boys, but most male adolescents are capable of fathering children as early as 12 years old.

Puberty is a time of many changes for both boys and girls. For a more thorough review of the growth and development of adolescents, you are encouraged to consult a text on pediatric nursing.

Psychosocial Development

The term *psychosocial* refers to the nonphysical realms or areas of human functioning. Adolescents experience many changes in each area of functioning during their passage into adulthood. There are periods in teenagers' lives when they feel awkward, inadequate, and unworthy. Adults who are aware of these changes are better able to offer the emotional support and acceptance so needed by an adolescent. This section briefly explores the major developmental tasks for each psychosocial area of functioning.

Intellectual changes (cognitive development) involve learning to use abstract thinking (Hagerman, 1994). Children's thinking is concrete, that is, based on what is observed or experienced in the present time. Young adolescents (10 to 13 years) have trouble thinking realistically about the future. However, as teens grow, their thinking moves from what is actually present and real (concrete) to the future and what is possible. They begin to look at the world in new and exciting ways, to think beyond the present time, to consider a sequence of events or relationships, and to solve problems through the use of scientific reasoning and logic.

By the middle teens (14 to 17 years), abstract thinking is well entrenched. The ability to think abstractly also arrives with a feeling of power and self-centeredness. Many believe that they can change the world by just thinking about it. About 17 years of age, teens' abstract thinking becomes more realistic and they are able to plan reachable actions, goals, and careers.

Emotional development during adolescence is marked by rapid periods of change and adjustment. By 10 to 13 years of age, the emotional stability of childhood is replaced with a preoccupation about bodily changes. Changes in the physical area bring about changes in self-esteem, body image, and self-concept, which are confusing to the adolescent. Behaviors move from the pleasant, cooperative child to the moody, unpredictable, and emotional teenager.

Emotionally, early adolescence is marked by rapid shifts between disturbed behavior and relative calm. Moods swing from upbeat and happy to withdrawn and depressed. Emotional reactions to small events can trigger outbursts of acting out and aggressive behavior. Adolescents also daydream much of the time. Because of this daydreaming, they often miss many of the messages from other people within their environments and become labeled as sullen or withdrawn.

The emotions and mood swings of puberty become intense when teenagers are between 14 to 17 years of age. Teens at this age tend to stay alone, looking at themselves and how they fit into the world. For many adolescents, this is a troubled, lonely time. By about 18, most teens are in control of their emotions and have an established self-concept.

Social development is an important area for adolescents. Younger teens struggle to establish a group identity as well as a personal identity. Teenagers must belong to a group. Many needs are fulfilled by peer groups at this age, but the most important function of the group is to help adolescents define the differences between themselves and their parents. Dress, music, dancing, and language are all designed to display differences and to show how unique the group really is. Belonging to a group serves as a steppingstone in the process of establishing an individual identity and separating from the family.

Middle teens establish their identities by experimenting with different images of themselves. By this time, the peer group determines new standards for dress, behavior, and activities. Newly developed abilities to abstract allow teens to begin seeing themselves as others might see them. Most of a 14- to 16-year-old's social relationships are self-centered. Sexuality becomes more important, and by age 18 the majority of adolescents have engaged in sexual intercourse. Social relationships for adolescents over 17 years shift from the group to the individual. Caring more about others than oneself begins. Dating becomes more personal and intimate.

Spiritual development for adolescents begins with questioning family values and ideals. Some teens may cling furiously to family values during periods of conflict, whereas others completely disregard them. Adolescents also use their abilities of abstract thinking to question their childhood religious and spiritual practices. Often they will stop attending church services and choose to worship within the privacy of their rooms or other special space. Many teens are attracted to new religious sects or movements.

Most teenagers experience a great degree of inner emotional turmoil. Fearing that nobody will understand, teens become extremely private. Most adolescents have deep spiritual concerns and require acceptance, understanding, and patience as they struggle to find the spiritual rock that will anchor them in adulthood.

Adolescence is a time of rapid and uncontrollable change. Between the ages of 10 and 20, adolescents grow, develop, and mature within each area of functioning. Table 15-1 offers a brief explanation of the major changes experienced throughout adolescence. As adolescents mature, they begin to move away from the family and function independently. Society welcomes them as adults, with all the rewards and obligations of the adult role.

Common Problems of Adolescence

The world of today is large and complex. Even the most self-actualized people feel overwhelmed by the sheer amount of information and experiences that are currently available. Adolescents, who are just beginning to emerge from the security of childhood, are now faced with a double dilemma. They must gain

◆ **TABLE 15-1**
Growth and Development During Adolescence

Early Adolescence (11-14 yr)	Middle Adolescence (14-17 yr)	Late Adolescence (17-20 yr)
Growth		
Rapidly accelerating growth Reaches peak velocity Secondary sex characteristics appear	Growth decelerating in girls Stature reaches 95% of adult height Secondary sex characteristics well advanced	Physically mature Structure and reproductive growth almost complete
Cognition		
Explores newfound ability for limited abstract thought Clumsy groping for new values and energies Comparison of "normality" with peers of same sex	Developing capacity for abstract thinking Enjoys intellectual powers, often in idealistic terms Concern with philosophical, political, and social problems	Established abstract thought Can perceive and act on long range operations Able to view problems comprehensively Intellectual and functional identity established
Identity		
Preoccupied with rapid body changes Trying out of various roles Measurement of attractiveness by acceptance or rejection of peers Conformity to group norms	Modifies body image Very self-centered; increased narcissism Tendency toward inner experience and self-discovery Has rich fantasy life Idealistic Able to perceive future implications of current behavior and decisions; variable application	Body image and gender role definition nearly secured Mature sexual identity Phase of consolidation of identity Stability of self-esteem Comfortable with physical growth Social roles defined and articulated
Relationships with parents		
Defining independence-dependence boundaries Strong desire to remain dependent on parents while trying to detach No major conflicts over parental control	Major conflicts over independence and control Low point in parent-child relationship Greatest push for emancipation; disengagement Final and irreversible emotional detachment from parents; mourning	Emotional and physical separation from parents completed Independence from family with less conflict Emancipation nearly secured
Relationships with peers		
Seeks peer affiliations to counter instability generated by rapid change Upsurge of close idealized friendships with members of the same sex Struggle for mastery takes place within peer group	Strong need for identity to affirm self-image Behavioral standards set by peer group Acceptance by peers extremely important—fear of rejection Exploration of ability to attract opposite sex	Peer group recedes in importance in favor of individual friendship Testing of male-female relationships against possibility of permanent alliance Relationships characterized by giving and sharing

From Wong DL: *Whaley and Wong's nursing care of infants and children*, ed 5, 1995, St Louis, Mosby.

Continued

◆ **TABLE 15-1**
Growth and Development During Adolescence—cont'd

Early Adolescence (11-14 yr)	Middle Adolescence (14-17 yr)	Late Adolescence (17-20 yr)
Sexuality		
Self-exploration and evaluation	Multiple plural relationships	Forms stable relationships and attachment to another
Limited dating, usually group	Decisive turn toward heterosexuality (if is homosexual, knows by this time)	Growing capacity for mutuality and reciprocity
Limited intimacy	Exploration of "self appeal"	Dating as a male-female pair
	Feeling of "being in love"	Intimacy involves commitment rather than exploration and romanticism
	Tentative establishment of relationships	
Psychological health		
Wide mood swings	Tendency toward inner experiences; more introspective	More constancy of emotion
Intense daydreaming	Tendency to withdraw when upset or feelings are hurt	Anger more apt to be concealed
Anger outwardly expressed with moodiness, temper outburst, verbal insults and name-calling	Vacillation of emotions in time and range	
	Feelings of inadequacy common; difficulty in asking for help	

understanding and control of themselves and, at the same time, learn to cope with living and growing within an uncertain world.

Most of the common problems of adolescence fall into two categories: problems that arise from within oneself (internal sources) and those that are rooted outside the teen's personal sphere of control (external sources).

Internal (Developmental) Problems

Most of the difficulties of early adolescence arise from within the individual. Physical changes are beginning to take place. New sensations are being experienced: one's own body ceases to cooperate at times, and floods of intense feelings bring on dramatic emotional ups and downs.

An important developmental problem of adolescence is defining oneself, the problem of establishing an identity separate from one's family. At this stage, teens need to look into themselves and to engage in **introspection.** They need to consider who they are, how they see themselves, how they think others may see them, and how relationships with various people affect them. This process of looking inward helps teens to define themselves, but it also brings about many changes in mood, attitude, and behavior. Problems that threaten self-esteem or confidence routinely arise during the process of developing into an adult. It is important for teens to feel secure and emotionally

supported by the adults in their environments during these confusing periods. Just knowing that someone accepts and cares goes a long way toward helping teens through troubled times.

External (Environmental) Problems

Problems that arise outside the internal thoughts and feelings of the teen are called external problems. External problems fall into three basic areas: family, social, and environmental. Even teens who are blessed with the best of everything experience difficulties in these areas of functioning.

Family problems change as the adolescent develops independence. During early adolescence (11 to 14 years), teens experience the pull between wanting to stay dependent and moving toward independence. They begin to seek their freedom but still require the emotional ties provided by the family structure.

By midadolescence (14 to 17 years), the push for independence is in full swing and major conflicts over control motivate the adolescent to detach from the family. Conflicts slowly fade as the adolescent matures into an independently functioning adult.

Separating from the family and establishing independence are problems faced by every teen, but difficulties often arise from within the family that are not related to the adolescent's developmental stage. Families can range from the overprotective parents who give their children too much of everything to those

CASE STUDY

Carol was a bright, energetic 5-year-old when her parents divorced, forcing her mother to live on a welfare income. Between the ages of 6 and 13, Carol experienced a series of "fathers," who would live with the family for various periods of time. Some of these men were kind to Carol, but others physically and sexually abused her. Her mother was usually away from the home or entertaining other adults, and Carol soon learned to fend for herself.

By about 12 years of age, Carol had already experimented with different drugs, but she soon found alcohol more to her liking. By the time she was 14, Carol was too wise in the ways of the adult world. She had learned to drive and would often steal her mother's car after her mother was asleep for the night. Unprotected sex happened frequently. Soon Carol dropped out of school because "it really doesn't matter."

Clinical Decisions

1. List the factors in Carol's life that put her at risk.
2. Identify two of her problems.
3. Select several interventions that could assist Carol.

◆ **TABLE 15-2**
Peer Groups and Adolescents

Functions of Peer Groups
Helps to loosen family ties
Provides stability during times of change
Helps adolescents to define present and future social roles
Helps teens test their views of themselves
Helps teens learn to trust their own choices
Helps teens learn to make and stand by their commitments
Establishes behavioral and dress standards

Positive Aspects	Negative Aspects
Provides emotional support, a sense of belonging	Rules and standards of the group may be too rigid
Helps teens establish values and behavioral standards	Values and behavioral standards may not be in keeping with society's definition
Provides protection, safety	May encourage self-destructive behaviors and disregard for others outside the group
Allows teens to test and try out new behaviors	

---

whose children grow up on the streets with little or no sense of belonging.

Children do not choose the family into which they are born. They have no control over the methods of child rearing chosen by their parents, living conditions, or the environment in which they must grow. Many adolescents must cope with physical violence, parents who abuse alcohol or drugs, sexual abuse, or neglect (Bijur and others, 1992). These are the types of problems that cannot be solved by just waiting for the adolescent to outgrow them. They must be faced every day, and they require the energy that should be spent in self-discovery.

Many adolescents who do not have the luxury of a caring, supportive family are considered to be at risk because the conditions to which they are currently exposed may threaten further development (see box above).

Every adolescent has some degree of family problems because that is the nature of the maturing process. Those teens who are not blessed with a nurturing family face problems that would test the strongest adult.

Adolescents are also challenged with numerous social problems. Early teens seek out their peers and form intense bonds with certain groups. The **peer group** becomes the focus of the adolescent's life. Peer groups are important for the social growth of people. They serve many purposes and help teens cope with their life changes (Table 15-2).

Peer groups and **gangs** are essentially the same thing; both consist of adolescents of about the same age and circumstances. The difference between peer groups and gangs lies in the behaviors or actions of the group members. Gangs are usually associated with negative behaviors or destructive actions. Peer groups focus their energies in more constructive ways, like volunteer work and projects that benefit their communities. Adolescents choose to join groups. Concerned parents should support their teen's choice of a group but remain aware of the powerful influences groups exert on the developing individual.

Other social problems encountered by most adolescents relate to establishing their sexuality. Interactions and intimacy are limited in early adolescence. Same-sex friends are still of primary importance. However, as time passes, interest in people of the opposite sex begins to increase. By 14 years, teens begin to explore the concepts of "sex appeal" and "being in love." Dating may be limited to one person at a time, but many relationships are experienced as adolescents struggle to define themselves, both socially and sexually. Around 20 years of age, people begin to form stable, attached relationships that are based on a sense of giving rather than receiving.

Last, the environmental problems faced by adolescents have an impact on development. Problems in the environment can threaten basic needs. The dirty air of so many cities, the quality and quantity of foods eaten, and the purity of the water have an impact, however quiet or subtle, on developing human beings. Exposure to drugs, crime, prostitution, corruption, and violence are very real environmental problems for many teens.

Most adolescents, though, are concerned with the more immediate problems of learning to effectively function within their physical and social environments. Environmental problems can range from inadequate food and housing to adjusting to life at summer camp. They are the problems that "come with the territory" and are a part of one's daily life. Environments that foster growth offer fewer problems than surroundings that require a constant state of awareness just to live through the day. Environmental conditions and the problems that go along with them must be recognized and acted on by health care providers if we are to provide our teenagers with the tools for a successful transition to adulthood.

Mental Health Problems of Adolescence

Adolescence is the time for teens to develop the personal strengths and social skills that promote effective functioning within the adult world. It is a period that involves great emotional swings, a focus on oneself, and increasingly active sexual and aggressive drives. In an effort to cope with these changes, adolescents engage in a wide variety of behaviors. Some help adolescents to successfully adapt, whereas oth-

ers result in negative outcomes. This is a period of "trying out" new behaviors, and any definition of mental health must consider this fact.

The definition for mental health, especially for adolescents, is composed of two parts:

1. The absence of dysfunction in psychological, emotional, behavioral, and social spheres
2. Optimal functioning or well-being in psychological and social domains (Kazdin, 1993).

The word *dysfunction* means an impairment in everyday life. It means that the problems faced by the adolescent are so severe that he/she cannot or will not partake in the activities of daily living. When an adolescent's difficulties impair performance (school, social, work) or threaten physical well-being, a mental health problem exists. Table 15-3 lists several categories of mental health disorders that affect adolescents.

Adolescent mental health also includes the concept of well-being, which is the "presence of personal and interpersonal strengths that promote optimal functioning" (Kadzin, 1993). Well-being includes the ability to do the following:

1. Function well socially (social competence)
2. Have positive interactions with others
3. Cope with stress and troubled times (adversity)
4. Become involved in activities and relationships with others

Mental health services for adolescents must focus on promoting positive life skills as well as preventing and treating dysfunction (Finke, 1994).

Behavioral Disorders

Every child goes through periods of misconduct, of refusing to do as told, of "being bad." However, for some teens the misconduct continues to occur. Their behaviors begin to disrupt their families, social interactions, and performance at school. These teens soon become more difficult to manage, both at home and at school. "They may clash with friends and classmates, developing a reputation for being unruly, mean, or even dangerous. Other children may shun them; their schoolwork often suffers; they are frequently in the principal's office" (Goleman, 1992). When a persistent pattern of disruptive behaviors is present, mental health interventions are usually necessary. The category of disruptive behavioral disorders is divided into two basic diagnoses: attention-deficit hyperactivity disorder and conduct disorders.

Attention-deficit hyperactivity disorder (ADHD) is usually diagnosed earlier in childhood, but its impact lasts through adolescence and into adulthood. The two key features of ADHD are inattention and im-

◆ **TABLE 15-3**
Adolescent Mental Health Disorders

Classification of Disorders	Examples
Behavioral disorders	Conduct disorder, attention-deficit hyperactivity disorder
Emotional disorders	Anxiety disorder, mood disorders (e.g., depression, posttraumatic stress disorder, suicidal thoughts and attempts
Eating disorders	Anorexia nervosa, bulimia
Chemical dependency	Abuse of alcohol, amphetamines (speed), caffeine, cannabis, cocaine, nicotine, hallucinogens, inhalants, opiates, prescription drugs
Personality disorders	Antisocial disorder, borderline disorder, dependent disorder, obsessive-compulsive disorder, paranoid personality disorder
Schizophrenia	Paranoid type schizophrenia, disorganized type schizophrenia, delusional disorder
Sexual disorders	Gender identity disorder, inappropriate sexual behaviors
Other disorders of adolescence	Adjustment disorder, impulse-control disorders, problems related to abuse or neglect

pulsivity. ADHD teens experience problems in three major areas of development:

1. Focusing their attention
2. Self-control of behaviors
3. Relating to others

Because of these difficulties, many teens become chronically unhappy. They may begin to abuse chemicals or go on to develop conduct disorders. "Only about one-third of children with ADHD reach mid-adolescence with no diagnosable psychiatric disorder" (Clark, 1994).

Treatment for adolescents with ADHD requires a multidisciplinary approach. Small, structured classes and firm but nonjudgmental teachers are needed in the school environment. Positive reinforcement programs, which reward appropriate behaviors and task completion are helpful at both home and school. Behavioral therapy assists both teens and their parents. Parents are taught how to structure and enforce limits on the teen's behaviors without becoming overly harsh, inconsistent, or angry. If the adolescent has specific learning disabilities, special education may be necessary. Medications to treat ADHD include stimulants, tricyclic antidepressants, and clonidine (see box above, at right).

Conduct disorders are characterized by a defiance of authority and aggressive behaviors toward others. Often the behaviors of teens with conduct disorders violate the rights of other people or defy society's norms and standards. A common factor in the development of conduct disorders appears to be harsh parental discipline with physical punishment. Recent studies have demonstrated that early harsh discipline fostered more aggressive behaviors later in a child's life (Weiss and others, 1992).

DRUG ALERT

When assessing an adolescent, be sure to obtain a complete history of all drugs, herbs, medicines, or tonics taken. Write the names of each substance as they are given by the client. Many different names are used for the same item. Remember to ask about over-the-counter items too.

Adolescents who are taking their prescribed medications may also be using various other substances. Serious drug interactions can occur when street and pharmaceutical drugs are mixed. Be patient and do not judge the teen, but be sure to obtain a complete history of past and current use of chemically active substances.

The typical adolescent with a conduct disorder is a boy with a history of social and academic problems. Common symptoms include fighting, temper tantrums, running away from home, destroying property, problems with authorities, and failure in school. Stealing and fire setting may occur. Truancy, vandalism, and substance abuse are frequently encountered. Many teens with conduct disorders, especially those with violent histories, also have neurological problems, psychomotor seizures, ADHD, and various mental health problems (Jaffee, 1991).

Treatment for adolescents with conduct disorders is focused on first stabilizing the teen's home environment and then working to improve family interactions and disciplinary techniques. Individual and family therapy is used to help the family learn to communicate and problem solve effectively. A combination of behavioral, emotional, and cognitive therapies helps the teen learn self-control. "The success of these interventions hinges on including the family, teachers, and other adults who are involved with the child and on gaining their support and assistance in treatment plans" (Hogarth, 1991). Efforts are made to treat the adolescent within the home environment; however, residential (inpatient) treatment may be necessary when the adolescent becomes a danger to himself/herself or others.

The outlook for adolescents with conduct disorders is poor. Nearly 50% of children with antisocial behaviors or conduct disorders become antisocial as adults (Clark, 1994). These teens need nurses with patience, a willingness to set limits, and the courage to consistently enforce them.

Emotional Disorders

Disturbed feelings or moods from time to time are a normal part of everyday living. Adolescents, because of their many developmental tasks, experience frequent emotional changes. Periods of feeling "down" or "blue" are not uncommon with most teens. However, when the moods or feelings have an impact on the teen's daily activities, mental health care may be needed.

Problems that affect the emotional dimension of human functioning are divided into two basic categories: anxiety disorders and mood disorders. Although each is discussed in detail in later chapters, a brief description of how these problems affect adolescents is important here.

Anxiety disorders result when the adolescent's ability to adapt is overwhelmed. When teens are overstressed, anxiety (that vague, uneasy feeling of tension) may balloon into an ever-present emotional state. This condition triggers physical or somatic changes as the body responds in an attempt to adapt. The combination of these physical and emotional symptoms can result in such clinical diagnoses as panic disorder, phobias, obsessive-compulsive disorders, and posttraumatic stress disorder. Anxiety is also associated with the development of depression and substance abuse problems. It is important to recognize and treat anxiety in children as early as possible because long-standing problems with anxiety may become difficult to change.

Adolescents with affective or mood disorders display a wide range of behaviors from profound depression to racing hyperactivity. One's mood is the ever-present emotional state that colors one's perception of the world. Because adolescents are struggling with issues of self-image and confidence, their moods change rapidly. Teens are expected to have short periods of "the blues," but when sad moods are prolonged or the teen's behavior alternates between extreme highs and lows, an emotional disorder is suspected.

There are four primary signs/symptoms of depression in adolescents:

1. *Lowered mood:* mild sadness to intense guilt; worthlessness; hopelessness
2. *Loss of interest:* decreased social activity; decreased school performance; refusal to initiate social contacts and interactions; shy, withdrawn; becomes less involved in work and play
3. *Difficulty in thinking:* inability to concentrate, make decisions, ponder and solve problems
4. *Somatic complaints:* loss of energy, headache, stomachache, eating and sleeping problems

Other interpersonal difficulties are often present, such as problems with parents and siblings, the use of drugs, and fighting. *Acting out* one's depression through antisocial behaviors, such as theft, vandalism, and truancy, may result in involvement with the law and its criminal system. Sexual acting out is also common among teens with depression. "Most adolescents who are depressed exhibit acting-out behaviors. Once the adolescent can make the connection between acting-out behaviors and a depressed mood, clinicians will observe signs associated with depressed mood, such as crying, hopelessness, and suicidal ideas" (Hogarth, 1991). Depression in adolescence is "characterized by irritable moods and acting-out behaviors, in contrast to the classic 'depressed mood' and 'loss of interest' symptoms characteristic of adults" (Hogarth, 1991). In short, depressed adults lose interest; depressed teens act out.

Severe anxiety and depression are not average adolescent conditions. "It is now known that the majority of adolescents of both genders successfully negotiate this developmental period without any major psychological or emotional disorder, develop a positive sense of personal identity, and manage to forge adaptive peer relationships at the same time they maintain close relationships with their families" (Petersen and others, 1993).

The best prevention for emotional disorders in teens involves early recognition. Emotional problems left unrecognized and untreated in adolescence frequently develop into serious mental health disorders in adulthood.

Eating Disorders

Among the most frequently encountered adolescent health problems are eating disorders. Adolescents' eating patterns and food behaviors may follow the latest trend or change to reflect the preferences of the peer group, but as long as the teen is well nourished there is little cause for concern. Eating disorders are characterized by "severe disturbances in eating behavior" (American Psychiatric Association, 1994), which can result in a body that is far below or over its ideal weight.

The weight control practices of adolescents have been a cause for concern in today's society. The message of "slim equals attractive" bombards people throughout childhood; therefore weight control becomes an important concern for many teens. The box below describes a research study that demonstrates this concern.

Obesity is defined as a body weight that is 20% or more above the average weight for a person of the same height and build. Because the eating patterns of obese teens do not pose an immediate threat, chronic overeating is not considered as a mental health disorder. However, many people who become overweight in adolescence use food to help them through troubled times. In these cases, mental health interventions may be helpful in assisting individuals in finding more effective ways of meeting their needs.

It has been estimated that between 5% and 10% of all female adolescents suffer from eating disorders (Serdula and others, 1993). About 90% to 95% of teens with eating disorders are girls, but eating disorders do occur in male teenagers, usually athletes (Zerbe, 1995). The mortality rate for eating disorders is about

9%, and their cause is unknown. A possible genetic role is being investigated, but it is certain that eating disorders have a strong impact on an individual's growth and development.

The most common eating disorders in adolescence are anorexia nervosa and bulimia. **Anorexia nervosa** is a prolonged refusal to eat to keep body weight at a reasonable minimum. It is characterized by an intense fear of becoming fat and a relentless pursuit of thinness. **Bulimia** is the uncontrolled ingestion of large amounts of food (called binge eating) followed by inappropriate compensatory methods to prevent weight gain (called purging). In short, bulimia is a cycle of binge eating followed by purging. Anorexia is seen at early ages, from about 12 years old, with peaks around 13 to 14 and again at 17 to 18. Bulimia may not often present until 17 or so. Both disorders also occur in adults, but the incidence decreases sharply after the midthirties.

The typical picture of an anorectic teen is one of an overly cooperative, achievement-oriented girl who sees herself as overweight and begins to diet. There may be a history of eating or mood disorders in the family. Over a period of months, her concern with dieting evolves into an obsessive, all-consuming need to be thin. All her behaviors soon center around remaining thin. She may restrict calories, exercise excessively, induce vomiting, or use pills (laxatives, diuretics, diet pills, street drugs) to prevent even the smallest weight gain.

As the disorder continues to progress, the teen cuts back on her social activities and begins to avoid friends. She becomes increasingly anxious, irritable, and depressed. Now all her thoughts focus on food and weight loss to the exclusion of all else. Although it is glaringly apparent to everyone who sees her, the anorectic teen will deny that a problem even exists. Soon the physical and psychological effects of starvation begin to appear (Fig. 15-1). Long-term, even life-threatening, complications can result unless medical and mental health interventions are undertaken.

Bulimia is more difficult to detect than anorexia nervosa, perhaps because of the secretive nature of the problem. However, it is estimated that as many as 20% of college-aged women are bulimic. The road to bulimia begins with an intense interest in dieting. Her struggle with food results in secret binge eating episodes in which she consumes 5000 to 20,000 calories of high-carbohydrate foods. Binging is followed by feelings of intense guilt or depression, and the teen then makes extreme attempts to control weight gain through vomiting, exercise, or the use of drugs. Self-imposed starvation may occur between binges. Some weight loss may occur, but body weight usually re-

---

THINK ABOUT

During 1989 and 1990, researchers administered self-assessment surveys to over 11,000 high school students and 60,000 adults. The results reported that:

- 44% of female students were actively trying to lose weight
- 26% of female students were trying to prevent weight gain
- 15% of male students were trying to lose weight
- 15% of male students were trying to prevent weight gain

Furthermore, the high school students reported using the following weight control methods within the past 7 days before the survey:

Method	Female Students	Male Students
Exercise	15%	30%
Skipping meals	49%	18%
Using diet pills	4%	2%
Vomiting	3%	1%

Discuss how this information could be used to plan care for an adolescent client with an eating disorder.

Modified from Serdula MK and others: *Ann Intern Med* 119(7 pt 2):667, 1993.

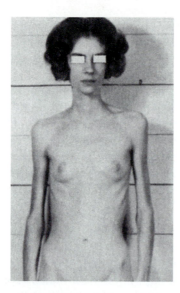

Fig. 15-1 Woman with anorexia nervosa. (From Ezrin D and others: *Systematic endocrinology*, ed 2, New York, 1979, Harper & Row.)

mains within 20% of normal. The medical complications of bulimia include erosion of tooth enamel, gastric dilation, pancreatitis, and electrolyte abnormalities. Most people with bulimia are aware of their behavior, but they are ashamed and afraid to admit that they are out of control. Binge episodes frequently follow a stressful life event.

Treatment for eating disorders has three goals:

1. Management of the medical dangers, such as metabolic disturbances, cardiac irregularities, dehydration, and hypotension
2. Restoration of normal nutrition and eating patterns
3. Meeting of the psychiatric treatment needs of the client and the family

Nursing diagnoses for eating disorders include activity intolerance, altered nutrition, altered thought processes, body image disturbance, chronic low self-esteem, defensive coping, denial, and ineffective family coping. Attempts are made to treat the teen within the family setting, but if the condition is severe, the teen is hospitalized. A plan to gradually improve the teen's nutritional intake (a refeeding program) is developed by the dietician and other treatment team members. Medical and nursing interventions are then designed to stabilize the client's physical condition. Total parenteral nutrition may be ordered. Force feeding is discouraged because the goal is to get the teen to choose to eat.

As the teen begins to feel physically better, she is encouraged to express her feelings. With both types of eating disorders, the primary issue is one of control, not of food. Psychotherapy is designed to help the teen recognize the underlying depression that is usually present and develop more effective coping skills.

Chemical Dependency

For adolescents, the temptation to "find out what it is like" is a strong motivator. Most teens who experiment with alcohol and drugs do not become dependent or addicted. However, for a growing number of teens, the use of chemicals is becoming a way of coping with the difficulties of life.

The problems associated with **substance abuse** are many: accidents caused by lack of judgment, interpersonal violence, depression, and worsening relationships with others. Young adolescents who use chemical substances usually become sexually active at an earlier age. Perhaps most important though is the fact that the use of chemicals interferes with an adolescent's normal growth and development.

Adolescents who are at risk for substance abuse problems include those who were abused as young children; teens from families who approve of, use, or promote the use of chemicals; and teens who suffer from other mental health problems. **Chemical dependency** is a state in which one's body physically and psychologically requires a drug. Identifying teens with substance abuse or chemical dependency problems is difficult. Many of the signs/symptoms of long-term abuse are absent. The teen may not have the maturity to define the situation or take the steps needed to problem solve.

Teens who become chemically dependent progress through four general stages: experimentation, active seeking, preoccupation, and burnout. During the experimentation stage, adolescents experience the pleasant moods and social belonging associated with drugs. Teens are social and usually experiment with chemicals for the first time within the comfort of their peer or other social group.

Teens who progress to the second stage, active seeking, begin to look forward to and actively seek out the mood changes brought about by the chemicals. They become experts in the use of chemicals to regulate their moods. Schoolwork and relationships with other family members begin to erode. Friends become limited to other teens who "use."

Preoccupation with the drug characterizes the third stage of adolescent chemical dependence. Teens in this stage believe that they cannot cope without their chemicals and have lost control over the use of their substance. Soon they develop a tolerance to the drug and may begin to use other substances. The chemical is now used to prevent withdrawal symptoms. At this stage, psychosocial functioning begins to fail. Friends are lost and may be replaced with antisocial, illegal, or violent behaviors.

The fourth stage is called burnout. Because chemical dependency develops over time, most of the individuals in this stage are late adolescents or young adults. The focus of drug use now is to prevent negative feelings. The euphoric, pleasant high that was sought in the beginning is no longer available. If the teen attempts to stop using the chemical at this time, withdrawal symptoms will appear. Adolescents who progress to this level of addiction are no longer able to function productively in society. Some are even unable to accomplish the activities of daily living.

Frequently, the most important clues to substance abuse in teens are small ones. A change in habits, mood, or personality is often the beginning hint of a problem. Sometimes a teen will suddenly become rebellious. More often though the adolescent will disappear with friends and take every necessary step to avoid contact with family members. The teen who becomes chemically dependent needs mental health intervention. Underneath a hardened, cocky exterior, there usually lies an individual who has few friends and little or no self-esteem.

Treatment for teens with alcohol-drug problems is focused on helping replace their use of chemicals with more effective coping skills. Many of the treatment programs in the United States, Canada, and Great Britain are modeled on the principles of Alcoholics Anonymous, whose goal is a chemical-free lifestyle. Settings for treating teens range from outpatient counseling to residential treatment programs and therapeutic communities. Individual and group psychotherapy is often combined with behavioral and cognitive therapies. Nursing care is focused on providing a safe environment because many of these teens are suicidal. Nurses also help teenaged clients identify and solve the problems related to their use of chemicals.

Drug and alcohol abuse is a complex problem that affects all aspects of an adolescent's life. Few teens seek treatment on their own, and the therapies for chemical dependency vary in their effectiveness. That is why prevention and early recognition remain the most effective tools for dealing with adolescent substance abuse.

Personality Disorders

One's personality is an important part of one's personal identity. Personality is the combination of behavioral patterns that each of us develops to cope with living. Our personalities characterize us as unique individuals and allow us to function effectively within society. However, there are some ado-

lescents who have long histories of inappropriate or maladaptive behaviors. These teens may be diagnosed as having a personality disorder. A **personality disorder** is defined as "an enduring pattern of inner experience and behavior that:

1. Deviates markedly from the expectations of the individual's culture,
2. Is pervasive and inflexible,
3. Has an onset in adolescence or early adulthood,
4. Is stable over time, and
5. Leads to distress or impairment" (American Psychiatric Association, 1994).

A major characteristic of the adolescent with a personality disorder is *impulsivity*—the drive or temptation to engage in an act that is harmful to oneself or others. These "spur-of-the-moment" decisions lead to inappropriate actions, such as overeating, casual sexual practices, shoplifting, and thrill-seeking behaviors. Intense emotional changes lead to anger and depression. Self-esteem and self-confidence are low. The ability to "look inward" (introspection) is minimal. These teens tend to develop "all-or-nothing relationships" in which others are either idealized or considered worthless. They flip between distance and closeness within their relationships and harbor a deep fear of being abandoned. Some become suspicious, and many attempt suicide. Frequently, a personality disorder will coexist with another mental health diagnosis.

Treatment for teens with personality disorders involves the use of psychotherapy and various medications. Recent studies have shown that personality disorders may be related to a problem with the neurotransmitter called serotonin. Treatment with selective serotonin reuptake inhibitors, such as fluoxetine hydrochloride (Prozac), has resulted in fewer impulsive actions, more stable moods, and less anger (Gabbard, 1995). Long-term individual therapy, in combination with selective medications, provides a promising outlook for teens who are suffering from personality disorders.

Sexual Disorders

One of the tasks during adolescence is to establish a sexual identity and role. To do this, many children and teens experiment with various sexual attitudes, outlooks, and behaviors. Attitudes about sexuality change as societies evolve. Sexual behaviors that were once considered inappropriate are now accepted. Because of these changing values, the definition of a **sexual disorder** must be characterized by significant distress and impaired ability to function.

Adolescents with sexual disorders relating to gender identity are still struggling with conflicts that began in childhood. Individuals with *gender identity dis-*

orders have a continual discomfort with their assigned sex. The child has a strong, persistent need to identify with the other sex and often insists on wearing clothing designed for the other sex. During play, the child identifies with or role plays the opposite sex. Playmates and activities are limited to those associated with the desired sex. For example, a boy might like to wear dresses, play house acting as the mother, and choose only girls as friends.

As such teens grow older, they become preoccupied with ridding themselves of their sexual characteristics and assuming those of the desired sex. They may request hormonal therapy, surgery, or other procedures that may produce characteristics of the desired sex. Treatment consists of medical and mental health therapies that are designed to relieve distress and help teens solve their problems.

Sexually acting out is not uncommon for teens. However, if their behaviors result in discomfort or harm for themselves or others, society defines the behaviors as inappropriate. Many of the sexual problems faced by adolescents can be solved with good communication skills. Sometimes just replacing ignorance with accurate knowledge can assist a teen along the road toward healthy sexual maturity.

Psychosis

The defining feature of **schizophrenia** and other psychoses is a grossly impaired ability to function. Psychotic disorders are discussed in detail in a later chapter, but here it is important to know that the onset of schizophrenia usually takes place in adolescence. The adolescent who suffers from schizophrenia is typically a good child who begins to develop a whole new set of sometimes bizarre behaviors and activities. "Psychosis can result from organic causes, head injury, illicit substance abuse, or extreme stress, or it may occur in the manic phase of bipolar disorder" (Hogarth, 1991).

The major characteristic of adolescent psychosis is loss of contact with reality. The teen may have hallucinations, delusions, and feelings of paranoia. He/she lacks judgment, behaves impulsively, and shows little insight. Behaviors may become inappropriate, ritualistic, or repetitive. Disordered thought patterns lead to communication problems and difficulties with peer relationships. Because of the loss of contact with reality, personal hygiene (even eating and drinking) may be neglected. The teen usually requires hospitalization and close supervision.

Treatment for psychosis includes a combination of psychotherapy and medications. Antipsychotics, antidepressants, and lithium may be ordered. Nursing care is focused on providing basic physical needs including feeding, bathing, and exercise; providing a safe environment; and developing skills for successful living. As the adolescent begins to respond to the treatment plan, education about the nature and control of the disorder is begun. Both adolescents and their families need ongoing support. Family members are often encouraged to join a support group for the emotional assistance required to cope with a teen who has a psychosis.

Suicide

The number of adolescents who take their own lives is growing at an alarming rate. From 1960 to 1990, the rate of **adolescent suicide** has more than doubled (Deykin and Buka, 1994). Adolescent girls attempt suicide three times more often than their male counterparts, but boys actually are more successful in their attempts. The leading cause of death for both sexes is from the use of firearms. Recent studies (Grossman, Soderberg, and Rivara, 1993) also suggest that teens who have been hospitalized for injuries or motor vehicle (especially single-car) accidents may be actually attempting suicide.

A suicide attempt by an adolescent is a call for help. Today's society is complex and has many influences on a developing adolescent. Factors that may influence suicidal behavior include more competition for fewer resources, exposure to child abuse and neglect (Randall, 1992), instability within the family, the presence of depression or other illness, the availability of handguns and other weapons, and an increased use of alcohol and drugs. The box on p. 219 lists the warning signs of adolescents who may be thinking about suicide.

Teenagers who attempt suicide usually fall into one of three groups: the teen with depression, the teen who is trying to influence others, and the teen with a serious mental health problem. Periods of depression are not uncommon during adolescence, but they are usually short lived. However, when a teen cannot keep up with school and social activities, withdraws from others, has problems eating or sleeping, and feels hopeless, then he/she is at risk for suicide resulting from depression.

The teen who uses a suicidal gesture as a way to get back at someone (usually parents or boyfriend/girlfriend) is attempting to influence someone. Often there is little or no depression and no longstanding wish to die. The teen is angry, and the gesture is done with the goal of gaining attention or scaring another person. Teenage girls engage in this type of suicidal behavior much more commonly than boys.

The third group of adolescents who attempt suicide are seriously ill. They can see no other way out of

---

WARNING SIGNS OF TEEN SUICIDE

- Change in grades at school
- Loss of interest, initiative
- Rapidly changing emotional highs and lows
- Defies rules, regulations, pushes limits
- May become secretive
- Withdraws from family interactions
- Changes in personal hygiene
- Isolates self from others
- Discusses suicide with peers, close friends
- Gives away prized possessions
- Hints about intentions (e.g., "After I'm gone. . . .")

---

their discomfort and actually welcome the relief they expect death to bring.

The highest risk group for suicide is the older white adolescent boy who has expressed his intention to die. Previous attempts, written plans, and available tools for committing suicide all heighten the risk for future attempts. Nurses who work with adolescents must assess every teen for his/her suicidal risk. Chapter 27 takes a more in-depth look at this problem.

The goals of treatment for suicidal adolescents are to protect them from harm, build trusting therapeutic relationships, and assist them to develop self-awareness and alternate coping skills. The box on p. 220 illustrates a nursing care plan designed for a suicidal adolescent.

Therapeutic Interventions

Adolescents require special care because they are developing and maturing at the same time they are experiencing mental health problems. Although each adolescent is unique, several nursing interventions can serve as strategies for working with all teens. The therapeutic relationship between client and nurse serves as the instrument for understanding and helping each teen. Nurses use their empathy to help adolescents define their problems and then develop new and more effective ways of solving their problems. Therapeutic communication skills help to establish the trust that is vital for self-disclosure; and the nurses' strength allows teens to continue trying even when things look bleak. Specific nursing interventions for adolescents center around five basic strategies: surveillance, limit setting, building self-esteem and confidence, role modeling, and skill development.

Surveillance and Limit Setting

Surveillance is defined as "the process of watching over adolescents to determine if they are safe, keeping their rules, making good decisions, or if they need adult intervention" (Hogarth, 1991). The amount of surveillance is determined by the degree of the problem. Some adolescents need only minimal supervision, whereas others may require 24-hour-a-day observation. The goal of surveillance activities is to assist teens in developing new skills and coping methods as well as to protect them from harm. The alert nurse can turn a potential crisis situation into an opportunity for growth.

Setting limits is also essential for adolescents. Part of the process of growing up is to test the limits of authority. Teens are struggling with learning to control their emotions. Nurses work to change the focus of control from external to internal (self-control). Situations in which the teen attempts to exceed the limits are treated as learning experiences.

When limits are set on an adolescent's behaviors, it is important that the teen understand the rules of acceptable behavior and the consequences of inappropriate behaviors.

Quite often, adolescents do well with the problem-solving approach. Here the nurse asks the teen what he/she is feeling and doing. Then the teen is asked if the behavior is helping him/her get what he/she wants (meeting the goal). The teen then develops a plan for meeting the goal or coping with the feelings and follows it through. This process helps adolescents learn to solve problems and gain some control over their situations. Positive actions are praised and reinforced, and the teen is encouraged to apply the process to other situations.

Building Self-Esteem

Adolescents, even the most well-adjusted, experience the discomfort of low self-esteem at some time or another; but for the teen with mental health problems, these discomforts can be great. Nurses who work with adolescents direct every interaction toward building the teen's self-esteem.

Teenagers are masters at reading nonverbal behaviors. Nurses who use eye contact, address each teen by name, and actively listen make adolescents feel accepted and valued. Do not lecture or give advice. Teens hate lectures. Instead, direct teens toward problem solving and assuming responsibility for their own feelings. Convey respect by requesting rather than ordering and by thanking them for their help. Praise each small effort toward success, and point out the adolescent's progress. If limits must be enforced, do so without anger or embarrassment for the teen. Remember that the goal of setting limits is to encourage responsibility.

Self-esteem is also fostered through the use of role models. We all serve as models of healthy, functional

SAMPLE CLIENT CARE PLAN
SUICIDAL ADOLESCENT

Assessment

History: Rita is a 15-year-old girl admitted to the medical unit of the local hospital for suicidal attempts. About 4 hours ago, she consumed approximately 35 tablets of diazepam (Valium) and was lavaged in the emergency room. Three earlier suicidal attempts have involved drug overdoses and slashed wrists.

Current Findings: A sleepy teenaged girl in no acute distress. Answers questions with one-word statements. States she attempted suicide to "get everyone off my back." Skin on wrists and forearms has numerous jagged scars. Rita refused further physical assessment.

Nursing Diagnosis

Violence, self-directed related to family and developmental conflict

Planning/Expected Outcomes

Rita will contract with staff for no suicidal behaviors. Rita will verbalize an awareness of her pattern of self-harm by May 7.

Nursing Interventions

Intervention

1. Assess potential for self-harm.

2. Ensure safety; place on suicidal precautions.

3. Monitor activities continually for first 24 hours.
4. Establish a verbal or written contract not to harm self; renew every 24 hours.
5. Establish rapport; offer support; be available to listen; ensure confidentiality.

6. Encourage Rita to keep a diary and write in it daily.

Rationale

1. Helps prevent harm or injury; helps determine level of surveillance needed.
2. Prevents impulsive reactions to stressful situations.
3. Helps assess level of suicidal intention, effectiveness of behaviors.
4. Demonstrates respect; prevents suicidal behaviors.
5. Acceptance of Rita's feelings shows respect and encourages self-worth even though her behavior is unacceptable.
6. Helps Rita identify her behavioral reactions and behavior.

Evaluation

Rita willingly contracted each day for no self-harm. By May 1, Rita was seeking Mary P., LPN, for interaction. By May 7, Rita was able to identify one area in which she was having problems.

---

adults for the teens with whom we work. The impression nurses present will have an impact on the effectiveness of therapeutic actions. Adolescents watch how their therapists and care providers interact with each other and solve the problems that arise among them. It is important to remember that nurses are always being watched and evaluated. If teens feel that your behaviors are effective, they will often adopt them for use in similar situations. Acting as a role model for healthy behavior requires a lot of energy,

but it is a highly effective way of helping an adolescent learn to cope.

Skill Development

One of the most important therapeutic interventions involves assisting adolescents in developing the skills that are essential for functional living. Nurses help their teen clients with cognitive (intellectual) skills, such as applying the problem-solving process to actual problems. They help young clients practice appropriate social skills. Working cooperatively within a group, learning how to listen to others, and exploring new methods for controlling anger or aggression are other nursing actions designed to help adolescent clients develop effective living skills. Working with adolescent clients is demanding and rewarding, but effective therapeutic interventions at this stage of life are extremely important if we are to prevent problems in the future.

❖ KEY CONCEPTS

- The passage from childhood to adulthood is a time of physical and psychosocial growth.
- Many common problems of adolescence can be classified into two categories: internal sources and external sources.
- A mental health problem exists when an adolescent's problems impair performance or threaten physical well-being.
- The category of disruptive behavioral disorders is divided into two basic diagnoses: attention-deficit hyperactivity disorder and conduct disorders.
- Although emotional ups and downs are a normal part of adolescence, many teens suffer from anxiety and mood disorders.
- Anorexia nervosa and bulimia are eating disorders characterized by severe disturbances in eating behavior, which can result in a body that is far below or above its ideal weight.
- Teens who become chemically dependent or addicted progress through four general stages: experimentation, active seeking, preoccupation, and burnout.
- Adolescents with long histories of inappropriate or maladaptive behaviors may be diagnosed with a personality disorder.
- A sexual disorder is diagnosed when problems cause the teen significant distress and impair his/her ability to function.
- The major characteristic of adolescent psychosis, such as schizophrenia, is a loss of contact with reality.
- Teenagers who attempt suicide usually fall into one of three groups: the teen with depression, the teen who is trying to influence others, and the teen with a serious health problem.
- In addition to the use of therapeutic relationships and communications, nursing interventions for adolescents center around five basic strategies: surveillance, limit setting, building self-esteem and confidence, role modeling, and skill development.

❖ SUGGESTIONS FOR FURTHER READING

For a thorough explanation of the mental health care of teens, read *Adolescent psychiatric nursing* by Christina R. Hogarth (St. Louis, 1991, Mosby).

❖ REFERENCES

American Psychiatric Association: *Diagnostic and statistical manual of mental disorders,* ed 4, Washington, DC, 1994, The Association.

Bijur PE and others: Parental alcohol use, problem drinking, and children's injuries, *JAMA* 267(23):2166, 1992.

Clark RB: Psychosocial aspects of pediatrics and psychiatric disorders. In Hay WW and others, editors: *Current pediatric diagnosis and treatment,* ed 12, Norwalk, CT, 1994, Appleton & Lange.

Deykin EY, Buka SL: Suicidal ideation and attempts among chemically dependent adolescents, *Am J Public Health* 84(4):634, 1994.

Finke LM: Child psychiatric nursing: moving into the 21st century, *Adv Nurs Sci* 29(1):43, 1994.

Gabbard GO: Researchers study causes and treatment of borderline personality disorder, *Menninger Lett* 3(5):1, 1995.

Goleman D: Psychotherapy and your child, *The New York Times Magazine* (10):10, Oct 4, 1992.

Grossman DC, Soderberg R, Rivara FP: Prior injury and motor vehicle crash as risk factors for youth suicide, *Clin Rev* 3(5):63, 1993.

Hagerman RJ: Growth and development. In Hay WW and others, editors: *Current pediatric diagnosis and treatment,* ed 12, Norwalk, CT, 1994, Appleton & Lange.

Hogarth CR: *Adolescent psychiatric nursing,* St Louis, 1991, Mosby.

Jaffee ES: Working with troubled teens, *RN* 54(2):58, 1991.

Kaplan DW, Mammel KA: Adolescence. In Hay WW and others, editors: *Current pediatric diagnosis and treatment,* ed 12, Norwalk, CT, 1994, Appleton & Lange.

Kazdin AE: Adolescent mental health: prevention and treatment programs, *Am Psychol* 48(2):127, 1993.

Petersen AC and others: Depression in adolescence, *Am Psychol* 48(2):155, 1993.

Randall T: Adolescents may experience home, school abuse; their future draws researchers' concern, *JAMA* 276(23):3127, 1992.

Serdula MK and others: Weight control practices of U.S. adolescents and adults, *Ann Intern Med* 119(7 pt 2):667, 1993.

Weiss B and others: Some consequences of early harsh discipline: child aggression and a maladaptive social information processing style, *Child Dev* 63:1321, 1992.

Wong DL: *Whaley and Wong's nursing care of infants and children* ed 5, St Louis, 1995, Mosby.

Zerbe KJ: Eating disordered men require diverse treatment, *Menninger Lett* 3(9):4, 1995.

16

PROBLEMS OF ADULTHOOD

LEARNING OBJECTIVES

1. List two developmental tasks of the young adult.
2. Explain the importance of having a strong sense of personal identity.
3. Identify three characteristics of a successful adult.
4. Discuss three developmental problems faced by most adults.
5. Name four stresses associated with parenting or guiding the next generation.
6. Describe how environmental problems such as poverty can limit an adult's ability to function effectively.
7. Identify two effects of a lack of social support for adults.
8. Explain how the fear of HIV/AIDS is affecting young adults.
9. Name three nursing interventions designed to help the psychosocial functioning of adults with problems.

KEY TERMS

acquired immunodeficiency
syndrome (AIDS)

adulthood
mortality

poverty
social isolation

For many years, adulthood was considered the end of the line for growth and development. Once an adolescent reached the age of 21 years or so, he/she was viewed as an adult, completely matured and ready to assume a full place in society. Adulthood was looked on as a time of stability with little or no change. Today, however, we see the period of life that follows adolescence as a dynamic one, filled with learning, struggle, rewards, and change. Adulthood is a time of personal, professional, and social development. It is the time to nurture and guide the next generation, and it is a time for individuals to move beyond themselves and direct their energies for the benefit of others.

The period of life labeled **adulthood** lasts from about 18 to around 65 years of age. Remember that these divisions are just for the sake of discussion. In reality, each adult is an individual who ages at his/her own particular pace.

Adulthood, like every other age, is filled with tasks, problems, and opportunities for learning. All young adults are faced with the challenge of establishing their careers, their identities, and the relationships that will emotionally support them throughout their lives. As they age, adults must learn to cope with changes in families, careers, and relationships. All this is accomplished within a society so complex that no single person is able to understand its workings.

Adult Growth and Development

Physical growth for men is complete by about 21 years of age. Women mature earlier, reaching their full growth around 17 years of age. Physical abilities are at their peak efficiency in young adulthood. Body systems have a remarkable ability to compensate, so the young adult is able to maintain a healthy state with little interruption, even during periods of illness (Edelman and Mandle, 1994). Because of this remarkable ability, young adults usually have few if any concerns about their health. After 30, many adults begin to show signs of aging, but with a healthy lifestyle and the absence of any chronic conditions, they usually enjoy good health well into later maturity.

Although physical growth may be complete, both young and middle adults continue to develop. The emotional, intellectual, sociocultural, and spiritual dimensions of one's character begin to receive attention. Young adulthood is a time to establish oneself as independent, fully functional, and capable of living and thriving independently. Middle adulthood sees the growth and maturity of one's family unit and profession.

The developmental tasks for young adults are many. Although growth may be completed, much is left to be done regarding the emotional, social, cultural, and spiritual realms. Young adults also face the realities of choosing a career or vocation that provides them with the ability to secure the basic necessities of daily life, establishing long-term goals, and committing themselves to personal relationships with others. For many, adulthood is also a time of marriage, creation of a family, and parenting. As individuals encounter each life change, they rely on previously learned behaviors to help them cope. If one has learned to cope effectively as a child, then adulthood will pose fewer crises. However, the problems of childhood, if not resolved, can follow throughout one's life.

Emotional development of young adults is centered around learning to function within a stressful environment. Work and school offer many opportunities to cope with stress. When used positively, stress motivates young adults to achieve their goals, some of which are long term. When ignored, stress leads to the many problems that come with heightened anxiety. Young adults still have occasional emotional outbursts, but they attempt to find new ways of coping with the many emotions experienced during this time. Feelings of loneliness, guilt, and anger can lead to despair and depression. Nurses who care for young adults must be willing to explore inappropriate or troublesome feelings with them. Assessments of the emotional status for all adults should also include "the client's perception of how his emotions affect his ability to develop satisfactory relationships or achieve professional goals" (Rawlins, Williams, and Beck, 1993).

Later in adulthood, emotional development deals with the struggle of seeing oneself age. Individuals who have successfully coped with life's problems until now gracefully accept and adapt to the fact that they are growing older. The anxiety generated by the prospect of a limited time on this earth motivates many middle adults to make the best of the benefits of middle age.

Fear of poor health, death, and loss of financial security causes anxiety in many adults. This anxiety often results in the appearance of stress-related illness and behavioral problems. Feelings of anger can arise when interactions with work and family members are not as expected. Guilt can be experienced over parents, children, and the failure to meet personal goals. Health care providers should always assess their adult clients for signs of stress, anxiety, and depression. About 15% of adults "will suffer from a major depressive disorder in their life, but the disorder will be accurately diagnosed and treated in fewer than one in three" (Discussion Guideline Panel, 1994).

Intellectual development focuses on the young adult's ability to solve cognitive (intellectual) and abstract problems. Young adults must process large amounts of information and learn many new skills to be successful in education or employment. As young adults effectively cope with their situations, their horizons broaden and they develop flexibility, the ability to adapt to change. This flexibility, combined with the willingness to take risks, encourages them to respond to available personal and career opportunities.

Adults continue to grow intellectually if they use their abilities to think. People who exercise their intellects "have little, if any, loss of mental ability, whereas those who do not engage in productive mental activities may experience a decline in intellectual performance" (Rawlins, Williams, and Beck, 1993). It seems that the "use it or lose it principle" also applies to the use of intellectual abilities.

Social development for young adults focuses on interactions and relationships with others. If the sense of personal identity is strong and well established, individuals learn to form close personal relationships and become willing to make lasting commitments.

Habits learned in childhood are likely to become lifelong. Patterns of communicating and interacting with others establish young adults' interactional styles, which have a strong impact on jobs, relationships, and choice of goals. Low self-esteem and withdrawal from social situations may result from inadequate social or communication skills.

Establishing sexual intimacy is an important task for young adults. Those who have strong senses of personal identity are able to merge themselves with another in a marriage or long-term relationship. Individuals who are still struggling with their identities may seek relationships to fill their unmet psychosocial needs.

Parenting is a major challenge for most adults. The responsibilities of parenthood force an individual to shift energies from self to caring for another. Parenthood is a 24-hour-a-day career. Its demands may create anxiety, feelings of inadequacy, and a sense of isolation and helplessness. Women who must manage both parenting and working outside the home are especially vulnerable. As the family unit gradually stabilizes and children begin to gain independence, parents often expand their focus beyond the immediate family or work situation and become involved in community activities.

The social tasks for adults also relate to the change from parent back to the role of partner. As children prepare for their careers and move out of the home, the middle-aged couple has the opportunity to redefine their marriage relationship. With the responsibilities of parenting over, the couple begins to explore their relationship based on three basic factors: commitment, communication, and compromise (Donohough, 1981).

Marriages that have weathered the challenges of career and parenting are based on a solid foundation. Each partner recognizes the individuality of the other and his/her need to achieve personal growth. They reaffirm their commitment to each other and the relationship.

Couples who have effective communications are able to freely share their attitudes, opinions, and emotions. Couples who find themselves unable to communicate are frequently faced with the possibility of divorce or separation.

Compromise involves the willingness to negotiate and to enter into interactions in which neither person wins or loses. Conflicts are resolved by defining and solving the problem. The focus is kept on the issue. Couples who compromise communicate openly, listen carefully, and try to understand their partner's point of view. Their relationship is respected and cherished.

Development within the spiritual dimension focuses on defining one's value system and belief system. Young adults often challenge their current religious practices by changing churches or refusing to attend services. As individuals become established within the community and begin to raise families, they reexamine their values. Children offer many opportunities for parents to reflect on their values, beliefs, and ethics.

Many people feel the need to define (or redefine) the meaning of their lives during the middle years. It is not uncommon for middle-aged adults to dramatically change their lifestyles. The 40-year-old wealthy businessman who sells everything and volunteers at a homeless shelter and the mother who leaves home to study for a college degree are examples.

The spiritual tasks of adults are concerned with finding meaning in life. Religious and spiritual beliefs are reexamined in light of one's own **mortality** (eventually having to die). Religious, social, and community activities become important. Volunteering to help others enriches their lives and provides many opportunities for socialization. Those adults who do not or cannot care for themselves or others become stagnant, self-absorbed, and isolated. The potential for serious mental health problems is greater for the unhappy, self-focused adult, no matter what the age.

To summarize, adults with good mental health are able to successfully adapt to life's changes. Once their personal identities have been established, they are capable of using each life experience as a lesson in personal growth. They develop the ability to problem solve and learn. Healthy adults are able to set priorities and reasonable expectations for themselves. They form bonds with other people and are willing to devote their energies to guiding the next generation or making the world a better place in which to live. They are able to give of themselves in both intimate and social situations, and their self-confidence remains unaffected by the whims and opinions of others. There is a balance between give and take. In short, successful adults have developed the inner strength to carry them through the joys, sorrows, and everyday activities of daily living (see box below).

Common Problems of Adulthood

Diagnosable mental health disorders that affect adults are described in detail in later chapters. Here we consider some of the risk factors and difficulties faced by many adults in today's society. All adults are faced with situations that produce anxiety. The stresses that accompany everyday living are many, and stress-related problems can develop when individuals become too anxious. One's personal outlook helps define stressful or anxious situations. One's environment plays an important role in determining the opportunities for jobs, education, and living conditions, and research results are leading us to consider the role that one's biochemical makeup plays in determining a person's behaviors. The common difficulties that challenge adults are divided into internal and external types of problems.

CHARACTERISTICS OF A SUCCESSFUL ADULT

- Accepts self
- Adapts to changes, is flexible
- Establishes priorities
- Sets realistic goals and expectations
- Learns from past experiences
- Functions in stressful circumstances
- Has achieved emotional control
- Solves problems and thinks abstractly
- Makes sound decisions
- Establishes and maintains intimate and social relationships
- Guides next generation
- Finds meaning in life
- Finds balance between give and take
- Has inner strength to effectively adapt to new situations

Internal (Developmental) Problems

Because life is a dynamic process, people must cope with change. As they do, they learn and (hopefully) develop more effective ways of living. As children, our developmental problems are clear. As adolescents, we discover that a unique individual lies within a seemingly ever-changing body.

Adults experience developmental problems too, but theirs are not so obvious. Choices made about oneself, relationships, education, occupation, marriage, and family have an effect on one's life. When adults feel they have made the right choices, they develop the inner strength to weather future storms. When they allow anxiety, anger, or other emotions to be the focus of an experience, effective adaptation does not occur as easily. Nurses and those who provide health care for adults should be aware of clients' problems and coping skills. Intervening early is a good form of preventative mental health care.

Personal identity.   Problems with establishing a strong personal identity begin in childhood. People who were not guided, nurtured, or unconditionally accepted in childhood find it more difficult to feel good about themselves as adults. Overcoming a childhood filled with negative examples is a difficult task for many young adults. It requires the willingness to look at one's own behaviors and learn new methods of coping. With the support and examples of effectively functioning people, many young adults are able to overcome the difficulties of their pasts and mature into capable individuals with strong senses of personal identity and self-worth.

Nurses have many opportunities to assist young men and women by offering the emotional support and encouragement to problem solve. They can act as resources, directing their clients to support groups and other community resources. Helping a young adult develop a positive personal identity will lessen the possibility of future mental health problems.

Problems of personal identity can also be related to a person's intellectual abilities: how one solves problems, makes decisions, and interprets stress. When an individual's ability to solve problems in effective ways is limited, behavioral and personality difficulties are much more common.

Emotional problems plague all adults, but those who are able to look at things in perspective cope with few stress-related effects. Mentally healthy adults can identify and accept their emotions without acting inappropriately on them. Unfortunately, anger-control problems plague many adults, especially those who were exposed to aggressive acts as children (O'Keefe, 1995). Drug and alcohol abuse may also be the result of a person's need to deal with emotional problems.

Interpersonal relationships.   Human beings are complicated creatures, always changing and moving in new ways. Young adults, who are still discovering their unique natures, are also searching for the relationships that will fulfill their needs and encourage their personal growth.

Adulthood is a time for commitment to others, be it through marriage or career. The need for intimacy and belonging is great throughout life, and adults usually form many relationships (Fig. 16-1). Young adults often seek relationships in an attempt to fill a personal void or escape an unhappy situation. Sometimes errors in judgment have enormous consequences for their future.

Many adults commit themselves solely to another with the vows of marriage. In this society, marriage is a legal state that bonds two people as a single family unit. Most often, children are produced, and the responsibilities of life focus on nurturing and providing for the offspring. As children mature and leave home, the marriage relationship is reevaluated, and decisions are made to continue or end the relationship.

Problems with interpersonal relationships can extend outside the family to work and social environments. Individuals who have little or no ability to look at how their attitudes and behaviors affect other people often have difficulties with long-term relationships. They become superficial and unwilling to consider the feelings of others. Small problems with social relationships can balloon into serious mental health problems. Learning effective communication and interpersonal skills can spell the difference between a functional adult and an unhappy, unfulfilled individual. Nurses can play an important role in preventing mental illness by identifying those clients with interpersonal problems and offering them support, education, and resources.

Guiding the next generation.   Most adults, married or not, have children. Children are not isolated events. They arrive as package deals, along with responsibility, fatigue, self-doubt, love, and joy. If pregnancies are planned, the children are anticipated with joy. Unplanned pregnancies are often unwanted, and the decisions faced by the two adults will have an impact on the rest of their lives. Nurses play a critical role in helping adults make responsible choices about parenthood.

The child-rearing practices of adults vary considerably. Most parents raise their offspring based on how they were treated as children. Parents who were dis-

ciplined physically as children tend to resort to such practices as spanking or hitting when correcting their own children. Adults who were nurtured and guided as children provide the same for their offspring. Factors such as money, family relationships, safety, housing, health practices, and spiritual beliefs all affect the family, parenting practices, and children. Relationships between individuals, interactions with extended family members, and social relationships can support or discourage certain child-rearing habits.

The rise of single-parent families must be considered. Today, it is estimated that over 14% of all households in the United States are headed by women alone (U.S. Bureau of Census, 1993). In these families, the single parent must function as father, mother, and provider. The joys of children can become overshadowed by the work and stress of providing for them. Without support and intervention, these families have a high potential for developing several mental health problems.

Childless adults contribute to the next generation through devotion to a career or volunteer activities. The need to share and leave one's mark increases by middle adulthood.

Economics.   One of the greatest stressors for adults of all ages is financial security. Young adults must choose a vocation or profession that offers an opportunity to provide the necessities of life. Food, shelter, and clothing cost money, a fact that many young adults fail to learn until they leave the security of the family. Decisions about education and training, made young in life, will affect the quality of living far into the future.

Unemployment is a multisided problem. When a parent does not work, he/she becomes unable to provide for the children. This absence of income begins the family on a downward spiral that may include poverty, physical illness, and psychosocial disorders. "Several studies have demonstrated that a stressful environment shared by families with an unemployed head of household is associated with child neglect, maltreatment, and abuse" (Zlotnick and Cassanego, 1992).

Adults are challenged with numerous problems. Fortunately, as they grow, they cope with each difficulty and apply lessons learned to the next problem. As time passes, the inner strength built through experience becomes a part of who they are. This inner strength provides encouragement to grow and expand beyond the limits of who they are today.

External (Environmental) Problems

The environment plays a strong role in the development of an individual during childhood. In adult-

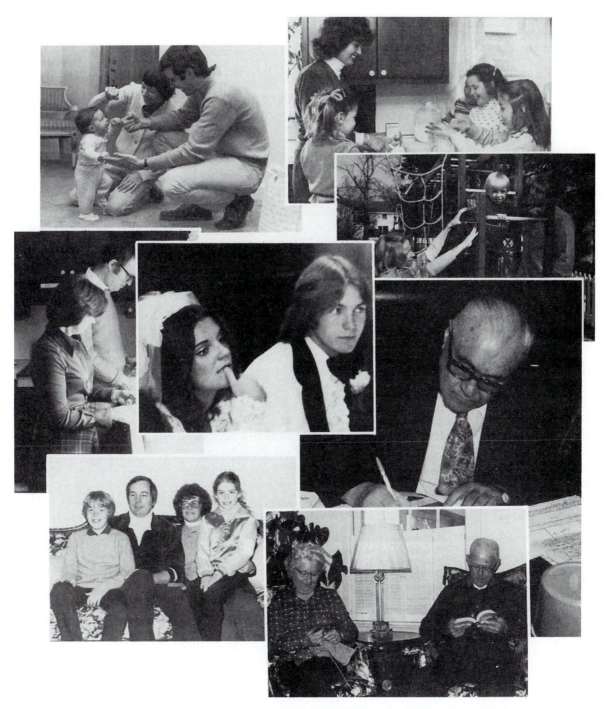

Fig. 16-1 The many aspects of adulthood. (From Edelman CL, Mandle CL: *Health promotion throughout the lifespan*, ed 3, St Louis, 1994, Mosby.)

hood, one's environment can limit or encourage further development. Some of the major environmental problems affecting adults today include a lack of education, poverty, homelessness, substance abuse, HIV/AIDS, and lack of social support. Each of these problems can have a strong impact on the mental health of adults. Health care providers, especially

nurses, must be aware of these problems if mental health interventions are to be effective.

Lack of education.   An individual's training or education is closely associated with his/her economic status. Less educated people tend to be poorer, with few savings or financial reserves. Many families live "from paycheck to paycheck," where one small financial demand (e.g., car breaking down or a sick child) can throw the family into turmoil. Adults who are vocationally trained or educated are more able to cope with the problems of everyday life because they have more financial and available health care resources. Encourage your clients to seek further education or training. Refer them to various community agencies that offer help or training. A lack of education limits abilities and fosters disabilities.

Poverty. The result of unemployment (or underemployment) is poverty. **Poverty** is the lack of resources necessary for reasonable comfortable living. Being poor means not having enough: not enough to eat, to wear, to learn, or to grow. Poverty means unstable housing, poor educational opportunities, work problems, and an increased risk of becoming a victim. Adults who survive below the poverty line often have children, and these children suffer as a result of their parents' misfortune.

Homelessness. Poverty, homelessness, and a lack of education go hand in hand. Adults who must cope with this three-pronged dilemma almost always need some kind of support and intervention.

The homeless are a diverse group. Many are single men, but a surprising 30% are families: homeless women and children (Milburn and D'Ercole, 1991). Many chronically mentally ill people inhabit the streets because they are unable to protect themselves or use their resources wisely. Discouraged by their prospects, homeless individuals run a much greater risk for depression, drug abuse, and other mental health disorders. Good health and effective living are only a dream for most of the homeless.

Remember that homeless people have special needs. Tailor nursing care to lifestyle and consider their individual situations. Nursing actions will be more effective when they are realistic and doable (see box below).

Lack of social support. Perhaps one of the most distressing problems for adults is **social isolation.** Before the time of rapid transportation, families tended to remain in one geographic area for generations. Small communities would often be composed of relatives and extended family members. Strong emotional and social support was always available during difficult times. People shared their anxieties, hopes, and difficulties with each other and derived the emotional support and energy to cope with their problems.

Today, families live apart from each other, each surviving as a single unit. The social interconnectedness that bonded people together is no longer intact. Adults must establish new connections, new relationships, and new support systems every time they move to a different community. This practice results in many people feeling socially isolated and disconnected with their fellow human beings.

Social support is the friendship from others that helps carry individuals through life's more difficult moments. With trusted friends, adults can share their problems, concerns, and stresses. These interactions—

CASE STUDY

Joan is a nurse in a center for homeless people located in a large U.S. city. She describes the qualifications necessary for her position: patience, persistence, and the ability to apply creative approaches to client care problems. Her role is one of facilitator/advocate who helps her clients gain access to other services in the community. She ensures that each person is clean and presentable when they request services. To do this, the shelter provides shower and laundry facilities, but Joan makes sure everyone uses the toothbrushes, deodorant, soap, and razors.

She reschedules missed appointments for her homeless clients, providing for transportation if necessary. Clarifying instructions from other agencies and helping her clients fill out job applications are also on her list of nursing interventions. Every opportunity for client education is taken. Joan in-structs her homeless clients on the importance of good nutrition, safe sexual practices, communicable diseases, and other health-related subjects. She works with each individual to set and reach realistic goals. She sees every person as worthy of respect and dignity. Although her successes may be small, "hearing someone express that since he was able to get help for his problems, he now feels better about himself and is motivated to change his lifestyle provides this nurse's personal reward and professional satisfaction in working with the homeless" (Foster, 1992).

Clinical Decisions

1. Does Joan think her work is rewarding?
2. Do you think that you would like to do Joan's job?

this social support given by friends—can make the difference between mental health and illness. Be sure to assess clients' social support systems. Refer to various support or community groups as needed. Remember that social isolation is not healthy for human beings. Acknowledging this fact can help prevent many future mental health difficulties.

AIDS. **Acquired immunodeficiency syndrome (AIDS)** was first recognized in the United States in 1981. Since then, millions of people, especially adolescents and young adults, have been exposed to this devastating disease. AIDS is caused by human immunodeficiency virus (HIV). It is spread through sexual activities, the sharing of needles, or exposure to blood and body fluids. AIDS prevents the body from fighting off infectious diseases, and its signs/symptoms are not often recognized for many years in some cases.

People with AIDS often present themselves with vague physical complaints, such as night sweats, cough, weight loss, or fever. Other problems can include ear, nose, or throat complaints and gastrointestinal or skin changes. Often their only complaints are psychiatric: anxiety, depression, or lapses in memory. In fact, several studies revealed that perhaps one in three symptom-free HIV-infected people experience mild loss of attention, memory, and reaction times (Bower, 1994).

AIDS has an impact on all members of society, but it is especially felt among sexually active young adults. People this age are more vulnerable to contracting the disease because they (1) lack the emotional maturity and judgment to make sound decisions and (2) feel the invulnerability of youth—the "it will never happen to me" attitude. It is only when a friend or loved one contracts the disease that its reality strikes home.

Adults who can appreciate the seriousness of the disease have either made changes in their lifestyles or suffer the anxieties associated with high-risk behaviors.

Fear of AIDS has spread to persons whose lifestyles mean little likelihood of contracting the disease. The term AFRAIDS (*Acute Fear Regarding AIDS*) has been coined to describe an anxiety-related condition caused by a fear of AIDS. Individuals with poor or marginal coping skills may find it difficult to deal with the emotional aspects of this epidemic (Cook and others, 1994).

Every health care provider, from physicians and nurses to technicians and therapists, has a responsibility to educate clients about AIDS. The most important tool in the treatment of this devastating disease is education. Knowledge can be a powerful weapon if it leads adolescents and adults toward making health-promoting decisions. Knowledge can decrease the fear and anxiety felt by those who do not know the facts but choose to react based on emotional experiences, and knowledge can help in detecting the need for diagnosis and treatment. It is true that AIDS has many physical consequences, but remember that its psychosocial and emotional effects can be equally devastating.

There are many potential health problems, both physical and mental, in the adult world. Drug use is increasing as it becomes a way of coping with the difficulties of life. Decisions made regarding oneself and one's environment have greater consequences than they did during earlier years. Nurses working with adult clients can find many opportunities to encourage healthy living practices, which in turn can prevent many future problems from ever developing.

Mental Health Problems of Adults

A great number of the mental health disorders suffered by adults have their roots in childhood. "It is striking to think that in a given year, 22% of the adult population in the United States has some diagnosable mental disorder or that 5 million people meet the criteria for severe mental illness" (Garritson, 1994). Add to the millions of adults who are struggling to cope with the problems and crises of everyday living, and you can see why nurses, therapists, and other health care providers have opportunities to provide the psychosocial care so needed by so many.

According to the *Diagnostic and Statistical Manual of Mental Disorders* (DSM-IV), there are 15 classifications of mental disorders. The box below lists each category.

DSM-IV CLASSIFICATION OF ADULT MENTAL DISORDERS

- Cognitive disorders: delirium, dementia, amnesia
- Mental disorders resulting from a general medical condition
- Substance-related disorders
- Schizophrenia and other psychotic disorders
- Mood disorders
- Anxiety disorders
- Somatoform disorders
- Factitious disorders
- Dissociative disorders
- Sexual and gender identity disorders
- Eating disorders
- Sleep disorders
- Impulse-control disorders
- Adjustment disorders
- Personality disorders

SAMPLE CLIENT CARE PLAN

INEFFECTIVE COPING

Assessment

History: Jed is a 33-year-old man who has recently lost his job and his wife and is now being sued. Last night, he had several drinks before driving home. His car ran off an embankment and rolled into an irrigation ditch. Jed was found uninjured, sleeping in the car early this morning. He has been referred to the clinic for evaluation of his recent problems.

Current Findings: In no acute distress; several bruises on arms and face; odor of alcohol. Jed states that 6 months ago his business as a roofer failed. After 4 months of trying to find employment, Jed began to drink. One evening he and his wife had an argument. When he returned later that night, she had moved her personal belongings out of the house and left a note saying that his drinking was becoming more than she could take. For the past 2 months Jed has been spending his time "getting drunk and sobering up."

Nursing Diagnosis

Ineffective individual coping related to loss of support systems

Planning/Expected Outcomes

Jed will stay sober throughout treatment.
Jed will recognize his maladaptive behaviors and take action to solve his identified problems.

Nursing Interventions

Intervention

1. Establish a trusting relationship with Jed.

2. Assess for degree of anxiety, depression, intent to do self-harm.
3. Help Jed identify each of his problems and current coping mechanisms.
4. Have Jed make a list of what resources and support systems he has.
5. Replace the use of alcohol with crisis support person and phone number to call at any time.

6. Help Jed devise new, more effective coping responses.
7. Refer to Social Services for placement in the employment program.

Rationale

1. Trust must be present if problems are to be solved.
2. To determine levels of intervention needed; to understand Jed's viewpoint.
3. Problems must be defined before they can be solved.
4. Use of previously successful coping mechanisms helps develop multiple skills.
5. Jed knows that his drinking is an excuse to forget about his problems and is willing to call his support person when he wants a drink.
6. Builds on Jed's current problem-solving abilities.
7. Provides new resources for exploring job opportunities.

Evaluation

During the first 3 weeks of clinic visits, Jed had been drinking. By the fourth week, he had decided to quit drinking so that he could concentrate on "getting (his) life back together." By the sixth week, Jed was able to identify his most pressing problems.

Remember, though, that beyond the diagnostic label lies an individual. If nurses are willing to see through their own biases and values to their clients, then they will do much to encourage the highest possible level of functioning in each client.

Therapeutic Interventions

Although specific nursing interventions for each mental health disorder are described in later chapters, a look at the interventions available to nurses in every practice setting may be helpful. The focus of most therapeutic mental health nursing interventions relate to treatment (assisting clients to cope) or prevention.

Health Care Interventions

When working with adults, nurses can use their assessment skills to uncover clients' descriptions of their difficulties. Frequently, the physician or nurse will be actively intervening with a problem that is not as important to a client as it is to the health care provider. Make sure to elicit clients' definitions of their problems. Nursing actions will have greater results if the goals of care are as important to the client as they are to the health care provider. The box on p. 230 offers a sample client care plan for an adult with situational problems.

Work within the client's reality. Learn about the living conditions of the client. It does no good to instruct a client to take his/her medication four times a day if he/she has no watch or means of telling the time. Too many nursing interventions fail because the client's total situation is not considered.

Last, give clients written instructions if you expect any educational efforts to be effective. Everyone experiences anxiety when interacting with the health care system. People do not remember information when they are under stress. Written instructions allow them to refer back to the information when they are less anxious and more willing to follow instructions.

Preventing Mental Illness

Health care providers in every setting can do much to prevent mental-emotional disorders. Always remember that it is the whole person who receives our care. We may separate the human being into physical, mental, social, cultural, intellectual, and emotional parts, but we must consider and treat the entire person.

Each physical illness has emotional components, and each mental disorder is accompanied by physical changes. Nurses who remember this fact structure their interventions to include both. A positive step toward preventing mental illness is for health care providers to recognize the need for making mental health interventions available for all individuals, not just those persons who are "diagnosed" with a mental disorder.

❖ KEY CONCEPTS

- Adults continue to develop the emotional, intellectual, sociocultural, and spiritual dimensions of their characters.
- Parenting provides many challenges for most adults.
- The social tasks for middle adults relate to the change from being a parent back to the role of partner.
- Adults with good mental health are able to successfully adapt to life's changes.
- Adults experience developmental problems, but they are not as obvious as those of children or adolescents.
- Problems of personal identity may be related to negative childhood experiences or a person's intellectual abilities.
- Anger-control problems plague many adults, especially those who were exposed to aggressive acts as children.
- Factors such as money, family relationships, safety, housing, health practices, and spiritual beliefs affect the family, parenting practices, and children.
- Some of the major environmental problems affecting adults today include a lack of education, poverty, homelessness, substance abuse, and lack of social support.
- The term AFRAIDS (*acute fear regarding AIDS*) has been coined to describe an anxiety-related condition caused by fear of AIDS.
- Each physical illness has emotional components, and each mental disorder is accompanied by physical changes.
- Health care providers must recognize the need for making mental health interventions available for all clients, not just those persons who are "diagnosed" with a mental disorder.

❖ SUGGESTIONS FOR FURTHER READING

Please read "The Gentle Art of Nurturing Yourself" by Heinrich and Killeen (*Am J Nurs* 93[10]:41, 1993) because the ability to care for oneself is essential if we are to care for others.

❖ REFERENCES

Bower B: HIV-linked mental loss takes job toll, *Sci News* 154(9):132, 1994.

Cook JA and others: HIV-risk for psychiatric rehabilitation clientele: implications for community-based services, *Psychosoc Rehabil J* 17(4):105, 1994.

Discussion Guideline Panel: Depression in primary care: detection, diagnosis, and treatment, *J Am Acad Nurse Pract* 6(5):224, 1994.

Donohough DL: *The middle years,* Philadelphia, 1981, WB Saunders.

Edelman CL, Mandle CL: *Health promotion throughout the lifespan,* ed 3, St Louis, 1994, Mosby.

Foster J: The nurse in a center for the homeless, *Nurs Management* 23(4):38, 1992.

Garritson SH: Comments on health care reform for Americans with severe mental illness: report of the National Advisory Mental Health Council, *Cap Comm Psychiatr Nurs* 1(1):31, 1994.

Milburn N, D'Ercole A: Homeless women, children, and families, *Am Psychol* 46(11):1159, 1991.

O'Keefe M: Predictors of child abuse in maritally violent families, *J Interpers Viol* 10:3, 1995.

Rawlins RP, Williams SR, Beck CK: *Mental health-psychiatric nursing: a holistic life-cycle approach,* ed 3, St Louis, 1993, Mosby.

U.S. Bureau of Census: *Statistical abstract of the U.S.: 1993,* ed 113, Washington, DC, 1993.

Zlotnick C, Cassanego M: Unemployment and health, *Nurs Health Care* 13(2):78, 1992.

17

PROBLEMS OF LATE ADULTHOOD

LEARNING OBJECTIVES

1. Name six physical and three mental changes of older adults.

2. Explain how a lack of finances or access to health care affects the mental health of older adults.

3. Describe the drug misuse (abuse) patterns of older adults.

4. Define the term *elder abuse* and describe a typical victim.

5. Explain how depression can affect older adults' abilities to function.

6. Describe the signs/symptoms seen during the progression of Alzheimer's disease.

7. List three nursing goals for the care of clients with Alzheimer's disease, dementia, or confusion.

8. Discuss how the standards of geriatric nursing care are used in practice.

9. Identify three therapeutic interventions that promote good mental health in older adults.

KEY TERMS

adaptation
affective losses
aging
Alzheimer's disease (AD)
catastrophic reactions

conative loss
delirium
dementia
elder abuse
functional assessment

gerontophobia
hoarding
integrity
memory loss

Aging is the process of growing older. Older adulthood, or maturity, is defined as the period in life from 65 years of age until death. Until recently, everyone older than 65 was considered "old," but as people have begun to live longer, our concepts of aging are changing. Ideas of aging are no longer based on the number of years an individual has been alive. This chapter focuses on the psychosocial adaptations made by older adults and the mental health disorders that affect this age group.

Overview of Aging

The aging process begins at birth, but few signs are noticed until well into middle age. With the passage of enough time, however, changes become apparent, and physical maturity begins to be replaced by the aging process. These are the senior citizen, geriatric, or elderly years (Fig. 17-1), a time of deep satisfaction and happiness to despair and sadness.

There are several theories or ideas about the aging process. Biological theories attempt to explain why we age physically. Psychosocial theories focus on the mental health aspects of aging.

The number of people 65 years old and older is growing dramatically. Today, because of scientific, medical, and technological advances, people are living longer and enjoying better health than their ancestors. The number of older Americans has nearly quadrupled (grown by four times) since the early 1900s. In 1980, there were about 24 million adults over the age of 65 in the United States. By 1995, that number had grown to over 34 million Americans (Associated Press, 1995). Nearly one of every eight adults in the United States is 65 or older. American elderly also appear to live longer than their counterparts in Europe and Japan (Associated Press, 1995).

Older adults are fast becoming an important segment of the population. Many continue to remain active members of their communities. Such organizations as the Grey Panthers and the American Association for Retired People have strong economic and political influences in the United States today. In 1990, over 11% of people over 65 were still employed (U.S. Bureau of Census, 1993). The "graying of America" will offer many challenges and rewards for the health care providers who work with our older citizens.

Facts and Myths of Aging

Many people carry mental pictures or myths of older adults as people who are wearing out, biding their time until the unescapable end arrives. This is a myth, a story based on little or no fact. In reality, the majority of older adults are dynamic individuals, living within their homes and functioning successfully within their communities (Edelman and Mandle, 1994).

Another myth of aging is that elders live in nursing homes. The facts show that only about "5% of them are in institutional settings, except in the 85-year-and-older age group, in which approximately 20% are in institutions" (Hogstel, 1995). More than half the adults older than 65 are still living at home with a husband or wife, and many maintain their own households alone. New living arrangements are being designed as the elder population continues to expand. Independent living centers, life contract facilities, foster homes, subsidized housing, and group

Fig. 17-1   Older adulthood can be a rewarding time. (From Edelman CL, Mandle CL: *Health promotion throughout the lifespan,* ed 3, St Louis, 1994, Mosby.)

living situations are all being explored as options for housing the elderly.

"The majority of the elderly are poor" or "the majority of the elderly are rich" are two myths that explode on further examination. Actually, the economic status of older adults is as varied as that of any other age group. Incomes for the majority of people older than 65 fall somewhere between the 500,000 millionaires and 12% of older adults who are living in poverty.

Perhaps the cruelest myth though is that young and attractive is "good," whereas old and imperfect is "bad." Today's modern society places little value on its elders. Other cultures hold older adults in high esteem and value their wisdom and experience (Giger and Davidhizar, 1995) (see box below).

It is difficult for young people to imagine growing old. As they mature, adults and children alike are repeatedly exposed to the negative or "bad" aspects of aging. Over a period of years, a fear of growing old develops, and anything associated with aging is avoided. "This fear of aging and refusal to accept the elderly into the mainstream of society is known as **gerontophobia**" (Wold, 1993). This attitude leads to stereotyping older adults as unattractive, dull, and useless, and it can affect both old and young alike. It is important for health care providers who work with older adults to look at their own attitudes and values about aging. The journey through life is for the most part taken as an adult, living in the currents of change.

Physical Health Changes

As an individual ages, so does every body system. The physical changes of aging are not noticeable until the late 30s. By the 50s, one cannot deny the effects of time. Signs of aging continue to show themselves until around 85. After that, people appear to age little until their deaths.

The physical aging process varies greatly. It is affected by genetics, early physical and mental health care, current lifestyle practices, and attitude. Refer to a basic nursing text for a discussion of the physical changes that are associated with normal aging. Fig. 17-2 shows one effect of decreasing sensory abilities in an elderly woman.

Mental Health Changes

Older adulthood is a time for **adaptation,** for adjusting to change. Developmental tasks at this stage are just as challenging as those of earlier stages. According to the theorist Erikson, older adults who have developed a sense of personal **integrity** (state of wholeness, of being complete) accept the worth and uniqueness of their own lifestyles. They are able to find order and meaning in their lives. A sense of the

 CULTURAL ASPECTS

In traditional Korean families, elders hold a high place of honor. The responsibility of caring for them in old age falls to the first-born son, who inherits the family leadership and most of the property.

Japanese people have close ties between the generations. Care of the elderly traditionally falls to the oldest son or an unmarried adult in the family. It is interesting to note that until recently there were few nursing homes (long-term care facilities) for the aged in Japan.

Native Americans value the wisdom of their older adults. Historically, most of their tribal leaders had attained a large amount of experience and knowledge before assuming leadership positions. Native American families were large, extended groups, and the care of the elderly was shared by every family member.

Fig. 17-2 Decreased sensory abilities and function. (From Edelman CL, Mandle CL: *Health promotion throughout the lifespan,* ed 3, St Louis, 1994, Mosby.)

flow of time (past, present, future) allows them to face life's challenges with grace and inner strength. They know they will survive because they have so many times in the past. If their relationships with their children have been positive, they experience love and respect from their offspring. In short, the elder is able to accept his/her own life (as it actually was and is) and value the contributions that he/she has made.

For older adults who have not reached a sense of wholeness, life is viewed with despair. Individuals become unhappy, feel that life has been a waste, and focus on "what might have been." They blame others for life's misfortunes. A sense of loss and contempt for other people leads these individuals to a sad and lonely lifestyle.

Mental health changes in older adults have been the subject of much study in recent times. The popular belief was that mental abilities decrease slowly with advancing age. The truth, we are learning, is not so simple.

Some mental functions peak in childhood, others in adolescence. Although short-term memory and speed begin to decline in the 40s, such mental capabilities as judgment and wisdom continue to improve as one grows older (Table 17-1). "What's more, research over the past decades shows that the mind constantly adjusts its way of doing things and compensates nicely for the many losses in efficiency" (White, 1993).

Common Problems of Older Adults

Older adults must cope with many changes. They are required to adjust to physical changes that accompany the passage of time. Often they will attempt to do tasks beyond their physical limits because it is difficult to see themselves as aging.

Older adults are faced with loss through the death of spouse, family, and friends. Retirement brings a loss of income and opportunities for socialization. Living arrangements may need to be changed, and relationships with adult children are often redefined. Older adults "must also learn to acquire new activities and interests to maintain the quality of life" (Potter and Perry, 1995). These challenges are common to many older adults. For some, adaptation to change comes easily and without discomfort. For others, however, each life change is stormy and produces major stresses.

Health care providers, especially those in the nursing profession, play a major role in caring for older adults. The problems encountered by elderly clients challenge and test our resources. As the population continues to age, nurses will be called on to assist many clients in coping with the changes of growing older.

Physical Adaptations

Because of normal changes associated with aging, many people believe that an inability to do physical activity is the natural result of growing older. However, much research has pointed to the importance of remaining physically active throughout life. Aerobic and muscle-strengthening exercises can prevent many of the physical problems associated with aging. Although the 70-year-old man cannot perform the same amount of physical labor in the same time a 30-year-old man does, he *can* perform the same amount of work if given extra time. The task will be done, it just takes longer. It is important, as nurses, to encourage daily physical activity in every client. A sound physical body usually houses a sound psychosocial "body."

In addition to adapting to changes in endurance and the ability to do physical work, older adults must cope with a body that wants to adjust itself to a new routine. Changes in eating and sleeping patterns take place as one ages. Once, one was able to sleep through the night. Now some need or another often awakens the older adult. One used to be able to eat anything; now antacids are placed at strategic locations throughout the house. The volume on the television creeps up; lights are adjusted to decrease the glare, and the odors drifting from the kitchen while awaiting dinner seem to be less inviting. Even without the problems of a chronic illness, adjusting to the small, everyday physical changes of aging is not an easy process.

Older adults face many alterations in their lifestyles that may affect them physically. Aged individuals who live alone, for example, tend to neglect their nutritional needs. They may eat too much or not enough or use their limited finances to buy less costly, empty-calorie foods. Many elders are not physically able to prepare their meals. Others suffer from sensory, dental, or digestive problems. Over time, the lack of adequate food intake results in chronic malnutrition. Resistance to the effects of stress and disease drops, and the risk for serious health problems increases. The box on p. 238 presents a typical case study.

Sexuality remains important for many older adults. The focus shifts from having children to an expression of caring, of intimate communication, of sharing. Adaptations may have to be made in the expression of sexuality because of physical limits or the presence of chronic health problems. A decrease in hormone secretions brings about some physical changes in the reproductive systems of older adults, but both men and women are capable of remaining sexually active well into their 90s.

Physical adaptations to aging include the loss of one's ability to move about freely. The loss of a driv-

◆ **TABLE 17-1**
Normal Mental Changes of Aging

Area of Function	Changes Associated With Aging
Attention: alertness, maintaining focus, noticing	Attention is fully developed by college age; declines slowly after age 70; easy to distract
Cognitive style: ability to adapt, to roll with punches of life	Mental decline is more rapid in people who are rigid; flexibility in midlife reduces risk of mental decline
Crystallized intelligence: specialized accumulated knowledge (nursing, engineering, technical skills)	Remains intact until 75 or older; may possibly remain intact until death
Episodic memory: ability to register and store memories of events in time and space, to retrieve memories	Retains memories of recent events when able to anchor them to own experiences, knowledge base
Information processing: ability to relate to, store, and retrieve information	Processing speed decreases with age; may take longer to retrieve information
Learning new tasks	Learning enhances many mental functions; people who do not continue to learn experience slowing and decline in many areas (which is reversible when one resumes learning)
Memory: names and faces	Decreases fairly rapidly in middle age; often considered worse than truly is; like people of all ages, older adults must process information by associating it to related data
Metamemory: judgment of one's ability to monitor and control one's own mental processes	After 40, older adults make conscious efforts to learn, manage, store, and remember new information; metamemory remains active in older adults who use their intelligence and lead active lives
Mood: emotions, feelings	People with frequent negative emotions have higher incidence of depression; depression is common in older adults
Perceptual speed: ability to become alert and respond	Perceptual speed slows after age 50 but may not be noticed; elderly score lower on timed tests but better on others
Personality: behavioral traits that make a person a unique individual	Personality is established in childhood and remains stable throughout life; if one was happy child, one is usually happy older adult; a cranky elder was often an obnoxious child
Reasoning: ability to solve problems and make choices, comparisons, and judgments	Great individual differences between 60 and 80; after 80, some loss noticed; people with active mental lives decline more slowly
Retrieval of information: ability to bring stored information into active consciousness	Takes longer after 50; more errors in retrieving; as persons age, there are more data to match up; slower information retrieval is sign of rich, well-stocked memory
Working memory: random access memory; memory to which one refers	Increases through childhood and peaks during early adulthood; strengthens with use through connecting of neurons that occurs with learning

Modified from White K: *Psychol Today* 26(6):38, 1993.

er's license can have a strong impact on one's independence and abilities to provide for the necessities of living. Without private or public transportation, many of our elderly are severely restricted in their abilities to move freely about the community.

Adapting to the physical changes of aging can pose many problems that place an individual at higher risk for mental health disorders. Physical problems can lead to changes in mental status. Older adults commonly have vague, generally nonspecific physical signs/symptoms that may mask a mental health disorder. Drug-drug interactions, food-drug interactions, or drug side effects can cause both physical and psychological problems. Every health care provider who works with older adults must be alert for the existence of physical problems. Early assessment and intervention are the key for keeping older adults' minor physical problems from becoming major ones.

CASE STUDY

Ned was 70 years old when he lost his beloved Molly, his wife of 50 years. They met while they were still in high school, married soon after the War, and swore never to be apart again. Four children filled the years with joy and hard work, and retirement was packed with new friends and experiences.

But once Molly was gone, life for Ned became filled with gloom. He no longer sought out his long-time friends. He stopped playing golf and horseshoes. He sold the motor home and retired into his darkened living room. Well-meaning friends often stopped by, but by the time they departed, they had taken on Ned's gloom instead of cheering him.

Soon Ned stopped eating. Molly had always prepared his meals, and he felt lost and unhappy every time he walked into the kitchen where Molly had spent so many hours. By the time his daughter visited Ned, he was confused and unable to care for himself. Assuming he had suffered a stroke, Ned's children admitted him to a long-term care facility.

Clinical Decisions

1. Could early nursing interventions have prevented Ned from being removed from his home?

2. Do you think Ned is better off at home or in the long-term care facility?

Psychosocial Adaptations

Until the ability to transport people across great distances was established, the psychosocial adaptations of people were less complex. Before the 1920s, it was not uncommon for individuals to grow up, marry, raise a family, and grow old within one community or group of people. People were cared for in their own homes as they aged, with relatives or friends attending to their well-being. If they became confused or forgetful, friends and surroundings were a source of comfort and familiarity.

Today, growing old has become more impersonal. The comforts of family and friends may lie miles away. Older adults may be saddled with problems relating to money, adequate food and housing, or health care. The loss of loved ones, social status, and earning power withers social support systems, and decreasing sensory abilities leave many elders questioning the soundness of their judgments.

The majority of older adults benefit from health care interventions. Nurses, because of their focus on the activities of daily living, are able to meet many of the elderly's needs. Nurses and other health care providers who work with older adults also help to fill the gap for missing family members by providing emotional and social support. The following section discusses a few of the most important problems faced by the elderly and some basic interventions (nursing actions).

Economics

The outlook of older adults in regard to money and financial security differs greatly from that of young adults. People in their 80s were born at least 15 years before the Great Depression of the 1930s. They were old enough to feel the pangs of hunger that arrive when food is scarce. They remember men selling ap-

ples on the street corners of large cities, and they have experienced the uncertainty of wondering how they were going to survive tomorrow. Many of these people even raised children during the Depression, sacrificing food from their own mouths to feed their offspring. The Depression years of the 1920s and 1930s forged an indelible memory on our older adults. Many of their seemingly strange behaviors such as **hoarding** are the result of attitudes learned during those difficult years. The 90 year old who takes doggie bags home from the restaurant to wither in the refrigerator remembers the Great Depression and cannot bear to waste food. The collections of newspaper, clothing, string, old magazines, and other assorted odds, ends, and useless items are protection for leaner days that may lie ahead.

Because of inflation, the value of a country's currency (e.g., dollar, pound, mark) changes, sometimes dramatically. Older adults in the United States have seen the price of a loaf of bread go from 5 cents to 2 dollars. During this time, many elderly people have followed savings plans or invested for their later years. Some are now financially comfortable, whereas others, not having realized the change in the actual value of a dollar, are coping with fewer resources than they had expected. People who made no preparations for later life often find themselves at the mercy of an impersonal system, living on meager resources with little quality in their lives.

The elderly are also faced with the problem of being financially vulnerable. Older people were taught to trust their fellow men, to take a person "at their word," and to believe that people spoke the truth. This background, combined with diminishing sight, hearing, or understanding, leaves older adults vulnerable to the scams, deceptions, and threats of con men and criminals. Many older adults have lost their life's savings because they could not understand the language on a contract or allowed themselves to be charmed or intimidated out of their money.

Although actual interventions relating to money are most often provided by social workers, nurses can assess for indications of financial problems and refer clients to the appropriate resource. Remember to monitor elderly clients. Worry about money can lead to mental health problems such as depression, anxiety, or paranoia.

Housing

Problems with housing for older adults range from having "too much house" to having none at all. In the United States during 1992, the majority of adults older than 65 lived in their own homes (54%) with their spouses, 31% of older adults lived alone, and about 15% resided with someone else (U.S. Bureau of Census, 1993). These statistics, of course, do not take into account the number of elderly who have no homes because homeless people are difficult to count.

The problems of "too much house" usually arise when one spouse passes away and the remaining person is unable to care for the property. Because women tend to outlive men, the most common scenario is that of a newly widowed woman who is faced with the care of a house about whose maintenance she knows nothing. She may live there for many years of widowhood, but eventually she will be forced to move to a safer environment that requires less responsibility and upkeep.

The problems of "too little house" are homelessness and despair. Older homeless adults make up from 4% to 15% of the homeless population in the United States (based on data collected from various federal and state programs). Many are mentally ill. "Older people are especially vulnerable in the streets, shelters, abandoned buildings, and subways. Although there are fewer older homeless mentally ill persons, they are usually sicker and have more needs for health services than the younger homeless" (Hogstel, 1995).

As the population of older adults increases, new arrangements in housing are being developed. Housing options for those older adults who did not have their own home were once limited to senior hotels, nursing homes, or isolated apartments. Today, inventive new plans and living arrangements are evolving for older adults.

Health Care

The availability of health care is an important factor in maintaining both physical and mental health of older adults. In the United States, persons older than 65 are covered by a national health program called Medicare. Canadian and British citizens have national health insurance for people of all ages.

Older adults in the United States must pay premiums for their medical insurance. In addition, they are required to cover other out-of-pocket expenses, such as medication costs and associated deductible and coinsurance costs. Because of these expenses, many older adults either do not seek medical care or are unable to afford the costs of their medications and treatments. Do not assume that older clients are receiving medical care. Many elderly place their health care needs in the background when they are unable to afford the costs.

Health services may be available and affordable, but without transportation, visits to health care providers are few. Older adults who live alone or have sensory problems often find it difficult to obtain health services because of the obstacles they must overcome. Periods of confusion and forgetfulness may cloud an elder's ability to follow therapeutic instructions, and many confused people attempt to disguise or cover up the problem by being very cooperative and voicing understanding.

Not all older adults use health care services equally. The majority of services are used by the seriously or terminally ill, many of whom happen to be elderly. "Studies done by the Health Care Financing Administration (HCFA) indicate that 2% of the over-65 population receiving Medicare account for 34% of all the costs. Overall, 72% of the total resources are used by only 10% of the aging population" (Wold, 1993).

Because of the high costs associated with treating these clients, many serious questions are being raised about how health care dollars are being spent. Nurses and every health care provider involved with older adults must become aware of the expenses involved in delivering health care. If we become careful and practical with the use of supplies and spend our clients' health care dollars as if they were our own, then the health care profession can go a long way in controlling the skyrocketing costs of health care for older adults.

Loss and Death

Elderly people can cope with many of life's problems, but perhaps their greatest mental health challenge is coping with the loss of loved ones and friends. We tend to travel life's paths with companions, friends, relatives, and people who have become important in our lives. With the passage of time, many older adults lose those individuals who are important for their emotional support and well-being. When a spouse of many years is lost, the remaining partner is

THINK ABOUT
◆ How do you picture yourself at 80 years old?
◆ How physically active do you expect to be?
◆ Have you thought about or made any plans for re-
  tirement?
◆ At what age do you think a person should think
  about retirement?

left to cope alone. Not infrequently, couples who have been together for many years will die within months of each other. It seems the will to carry on without the loved one is lost, and death becomes an opportunity to be reunited with those one loves.

Losses during the older years also arrive in various other forms. The loss of physical stamina and endurance and the loss of sharp senses with which to enjoy the world present problems and challenges for older adults. Although the concept of loss is described in a later chapter, it is important to remember that coping with loss is one of the most difficult problems of older adults. They need compassion, understanding, and support if they are to reestablish the psychosocial connections that bind us together (see box above).

Substance Abuse

The misuse or abuse of chemicals is a complex issue for older adults. The elderly receive a great number of prescription drugs to treat multiple and chronic health problems. "Seventy-five percent of persons over the age of 65 use some kind of medication, one-third of which are over-the-counter medications; 25% of all prescriptions are written for persons over age 65" (Hogstel, 1995). Older adults also metabolize and excrete drugs more slowly. Their decreased tolerance for most drugs can result in overdoses and more severe interactions with other medications and foods.

Older adults with several health problems may visit with many specialists, with each one prescribing a different medication. The purchase of over-the-counter drugs compounds the situation by increasing the potential for adverse reactions. In addition, many of the elderly use several pharmacies, share their prescriptions with friends, and follow the recommendations of those offering a new "cure" or relief from their discomfort.

Hoarding drugs is common because of the expense and the possible need for them in the future. Many will underdose themselves to save money and make medications last longer. Outdated medications are seldom thrown away.

Nurses have a special responsibility to ensure that their older clients are using their medications correctly. This responsibility includes a thorough assessment of a client's drug history, current drug use (prescribed, over the counter, and recreational), and an understanding of the medications currently being taken (see box on p. 241).

Although the use of recreational or street drugs decreases with age, some drugs, especially alcohol, still cause problems for many older adults. Alcohol use helps to provide a substitute for social interactions, and many of the elderly drink to dull the discomforts associated with isolation. Older adults who were heavy drinkers in the past often show the results of long-term alcohol abuse.

The use of opiates (heroin, opium) is even more invisible than the use of alcohol. Older Asian-Americans with opium addictions or retired white-collar workers addicted to cocaine seldom reach the attention of health care providers because their habits do not usually result in the serious medical complications usually associated with alcohol.

Nurses should assess older adults for signs of substance abuse whenever an unusual accident or event occurs. Often a history of minor accidents and injuries signals a problem with drugs. If problems with drug or alcohol use are suspected, the client is referred to a physician for a medical assessment.

Mental Health Problems of Older Adults

People older than age 65 suffer from the same mental health disorders as adolescents and younger adults. In addition, older adults are faced with the mental health problems of vulnerability and abuse, memory loss, dementia, and Alzheimer's disease. Mental health difficulties can result from physical or biochemical disorders, such as diabetes or electrolyte imbalances. Many threats to an older adult's mental health arise from loneliness and social isolation. Psychological problems with which individuals have struggled throughout their lives follow them into old age. Although all major mental health disorders can occur in older adults, by far the most common disorders relate to depression and loss.

Elder Abuse

Older adults view the world from a different point of view than younger people. Many are lonely and easily trust an individual who is kind or interested in them. Older adults without adequate support are a vulnerable population—those persons who are open

DRUG ALERT

NURSING PROCESS

Assessment

1. Obtain a complete drug history: name of drug, reason prescribed, amount taken, how often taken. Is drug taken with other medications, on an empty or full stomach, at a certain time? What is your client's knowledge about the drug's side effects, drug-food interactions?
2. Instruct the client to put every medication he/she has into a paper bag and bring them to you. Check each medication for expiration date. Be alert for several bottles of the same medication. Do not forget to include all over-the-counter products, vitamins, and herbal or natural remedies.
3. Assess the client's ability to follow verbal and written instructions and the client's willingness to learn about each medication.

Planning

1. Based on the client's abilities to understand and cooperate, develop a plan for teaching and monitoring the client's use of the drug.
2. Arrange for the client to return-demonstrate the steps in identifying and taking the medication if necessary. Include family members in the teaching process when possible.

Nursing Diagnoses

Possible nursing diagnoses include:
Knowledge deficit relating to use, administration, and monitoring of prescribed medications
Ineffective management of therapeutic regimen because of sensory loss
Noncompliance related to altered thought processes

Nursing Interventions

1. Teach the client and significant others about the proper use and dosage of each medication, side effects and what to do about them, and expected therapeutic actions.
2. Devise a system for taking daily medications. Pill dispensers are available at most pharmacies. These multiboxed units can hold up to 1 week's medications. They usually consist of a series of small compartments, which are filled with all the drugs that must be taken at a certain time. The client opens the compartment at the prescribed time and takes every medication in the box. Having the client return weekly with his/her medications and pill dispenser allows the nurse to monitor the medications taken and refill the dispenser with the appropriate medications.

Evaluation

1. Assess the client's therapeutic response to the medications. Is the blood pressure down? Has the pain been relieved? Did the drug do what it was intended to do?
2. Evaluate the client's willingness and ability to cooperate. Has there been any change in the client's alertness, level of understanding, or memory?

---

to assault or attack by others. They are the abused elderly.

Elder abuse is defined as any action on the part of a caregiver to take advantage of an older person, his/her emotional well-being, or property (Minakar and Frishman, 1995). Elder abuse can appear in various forms, ranging from physical neglect to stealing money and exploiting the older person's resources. Table 17-2 lists several ways in which elder abuse occurs.

The victims of elder abuse are divided into "two broad categories: (1) those in which the elder has physical or mental impairment and depends on the family for daily care needs and (2) those in which care needs are minimal or overshadowed by the pathologic behavior of the caregiver" (All, 1994). The typical abused elder is a woman at least 75 years old with physical or mental problems who is living with a relative. Often the responsibilities of care can lead even well-intentioned family members or caregivers to lose their tempers when they are stressed, pressured, or exhausted. However, losing control assists neither the victim nor the caregiver.

Abuse of the elderly is not new, but it has just begun to receive public attention. Although the actual numbers of abused elderly are unknown, in 1994 over 241,000 incidents involving the mistreatment of persons older than age 65 were reported in the United States (*Harvard Mental Health Letter,* 1995). Experts agree that this figure is only the tip of the iceberg and that the actual numbers of abused elderly are far greater. Nurses must be aware of and alert for the indications of abuse in every older client. Chapter 26 focuses on the recognition, prevention, and treatment of this problem.

Depression

In addition to the losses experienced through death, retirement, and relocation, many older adults are faced with losing their social supports. As stresses mount and resources are lost, many older individuals become saddened. This emotional state continues, and unless it is interrupted by the attentions of others, the only remaining outlook is bleak and hopeless. The mood becomes overpowering and reaches into every aspect of one's life. Individuals feel hopelessness and powerless to do anything about it. The fu-

◆ **TABLE 17-2**
Forms of Elder Abuse

Type of Abuse	Description and Examples
Exploitation	Improper use of a person for one's own profit. *Examples:* theft of objects, diversion of elder's money into own pocket, use of legal power assigned by the older adult for own gain. An estimated 10% of the elderly are exploited.
Neglect	Refusing to meet basic physical and mental health needs. *Examples:* depriving food, drink, clothing, shelter, hygiene, corrective and remedial devices (e.g., glasses, hearing aids); refusal to seek medical care, even when urgently needed; refusing to interact, to provide for love, belonging, social needs. About 65% of abused elderly are neglected.
Physical abuse	Physical harm caused by the actions of another person. *Examples:* beating, whipping, scalding, cigarette burns, bruises, fractures.
Psychological abuse	Threats to mental health caused by another person. *Examples:* poor personal hygiene, grooming, environmental conditions; threats of nursing home placement; being humiliated, threatened, or socially isolated; verbal assaults, name calling; being treated like a child; being placed in seclusion.
Violation of rights	The refusal to allow another the exercise of individual rights. These rights include the right to consent for medical treatment or surgery, refuse treatment, live in a safe environment of choice, privacy, and the right to use personal financial resources as desired.

Modified from Hogstel MO: *Geropsychiatric nursing,* ed 2, St Louis, 1995, Mosby.

ture holds no joy, only the possibility of suffering more tomorrow than today. This is the face of depression in older adults.

Depression is probably the most common mental health disorder of late adulthood. It is estimated that over 15% of older adults in the community have depressive signs/symptoms (Blixen, Wilkinson, and Schuring, 1994). Older adults in long-term care institutions or hospitals have even higher rates of depression. It is commonly underdiagnosed and undertreated because it can be difficult to detect. Sometimes vague complaints are the only clue. Other times, depression will mask itself as a physical illness. Knowing clients' lifestyles, preferences, social habits, and attitudes toward life is important. With this knowledge, nurses can assess for the signs/symptoms that signal the onset of depression. Offering emotional support and interest in older clients helps to prevent depression by reestablishing the human connection that elders so often need. Remember that a single person can make a difference in the quality of an elderly individual's life.

Dementia and Alzheimer's Disease

Dementia relates to those mental health problems caused by a medical condition or substance (e.g., abused drug, medication, toxin). Problems of this nature were referred to as organic brain syndromes in the past.

The cognitive (intellectual) changes of older adults may range from mild lapses in memory to multiple, severe behavioral changes. **Memory loss** is the inability to recall a certain detail or event. It is a natural part of the aging process and affects most people older than 70. **Delirium** is a change of consciousness that occurs over a short period of time. It can be caused by various medical conditions, a variety of drugs and their interactions, or other problems. **Dementia** is a loss of multiple abilities, including short-term and long-term memory, language, and the ability to conceptualize (understand).

Dementia is a broad term that describes a group of symptoms relating to a severe loss of intellectual functions (Hamdy and others, 1994). The condition may be reversible if the cause is discovered and treated early. There are more than 60 causes associated with dementia (Lamy, 1993). They include metabolic problems; hormonal abnormalities; infections; cardiovascular disorders; brain traumas, infections, or tumors; pain; sensory deprivations; toxic alcoholic reactions; anemia; chemical intoxications; drug interactions; and nutritional deficiencies such as vitamin B_{12}, folic acid, or niacin.

Remember to assess older clients thoroughly and completely. The minor observations of one nurse can prevent a client from suffering the consequences of dementia. Do not automatically assume that clients are unable. The label "dementia" should never be an excuse for considering a client helpless.

Dementia of the Alzheimer's type presents special challenges. "As many as 4 million Americans are affected by **Alzheimer's disease (AD),** a progressive, degenerative disorder that impedes the functioning of brain cells and synapses and results in impaired memory, thinking, and behavior" (Phelps, 1993).

The unique characteristics of this condition were first described by a German psychiatrist, Alois Alzheimer, in 1907. He related the case of a 51-year-old woman who had a severely impaired ability to encode information, compromised language functions, and delusions. When she died from this severe form of progressive dementia, an autopsy of her brain revealed that it was shrunken, contained abnormal tangles of nerve fibers, and had clusters of degenerated nerve endings throughout the cortex. Since this first description, the pathological findings of AD have been the subject of intense study and research.

The number of older adults with dementia increases with age. Approximately 5% of 65 year olds and about 80% of 80 year olds experience some degree of dementia (Miceli, 1993). Over 50% of these persons suffer from AD. Each year more than 250,000 new cases of AD are diagnosed; as life expectancy continues to increase, the number of people with AD will grow considerably. Because people with AD can live more than 20 years after diagnosis, many elderly people need extensive care. In fact, AD is "the single largest cause of institutionalization of aged people in the United States and other Western nations" (Lamy, 1993). Nurses must be knowledgeable about the effects of AD and other dementias for we will be caring for many of these people.

The diagnosis of AD is not clear cut. Today, the only way to surely diagnose AD is through an analysis of the brain tissue (from biopsy or autopsy). Therefore a diagnosis is usually made by exclusion—that is, by exploring and ruling out all other causes of dementia (Fackelmann, 1995).

Many times a client's dementia may be the result of a drug interaction or reaction. Other times, dementia occurs as the result of a medical condition. Careful and thorough history, physical examination, and mental status examinations are performed and the diagnosis of AD is made after all the findings are considered (Newbern, 1991). Today, researchers are working intensively to develop a diagnostic test for AD.

Promising results have been seen with a type of skin testing, brain imaging techniques, and genetic studies (Fackelmann, 1995).

AD involves a gradual, progressive death of one's brain and its functions. It is found in persons as young as 40, but the incidence increases with advancing age. AD progresses slowly and involves a loss in every area of functioning.

In normal aging, cognitive (intellectual) and psychomotor (physical) changes are to be expected. Reaction times slow and lapses of memory commonly occur. Learning new skills requires more time and practice, but intelligence and understanding (cognitive functions) remain intact (Fawcett, 1993).

Persons with AD, however, lose their cognitive (intellectual) abilities and suffer many intellectual losses. They cannot recall any recent events or process new information. They become increasingly forgetful and may display personality changes. Slowly, other changes take place. As the disease progresses, individuals usually develop one or more of the following:

aphasia: a loss of language
apraxia: loss of ability to perform everyday actions, activities
agnosia: loss of recognition of previously known or familiar people and objects

Soon individuals with AD become unable to make even the simplest decisions or choices. Following a conversation eventually becomes impossible because speech becomes disjointed, simplified, and empty. As the disease continues, many people develop mutism (inability to speak) or speak in guttural tones or grunts.

The intellectual losses of AD are accompanied by the slow drain of one's own personality **(affective losses).** The power to control one's emotions declines as the person with AD fades into childlike, antisocial, or emotionally labile behaviors. As the disease progresses and the ability to interpret data (process information) is lost, individuals with AD become lost and absorbed in themselves. Some may even experience delusions, hallucinations, and feelings of paranoia.

Another loss for persons with AD relates to the ability to make and carry out plans **(conative loss).** People who have AD lose the ability to plan and then follow through on even the simplest activities. The everyday tasks of living, such as dressing, grooming, and bathing, become overwhelming challenges. The harder they concentrate on the activity, the more difficult the activity becomes to perform. Stress, anger, and frustration increase fatigue levels because everything requires so much energy. "Remember that their short-term memory is diminished or gone, so everything that happens seems to be happening for the first time" (Stolley, 1994).

The last loss focuses on the loss of the ability to withstand stress. Persons with AD become less and less able to cope with stress as the disease progresses. What once were minor anxieties cascade into full **catastrophic reactions,** in which the person becomes increasingly confused, agitated, and fearful. They may wander, become noisy, act compulsively, or behave violently. Because of the lowered stress threshold, it takes fewer and fewer stimuli to produce these overwhelming behavioral reactions. For this reason, the nursing care for clients with AD disease centers around providing a low-stimuli environment with as few as possible stress-provoking situations (Tackenberg, 1992).

Treatments for AD are presently limited to providing physical and emotional support. Drug therapy is beginning to show promise with the medication tactrine (Cognex) (*Harvard Mental Health Letter,* 1995). Lately, researchers have demonstrated that certain antiinflammatory drugs "may forestall or slow the devastation of Alzheimer's disease" (Fackelmann, 1994). Until definite diagnostic and treatment measures are discovered, the care of persons suffering from AD is focused on providing the highest quality of life possible during the slow progression of the disease.

Most persons with AD are cared for in the home by friends or family members until the demands of care become too great or the individual's safety is threatened (e.g., wandering, smoking). Many are admitted to long-term care facilities in the final stages of the disease. Others arrive earlier if family support is unavailable because persons with AD cannot be left alone for any period of time. Once the client adjusts to his/her new surroundings, the quality of life often improves. Family members are frequently relieved as the tremendous responsibility of providing for every need of their loved one (without recognition or thanks) is lifted off their shoulders.

Nurses who work with clients with AD should first perform a **functional assessment,** an analysis of each client's abilities to perform the activities of daily living. How do they eat, bathe, move, and provide for their own hygiene? This information helps to establish an important baseline for comparisons later as the client deteriorates.

Nursing care for clients with AD has three major goals:

1. Provide for clients' safety and well-being
2. Manage client behaviors therapeutically
3. Provide support for family, relatives, and caregivers

Persons with AD are unable to care for themselves, even in the most basic ways. They have no sense of safety or concept of danger. When they wander, they may walk in the street, step out in front of moving vehicles, or sit on the railroad tracks. Because of this ab-

---

TIPS FOR MANAGING CONFUSION

- Determine physical, social, and psychological history of client before confusion.
- Identify potential dangers to client in environment.
- Place identification bracelet on client.
- Touch client to convey acceptance if appropriate.
- Identify strategies used by home caregiver to provide comfort as appropriate.
- Monitor cognitive functioning using an appropriate screening tool.
- Avoid unfamiliar situations when possible.
- Identify usual patterns of behavior for such activities as sleep, medication use, elimination, food intake, and self-care.
- Allow client to eat alone if appropriate.
- Provide finger foods to maintain nutrition for client who will not sit and eat.
- Provide client a general orientation to season of year by using holiday decorations.
- Decrease noise levels by avoiding paging systems and call lights that ring or buzz as appropriate.
- Select one-to-one activities geared to client's cognitive abilities and interests.
- Label familiar photos with names of individuals.
- Limit visitors to one or two people at a time.
- Instruct visitors as to appropriate topics to discuss with client.
- Give one simple direction at a time.
- Address client by name when initiating interaction.
- Provide boundaries, such as red or yellow tape on the floor, when low-stimulus units are not available.
- Place client's name in large block letters in his/her room and on his/her clothing.
- Use symbols rather than written signs to assist client to locate room, bathroom, or other equipment.
- Refrain from using physical restraints.
- Monitor carefully for physiological causes for increased confusion.

Modified from McCloskey JC: *Classification of nursing interventions (NIC),* St Louis, 1992, Mosby.

sent sense of danger, many facilities that care for AD clients have restricted or locked environments. Here, clients are safe from both the threats of physical harm and overstimulation.

Nurses also protect their AD clients by providing for their daily needs. Bathing, grooming, eating, and physical activity for persons with AD all require nursing interventions tailored to the individual. When clients behave inappropriately, they are gently redirected in less stressful activities. The box on p. 244 offers a few tips for managing confusion in the elderly.

Family members and friends who visit often are included in planning care, and many nursing actions are directed at providing support and understanding for them. It has often been said that AD is worse on the caregivers, who must stand by helplessly as they watch the person they love lose himself/herself and fade into a vague, unconscious existence. Never forget

---

SAMPLE CLIENT CARE PLAN
DYSFUNCTIONAL GRIEVING

Assessment

History: Moe and Mary were married for over 40 years when Mary died last month. Since her death, Moe has refused to leave his home. His days are spent in front of the television, eating snack food. Friends no longer visit because Moe refuses to turn off the TV, and it is too difficult to converse above the noise. For the past week, Moe has not bathed or changed his clothes.

Current Findings: A sad-looking man, untidy, with a strong body odor. Speech is slow, answers with one word. When asked, states that "life is no longer worth living without Mary."

Nursing Diagnosis

Dysfunctional grieving related to loss of long-time spouse

Planning/Expected Outcomes

Moe will acknowledge his loss and express emotions appropriate to the grief process.

Nursing Interventions

Intervention

1. Identify which task of mourning must be accomplished (acknowledge loss, work with pain, adjustment to loss).
2. Help Moe express his feelings about Mary's death.
3. Assure Moe that his emotions are normal expressions of grief.
4. Encourage Moe to talk about both positive and negative qualities of their relationship.

5. Engage Moe in social activities and refer to senior support group.

Rationale

1. Helps place client on the grief continuum to begin grief work and reintegration into life.

2. To prevent unexpressed emotions from being directed inward.
3. Provides reassurance, acceptance of feelings.

4. Realistic appraisal of loss gives clearer perspective and promotes acceptance of current situation.
5. Decreases isolation and withdrawal; helps regain trust that "life will go on."

Evaluation

After 3 weeks, Moe was able to discuss his feelings of loss, anger, and hopelessness associated with Mary's death.

that clients' loved ones need your attention as much as the client. AD and other dementias are serious problems, but with continued research and good nursing care, we may someday be able to lessen the sad effects of these devastating conditions.

Therapeutic Interventions

Nursing care for older adults cannot effectively be accomplished unless a special ingredient is present. That special ingredient is *respect:* the courtesy, consideration, and esteem due each individual who has reached this stage of life. Every older adult, alert or not, cooperative or not, deserves respect, and this respect is demonstrated by each nursing action and each interaction we perform. Treat clients as you would like to be treated if *you* were in their situation.

Standards of Geriatric Nursing Practice

The American Nurses Association has developed guidelines (standards) for nurses who work with older adults. These standards offer nurses a means for providing and measuring the nursing care they deliver to older adults. Every nurse who works with older adults is responsible for following the standards of geriatric nursing practice.

Mental Health Promotion and Prevention

Many of the problems of older adults can be prevented or minimized if they are discovered early. Because of this, nurses must grasp every opportunity to promote healthful practices in their older clients. They should assess clients for changes in social, emotional, behavioral, and physical functioning and intervene early. When caring for older adults, nurses should not hesitate to meet clients' needs, even though it may take some creative planning. Newer nursing interventions, such as using dolls and stuffed animals to provide comfort (doll therapy) and life review (reminiscence therapy), are proving effective with many older adults (Bailey, 1992; Burnside and Haight, 1994). The box on p. 245 offers a description of a client care plan for an older adult who is having trouble recovering from a significant loss. As nurses continue to play a major role in the care of the elderly, they have the opportunity to make a significant difference in the direction of public policies regarding older adults and the lives of all persons they touch.

❖ KEY CONCEPTS

- Older adulthood, or maturity, is defined as the period of life from 65 years of age until death.
- According to the theorist Erikson, older adults with a well-developed sense of personal integrity accept the worth and uniqueness of their own lifestyles.
- Although short-term memory and speed begin to decline in the 40s, such mental capabilities as judgment and wisdom continue to improve as one grows older.
- Physical problems can lead to changes in mental status.
- Older adults experience several physical and social losses.
- Problems with housing for older adults range from having too much house to having none at all.
- The availability of health care for the elderly is an important factor in maintaining both physical and mental health.
- One of the greatest mental health challenges is coping with the loss of loved ones and friends.
- The misuse or abuse of drugs and alcohol is a complex issue for older adults who receive a great number of prescription drugs to treat multiple and chronic health problems.
- Elder abuse is defined as any action on the part of a caregiver to take advantage of an older person, his/her emotional well-being, or property.
- Depression is one of the most common mental health disorders of late adulthood.
- Alzheimer's disease and other dementias are behavioral or mental health problems caused by a medical condition.
- Dementia is a loss of multiple abilities, including short-term and long-term memory, language, and the ability to understand.
- Nursing care for older adults cannot be effective without respect, courtesy, consideration, and the esteem due each individual who has reached this stage of life.
- Nurses play a major role in the care of the elderly.

❖ SUGGESTIONS FOR FURTHER READING

"How to assess the older mind," by G.P. Anderson (*RN* July 1992, pp. 34-40) presents a simple but very important method for assessing the cognitive status of older clients.

❖ REFERENCES

All AC: A literature review: assessment and intervention in elder abuse, *J Gerontol Nurs* 20:25, 1994.

Associated Press: U.S. seniors live longer than those in Europe, Japan, *The Oregonian,* Nov 17, 1995.

Bailey J, Gilbert E, Herweyer S: To find a soul, *Nurs 92* 22(7):63, 1992.

Blixen CE, Wilkinson LK, Schuring L: Depression in an elderly clinic population: findings from an ambulatory care setting, *J Psychosoc Nurs Ment Health Serv* 32(6):43, 1994.

Burnside I, Haight B: Reminiscence and life review: therapeutic interventions for older people, *Nurse Pract* 19(4):55, 1994.

Edelman CL, Mandle CL: *Health promotion throughout the lifespan,* ed 3, St Louis, 1994, Mosby.

Fackelmann K: Brain changes may foretell Alzheimer's, *Sci News* 147(12):180, 1995.

Fackelmann K: Anti-inflammatories: new hope for Alzheimer's? *Sci News* 145(8):116, 1994.

Fawcett CS: *Family psychiatric nursing,* St Louis, 1993, Mosby.

Giger JM, Davidhizar RE: *Transcultural nursing: assessment and intervention,* ed 2, St Louis, 1995, Mosby.

Hamdy RC and others: *Alzheimer's disease: a handbook for caregivers,* ed 2, St Louis, 1994, Mosby.

Hogstel MO: *Geropsychiatric nursing,* ed 2, St Louis, 1995, Mosby.

Lamy PP: Understanding and managing Alzheimer's disease, *J Pract Nurs* 6:45, 1993.

Miceli DG: Evaluating dementia, *Adv Nurse Pract* 1(3):8, 1993.

Minakar KL, Frishman R: Elder abuse: love gone wrong, *Harvard Health Lett* special supplement, October 1995.

Newbern VB: Is it really Alzheimer's, *Am J Nurs* 91(2):51, 1991.

Phelps CH: The complex pathogenesis of Alzheimer's disease, *Adv Nurse Pract* 1(1):10, 1993.

Potter PA, Perry AG: *Basic nursing: theory and practice,* ed 3, St Louis, 1995, Mosby.

Stolley JM: When your patient has Alzheimer's disease, *Am J Nurs* 94(8):34, 1994.

Tackenberg J: Teaching caregivers about Alzheimer's disease, *Nurs 92* 22(5):75, 1992.

Update on Alzheimer's disease: part 1, *Harvard Ment Health Lett* 11(8):1, 1995.

U.S. Bureau of Census: *Statistical abstracts of the U.S.: 1993,* ed 113, Washington, DC, 1993.

White K: How the mind ages, *Psychol Today* 26(6):38, 1993.

Wold G: *Basic geriatric nursing,* St Louis, 1993, Mosby.

UNIT 4

CLIENTS WITH PSYCHOLOGICAL PROBLEMS

18

ILLNESS AND HOSPITALIZATION

Remember the first time you visited a hospital? Perhaps you were a visitor or maybe even a patient. Can you recall how you felt? First, the hospital appeared to be huge. Even small hospitals are confusing, with their mazes of hallways and mysterious little rooms everywhere. The odors were extra clean, antiseptic smells, like no odor you ever encountered "on the outside," and the people who worked there were all dressed the same color. White-coated doctors, white-clad nurses, and hospital workers everywhere—all dressed in ceremonial garb—paraded through the hallway mazes with business-like efficiency. Then there is the equipment, the dreaded machines and contrivances that do one thing or another. It seemed that every piece of hospital equipment came with a bell, whistle, or other annoying tone to periodically remind us of its presence. All in all, a hospital can be a scary, intimidating place, not one in which the majority of people choose to spend their time.

However, for those of us in the health professions, the hospital (or nursing home or clinic) is a known, comfortable environment, filled with the familiar. We often forget that many people have never even walked through the doors of a health care institution. The thought of "going to the hospital" brings immediate anxiety and fear of the unknown to the hearts of many. For these people, hospitalization can be an overwhelming and threatening experience (see box below).

This chapter explores the mental health aspects of illness and the situational crisis of hospitalization. It describes the process of illness and its psychosocial adaptations, and it offers several therapeutic interventions for decreasing or eliminating the anxieties that accompany the illness and hospitalization experiences. Most important, though, it reminds us of the discomforts shared by the individuals who must cope with and adapt to the hospital environment that we health care providers take for granted. Remember, the hospital is *our* reality, not theirs; and being there, for the average person, is like making a visit to another world.

The Nature of Illness

As you learned earlier, **health** is a dynamic state of physical, mental, and social well-being as well as the

---

CASE STUDY

Bob was an 82-year-old retired printer, living in a small retirement mobile home village with his diabetic wife. Although troubled with pneumonia as a child, Bob has enjoyed excellent health throughout his life. Other than periodic visits to his physician, he has had no contact with the medical community.

One evening, Bob noticed that he was bleeding when he urinated. After he was referred to a specialist, it was decided that he required a simple operative procedure to remove the extra tissue impeding the flow of urine and causing the bleeding. Bob and his wife were instructed to arrive at the local hospital early the following morning.

On admission, the nurse, noting Bob's age, assumed that he had some experience in a hospital—after all, he was older than 80. He could not have lived this long without at least one experience in a hospital, she thought. Wrong assumption!

The surgical procedure was completed without problems. Bob was taken to the recovery room in good condition with a Foley catheter to straight drainage and an intravenous line in his right forearm. The first hour following the procedure was uneventful; however, the minute Bob regained consciousness, he insisted on going home. The nurse reassured him that he would be discharged as soon as the doctor saw him. He nodded and then dozed off. The nurse, seeing him sleeping, turned her attention to other clients.

The moment her back was turned, Bob hopped off the gurney and proceeded to detach himself from the intravenous line and Foley catheter. He was last seen walking out the door to his car in his hospital gown and bleeding from the urethra. As a result of this mishap, Bob was chased down, "captured" against his will, and hospitalized for 3 days to control the bleeding from the traumatic catheter removal. You can imagine what a challenging time that was for Bob and his wife, not to mention his nurses and other care providers.

No one, not one physician or nurse, bothered to assess this man's previous experiences relating to hospitalization or medical treatment. Bob was under the assumption that, once the task was completed, he was free to return home.

The lesson here: *Never assume your client is knowledgeable.* Assess first. The complex situation described here could have been prevented if the nurses had taken the time to explore the client's experiences and perceptions of his hospitalization.

Clinical Decision

1. What lessons from this case study can be applied to your nursing practice?

absence of disease or abnormal conditions (Potter and Perry, 1995). Our state of health is constantly changing as we respond and adapt to the challenges of life. This constant change process is called *homeostasis,* and it serves us well throughout our lives. However, when individuals become unable to adapt, to regain the balance of homeostasis, they become ill and must mobilize needed energies to return to a state of health.

Illness is a state of disequilibrium and imbalance. It is an "abnormal process in which aspects of the social, physical, emotional, or intellectual condition and function of a person are diminished or impaired, compared with that person's previous condition" (Anderson, Anderson, and Glanze, 1994). When you are ill, sick, or indisposed, you feel poorly. The body is not working correctly, energy is sapped, and spirits are low. The activities performed without a thought yesterday now loom as insurmountable obstacles. Getting dressed for work becomes such a challenge that you seriously wonder how (or if) you will make it through the day. The body is screaming to give it some rest, but the will is reminding you of your commitments and obligations. Sound familiar?

All of us have personally experienced the situation of an acute illness. Perhaps it was a bad cold or the flu. Perhaps it was something more serious, but we have all felt the discomforts and limitations that are part of the package of illness.

Illness is the body's way of communicating its need for attention. If the illness is of a physical nature, the body will attempt to restore homeostasis, to bring itself back into balance, until it exhausts its reserves and falls over, unable to continue. If the illness is psychological (a dysfunction in the emotional, intellectual, social, or spiritual dimension of functioning), the body will adjust to the demands placed on it until it is no longer capable of compensating. Eventually, the individual becomes too exhausted to carry on without some attention. The example of the man with hallucinations who collapses in the street from malnutrition because his visions told him he was too crazy to accept food from others reminds us of the complexity of the mind-body interaction.

Stages of the Illness Experience

The subjective experiences associated with illness or disability are highly individual and personal. Some persons consider being ill a minor annoyance, whereas others analyze their sickness for hidden evidence of certain doom.

The illness experience is roughly divided into five stages. Each stage is associated with certain perceptions, decisions, and behaviors (Fig. 18-1). Because nurses support clients throughout their institutional stays, it is important to be familiar with the emotional and behavioral reactions during each phase of the illness experience.

Stage 1: symptoms. The illness experience begins when a person becomes aware that something is not right. It may be a physical feeling or an emotional dis-

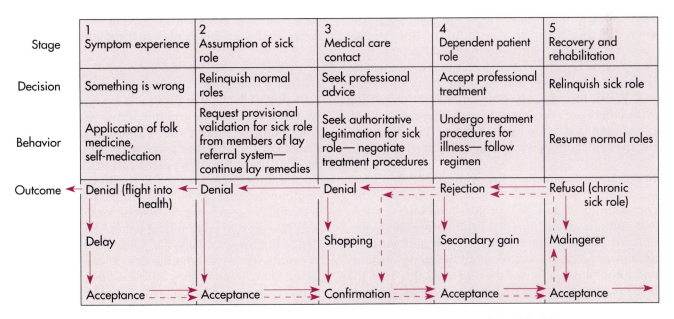

Stage	1 Symptom experience	2 Assumption of sick role	3 Medical care contact	4 Dependent patient role	5 Recovery and rehabilitation
Decision	Something is wrong	Relinquish normal roles	Seek professional advice	Accept professional treatment	Relinquish sick role
Behavior	Application of folk medicine, self-medication	Request provisional validation for sick role from members of lay referral system—continue lay remedies	Seek authoritative legitimation for sick role—negotiate treatment procedures	Undergo treatment procedures for illness—follow regimen	Resume normal roles
Outcome	Denial (flight into health)	Denial	Denial	Rejection	Refusal (chronic sick role)
	Delay		Shopping	Secondary gain	Malingerer
	Acceptance	Acceptance	Confirmation	Acceptance	Acceptance

Fig. 18-1 Stages of the illness experience. (Redrawn from Suchman EA: *J Health Hum Behav* 6:114, 1965.)

comfort, but something is perceived as wrong. During this experience, an individual does the following:

1. Becomes aware of an undesirable change
2. Analyzes and evaluates the change
3. Makes a decision that the change indicates an illness
4. Acts to remedy the situation based on the decision and the accompanying emotional response

Many factors, such as the nature of the symptoms, the knowledge level of the individual, and the availability of treatment resources, come into play when the person is determining if an illness exists.

Many times emotional responses govern one's behavior during this stage. If signs/symptoms of illness are mild, one may self-medicate with various over-the-counter drugs, visit a local cultural folk healer, pray/meditate, or ignore the whole situation. If signs/symptoms are more serious, the individual may seek medical care or continue to deny a problem exists. When an individual *recognizes* the presence of a health problem, he/she begins to move into the second stage—assuming the role of being ill, of being the client, the sick one.

Stage 2: the sick role. Once a person acknowledges the presence of an illness, he/she seeks to confirm it by talking with other people. Family members, fellow workers, and friends are consulted for their opinions. The social group supports the presence of an illness, and the individual either assumes the **sick role** or continues to deny the illness.

Assuming the sick role serves several purposes. First, because of the illness, a person is excused from everyday duties and responsibilities. Other people "take up the slack" by assuming the ill person's duties at work. Second, permission is given by others for the individual to rest and conserve energy for healing. Third, the social responsibilities of interacting with others are relieved during the illness. In short, permission is given to focus one's energies on restoring the balance between health and illness.

Stage 3: medical care. If symptoms of the illness persist and home remedies fail, the person usually becomes motivated to seek professional intervention. The authoritative advice of a health professional validates the presence of the illness, provides treatment, and informs the individual about the causes, course, and future implications of the illness. At this time, the individual can either accept the diagnosis and follow the plan of treatment or continue to deny the problem (Ness and Ende, 1994). Many people consult several different health care professionals in an attempt to re-

ceive a diagnosis more to their liking or until they finally accept the initial professional's opinion.

Stage 4: dependency. In the dependency stage, the ill individual must be willing to accept the attentions of other people. A dependent role is assumed in which one must rely on the kindnesses and energies of others. "Care, sympathy, and protection from the demands and stresses of life" (Potter and Perry, 1995) are provided by family, friends, or caregivers. The individual is relieved of obligation, allowed to be passive and dependent, but expected to get well. More often than not, the person feels ambivalent: grateful for the help but resentful of the limitations. People in this stage have a particular need to be informed and emotionally supported.

Stage 5: recovery and rehabilitation. Movement into the recovery and rehabilitation stage can occur suddenly (e.g., a response to drug therapy or the breaking of a fever) or more slowly (e.g., recovery from a stroke or mental disorder). If recovery is rapid and complete, the individual gradually gives up the sick role and resumes his/her normal obligations and duties. For those whose recoveries are prolonged, arrangements for long-term care are made. Whenever possible, arrangements are made for individuals to recover in their homes. When this is not an option, the person is usually transferred to another institution for further rehabilitation or care.

Not all people pass through every stage of the illness experience, and progression through the stages occurs at a very individual rate. However, nurses who understand the emotional aspects of the illness experience are better able to plan and implement effective client care.

Illness Behaviors

During each stage of the illness experience, people are faced with several emotional choices. Some emotions serve to protect the individual from further stresses or mobilize resources to be devoted to healing, but other emotions can be destructive if they block efforts toward resolving health problems. The emotion of denial can be useful or paralyzing.

Denial is a psychological defense mechanism. In illness, it is used to ward off the painful feelings associated with problems (Ness and Ende, 1994). Denial can be helpful when it allows the time to collect and reorganize thoughts and plans, but it can be deadly when it clouds judgments and prevents individuals from taking the needed steps to restore themselves to health.

During the recognition of symptoms, denial helps people to ignore their responses to illness. They may even increase their usual activity levels in an attempt to "prove" to themselves that they are not really sick. Frequently, this denial leads to a delay in seeking treatment and a worsening of the actual health problem.

In stage 2 of the illness experience, denial is used to explain away the comments of others who validate the illness or give one permission to assume the sick role. In stage 3, the symptoms cannot be ignored any longer, and health care is sought, but denial can still play a role. People who deny the illness experience at this stage often "shop around," consulting various health professionals, healers, or friends who have "had the same thing." The dependency of stage 4 is denied when one refuses to rest, to take care of the body, and to devote the time and energy required for healing. Here, denial evolves into rejection of treatment and refusal to cooperate with the treatment plan. Clients in denial require patience and understanding. They are struggling with the emotional aspects of illness and attempting to restore themselves to a more comfortable state of functioning.

Fortunately, most people experience illness, recover to their previous levels of functioning, and move on with their lives. During their ordeal they have assumed the roles of detective, consultant, consumer, patient, dependent, and self-healer. They have actively or passively taken part in returning themselves to a state of balanced functioning, and to accomplish this homeostasis, they have engaged in various behaviors. Becoming ill and experiencing disability is not pleasant, and nurses must remember that one's illness is the most important priority to the individual who is suffering from it.

Impacts of Illness

Sickness affects the activities of the individual suffering from the illness as well as the activities of every person who comes in contact with the ill person. Illness never occurs when it is expected and it is not an isolated event. When illness does occur, it challenges resources and changes the activities of all those involved with the sick person.

Illness has an impact on the individual. Short-term acute illnesses, such as the flu or a cold, have little effect on behavior, but a serious health problem (physical or mental) can lead to major emotional and behavioral changes. Individuals may react to illness with anxiety, anger, denial, shock, or withdrawal (see box above, at right).

If the illness involves a change in physical appearance it will have a strong impact on the individual's **body image** (one's concept of his/her body). Threats to body image occur with surgery, extensive diagnostic procedures, chronic dysfunctions, and acute ill-

---

BEHAVIORAL AND EMOTIONAL CHANGES WITH ILLNESS

ANXIETY
Feelings of apprehension, stress, and uncertainty about the illness. Responses to anxiety vary with the individual and the stage of the illness.

ANGER
A response to feeling mistreated, injured, or opposed. Anger may be directed inward at oneself or outward toward others. It may be irrational (have no basis in fact), and it may affect the person's social functioning.

DENIAL
The refusal to acknowledge painful facts. Short-term denial helps the person mobilize resources, but longstanding anger usually results in maladaptive behaviors.

SHOCK
An overwhelming emotional state in which the individual is unable to process the information within the environment. Shock may trigger both effective and maladaptive behaviors.

WITHDRAWAL
The removal of self from others whereby the individual refuses to interact with others. Withdrawal is often a sign of depression. Family members can withdraw from the ill person, and the ill person can withdraw from the family.

Modified from Potter PA, Perry AG: *Basic nursing: theory and practice*, ed 3, St Louis, 1995, Mosby.

---

ness. One's self-concept also becomes threatened if the illness progresses beyond the expected time. Tension and conflict with other family members can further erode the ill person's confidence, and depression may begin to take hold.

Psychosocially, illness impacts the family. Changes in routine, required to provide care for the sick family member, add more pressure to an already threatened family. Because the obligations and responsibilities of the ill individual cannot be met, family members often take on heavier work loads during times of illness (Starck and McGovern, 1992). If the illness is prolonged, family members may have to establish new roles and patterns of functioning.

Illness has many faces. It has an impact on every area of a person's functioning and affects a person's loved ones as well. Remember that when assessing the physical signs/symptoms of illness, nurses are touching only the tip of the iceberg. Underneath the physical illness lie all the other emotions, reactions, and behaviors that arrive with the package called "illness."

The Hospitalization Experience

The great majority of illnesses are treated successfully in the home. However, when the condition does not respond to home care or becomes serious, individuals are usually placed in a hospital or medical center for treatment. **Hospitalization** is the placing of an ill or injured person into an inpatient health care facility that provides continuous nursing care and an organized medical staff.

Throughout their lives, people have vastly different experiences relating to stays in a hospital. The elderly woman with a chronic disorder and history of multiple surgeries views hospitalization differently than the elderly woman who bore her children at home and has never experienced a night in the hospital. Attitudes are also affected by what one hears. The relative who drags out minor historical facts about the assorted hospital experiences of every family member for three generations at every holiday get-together and the horror stories from tabloid newspapers add to one's concerns about receiving care in a hospital.

People who are hospitalized experience several emotional threats to their well-being and progress through different stages throughout the course of their hospital stays (Robinson, 1984). During each stage, certain anxieties and emotional issues about the illness surface and challenge the client's coping abilities. Nurses must be aware of these issues and include them in the client's plan of care. Persons who are hospitalized are faced with physical, emotional, and environmental problems all at the same time. For most individuals, being hospitalized is seen as a crisis, an event with which they are unable to cope.

Situational Crisis

People are generally hospitalized in one of two ways: either the admission is planned in advance for a special purpose or an emergency situation that requires special health care resources has arisen. In the case of the planned admission, one has time to experience the anxieties and work through the complications that occur as a result of the individual's absence. Although emotional reactions may be intense and the event may be viewed as a crisis, persons who elect to be hospitalized have the luxury of time—time to prepare themselves and their loved ones, both physically and emotionally.

The story for those individuals brought to the hospital through the emergency room, however, is quite different. In these situations, no time is allowed for preparation. Their lives have suddenly and totally been disrupted and torn apart. If the health problems are serious or require complicated, long-term treatment, major adjustments in lifestyles must be made quickly.

Review the principles of crisis intervention discussed earlier and apply them to the crisis of being hospitalized. Remember, a **situational crisis** is one that relates to outside or environmental factors, not inner emotional or maturational problems. In the case of the client who has been coping with an illness or dysfunction for a period of time before admission, the precrisis behaviors consist of efforts to deal with the health problem. For the individual whose admission was an emergency, the precrisis behaviors were a healthy person's usual activities of daily living with no thought of illness or injury.

The actual crisis in both cases though is about being removed from one's familiar home environment to be cared for by strangers in an impersonal, uncomfortable setting (Aguilera, 1994). If nurses who care for these individuals are sensitive to the fact that their clients are experiencing a crisis, therapeutic interventions will meet with greater success. All hospitalized clients have one thing in common—the feeling of being out of control and dependent on the mercy, knowledge, and expertise of unknown health care providers.

The Person Becomes a Patient

The process of becoming a patient is peppered with problems. The dilemma becomes more anxiety provoking as the admission process slowly transforms an individual into a "patient." The name band around the wrist provides a means of identity that removes the requirement of a vocal inquiry. The demand for the paperwork diminishes a person into an account number and saps what little energy is present. "Next, an institutional gown helps the sick person to exchange his role as a functioning adult for that of a patient" (Robinson, 1984) (Fig. 18-2). Then the individual must go to bed and assume the attitude of an infant surrounded by caregiving people. In this vulnerable position, a person is expected to passively submit to the poking, prodding, and scrutiny of his/her body and its various products. All this is expected to be done gracefully and cooperatively, denying the fear, anger, and humiliation that are actually being experienced. The sick individual has made an agreement, a deal of sorts, whereby the body is offered in exchange for treatments and interventions that will return him/her to wellness. Although the focus of treatment is on the physical body, care providers must not deny

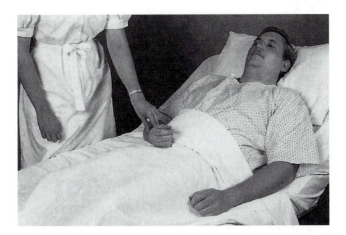

Fig. 18-2 Becoming a patient. (From Potter PA, Perry AG: *Basic nursing: theory and practice,* ed 3, St Louis, 1995, Mosby.)

the psychosocial aspects of the client's health problems and hospitalization experiences.

Individuals who are experiencing hospitalization progress through three steps. The first stage is the sense of being *overwhelmed.* Becoming a patient can be threatening. The intensity of being separated from loved ones and left alone in an unfamiliar environment leaves many individuals exhausted. The energies required to cope with the illness were diverted to surviving the admission process, separating from the family, and tolerating various diagnostic procedures. As a result, many clients withdraw into themselves and interact only when necessary. They must focus their attention inward in an effort to replenish (replace) the energies that have been drained by the experiences of illness, crisis, and hospitalization.

During the second stage, *stabilization,* the hospitalized person gradually gains the physical and emotional strength to reestablish some personal identity. Individuals can become self-centered in this phase. The intellectual understanding that one is not the only (or the most ill) person requiring care is there, but the emotional needs for reassurance and personal interest frequently need to be asserted.

Adaptation marks the third stage. In this stage, the individual has regained enough of a personal identity to adapt. He/she often becomes interested and willing to learn about health problems, coping techniques, or preventive measures. His/her energies are replenished, the body is feeling better, and the emotional responses are fading. Reorganization has taken place, and most people are once again able to function effectively after discharge. For those persons who are transferred or discharged to another institution, the crisis begins again.

Common Reactions to Hospitalization

The rule of thumb for clients' reactions to their confinement is "every person will react in his/her own way." The manner in which individuals respond to the stresses of being hospitalized is in large part determined by how they react to every other threat or crisis. The executive who controls a large company commonly reacts by attempting to gain control over his/her hospital environment. The mother who is dominated by her spouse makes few decisions without his opinion; and the helpless individual often becomes more so in the hospital. Please remember that even though you may find some of your clients' behaviors distasteful, the clients are coping with their situations to the very best of their abilities.

Hospitalization may also hold some symbolic meaning. For some persons, hospitalization confirms the fear that this is no ordinary illness, that there may actually be something seriously amiss. For others, especially the elderly, the hospital is the place where one goes to die. It is a place where all independence and autonomy are checked at the door on admission. Add the periods of separation from family and friends and it is easy to understand the need for some clients to express their discomforts. A client's behaviors may test the patience of the entire nursing staff, but try to look beyond the actions and find the real person.

The Experience of Surgery

People face many stresses, physical and psychological, when confronted with surgery. All surgeries are invasive. The very nature of surgery is to enter the body, fix or remove whatever is wrong, then sew up the client and send him/her home as soon as he/she is able. This process, no matter how many times one has experienced surgery, produces high anxiety and numerous stressors in every client.

The experience of undergoing a surgical procedure requires trust in the physician and nursing staff and a willingness to become totally dependent (even to the point at which breathing is controlled by someone else). Because most individuals who must undergo surgery are in control of their behavior, nurses may witness little of their anxieties. However, it is important for clients to be emotionally supported throughout the surgical experience (Good, 1995). Any medical/surgical nurse will tell you that the more anxious the individual is before surgery, the greater the number of postoperative problems.

Persons who experience surgery must cope with several psychosocial problems. Intellectually, they must admit that their own knowledge about the body and its functions is inadequate. Emotionally, clients are apprehensive and fearful of the future. The "What if . . . ?" syndrome begins, and soon the clients are caught in the web of conflict, struggle, and control. Socially, hospitalized persons are removed from every routine source of support in their environment. Spiritually, they may be questioning their faith, and culturally, the experience of hospitalization may be very different from what was expected.

When the actual moment of surgery arrives, a person is stripped of all nonpermanent items. The removal of wedding rings, dentures, and watches, added to the fact that the individual is secured to a gurney and wheeled away by an unfamiliar face, can transform anxiety into sheer terror.

In addition, people have emotional reactions to specific aspects of surgery. The individual who must become dependent on a mechanical device, such as a cardiopulmonary bypass machine during open heart surgery or a respirator, may feel anger, helplessness, and fear. The loss of a body part, especially if it is noticeable, brings about feelings of loss and grief. The surgical procedure that was expected to bring greater gains than it actually did leads to feelings of despair and frustration.

All these aspects of the surgical experience must be recognized and remembered by the nurses who care for surgical clients. Nurses can "demonstrate a caring attitude about the individual by an unhurried approach; by attentive, perceptive listening; and by anticipation of physical needs" (Taylor, 1994). Surgery is a crisis situation for most people. A concerned, caring nurse can make a significant difference in each person's surgical experience.

Therapeutic Interventions

Nurses play a vital role in the care of the sick within the hospital setting. Clients remember the nurses who cared for them. The nurse who went that extra mile for a personal favor, the nurse who made sure his/her client's pet was fed, and the nurse who sat at the bedside when a client was too anxious too sleep are remembered clearly. Unfortunately, the opposite is also true. Clients remember the short temper, the cutting words, and the nonverbal messages of disapproval just as easily as they do the acts of kindness and concern. Therefore nurses and all health care providers who interact with clients must remember that psychosocial attention is just as important as good physical care. We must be willing to meet both the physical and nonphysical needs of all clients. The box above, at right, lists several nursing diagnoses that apply to the experience of illness and hospitalization.

NANDA NURSING DIAGNOSES

- Activity intolerance
- Adjustment, impaired
- Anxiety
- Body image disturbance
- Communication, impaired
- Coping, ineffective, individual, family
- Decisional conflict
- Denial
- Diversional activity deficit
- Family processes, altered
- Fear
- Grieving, anticipatory
- Growth and development, altered
- Hopelessness
- Self-esteem disturbance
- Sexual patterns, altered
- Sleep pattern disturbance
- Social interactions, impaired
- Spiritual distress

Psychosocial Care

"Good physical care is always the first place to start in meeting the emotional needs of persons who have physical illness" (Taylor, 1994). Nursing care communicates a willingness to focus attention on the client, offers opportunities for interaction, and allows nurses to assess the client's adaptation to the changes resulting from treatment.

Good psychosocial care begins with an assessment of the client's coping status (Ferszt, 1995). Perform a crisis assessment using the criteria listed in Table 18-1. This evaluations allows you to identify possible problems *before* a crisis develops and plan preventive interventions.

Next, get to know your clients as individuals and real persons. Use your active listening skills to encourage clients to discuss their anxieties and concerns. Listen more than you talk because most clients need to share their emotions about the illness or surgical experience. No matter what *your* personal opinions are, do not pass judgment on clients' emotions and behaviors. Creating an accepting environment gives clients permission to share themselves, thereby beginning to establish trust in the therapeutic relationship.

Assist clients to cope with the fight-flight response brought about by the anxieties of illness or hospitalization. Teach and encourage clients to practice muscle relaxation techniques, imagery, and conscious sedation techniques to help ease their stresses. If the client practices a certain spiritual belief, make sure to notify the appropriate priest, minister, or spiritual

◆ **TABLE 18-1**
Crisis Assessment

Assessment Steps	Description
Assess client's history of loss	What types of losses (physical, psychological, social, or spiritual) has client experienced in past?
	Who or what has helped client through crises in past?
	Older and younger persons have more difficulty coping with crisis.
Assess what illness means to client	What is client's understanding of current situation?
	What has client been told about condition, treatment, chances for recovery?
	How has client and family been affected?
Assess for other risk factors	Assess client's level of support from supportive significant others and friends.
	How easily does client adapt to new situations?
	Assess for other crises. Other problems can exist in addition to the crisis.
	Older adults and children have more trouble cooperating and following therapeutic plans.

Modified from Ferszt GG: *Nurs 95* 25(5):88, 1995.

practitioner. Also, be alert for any cultural practices that bring emotional support and comfort to clients.

Remember to emotionally support clients throughout each stage of the illness or surgical experience. Be aware of the behaviors associated with each stage of illness and hospitalization. Assist clients to cope with the emotional discomforts of illness, whether these discomforts are associated with a physical or a psychological diagnosis. The box on p. 258 presents a client care plan that addresses these factors. In reality, the line between the physical and the mental does not even exist.

Supporting Significant Others

An individual's family is the most important group in one's life. It matters little who the family members are. The family of the traditional mother, father, siblings, and relatives is being replaced by newer forms of the family, such as the single-parent family, the same-sex couple family, and the blended family in which the children of previous relationships are blended into a new family group. The point to remember is that clients' families can have a significant impact on the outcome of their illnesses.

In many societies, the man is a symbol of strength and stability. When men from these societies are ill or hospitalized, their roles as providers of emotional support change and they become receivers. Because they are unable to fulfill their roles, they feel inadequate and humiliated. This change of roles leaves family members bewildered and uncertain. The strength that everyone has depended on now lies helplessly in a bed. If the condition is serious or chronic, loved ones are also faced with the issues of long-term care placement or death. In addition, each family member is trying to cope with all the internal emotional problems associated with the illness.

Nurses should be alert for how the family's interactions affect their clients. Family members should be included in client care whenever an interest is expressed (Becker and Fendler, 1994). They should be consulted for details about the client's care, and all family members should be kept informed about the client's progress.

Last, remember that family members are people in crisis themselves, and gentle nursing interventions provide some much-needed emotional support. When family members are satisfied that their loved one is receiving good nursing and medical care, the decrease in anxiety can help promote clients' recoveries.

Pain Management

An important component of any illness, hospitalization, or surgery relates to the concept of pain, that unpleasant sensation of nerve endings being unkindly stimulated. Pain is associated with many illnesses and most hospital stays. It is a subjective experience and can be felt only by the individual experiencing it. People view pain individually based on their own experiences, attitudes, and anxieties.

SAMPLE CLIENT CARE PLAN
HOSPITALIZATION

Assessment

History: Mac is a 72-year-old man who has enjoyed excellent health until approximately 6 weeks ago when he noticed a lump in the right abdominal area. Because of the possibility of extensive surgery, the physician would prefer to perform the biopsy at the hospital. Mac is being admitted the evening before surgery for preparation.

Current Findings: A nervous, pale man, appearing his stated age. Appearance, speech, and motor activity are all within normal limits. Mac states he is "a little concerned" about the surgery. Although alert, oriented, and cooperative, he has difficulty following instructions.

Nursing Diagnosis

Anxiety related to situational crisis of hospitalization and outcome of surgery

Planning/Expected Outcomes

Mac will verbalize his concerns over his illness, outcome, and management of care. Mac will understand and cooperate with his care.

Nursing Interventions

Intervention

1. Address client by his preferred name.

2. Obtain nursing history of all previous hospitalizations.
3. Actively listen to and accept Mac's feelings of anxiety and the threat it poses to his self-esteem.
4. Explain each procedure and gain cooperation before beginning.
5. Assist Mac to identify and build on previously successful methods of coping.
6. Help Mac identify new ways to cope with his anxiety.
7. Inform Mac frequently of his status and progress made during hospitalization.

Rationale

1. Demonstrates respect and ensures that his dignity will be maintained.
2. Helps plan nursing care based on individual needs and experiences.
3. Conveys respect, self-worth; assures him that his concerns will be addressed.

4. Helps decrease anxiety and fear of the unknown.
5. and 6. Coping mechanisms that were successful in the past, when added to newly learned ones, equip Mac with more skills to manage anxiety.
7. Knowledge of one's condition decreases anxieties associated with the lack of control during the hospital experience.

Evaluation

By the morning of surgery, Mac was able to discuss his concerns with the nurse. Recovery from anesthesia was uneventful.

To manage clients' pain effectively, nurses must discover their clients' expectations of pain, what they think may happen to them, and how much they expect it will hurt. Many "have low expectations about pain relief" (Gordon and Ward, 1995) and believe that, if they complain, the doctors and nurses will be distracted from their real job—helping them to heal. Taking the time to learn about the clients' viewpoints will help you plan and implement more effective pain relief measures.

An essential step in helping clients control their pain (**pain management**) is mutual goal setting. Using a pain scale of 1 to 10, the client is asked to pick a target, a pain score. The objective is to keep pain at or below the pain score level throughout the illness or hospital stay. This concrete goal helps both nurses and clients set realistic, attainable goals for pain management.

Assess your client's pain frequently. Try nondrug or natural remedies to decrease the discomforts *before* resorting to pain medications. Massage, visualization, and therapeutic touch have all been found helpful in relieving pain (Dossey, 1995). Remember, all pain has an emotional component attached to it. If nurses can decrease the anxiety associated with pain, the chances of a speedy recovery are much greater. Energy that was once used to control pain can now be used to focus on healing.

Discharge Planning

To help clients cope with the hurdles of illness or surgery, early identification and intervention of their potential problems following hospitalization are essential. This process is called **discharge planning.** After the initial admission assessment, possible home care needs are identified (Dellasega and Shellenbarger, 1992). Then referrals are made to appropriate resources. For example, home health nursing is arranged for the client who must recover from a fractured femur at home, or the social worker is notified of a client's need for housing. For clients who are living with others, discharge planning helps discover educational needs relating to the care of the recovering individual.

Illness affects the entire family group (Danielson, Hamel-Bissel, and Winstead-Fry, 1993). Changes in routine have led to stress, and new anxieties about the individual returning home must be addressed *before* release from the hospital. During your client's hospitalization, make an effort to discuss home care requirements with the family. Note and correct any misleading or inaccurate information. Use time with family members to teach health care practices related to client care. Most loved ones are more than willing to learn about good nursing care.

For people living alone, especially older adults, discharge planning is vital if individuals are to return to their own homes after leaving the health care institution. Basic needs are a high priority for persons living alone, especially if they are aged. When those needs are met, anxieties are diminished, and people can get on with the business of living. Discharge planning is an important component of every client's care plan and a valuable tool for assessing and meeting clients' posthospitalization needs.

Illness and hospitalization are stressful. Although many thousands of people are treated in hospitals yearly, every admission is a crisis for someone. Do not become so comfortable in your hospital work environment that you cannot appreciate your clients' emotional reactions to their situations.

❖ KEY CONCEPTS

- Health is a dynamic state of physical, mental, and social well-being.

- Illness is an abnormal process in which aspects of the social, physical, emotional, or intellectual condition and function of a person are diminished or impaired compared with that person's previous condition.

- The illness experience is roughly divided into five stages, with each stage associated with certain perceptions, decisions, and behaviors.

- During each stage of the illness experience, people are faced with several emotional choices and with reactions frequently involving feelings of denial, anger, frustration, shame, and helplessness.

- Hospitalization is the placing of an ill or injured person into an inpatient health care facility that provides continuous nursing care and an organized medical staff.

- The situational crisis of hospitalization is about being removed from one's familiar home environment to be cared for by strangers in an impersonal, uncomfortable building.

- It is important for clients to be emotionally supported through the surgical experience because the more anxious the individual is before surgery, the greater the number of postoperative problems.

- Nurses and all health care providers who interact with clients must remember that psychosocial attention is just as important as good physical care.

- Pain has an emotional component. If nurses can decrease the anxiety associated with pain, the chances of a speedy recovery are much greater because the energy that was once used to control the pain can now be used to focus on healing.

- Psychosocial nursing care for hospitalized clients focuses on supporting clients and their families throughout their illness or hospital experience.

❖ SUGGESTIONS FOR FURTHER READING

"Using Imagery to Help Your Patient Heal" by Barbara Dossey (*The American Journal of Nursing* 95[6]:40, 1995) states that the images we focus on can evoke physical changes throughout the body and offers us a powerful technique for guiding our clients' images and energies in a positive, healing direction.

❖ REFERENCES

Aguilera DC: *Crisis intervention: theory and methodology,* ed 7, St Louis, 1994, Mosby.

Anderson KN, Anderson LE, Glanze WD: *Mosby's medical, nursing, and allied health dictionary,* ed 4, St Louis, 1994, Mosby.

Becker BG, Fendler DT: *Vocational and personal adjustments in practical nursing,* ed 7, St Louis, 1994, Mosby.

Danielson CB, Hamel-Bissel B, Winstead-Fry P: *Families, health and illness: perspectives on coping and intervention,* St Louis, 1993, Mosby.

Dellasega C, Shellenbarger T: Discharge planning for cognitively impaired elderly adults, *Nurs Health Care* 13(10):526, 1992.

Dossey B: Using imagery to help your patient heal, *Am J Nurs* 95(6):40, 1995.

Ferszt GG: Performing a crisis assessment, *Nurs 95* 25(5):88, 1995.

Good M: Relaxation techniques for surgical patients, *Am J Nurs* 95(5):39, 1995.

Gordon DB, Ward SE: Correcting patient misconceptions about pain, *Am J Nurs* 95(7):43, 1995.

Ness DE, Ende J: Denial in the medical interview, *JAMA* 272(22):1777, 1994.

Potter PA, Perry AG: *Basic nursing: theory and practice,* ed 3, St Louis, 1995, Mosby.

Robinson L: *Psychological aspects of the care of hospitalized patients,* ed 4, Baltimore, 1984, FA Davis.

Starck PL, McGovern JP, editors: *The hidden dimensions of illness: human suffering,* New York, 1992, National League for Nursing Press.

Taylor CM: *Essentials of psychiatric nursing,* ed 14, St Louis, 1994, Mosby.

19

LOSS AND GRIEF

LEARNING OBJECTIVES

1. Describe two characteristics of loss.
2. List four behaviors associated with loss.
3. Explain the difference between healthy and unresolved grief.
4. State three techniques that help nurses and other health care providers cope with their own feelings of grief.
5. Describe how cultural factors can influence attitudes about death, grief, and mourning.
6. Compare the reactions of being diagnosed with a potentially fatal illness to those of having a terminal diagnosis.
7. Explain the stages of the dying process.
8. Explain the meaning of a "good death."
9. Describe the support provided by nurses who provide hospice care for terminally ill persons.

KEY TERMS

bereavement
bereavement-related depression
complicated grief
dying process

external losses
grief
grieving process
hospice

internal losses
mourning
terminal illness

Life is a series of situations, challenges, joys, and losses; it is a dynamic process that requires continual adaptation and adjustment for survival. Life is filled with gains and losses on every level of functioning. Although change is an interwoven part of every human being's life, reactions to change and its accompanying losses vary according to our sociocultural perceptions. In short, we each tend to react to our worlds *as we were taught*. Culture influences attitudes about proper living, relationships with others, and what is considered important in life. Emotional reactions and their resultant behaviors were learned from childhood observations and experiences. How individuals cope with problems, successes, and losses is influenced by the success or failure of past experiences and present attitudes. Culture also has a strong influence on a society's attitudes and practices relating to loss, the expression of a loss, and the dying process (Koenig and Gates-Williams, 1995) (see box below). Our lives occur within a cultural and social environment.

This chapter explores the human reactions to loss. It offers several suggestions for assisting clients and their loved ones through the emotions associated with their losses, and, most important, it encourages you to consider a "good death" as an appropriate nursing goal.

The Nature of Loss

The word *loss* has several meanings. It is a form of the verb *to lose*, which means to bring about the ruin or destruction of; to become unable to find, to misplace; a failure to keep, win, or gain; and to have taken from one by accident, separation, or death. Add to this the emotional perceptions attached to loss, and one can see how loss becomes a very individual and personal experience.

 ## CULTURAL ASPECTS

In Sri Lanka, a small island off the southeastern tip of India, quality of life is strongly preferable to quantity of life. The majority of Sri Lanka's citizens are Buddhist (69%) and believe in reincarnation (the rebirth of a soul in a different body). They believe the suffering of this life will be relieved in the next incarnation, so there is no need for heroic life-saving measures.

Dying persons in this culture are prepared for death by helping them remember the past good deeds of their lives and achieve a comfortable mental state. As the body is no longer required after death, cremation is the preferred burial custom.

Because losses are an unavoidable part of life, everyone must cope with them. How people react and behave during times of loss, however, is highly individual. Responses to loss can range from quiet withdrawal to angry rampages depending on how the loss is perceived, valued, and supported by others.

Losses can be classified as external or internal (self) losses. **External losses** include those outside the individual: losses that relate to objects, possessions, the environment, loved ones, and support. **Internal losses** are more personal and include the losses that involve some part of oneself: the loss of physical, emotional, sociocultural, or spiritual self. An understanding of the characteristics of loss is important if nurses are to provide the psychosocial interventions that are so important in helping clients (and themselves) cope effectively during the emotional times associated with loss.

Characteristics of Loss

In the health care professions, loss has a special meaning. It is defined as "an actual or potential state in which a valued object, person, or body part that was formerly present is lost or changed and can no longer be seen, felt, heard, known, or experienced" (Rawlins, Williams, and Beck, 1993). This broad statement requires some analysis.

First, loss is an actual or potential state. A loss can be real—an actual threat or a situation based in reality. For example, the family whose home burns in flames is experiencing an actual loss. Potential losses are perceived or defined by the individual experiencing them. The industrial worker who is facing a layoff is coping with the possibility of losing his means of providing for his family. A college student who loses her confidence is faced with a less overt but still important potential loss.

Losses can also be imagined. The case of a newlywed who loses her breast to cancer and imagines that her husband will reject her (even though that is not actually the case) illustrates an imagined loss that resulted from an actual loss.

Consider the next portion of the definition—"in which a valued object, person, or body part . . . is lost or changed." The key word here is *valued*. How a loss is defined depends on the value, importance, and significance of the item to the individual. This point is important for nurses to keep in mind. Often the significance of a loss will be different for the client and the nurse. For example, the young mother who has just experienced her fourth miscarriage may define her loss differently than the nurse who has never been pregnant. Remember to assess the meaning of loss for each client.

The last portion of the definition, "and can no longer be seen, felt, heard, known, or experienced," explains the state of loss. When the valued person, object, or concept is gone, something is changed. This change leads to certain emotional reactions and responses that we call grief.

Losses may also be temporary or permanent, expected or unexpected. They may occur suddenly or gradually. Illness, for example, results in the temporary loss of roles and obligations, but the loss of a limb is definitely a permanent loss.

Expected losses arrive with many situations. For example, a chronically ill 60-year-old does not expect to compete in the Senior Olympics because he knows he has gradually lost physical abilities. The individual diagnosed with a terminal illness is coping with an expected loss. Unexpected losses are just that. They are the unknown occurrences that arrive suddenly and without warning. The automobile accident, the diagnosis of HIV, and the suicide of a cherished friend illustrate unexpected losses.

Losses can also be maturational, in which an individual must give up something to gain a higher level of development. The 18-year-old who is moving into her own apartment is leaving the comfort and security of family behind to establish herself as an independent adult. The loss here is ideally offset by the gains in self-development and maturity.

Situational losses occur in response to external events. In a situational loss, the individual has no control over the event leading to the loss. The death of a loved one, a natural disaster, and the divorce of family members are typical of situational losses.

Behaviors Associated With Loss

Each person reacts to loss based on his/her level of development, past experiences, and current support systems. To support clients in coping with their losses, it is important to understand how people at various developmental stages react to loss.

Children's understanding of and reactions to loss change as they grow and develop (Wong, 1995). Newborns and infants feel the loss of their caregivers but show little emotional reaction to the loss as long as their basic needs are being met. Toddlers are concerned with themselves. Although they may repeat phrases such as "Daddy is gone," they have no grasp of the real meaning of loss.

Because of their sense of time, preschoolers cannot understand a permanent loss such as death. Preschoolers use magical thinking (they believe that their thoughts can control events) to explain their losses. This can result in a child carrying the burdens of shame, doubt, and guilt when his/her thinking is

associated with the loss. To illustrate, Jerry, a 3-year-old, believes that if he were not such a bad boy, his mother would not have gone away. Younger children may react to the same loss more intensely than older children or adults because they have fewer coping mechanisms.

School-aged children have some idea about causes and events, but they still associate bad thoughts or misdeeds with losses. At this age, children experience great feelings of grief over the loss of a body part or function. They may feel overwhelming responsibility and guilt about an event, but they respond well to simple, logical explanations. Children around 6 or 7 often apply a broad definition to loss, especially death, by giving responsibility for the loss to the devil, God, or the bogeyman.

By 9 or 10 years of age, most children have an adult concept of loss and death. They realize that some losses such as death are permanent, whereas others are only temporary. Their attitudes, reactions, and responses to their losses are now firmly established.

Adolescents react to loss with adult abstract thinking and childlike emotions. Although they can understand the concepts of loss and death, they are the age group least likely to accept the situation. Adolescents grieve acutely over the loss of a body part or function and fear rejection from their peers. Death is particularly difficult to accept at this age because the developmental task of adolescence is to define who they are and to establish an identity. Threats of loss at this age may make a person stand out from the crowd or peer group, so many adolescents ignore their losses or minimize their differences.

Adults facing loss are able to perceive events more abstractly than younger persons. They can tell the difference between temporary and permanent losses. Most are able to accept their losses and grow from the experiences. As they continue to encounter and cope with various losses, most adults develop a "hardiness," a sense of self-confidence and motivation about life and death, which staves off the depression so common in older adults who have experienced significant losses. Hardy people are in control of their emotions, their lives, and their reactions to loss. By the time most individuals have reached old age, their emotional hardiness has carried them through many of life's losses.

The Nature of Grief and Mourning

Although the terms *grief* and *mourning* are used interchangeably, each has a separate meaning. **Grief** is the set of emotional reactions that accompany a loss. **Mourning** is the process of working through or resolving one's grief, and **bereavement** is the emotional and behavioral state of thoughts, feelings, and activities that follow a loss. The period of grief and mourning after a loss can be intense and painful. It may last only a short period of time or remain as a deep emotional scar for the remainder of one's life. Feelings of loss, grief, and mourning are deeply personal, and each of us has our own way of coping with these emotions. There is no right or wrong way to grieve.

The experience of coping with a significant loss is called the **grieving process.** Note the word "process," which describes a series of events or situations. Grieving is a process, a method for resolving losses and a way of healing or recuperating. Grief is a normal reaction to loss. It affects family and friends of the grieving person and colors the interactions and communications of those related to the loss.

Several theories have been offered to explain the concept of grief, but until recently, the complexity of grieving has not been fully appreciated. It is now thought that an individual can experience the grieving process, adapt, and function well even though the grieving may continue indefinitely (Taylor and Ferszt, 1994).

Grieving serves several purposes. First, it allows individuals to work through the feelings of anger, helplessness, and emptiness that result from the loss. Second, it offers a socially acceptable avenue for receiving physical and emotional support. The church members who bring food, companionship, and other necessities to recently widowed persons illustrate the point. Third, grieving helps to put the loss into perspective and to see it within a bigger picture (Fortinash and Holoday-Worret, 1995). Although one may never understand why the loss had to occur, one learns to accept it and eventually to live with it.

The Grieving Process

To work through the emotional responses to loss, one must experience the grieving process. Grieving, mourning, and bereavement are normal, healthy responses to loss. Working through the grieving process allows people to "piece themselves back together," to reintegrate their lives, to find meaning in new relationships, and to reestablish a positive picture of themselves. It is a healing process that encourages people to continue even after the loss. Although each of us experiences grief in our own way, the process of grieving is much the same. "The nurse's role in the grieving process is to provide an atmosphere for clients to accomplish the painful work of grieving" (Rawlins, Williams, and Beck, 1993).

The grieving process was first studied by Sigmund Freud in the early 1900s. Since then, many theories have been developed to explain the work of grieving. Although various theories consider different aspects of grieving, all include stages that individuals experience while resolving their grief.

The first step in the process of grieving begins with a feeling of shock, disbelief, and denial. One wants to deny the loss, to say "no," and to refuse to give up the cherished object and accept the loss. During this first stage, individuals may refuse to acknowledge that a loss has even occurred. They may behave as if nothing has happened or pretend that the loved object is still present. Denial at this stage provides an emotional buffer that gives grieving persons time to mobilize their resources for the work ahead.

As the realization that the loss can no longer be ignored sets in, denial turns to yearning, protest, and anger. During this stage, the reality of the loss begins to sink in and the griever becomes overwhelmed. Crying, self-blame, and anger are common behaviors. Some persons may even strike out at themselves or others. The griever "falls apart" and becomes disorganized, depressed, and unable to complete daily living activities. He/she may try to postpone coping with the loss by ignoring it or feel that life is not worth living and consider or attempt suicide (see box below). This is an extremely difficult time for people. They need the emotional support and caring of friends and family to remind them of all that still remains, even after loss and suffering.

As the impact of the loss becomes felt in daily living, a depression and identification with the lost object settles over the grieving individual. The work of mourning begins as the full impact of the loss is realized. Feelings of guilt and remorse are frequent as attempts are made to cope with the large, painful void left from the loss. The grieving individual may withdraw from social interactions, engage in unhealthy behaviors, or experience overwhelming loneliness. As time passes, however, most people become willing to share their memories and rely on the emotional support of others.

DRUG ALERT

Individuals who are experiencing acute emotions of grief and loss often feel that life is not worth continuing. Any medications, over-the-counter drugs, or other chemicals in the environment have the potential of being used for a suicide attempt. Grieving persons have been known to ingest medications prescribed for the deceased with the purpose of committing suicide during the grieving process.

Acceptance and reorganization begin when grieving individuals begin to focus their energies away from the loss toward the living. The loss is a reality, but people must continue with life, so they begin to reinvest their feelings in others and nurture their remaining relationships. They take steps to reorganize their lives, filling the void created by the loss. Eventually, a new self-awareness and inner strength evolve from the grieving experience. The good times start to outweigh the bad; life once again slowly stabilizes.

The actual length of time required for the work of grieving varies considerably, depending on the severity of the loss and coping resources available. Some theorists state that the intense reactions of grief gradually decrease within 6 to 12 months, but active mourning may continue for up to 5 years after the loss. Recent evidence suggests that the grief and mourning process "is much more complicated than we know and that when a 'high-grief' death occurs a griever may adapt, adjust, and function well but the grieving continues indefinitely in an infinite variety of presentations" (Ebersole and Hess, 1994).

Grieving and mourning are natural, healthy responses to loss. Because resolving an important loss occurs slowly, time is allowed for people to mourn and to sort through and cope with their feelings. When the grieving process and its accompanying mourning behaviors are experienced successfully, people emerge with hope and a new sense of involvement with life. The loss has been recognized, accepted, and placed in memory. Although life may never be the same, a new appreciation and interest in current activities gradually replace the grief. One becomes healed and able to continue.

Unresolved Grief

When the grieving process is prolonged or impairs functioning over time, mental health problems can result. *Unresolved grief, dysfunctional grief,* and *complicated bereavement* are terms used to describe unhealthy or ineffective grief reactions. Although everyone who experiences a great loss grieves, people who are suffering from unresolved grief are unable to shift their attention from their loss to the realities of everyday life. They become so preoccupied with the loss that they are unable to function effectively (Edwards, 1994).

There are two types of dysfunctional (unresolved) grief: bereavement-related depression and complicated grief. Both are associated with expressions of distress about the loss, changes in eating or sleeping patterns, and changes in activity levels.

With **bereavement-related depression,** the griever feels the loss so intensely that feelings of despair and worthlessness overwhelm everything else in life. Every day is a gray fog with no light as one looks toward the future. Life becomes a burden, and each new day is faced with remorse. This attitude overshadows all else, and the griever experiences changes in eating, sleeping, and activity levels; angry, hostile moods; and an inability to concentrate or complete work tasks. To complicate matters, individuals often become more and more socially isolated and react with hostility or anger when friends express concern. This type of grief commonly leads to the despair of suicide.

Bereavement-related depression responds well to treatment when it is recognized and interventions are begun early. A combination of psychotherapy and drug therapy has been effective, but emotional and social support are always important factors.

Complicated grief is "a persistent yearning for a deceased person that often occurs without the signs of depression. Although the symptoms appear to be those of normal grieving, they are associated with impaired psychological functioning and disturbances of mood, sleep, and self-esteem. The griever becomes preoccupied with the loss and may idealize and search for the lost person or object, relive past experiences, and yearn for the past. Because life in the present is not as desirable as past memories, the individual may become intolerant of others and socially isolated.

Treatment for unresolved grief depends on the presence of depressive symptoms. A psychotherapeutic and psychopharmacological approach treats depression, whereas grief is helped by emotional support and a responsive ear. Support groups and opportunities for social interactions add to the effectiveness of treatment in most cases (see box below).

The therapeutic nursing interventions for both types of unresolved grief involve listening, providing emotional support, and referring to appropriate resources. Nurses are often the first to identify the signs/symptoms of dysfunctional grieving because of their focus on clients' activities of daily living. Therapeutic listening helps in understanding the needs of

> ### THINK ABOUT
> Your client displays all the signs/symptoms of complicated grief. You have recommended that she start attending a support group for widows. She refuses. With gentle questioning, she confides in you that she has no money for transportation to the meetings and is too proud to ask for help.
>
> What nursing interventions would help this client meet the goal of regularly attending the support group meetings?

the grieving individual (Brown, 1994). It also offers an opportunity to provide emotional support and comfort. Sometimes, when grievers are encouraged to verbalize their feelings, the real healing begins. Nurses are also instrumental in referring their clients to the therapists, support groups, and educational opportunities that assist in effectively working through the grieving process.

Nurses' (Caregivers') Grief

Nurses experience the same grief as others when faced with loss. The profession of nursing involves the joys of birth to the sorrows of death and all stages in between.

Many nurses work with dying clients, some on a daily basis. Relationships are formed. Nurse and client develop an understanding and a rapport. The focus is on the client, and the nurse acts therapeutically, but the bond between individuals grows with the relationship. When that relationship is lost, even if it was an expected loss, the nurse grieves, and that is a *necessary* process for the health of nurses.

However, the nurse's role in offering support and comfort to grieving loved ones can become complicated if the nurse's grief overshadows his/her effectiveness. Nurses should share in the grief experience with the remaining loved ones, but they should remember that the primary goal is to provide support for the grievers. Nurses should also be aware of relationships with their client's significant others and how their own grieving may affect these relationships. Many health care facilities offer support groups for nurses who work with dying clients in an effort to assist them with their own grief experiences.

Learn to appreciate the experiences of dying and grieving clients (Grassman, 1992). Understand the steps of the grieving process (denial, anger, bargaining, depression, and acceptance) and how *you* cope with losses. Last, do not forget to find a way to renew your energies. When we know and accept our own attitudes and feelings about loss and grieving, we can provide the therapeutic interventions that are so needed by others.

The Dying Process

Dying is the last stage in growth and development. Like birth, it is an intensely personal process. Unlike birth, however, an individual is often aware and consciously takes part in the process. Death means different things to each of us. For some, it is a welcome relief from the suffering of the body. For others, it is the ultimate fear. The process of dying remains unchanged, but attitudes, beliefs, and behaviors surrounding death are as variable as the individuals who practice them.

Death may occur suddenly or gradually. It may be expected or arrive as a total surprise. One may be fortunate enough to die in familiar surroundings, attended to by loved ones and friends, or be faced with the fate of dying alone and unloved.

During earlier days in American history, most families cared for their aged and ill at home. Children witnessed the births of their siblings and deaths of their grandparents at home. It was all accepted as a part of living. Today, though, children know little about dying because elders no longer live in the family home. As a society, we tend to isolate our old and infirmed, "not only for care and protection but because their dying processes are emotionally disruptive and offensive to most people" (Ebersole and Hess, 1994). In fact, more than two thirds of all deaths now occur in health care facilities, hospitals, and nursing homes.

Cultural Factors, Dying, and Mourning

Although death is a personal experience, it occurs within a cultural and social context. Cultural practices regarding dying, grief, and mourning have a strong influence on behaviors. To illustrate, many modern North Americans see death as the final loss in life. East Indian Hindus believe that all creatures are in a process of spiritual evolution that extends through the boundaries of time and space. They view death as a passage from one existence to another (Giger and Davidhizar, 1995).

Culture also dictates many funeral, burial, and mourning practices. The length of time for mourning and public displays of grief are determined by culture. Clothing is often worn during the grieving process to symbolize the loss. To illustrate, traditional Chinese wear white as a sign of mourning, whereas black is the required color for mourning in North America and Russia.

The beliefs, rituals, and practices of one's culture may be very important to one individual and barely matter to another member of that same culture. Nurses must be careful to assess and understand the meaning of each client's cultural, religious, and social practices (Geissler, 1994). Many variations exist in every group of people, no matter which culture. Do not assume how a client feels about his/her cultural beliefs and practices. Find what is important and, if at all possible, incorporate it into the client's plan of care. Never take a person's cultural background for granted.

Terminal Illness

A **terminal illness** is a condition in which the outcome is death. The diagnosis of a terminal illness is perhaps one of the most difficult challenges an individual must face in his/her lifetime, especially if that diagnosis relates to an adolescent or young adult. In today's world, the diagnosis of HIV/AIDS is especially devastating for young adults. The course of the disease is long and marked by periods of physical improvement and hope alternating with times of illness and suffering. Grieving occurs throughout the course of the illness.

How a person responds to and prepares for death depends on two factors: what death means and the coping mechanisms used throughout life to deal with problems. If the individual is comfortable and satisfied with life, death is usually accepted without fear; but if the person lived life struggling and fighting, the experience of dying will be much the same. In short, people tend to cope with dying in the same ways in which they coped with living.

The diagnosis of a fatal illness or condition is received with disbelief and shock—true crisis. This is a time of great uncertainty because client and family are struggling to cope with the illness, its effects and its final outcome. Crisis interventions can be very effective at this stage.

As the condition progresses, denial and hope allow the client and family to slowly adjust to the reality of the situation. Hope is future oriented and helps individuals endure the suffering of the present because it offers the possibility that soon things will be better. Denial offers a way of coping with each little loss until the reality of the situation is finally accepted. During this time, the individual is encouraged to continue with daily activities until he/she is no longer able. As time goes by, both the family and individual either accept the final outcome and make preparations or continue to deny the reality of the situation, sometimes until the moment of death.

Receiving the diagnosis of a potentially fatal illness, along with the possibility of death, can bring forth a variety of reactions. Individuals who are young and feel healthy may refuse to accept that a problem exists. For others, the diagnosis of a potentially terminal condition acts as a wake-up call and motivates them to make major lifestyle changes. The box below illustrates such a case. The reactions to facing a terminal or potentially terminal illness vary with the individual.

Many people often make the major changes necessary to prevent the condition from becoming fatal. Others value their present ways of living too much to make the necessary changes or feel that the work is not worth the extra time gained. The decisions about

---

CASE STUDY

Brittany was just 35 years old when she received the diagnosis of severe coronary artery disease. She became short of breath one day while doing household chores a few days ago and decided that she must be hanging on to the cold her 8-year-old presented her with last week. Because it was time for her regular checkup, she decided to schedule an appointment with her family physician.

Dr. Dunn had worked with Brittany's family for many years. He knew about her smoking, eating, and exercise habits. He had encouraged her to consider weight loss and attempted to refer her to a smoking cessation program several times in the past few years but to no avail. Today, when Brittany appeared for her appointment, he feared the worst.

After a thorough physical examination and an electrocardiogram, Dr. Dunn scheduled Brittany for a cardiac catheterization at the local hospital the following day. Brittany left the office in shock, stunned by the realization that she may actually not live long enough to see her children grow into adults. She knew deep inside her heart that this was the warning call to take her life and health more seriously.

She only hoped that she had the strength to make the changes she knew would be required if she wanted to live a while longer.

The results of Brittany's cardiac catheterization showed that three of her coronary arteries were seriously blocked and the blood supply to the heart was inadequate. Her physician recommended surgery to restore the blood supply to the heart but firmly stated that this was only a temporary measure. Without major lifestyle changes, the problem will reappear again and again. At this point, Brittany had to make some life-and-death decisions. As she saw it, she had two options: to continue with her easygoing, comfortable lifestyle, full of tobacco, alcohol, fun, and fatty foods and run the risk of dropping over with a heart attack at too young an age or to change her diet, stop her unhealthy habits, begin to exercise, and learn to defuse her stress.

Clinical Decision

1. What nursing interventions would help Brittany make a decision?

one's remaining time belong to and should be made by the individual. Nurses should accept and support clients' decisions about terminal illness and structure the goals of care to provide the best possible interventions within the realities of each situation.

Stages of Dying

Unless death arrives suddenly, both individuals and family members progress through several psychological stages. These stages or phases, called the **dying process,** allow people to cope with the overwhelming emotional reactions associated with dying and losing loved ones.

Several theories about the process of dying have been developed during the past few years. The most well known is Elizabeth Kübler-Ross's five stages of dying: denial, anger, bargaining, depression, and acceptance (Kübler-Ross, 1969) (Fig. 19-1). Later theorists simplified Ross's five stages into three basic phases of resistance, working, and acceptance.

During the resistance stage, the individual experiences denial, anger, bargaining, and avoidance and fights the issue. The working or review stage broadens the consciousness of the individual as one's life is reviewed: "the struggle or resistance disappears and the individual begins to deal with unfinished business and reclaims a part of himself, becoming more in tune to himself of the present rather than of the past" (Hess, 1994). The last stage is labeled acceptance or the unconscious. Although these two terms appear to be unrelated, during this last phase of the dying process, the individual is comfortable and accepting of death. He/she can discuss death with peace and calm. Increasingly greater amounts of time are spent focusing inward, moving one's energies away from this reality. Some individuals have near-death experiences that they describe as a "passage to another realm of consciousness that we can only begin to imagine" (Schoenbeck, 1993). Eventually, the dying person fades from this life, leaving only a body behind.

A broader perspective of the dying process is offered by Glaser and Strauss (1963), whose four models of awareness dying can be applied to family, friends, and health professionals who care for the dying indi-

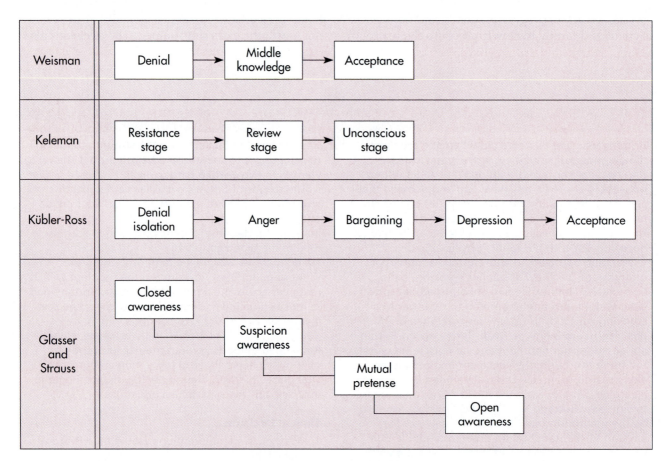

Fig. 19-1 Theories of the stages of dying and grieving. (Redrawn from Ebersole P, Hess P: *Toward healthy aging: human needs and nursing response,* ed 4, St Louis, 1994, Mosby.)

vidual. They describe the closed awareness model as one in which medical personnel know that the condition is fatal but still "keep the secret" or withhold the information from the client. Once the dying individual becomes suspicious of the truth, a battle for control of information ensues.

This type of closed awareness was commonly practiced by health care providers in the past. Frequently, clients were not told of the seriousness of their illness because it was believed that the news was too upsetting. Although most terminally ill persons know that they are dying, many still experience death locked into a health care provider–supported denial.

The mutual pretense model is a "let's pretend" kind of awareness. Both caregivers and the dying individual are aware of the impending death, but nobody talks about it. Although no one really expects the client to recover, it is easier to pretend that things will get better. Unfortunately, the true feelings of everyone remain hidden and unable to be expressed.

In the open awareness model, the approaching death is openly acknowledged and accepted. The client is resigned to dying and accepts each day as it can be lived. Family members, health care providers, and the dying have permission to discuss their fears, concerns, and experiences. The open awareness method of coping allows mutual support and comfort to be given and received. It also encourages loved ones to grieve *with* the dying instead of for them (Miles, 1993).

Age Differences and Dying

The impact of death is only as strong as one's understanding of it. Before the age of 8, most children do not understand the permanency of death, but they do experience a sense of doom and danger associated with dying. By age 12, most children are aware that death is irreversible. Adolescents and young adults do not relate to death unless forced. As people grow older they begin to lose family and friends, and so they must begin to face their own mortality.

A special word about the dying child is needed here. Children are remarkably observant, and they have an intuitive ability to understand the seriousness of their illness and its outcomes. However, their immediate concerns focus on how the illness affects the activities of daily living and limits their abilities. Children are also very aware of the family's reactions and they are "reluctant to bring up issues they know are upsetting to their parents" (McIntier, 1995).

Whenever possible, parents should be encouraged to communicate with their dying child. Open discussions of the illness and its outcome help the child to cope with the feelings of isolation, anxiety, and guilt over causing distress in the family. Sharing feelings and insecurities helps to bond family members to-

gether and gain strength from each other. Children who are able to share their emotions have fewer behavioral problems, less depression, and higher self-esteem than those who suppress their feelings (Calandra, 1993). They adapt to the difficulties of their disease and its treatment better than those who must cope with the emotional isolation of dying emotionally alone. Siblings of the dying child also need extra attention during this time because feelings of jealousy, anger, and guilt are often present.

Therapeutic Interventions

One of the most rewarding experiences in nursing is assisting an individual to experience a "good death," one in which the dying and the living participate fully and completely. In a good death, individuals control their own destiny. Clients are the ones to decide when to stop aggressive treatments, to refuse the one last surgical procedure, or to end the discomfort of a painful therapy. With a good death, peace, serenity, and acceptance replace denial, fighting, and anger. Individuals value and cherish each day but look forward to the day when their suffering will end. They are not afraid of death. It is the last step of the growth process, which draws a productive and fruitful life to a close (Houlberg, 1992).

Nurses bring their own sets of attitudes, values, beliefs, and biases to the care of the dying. The way caregivers view or perceive "the act of dying, as painful, upsetting, indifferent, or a blessing, influences the treatment the dying patient will receive in the last days, whether in the hospital or nursing home" (Ebersole and Hess, 1994). Explore your own attitudes about death; the quality of your client's care depends on it.

Today, dying occurs in either an institution or the home. Because institutional processes tend to reduce everything to segments, the whole individual tends to become lost in a heap of component parts. Nurses and their peers tend to categorize clients into theoretical niches.

Remember, never limit your clients by placing labels on them. It is easy for nurses to focus on the dying person's biological or physical needs. It is nonthreatening to help relieve the physical symptoms associated with dying, but it is another thing to become involved in a meaningful therapeutic relationship that supports the dying individual. The box on p. 270 lists several nursing diagnoses that relate to dying clients. This section offers interventions for coping with the dying experience.

Hospice Care

In the past, most of the dying were cared for in the home by family and friends. With the advent of mass transportation, travel for everyday people became possible. As society gradually became more mobile, families were separated from their relatives as they moved to different locations. Dying at home was no longer an alternative for many people, so they were sent to hospitals and nursing homes. For many years, nurses assisted their clients through the dying process, providing comfort where they could but realizing that there must be better ways to meet life's final challenge.

Finally, during the 1960s, a model for humane care of the dying (which was centered in the home) was developed and tested at Saint Christopher's Hospice in London, England. Since then, the number of hospices has grown tremendously, with over 2000 in the United States alone (U.S. Bureau of Census, 1993).

The term **hospice** has come to mean a philosophy of care for people with terminal illnesses or conditions and their loved ones (Zerwekh, 1994). Guidelines for hospice care have been developed by the National Hospice Organization (NHO), which is dedicated to promoting the principles and standards of high-quality hospice care.

Nursing is the cornerstone of hospice care just as it is with the institutional care of the dying. The goal of hospice care is to make the remainder of an individual's life as meaningful and comfortable as humanly possible. Hospice care differs from institutional care in several ways. The focus of health care reorients from the institution to the home, where hospice services are available 24 hours a day. Hospice care redefines family relationships because care of the dying individual requires the energies of loved ones and friends. Hospice care helps the family retain control for the dying individual, and it allows people to experience death with the dignity they deserve. Many nurses are choosing to specialize in hospice care today because it is such a rewarding area of nursing.

Meeting the Needs of Dying Persons

Dying clients have special needs during their final days (Fig. 19-2). One of the most urgent needs for many of the dying is to be free from pain and discomfort. This can usually be accomplished by around-the-clock administration of pain-relieving medications. Addiction is not an issue in caring for the terminally ill.

NANDA NURSING DIAGNOSES

- Adjustment, impaired
- Anxiety
- Caregiver role strain
- Coping, ineffective
- Decisional conflict
- Denial, ineffective
- Grieving, anticipatory, dysfunctional
- Hopelessness
- Knowledge deficit
- Nutrition, altered: more, less than body requirements
- Powerlessness
- Self-esteem disturbance
- Sleep pattern disturbance
- Social interactions, impaired
- Social isolation
- Spiritual distress
- Violence, risk for: self-directed

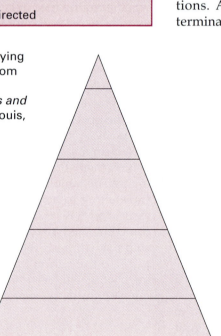

Fig. 19-2 Hierarchy of the dying person's needs. (Redrawn from Ebersole P, Hess P: *Toward healthy aging: human needs and nursing response,* ed 4, St Louis, 1994, Mosby.)

To share and come to terms with unavoidable future
To perceive meaning in death

To maintain respect in face of increasing weakness
To maintain independence
To feel like normal person, part of life right to end
To preserve personal identity

To talk
To be listened to with understanding
To be loved and to share love
To be with caring person when dying

To be given opportunity to voice hidden fears
To trust those who care for him/her
To feel that he/she is being told truth
To be secure

To obtain relief from physical symptoms
To conserve energy
To be free of pain

Freedom from loneliness is not always so easily accomplished. Loneliness can arise from within oneself and from the outside. Many dying individuals have already suffered numerous losses, both physical and emotional. The strange surroundings of an institution and unfamiliar caregivers can add to a person's sense of isolation and loneliness. Dying clients need to know that someone who really cares for their welfare is there to help. Nurses must assess for loneliness in clients and offer a little of themselves.

Individuals with terminal illnesses also need to preserve their self-esteem (Cataldo, 1994). The pride of a lifetime of work and struggle can be easily shattered by the thoughtless words or actions of a nurse or other care provider. Remember, respect is always an important factor in caring for clients, especially the aged.

One of the most important principles to remember when working with dying people is that a dying person lives with the same needs as the rest of us (Potter and Perry, 1995). Life and its needs for love, friendship, and self-esteem continue, even when an individual is in the process of dying.

As death approaches, many physical and emotional changes begin to take place (Tables 19-1 and 19-2). This is a time to provide comfort and solace and to meet the physical needs of care, but most important, it is a time to support those who must say goodbye and those who are left behind.

◆ **TABLE 19-1**
Physical Signs/Symptoms Associated With the Final Stages of Dying: Rationale and Interventions

Symptoms	Rationale	Interventions
Coolness, color and temperature change in hands, arms, feet, and legs	Peripheral circulation diminishes to facilitate increased circulation to vital organs	Place socks on feet. Cover with light cotton blanket.
Increased sleeping	Conservation of energy	Spend time with the client; hold client's hand; speak normally to the client even though there may be a lack of verbal response or consciousness.
Disorientation, confusion of time, place, or person	Metabolic changes	Identify self by name before speaking to client; speak softly, clearly, and truthfully.
Incontinence of urine and feces	Increased muscle relaxation and decreased consciousness	Maintain vigilance and change bedding as appropriate.
Congestion	Poor circulation of body fluids, immobilization, and inability to expectorate secretions causing gurgling, rattles, bubbling	Elevate the head and gently turn the head to the side to drain secretions.
Restlessness	Metabolic changes and a decrease in oxygen to the brain	Calm the client by speech and action. Reduce light; gently rub back, stroke arms, or read aloud, play soothing music. DO NOT USE RESTRAINTS.
Decreased intake of food and liquids	Body conservation of energy for function	Do not force client to eat or drink. Give ice chips, soft drinks, juice, and popsicles as appropriate. Apply petroleum jelly to dry lips. If client is a mouth-breather, apply protective jelly more frequently as needed.
Decreased urine output	Decreased fluid intake and decreased circulation to kidney	None
Altered breathing pattern	Metabolic and oxygen changes to respiratory centers	Elevate the head of bed; hold hand, speak gently.

Modified from Beare PG: *Principles and practice of adult health nursing,* ed 2, St Louis, 1994, Mosby.

◆ **TABLE 19-2**
Emotional/Spiritual Symptoms of Approaching Death: Rationale and Interventions

Symptoms	Rationale	Interventions
Withdrawal	Prepares the client for release and detachment and letting go of relationships and surroundings	Continue communicating in a normal manner using a normal voice tone. Identify self by name; hold hand, say what you want person to hear from you.
Visionlike experiences (dead friends or family, religious vision)	Preparation for transition	Do not contradict or argue regarding whether this is or is not a real experience. If the client is frightened, reassure that he/she is not crazy, but that these aberrations do occur.
Restlessness	Tension, fear, unfinished business	Listen to client express fears, sadness, and anger associated with dying. Give permission to go.
Decreased socialization	As energy diminishes, the client withdraws and begins to make the transition	Express support; give permission to die.
Unusual communication: out of character statements, gestures, requests	Signals readiness to let go	Say what needs to be said to the dying client; kiss, hug, or cry with him/her.

Modified from McCracken AL, Gerdsen L: *J Gerontol Nurs* 17(12), 1991.

Loss, Grief, and Mental Health

Loss is a part of living. The behaviors associated with grief and mourning allow us to heal and to become whole after suffering a loss. For many people, death represents the ultimate loss. How effectively individuals cope with their losses has a large effect on their mental and emotional health. The box on p. 273 offers a sample client care plan for an individual who is coping with grief.

Many of the behaviors associated with the grieving process could be diagnosed as mental health disorders except for the fact that they are short lived. Mental health problems arise only when a person is stuck or immobilized during a stage of the grief reaction. Clinically, the *Diagnostic and Statistical Manual of Mental Disorders* (DSM-IV) diagnoses of bereavement and bereavement-related depression are applied to those grievers who are significantly impaired in their abilities to accomplish the activities of daily living for more than 2 months (Rawlins and Heacock, 1993a).

For persons who currently suffer from a mental health disorder, the stresses of loss and grief can overwhelm delicate coping mechanisms and lead to further problems. For example, the 23-year-old with schizophrenia who has lived with her family all her life will have great difficulties in grieving for the loss of her mother. Nurses who work with mental health clients must remember that they require extra emotional support during periods of loss or grieving.

How each human being copes with loss is unique and individual. Coping mechanisms may be effective and result in growth and healing. They may also be inadequate or inappropriate, resulting in distress, depression, or other mental health problems. Nurses need to assess their clients' abilities and resources to cope with their losses. By encouraging effective coping skills and providing physical and emotional support, nurses are able to help their clients and themselves work successfully through life's losses and griefs.

❖ KEY CONCEPTS

- Life is filled with gains and losses on every level of functioning.
- Grief is the set of emotional reactions accompanying loss, whereas mourning is the process of working through or resolving one's grief.

▌▌▌▶ **SAMPLE CLIENT CARE PLAN**
GRIEVING

Assessment

History: Jerry was 14 when he lost his leg because of a crush injury sustained in an automobile accident. His attitude toward the loss of his leg was casual at first, but soon he became angry and withdrawn. Complaints of chronic fatigue, poor appetite, and an inability to concentrate have prompted his mother to seek health care.

Current Findings: An alert but sullen adolescent boy who complains that he is unable to sleep. Speech is slow with delayed responses. Left leg is amputated above the knee. Uses crutches for mobility.

Nursing Diagnosis

Dysfunctional grieving related to loss of body part and physiological functioning

Planning/Expected Outcomes

Jerry will attend each counseling session. Jerry will identify his feelings of loss and anger by February 21.

Nursing Interventions

Intervention

1. Establish trust and open communication.

2. Assure Jerry that his feelings are important and give permission to discuss them.
3. Assist Jerry to acknowledge his feelings associated with losing his leg.
4. Help Jerry and family understand that anger is a normal response to loss.
5. Assist Jerry to find appropriate outlets for his anger rather than projecting it onto others.

6. Encourage Jerry to make plans for the future and set goals.

Rationale

1. Adolescents must trust in the relationship before they commit themselves.
2. Shows interest and respect; helps maintain self-worth and dignity.
3. Helps Jerry to connect his anger with the loss and begin the work of grieving.
4. Assures him that his emotions are a normal part of the grieving response.
5. Provides structure, gives a sense of control, and helps him focus on more effective ways of emotional expression.
6. Goals help change the focus from the past to the future.

Evaluation

Jerry missed the first two appointments but has kept every one for the past month. Jerry is able to identify three reasons why he feels angry and frustrated. Jerry was unwilling to make any plans for the future.

- Bereavement is the emotional and behavioral state of thoughts, feelings, and activities that follow a loss.
- The steps of the grieving process are shock, disbelief, and denial; anger, bargaining, reviewing; depression; and acceptance.
- Two types of dysfunctional (unresolved) grief are known as bereavement-related depression and complicated grief.

- The nurse's role in offering support and comfort to grieving loved ones can become complicated if the nurse's personal grief overshadows his/her effectiveness.
- Dying is the last stage in the growth and development of an individual.
- How an individual responds to and prepares for death depends on what death means and the coping mechanisms used throughout life.

- Terminally ill children who are able to share their feelings have fewer problems and adapt better than those who must cope with emotional isolation.

- One of the most rewarding experiences in nursing is assisting an individual to experience a "good death," one in which the dying and the living participate fully and completely.

- The term *hospice* has come to mean a philosophy of care for people with terminal illnesses or conditions and their loved ones.

- Dying clients have special needs during their final days, including the need to be free from pain and discomfort, freedom from loneliness, and preservation of self-esteem.

- One of the most important principles to remember is that a dying person lives with the same needs as the rest of us.

❖ SUGGESTIONS FOR FURTHER READING

"When the Family Can't Let Go" by Barbara Springer Edwards (*American Journal of Nursing*, 94:52, 1994) discusses the ethical issues regarding a family's inability or unwillingness to let go of their loved one.

❖ REFERENCES

Brown MA: Lifting the burden of silence, *Am J Nurs* 94(9):62, 1994.

Calandra B: A death in the family: helping children cope, *Adv Nurse Pract* 1(3):17, 1993.

Cataldo JK: Hardiness and death attitudes: predictors of depression in the institutionalized elderly, *Arch Psychiatr Nurs* 8:326, 1994.

Ebersole P, Hess P: *Toward healthy aging: human needs and nursing response*, ed 4, St Louis, 1994, Mosby.

Edwards BS: When the family can't let go, *Am J Nurs* 94(2):52, 1994.

Fortinash KM, Holoday-Worret PA: *Psychiatric nursing care plans*, ed 2, St Louis, 1995, Mosby.

Geissler EM: *Pocket guide to cultural assessment*, St Louis, 1994, Mosby.

Giger JM, Davidhizar RE: *Transcultural nursing: assessment and intervention*, ed 2, St Louis, 1995, Mosby.

Glaser B, Strauss A: *Awareness of dying*, Chicago, 1963, AVC, Inc.

Grassman D: Turning personal grief into personal growth, *Nurs 92* 22(4):4-47, 1992.

Hess PA: Loss, grief, and dying. In Beare P, Meyers J, editors: *Principles and practices of adult care nursing*, ed 2, St Louis, 1994, Mosby.

Houlberg LH: Coming out of the dark, *Nurs 92* 22(2):43, 1992.

Koenig BA, Gates-Williams J: Understanding cultural differences in caring for dying patients, *West J Med* 163(3):244, 1995.

Kübler-Ross: *On death and dying*, New York, 1969, MacMillian.

McIntier STM: Nursing the family when a child dies, *RN* 58(2):51, 1995.

Miles A: Caring for the family left behind, *Am J Nurs* 93(12):34, 1993.

Potter PA, Perry AG: *Basic nursing: theory and practice*, ed 3, St Louis, 1995, Mosby.

Rawlins RP, Heacock PA: *Clinical manual of psychiatric nursing care plans*, ed 2, St Louis, 1993, Mosby.

Rawlins PR, Williams SR, Beck CK: *Mental health-psychiatric nursing: a holistic life-cycle approach*, ed 3, St Louis, 1993, Mosby.

Schoenbeck SB: Exploring the mystery of near-death experiences, *Am J Nurs* 93(5):43, 1993.

Taylor PB, Ferszt GG: Letting go of a loved one, *Nurs 94* 24(1):55, 1994.

U.S. Bureau of Census: *Statistical abstract of the U.S.: 1993*, ed 133, Washington, DC, 1993.

Wong DL: *Whaley and Wong's nursing care of infants and children*, ed 5, St Louis, 1995, Mosby.

Zerwekh J: The truth-tellers: how hospice nurses help patients confront death, *Am J Nurs* 94(2):31, 1994.

20

ANXIETY DISORDERS

1. Describe the continuum of responses to anxiety.

2. Identify three types of coping mechanisms.

3. Explain how anxiety is experienced through each life cycle.

4. Describe the difference between normal anxiety and an anxiety disorder.

5. Discuss the difference between phobic and obsessive-compulsive behaviors.

6. Name three features of posttraumatic stress disorder.

7. List two important nursing interventions for the client with rape trauma syndrome.

8. Explain the importance of monitoring medication use for clients with high levels of anxiety.

9. Identify three methods for recognizing and preventing anxiety.

KEY TERMS

addictive behaviors
agoraphobia
anxiety
anxiety state
anxiety trait
avoidance behaviors

compulsion
coping mechanisms
fear
flashbacks
free-floating anxiety
obsession

panic attack
phobia
signal anxiety
traumatic stress reaction

Anxiety is a vague feeling of uneasiness, uncertainty, and helplessness. It is a state of tension that is sometimes associated with feelings of dread or doom. Anxiety is the normal emotional response to a threat or stressor, whereas **fear** is an intellectual appraisal of a dangerous stressor.

Anxiety occurs as the result of a perceived threat to one's physical or psychological self. The threat itself may be real or a response to what one *thinks* may be happening. The actual object of one's anxiety often cannot be identified, but the feelings associated with the experience are all too real.

For the sake of discussion, anxiety has been described by type. **Signal anxiety** is a learned response to an anticipated event. The usually calm student who becomes nauseated when examinations are returned is an example of signal anxiety. **Free-floating anxiety** is associated with feelings of doom and dread. The cause of this type of anxiety cannot be identified, and it often leads to ritualistic, phobic behaviors. An **anxiety state** occurs when an individual's coping abilities are overwhelmed and emotional control is lost. Many emergencies, accidents, and traumas are associated with anxiety states. Last is an **anxiety trait,** a learned component of the personality. Persons with anxiety traits react to relatively nonstressful situations with anxiety. The teen who is always explaining why he did or did not do something is an example of trait anxiety.

Anxiety has several useful purposes. Anxiety commonly served as a warning of impending danger for our ancestors, who were always concerned with surviving the day. Mild anxiety can increase learning by helping a person focus and concentrate, or anxiety can serve to motivate an individual. However, uncontrolled anxiety can often lead to ineffective and maladaptive behaviors. Anxiety is necessary for survival and growth. How individuals control and use anxiety is one of the measures of mental health or mental illness.

Continuum of Anxiety Responses

Reactions to anxiety occur along a continuum of behavioral responses (Stuart and Sundeen, 1995) (Fig. 20-1). Adaptive responses to anxiety result in positive outcomes, new learning, and greater self-esteem. Here anxiety is focused positively; the individual adapts, learns, and grows. In short, he/she copes successfully. Maladaptive responses to anxiety are ineffective attempts to cope; they do nothing to resolve the problem or eliminate feelings of anxiety.

Most individuals deal with anxiety by using a number of behaviors or **coping mechanisms** that help to decrease discomfort. Coping mechanisms in the physical realm of functioning include efforts to directly face and handle the problem. The woman who fights the thief who is attempting to snatch her purse, for example, is directly dealing with the source of her anxiety. Intellectual coping mechanisms are aimed at making the threat less meaningful by changing the definition of the threat, whereas emotional responses to anxiety use ego defense mechanisms to reduce anxiety.

Responses to anxiety occur on four levels, ranging from mild to severe (Table 20-1). During periods of anxiety, many physical, intellectual, emotional, and behavioral responses are called on to help an individual cope with the distress being experienced. In periods of severe anxiety, the autonomic nervous system stimulates the "fight-flight" response, which triggers many physical changes.

Self-Awareness and Anxiety

A basic characteristic of anxiety is that it is contagious. Like a cold or flu virus, anxiety is easily transmitted to others. Clients have an uncanny ability it seems to focus on the anxiety levels of their health care providers. Sometimes the client becomes the therapeutic agent for an anxious caregiver. For this reason, it is important for nurses to recognize and effectively cope with their own anxieties.

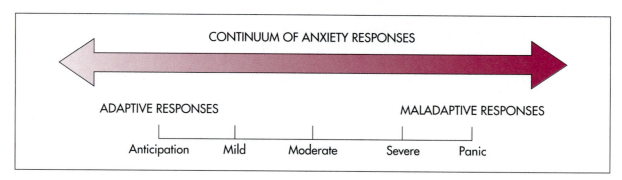

Fig. 20-1 Continuum of anxiety responses. (Redrawn from Stuart GW, Sundeen SJ: *Principles and practice of psychiatric nursing,* ed 5, St Louis, 1995, Mosby.)

The therapeutic relationship is built on trust. Inherent in that trust is the nurse's responsibility to listen and communicate effectively. High levels of anxiety impair a nurse's ability to therapeutically interact with the client. Remember, we may not choose our anxieties, but we *do* choose how to deal with them. The box on p. 278 provides an example of how a care provider's anxiety can affect the therapeutic relationship.

Anxiety Throughout the Life Cycle

Anxiety is a universal experience. It begins early in life, as soon as an individual is capable of realizing that something could go wrong. Responses to anxiety grow and evolve with the individual. Behavioral reactions to anxiety change as effective actions are added to the present coping mechanisms. Those responses or behaviors that are ineffective or serve no purpose are discarded as useless. An understanding

◆ **TABLE 20-1**
Levels of Anxiety

Anxiety Level	Physiological	Cognitive/Perceptual	Emotional/Behavioral
Mild	Vital signs normal. Minimal muscle tension. Pupils normal, constricted.	Perceptual field is broad. Awareness of multiple environmental and internal stimuli. Thoughts may be random, but controlled.	Feelings of relative comfort and safety. Relaxed, calm appearance and voice. Performance is automatic; habitual behaviors occur here.
Moderate	Vital signs normal or slightly elevated. Tension experienced; may be uncomfortable or pleasurable (labeled as "tense" or "excited").	Alert; perception narrowed, focused. Optimum state for problem solving and learning. Attentive.	Feelings of readiness and challenge, energized. Engage in competitive activity and learn new skills. Voice, facial expression interested or concerned.
Severe	Fight or flight response. Autonomic nervous system excessively stimulated (vital signs increased, diaphoresis increased, urinary urgency and frequency, diarrhea, dry mouth, appetite decreased, pupils dilated). Muscles rigid, tense. Senses affected; hearing decreased, pain sensation decreased.	Perceptual field greatly narrowed. Problem solving difficult. Selective attention (focus on one detail). Selective inattention (block out threatening stimuli). Distortion of time (things seem faster or slower than actual). Dissociative tendencies; vigilambulism (automatic behavior).	Feels threatened; startles with new stimuli; feels on "overload." Activity may increase or decrease (may pace, run away, wring hands, moan, shake, stutter, become very disorganized or withdrawn, freeze in position/unable to move). May seem and feel depressed. Demonstrates denial; may complain of aches or pains; may be agitated or irritable. Need for space increased. Eyes may dart around room or gaze may be fixed. May close eyes to shut out environment.
Panic	Above symptoms escalate until sympathetic nervous system release occurs. Person may become pale, blood pressure decreases, hypotension. Muscle coordination poor. Pain, hearing sensations minimal.	Perception totally scattered or closed. Unable to take in stimuli. Problem solving and logical thinking highly improbable. Perception of unreality about self, environment, or event. Dissociation may occur.	Feels helpless with total loss of control. May be angry, terrified; may become combative or totally withdrawn, cry, run. Completely disorganized. Behavior is usually extremely active or inactive.

From Fortinash KM: *Psychiatric nursing care plans,* ed 2, St Louis, 1995, Mosby.

of how individuals at various developmental stages perceive and cope with anxiety helps nurses and other health care providers plan and implement individualized care for all clients experiencing anxiety.

Anxiety in Childhood

Anxiety is experienced in relation to a child's developmental level. Infants feel a sense of discomfort if their basic needs are not met immediately. Toddlers become anxious when they perceive something that is larger or more ferocious than themselves and capable of harming them. Their anxiety relates to power and lasts until the balance of power can be restored. To illustrate, an encounter with the neighborhood bully can be terrifying when one is alone, but hardly worth noticing when surrounded by six friends.

Children learn to cope with anxiety by watching and imitating others in their environments. Most children are happy, active persons with few anxieties; but if their needs for love, belonging, and nurturing are not met, high levels of anxiety can result. Children's needs for love and belonging are so great that, in later life, "emotional problems for which people seek help, such as anxiety, depression, grief, and loneliness, are often related to a failure to satisfy the need to belong" (Baumeister and Leary, 1995) in childhood.

"Although children are not strangers to stress, some children appear to be more vulnerable than others" (Wong, 1995). Recognizing the signs of childhood stress and intervening early prevents anxiety from becoming overwhelming and help teach children how to cope successfully.

Anxiety in preschool children revolves around the experience of separating from the security of parents. As children learn that their separation is not permanent, anxieties lessen and coping abilities improve.

School-aged children learn to cope with the anxieties of becoming members of a group.

The development of certain behavioral habits early in childhood appears to help children relieve their anxieties. Thumb sucking, nail biting, hair pulling, and rhythmic body movements are examples of behaviors that seem to soothe and lessen the anxiety of young children. Excessive anxiety appears to develop when children resist their feelings of anxiety and focus them elsewhere. Problems associated with anxiety in childhood include compulsions, phobias, separation anxiety disorder, overanxious disorder, and avoidant disorders.

Separation anxiety disorder is diagnosed when children are unable to be without their parents for any length of time. By about 6 months of age, infants are able to recognize their mother's absence from the room and protest. They soon become very aware of mother's activities and learn to identify the behaviors indicating mother is leaving the area. By 11 months, most children learn to protest *before* their mother leaves. During the next 4 years, children learn to tolerate varying degrees of separation from parents. By school age, most children separate from parents easily, and the focus of their anxieties changes to coping with school life.

Children with separation anxiety disorder, however, experience severe anxiety that may even develop into panic when left by their parents or significant others. Physical complaints such as headaches, nausea, or vomiting are common when children anticipate separation. Nightmares occur frequently. Associated fears of death, animals, monsters, and harmful situations are seen in children with separation anxiety disorder.

Overanxious disorder appears during childhood. Its predominant feature is unrealistic levels of anxiety lasting longer than 6 months, a long time in the life of a child. These children worry about everything, from past events to future expectations. Overanxious disorder is often seen in children whose parents focus on overachievement and downplay their children's actual accomplishments.

Children can also experience severe anxiety during times of great change in the family. Reactions to divorce, death, or separation from loved ones and friends often lead to situational anxiety or **avoidance behaviors** in which the child refuses to cope with the anxiety-producing situation by ignoring it.

Sadly, children are not immune to the effects of unresolved anxiety. Occurrences of posttraumatic stress disorder, depression, and suicide are on the rise in children. "It is estimated that over 400,000 children suffer from depression each year in the United States" (Clunn, 1995).

If we are to give children the opportunities to grow and mature into effective, adaptable individuals, we must learn to recognize and treat the signs of anxiety early. The old adage "A stitch in time saves nine" is a saying worth remembering when working with children.

Anxiety in Adolescence

The coping skills learned in childhood continue to be practiced and refined throughout adolescence. If adolescents have successfully handled their anxieties in childhood, the distresses of becoming an adult offer opportunities for personal growth and maturation. Adolescents who ineffectively cope with anxiety often express themselves by running away from home; becoming angry, defiant, aggressive, or manipulative; experimenting with drugs; and engaging in high-risk behaviors (Hogarth, 1995). They frequently use denial to cope with their stresses and resist attempts to explore the anxiety-producing aspects of themselves that lead to understanding. When anxieties are extreme, adolescents may engage in self-mutilating behaviors or develop the characteristics of anorexia nervosa or bulimia. Many beginning symptoms of schizophrenia and other psychoses begin in adolescence.

Unfortunately, adolescents are a forgotten population when it comes to mental health care. "According to recent studies, large numbers of children and adolescents with serious emotional or behavioral disorders receive either no mental health treatment or treatment inappropriate to their needs" (Collins and Collins, 1994). Health care providers who work with adolescents must learn to recognize clients' anxiety levels and offer interventions and education early, *before* anxiety becomes the fuel for more serious mental health problems.

Anxiety in Adulthood

By young adulthood, one's coping behaviors are well established. Adults are more likely to encounter crises and situations that provoke anxiety as they move through their worlds of work, family, and community. Some adults appear to lead a "charmed life" with few stresses and anxieties. Others seem to continually struggle, only to rebound from one misfortune after another. Like their younger counterparts, adults handle anxiety based on earlier, established coping mechanisms.

Adults must cope with many anxiety-producing situations. Developmental tasks, such as establishing a career and family, present numerous stressors. The loss of income, spouse, or physical ability can lead to severe anxiety. Uncontrollable situations, like fires, floods, war, or earthquakes, often result in long-lasting anxiety, which, unless resolved, can evolve into posttraumatic stress syndrome.

When adult anxieties are not focused or controlled, a number of mental health problems may result. Generalized or situational anxiety disorders are diagnosed when individuals become overwhelmed and nonfunctional as a result of their anxieties. Other maladaptive responses to anxiety in adults include panic disorders, phobias, behavioral addictions, obsessions, and compulsive activities.

Anxiety in Older Adulthood

Older adults face a combination of unique, anxiety-producing life hazards. Because of physical and possibly mental changes, older adults express their anxieties in less overt ways than younger persons. "Older people tend to deny or somatize (express physically) feelings of depression, anxiety, and tension, either because of social desirability factors such as 'looking good' to others and projecting an image of self-reliance, or a lack of self-awareness as to what they really are experiencing" (Hogstel, 1995).

Although few actual statistics are available, anxiety appears to be a common problem for many older adults. Elders face an uncertain future and must cope with a number of problems in the present. Issues about loss of self-determination and control can cause much anxiety in the elderly.

Because older adults are less likely to directly share their feelings of anxiety, it becomes more difficult for nurses to recognize the signs of anxiety in their elderly clients. Behaviors indicating the presence of anxiety include apathy; changes in eating, sleeping, and ability to concentrate; impatience; and fatigue. One of the most effective methods for assessing anxiety in older adults is simply to ask the client to explain his/her anxious feelings. The elderly appreciate the interest and concern of the nurse who is willing to inquire.

Theories Relating to Anxiety

A number of theories have been developed to explain anxiety and its responses since Sigmund Freud first listed anxiety as a defense mechanism. Today, the causes of anxiety are still uncertain, but research indicates that a combination of physical, psychosocial, and environmental factors are involved. A few of the more well-known theories (models) of the origin and development of anxiety are discussed here.

Biological Models

The group of theories receiving the most recent attention attempts to find a biological or physical basis for anxiety. The work of Charles Darwin first posed the possibility of a link between emotions and the ability to adapt. Later, Hans Selye demonstrated a connection between the perception of stress and physical changes in the body with his "fight-flight" response. Today, thanks to modern technology and science, we are beginning to gain an understanding of the role emotions play in health and illness as researchers unveil another bit of new information.

One of the most popular current theories of anxiety relates to the role of the body's elusive neurochemicals. Research into the role of these body chemicals, called *neurotransmitters,* has resulted in "increasing evidence that anxiety has neurobiological origins" (Salzman and others, 1993). Anxiety is thought to result from the dysfunction of two or more neurotransmitters. Further research is being done to investigate the possibility of treating anxiety with specific medications designed to alter neurotransmitter activity. Other ongoing studies are investigating the role of the autonomic nervous system in the development of anxiety.

Psychodynamic Model

According to Freud's psychoanalytical point of view, anxiety results from a conflict between two opposing forces within the personality—the ego and the id. Neurotic or maladaptive behaviors are the result of attempts to defend oneself against anxiety, just as adaptive behaviors succeed in doing. Today, many psychotherapists have broadened the psychoanalytical theory to define anxiety as the result of a conflict between two opposing forces within an individual.

Interpersonal Model

With the interpersonal model, anxiety is explained in terms of interactions with others. Anxiety develops when early childhood interactions with parents and significant others result in negative outcomes, such as disapproval. Over a period of time, an individual's experience of and responses to anxiety form the basis for low self-esteem and poor self-concept.

Interpersonal theorists work with a broad definition of anxiety. Its most famous theorist, Harry Stack Sullivan "saw individuals striving for security and relief from anxiety to protect their self-systems" (Keltner, Schwecke, and Bostrom, 1995). Sullivan believed that children take on the values of their parents because they are dependent on others for approval or disapproval. In adulthood, individuals cope with anxiety based on their perceptions and on how they were taught to cope with conflict as children. Using this interpersonal model, one can see the importance of early assessment and intervention for children who are anxious.

Behavioral Model

The behavioral theories consider anxiety a learned response. Children who experienced anxiety in one situation link those feelings to more general, nonthreatening situations. Anxiety results when individuals encounter a signal that reminds them of earlier anxious times. Thus, individuals *learn* to react with anxiety.

Other Models

Other theories explain anxiety as the result of a loss of life's meaning (existential theory). Environmental models tie anxiety with uncontrollable events or situations. Fires, floods, or other natural disasters, along with assaults and man-induced traumas, all serve as stressors for the modern human being.

Many nurses and other health care providers have chosen to view anxiety from a holistic model. With this point of view, anxiety is seen as having an impact on every realm of human functioning. Physical reactions, like the 'fight-flight' reaction, result from anxiety. In fact, "researchers studying a group of more than 2,000 men over a period of 32 years have found a correlation between high anxiety and sudden cardiac death" (Ichiro and others, 1994). Strong emotional responses occur when one is anxious. Social areas of functioning can become impaired as a result of anxiety, and even one's spirituality comes into question during times of great or prolonged anxiety. By considering each area of functioning, nurses are better able to plan and implement effective therapeutic interventions for the relief of anxiety.

Anxiety Disorders

"Up to 48% of patients seeking care from primary care providers may have emotional problems . . . . About 10% of adult primary care patients may have unrecognized and untreated anxiety" (Fifer and others, 1994). It appears that the effective control of anxiety is a problem for many people.

If anxiety is a normal human response, when does its expression become a disorder? An anxiety disorder exists when anxiety is expressed in ineffective or maladaptive ways and one's coping mechanisms (behaviors) do not successfully relieve the distress. People cope with or handle anxiety using skills from every area of functioning. In the physical realm, one attempts to cope directly with the source of the anxiety. Intellectual efforts are directed at analyzing the situation, problem solving, or changing the meaning of the problem. When efforts in these areas fail, ego defense mechanisms attempt to reduce the emotional distress associated with anxiety, and many individuals call on their spiritual resources in an effort to cope with anxiety-producing problems. The spectrum of coping behaviors is broad, but coping behaviors that do nothing to deal with the *source* of the anxiety are considered ineffective and maladaptive.

The diagnosis of an anxiety disorder is based on a description of the behaviors used to express distress. The *Diagnostic and Statistical Manual of Mental Disorders* (DSM-IV) classifies anxiety disorders as generalized, panic, phobic, obsessive-compulsive, behavioral, and posttraumatic. Because these disorders are commonly encountered in every culture, society, and health care setting, it is important for nurses to understand their nature (see box below).

Generalized Anxiety Disorder

Anxiety disorders usually manifest in adolescence or early adulthood. A generalized anxiety disorder is diagnosed when an individual's anxiety is broad, long-lasting, and excessive. It is primarily a disturbance in the emotional area of functioning that eventually affects every other aspect of one's world.

People with generalized anxiety disorder are worried and anxious more than they are not. They tend to fret about numerous things and find it difficult to control their worry. Often, they are so anxious they find it difficult to concentrate on a task long enough to complete it. Responses are far out of proportion with the actual situation or impact of the feared event. Physical signs/symptoms usually accompany the anxiety and can range from muscle tension to full "fight-flight" responses. Generalized anxiety disorder is often seen in persons with irritable bowel syndrome, headaches, sleep disturbances, and substance abuse.

When generalized anxiety is seen in children, it is diagnosed as *overanxious disorder of childhood*. Children with this maladaptive anxiety tend to worry about their performance in school and social interactions. Adults with generalized anxiety concentrate on worrying about the everyday, routine events.

Panic Disorders

Panic disorders offer a challenge to health care providers because their signs/symptoms are difficult to distinguish from actual physical dysfunctions. A **panic attack** is a brief period of intense fear or discomfort. It is always accompanied by various physical and emotional reactions (see box below). The duration of the actual attack is short (1 to 15 minutes), with a peak in anxiety after about 10 minutes.

Panic disorders are more common than once thought. Research has shown that over 6% of clients seen in primary care settings suffer from panic disorders. Nearly 50% of these disorders are either undiagnosed, misdiagnosed, or inadequately treated (Laria, 1995). Panic disorders are more common in women (70%), people who are separated or divorced, and persons of both sexes between ages 24 to 44 (American

CULTURAL ASPECTS

Anxiety appears to occur in most if not every culture. The expressions of anxiety, however, differ greatly:
- Japanese people tend to somatize or handle anxiety by becoming physically ill.
- Mothers in the Dominican Republic cope with the anxiety of the "evil eye" by wearing red and saving the infant's umbilical cord.
- Greek men consider body hair a sign of manhood. Shaving their hair in preparation for a surgical procedure can result in great anxiety.

PANIC ATTACK CRITERIA

A panic attack is a discrete period of intense fear or discomfort in which at least four of the following symptoms develop abruptly and reach a peak within 10 minutes:
1. Palpitations, pounding heart, or accelerated heart rate
2. Sweating
3. Trembling or shaking
4. Feelings of shortness of breath, smothering
5. Feeling of choking
6. Chest pain or discomfort
7. Nausea or abdominal distress
8. Feeling dizzy, unsteady, light-headed, or faint
9. Derealization (feelings of unreality) or depersonalization (being detached from oneself)
10. Fear of losing control or going crazy
11. Fear of dying
12. Paresthesias (numbness, tingling sensations)
13. Chills or hot flushes

From Stuart GW, Sundeen SJ: *Pocket guide to psychiatric nursing*, ed 3, St Louis, 1995, Mosby.

Psychiatric Association, 1994). Typically, an individual with a panic attack presents with physical complaints that may indicate a life-threatening situation.

There are two kinds of panic disorders: those associated with agoraphobia and those that are not. **Agoraphobia** is anxiety about possible situations in which a panic attack may occur. People with agoraphobia avoid people, places, or events from which escape would be difficult or embarrassing. Fear accompanies a sense of helplessness and embarrassment with the thought of a panic attack occurring and no help being available. Typically, agoraphobia is associated with public situations, such being in a crowd, standing in line, traveling on a bus or plane, standing on a bridge, or being afraid to leave the house alone. Recent studies (Wade, Monroe, and Michelson, 1993) have shown that the presence of chronic stressors complicates the picture for treatment and improvement.

Treatment for panic disorders focuses on educating clients about the nature of the disorder, blocking the panic attacks pharmacologically, and assisting clients to develop more adaptive ways of coping with their anxieties. Cognitive therapy helps individuals identify their emotions and behaviors, whereas psychotherapy allows them to explore social or personal difficulties. Education, emotional support, and reassurance are important nursing measures for the care of clients who suffer with panic disorders.

Phobic Disorders

A **phobia** is an unnatural fear. Phobias may be expressed as a fear of people, animals, objects, situations, or occurrences. For example, a *social phobia* is characterized by an unrealistic and persistent fear of any situation in which other people could be judging them (*Harvard Mental Health Letter*, 1994). These individuals are constantly worried about being made to look foolish. They fear their hands will tremble if they try to write, their voice will quaver if they attempt to talk, or they will vomit if they start to eat. Some are especially anxious in the presence of authority figures or persons with high social contacts. Even eye contact (or the lack of it) from others can be misunderstood as scrutiny and rejection. When the anxieties associated with the social phobia are intense, a full-blown panic attack often results. Persons with severe social phobias often avoid contact with anyone outside their immediate family. Life for many socially phobic individuals is a lonely and isolated existence.

Phobias differ from normal fear. First, phobias are obsessive in nature. Individuals with phobias tend to dwell on their object of fear almost to the point of fascination. Thinking may take the form of fantasies about the fear, such as the person with *thanatophobia* (fear of dying) rehearsing her funeral.

People with phobias handle their anxieties differently. "A phobia typically produces so high a level of anxiety that it is immobilizing, preventing the person from acting in a way that could prove effective in alleviating the anxiety" (Corsini, 1994). The experience of great anxiety or fear that normally protects a person immobilizes the individual with a phobia.

The characteristics of phobias vary with the culture. In some cultures, the fear of hexes, spells, magical spirits, and unseen forces results in phobic reactions. Health professionals should remember cultural backgrounds when assessing clients for phobic responses to anxiety (see box below).

Obsessive-Compulsive Disorder

An **obsession** is a distressing persistent thought. A **compulsion** is a distressing recurring behavior. For behaviors to be called obsessions and compulsions, they must meet certain criteria (see box on p. 283). An obsession must be persistent, recurring, inappropriate, and distressing. Compulsions are not just habits. They are specific behaviors that *must* be performed to reduce anxiety.

Although all of us have repeated worries or routines that we recognize as not entirely sensible, persons with *obsessive-compulsive disorder (OCD)* are consumed by self-destructive, anxiety-reducing thoughts and actions.

OCDs were once thought to be relatively rare, but recent studies by the Resource Catchment Area have demonstrated that OCD occurs in 2.5% of Americans (United States and Canada) at any given time. Simi-

---

◆ THINK ABOUT

Your client believes that his abdominal abscess was caused by a hex placed on him by his neighbor. It seems that he and his neighbor had an ongoing dispute over the correct placement of the shared fence. Last week a particularly angry interaction took place. At that time, his neighbor shouted curses and threatened to have a hex placed on him. Less than 24 hours later, the client began to experience abdominal pain, which he endured for 3 days before seeking treatment.

At this time, you are preparing the client for surgery to drain the abscess. Noting his anxious expression, you ask what is bothering him. He replies by telling you that the surgery will not cure his condition until the hex is removed, and the only way to do that is to appease his neighbor.

Are this client's fears real and justified?

Which nursing interventions would you choose if you were this client's nurse?

lar results are seen in other countries, such as Great Britain, Germany, Korea, and New Zealand (*Harvard Mental Health Letter,* 1995).

Symptoms of OCD can occur as early as 3 years of age, but usually they begin in adolescence. Men and women appear to be equally affected, although symptoms frequently appear an average of 5 years earlier in men. A high rate of OCD occurs in persons with other mental health problems, especially depression.

The most common obsessions relate to cleanliness, dirt, and germs; aggressive and sexual impulses; health concerns; safety concerns; and order and symmetry. Obsessions can take the form of thoughts, doubts, fears, images, or impulses. Individuals with obsessions are aware of their unreasonableness. They know intellectually that their attempts to relieve anxiety are maladaptive but feel compelled emotionally to yield to their distressing obsessions.

Compulsive behaviors help to reduce anxieties generated by the obsession for a time. Persons with OCD use the ego defense mechanisms of *repression* to cope with distressing obsessions. They focus their anxieties into compulsive actions *(displacement)* and engage in undoing behaviors to relieve guilt and stress.

Persons with OCD reassure themselves with repetition. They constantly check, rehearse, pray, count, or repeat single words. Their compulsive behaviors neutralize the obsessive thoughts, thereby relieving anxiety. During times of increased stress, many ritualistic behaviors become more intense. Soon the compulsive behavior becomes more important than other aspects of life. Many persons with OCD are unable to maintain social relationships because their compulsions are too time-consuming or inappropriate.

OCD is seen in families, and many studies are exploring possible genetic and hormonal causes. "Recently researchers using magnetic resonance imaging (MRI) and positron emission tomography (PET) have discovered abnormal brain structure and function in patients with obsessive-compulsive disorder (OCD)" (*Harvard Mental Health Letter,* 1995). Treatment for OCD consists of a combination of drug and behavioral therapy (Dattilio, 1993). A number of antidepressants and SSRI-antidepressant medications have been successfully used to treat clients with OCD.

Behavioral Addictions

Obsessive-compulsive activities may also take the form of certain **addictive behaviors,** such as gambling, shopping, working, or engaging in excessive sexual activity. Compulsive gambling or wagering is fast becoming a problem for many people as more and more states legalize gambling and open casinos. Estimates put the number of compulsive gamblers in the United States at more than 6 million people (Meintz and Larson, 1994).

Compulsive gambling, shopping, and working behaviors have great effects on others. If left unchecked, they can destroy personal, professional, and financial relationships. Compulsive sexual activity has the added factor of increased risk of contracting and spreading sexually transmitted diseases.

Traumatic Stress Reaction

A **traumatic stress reaction** is a series of behavioral and emotional responses following an overwhelmingly stressful event. People at high risk for being exposed to traumatic stress are persons with current mental health problems, victims or observers of violence, victims of sexual assault (especially as a child), victims of spouse abuse, and homeless persons.

Traumatic stress reactions are always considered with women who have been sexually assaulted. Like reactions to other types of trauma, individuals with the nursing diagnosis of *rape trauma syndrome* follow a predictable clinical course: fear and anguish, recovery and repair, and adaptation.

OBSESSIONS AND COMPULSIONS CRITERIA

OBSESSIONS

1. Recurrent and persistent thoughts, impulses, or images that are experienced at some time during the disturbance as intrusive and inappropriate and cause marked anxiety or distress
2. The thoughts, impulses, or images are not simply excessive worries about real-life problems
3. The person attempts to ignore or suppress such thoughts or impulses or to neutralize them with some other thought or action
4. The person recognizes that the obsessional thoughts, impulses, or images are a product of one's own mind

COMPULSIONS

1. Repetitive behaviors (e.g., hand washing, ordering, checking) or mental acts (e.g., praying, counting, repeating words silently) that the person feels driven to perform in response to an obsession or according to rules that must be applied rigidly
2. The behaviors or mental acts are aimed at preventing or reducing distress or preventing some dreaded event or situation; however, these behaviors or mental acts either are not connected in a realistic way with what they are designed to neutralize or prevent or are clearly excessive

From Stuart GW, Sundeen SJ: *Pocket guide to psychiatric nursing,* ed 3, St Louis, 1995, Mosby.

Following a traumatic event, "the initial response generally consists of an outcry of anguish or fear. Then the patient tries to recover from the traumatic event and repair the immediate damage" (Forster and King, 1994). During the repair and recovery stage, most individuals make reasonably adaptive responses but some will react ineffectively and go on to develop chronic stress reactions or posttraumatic stress disorder. The adaptation phase is heralded by a return to real-world situations and appropriate coping behaviors. Providing psychological stability, emotional support, and advocacy is the most important nursing intervention for clients with traumatic stress reactions.

Posttraumatic Stress Disorder

Individuals with posttraumatic stress disorder have at sometime in their lives been exposed to a traumatic experience outside the realm of normal life experiences in which intense fear, horror, or helplessness was experienced. Posttraumatic stress disorder (PTSD) is the reexperiencing of the traumatic events or situations. Persons involved in natural or man-made disasters, combat, motor vehicle accidents, crime, rape, or abuse are the most likely candidates for developing PTSD.

The symptoms of PTSD include **flashbacks,** vivid recollections of the event in which the individual re-

---

◆ TABLE 20-2
Side Effects of Benzodiazepines and Nursing Care

Side Effects*	Nursing Interventions
Central nervous system	
Dizziness, drowsiness, sedation, headache, tremors, depression, insomnia, hallucinations	Ensure safety, prevent falls, assist with ambulation, use side rails. Reassure that symptoms are common when first beginning the medication. Assess mental status routinely.
Gastrointestinal	
Dry mouth, anorexia, nausea, vomiting, constipation, diarrhea	Give with food or milk. Ensure frequent oral care. Offer hard candy, gum, sips of water frequently.
Cardiovascular	
ECG changes, *orthostatic hypotension, tachycardia*	Monitor intake and output if anorexia, vomiting, diarrhea occurs. Assess blood pressure, pulse (lying and standing); if systolic blood pressure drops 20 mm Hg, hold drug and notify physician. Monitor complete blood count and other laboratory studies during long-term therapy.
Eyes, ears, nose, throat	
Blurred vision, ringing in ears	Provide reassurance. Ensure safety.
Integument (skin)	
Itching, rash, dermatitis	Encourage use of tepid baths without soap. Assess rash and report to physician.
Emotional	
Feelings of detachment, irritability, increased hostility	Encourage social interactions. Assess for loss of control over emotions and aggression.
Long-term effects	
Increased drug tolerance, physical and psychological dependency, rebound anxiety and insomnia	Drug dose is tapered slowly after 4 months of treatment. Help client identify difference between symptoms of drug withdrawal and original feelings of anxiety.

*The most common side effects are in italics.

lives the frightening experience. Flashbacks can last from a few seconds to longer than ½ hour. During a flashback, the experience is vividly real and *life-threatening* to the individual. Health care providers must remember this fact when coping with a client who is experiencing a flashback. Interventions are to ensure everyone's safety and reorient the client to his/her present surroundings.

Anxiety, depression, and nightmares can complicate the picture and soon individuals reduce their involvement with the outside world as their responsiveness to life numbs. Frequently, people with severe PTSD isolate themselves from society by living in sparsely populated rural areas. Children with PTSD express themselves through disorganized or agitated behaviors. Long-term interventions include pharmacological and psychological therapy (Cumbie, 1994).

Therapeutic Interventions

The most effective way to cope with anxiety is to prevent it. Learn to recognize the signs/symptoms of anxiety. Include an anxiety level assessment for every client. Be especially alert to the signs of anxiety in children. Teaching children how to appropriately cope with their anxieties at a young age can prevent a number of mental health problems later in life.

Therapeutic interventions for individuals with maladaptive responses to anxiety involve a combination of mental health therapies and medications. Psychotherapy helps clients to uncover the core of their anxiety. Two behavioral therapies that are successful in treating phobias are systematic desensitization and flooding (Dattilio, 1993).

With *systematic desensitization,* clients learn to cope with one anxiety-provoking stimulus at a time until the stressor that brings about the greatest reaction is no longer associated with anxiety. This step-by-step method gradually removes the anxiety from the distress-causing event and allows clients to develop more effective ways of perceiving their anxiety.

Flooding is just the opposite. This method for treating phobias rapidly and repeatedly exposes clients to the feared object or situation until anxiety levels diminish. Other treatments, such as *rational-emotive therapy,* are designed to help clients learn how their illogical thinking leads to maladaptive behaviors.

Anxiety is also treated with various medications, including benzodiazepines, tricyclic antidepressants, and monoamine oxidase inhibitors (MAOI) and SSRI antidepressants (Blair and Ramones, 1994). Because each type of drug is associated with possibly severe side effects, nurses must monitor their clients' responses to drug therapy. Table 20-2 lists the side effects of the most commonly used antianxiety agents, benzodiazepines, and suggested nursing interventions.

Nursing Interventions

After a complete nursing history and thorough physical examination, the most appropriate nursing diagnoses are selected (McCloskey and Bulechek, 1996) (see box below). Next, client goals are established and interventions are chosen.

One of the first priorities of care is to protect the client from possible injury to self and others. Establishing a trusting therapeutic relationship helps clients to explore their distresses and learn to link their behaviors to the sources of their anxiety (Badger, 1994). Problem-solving techniques assist clients in developing more effective coping mechanisms. Relaxation techniques, such as meditation, and stress-reducing exercises help clients counter the anxieties being experienced. The box on p. 286 provides a sample of a client care plan for anxiety responses.

Nurses are in an excellent position to help clients cope effectively with the effects of stress and anxiety. Handling small, everyday distresses successfully is key to preventing complicated mental health problems that arise as maladaptive expressions of anxiety.

NANDA NURSING DIAGNOSES RELATED TO ANXIETY RESPONSES

- Adjustment, impaired
- Anxiety*
- Breathing pattern, ineffective
- Communication, impaired verbal
- Coping, ineffective individual*
- Diarrhea
- Energy field disturbance
- Fear*
- Health maintenance, altered
- Incontinence, stress
- Injury, risk for
- Nutrition, altered
- Posttrauma response
- Powerlessness
- Self-esteem disturbance
- Sensory/perceptual alterations (specify)
- Sleep pattern disturbance
- Social interaction, impaired
- Social isolation
- Thought processes, altered
- Urinary elimination, altered

From North American Nursing Diagnosis Association: *NANDA nursing diagnoses: definitions and classification 1995-1996,* Philadelphia, 1994, The Association.
*Primary nursing diagnosis for anxiety.

SAMPLE CLIENT CARE PLAN
ANXIETY

Assessment

History: Joe is a 44-year-old man who has lost his wife, job, and car within the past 3 months. Last night, after Joe and his buddies "had a few drinks," Joe became suspicious and accused his friends of trying to steal "what little I have left. I just know something awful is going to happen. It's happened twice, and you know things always occur in threes." Today, Joe is seeking treatment for his upset stomach and inability to sleep.

Current Findings: An untidy man who appears older than his stated age. There is an odor of alcohol about him. Vital signs are increased, with a pulse rate of 116 beats/min. He complains of shortness of breath, upset stomach, frequent urination, and lack of sleep. When questioned about the recent changes in his lifestyle, he replies, "It's no big deal. I'll get by."

Nursing Diagnosis

Anxiety related to loss of wife and job

Planning/Expected Outcomes

Joe will identify the causes of his anxiety and make two attempts to decrease the level of anxiety he is experiencing.

Nursing Interventions

Intervention

1. Establish trust with Joe.

2. Contract with him to refrain from hurting himself and others for the duration of therapy.
3. Use active listening to gently encourage Joe to link his anxiety with his recent experiences.

4. Assess Joe's statements of self-worth and reinforce personal strengths that he has identified.
5. Help Joe identify areas of his life over which he has control.

6. Give positive feedback for attempts to reduce anxiety.
7. Encourage Joe to continue already established relationships.
8. Help identify areas of strength and limitations in social interactions.

Rationale

1. Trust helps client to explore new ways of coping.
2. To ensure safety of Joe and others during expressions of anxiety.
3. Allows time to assess Joe's perspective; helps Joe to connect his emotions with his feelings of anxiety.
4. Helps determine Joe's perception of himself; energy flows where it is focused.
5. Learning to direct one's energies decreases anxiety, promotes relaxation, and increases sense of control.
6. One small success builds on another when recognized.
7. Established relationships can be source of comfort and support.
8. Positive reinforcement encourages appropriate actions; the first step in changing behaviors is identifying them.

Evaluation

Joe attended four counseling sessions before he recognized that he was anxious. By the seventh session, Joe was able to reduce his anxiety by practicing 10 minutes of relaxation exercises.

❖ KEY CONCEPTS

- Anxiety is a vague feeling of uneasiness, uncertainty, and helplessness, which is a normal emotional response to a threat or stressor.

- Adaptive responses to anxiety result in positive outcomes, new learning, and greater self-esteem.

- Maladaptive responses to anxiety are ineffective attempts to cope that do nothing to resolve problems or eliminate feelings of anxiety.

- An understanding of how individuals at various developmental stages perceive and cope with anxiety is important for nurses and other health care providers.

- The specific causes of anxiety are still uncertain, but research indicates that a combination of physical, psychosocial, and environmental factors are involved.

- An anxiety disorder exists when anxiety is handled in ineffective or maladaptive ways (when one's coping mechanisms or behaviors do not relieve anxiety's distress).

- A generalized anxiety disorder is diagnosed when anxiety is broad, long-lasting, and excessive.

- A panic attack is a brief period of intense fear or discomfort accompanied by physical and emotional reactions.

- A phobia is an unnatural fear of people, animals, objects, situations, or occurrences.

- An obsession is a distressing, recurring, persistent thought.

- A compulsion is a distressing recurring behavior.

- Posttraumatic stress disorder (PTSD) is the reexperiencing of previously experienced traumatic events or situations.

- One of the first priorities of nursing care is to protect the client from possible injury to self and others.

- Establishing a trusting therapeutic relationship is a nursing intervention that helps clients to explore their distresses and learn to connect behaviors with the sources of their anxiety.

- Problem-solving techniques assist clients in developing new, more effective coping mechanisms.

- Relaxation techniques help clients counter the anxieties currently being experienced.

- Nurses are in an excellent position to help their clients cope effectively with the effects of stress and anxiety.

❖ SUGGESTIONS FOR FURTHER READING

An important article that discusses interventions for PTSD is "Treating a PTSD flashback," by B. Cumbie (*Nurs 94* 24[2]:33, 1994).

❖ REFERENCES

American Psychiatric Association: *Diagnostic and statistical manual of mental disorders,* ed 4, Washington DC, 1994, The Association.

Badger JM: Calming the anxious patient, *Am J Nurs* 94(5):46, 1994.

Blair T, Ramones VA: Psychopharmacologic treatment of anxiety, *J Psychosoc Nurs* 32(7):49, 1994.

Baumeister RF, Leary MR: The need to belong: desire for interpersonal attachments as a fundamental human need to belong, *Psychol Bull* 117(3):497, 1995.

Collins BG, Collins TM: Child and adolescent mental health: building a system of care, *J Couns Dev* 72(3):239, 1994.

Corsini RJ, editor: *Encyclopedia of psychology,* ed 2, New York, 1994, John Wiley.

Clunn P, editor: *Child psychiatric nursing,* ed 2, St Louis, 1995, Mosby.

Cumbie B: Treating PTSD flashback, *Nurs 94* 24(2):33, 1994.

Dattilio FM: A practical update on the treatment of obsessive-compulsive disorders, *J Ment Health Counsel* 15(3):244, 1993.

Fifer SK and others: Untreated anxiety among adult primary care patients in a health maintenance organization, *Arch Gen Psychiatry* 51:740, 1994.

Forster P, King J: Traumatic stress reactions and the psychiatric emergency, *Psychiatr Ann* 24:603, 1994.

Hogarth CR: *Adolescent psychiatric nursing,* ed 2, St Louis, 1995, Mosby.

Hogstel MO: *Geropsychiatric nursing,* ed 2, St Louis, 1995, Mosby.

Ichiro K and others: Symptoms of anxiety and risk of coronary heart disease: the normative aging study, *Circulation* 90(11):2225, 1994.

Keltner NL, Schwecke LH, Bostrom CE: *Psychiatric nursing,* ed 2, St Louis, 1995, Mosby.

Laria MT: Panic disorder, *Adv Nurse Pract* 3(12):24, 1995.

McCloskey JC, Bulechek GM: *Nursing interventions classification,* ed 2, St Louis, 1996, Mosby.

Meintz SL, Larson C: Can you spot this kind of addiction? *RN* 57(7):42, 1994.

Obsessive-compulsive disorders—part one, *Harvard Ment Health Lett* 12(5):1, 1995.

Salzman C and others: Neurobiologic basis of anxiety and its treatment, *Harvard Rev Psychiatry* 1(2):197, 1993.

Social phobia—parts 1 and 2, *Harvard Ment Health Lett* 11(4):1, 1994.

Stuart GW, Sundeen SJ: *Principles and practice of psychiatric nursing,* ed 5, St Louis, 1995, Mosby.

Wade SL, Monroe SM, Michelson LK: Chronic life stress and treatment outcome in agoraphobia with panic attacks, *Am J Psychiatry* 150:1491, 1993.

Wong DL: *Whaley and Wong's nursing care of infants and children,* ed 5, St Louis, 1995, Mosby.

DEPRESSION AND OTHER MOOD DISORDERS

LEARNING OBJECTIVES

1. Describe the continuum of emotional responses.
2. Identify how emotions affect individuals throughout the life cycle.
3. Explain four theories relating to emotions and their disorders.
4. State the difference between a depressive episode and a depressive disorder.
5. List the diagnostic criteria for bipolar disorders.
6. Describe behaviors associated with postpartum depression.
7. Explain seasonal affective disorder.
8. Name three drug classes used for the treatment of depression and other mood disorders.
9. Identify four nursing interventions for clients with mood disorders.

KEY TERMS

affect
bipolar disorder
cyclothymic disorder
depression
dysthymia

emotion
hypomania
mania
manic depression
mood

mood disorder
postpartum depression
religiosity
seasonal affective disorder
situational depression

The emotional realm or dimension of human functioning affects all areas of human behavior. We all have experienced how emotions can result in physical changes, new intellectual perspectives, and altered social roles. It is safe to say that emotions play an important role in the lives of human beings.

An **emotion** is a feeling, a nonintellectual response. Emotions are reactions to various stimuli based on individual perceptions. The box below presents an example of how perceptions affect emotional reactions.

Continuum of Emotional Responses

The spectrum of human emotion ranges from elation to despair. Emotional responses can be growth promoting and adaptive, or they can lead to ineffec-tive behaviors that could soon become maladaptive. Fig. 21-1 illustrates the continuum of emotional responses (Stuart and Sundeen, 1995).

Characteristics of Mood Disorders

A **mood** is described as a "prolonged emotional state that influences one's whole personality and life functioning" (Rollant and Deppoliti, 1996). **Affect** is the outward expression of one's emotions. Affects can be described as blunted (restricted), flat, inappropriate, and labile (rapidly changing).

A **mood disorder** is defined as a disturbance in the emotional dimension of human functioning. Mood disorders are also called affective disorders. Problems with emotions occur when one is extremely happy or intensely sad. Most of us experience emotional extremes; but when one's feelings (emotions) interfere with effective living, they become maladaptive.

Problems with emotions range from mania to depression. **Mania** refers to an emotional state in which a person has an elevated, expansive, irritable mood accompanied by a loss of identity, hyperactivity, and grandiose thoughts and actions. **Depression,** the opposite of mania, is an emotional state characterized by feelings of sadness, disappointment, and despair.

Most people have experienced both these emotional states. Sometimes, people are unable to carry out their daily activities because of mania or depression, but these situations are most often short-lived. Individuals with mood disorders, however, can suffer for months or even years without relief. Long-term depression also affects one's physical state. "Many studies show that depressed people feel worse and even more limited in their daily activities than patients with such serious chronic medical conditions as diabetes and arthritis" (*Harvard Mental Health Letter*, 1995).

"Depression is more than a state of mind: it is an illness. Depression affects 11.5 million people—or about

---

THINK ABOUT

It is a warm summer Saturday, and people in the neighborhood are enjoying the outdoors. Ted and Fred, two neighborhood teens, are working on building a model airplane in Fred's backyard.

Suddenly, a piece of the model breaks. Fred blames Ted, and Ted blames it on Fred's clumsi-ness. They begin to scuffle and swear at each other. Soon they are exchanging blows and fighting.

The commotion brings both fathers to the back doors of their homes. Fred's father, noting the scuffle, shakes his fist and shouts, "That's a boy! Punch him good. No son of mine is going to let someone get the best of him. Hit 'em again!"

Ted's father, seeing the scene, reacts with, "Boys! Stop fighting! There are better ways to solve your problems than beating each other up."

Were both fathers witnessing the same event?

If so, what do you think caused the difference in their reactions?

What lesson do you think the reactions of each father taught Fred and Ted?

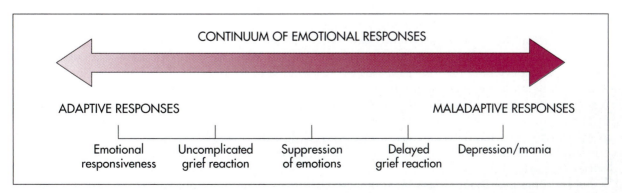

Fig. 21-1   Continuum of emotional responses. (Redrawn from Stuart GW, Sundeen SJ: *Principles and practice of psychiatric nursing,* ed 5, St Louis, 1995, Mosby.)

1 in 20—every year, and it is said that the incidence of depression is second only to the common cold" (Kronberg, 1995). Depression is found in all races, ethnic groups, age groups, and socioeconomic levels. It commonly affects twice as many women as men. When the effects of depression are added to those of other mood disorders, it is easy to see that emotional problems are a large part of the distresses suffered by human beings.

Emotions Throughout the Life Cycle

Because emotional responses are one of the realms of human functioning, they grow and develop as the individual does. When we are young, emotions are often experienced but seldom controlled. With growth and maturity, emotional control is slowly gained as individuals test and learn about the appropriateness of their emotionally expressive behaviors. By adulthood, most societies expect people to control their emotions and express them in appropriate ways.

Emotions in Childhood

When infants' basic needs are met, they usually feel a sense of contentment. Any delay in meeting those needs, however, is often announced by expressions of frustration or even anger. Toddlers struggle to cope with many newly experienced emotions, such as fear, helplessness, and anxiety. Many of these feelings are acted out rather than identified because young children are often unable to express themselves verbally.

Most depressive responses in children are tied to a specific event or situation, such as the loss of a parent or significant other. Once the stressors are removed or decreased, the depression is relieved. This type of depression is called acute depression or **situational depression** because it can be traced to a recognizable cause. Situational depression is seen in all age groups.

Children who are depressed have a distinct way of thinking that involves feelings of hopelessness, low self-esteem, and a tendency to take the blame for every negative event (Wong, 1995). They often respond with irritability, tearfulness, and sadness. Schoolwork and friendships suffer as more and more time is spent in solitary activities, especially watching television. Some children become clinging and dependent, whereas others engage in aggressive or disruptive behaviors. Many show changes in eating and sleeping behaviors. Fortunately, most acute episodes of childhood depression fade with family nurturing and social support.

During childhood, individuals establish their self-esteem, coping mechanisms, and problem-solving abilities. If they have been successful in developing these skills, they are well prepared to handle the emotional distresses of later life. If they have not, mental health problems may arise. The incidence of depression in childhood is increasing, and health care providers should include an assessment of mood for all young clients.

Emotions in Adolescence

During the teen years, individuals struggle to identify, gain control over, and express emotions. The moods of adolescents commonly swing from feeling vulnerable and dependent to knowing that they are smarter than everyone else in the family.

Most adolescents establish their personal and social identities without significant psychological problems or emotional disorders, but a growing number of teens are showing evidence of depression. Estimates based on several studies report that as many as 21% of high school students reported mild to moderate signs of depression, and 7% reported their depressive feelings as severe (Brage, Campbell-Grossman, and Dunkel, 1995).

Depression in adolescence appears to be related to four factors: self-esteem, loneliness, family strengths, and parent-adolescent communications. Age and gender are lesser factors, but women with depression outnumber men by two to one. When self-esteem is low, individuals have "a tendency to react to frustration with a sense of helplessness and feelings of depression" (Brage, Campbell-Grossman, and Dunkel, 1995). They begin to see the world as bleak, and themselves as small and insignificant. Feelings of self-esteem feed further negative emotions, and a cycle of depression and low self-esteem is established. Grades drop as interest in school activities wanes.

Loneliness is highly associated with depression in all age groups, but especially in adolescence. People need the companionship of others; as loneliness increases, so does depression. The emotionally isolated teen may be surrounded by others yet still feel like an outcast.

Family relationships also have an influence on adolescent depression. In one study, mothers of depressed adolescents were much stingier with their praise than those of nondepressed adolescents. They tended to set and expect higher standards of achievement for their children but seldom rewarded them for their efforts (Marton and others, 1993). Often, adolescents rebel against impossible standards by withdrawing into depression. Parent-adolescent communication patterns also have an impact on the teen's ability or willingness to discuss problems. Teens who can discuss their concerns with understanding parents have lower rates of depression.

The occurrence of depression and other mood disorders in adolescence reaches across ethnic and cultural lines. Table 21-1 offers some interesting information about the incidence of depression in different cultural groups of adolescents. Depression in adolescence must be recognized as serious. "Depressions arising during adolescence persist longer than those arising in adulthood, have a high rate of recurrence, and are associated with longstanding interpersonal difficulties" (Marton and others, 1993). Teaching adolescents to cope effectively is essential if we are to protect the mental health of our greatest "natural resource," our children.

Emotions in Adulthood

During adulthood, society expects people to practice emotional control. Individuals who observed, developed, and integrated effective problem-solving and coping skills as children mature into effective adults capable of identifying and handling their emotions in a healthy manner. Unfortunately, many adults have difficulties with emotional control, and mood disorders are among the most common serious mental health problems today.

Approximately 17% of U.S. citizens suffer from depressive illnesses (Foster, Siegel, and Landes, 1995). In adults, depression is more frequently found in (1) women, (2) persons between 35 and 44, (3) whites and Hispanics, (4) individuals with fewer than 12 years of school, (5) people who live in major urban areas, and (6) people who live in the Western region of the United States (Keltner, Schwecke, and Bostrom, 1995).

Adults must cope with situations, events, developmental tasks, and numerous personal responsibilities in addition to the emotional reactions that accompany each. Not infrequently, adults are also challenged with the problems of physical illness or dysfunction. Sometimes, the practice of certain behaviors, such as drug use, dieting, or refusal to seek help for distressing symptoms, can result in the development of a mood disorder.

Unfortunately, mood disorders are viewed by the public (and clients themselves) as "evidence of a character defect or lack of will power" (Depression Guideline Panel, 1994). Thus those adults who suffer from depression or mania must endure the additional burden of being stigmatized and stereotyped as "mentally ill." A sensitivity to this issue assists care providers in providing support for adults with emotional difficulties.

Emotions in Older Adulthood

Depression is very common in the elderly. To illustrate, "major depression or depressive symptoms affect 20% to 40% of older Americans" (Valente, 1994). The highest rates are found in elderly women, those who are medically ill, and individuals who receive long-term care.

Depression is *not* a normal consequence of aging. Most older adults live full, active, and rewarding lives. When depression or another mood disturbance occurs *suddenly* in an older adult, it is most likely linked to a physical cause. Depression can be treated, but failure to recognize its symptoms prevents many elders from receiving therapy.

Older adults often express their depression in more subtle ways than younger persons. Most do not complain or volunteer to share their feelings. Active listening, gentle questioning, and alert assessments assist nurses in detecting the signs of depression.

◆ TABLE 21-1
Ethnic and Gender Differences in Adolescent Depression

Group	Findings
Girls 14 years and older	Higher rates of depression than boys
African-American adolescents	Higher rates of depression and depressed mood than white adolescents
White and Asian-American youth	More depressive symptoms than African-Americans or Hispanic-Americans
Native American youth, especially those in boarding schools	Higher rates of depression and suicide than other adolescents
Adolescents living in rural areas	Greater risk for depression than adolescents living in urban or suburban areas
Gay and lesbian adolescents	Twofold to threefold risk of suicide; rates of depression higher
Adolescents with depression	Depression is often accompanied by other mental health disorders
Depressed adolescent girls	Have pregnancy rates three times higher than nondepressed teens

Modified from Peterson AC and others: *Am Psychol* 48(2):155, 1993.

The symptoms of depression in the elderly include changes in daily routine, eating, sleeping, or activity patterns; decreased concentration, communications, and motivation; feelings of envy, failure, indecision, guilt, and hopelessness; loss of interest, self-confidence, and self-esteem; and worry or talk about death. Remember, depression in older adults *is treatable* and everyone deserves the opportunity to live without emotional distress, no matter what the age or state of health.

Theories Relating to Emotions and Their Disorders

Mood disorders were once considered as simple, correctable imbalances in behavior. Today, evidence suggests that a combination of physical, psychological, and environmental factors is involved in the development of mood disorders. Many theories about the cause of mood disorders have been presented throughout the years, but none fully explains the complexities of these conditions.

Biological Evidence

Over the past decade, much has been learned about the physical nature of mood disorders. Studies of the effects of neurochemical messengers (neurotransmitters) and hormones on behavior have revealed that behaviors and body chemistries are interrelated. Defects in the immune system have been implicated in depression. One research study (Birmaher and others, 1994) demonstrated that adolescents who must cope with adverse life events have lower levels of killer cell activity. Genetics may also be a factor in mood disorders because high rates of depression and bipolar illness are seen in individuals who have relatives with mood disorders. Investigators have also found that the biological rhythms of depressed persons are different from those of nondepressed persons.

Other Theories

Psychoanalytical theories see mood disorders as anger turned inward. Behaviorists view depression as a group of learned responses, whereas social theorists consider depression the result of faulty social interactions. For health care providers, a holistic viewpoint incorporates all aspects of human functioning and provides a framework from which to work with the whole person, not just the emotional problem.

Many factors have an influence on the development of mood disorders. Adults who were not nurtured as children are at higher risk for depression. Losses, real or imagined, role changes, and physical illnesses have an impact on the development of emotional problems. Poor social support, such as few friends and no significant others, heightens the loneliness of individuals, and repeated reactions to stress and crises wear down one's emotional resistance. Although the exact cause of depression and other mood disorders remains unclear, we do know that early recognition and treatment greatly improve the lives of people who suffer from severe and prolonged emotional problems.

Mood (Affective) Disorders

According to the *Diagnostic and Statistical Manual of Mental Disorders* (DSM-IV), mood disorders are divided into two basic categories: depression and mania (Fig. 21-2). Depression is further divided into depressive episodes and depressive disorders based on length of time and recurring patterns of the behaviors. Mania is now referred to as **bipolar disorder,** and it is further divided into three groups: bipolar I, bipolar II, and cyclothymic disorders.

Depression is a "whole body" illness that involves emotional, physical, intellectual, social, and spiritual problems. It can be transitory (lasting only a few days) or it can plague an individual for many years. Table 21-2 lists many of the behaviors associated with depression. Study it carefully because many times a client's nonverbal messages may be the only clues to the presence of this mood disorder.

Depression can occur on several levels. Mild depression is short-lived and usually triggered by life events or situations outside the individual. For example, mild depression following the grief reaction is common after suffering an important loss. With mild depression, individuals frequently complain of feeling lost, let down, or disappointed. Drug or alcohol use may increase during this time. Mild depression is usually self-limiting and subsides as interest in life returns to normal.

Moderate depression **(dysthymia)** persists over time; the feelings of depression begin to seriously interfere with activities of living. Individuals with moderate depression lack the energy in every sense to make it through the day. Physically, they are fatigued and drag themselves around. Eating and sleeping difficulties and changes in sexual functioning and menstrual cycles begin to surface. Emotionally, these individuals are drained of energy. They feel despondent, dejected, and gloomy. Feelings of helplessness, low self-esteem, and ineffectiveness reinforce their negative outlooks. Judgment and decision making are clouded by gloom.

With moderate depression, the intellectual realm of functioning is focused on proving how really bad the

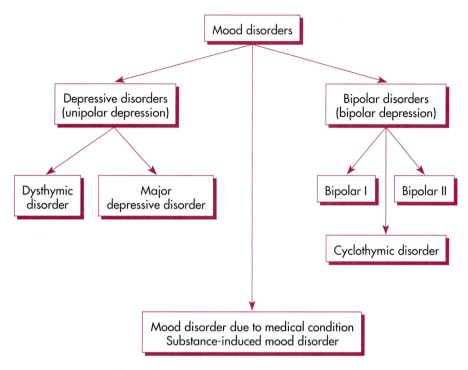

Fig. 21-2 Classification of mood disorders.

◆ TABLE 21-2			
Behaviors Associated With Depression			
Emotional	**Physical**	**Intellectual**	**Behavioral**
Anger	Abdominal pain	Ambivalence	Aggressiveness
Anxiety	Anorexia	Confusion	Agitation
Apathy	Backache	Inability to concentrate	Alcoholism
Bitterness	Chest pain	Indecisiveness	Altered activity level
Dejection	Constipation	Loss of interest and	Drug addiction
Denial of feelings	Dizziness	motivation	Intolerance
Despondency	Fatigue	Pessimism	Irritability
Guilt	Headache	Self-blame	Lack of spontaneity
Helplessness	Impotence	Self-depreciation	Overdependency
Hopelessness	Indigestion	Self-destructive thoughts	Poor personal hygiene
Loneliness	Insomnia	Uncertainty	Psychomotor retardation
Low self-esteem	Lassitude		Social isolation
Sadness	Menstrual changes		Tearfulness
Sense of personal	Nausea		Underachievement
worthlessness	Overeating		Withdrawal
	Sexual nonresponsiveness		
	Sleep disturbances		
	Vomiting		
	Weight change		

Modified from Stuart GW, Sundeen SJ: *Principles and practice of psychiatric nursing,* ed 5, St Louis, 1995, Mosby.

individual is. Slowed thoughts and impaired concentration add to the picture of ineptness. Problem-solving skills fall by the wayside as individuals begin to believe that they are in an unescapable situation of sadness and gloom. Persons who suffer from moderate levels of depression are at higher risk of suicide as their depression increases.

Major Depressive Episode

When depression is severe and lasts more than 2 weeks, it is called a major depressive episode. Severe depression encompasses one's whole being, every realm of human functioning. "The zest for life has vanished. It left without notice. Hours, days drag into weeks, months, even years. The simplest tasks loom over us like impossible demands. Energy is gone. Hope and joy are only meaningless words. Truly, darkness rules" (NDMDA, 1993).

Behaviors associated with severe depression range from paralysis to agitation. Feelings of worthlessness, guilt, and despair are expressed in every thought, every movement, and every activity. Physical appearance declines. Eating and sleeping become distasteful chores. Poor concentration and an inability to follow through on tasks lead to feelings of powerlessness and helplessness. Suicidal thoughts are entertained, and suicide is seen as the only way out of the misery. Individuals suffering a major depressive episode literally drag through the day, unable to function, caring about nothing, and interested only in their suffering. They are truly distressed human beings, caught in a downward emotional cycle. Major depressive episodes can occur in response to situations, events, and developmental tasks. They are frequently seen in combination with other mental health problems.

Major Depressive Disorder

When major depressive episodes routinely repeat themselves (for more than 2 years), a *depressive disorder* is diagnosed. Persons with major depressive disorders have a high mortality rate. "Up to 15% of individuals with severe major depressive disorder die by suicide. Statistical evidence also suggests that there is a fourfold increase in death rates in individuals with major depressive disorder who are over age 55 years" (American Psychiatric Association, 1994).

Major depressive disorder occurs twice as often in adolescent girls and adult women than in men. Symptoms may begin at any age, but the average age of symptom onset is in the early 20s. The course of the disorder is variable. Some individuals experience isolated depressive episodes separated by many years, whereas others may have more frequent episodes as they grow older. Families with one depressed member have an increased risk of other members developing the disorder.

Severe, prolonged depression results in many physical changes and increases one's risk for illness. Studies have demonstrated "an association between stress or depression and low activity of helper T cells, one of the most important components of the immune system" (Evans and others, 1995). Researchers who follow depressed individuals over time (Hays and others, 1995) have found that "someone who is depressed faces similar or even worse physical and mental functioning" than those individuals with chronic illnesses. Major depressive disorders are truly debilitating.

Dysthymic Disorder

A dysthymic disorder is daily moderate depression that lasts for longer than 2 years. People with dysthymic disorder are chronically sad and self-critical. They see themselves as incapable and uninteresting. Usually, they experience many symptoms of moderate depression, such as low energy levels, poor decision-making skills, and eating or sleeping difficulties.

Because the feelings of depression have lasted so long, they become a part of everyday experiences. Individuals with dysthymia have learned to see the world from a negative, pessimistic point of view and will often tell you that they "have always been this way." During periods of intense stress, these persons may experience a major depressive episode in addition to the existing dysthymia. This "double depression" almost always requires professional intervention.

Dysthymic disorders can begin in childhood or as late as early adulthood. Because they develop slowly, dysthymic disorders are often difficult to recognize and diagnose. Persons with dysthymia can often carry out their daily living activities, but they are unable to enjoy them.

Bipolar Disorders

The hallmark of a bipolar disorder is sudden, dramatic shifts in emotional extremes. Persons with bipolar disorders live in a world that seesaws between the emotional extremes of mania and depression. Thoughts, moods, and behaviors swing from normal to grandiose to depressed. Then a return to normal functioning follows, the "in-between time," before the cycle begins again.

Mania is defined as "an abnormally and persistently elevated, expansive, or irritable mood" (American Psychiatric Association, 1994). During periods of mania, behaviors build in intensity as the individual moves through three stages or levels of mania (Table 21-3). **Hypomania,** an exaggerated sense of cheerfulness, begins the cycle. Soon cheerfulness progresses to the unstable "high" of mania. If allowed to continue, the extreme excitement of delirium may result.

During the manic phase, the individual's behaviors become more and more impaired. If not treated, the manic phase of bipolar illness "can last for as long as three months. But eventually, the depressive phase of the illness sets in" (NDMDA, 1993). Hospitalization is often required to break the cycle of mania and to protect the person from the negative consequences of his/her poor judgments and actions. The box on p. 296 presents a case study of an episode of mania.

Bipolar disorders (also called **manic depression**) exist in two forms. Bipolar I disorder is characterized by episodes of depression alternating with episodes of mania. It is the more severe and incapacitating form of bipolar illness. Delusions and hallucinations are not uncommon during periods of mania.

With bipolar II disorder, individuals suffer major episodes of depression alternating with periods of hypomania. Bipolar II disorder "often sends individuals careening from 1 to 2 weeks of severe lethargy, withdrawal, and melancholy to several days of elevated or irritable mood, constant activity, and risky decision making" (*Science News,* 1995). Although the depths of depression and mania may not be as severe as with bipolar I disorder, the effects of bipolar II disorder are just as devastating.

Cyclothymic Disorder

The extreme emotional swings of bipolar disorders are less intense in persons with cyclothymic problems.

As the name implies, a **cyclothymic disorder** is a pattern that involves repeated mood swings alternating between hypomania and depressive symptoms. With cyclothymia, there are no periods of "normal" functioning. No day is free of symptoms because individuals bounce from too high to too low. Many persons with cyclothymic problems eventually progress to full-blown (clinically definable) bipolar disorders.

Other Problems With Affect

Many other emotional problems exist in society today. **Seasonal affective disorder** (also known as winter depression) has been found in many individuals from October to April. Levels of mild and moderate depression are experienced during long winter days, and the symptoms begin to lift with the coming of spring. Recent studies (Teicher and others, 1995) have demonstrated that daily exposure to full-spectrum light (phototherapy) lessened the symptoms of sadness and social withdrawal in persons with seasonal affective disorder.

Phototherapy or light therapy has also found to be useful in treating women with late luteal phase dysphoric disorder, the depression associated with the onset of menses. Every month, these women experience the melancholy and sadness of depression, only in these cases the cause lies within the rhythms of their hormone cycles.

A connection between hormonal balance and emotions is implicated as a possible cause of **postpartum depression.** This condition is characterized by "symptoms of tearfulness, irritability, hypochondria, sleeplessness, impairment of concentration, and headache in the days and weeks following childbirth"

◆ TABLE 21-3
Levels of Manic Behavior

Level of Mania	Description of Behaviors
Hypomania	Extroverted, happy-go-lucky, free of worry; catchy euphoria (observers feel euphoric), confident, uninhibited; unconcerned about feelings of others; increased motor activity, sexual drives, distractibility, sense of importance; decreased ability to concentrate; moves quickly from one topic to another (flight of ideas); becomes easily irritated
Mania	"High," expansive, unstable affect; angers quickly; pressured speech, flight of ideas, delusions of persecution and grandiosity; dresses inappropriately (layers of clothing, bizarre outfits, excessive makeup and jewelry); inappropriate behaviors (meddles in other's affairs, spends money recklessly, engages in risky activities); sexually driven; little food or sleep but still hyperactive
Delirium	Period of extreme excitement, anger, elation; has grandiose or religious delusions; becomes disoriented, incoherent, agitated; may injure self or others; poor hygiene, disheveled, physically drained; death from exhaustion may occur if mania goes untreated

Modified from Rollant PD, Deppoliti DB: *Mosby's review series: mental health nursing,* St Louis, 1996, Mosby.

CASE STUDY

Kevin was ordinarily a quiet and reserved man, but today he felt extraordinarily good, full of confidence and vigor. He even felt himself believing that this would be his lucky day. By the time he started dressing, he had planned the day. Never mind going to work. He was going to the casino because he could do no wrong today. Too impatient to eat or finish dressing, he bolted from the house and jogged the 4 miles to the casino.

By noon, his pocket money was gone, and Kevin had consumed four scotch and sodas. He became angry with the cashier when she refused to cash a check without identification. "She should certainly know who I am. Why should I need identification? Everyone in town knows who I am! How dare they demand to see my identification!" Kevin screamed as he paced agitatedly.

After being forcibly removed from the casino, Kevin began a tour of every business in town. He demanded to see the owners and then offered them a contract sharing a portion of his winnings if they financed his gambling now. By the time he visited the fourth establishment, the police were waiting.

Kevin made his offer to both waiting policemen and was promptly admitted to the local hospital for mental health care. After 3 days of hospitalization, Kevin traded his extraordinarily good feelings for depressive ones.

Clinical Decision

1. What clues (signs/symptoms) did Kevin present that would lead you to believe that he was in the manic phase of bipolar illness?

(NDMDA, 1993). Mild postpartum depression often clears within days, but symptoms lasting longer than 2 weeks should be investigated. Women who have experienced complicated pregnancies or difficult deliveries and women who are not emotionally prepared for motherhood are at higher risk for postpartum depression.

A *substance-induced mood disorder* is defined as a persistent emotional disturbance that can be directly traced to the physiological effects of a chemical. Many illegal chemicals (street drugs), such as amphetamines, cocaine, and heroin, as well as alcohol, are associated with changes in mood. Also, many therapeutic medications are related to the development of mood disorders. The box on p. 297 lists common medications that have depressive effects.

Mood Disorders Caused by Medical Problems

The experience of being ill or disabled is an unpleasant one for most people. Depression is a common condition among hospitalized persons, and up to "85% of all physically ill people are depressed to some degree" (Messner and Lewis, 1995). Because the whole person is involved, a physical illness always has emotional consequences.

Many physical problems and medical conditions are associated with mood disorders. It is common for people to feel depressed when ill or feeling poorly. Depression is a response to the news of chronic illness or lingering disability because people anticipate their losses and lifestyle changes. Because depression is of-

ten encountered within health care settings, it is an important responsibility of each health care provider to assess for signs/symptoms of mood disorders in every client, from the youngest to the oldest.

Therapeutic Interventions

Mood disorders present many treatment challenges. Perhaps the greatest is the fact that "fewer than half of the people with mood disorders receive treatment" (*Harvard Mental Health Letter*, 1995). Feelings of hopelessness and the stigma of having a mental illness prevent many people from seeking treatment. Others are misdiagnosed or treated for a medical illness because their symptoms are mainly physical. Also, men are less likely to receive treatment because they often hide their emotions behind alcohol, drugs, or aggression. Some problems, such as early mild depression, respond well to treatment. The more serious disturbances of severe depression and bipolar disorders remain difficult to treat even after many years of therapy.

Treatment and Therapy

The therapeutic plan for clients with mood disorders is arranged into three phases. The acute treatment phase lasts 6 to 12 weeks. The goal during this phase is to reduce symptoms and inappropriate behaviors. Inpatient hospitalization may be required when clients are too impaired to continue with the activities of daily living or too suicidal to be left alone.

The goal of the continuation phase is to prevent relapses into distressing emotional states. This period

💊 DRUG ALERT

DRUGS AND TOXINS THAT MAY INDUCE DEPRESSION

Analgesics
Phenacetin
Pentazocine

Antibiotics
Aminoglycosides
Chloramphenicol
Sulfonamides

Anticonvulsants
Carbamazepine (rare)
Clonazepam
Phenytoin
Phenobarbital
Primidone
Succinimide

Antihypertensives
Alpha-Methyldopa
Calcium channel blockers (possibly)
Clonidine
Hydralazine (possibly)
Propranolol
Reserpine

Antiinflammatory Agents
Corticosteroids
Indomethacin

Cardiovascular Agents
Digitalis
Disopyramide
Procainamide

Psychotherapeutic and Central Nervous System Agents
Aliphatic phenothiazines
Amphetamines
Appetite suppressants
   Fenfluramine
   Phenmetrazine
Barbiturates
Benzodiazepines
High-potency neuroleptics*

Miscellaneous
Baclofen
Choline
Cimetidine
Disulfiram
Phenylephrine
Physostigmine

Antituberculosis Agents
Ethambutol
Isoniazid

Antineoplastic Agents
Asparaginase
Corticosteroids
Nonsteroidal antiinflammatory drugs
Phenylbutazone

Antiparkinsonian Agents
Amantadine
Levodopa
Cycloserine
Vinblastine sulfate

Modified from Ford CV, Folks DG: *South Med J* 78(4):397, 1985.
*May cause akinesia as a form of secondary depression.

usually lasts from 4 to 9 months and is carried out on an outpatient basis. Medications and psychotherapy are continued. Clients are educated about the nature of their conditions and their medications and encouraged to try new coping behaviors.

The maintenance treatment phase concentrates on preventing recurrences in clients with prior episodes of depression and/or mania. "Maintenance medication prevents a new episode (recurrence). Maintenance psychotherapy may delay the next episode" (Depression Guideline Panel, 1994).

Current standard treatments for mood disorders include psychotherapy, pharmacological therapy, and electroconvulsive therapy. During each phase of treatment, nurses play an important role because they are the ones who help teach, encourage, and guide clients toward living effectively with their disorders.

Psychotherapies

Various psychotherapies are effective in treating mild and moderate depression. Cognitive-behavioral therapy is used to help clients identify and correct self-defeating thoughts and actions. Interpersonal therapy assists clients with relationships and interactions, and psychodynamic therapy encourages the growth of personal insight. Support groups and organizations have also been found to be very helpful for clients and families coping with mood disorders.

Pharmacological Therapies

Medications are a mainstay in the treatment of mood disorders. However, their use must be carefully assessed, monitored, and evaluated because of the possibility of side effects and drug misuse. The most commonly used drug classes for treating mood disorders are the antidepressants and the antimanics (lithium).

Based on their chemical composition, *antidepressants* are divided into five categories: tricyclics, nontricyclics, monoamine oxidase inhibitors (MAOIs), selective serotonin reuptake inhibitors (SSRIs), and nonselective serotonin reuptake inhibitors (NSSRIs). Each type of antidepressant alters a part of the brain's neurochemical balance or function. Many antidepressants require from 2 to 4 weeks before their effects are noticed and the client's well-being improves. For this reason, some clients believe that antidepressants are ineffective. They require reassurance that these drugs require time to take effect and encouragement to continue taking their medications.

Tricyclic antidepressants are usually the first choice for the treatment of depression. The selective serotonin reuptake inhibitors (SSRIs), a relatively new class of antidepressants, are gaining popularity because of their low incidence of side effects. Last choice for use are the monoamine oxidase inhibitors (MAOIs) because of their severe and potentially fatal side effects. New antidepressants, which are chemically unrelated to the other classes, are currently being introduced into the market. Nurses who administer these chemicals are responsible for maintaining current knowledge about their uses and effects.

Tricyclic antidepressants can produce severe central nervous system (CNS) depression when they interact with the barbiturates, certain anticonvulsants, drugs, and alcohol. When MAOI antidepressants are combined with certain substances, hyperexcitability of the nervous system results. This can lead to severely elevated blood pressure levels and hypertensive crisis. Other interactions may result in profound CNS depression or severe anticholinergic effects.

Basically, antidepressants exert their unwelcome side effects on both the central and peripheral nervous systems (Table 21-4). Nursing care measures are often necessary to assist clients in adjusting to their medications.

Because antidepressants may alter liver and kidney functions, hepatic and renal studies should be obtained monthly. Review all laboratory results for each client. Often, blood levels of certain drugs are measured to determine the amount of drug still in the system. Toxic antidepressant levels can result if clients are not carefully monitored. Headaches, palpitations, and stiffness in the neck should be reported to the physician immediately.

Lithium is a naturally occurring salt that helps to control the exaggerated thoughts and behaviors associated with mania. Because lithium does not bind to body proteins (as many other drugs do), it does not need to be metabolized by the liver. Lithium is distributed throughout the body fluids, where it competes with sodium. It is excreted by the kidneys more rapidly than sodium; therefore an important interaction between the level of lithium in the blood and common table salt exists.

When clients who are taking lithium ingest large amounts of salt, lithium levels usually drop (the kidney excretes lithium more rapidly than it excretes salt). The opposite is also true. When clients decrease their salt intake or lose salt through sweating, diarrhea, or altered kidney function, lithium levels in the blood are likely to increase. Because the range between therapeutic response and toxic effects is very narrow, clients must be instructed not to change their diet or activity habits abruptly.

The "narrow therapeutic index" of lithium requires close observation of client responses. If blood levels of the drug are too low, manic behavior returns; if levels are too high, an uncomfortable and possibly life-threatening toxicity may result.

Most side effects of lithium are directly related to dosage and blood serum levels (Table 21-5). Polyuria (large urinary output) and polydipsia (increased thirst) are frequently seen in people beginning lithium therapy. Common unwanted gastrointestinal tract reactions include a metallic taste, dry mouth, thirst, nausea, diarrhea, a bloated feeling, and weight gain. Sleepiness, light-headedness, drowsiness, and a mild hand tremor are seen frequently at the beginning of therapy.

Because the signs/symptoms of lithium toxicity are the same as the side effects during the first weeks of therapy, nurses must be aware of clients' responses to their lithium therapy. Most side effects disappear or decrease to a tolerable level by the sixth week of treatment. If they continue, be alert for the possibility of early lithium toxicity.

Toxic reactions occur when lithium levels in the blood are greater than 1.5 mEq/L (Table 21-6). Therapeutic blood levels of lithium range from 0.6 to 1.2 mEq/L. Lithium toxicity can be life-threatening, and no specific antidote exists. Therefore it is one of the nurse's most important responsibilities to frequently assess each client's response during treatment with lithium or any other antimanic medication and monitor for signs/symptoms of toxicity. Review Chapter 7 for more information about client care and education for persons taking lithium. Study the procedure for a prelithium workup. Be alert to the special educational needs of clients who require lithium.

Once the client is no longer manic, the need for lithium drops dramatically. "In fact, toxicity may set in rapidly unless the dose is reduced immediately by as much as half" (Harris, 1989). Clients must be carefully monitored during the first weeks of lithium therapy. If little response is seen by the sixth week of treatment, the physician usually considers other therapies.

◆ **TABLE 21-4**
Side Effects of Antidepressants and Nursing Care

Side Effects	Nursing Care
Tricyclic antidepressants	
Fatigue, sedation, slow psychomotor reactions, poor concentration, tremors, ataxia	Give h.s.; increase dose slowly; teach caution when using machinery; write instructions; document behaviors.
Suicidal gestures	Institute suicide precautions; drug increases energy for suicide.
Anticholinergic effects: dry mouth, decreased tearing, blurred vision	Encourage frequent oral care, water, gum; use artificial tears; ensure that vision clears in 2 weeks; report eye pain immediately.
Constipation, urinary hesitancy or retention, excessive sweating	Monitor food and fluid intake; promote high-fiber diet (more than 30 mg/day); encourage water intake of at least 2500 ml/day; teach importance of adequate fluids, clothing, and sensible exercise; avoid hot showers, baths, dehydration.
Nontricyclic antidepressants	
Dizziness, drowsiness, anxiety, confusion, tremors, weakness, dry mouth, nausea, diarrhea, increased appetite, paralytic ileus, urinary retention	Ensure safety; monitor mental status, moods, affect, level of consciousness, increased symptoms; weigh weekly; monitor for weight gain; encourage fluids to 2500 ml/day; monitor intake and output.
Orthostatic hypotension, tachycardia, palpitations	Teach client to rise slowly; monitor and report vital signs.
Monoamine oxidase inhibitors (MAOIs)	
Increased CNS stimulation	Reassure client; monitor for psychosis, seizures, hypoactivity.
Postural hypotension	Teach client to rise slowly; assure client that symptoms will decrease.
Muscle twitching	Vitamin B$_6$ (300 mg/day) is helpful.
Fluid retention, urinary hesitancy	Monitor intake and output; administer thiazide diuretics as ordered.
Insomnia	Give last dose as early as possible; encourage relaxation in evening.
Food-drug interaction with tyramine (common amino acid)	Avoid tyramine-rich foods; avoid drugs with epinephrine or stimulants.
Selective serotonin uptake inhibitors	
Dry mouth	Encourage fluids, good oral care.
Nausea, diarrhea	Give drug with meals; maintain bland diet; encourage good hydration; administer lower dose.
Drowsiness, dizziness, nervousness	Give h.s.; keep active during day; institute safety precautions; instruct client to avoid machinery.
Sweating	Maintain good hygiene; wear cotton clothing; encourage fluids.
Headaches	Teach relaxation techniques; administer mild analgesic for headache.
Insomnia	Give medications early; encourage good sleep habits and relaxation.
Nonselective reuptake inhibitors (venlafaxine)	
Increased blood pressure	Monitor vital signs; report to physician if blood pressure stays high; may reduce dose.
Weakness, sweating, sleepiness, dry mouth, nausea, vomiting, constipation, anorexia, blurred vision, anxiety, tremors	Refer to nursing care for other drug classes of antidepressants.

◆ **TABLE 21-5**
Side Effects of Lithium and Nursing Care

Side Effects	Nursing Care
Abdominal discomfort, nausea, soft stools, diarrhea	Give lithium with food or milk; reassure that signs/symptoms are temporary and should subside.
Edema, especially feet	Reassure that signs/symptoms are temporary; check with physician about salt restriction.
Hair loss, hypothyroidism	Obtain thyroid function tests; reassure that condition is temporary; if continues, notify physician, who may discontinue drug.
Muscle weakness, fatigue	Provide reassurance; give more frequent divided doses per physician order.
Polyuria (can progress to diabetes insipidus)	Provide reassurance; increased output is expected; monitor intake and output; report if output greater than 3000 ml/24 hr.
Thirst	Encourage client to quench thirst but maintain stable fluid intake.
Tremors	Provide reassurance; eliminate caffeine; give slow-release form per physician order.
Weight gain	Provide reassurance that weight gain is common; moderately restrict calories; advise client against restricting fluids or salt.

◆ **TABLE 21-6**
Signs/Symptoms of Lithium Toxicity

Level of Toxicity	Signs/Symptoms
Mild toxicity	
Blood serum levels 1.5 mEq/L	Apathy, sluggishness, drowsiness, and lethargy; diminished concentration; mild incoordination, muscle weakness, muscle twitches, coarse hand tremors
Moderate toxicity	
Blood serum levels 1.5 to 2.5 mEq/L	Nausea, vomiting, severe diarrhea; slurred speech, blurred vision, ringing in the ears; apathy, drowsiness, lethargy, moderate sluggishness; muscle weakness, irregular tremors, ataxia, frank muscle twitching, increased tonicity
Severe toxicity	
Blood serum levels above 2.5 mEq/L	Nystagmus; irregular muscle tremors, fasciculations (twitches of single muscle groups), hyperactive deep tendon reflexes; oliguria, anuria; confusion, severe changes in level of consciousness, hallucinations; grand mal seizures, coma, death

Electroconvulsive Therapy

Introduced in the 1930s as a treatment for severe depression, electroconvulsive therapy (ECT) is the introduction of a controlled grand mal seizure by passing an electrical current through the brain. Although the exact action is not known, some experts believe that ECT works by raising the levels of the neurotransmitter norepinephrine, which are low in many people with depression. ECT is used only after attempts to stabilize the depression with medications have failed.

Each ECT treatment requires about 15 minutes, but the actual shock lasts for only a few seconds. Generally, six to twelve treatments are administered over a course of several weeks. Most individuals receive ECT two to three times a week.

ECT is contraindicated in clients with "a recent MI [myocardial infarction], severe cardiac disease, hypertension, hypotension, aortic aneurysm, or congestive heart failure" (Kotin, 1993) because the treatment triggers bradycardia and hypotension followed by a reflex tachycardia and rise in blood pressure. Each client is evaluated for ECT on an individual basis, and the benefits must outweigh the risks before treatment is prescribed.

ECT may be administered on an outpatient or inpatient basis. The preparation of the client includes physical and emotional care. Consent for treatment forms are signed, and the client is reminded that confusion and memory loss are common after treatment. If the client is an outpatient, he/she must be accompanied by someone who can care for him/her following treatment.

Clients must eat nothing by mouth for at least 8 hours before treatment. Once the client is admitted, baseline vital signs are obtained, and the nurse attaches cardiac, blood pressure, and oxygen monitors to the client. An intravenous line is started, and short-acting intravenous muscle relaxants, sedatives, and an anesthetic agent are administered.

Once the client is sedated, electroencephalogram (EEG) monitors and electrodes are positioned at certain points on the head by the physician. An airway is established, and an electrical shock, lasting a few seconds, is delivered. This shock results in a controlled seizure of about 30 to 60 seconds. Often the only evidence of a seizure is a flexing of the client's big toes. Brain waves are monitored throughout the procedure, and the client sleeps for about an hour following the treatment.

Common side effects of ECT include headache, confusion on awakening from the treatment, and short-term amnesia, but the client's mood improves rapidly. Many individuals can be managed on an outpatient basis with good postprocedure nursing management and appropriate client teaching. The box at right provides client instructions for undergoing ECT. The responsibilities of the nurse when working with clients undergoing ECT include initiating intravenous therapy, administering ordered medications, and monitoring the client's responses before, during, and after treatment.

Nursing Process

The nursing care for clients with disturbances in mood relates to the whole person. Clients are first assessed for level of depression or mania. Then a thorough nursing history and physical examination help to establish the database. Nursing diagnoses are then chosen based on the individual's most distressing problems (see box on p. 302).

Nursing interventions for the physical realm focus on helping clients with personal hygiene, maintaining adequate nutrition, and encouraging physical activity. If clients are suicidal, special precautions and observations are implemented.

Nursing care in the emotional realm revolves around the therapeutic relationship. Acceptance and support are the nurse's powerful tools in this area.

ELECTROCONVULSIVE THERAPY (ECT)

The series of treatments you are about to undergo is safe and effective. It's likely to make you feel better even if medication did not. Like all treatments, however, ECT can cause side effects and has both benefits and possible risks. Your doctor will explain them to you before your first treatment and will describe the procedure.

When you arrive at the hospital, a nurse will ask you to lie on a bed, where she'll attach equipment that monitors your heart and blood pressure. A nurse or doctor will insert an IV in your arm, which will be used to administer anesthesia. Once you're asleep, the electrodes that will produce the shock—and monitor your response to it—will be attached.

Each treatment will last no more than 15 minutes, but you'll stay asleep for several minutes after the procedure. You may feel confused when you awaken, and you may not remember coming to or leaving the hospital. It can take some time for your memory to return to normal—as long as six months after you complete the entire course of treatment.

Headache is common as well in the first few hours following ECT. If it persists, take acetaminophen (Tylenol, Anacin-3, others) in order to get relief.

To keep problems to a minimum, follow these instructions:

- Do not eat or drink anything after midnight on the day you'll be coming for treatment.
- Arrange for a responsible adult to accompany you to and from the hospital. If you come alone, the doctor will cancel your treatment.
- Do not drive or operate machinery for at least a day after each treatment.
- Avoid making major decisions—about your job, relationships, or finances, for instance—until you have completed the entire course of treatment.
- Call to report adverse effects of ECT and any changes in your medical condition to your doctor or treatment team as soon as they occur.
- Take any medication prescribed at the right time and in the right dosage. If your doctor calls for any adjustments on the day of treatment, be certain to follow them.
- If you have to see another doctor or visit a hospital emergency room for any reason, let the staff know that you are undergoing electroconvulsive therapy.
- Call your doctor if you have any problems or questions about your treatment.

From Kotin B: *RN* 56(7):29, 1993.

NANDA NURSING DIAGNOSES RELATED TO EMOTIONAL RESPONSES

- Anxiety
- Communication, impaired verbal
- Community coping, ineffective
- Coping, ineffective individual
- Grieving, anticipatory
- Grieving, dysfunctional*
- Hopelessness*
- Injury, risk for
- Loneliness, risk for
- Nutrition, altered
- Powerlessness*
- Self-care deficit
- Self-esteem disturbance
- Sexual dysfunction
- Sleep pattern disturbance
- Social isolation
- Spiritual distress*
- Thought processes, altered
- Violence, risk for: self-directed

From North American Nursing Diagnosis Association: *NANDA nursing diagnoses: definitions and classification 1995-1996*, Philadelphia, 1994, The Association.
*Primary nursing diagnosis for disturbances in mood.

Once trust is established, clients feel the encouragement to cope with their problems.

In the intellectual realm, extreme emotional responses alter one's ability to think logically long enough to complete anything. Nurses must remember that these clients need extra patience and nonjudgmental guidance when attempting to follow through on tasks. Give instructions slowly and clearly. Repeat them as needed, but do not become impatient. Remember, it is difficult to cope when one cannot think straight.

Socially, most persons with mood disorders are lonely and afraid of associating with others. Once medications have begun to stabilize the client's moods, gentle encouragement to begin interacting with others may be needed.

Mood disorders involve the spiritual realm too. Many individuals with depression often question their spiritual beliefs. Manic clients commonly have delusions of **religiosity,** believing they have powers to communicate with God or become a spirit. Therapeutic listening is a helpful intervention, but do not hesitate to contact a clergyman or clergywoman if the client so requests. A sample client care plan for clients with a mood disorder is included in the box on p. 303. Remember, each actual plan will be unique according to the needs of the individual client.

Emotions, both positive and negative, add texture and meaning to the tapestry of our lives. Although we may not understand the exact connections between mind and body, we do know that our emotions are determined in large part by the way we think, the way we perceive the world, our "self-talk." "So powerful is this optimistic or pessimistic 'self-talk' that it determines not only our emotions, but the very condition of our physical and mental health" (Sobel and Ornstein, 1996). Stay healthy by thinking positively. You and your clients will *both* benefit.

❖ KEY CONCEPTS

- An emotion is a nonintellectual response in the affective realm of human functioning.
- A mood disorder (also called affective disorder) is defined as a disturbance in the emotional dimension of human functioning.
- Emotional responses grow and develop with the individual.
- Current evidence suggests that a combination of physical, psychological, and environmental factors are involved in the development of mood disorders.
- Depression is a "whole body" illness that involves emotional, physical, intellectual, social, and spiritual problems.
- Depression can be experienced as mild, moderate, or severe.
- When depression is severe and lasts more than 2 weeks, it is called a major depressive episode.
- When major depressive episodes routinely repeat themselves (for more than 2 years), a depressive disorder is diagnosed.
- A dysthymic disorder is daily moderate depression that lasts for longer than 2 years.
- The hallmark of bipolar disorders is sudden, dramatic shifts in emotional extremes.
- Bipolar I disorder is characterized by episodes of depression alternating with episodes of mania.
- With bipolar II disorder, individuals suffer major episodes of depression, alternating with periods of hypomania.
- Other problems with depression include seasonal affective disorder, postpartum depression, and depression associated with menses, medical conditions, or substance use.
- The therapeutic plan for clients with mood disorders is arranged into three phases: acute treatment phase, continuation phase, and maintenance phase.
- Various psychotherapies are effective in treating mild and moderate depression.

SAMPLE CLIENT CARE PLAN

DEPRESSION

Assessment

History: Leanne is a 22-year-old woman with a diagnosis of major depressive episode following the loss of her infant son. Her childhood was uneventful except for a domineering father. She was not abused during childhood but does admit to being intimidated by her father's loud voice and gruff manner.

During her first year in junior college, she met and married Mark, a senior majoring in marketing. The first 10 months of the marriage went well, until Leanne discovered she was pregnant. The news of her pregnancy infuriated Mark, who insisted that she "do something." Leanne insisted on keeping the baby but was plagued by the guilt of adding an extra burden to Mark's load throughout the pregnancy. On May 10, she delivered a son.

Leanne's postpartum course was difficult. She was trying to care for her son, attend school, and appease her husband, who had become somewhat more interested in the baby. One morning she noticed that her son was too quiet. Attempts to revive him were unsuccessful, and the diagnosis of sudden infant death syndrome was made on autopsy. Three weeks later, Mark filed for divorce, stating that Leanne was not a "good mother."

Current Findings: A disheveled-appearing young woman with uncombed hair and wrinkled clothes. Speech is soft, almost inaudible. Does not maintain eye contact. Eyes red and swollen. Offers no information but when questioned admits to "being a complete failure," "not worth the space I'm taking up." She describes her history as "filled with failures."

Nursing Diagnosis

Hopelessness related to loss of significant others as evidenced by an inability to perform activities of daily living

Planning/Expected Outcomes

Leanne will use effective coping methods to counteract her feelings of hopelessness by November 29. Leanne will express hopeful thoughts by December 15.

Nursing Interventions

Intervention

1. Assess risk for suicidal behaviors.
2. Establish a no-self-harm contract with Leanne.

3. Assist with activities of daily living as needed.

4. Monitor fluid and food intake.
5. Use active listening to encourage her to identify and express feelings.
6. Assess progress through the grief reaction and offer appropriate support.

7. Help her to focus on the positive aspects of her life.

Rationale

1. Suicide rates are high in depressed persons.
2. Demonstrates caring; helps to prevent suicidal gestures.
3. Supports Leanne until she is able to care for herself.
4. Depressed persons often do not eat or drink.
5. Gives her an opportunity to explore and vent her emotions realistically.
6. Unresolved grief can cause depression; Leanne may not have grieved for the loss of her child yet.
7. When energies are positively focused, success is encouraged.

Evaluation

After 5 days on the unit, Leanne assumed self-care activities and appeared well-groomed throughout her stay. By December 1, Leanne was able to discuss her feelings with two staff members. On December 14th, Leanne joined a support group for mothers who have lost children.

- The most commonly used drug classes for treating mood disorders are antidepressants and antimanics (lithium).
- Electroconvulsive therapy (ECT) is used to relieve depression by inducing a controlled grand mal seizure via passing an electrical current through the brain.
- The nursing care for clients with disturbances in mood relate to each realm of functioning.
- Stay healthy by thinking and focusing positively.

❖ REFERENCES

American Psychiatric Association: *Diagnostic and statistical manual of mental disorders,* ed 4, Washington, DC, 1994, The Association.

Birmaher B and others: Cellular immunity in depressed, conduct disorder, and normal adolescents: role of adverse life events, *J Acad Child Adolesc Psychiatry* 33:671, 1994.

Brage D, Campbell-Grossman C, Dunkel J: Psychological correlates of adolescent depression, *J Child Adolesc Psychiatr Nurs* 8(4):23, 1995.

Depression and health: long-term effects, *Harvard Ment Health Lett* 12(2):7, 1995.

Depression Guideline Panel: U.S. Department of Health and Human Services, Public Health Service, and Agency for Health Care Policy and Research: depression in primary care: detection, diagnosis, and treatment, *J Am Acad Nurse Pract* 6(5):224, 1994.

Evans DL and others: Stress-associated reduction of cytotoxic T lymphocytes and natural killer cells in asymptomatic HIV infection, *Am J Psychiatry* 152:543, 1995.

Foster CD, Siegel MA, Landes A: *Health: a concern for every American,* ed 7, Wylie, TX, 1995, Information Plus.

Harris E: Lithium: in a class by itself, *Am J Nurs* 89(2):190, 1989.

Hays PD and others: Functioning and well-being outcomes of patients with depression compared to chronic general medical illnesses, *Arch Gen Psychiatry* 52(1):11, 1995.

❖ SUGGESTIONS FOR FURTHER READING

"Double Trouble: Managing Chronic Illness and Depression" by Roberta Messner and Susan Lewis (*Nurs 95* 25[8]:46, 1995) is an excellent reminder of the fact that many of our chronically ill clients suffer from emotional distresses too.

Keltner NL, Schwecke LH, Bostrom CE: *Psychiatric nursing,* ed 2, St Louis, 1995, Mosby.

Kotin B: Shock therapy: facts, not myths, *RN* 56(7):29, 1993.

Kronberg ME: Down in the dumps: depression in the primary care setting, *Adv Nurse Pract* 3(5):31, 1995.

Marton P and others: Cognitive social skills and social self-appraisal in depressed adolescents, *J Am Acad Child Adolesc Psychiatry* 32:739, 1993.

Messner RL, Lewis S: Double trouble: managing chronic illness and depression, *Nurs 95* 25(8):46, 1995.

National Depressive and Manic-Depressive Association (NDMDA): *Depression and bipolar illness,* Chicago, 1993, The Association.

Rollant PD, Deppoliti DB: *Mosby's review series: mental health nursing,* St Louis, 1996, Mosby.

Sobel DS, Ornstein R: Thinking healthy, *Ment Med Update* 4(4):3, 1996.

Stuart GW, Sundeen SJ: *Pocket guide to psychiatric nursing,* ed 3, St Louis, 1995, Mosby.

Teicher MH and others: The phototherapy light visor: more than meets the eye, *Am J Psychiatry* 152(7):1197, 1995.

Temperament, depression make volatile mix, *Sci News* 147(8):118, 1995.

Valente SM: Recognizing depression in elderly patients, *Am J Nurs* 94(12):19, 1994.

Wong DL: *Whaley and Wong's nursing care of infants and children,* ed 5, St Louis, 1995, Mosby.

22

PHYSICAL PROBLEMS, PSYCHOLOGICAL SOURCES

For centuries, mankind has questioned the interactions of mind and body and the role emotions play in health. In ancient China, 2000 years before the birth of Christ, the emperor Huang Ti recorded his keen observations of the physical illnesses arising from emotional causes in his book *Classic of Internal Medicine.* The central theme of the herbal doctors of Babylonia (2500-500 BC) was the mind-body interaction because they believed that the cause of all physical illness was sin. Hippocrates instructed people to care for the spirit as well as the body. Throughout the Middle Ages, magical and symbolic thinking kept the body and mind inseparably linked. People whose behavior or physical appearance differed were and condemned as witches and workers of the devil.

Toward the end of the nineteenth century, scientific advances were made in biology, chemistry, and microbiology. These advances shifted the emphasis of research to the cause and treatment of physical disease. By the time Freud's theories of consciousness were introduced, the study of human beings had evolved into two distinct divisions: the biological (or physical) and all other aspects of human functioning (or the psychological). The complex creature known as man was now officially boxed, categorized, and divided into convenient sections for study, discussion, research, and treatment.

Today, however, researchers and practitioners alike are discovering that in reality no such divisions between the mind and body exist. Human beings are dynamic, complicated physical organisms that are affected by many nonphysical events. Each of us is a unique individual—a combination of genetics, culture, and past experiences. Each of us has psychological aspects to our being, and each of us has our own way of coping with the stresses of life and transferring our emotions into physical symptoms.

This chapter explores the connection between the physical and psychological aspects of people. This chapter is important because clients with psychologically based physical problems are encountered in every practice setting. An understanding of the role emotions play in the development of both physical and mental health problems helps nurses and other health care providers to plan the most effective client care.

Role of Emotions in Health

Health is a concept embodying the whole person. Health is a state of physical, emotional, sociocultural, and spiritual well-being. It is a state in which the psychological realms are in balance with the physical self in a state of homeostasis.

All animals, including humans, must live with and adapt to stress. The antelope on the African savanna must deal with the stress of becoming some carnivore's lunch every day of its life. To do this, the antelope is equipped with a delicate internal mechanism of hormones and other biochemicals, all wired to the appropriate organs. When the animal is stressed, a response is activated and the antelope can run faster, jump higher, and endure the rigors of the chase longer. In short, animals have evolved a stress response mechanism that protects them during times of threat or illness. It is called the fight-flight response, and it is an essential part of every animal's survival mechanisms.

Anxiety and Stress

Human beings are also equipped with a **physiological stress response** mechanism, a biochemical fight-flight system. It is a biological survival tool designed to provide the energy for fighting opponents or running to save one's skin. The physiological (physical) stress response served early man effectively, but as people became civilized and adopted rules for behavior, fighting and running were replaced by more socially acceptable (but biochemically stifling) behaviors. Today, the stressors of modern life are many, but outlets for the stress response are few.

In his book *Stress of Life,* Hans Selye "proposed that all humans show the same general bodily response to stress" (Corsini, 1994). He studied the biochemical reactions of the stress response and their effects on various body systems and called these reactions the *general adaptation syndrome.* Today, we know that stress "activates primitive regions of the brain, the same areas that control eating, aggression, and immune responses" (Carpi, 1996). Our responses to the stresses of modern life are biochemically identical to the responses that our ancestors experienced when they were fighting to stay alive. The problem today is that the fight-flight response occurs in non–life-threatening situations, stimulating the body for actions that never occur. In fact, the stress response mechanism can work overtime when individuals are exposed to such modern stressors as the approaching deadline, the traffic snarl, or even overexercise.

When an individual perceives stress, tension, or anxiety, the body begins a cascade of biochemicals. The central command post, the hypothalamus, communicates to the pituitary gland, which in turn notifies the adrenal glands. The adrenal glands manufacture and release the body's four major stress hormones—dopamine, epinephrine, norepinephrine, and cortisol. The basic functions of the body are so responsive to the release of these chemicals that even small changes in their levels can have a significant impact on one's state of health.

We now know, for example, that the immune system is affected by one's level of stress. Studies done at Ohio State University (Kiecolt-Glasser and others, 1993) demonstrated that significant immune function and blood pressure changes were identified in couples who displayed hostile or negative behaviors during periods of marital conflict. Simply put, the married couples who argued had less effective immune systems. Other studies have demonstrated the importance of a positive attitude in healing after surgical procedures or after being diagnosed with breast cancer (Cooper and Faragher, 1993).

The psychological side of an individual has a strong impact on the ability to identify and successfully cope with stress. People who are able to recognize and defuse their stressors early seldom suffer from the physical effects of stress. Most of us, however, struggle to counteract our stressors but still feel the body's response to its effects. Some individuals focus their stress into bodily activities and functions, thus developing physical problems that arise from psychological sources. These problems are called *somatoform* or *psychosomatic illnesses*.

Childhood Sources

How an individual perceives and responds to stress is established in childhood (Fig. 22-1). Biochemical reactions to stress alter the physical patterns of the brain and sensitize children to future stressors. Children who have experienced an unstable home environment, for example, may react to stress with exaggerated hormonal mechanisms as adults.

The link between mind and body is made early in infancy. Infants require the routine attentions of a consistent caregiver, someone who feeds, cuddles, and protects them. As children cope with stresses, the brain becomes sensitized and patterned. This patterning sets up an automatic chemical response to stress; every time the individual is exposed to stress, the body responds with its biochemical program, even though the individual may not consciously feel stressed.

People can experience stress relating to levels of development. In infancy, mechanisms for coping with stress are limited. The only means of expression is through the body, so infants create physical signs/symptoms in an effort to cope with their stresses. Problems such as colic, atopic dermatitis, allergic reactions, and obesity may all arise from the effects of stress. It is not uncommon in family practice to encounter infants with physical problems that are caused by high levels of stress.

Fig. 22-1 The stress response is established early in childhood. (From Sundeen SJ and others: *Nurse-client interaction: implementing the nursing process,* ed 5, St Louis, 1994, Mosby.)

Children express their stresses through different body systems. They may develop allergic skin reactions, asthma, gastrointestinal tract complaints, or joint aches and pains. An interesting study by Burke and others (1994) clearly indicates a connection between stress and the development of inflammatory bowel disease in the children of mothers with anxiety disorders and depression.

The way in which an individual is patterned to respond to stress exhibits itself early in life (Fig. 22-2). In households in which children are emotionally supported and encouraged to effectively cope with their stresses, few physical complaints exist. Families filled with conflict and uncertainty live with numerous physical problems as well as psychological distresses. Most psychosomatic problems and somatoform disorders (physical problems with emotional sources) start in childhood and become established during adolescence. By adulthood, many people are significantly impaired in their daily living activities.

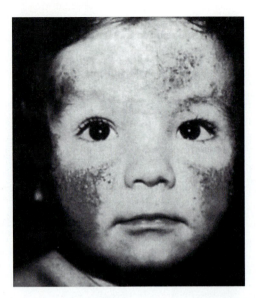

Fig. 22-2   Infantile atopic dermatitis, which can be a manifestation of stress. (From *Mosby's medical, nursing, and allied health dictionary,* ed 4, St Louis, 1994.)

PHYSICAL CONDITIONS AFFECTED BY PSYCHOLOGICAL FACTORS

CARDIOVASCULAR
Migraine
Essential hypertension
Angina
Tension headaches

MUSCULOSKELETAL
Rheumatoid arthritis
Low back pain (idiopathic)

RESPIRATORY
Hyperventilation
Asthma

GASTROINTESTINAL
Anorexia nervosa
Peptic ulcer
Irritable bowel syndrome
Colitis
Obesity

SKIN
Neurodermatitis
Eczema
Psoriasis
Pruritus

GENITOURINARY
Impotence
Frigidity
Premenstrual syndrome

ENDOCRINOLOGICAL
Hyperthyroidism
Diabetes

From Stuart GW, Sundeen SJ: *Pocket guide to psychiatric nursing,* ed 3, St Louis, 1995, Mosby.

Common Psychophysical Problems

The physical signs/symptoms of psychic or emotional distress are very real to the individual who is suffering from them. The discomfort of an upset stomach is the same, whether it is caused by too much pizza or a disturbing piece of news. The effects of an emotionally caused illness are the same as those arising from a physical source.

When the body is under continual or repeated stress, it responds by over-activating its stress response mechanism, which can result in many of the physical signs/symptoms of an illness, disease, or disability. In the past, these symptoms were often referred to as **psychosomatic illnesses,** meaning emotionally (psycho) related physical (somatic) disorders. Unfortunately, this term has come to mean an imaginary illness in popular vocabulary. The more recent term, **psychophysical disorders,** was coined to refer to the stress-related problems that result in physical signs/symptoms.

The physiological stress response affects many body systems (see box above, at right). One of the systems that receives the lion's share of the stress response is the gastrointestinal tract. In addition to the usual stress-related indigestion, vomiting, constipation, and diarrhea, more serious illnesses are related to stress. Ulcerative colitis and gastric, peptic, and duodenal ulcers can occur when the gastrointestinal tract is the focus of one's stress. The respiratory sys-

tem can develop asthma, and the cardiac system can raise blood pressure when subjected to prolonged stress.

Theories of Psychophysical Disorders

Although it is known that emotions play an important role in the development or prevention of illness, just how this connection works is uncertain. Several theories attempt to explain this relationship.

The *stress response theory* states that individuals are biochemically patterned to react to stress in childhood. During stress, the autonomic nervous system prepares the body for fight or flight. When emotional conflict is the basis for stress, the physical responses of the fight-flight mechanism are unconscious. Because the threat is not external, no physical outlet for the biochemical response is possible. Consequently, the state of stress does nothing to relieve the underlying emotional conflict, and soon a cycle of biochemical stimulus-response is established. This pattern eventually results in physiological disturbances within the body.

A second theory focuses on the *symbolism* attached to a symptom or illness. For example, the angry young executive who needs to vent his rage but feels that displays of anger are inappropriate may soon develop ulcerative colitis or high blood pressure as a way of coping with his emotions.

Another theory states that certain *personality types* are prone to developing certain illnesses. The hard-working, independent, overly ambitious businessman is considered at high risk for the development of cardiac problems because of his aggressive personality. The quiet, uncomplaining, overburdened clerk may suffer from ulcers, joint problems, or skin rashes.

Last is the theory of *organic weakness,* which states that every individual has one body system that is more sensitive or less healthy than other systems. When a person has underlying emotional problems that affect functioning "but at the same time has sufficient ego strength so that a flight from reality is not necessary, this person may develop a physical illness as a means of coping with the unconscious problem" (Taylor, 1994).

Although each theory may appear unrelated, all of them have several concepts in common:

1. Unconscious emotional conflict that increases anxiety and interferes with daily living activities is the basis for many psychophysical problems.
2. The development of physical symptoms is the result of attempts to lower anxieties associated with unconscious conflict.
3. The illness is real to the person, whether or not organic changes exist. In some cases, physical changes can be life-threatening, so never treat a client's complaints casually.
4. Most often, the onset of the illness or problem is related to an actual or perceived stressful event.

The physical signs/symptoms of an illness often relieve an individual's anxieties by masking their inner emotional turmoil. This anxiety-reducing benefit is called **primary gain** because the symptoms reduce anxiety. However, there are other benefits to assuming the sick role. They are termed **secondary gains** and include such factors as being relieved of responsibilities, receiving the special attentions of others, and having dependency needs met. Not infrequently,

these gains tend to reinforce the pattern of psychophysical symptoms and encourage illness behaviors to continue.

Somatoform Disorders

Somatization is "the official term for feeling physical symptoms in the absence of disease or out of proportion to a given ailment" (Corr, 1992). It is a common stress-reducing mechanism that may or may not result in pathological functioning. However, the person suffering from a **somatoform disorder** demonstrates no objective organic causes or physiological dysfunctions for their signs/symptoms. In fact, the most common feature of somatoform disorders is the "presence of physical symptoms that suggest a general medical condition (hence the term *somatoform*) and are not fully explained by a general medical condition, by the direct effects of a substance, or by another mental disorder" (American Psychiatric Association, 1994).

The diagnosis of a somatoform disorder is made by first excluding any possible physical causes or dysfunctions, the presence of drugs or other toxic substances, or other mental health problems that may be related to the symptoms. Finally, when there is no diagnosable medical condition that accounts for the client's physical symptoms, a diagnosis of one of the somatoform disorders is made.

Somatization is common in the United States. Almost 80% of basically healthy people demonstrate somatic symptoms in any given week. Many health care dollars (about one in five) are spent treating nonphysically based complaints, and "nearly half of the patients seen in physicians' offices are the 'worried well'" (Corr, 1992).

Somatization costs more than just money. Not uncommonly, individuals with somatoform disorders will subject themselves to painful or dangerous diagnostic procedures and treatments. Cardiac pain, for example, must be investigated. Whether its origin is emotional or physical is unimportant to the person experiencing the discomfort.

The signs/symptoms of illness are the client's way of coping with emotional distress. Emotional distress costs the body energy and results in decreased immune functions, which can make the person more susceptible to illness and disease. Remember, though, that people with somatoform disorders also fall ill to the same maladies as everyone else. Do not dismiss these clients' complaints as trivial.

Cultural Influences

Cultural differences are associated with certain illnesses, both physical and mental. Many somatization disorders are culturally related, and their treatment depends on understanding the problem within the client's cultural context or framework (Table 22-1).

Nurses who work with clients from different cultures must be aware of the meaning or importance that the problem holds for the person (Giger and Davidhizar, 1995). Many somatic illnesses are based in cultural or spiritual beliefs. Assessments and treatment plans must not threaten or challenge these beliefs if therapeutic interventions are to be effective. Culturally appropriate nursing interventions are based on knowledge of and respect for another's way of living (Geissler, 1994). Do not hesitate to learn as much as possible about other cultures.

Criteria for Diagnosis

Expressing emotions through the body (somatization) is a common coping mechanism for many people. It fulfills needs and relieves anxiety. Because every physical sign/symptom may have a biological cause, each complaint must be investigated thoroughly before it is labeled emotionally based. So the first criteria for diagnosis is that no diagnosable organic medical condition to explain the symptoms can be found.

The second condition for diagnosis is that the disorder significantly disrupts or impairs one's level of functioning. Because of the somatoform problem, the person is unable to engage in the activities of daily living, perform his/her work, or engage in social activities. This adds significant distress to an already emotionally charged situation.

The third criteria for diagnosis is that the client is unaware of or unable to express his/her emotional distress. Acknowledging emotional distress may be seen as a weakness, especially for men. Experiencing physical problems, however, enables individuals to accept the attention and the sympathy that anxiety or emotional expression would not elicit. Somatization is a common way for many emotional problems to make themselves known.

The *Diagnostic and Statistical Manual of Mental Disorders* (DSM-IV) lists five types of somatoform disorders: somatization disorders, factitious disorders, conversion disorders, hypochondriasis, and body dysmorphic disorders. Eating and sleeping disorders can arise from emotional sources, and they are considered in the next chapter. Because most of these clients are seen in general medical settings, such as clinics and physicians' offices, it is important for nurses to be familiar with somatoform disorders.

Somatization Disorder

Somatization disorder has been historically referred to as Briquet's syndrome or hysteria. It is a polysymptomatic disorder; that is, the disorder is associated with many signs and symptoms. It begins before age 30, sometimes as early as adolescence or childhood, and can persist for many years.

Somatization disorder occurs more frequently in women and appears to have a familial pattern. It is observed in 10% to 20% of the daughters of women diagnosed with the disorder. The male relatives of these women show an increased risk of antisocial personality disorders and substance-abuse problems (American Psychiatric Association, 1994). Both genetic and environmental factors contribute to the risk of developing a somatization disorder.

Individuals with somatization disorder often arrive with a long history of vague complaints. They com-

---

◆ TABLE 22-1
Culturally Related Somatoform Disorders

Cultural Group	Description
Japanese	*Gaman* means to internally suppress emotions, especially anger. Client tends to express emotional distresses through physical signs/symptoms. Illness is a socially acceptable way of receiving care. Client worries about body functions, especially blood pressure. Headaches are related to depression.
Southeast Asians	Mental distress is not discussed but expressed via various physical ailments. *Koro* is fear of penis shrinking into abdomen, which results in death.
Mexicans	*Mal ojo* (the evil eye) is associated with fever, headaches, diarrhea, restlessness, irritability, weight loss.
East Indians (India)	*Dhat* syndrome, male reproductive signs/symptoms caused by fear and concern about losing semen.
Koreans	The body is the property of the ancestors. Mental and emotional illnesses are expressed as physical (somatic) complaints.

monly describe their complaints in colorful and exaggerated terms but offer few facts. Although the descriptions of their illnesses may be vivid, they actually give a poor history of their medical problems.

In addition, it is not uncommon for individuals with somatization disorder to seek treatment from several physicians at the same time. This dangerous practice can lead to hazardous events for these clients if the combination of drugs and therapies are not compatible. Make sure to ask all clients if they are currently seeing any other health care providers, natural healers, or any other practitioners.

The most common complaints are a combination of gastrointestinal tract and sexual problems, combined with pain and false neurological (pseudoneurological) symptoms. The box below explains a typical case.

For a diagnosis of somatization disorder to be made, the client must meet the following criteria:

1. There must be a history of pain related to at least four different sites (e.g., headache, backache, joint, extremity, chest, or abdominal pain) or functions (menstrual, sexual, urinary dysfunctions).
2. There must be a history of at least two gastrointestinal tract symptoms (other than pain), such as nausea, abdominal bloating, vomiting, diarrhea, and food intolerance.
3. There must be a history of one sexual or reproductive problem other than pain. For women, these include irregular or difficult menses, heavy menstrual bleeding, or vomiting throughout pregnancy. For men, there may be erectile or ejaculatory problems. Both men and women are often sexually indifferent.
4. There must be a history of at least one symptom that suggests a neurological disorder, such as impaired coordination, localized weakness, and double vision.

Signs of anxiety and depression are very common in people with somatization disorders. They may also behave in impulsive, antisocial, or suicidal manners. Very often their lives are associated with chaos, marital discord, and social problems. Their lifestyles can be as complicated as their medical histories.

Three features help health care providers differentiate a somatization disorder from a medical problem (Kirmayer, Robbins, and Paris, 1994). First, the involvement of multiple organ systems suggests somatization disorder. Second, the disorder is characterized by an early onset and chronic course that continues *without* the development of any physical, structural, or functional abnormalities. In short, no physical changes occur over time. Third, the absence of any significant laboratory values indicates that the underlying problems may be emotionally based. It is important to remember that the onset of multiple complaints in an older person is *almost always* caused by a medical condition, not somatization. Also, having a somatization disorder does not protect individuals from developing a physical illness or dysfunction.

CASE STUDY

Sarah was a single 31-year-old woman who came to the clinic with complaints of diarrhea, nausea, pain, and weight loss over a period of 5 years. During the nursing history, Sarah revealed that she was the only one of five children still living at home with her mother. Sarah described herself as a youngster as always being "sickly," but she could not identify any specific health problems.

Her father, whom Sarah described as "silent and cold," died when she was 15. She remembers feeling little loss at her father's death and only growing closer to her mother. Sarah's relationship with her mother became very important after the death of her father. Sarah and her mother did everything together, even to the point of sharing the same bed.

On graduation from high school, Sarah worked in a candy shop for a few years but found the work too demanding and quit. She has not been employed in over 7 years and continues to live with her mother.

It seems that just before the symptoms of her illness began, Sarah's mother's sister became widowed and decided to move in with Sarah and her mother. Aunt Sally arrived with much of her furniture, including a pair of twin beds. Soon thereafter, the mother sold the large double bed and substituted the twin beds, forcing Sarah to sleep alone. Although she did not protest, Sarah felt angry and deserted. A few weeks later she developed abdominal pain, diarrhea, and nausea.

Clinical Decisions
1. How do you think the onset of Sarah's symptoms relates to her family situation?
2. If Sarah's physical problems disappeared, would her problem be solved?

Clients with somatization disorder are difficult to diagnose and even more challenging to effectively treat. Most of the time, these individuals are not consciously aware of the emotional conflicts or reactions responsible for their difficulties. Long-term therapy is usually indicated when clients are willing to recognize and work with the emotional conflicts that are at the basis of their physical problems.

Conversion Disorder

The term *conversion* is derived from Freud's theory of conversion hysteria, which stated that a psychosexual conflict is focused or converted into a physical disturbance. Today, this relatively uncommon condition, called a **conversion disorder,** is considered to be a somatoform disorder in which the individual presents with problems related to the sensory or motor functions (Table 22-2).

Conversion disorders appear more commonly in persons of lower socioeconomic status, those living in rural areas, and people with little health care knowledge. Approximately 1% to 3% of referrals to mental health clinics involve clients with conversion reactions (Kirmayer, Robbins, and Paris, 1994). When clients with conversion disorders are assessed, it is important to consider their social and cultural backgrounds.

Men and women differ in relation to conversion disorders. The disorder is much more common in women. As many as ten women for every one man are diagnosed with conversion disorders. Conversion disorders in men are often associated with military service or industrial accidents. Antisocial personality disorders are also associated with conversion disorders, especially in men.

The onset of problems is usually during late childhood through early adulthood, but conversion reactions almost always appear after 10 and before 35 years of age. There have been reports, however, of conversion reactions in persons in their 90s. Symptoms often appear suddenly, but they can begin slowly and increase over time. The symptoms typically last only a short time. In hospitalized clients, symptoms often disappear within 2 weeks. Recurring episodes are common. As many as 25% of clients have a return of symptoms within 1 year.

Conversion symptoms are thought to be the result of an emotional (psychic) conflict. The appearance of physical symptoms allows the person to avoid emotional conflict (primary gain). Secondary gains are also realized when the individual's symptoms prevent normal activities or elicit attention and emotional support that would otherwise be unavailable. Situational factors, such as environmental stressors or in-terpersonal conflicts, can frequently trigger the appearance of conversion signs/symptoms.

Children younger than 10 years of age usually present with gait problems or seizures. In older individuals, the signs/symptoms usually appear as sensory or motor disturbances.

For a conversion disorder to be diagnosed, the client must meet four criteria:

1. At least one of the signs/symptoms involves the voluntary motor or sensory system and suggests the presence of a neurological problem.
2. The signs/symptoms are brought on or exacerbated (worsened) by the presence of a conflict or other stressor.
3. The signs/symptoms are not intentionally produced.
4. The signs/symptoms cause significant distress and impairment in daily functions.
5. After extensive investigation, the signs/symptoms cannot be explained by a pathological condition, the effects of a substance, or a culturally appropriate behavior.

Conversion signs/symptoms do not usually follow normal anatomical and physiological pathways. The symptoms tend to be more in keeping with the individual's ideas of what the problems should be. For example, a "paralyzed" arm that is raised over the head by the nurse, remains suspended for a moment, and then falls to the side rather than on its owner's head or an extremity that is "paralyzed" moves automatically when the client is dressing or not paying attention to the arm. Individuals with conversion "seizures" vary in their seizure activity and usually few if any changes are noted on an electroencephalogram (EEG). In short, the course of the signs/symptoms or condition is not in keeping with physically based disease processes but rather the client's ideas.

One of the interesting features of conversion disorders is **la belle indifference,** which is a lack of concern or indifference about the nature or the implications of the signs/symptoms. Many individuals with conversion disorders appear totally indifferent to their symptoms, whereas others present their complaints in dramatic or hysterical manners. Symptoms are more apparent during times of extreme psychological stress, such as the loss of a loved one or change in fortune. People with conversion disorders are often very suggestible, and their symptoms can be modified or intensified by the reactions of others in their environments. Laboratory and other diagnostic examinations show no specific abnormalities. In fact, it is the absence of diagnostic findings that helps to establish the diagnosis.

Treatment goals focus on eliminating the possibility of any physical causes and then assisting clients in identifying the conflicts responsible for their signs/symptoms. Individuals and their families are frequently referred for psychotherapy. Antidepressants and antianxiety agents are often prescribed. Behavior modification techniques are successful in some cases.

Hypochondriasis

Hypochondriasis is a somatoform disorder in which one has an intense fear or preoccupation of having a serious disease or medical condition based in a misinterpretation of body signs/symptoms. Hypochondriasis is a persistent fear that something is physically wrong, even when all diagnostic test results are negative and reassurances have been given by various physicians. Although the individual can acknowledge the possibility that the symptoms are being exaggerated or blown out of proportion, he/she continues to hold onto the belief that something is physically wrong.

Symptoms commonly relate to minor abnormalities (a sore on the skin, a cough), body functions (heartbeat, sweating), or vague physical sensations, such as "tired blood" or "aching veins." The meaning, source, and nature of the symptoms continue to cause great concern to the client despite repeated negative test results and reassurances from health care providers. These people commonly "doctor shop," seeing several physicians or health care providers at the same time. Often their relationships with health care providers become strained because clients with hypochondriasis feel they never receive the proper medical care and usually resist referral to mental health care settings.

Hypochondriasis can begin at any age, but the most common time for the appearance of symptoms is in early adulthood. It appears more frequently in persons who were exposed to a serious illness or life-threatening condition in childhood (Barsky and others, 1994). The course of the disorder follows a seesaw pattern and tends to become chronic in nature. In some cases, the disorder is first diagnosed after a severe stressor, such as the death of a loved one. Although exact statistics are not available, it is estimated that from 4% to 9% of the clients seen in a general medical practice are suffering from hypochondriasis.

People with hypochondriasis often have strained interpersonal relationships. Because they are so focused on themselves, many expect special consideration and treatment from others. Family and social lives can become quite disturbed as they center around clients' pictures of their state of health. Individuals may be able to remain employed if the appearance of symptoms is limited to nonwork time. Time is frequently missed from work. In the most severe cases, people become complete invalids.

For a diagnosis of hypochondriasis to be made, the client must meet five criteria:

1. There must be a preoccupation with fears of having a serious disease based on a misunderstanding of body messages.
2. The preoccupation is not delusional (clients can admit that they have an unreasonable concern).
3. The preoccupation persists despite negative diagnostic testing and workup results.
4. The preoccupation causes significant distress or impairment in the client's activities of daily living.
5. The preoccupation has been present for at least 6 months.

Remember, clients with hypochondriasis do actually become ill on occasion. The problem with hypochondriacal clients is like the boy who cried "Wolf!" too many times: no one believes the real message when all the others have been false.

Anxiety, depression, and compulsive personality traits are often present along with hypochondriasis. These clients are frequently demanding and a challenge to treat because they can be critical and suspicious of all medical or nursing care they receive. Your patience, therapeutic communication skills, and alert observations are needed when caring for individuals with hypochondriasis.

Because of the chronic nature of the disorder and the fact that these clients are "doctor shoppers," hypochondriasis is difficult to treat. Many times clients show poor insight or little concern about the source of their preoccupations. Psychotherapy and emotional support assist some clients in identifying the sources of their problems. Antianxiety and antidepressive medications may be prescribed. Because of the chronic and interfering nature of the disorder, long-term therapy and support are indicated. Table 22-2 presents a summary of the essential features of the three most common somatoform disorders.

Other Somatoform Disorders

Two less common but important somatoform disorders relate to the perceptions of pain and disfigurement. *Somatoform pain disorder* may be diagnosed when pain or discomfort is the major focus of distress *and* no other cause of the pain can be identified. Many times these individuals benefit from attending pain clinics.

◆ **TABLE 22-2**
DSM-IV Medical Diagnoses for Somatoform Disorders

DSM-IV Diagnosis	Essential Features
Somatization disorder	A history of many physical complaints beginning before the age of 30, occurring over a period of several years, and resulting in treatment being sought or significant impairment in social or occupational functioning. The patient must display at least four pain symptoms, two gastrointestinal symptoms, one sexual symptom, and one symptom suggesting a neurological disorder.
Conversion disorder	One or more symptoms or deficits affecting voluntary motor or sensory function suggesting a neurological or general medical condition. Psychological factors are judged to be associated with the symptom or deficit because the initiation or exacerbation of the symptom or deficit is preceded by conflicts or other stressors. The symptom or deficit cannot be fully explained by a neurological or general medical condition and is not a culturally sanctioned behavior or experience.
Hypochondriasis	Preoccupation with fears of having, or ideas that one has, a serious disease based on the person's misinterpretation of bodily symptoms. The preoccupation persists despite appropriate medical evaluation and reassurance and has existed for at least 6 months. It causes clinically significant distress or impairment in functioning.

Modified from American Psychiatric Association: *Diagnostic and statistical manual of mental disorders,* ed 4, Washington, DC, 1994, The Association.

Body dysmorphic disorder is characterized by a preoccupation with a physical difference or defect in one's body. The most common site of concern is the face or head. Clients may be concerned about their ears, noses, thinning hair, drooping chin, crooked teeth, or numerous other imperfections. They describe their distress as tormenting, devastating, or intensely painful. Because of their concern and embarrassment over their perceived defect, these individuals often describe themselves as "ugly" or "unacceptable" and often avoid work, social, or public gatherings. Their distress can lead to repeated hospitalizations for treatment of the perceived defect as well as suicide attempts.

Factitious Disorders and Malingering

Factitious disorders and malingering differ from somatoform disorders in that signs/symptoms are intentionally produced. Individuals with somatoform disorders are unaware that the roots of their complaints lie in a deep, internal emotional conflict. However, people who are malingering or engaging in factitious behaviors are purposefully and willfully producing the signs/symptoms of illness to realize some form of gain.

Both psychological and physical signs/symptoms can be expressed. Persons with psychological symp-toms may be using psychoactive drugs to produce the symptoms of a psychosis, whereas those with physical symptoms may be abusing prescription drugs with the goal of altering certain diagnostic test results.

Clients are rarely diagnosed with factitious disorder because they tend to move from physician to physician and undergo various operative procedures in different facilities. Some spend the major focus of their lives seeking admission or staying in health care facilities.

Clinical Presentations

The difference between a factitious disorder and malingering lies with the intent of the individual.

The most important feature of a **factitious disorder** is that symptoms are purposefully produced to assume the sick role. Presenting complaints include psychological signs/symptoms, self-inflicted illnesses or injuries, and exaggerated symptoms of actual physical problems. Examples include complaining of acute abdominal pain, producing abscesses by injecting saliva under the skin, ingesting medications to produce dramatic side effects, or pretending to have a seizure with no actual history of epilepsy. The motivation for their behaviors is to assume the sick role.

The medical history of individuals with factitious disorders may be dramatic and colorful, but clients are vague and inconsistent when questioned. Often they lie entertainingly about any aspect of their condition. Some may have extensive knowledge of hospital routines, diagnostic testing, and medical terminology. When the cause of the original symptoms is ruled out, individuals often develop new complaints and eagerly undergo invasive procedures. If they are confronted with evidence of their behaviors, they strongly deny it and discharge themselves from the institution or change health care providers.

On the other hand, the **malingering** individual produces symptoms to meet a recognizable goal. The student who fakes a stomachache to be excused from school for the day is a common example of malingering. Producing symptoms to avoid military service, the police, jury duty, or social obligations is another example. Not infrequently, clients will produce symptoms with the goal of receiving compensation, food, or shelter for the night. However, once the motive becomes apparent to others, the symptoms usually disappear because they no longer serve a purpose.

Implications for Care Providers

Caring for clients with somatoform disorders is challenging and rewarding. The first goal of care in every case is to rule out the presence of any physical disease or dysfunction. As physicians order and interpret diagnostic tests, nurses observe and assess clients and their activities. As data are gathered and analyzed, physical dysfunctions are ruled out, and nursing diagnoses are established (see boxes at right).

The development of trust is an important goal in the treatment of clients with somatoform disorders. Clients' pain and suffering are very real to them, and nurses must be aware of how their behaviors and attitudes affect the clients for whom they care (see box on p. 316). Nurses should attempt to understand the purposes served by clients' symptoms and work to encourage a trusting relationship with clients. Encourage the expression of feelings and emotional states rather than physical complaints.

Also, teach the importance of good nutritional, exercise, and sleep habits using the client's anxiety level as a guide for teaching. Meet physical needs when necessary but encourage independence. Help clients fill their social needs and encourage them to explore more adaptive ways of handling their stresses. Refer to the box on p. 317 for a summary of key nursing interventions for clients with somatoform disorders. Last, acknowledge clients as individuals and responsible adults who are capable of changing and developing more effective coping mechanisms.

NANDA NURSING DIAGNOSES PSYCHOPHYSIOLOGICAL RESPONSES

- Adjustment, impaired*
- Anxiety
- Body image disturbance
- Constipation
- Coping, ineffective individual
- Denial, ineffective
- Diarrhea
- Diversional activity deficit
- Family processes, altered
- Fear
- Gas exchange, impaired
- Health maintenance, altered
- Hopelessness
- Nutrition, altered: less than body requirements
- Pain, chronic*
- Physical mobility, impaired
- Powerlessness
- Self-care deficit
- Self-esteem, chronic low
- Self-esteem disturbance
- Self-esteem, situational low
- Skin integrity, impaired
- Sleep pattern disturbance*
- Social interaction, impaired
- Social isolation
- Spiritual distress

From North American Nursing Diagnosis Association: *NANDA nursing diagnoses: definitions and classification 1995-1996,* Philadelphia, 1994, The Association.
*Primary nursing diagnosis for maladaptive psychophysiological responses.

THINK ABOUT

Clients who have been diagnosed with somatoform disorders receive more than just a name for their symptoms. They are also the recipients of health care provider's attitudes.

Because many individuals with somatoform problems are demanding and difficult to care for, they test the patience and goodwill of nurses, therapists, and physicians alike. As a result, their caregivers engage in forced politeness and interact with these clients as little as possible. They soon become labeled as "uncooperative," and this label follows them through all areas of the health care system.

How would you feel about caring for these types of clients?

How do you think the negative labeling affects the health care received by this type of client?

SAMPLE CLIENT CARE PLAN
PSYCHOPHYSIOLOGICAL RESPONSES

Assessment

History: Jasmine is a 20-year-old college student. Last year, during final examination week, she developed frequent bouts of nausea followed by vomiting. Once final examinations were over, her symptoms subsided and have caused no further problems until 3 days ago.

Current Findings: A tense-appearing woman sitting stiffly in the chair and wringing her hands. On questioning, Jasmine reveals that she has "never had problems with her stomach." She believes that her nausea and vomiting are related to the "institutional food" she eats while on campus. She is here at the clinic to "get some of those nausea pills." Final examinations are scheduled for next week. Jasmine states that "they really have nothing to do with my stomach problems. It's the food that's the real problem here."

Nursing Diagnosis

Impaired adjustment related to anxiety about examinations

Planning/Expected Outcomes

Jasmine will express her feelings verbally rather than through the development of nausea and vomiting.

Nursing Interventions

Intervention

1. Assist Jasmine to identify stressful situations by reviewing the events surrounding the development of nausea and vomiting.
2. Help her see the association between thoughts, feelings, and behaviors.
3. Gently explore more effective ways of coping with her anxieties.
4. Help her choose two new coping mechanisms for dealing with the stress of examinations.
5. Actively encourage Jasmine to test the new coping mechanisms and provide positive feedback.
6. Encourage physical activity and relaxation exercises.
7. Assess eating and sleeping habits and encourage her to follow a routine schedule.

Rationale

1. Identifying the events relating to internal conflicts helps reduce the anxiety that results in nausea and vomiting.
2. Helps Jasmine to gain control over her expressions of emotions.
3. Preserves dignity and self-respect; encourages more effective coping behaviors.
4. Equips Jasmine with multiple ways to manage her anxieties and demonstrates more effective behaviors.
5. Change requires time, emotional support, and positive reinforcement from others.
6. Wellness requires a balance between physical and psychosocial needs.
7. A healthy, well-cared for body functions more effectively during stress.

Evaluation

During final examination week, Jasmine had two episodes of nausea but no vomiting. By the next examination period, Jasmine had replaced nausea and vomiting with a 1-mile walk and 10 minutes of relaxation exercise before each examination.

KEY INTERVENTIONS FOR CLIENTS WITH PHYSIOLOGICAL STRESS RESPONSES

- Convey an attitude of acceptance and understanding.
- Meet all physical needs of the client during acute exacerbations of the illness, even if doing so supports dysfunctional adaptations.
- Minimize secondary gains once the acute phase of the illness is resolved.
- Use the client's level of anxiety as a gauge to determine the amount and specificity of health teaching.
- Acknowledge the client as a responsible adult while indirectly addressing dependency needs.
- Encourage the client to talk about his/her feelings to the extent possible.
- Assist the client and family to enlarge their social network.

From Taylor CM: *Essentials of psychiatric nursing,* ed 14, St Louis, 1994, Mosby.

❖ KEY CONCEPTS

- No real divisions between mind and body exist because human beings are dynamic, complex physical organisms who are affected by many nonphysical events.
- The physical signs/symptoms of psychic or emotional distress are very real to the individual who is suffering from them at the time.
- When the body is under continual or repeated stress, it activates its stress response mechanism.

- Theories about stress include the stress response, symbolism, personality, and organic weakness theories.
- Somatization is the term for feeling physical symptoms in the absence of disease or out of proportion to a given ailment.
- Many somatization disorders are culturally related.
- A somatoform disorder is diagnosed when no diagnosable organic medical condition to explain the symptoms can be found, the disorder significantly impairs one's level of functioning, and the client is unaware of or unable to express his/her emotional distress.
- Clients with a conversion disorder present with problems related to sensory or motor functions.
- Hypochondriasis is an intense fear or preoccupation of having a serious disease or medical condition based on a misinterpretation of body signs/symptoms.
- The most important feature of factitious disorder is that symptoms are purposefully produced so that the individual can assume the sick role.
- The malingering individual produces symptoms to meet a recognizable external goal.
- The goals of care for every client with a somatoform disorder are to rule out the presence of any physical disease or dysfunction and to develop trust in the therapeutic relationship.

❖ SUGGESTIONS FOR FURTHER READING

"Somatization: mind over matter" by J.M. Corr (*Harvard Mental Health Letter* 17[6]:4, 1992) offers an excellent description of somatoform disorders and is written for the general public.

❖ REFERENCES

American Psychiatric Association: *Diagnostic and statistical manual of mental disorders,* ed 4, Washington, DC, 1994, The Association.

Barsky AJ and others: Histories of childhood trauma in adult hypochondriacal patients, *Am J Psychiatry* 151:397, 1994.

Burke PM and others: Correlates of depression in new onset pediatric inflammatory bowel disease, *Child Psychiatry Hum Dev* 24:275, 1994.

Carpi J: What to do about stress, *Psychol Today* 29(1):34, 1996.

Cooper CL, Faragher EB: Psychosocial stress and breast cancer: the inter-relationship between stress events, coping strategies, and personality, *Psychol Med* 23:653, 1993.

Corr JM: Somatization: mind over matter, *Harvard Ment Health Lett* 17(6):4, 1992.

Corsini RJ, editor: *Encyclopedia of psychology,* ed 2, New York, 1994, John Wiley.

Geissler EM: *Pocket guide to cultural assessment,* St Louis, 1994, Mosby.

Giger JN, Davidhizar RE: *Transcultural nursing: assessment and intervention,* ed 2, St Louis, 1995, Mosby.

Kiecolt-Glasser and others: Negative behavior during marital conflict is associated with immunological down-regulation, *Psychosom Med* 55:395, 1993.

Kirmayer LJ, Robbins JM, Paris J: Somatoform disorders: personality and the social matrix of somatic distress, *J Abnorm Psychol* 103(1):125, 1994.

Taylor CM: *Essentials of psychiatric nursing,* ed 14, St Louis, 1994, Mosby.

23

EATING AND SLEEPING DISORDERS

LEARNING OBJECTIVES

1. List three criteria for the diagnosis of an eating disorder.
2. Describe the difference between anorexia nervosa and bulimia.
3. Forecast the prognosis (outcome) for a client with an untreated eating disorder.
4. Explain why obesity can be considered an eating disorder.
5. List the main therapeutic goal for treating clients with eating disorders.
6. State four therapeutic nursing interventions for clients with eating disorders.
7. Explain three functions of sleep.
8. Describe the signs/symptoms of a client suffering from insomnia.
9. List four therapeutic nursing interventions to assist clients with sleeping problems.

KEY TERMS

anorexia nervosa
binge
bulimia
cataplexy
compulsive overeating
dyssomnias

eating disorder
insomnia
narcolepsy
obesity
parasomnias
pica

polysomnogram
purging
rumination disorder
sleeping disorder

Every person has his/her own *body image,* which is the collection of perceptions, thoughts, feelings, and behaviors that relate to one's body size and appearance. Body image is an important part of self-concept. Positive body images lead to behaviors that express confidence and self-assurance. Negative body images, on the other hand, can often lead to such problems as shyness and social isolation. Anxiety, depression, anorexia nervosa, bulimia, obesity, and other mental health problems are also interwoven with body image.

In the privacy of our thoughts, we all carry on dialogues or conversations with ourselves. Our internal dialogue that focuses on the body and appearance is our "private body talk." It is the content of our private body talk that helps to determine how we feel about our bodies.

Body image is also historically defined. Throughout European history, a large, fleshy body was considered a sign of wealth and prosperity. The wealthy could afford rich foods and extra pounds of body fat. Poor people were thin because they never got enough to eat. The same ideals followed our ancestors to the Americas. The wealthy and fat remained well-fed while the remainder of the population worked hard and carried little extra weight.

By the early 1900s, things began to change. Economic situations became more secure, and people ate better. The style and attitude evolved from "fat's where it's at" to "thin is in," and the day of the dieter began. Since the early part of this century, the emphasis on bodily appearance has centered around one's weight as a definition of beauty.

Today, anorexia nervosa is much more common in modern industrialized societies in which there is an abundance of food and a focus on being thin as a measure of attractiveness. In most Western societies, a high value is placed on the thin body. Little tolerance is shown for those individuals whose bodies are outside the range of "normal." Almost "one-third of Americans are dissatisfied with their weight" (Cameron, 1993).

A fear of obesity leads many persons to engage in unhealthy or destructive lifestyles. People who think of themselves as too thin try to gain weight. People whose body images portray them as too fat try to lose weight. It seems that few people in modern Western societies are content with how their bodies look.

Children learn early about which body images are desirable. It is not unusual to see boys imitating some popular, muscular hero or young girls dieting so that they may look like the latest underfed model. Because late childhood and early adolescence is a time for defining oneself, body image plays an important role. The desire for the perfect body can push young individuals toward many unsound physical and emotional habits.

This chapter focuses on the eating and sleeping problems considered mental health disorders. As with everything in life, moderation in eating and dieting is not a problem (Fig. 23-1). Occasional skipped meals or nights of lost sleep are not a problem; but when behaviors associated with eating or sleeping interfere with an individual's quality of daily life, they become mental health disorders.

Eating Disorders

An **eating disorder** is an ongoing disturbance in behaviors associated with the ingestion of food. The

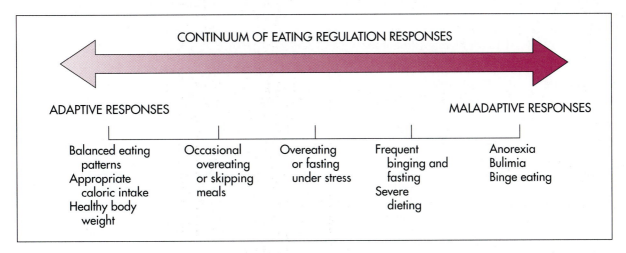

Fig. 23-1   Continuum of eating regulation responses. (Redrawn from Stuart GW, Sundeen SJ: *Principles and practice of psychiatric nursing,* ed 5, St Louis, 1995, Mosby.)

most common eating disorders are anorexia nervosa and bulimia. Although obesity is not officially classified as an eating disorder, it presents problems for almost 30% of our population. According to the Statistical Abstract of the United States (U.S. Bureau of Census, 1993), 27.5% of all adults consider that their *actual* weight is 20% or more than their *desirable* weight.

For adolescents, the statistics relating to weight loss behaviors are alarming. One large study demonstrated that attempts to lose weight were very common among adolescents and adults. Among the high school students surveyed, "44% of female students and 15% of male students reported that they were trying to lose weight" (Serdula and others, 1993). The weight control methods chosen by adolescents in the study were exercise, skipping meals, taking diet pills, and vomiting. Although the cause remains unknown, several theories and much research has attempted to explain the nature of anorexia nervosa (Table 23-1).

As you can see, our society is concerned with being thin. The desire for thinness leads many of our young people into unhealthy behaviors that can eventually lead to severe mental health problems and life-threatening situations. Eating disorders are one result of our nation's quest for the perfect body.

Anorexia Nervosa

One of the most serious eating disorders is **anorexia nervosa,** a condition in which an individual refuses to maintain a normal body weight because of an intense fear of becoming fat. Actually, the term *anorexia* (which in Greek means "want of appetite") is inaccurate because there is seldom an actual appetite loss associated with the disorder. The refusal to gain weight is a part of a strategy to solve a deep psychological problem or conflict and maintain some form of control.

Because of the secrecy and social stigma (shame) associated with eating disorders, the exact number of persons who suffer with these problems is unknown. It is known, however, that girls as young as 8 years old are dieting and the number of people with serious eating disorders is increasing.

Anorexia nervosa was first described over 100 years ago as a mania to be thin. Since then, the number of persons with this once rare disorder has steadily

◆ **TABLE 23-1** Theories About the Nature of Eating Disorders	
Theory	**Description**
Psychological	
Behavioral	Eating-disordered behaviors are attempts to reduce anxiety; discomfort with body image creates more anxiety, feelings of guilt and disgust, and loss of self-protecting boundaries.
Cognitive	Eating disorders are the result of deficits in attention, concentration, and vigilance related to underlying anxiety and depression.
Developmental	Individual fails to develop an appropriate sense of self and body; eating behaviors relate to problems with autonomy and self-identity; disorder is often brought about by a significant loss or crisis.
Sociocultural	Eating disorders are a response to a daily social emphasis on a stereotypical ideal of thinness; social stereotypes serve as stressors that drive women and girls to harmful dieting behaviors; anorexia nervosa is a way of mastering some control over the pressure on women to be successful in all areas of life (career, marriage, homemaking, and motherhood).
Neurobiological	The causes for eating disorders involve complex relationships among the body's neurotransmitters; persons with eating disorders show evidence of altered serotonin function; many of the same neuroendocrine findings are found in persons with depressive, bipolar, and eating disorders; cortisol levels are altered in depression and eating disorders; anorexia nervosa decreases levels of luteinizing hormone and follicle-stimulating hormone, which results in menstrual irregularities.

Modified from Irwin EG: *Arch Psychiatr Nurs* 7(6):342, 1993.

grown to about 1 in 250 persons. Today, approximately 90% to 95% of people with anorexia nervosa are female, but men are not immune to the disorder. Anorexia nervosa is seldom seen before puberty and rarely appears after 40 years of age. The average age of onset is around 17, but it is not uncommon to see anorectic behaviors in a 12-year-old. People who are concerned with their appearances for professional reasons, such as models, athletes, or flight attendants, are at a higher risk for developing anorexia nervosa. Early signs/symptoms of anorexia nervosa may be found in children with depressive symptoms and obsessive behaviors (Leon and others, 1993). Children from dysfunctional or abusive families are at a greater risk for developing the disorder.

Certain personality factors appear to be associated with anorexia nervosa (Irwin, 1993). The classic description of a person with anorexia nervosa is a tense, alert, hyperactive, rigid woman who thinks, talks, and walks rapidly. She is very ambitious and drives herself to perfection. She is sensitive, insecure, and serious with a conscience that works overtime. Her neatness, self-will, and stubbornness make her difficult to treat, and her lack of warmth and friendliness allows her to make few friends. As she struggles to gain a self-respecting identity, "the ritualistic control of food and weight provides a substituted sense of purpose and accomplishment" (Vitousek and Manke, 1994).

The main issue is one of control, and the female adolescent with anorexia nervosa becomes constricted, conforming, and obsessed with the need to control her body weight. Some teenagers have a fear of growing up and sexually maturing. Anorexia nervosa allows them to prevent the onset of adulthood by delaying menses and the development of secondary sexual characteristics.

Clinical presentation.   Weight concerns put adolescents (especially girls) at a high risk for developing anorexia nervosa. "Dieting behaviors, body dissatisfaction, body weight ideals below current body weight, and unusual eating patterns are quite prevalent in adolescent girls and college women" (Leon and others, 1993). These behaviors do not necessarily indicate an eating disorder, but when the quest for thinness results in the refusal to maintain a normal body weight, anorexia nervosa may be diagnosed.

To be diagnosed with anorexia nervosa, the individual must meet four criteria:

1. There is a refusal to maintain body weight that is more than 15% below normal.
2. Even though the individual is underweight, an intense fear of becoming fat exists.
3. There is a distorted (inaccurate) experience and significance placed on body weight and shape (person "feels fat" despite underweight).
4. There is an absence of at least three menstrual cycles in a female who has previously menstruated. Fig. 23-2 shows a typical anorectic woman before and after treatment.

People with anorexia nervosa have a self-esteem that is highly dependent on their body's size and shape. They often go to great measures to monitor their bodies, such as weighing three or four times a day, measuring body parts, and frequently looking in the mirror to check for areas of fat. The ability to lose weight is considered a sign of control and extraordinary self-discipline. Even the smallest gain in weight is seen as unacceptable, a threat, and a failure of self-control. Some individuals may actually acknowledge their extreme thinness, but they typically deny the seriousness of their condition.

Anorexia nervosa is a life-threatening disorder. Of the approximately 8 million people in the United States with anorexia nervosa, 3% to 6% will die (Carley and Rooda, 1995). This death rate is far higher than for any other mental illness. Death usually results from dehydration, loss of critical muscle mass, or electrolyte imbalances. Often, clients are not seen by health professionals until the disorder has resulted in some physical problem.

Behaviorally, many anorectic persons have a preoccupation with food. They may save recipes or prepare elaborate meals and then cut their own food into small pieces and push it around the plate without eating. Their obsessive behavior with food often extends into other obsessive-compulsive activities, such as a preoccupation with studying, exercising, or cleaning. Often the individual has poor sexual adjustment, with delayed sexual development or little interest in sex.

An inability to effectively cope or solve problems commonly exists. The past history frequently is positive for anxiety, depression, or substance abuse. People with anorexia nervosa need intervention, but they often deny the seriousness of their problems until extensive physical damage has taken place. We, as nurses in every care setting, must be alert for the clues of anorexia nervosa because early intervention will often save a life that otherwise would have literally wasted away.

Bulimia

Although anorexia nervosa may be a more dramatic problem, bulimia occurs more commonly. "The estimated incidence of anorexia nervosa in women is approximately 1%. Bulimia incidence rates vary

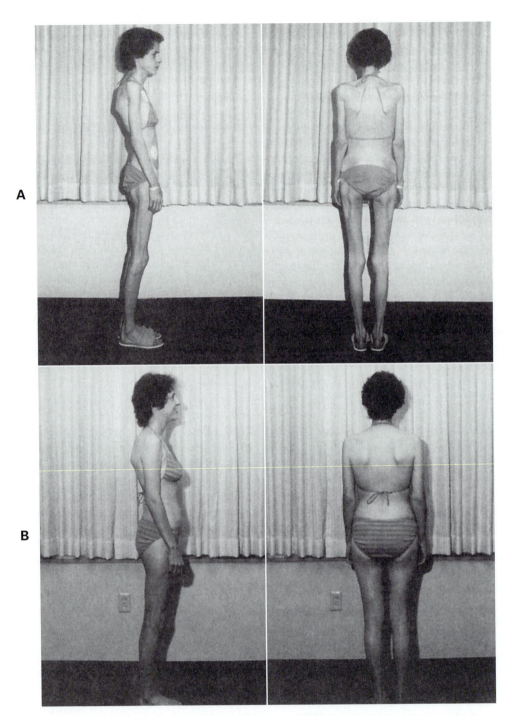

Fig. 23-2   **A,** Anorectic woman before treatment. **B,** Same woman after *gradual* refeeding, nutritional management, and psychological therapy. (From Williams SR: *Basic nutrition and diet therapy,* ed 10, St Louis, 1995, Mosby.)

among 4%, 8%, and 10.3%, depending on the population, method, and criteria used" (Carley and Rooda, 1995). Because it is more difficult to detect, many individuals with bulimia go untreated. Some studies have estimated the incidence of bulimia to be as high as 19% in college-aged women (Serdula and others,

1993). Like anorexia nervosa, bulimia appears to be more of a problem in modern industrialized countries.

Bulimia is a disorder of binge eating and the use of inappropriate methods to prevent weight gain. A **binge** is defined as eating (within a certain period of

KEY FEATURES OF ANOREXIA NERVOSA AND BULIMIA

ANOREXIA NERVOSA	BULIMIA
Rare vomiting or diuretic/laxative abuse	Vomiting or diuretic/laxative abuse
More severe weight loss	Less weight loss
Slightly younger	Slightly older
More introverted	More extroverted
Hunger denied	Hunger experienced
Eating behavior may be considered normal and source of esteem	Eating behavior considered foreign and source of distress
Sexually inactive	More sexually active
Obsessional features predominate	More hysterical or borderline features as well as obsessional features
Death from starvation (or suicide in chronically ill)	Death from hypokalemia or suicide
Amenorrhea	Menses irregular or absent
More favorable prognosis	Less favorable prognosis
Fewer behavioral abnormalities	Stealing, drug and alcohol abuse, self-mutilation, and other behavioral abnormalities

From Andersen AE: *Practical comprehensive treatment of anorexia nervosa and bulimia,* Baltimore, 1985, Johns Hopkins University Press.

time) an amount of food that is definitely larger than most individuals would eat in similar circumstances. During a binge, an individual often consumes large amounts of certain foods, usually carbohydrates. It is not unusual for the bingeing person to eat as much as 5000 calories in donuts, cakes, or other sweets. The binge lasts about 1 to 2 hours and then is followed by feelings of guilt and attempts to rid the body of the food just consumed.

Two subtypes of bulimia are classified according to the presence or absence of purging behaviors. **Purging** is an attempt to rid the gastrointestinal tract and body of unwanted food. The most common purging behaviors are vomiting and the use of diuretics and laxatives. Less commonly, some people use syrup of ipecac or enemas to purge.

The individual with "nonpurging type" of bulimia does not purge after a binge but uses other inappropriate methods to prevent weight gain, such as fasting between binges and exercising excessively.

The personality traits of persons with bulimia differ from those with anorexia nervosa. The average individual with bulimia is a woman who is slightly older and more outgoing than her anorectic counterpart. She is more socially and sexually active. She actually experiences hunger and feels distressed about her abnormal eating behaviors. Often her body weight is normal or even slightly above average. It is not uncommon for other mental health problems, such as substance abuse, self-mutilation, or hysteria, to be present at the same time. The box above offers a comparison of the key features of anorexia nervosa and bulimia.

Recent studies (Brouwers and Wiggum, 1993) have demonstrated that perfectionism is often seen with bulimia and contributes to maintaining bulimic behaviors. Bulimic women frequently have unrealistic expectations about themselves and how their lives should run. They become frustrated over and over by their own inabilities to reach unrealistic goals. If they experience failure, they conclude that they were unable to reach the goal because they were weak, not trying hard enough, inadequate, or unlovable or had some other negative failing. In short, these are the "I should have . . ." types who are never satisfied at their own efforts. Even when successful, they seldom can enjoy their accomplishments because they tell themselves that they should have done it better, sooner, or more efficiently.

When it comes to body image, people with bulimia typically view themselves as fat or thin. Being in the middle, or average, is not considered. Not infrequently, a woman with bulimia fears that she must follow a diet for the rest of her life if she gives up binge eating. The following is an example: "She assumed that her choices consisted of bingeing (all) or food deprivation through chronic dieting (nothing). She had never considered the alternatives of natural appetite, trusting her body, or of eating regular meals" (Brouwers and Wiggum, 1993).

The desire to become the perfect person commonly leads to feelings of failure and uselessness. When life is based on the all-or-nothing principle, anything short of perfect is considered to be a failure. Unfortunately, this means most of their time is spent in feeling that they are truly "nothing." Perfection, in reality, is not attainable.

Bulimia is most commonly found in young, white middle-class and upper-class women. Men account for about one out of nine cases. There is an increased frequency of anxiety, depression, and drug abuse among individuals with bulimia. About one third to one half also meet the diagnostic criteria for a personality disorder.

Clinical presentation.   To receive the diagnosis of bulimia, a person must meet four basic criteria:

1. The most essential feature is recurring episodes of binge eating. Individuals are usually ashamed of their binges and often do their eating in secret. Episodes of binge eating may or may not be planned in advance. During the bingeing episodes, the individual feels out of control and often attacks eating in a frenzied state.
2. Bingeing is followed by recurring inappropriate behaviors to prevent weight gain (purging). The most popular method of purging is to induce vomiting (80% to 90%), which relieves the physical discomfort of a full stomach and the emotional fear of gaining weight. "In some cases vomiting becomes a goal in itself, and the person will binge in order to vomit or will vomit after eating a small amount of food" (American Psychiatric Association, 1994). Other methods of purging include the misuse of laxatives, diuretics, enemas, and syrup of ipecac. Some people use a combination of methods to purge, engage in strenuous exercise at inappropriate times, or follow semistarvation diets after a bingeing episode.
3. The eating binges must occur at least twice a week for at least 3 months. Patterns of binge eating range from several episodes a day to a regular and persistent pattern. Often episodes are triggered by a stressful event or experience.
4. Individuals place excessive emphasis on body shape and weight in determining their self-esteem. They are dissatisfied with their imperfect bodies, have a fear of gaining weight, and often restrict their caloric intake or choose low-calorie foods between binge-eating episodes.

When purging behaviors are frequent, fluid and electrolyte abnormalities can result. The few persons who use syrup of ipecac are at risk for developing serious cardiac and skeletal myopathy (muscle wasting). Although death from bulimia is rare, the underlying psychiatric problems are often more severe than those seen with anorectic persons.

Obesity

According to the *Diagnostic and Statistical Manual of Mental Disorders* (DSM-IV), obesity is not listed as a mental health disorder because it has not been established that obesity is consistently associated with mental health or behavioral problems. However, obesity is linked to many physical and psychological problems that cause distress for most overweight individuals.

Obesity is defined as an excess of body weight. Clients are classified as mildly obese (20% to 40% above normal weight), moderately obese (41% to 100% above normal weight), and severely (morbidly) obese (over 100% above normal weight). Concern with being overweight is common in modern industrialized societies in which the luxury of chronic overeating and underexercising is available. Obesity is a relatively rare condition in less-developed societies. In some cultures, it is seen as a sign of wealth and prosperity (see box below).

Obesity is the result of too many calories consumed or not enough calories burned (Fig. 23-3). As with the person with bulimia or alcoholism, many overweight individuals lose control over their eating. Although the eating patterns of obese individuals do not pose an immediate threat, being chronically overweight can eventually result in severe physical and emotional problems. Today, much money and time are spent in the pursuit of losing weight throughout the industrialized world.

The causes of obesity are several. In addition to overeating, other factors have been discovered that may help explain obesity. Complicated neurochemical mechanisms that help to control appetite and eat-

 CULTURAL ASPECTS

The island nation of Nauru lies south of the equator in the western Pacific Ocean. Most Nauruans lead an inactive lifestyle because the island's phosphate mines are worked by immigrant miners. Almost all food and water is imported from Australia.

Eating processed foods is considered a sign of wealth. Obesity is seen as attractive, and overweight women are sought as wives. Nauru has the highest rate of diabetes in the world.

ing behaviors are being studied. Heredity appears to play a role in the development of obesity. The children of obese parents tend to be overweight themselves. Obese persons have larger fat cells in their bodies. The lack of sufficient exercise also contributes greatly to obesity.

Faulty eating behaviors appear to begin in childhood. Many overweight persons once relied on food to numb the emotional discomforts of growing up. Throughout childhood, they learned to cope by eating, which helped to relieve the emotional distresses of life. This pattern of lessening emotional pain by eating is called **compulsive overeating.** In time, food becomes like a drug, with a "fix" that temporarily lessens psychological discomforts of an ever-growing desire for more food.

As the individual continues to find comfort in food, he/she grows physically more obese and becomes less attractive to others. (Remember our cultural bias

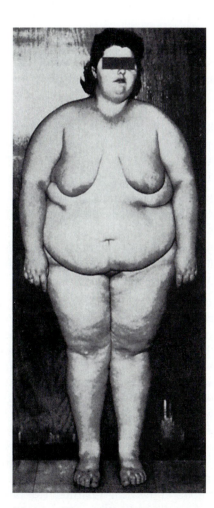

Fig. 23-3 Obesity. (From Seidel HM and others: *Mosby's guide to physical examination,* ed 3, St Louis, 1995, Mosby.)

against obesity.) This behavior serves only to increase feelings of worthlessness, and the person again eats to relieve the pain. A vicious circle soon becomes established, and the person begins to replace social relationships with the comforts of food. Compulsive overeating can become a lonely way of life.

Clinical presentation.   The first signs of obesity are seen early in life. An estimate may be made by comparing one's height and weight to a standardized chart. "Children who are 20% over normal for their height and weight should undergo further evaluation, including a height and weight history of the child, parents, and siblings, as well as eating habits, appetite, and hunger patterns, and physical activity" (Wong, 1995).

As overweight children grow and mature, they begin to sense society's disapproval of their obesity. Youngsters may begin to diet and exercise or react by continuing to find comfort in food. Dieting and other weight loss methods soon become a way of life for many overweight people at a young age (Centers for Disease Control, 1994).

During adolescence, weight becomes an important part of a newly forming body image. Teens may rebel against parental nagging to lose weight or become unwilling to control their caloric intake. They may resort to unhealthy methods, such as prolonged fasting or purging, to gain some control over their weight. Not infrequently, they will ignore their obesity and continue to eat as though a problem does not exist.

The cycle of "I'm not attractive, so I'll eat because it makes me feel better" becomes ingrained as a way of coping in childhood and early adolescence. Many overweight individuals become even more obese as they grow older. Eventually, the numerous chronic health problems associated with moderate or severe obesity begin to appear. These problems increase anxiety and further encourage the individual to seek the comfort that food has so frequently brought in the past. The cycle continues, and problems grow.

Other Eating Disorders

Two other but less common eating disorders are pica and rumination. **Pica** is the persistent eating of nonnutritive substances (nonfood items) that lasts for more than 1 month. Substances, such as clay, laundry starch, insects, leaves, or pebbles are chosen for ingestion. The person with pica still eats and enjoys food. He/she just has an overwhelming need to eat the nonfood item. Many times the cause of pica can be traced to a vitamin, mineral, or calorie deficiency. The box on p. 326 presents an interesting case history of pica. Treatment for the problem is to rule out the

CASE STUDY

Loren was assigned to rounds with the mobile clinic nurse, whose responsibility was to provide prenatal services for a group of poor women from a rural farming region. As he rode through the countryside, he was surprised to see how many pregnant women and children were working in the fields. He asked the clinic nurse how long field workers were expected to work during their pregnancies and was surprised to find that they were expected to be in the fields until the onset of labor. "How do they get enough to eat when they are working in the fields?" he wondered.

The mobile clinic nurse, sensing Loren's curiosity, assigned him to obtain dietary histories from as many of the farm workers as he could. By the time Loren had completed four histories, he was amazed. Not only were the workers' daily diets poor, but many of the pregnant clients made it a habit to carry laundry starch into the fields with them. During the day, as they became hungry, they would eat a handful of laundry starch and drink a few sips of water.

When Loren finally mustered enough courage to ask one of the women why she ate laundry starch, she told him that it "takes the edge off my hunger and lets me work a little longer. Some of the ladies even eat clay, if it's a good kind."

It seemed that eating the laundry starch provided these women with a substitute for more expensive calories. The need to eat clay may have indicated the presence of a mineral deficiency.

Clinical Decision

1. How do you think the infants will be affected by their mothers' dietary habits?

---

presence of any physical problem or deficiency and then to assist clients in establishing more healthful eating habits.

Rumination disorder is an uncommon problem that is most often seen in childhood. It is defined as the regurgitation and rechewing of food. According to the DSM-IV, "partially digested food is brought up into the mouth without apparent nausea, retching, disgust, or associated gastrointestinal disorder. The food is then either ejected from the mouth or, more frequently, chewed and reswallowed."

When rumination disorder affects infants, death from malnutrition can result. In older children and adults, malnutrition is less of a problem. This disorder can occur continuously or appear at intervals. Psychosocial problems, such as lack of attention, neglect, or a stressful environment, may be risk factors. Other feeding disorders of early childhood are discussed in Chapter 14.

Guidelines for Intervention

Basically, the main therapeutic goal for all eating disorders is to establish behaviors that promote health for the individual. Although it sounds simple, this is a lofty goal.

People with eating disorders have learned to cope with their stresses and troubles by focusing on food in one way or another. Those with anorexia nervosa attempt to cope by controlling, and the highest form of control is the ability to rule over one's body size. Individuals with bulimia learn to numb the emotional pain by eating large amounts of food, and then they suffer through overwhelming guilt. Many persons who experience the discomforts of obesity have developed compulsive overeating habits to fill their needs for love and belonging.

Treatments and therapies. The treatment for anorexia nervosa and bulimia requires medical and mental health interventions. The three immediate (short-term) goals of treatment are:

1. To stabilize existing medical problems
2. To reestablish normal nutritional and eating patterns
3. To help the client resolve the psychological or emotional issues that underlie the disordered eating behaviors

Medical care centers around nutritional management of the client. Individuals with severe weight loss may receive total parenteral nutrition (hyperalimentation) whereby all the necessary nutrients are administered through an intravenous line placed in a large blood vessel. For less severely malnourished clients, intravenous therapy or tube feedings may be ordered, but the main focus is to encourage the client to voluntarily consume food.

Clients are weighed daily, and supplemental vitamins are usually prescribed. Clients are closely observed for secret anorectic or bulimic behaviors. The long-term goals of medical treatment (for both underweight and overweight clients) focus on teaching clients about good nutrition and assisting them to develop appropriate eating habits.

DRUG ALERT

Administering antidepressants to clients with anorexia nervosa *before they regain* weight may be hazardous if the individual has a history of cardiac dysrhythmia or presently has a low serum potassium level. For this reason, the physician may order a trial dose of the antidepressant before ordering the medication.

Be sure to check the laboratory results of your clients with eating disorders. Withhold the medication and notify the physician if the potassium level drops below normal limits.

The goals of mental health care focus on helping clients improve their self-esteem and develop more effective coping skills. Once clients are physically stable, they can be encouraged to adopt proper eating habits. Behavior modification techniques may help to reinforce healthful eating behaviors. Signs of depression may be diagnosed and treated. Often family therapy is helpful. Individual or group therapy helps clients to focus on the psychological conflicts that underlie their inappropriate eating behaviors.

Drug therapy can be quite effective, but only if it is combined with some form of psychotherapy. Amphetamines have been successfully used to treat obesity. However, their potential for addiction is high, and they are not frequently prescribed. Antidepressants or lithium has been used with success in the treatment of bulimia (see box above).

Nursing interventions.   Nurses play an important role in caring for individuals with altered eating patterns in both the hospital and community setting. The main goals for nurses who care for persons with eating disorders are to assist their clients in identifying and coping with the problems that led them to their inappropriate eating behaviors. Nursing diagnoses relating to eating disorders include anxiety, body image disturbance, altered nutrition, powerlessness, self-esteem disturbance, risk for self-mutilation, and ineffective management of the therapeutic regimen.

To accomplish the goals of care, nurses first work to establish rapport and trust with clients. Then they assist their clients in identifying how food is used to provide comfort and reduce anxiety. During the working phase of the therapeutic relationship, nurses help clients replace the distorted ideas about their body images with thoughts and behaviors that build self-esteem. Problem-solving skills are taught, and clients are encouraged to identify the social support systems that encourage healthful practices. A sample client care plan summary for clients with eating dis-

orders is illustrated in the box on p. 328. Every individual suffering from an eating disorder needs the understanding and compassion of health care providers. Hopefully nurses can help make the struggles of clients with eating disorders a little less difficult by nurturing and supporting more effective coping behaviors.

Sleep Disorders

Sleeping patterns and routines change as we grow older and more mature. The 16 hours of nightly sleep required by the infant dwindles to less than 8 hours by adulthood. The afternoon naps of childhood are soon replaced by the all-day demands of school and work, while the ritual of the bedtime hour disappears altogether. By the time many persons reach adulthood their sleeping habits may have changed dramatically.

Most young adults have few difficulties with sleeping. However, sleep disorders begin to occur more frequently as adults grow older. By older adulthood, it is unusual to have a full night of uninterrupted sleep.

Although no one knows exactly why we must sleep every night, researchers have found that sleep serves several purposes. During sleep, bodily functions and metabolic rate slow, decreasing the workload on the heart. Muscles relax and the body conserves energy during sleep. One theory states that sleep is important for the renewal and repair of body cells and tissues. Sleep also "appears to be a critical cycle of brain activity important for learning, memory, and behavioral adaptation" (Potter and Perry, 1995).

The dreaming that takes place during sleep is also important for health. Dreaming allows us to gain insights, solve problems, work through emotional reactions, and prepare for the future. Many cultures place great meaning in dreams and use them to cope with the problems of everyday reality (see box on p. 329).

Sleep occurs in cycles of about 24 hours, depending on each individual's biological clock or personal body rhythms. There are two phases to sleep: nonrapid eye movement (NREM sleep) and rapid eye movement (REM sleep). NREM sleep is divided into four stages.

The average adult's sleep pattern begins with a presleep period, lasting from about 10 to 30 minutes. During this time, a gradual drowsiness develops until the individual "drops off to sleep" or enters stage 1 of NREM sleep. As the sleeper moves through each stage of NREM, the quality of sleep becomes deeper. During stage 4, the sleeper is most difficult to arouse. After reaching stage 4, the sleep pattern reverses, and the sleeper moves back through stages 3 and 2 where REM sleep takes place. Fig. 23-4 illustrates the normal adult sleep cycle and its stages.

SAMPLE CLIENT CARE PLAN
EATING DISORDER

Assessment

History: Erica is a 15-year-old girl who is 20 pounds under her usual body weight. She has always been a "chubby child" who had no problems eating until the beginning of this school year. Three months ago, Erica told her mother to stop fixing "all those fattening foods" and began refusing her meals.

Current Findings: A thin, tired-appearing adolescent girl who appears older than her stated age. Face is hollow, eyes sunken, and skin is dry. Hair is fine and brittle. Skin is covered with lanugo (fine hair). Skin turgor is poor. Vital signs are low for age and size.

When questioned, Erica states that she "feels fine" and does not "know what all the fuss is about." "Just because I choose to lose a few pounds everybody gets upset. Sounds like this is their problem more than mine. I'm really still too fat."

Nursing Diagnosis

Alteration in nutrition: less than body requirements related to distorted self-image

Planning/Expected Outcomes

Erica will voluntarily consume 2000 calories a day by July 4. Erica will gain 1 pound of body weight per week.

Nursing Interventions

Intervention

1. Establish trust and gain Erica's cooperation.

2. Perform a complete nutritional assessment.

3. Help Erica identify the positive and negative consequences of her eating behaviors.
4. Monitor physical status for signs of malnutrition.
5. Explore other ways to achieve control over the parts of Erica's life that are causing distress.

6. Involve family members in therapy if possible.

Rationale

1. Erica must first agree to work with the staff if other interventions are to achieve therapeutic results.
2. Establishes a baseline from which to judge progress.
3. Helps her acknowledge the problem and its effects on her life.
4. To prevent further physical problems and decline.
5. When control is achieved in one area, it tends to spread to other areas; control builds Erica's self-image and confidence.
6. Erica may benefit from supportive family members; offers an opportunity to assess family interactions.

Evaluation

During the first week, Erica consumed an average of 1000 calories/day with much encouragement. By July 3, Erica was voluntarily consuming about 1800 calories/day. Weight gain averaged ½ pound/wk.

If the sleeper is interrupted or awakened at any time during the cycle, he/she must return to stage 1 and begin the process again. If the disturbances occur frequently enough, the individual will suffer from the signs/symptoms of sleep deprivation.

Everyone has the occasional poor night's sleep. For people with sleeping disorders, however, this experience becomes an unwelcome and unwanted way of life.

A **sleeping disorder** is a condition or problem that repeatedly disrupts an individual's pattern of sleep. Problems with sleep are very common in the United States and other modern societies in which the pace of life is fast and demanding. Sleep disorders occur more frequently in the elderly, but all age groups can be affected.

◆ THINK ABOUT

It has been said that dreams are the result of reflection or suggestion. What do you think is meant by this statement?

Do you believe that dreams have meaning?

The diagnosis of a sleep disorder is based on a thorough history, physical examination, and the results of a nighttime **polysomnogram.** A polysomnogram monitors the client's electrophysical responses during sleep. It includes such measurements as brain wave activity (electroencephalogram [EEG]), muscle movement (electromyogram [EMG]), and extraocular eye movements (electroolfactogram [EOG]). Many hospitals and medical centers have specially designed sleep laboratories where clients can be monitored for the quantity, quality, and characteristics of their sleep.

Sleep disorders are divided into two basic types: primary sleep disorders and those related to other conditions (secondary sleep disorders) (Fig. 23-5).

Primary sleep disorders are thought to be related to abnormal functioning of the sleep-wake or timing mechanisms of the body. The two subdivisions of primary sleep disorders are called the dyssomnias and the parasomnias.

Dyssomnias

Dyssomnias are characterized "by abnormalities in the amount, quality, or timing of sleep" (American

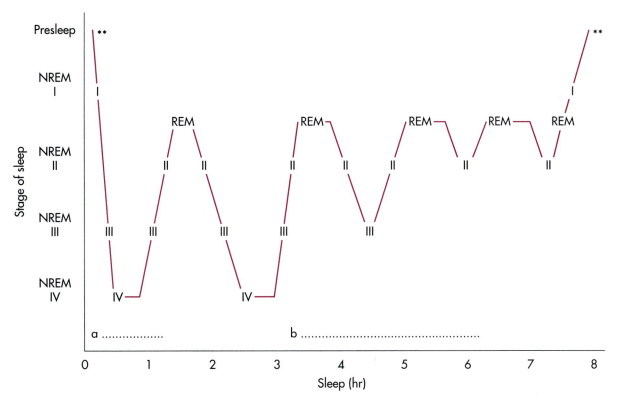

Fig. 23-4 Normal adult sleep cycle and the stages of sleep. (Modified from Biddle C, Oaster TRF: *J Am Assoc Nurs Anesthet* 58(1):36, 1990.)

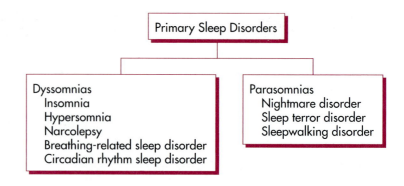

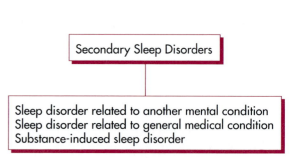

Fig. 23-5   Classification of sleep disorders.

Psychiatric Association, 1994). The dyssomnias include such problems as insomnia, hypersomnia, narcolepsy, and breathing-related and circadian rhythm sleep disorders. Insomnia occurs most frequently.

Insomnia is a disorder of falling asleep or maintaining a sound sleep (Allen, 1994). It is often associated with increased physical and mental alertness at nighttime and sleepiness during the day. The individual who cannot regularly fall asleep often becomes preoccupied and distressed. This contributes to the development of more anxiety about sleep and sets up a vicious cycle in which the harder they "try" to fall asleep, the more difficult it becomes. Often, people are worried, anxious, or concerned about something when they prepare for sleep.

As nights of interrupted sleep continue, individuals become negatively conditioned toward sleep and even begin to expect a poor night's sleep. Eventually, chronic insomnia develops and persists long after the problem that caused the sleep loss in the first place is solved. Chronic insomnia often leads to decreased feelings of well-being during waking hours. Individuals may complain of a lack of energy or motivation; decreased attention span, energy, and concentration; or a general worsening of moods and emotional reactions.

Insomnia is relatively rare in childhood and adolescence. Approximately 30% to 40% of adults have problems with insomnia, and the incidence increases with age. It is seen more often in women and usually begins in young adulthood or middle age with an initial period of poor sleep that progressively worsens over a period of months. Some people then experience periodic episodes of insomnia, whereas others develop a chronic ineffective sleep pattern that may last for years. Many individuals with insomnia have a history of being "light sleepers" who are easily disturbed by environmental noises or other distractions.

Primary hypersomnia is an excessive sleepiness. It usually begins between 15 and 30 years of age, slowly progresses over a period of weeks or months, and then becomes chronic and stable. To be diagnosed, hypersomnia must meet three criteria:

1. Prolonged sleep episodes or daytime sleeping that occurs daily for at least 1 month
2. Excessive sleepiness severe enough to cause significant distress or impairment in the activities of daily living
3. Excessive sleepiness that is not caused by any other physical or mental health disorder

In persons with hypersomnia, nighttime sleep may last from 8 to 12 hours, but it is often followed by difficulty awakening in the morning and excessive sleepiness during normal waking hours. During the day, these people may take long naps, which commonly last for more than an hour. Some naps are intentionally planned, whereas others occur as involuntary episodes of daytime sleep. After awakening from these naps, individuals do not feel more refreshed or alert.

Hypersomnia can lead to significant distress in a person's functioning. The long sleep and difficult morning awakenings make it nearly impossible to meet morning business or social obligations. Low levels of alertness result in decreased concentration, poor efficiency, and few memories of the day's events. Unplanned episodes of sleep can lead to embarrassing and even dangerous situations, such as falling asleep while driving a car or operating a dangerous piece of equipment. Daytime sleepiness can result in automatic behavior in which tasks are carried out with little or no memory of having done them. Family and social relationships can also be affected by hypersomnia. Sadly, people with excessive sleepiness are often thought of as lazy or indifferent.

Narcolepsy is an uncommon condition in which an individual has repeated attacks of sleep. Symptoms usually become apparent during adolescence, but a careful history often reveals a pattern of sleepiness dating back to preschool years. The onset of the disorder often follows a change in the person's sleep-wake schedule or a very stressful event.

The periods of sleepiness in narcolepsy are described as irresistible. Individuals fall asleep for about 10 to 20 minutes in any situation, whether it is appropriate to sleep or not. Episodes occur from two to six times a day. Some people with narcolepsy can "fight off" their sleep attacks, whereas others plan naps throughout the day to manage the condition.

Two other distressing features of narcolepsy are cataplexy and inappropriate rapid eye movement. **Cataplexy** is a sudden episode of muscle weakness and loss of muscle tone that lasts for seconds to minutes. These episodes are often brought about by an intense emotion. Inappropriate rapid eye movement occurs during the transition between sleep and wakefulness during which dreamlike hallucinations or paralysis of voluntary muscles occurs.

Breathing-related sleep disorders are more common than once thought. They are defined as sleep disruptions caused by abnormal ventilation during sleep. The most common form is called *obstructive sleep apnea syndrome*. During sleep, a partially obstructed upper airway causes periods of apnea that repeatedly awaken the individual.

Sleeping patterns are characterized by periods of loud snoring, followed by periods of apnea lasting as long as 90 seconds. The apneic event is ended when the individual gasps, moans, mumbles, or shakes with loud air-gulping snores. Although the person may not fully awaken during these events, sleep is disrupted enough to result in excessive sleepiness during the day. People who are extremely overweight are at risk for this disorder. The term *pickwickian syndrome* was coined to describe this disorder based on an obese character in a Charles Dickens' novel.

Another parasomnia is called *circadian rhythm sleep disorder*, a persistent pattern of sleep disruption that results from a mismatch between personal body rhythms and the demands of the environment. This disorder is most often seen in persons who do shift work or must travel frequently.

Disruptions in sleep can also be caused by environmental factors, restless leg syndrome, or nocturnal myoclonus. *Restless leg syndrome* is described as disagreeable sensations, such as pricking, tingling, itching, or crawling, that occur while falling asleep or during sleep. The sensations are relieved by moving the legs or walking and return when the legs are still. *Nocturnal myoclonus* is also called idiopathic periodic limb movements. These repeated, brief jerks occur mostly in the legs at the beginning of sleep and decrease during stage 4 NREM sleep. Because the movements take place every 20 to 60 seconds, they disturb normal sleep patterns.

Parasomnias

Sleep disorders characterized by abnormal behavioral or physical events during sleep are called **parasomnias.** It is believed that parasomnia sleep disorders are caused by the activation of certain physiological systems at inappropriate times. People with parasomnias most often complain of unusual behaviors during sleep instead of daytime sleepiness. The most common parasomnias are nightmare disorder, sleep terror disorder, and sleepwalking disorder.

The most important feature of *nightmare disorder* is repeated frightening dreams that lead to abrupt awakenings. The individual is fully alert on awakening and significantly distressed from the experience. Awakenings may be accompanied by fight-flight responses, such as sweating, rapid respirations, and rapid heart beat. Often, a sense of anxiety lingers after the individual is awake, and he/she finds it difficult to return to sleep. Nightmares occur during REM sleep and produce images that are often remembered in detail after awakening.

Sleep terror disorder is repeated nightmares and abrupt awakenings accompanied by a panicky cry or scream and intense fear. During the episode, the person cannot be comforted or awakened without difficulty. Usually, the individual does not awaken but returns to sleep. There is no memory of the event on morning awakening. Sleep terrors usually occur only once a night during stages 3 and 4 of NREM sleep. They are often accompanied by the physical signs of intense stress, such as increased heart rate, respirations, and muscle tone.

Sleepwalking disorder is characterized by episodes of complex motor movement during sleep. Individuals who sleepwalk rise from their beds and begin to walk around. They often have a blank stare and are not responsive to communication or efforts to awaken them. If awakened during or after an episode, they remember little about the event and may have a brief period of confusion until they become oriented. Sleepwalking is first seen between the ages of 4 and 8. It peaks by about age 12 and usually disappears by adolescence. First-time episodes rarely occur in adults.

Other Sleep Disorders

Other sleep disorders relate to problems that can be traced to specific causes. They include sleep disorders related to a general medical condition, a mental health condition, and the use of chemical substances. Sleep disorders can result from many physical problems. The presence of a neurological, cardiovascular, or respiratory disorder or an infection have a significant effect on sleep. Pain from musculoskeletal disease and anxiety related to coughing or difficult breathing can lead to prolonged periods of inadequate sleep.

Many mental disorders are associated with sleep-related problems. Insomnia or hypersomnia is often seen in clients with major depressive, mood, anxiety, adjustment, somatoform, panic, and personality disorders. During flare-ups of schizophrenia, people suffer from significant periods of insomnia.

Last are *substance-induced sleep disorders*. These sleeping problems occur during substance use (intoxication) or during periods of withdrawal. Many substances can produce a sleep disorder. Numerous prescription medications are associated with sleep disorders, including drugs that treat hypertension, cardiac problems, inflammatory processes, neurological conditions, and respiratory diseases. Chemicals such as alcohol, cocaine, and various street drugs affect sleep. Even the medications prescribed to induce sleep (hypnotics and sedatives) produce unwanted effects on the sleep cycle. Nurses must be aware of how various medications and chemicals affect each client's sleep.

Guidelines for Interventions

The first step in the treatment of sleep disorders is to teach prevention. Because many people do not regularly receive a good night's sleep, the need for good sleep hygiene habits is great. One of the best treatments for insomnia is to establish and maintain a regular sleeping routine by preparing both body and mind for the night's upcoming rest. Nurses and other health care providers are in ideal positions to educate clients about the importance of receiving enough quality sleep. The box below offers several suggestions for effective sleep practices.

The main goal of nursing care is to assist the client in obtaining a restful night's sleep. Short-term goals focus on helping clients establish a regular and healthy sleep pattern. Nursing diagnoses for sleep disorders include sleep pattern disturbance, high risk for injury, fatigue, altered thought processes, ineffective (individual, family) coping, ineffective breathing pattern, or knowledge deficit related to sleep hygiene practices.

Nursing interventions are aimed at promoting comfort, controlling physical disturbances, and maintaining a quiet, restful environment. Hypnotics (sleeping pills) may be administered as ordered, but only after all other methods of inducing sleep have failed. Special care must be taken when administering hypnotics or sedatives to older persons because they react

---

SLEEP HYGIENE STRATEGIES

- Set a regular bedtime and wake-up time 7 days a week.
- Exercise daily to aid sleep initiation and maintenance; however, vigorous exercise too close to bedtime may make falling asleep difficult.
- Schedule time to wind down and relax before bed.
- Avoid worrying when trying to fall asleep.
- Guard against nighttime interruptions. Earplugs may help with a noisy partner. Heavy window shades help to screen out light. Create a comfortable bed.
- Maintain a cool temperature in the room. A warm bath or warm drink before bed helps some people fall asleep.
- Excessive hunger or fullness may interfere with sleep. Avoid large meals before bed. If hungry, a light carbohydrate snack may be helpful.
- Avoid caffeinated drinks, excessive fluid intake, stimulating drugs, and excessive alcohol in the evening and before bedtime.
- Excessive napping may make it difficult for some people to fall asleep at night.
- Do no eat, read, work, or watch television in bed. The bed and bedroom should be used only for sleep and sex.
- Maintain a reasonable weight. Excessive weight may result in daytime fatigue and sleep apnea.
- Get out of bed and engage in other activities if not able to fall asleep.

From Stuart GW, Sundeen SJ: *Pocket guide to psychiatric nursing,* ed 3, St Louis, 1995, Mosby.

strongly to these classes of medications (Gorbein, 1993).

Recent research has demonstrated that morning bright light therapy improves the sleeping patterns of older adults with dementia by helping reestablish natural biological rhythms (Mishima and others, 1994) and has revealed that the body has a naturally occurring sleep hormone, called melatonin, which helps to control our biological clocks (Elias, 1993). These findings may prove to be promising developments in the treatment of sleep disorders.

Become aware of the importance of keeping client environment dark during sleep and brightly lit during daylight hours. Read about the new developments in the treatment of sleeping disorders and apply them to yourself and your clients because we are learning more every day about the mysteries of sleep.

❖ KEY CONCEPTS

- Body image is the collection of perceptions, thoughts, feelings, and behaviors that relate to body size and appearance.
- An eating disorder is an ongoing disturbance in behaviors associated with the ingestion of food.
- Although obesity is not officially classified as an eating disorder, it presents problems for almost 30% of our population.
- One of the most serious eating disorders is anorexia nervosa, a condition in which an individual refuses to maintain a normal body weight because of an intense fear of becoming fat.

- Bulimia is a disorder of binge eating and the use of inappropriate methods to prevent weight gain.
- Obesity is defined as an excess of body weight.
- The main therapeutic goal for treating all eating disorders is to establish eating behaviors that promote health.
- The main goals for nurses who care for persons with eating disorders are to assist their clients in identifying and coping with the problems that led them to their inappropriate eating behaviors.
- A sleeping disorder is a condition or problem that repeatedly disrupts an individual's pattern of sleep.
- Dyssomnias are characterized by abnormalities in the amount, quality, or timing of sleep.
- Sleep disorders characterized by abnormal behavioral or physical events during sleep are called parasomnias.
- Sleep disorders can also result from medical, psychological, or drug-induced conditions.
- The first step in the treatment of sleep disorders is to teach good sleep hygiene habits.
- Nursing interventions to promote sleep are aimed at promoting comfort, controlling physical disturbances, and maintaining a quiet, restful environment.

❖ SUGGESTIONS FOR FURTHER READING

You are encouraged to review your basic nursing texts in relation to the functions of food and sleep. See how the tools for conducting dietary and sleeping pattern assessments are helpful in mental health nursing.

❖ REFERENCES

Allen T: Sleepless in Seattle . . . and San Francisco, Syracuse, Shreveport . . . : evaluating and treating insomnia, *Adv Nurse Pract* 2(4):26, 1994.

American Psychiatric Association: *Diagnostic and statistical manual of mental disorders,* ed 4, Washington, DC, 1994, The Association.

Brouwers M, Wiggum CD: Bulimia and perfectionism: developing the courage to be imperfect, *J Ment Health Counsel* 15(2):142, 1993.

Cameron AM: Body image and weight control, *Dietet Curr* 20(1):1, 1993.

Carley J, Rooda L: Help for eating disorders, *Adv Nurse Pract* 3(9):31, 1995.

Centers for Disease Control: Prevalence of overweight among adolescents-United States, 1988-1991, *JAMA* 272(22):1737, 1994.

Elias M: Hormone research: the mysteries of melatonin, *Harvard Ment Health Lett* 18(8):6, 1993.

Gorbein MJ: When your older patient can't sleep: how to put insomnia to rest, *Geriatrics* 48(9):65, 1993.

Irwin EG: A focused overview of anorexia nervosa and bulimia: part 1—etiological issues, *Arch Psychiatr Nurs* 7(6):342, 1993.

Leon GR and others: Personality and behavioral vulnerabilities with risk status for eating disorders in adolescent girls, *J Abnorm Psychol* 102(3):438, 1993.

Mishima K and others: Morning bright light therapy for sleep and behavior disorders in elderly patients with dementia, *Acta Psychiatr Scandi* 89(1):1, 1994.

Potter PA, Perry AG: *Basic nursing: theory and practice,* ed 3, St Louis, 1995, Mosby.

Serdula MK and others: Weight control practices of U.S. teens and adults, *Ann Intern Med* 119(7):667, 1993.

U.S. Bureau of Census: *Statistical abstract of the U.S.: 1993,* ed 113, Washington, DC, 1993.

Wong DL: *Whaley and Wong's nursing care of infants and children,* ed 5, St Louis, 1995, Mosby.

Vitousek K, Manke F: Personality variables in anorexia nervosa and bulimia nervosa, *J Abnorm Psychol* 103(1):137, 1994.

24

DISSOCIATIVE DISORDERS

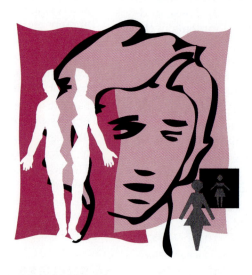

1. Explain the meaning of the term *self-concept.*
2. Describe the continuum of self-concept responses.
3. Discuss the development of self-concept throughout the life cycle.
4. List the main characteristic of dissociative disorders.
5. Identify and describe four types of dissociative disorders.
6. Name the outstanding feature of a dissociative identity (multiple personality) disorder.
7. State the main goal of treatment for clients with dissociative disorders.
8. List three nursing diagnoses for clients with dissociative disorders.
9. Develop a care plan for a client who has been diagnosed with a dissociative disorder.

KEY TERMS

ageism
amnesia
depersonalization
dissociation
dissociative disorder

dissociative identity disorder (DID)
fugue
identity diffusion
personal identity
role performances

self-concept
self-esteem
self-ideal
trance

uman beings differ from the most complex animals in a significant way: they are aware of themselves and have a concept of self. As children grow and develop, they learn to identify and define themselves as individuals. They develop a picture (a point of view) of who they are, and then they use that picture as a framework for perceiving, experiencing, and evaluating the world. This point of view becomes one's self-concept.

Self-concept is defined as all the attitudes, notions, beliefs, and convictions that make up a person's self-knowledge. "It includes the individual's perceptions of personal characteristics and abilities, interactions with other people and the environment, values, associated experiences and objects, and goals and ideals" (Stuart and Sundeen, 1995).

The development of self-concept is influenced by many factors. The culture into which an individual is born and the society in which one lives have a strong impact on self-concept. The attitudes and beliefs of parents, siblings, and other significant people influence how an individual defines himself/herself. The experiences of life also shape and influence one's picture of the self.

Self-concept is the frame of reference through which people view the world. It is the sum of several components, including body image, the attitudes and feeling one has for his/her body; **self-esteem,** an individual's judgment of his/her own worth; **self-ideal,** personal standards of how one should behave; **personal identity,** an awareness of oneself as an individual; and **role performances,** socially expected behavioral patterns. All these parts of an individual fuse and blend over time into the unique human characteristics called self-concept.

Continuum of Self-Concept Responses

People behave based in large part on their self-concept. The range of behavioral responses relating to self-concept can be seen as occurring on a continuum. At the adaptive end, a healthy self-concept leads one toward self-actualization. Low self-concept results in maladaptive behavioral responses as individuals struggle to define who they are (Fig. 24-1).

The Healthy Personality

Persons with healthy personalities are able to effectively perceive and function within their worlds (Fortinash and Holoday-Worret, 1996). They have achieved a sense of peace and harmony within themselves that allows them to successfully cope with life's anxieties, traumas, and crises. A realistic self-ideal and a clear personal identity help to provide these individuals with a sense of purpose and direction in life. High self-esteem and confidence provide them the strength to handle anxieties and learn from life's highs and lows. Socially they are satisfied with the roles they play in society. They have the ability to intimately relate to others and to share themselves without fear. In short, individuals with healthy personalities are able to struggle with life's problems while feeling good about living (see box below).

> **THINK ABOUT**
> Using the five components of a healthy personality, assess yourself.
> How do you compare to the description of a person with a healthy personality?

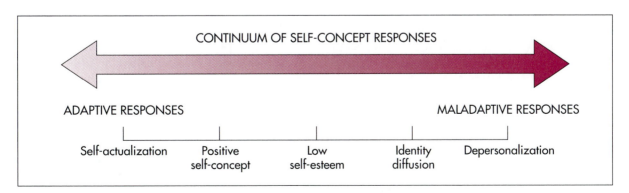

Fig. 24-1   Continuum of self-concept responses. (Redrawn from Stuart GW, Sundeen SJ: *Principles and practice of psychiatric nursing,* ed 5, St Louis, 1995, Mosby.)

Self-Concept Throughout the Life Cycle

Self-concept develops over time, shaped by the influences within one's environment. The theorist, Erik Erikson, in describing his eight stages of human development, stated that a psychosocial crisis or core task must be resolved for further personality development. As each task is completed, one's self-concept is affected. Mastery of core tasks builds self-confidence, worth, and esteem (Wong, 1995). If, however, one is unable to cope with a core task, ineffective or maladaptive behaviors result. This process, according to Erikson, continues throughout life.

Self-Concept in Childhood

Infants do not view themselves as separate from the rest of the world (Clunn, 1995). Only after a period of time do they begin to distinguish themselves as different from their mother or father. Infants learn to trust others when their needs are consistently met. After a series of social experiences, they develop stable relationships with other people and learn to feel good about themselves. Rejection by parents or significant others at this time has a strong negative effect on an individual's self-concept.

Toddlers' tasks are to explore the limits of their abilities, and these tasks include the nature of their impact on others. Toddlers learn to be independent by exploring their environments and testing their capabilities. They develop their autonomy and their sense of self by experimenting with a variety of behaviors. The actions that get results are effective, even if they are inappropriate, and they are added to the general knowledge of the child. Behaviors that are not rewarded or do not get results are discarded. In this way, children learn about "right and wrong," and they use this information as a framework for their self-ideal. When parental reactions are routine and consistent, children develop a stable sense of who they are and a stable self-concept. When the reactions of significant others change or differ, children become confused and have trouble establishing a positive personal identity and healthy self-concept.

School-aged children become aware of different perspectives of life. They learn about social norms, peer pressures, and moral issues. Skill building and broadening social relationships keep them constantly occupied with self-evaluations. Self-concept continues to develop as school-aged children assess their skills and interactions with others to form mental pictures of themselves. If the picture is positive, the move into adolescence is graceful; but if self-concept is low or threatened, adolescence is filled with anxiety and turmoil.

Self-Concept in Adolescence

By the early teen years, the comfortable self-concept of childhood is challenged. As adolescents mature, they begin to develop a more complex picture of themselves. Self-concept becomes more individual and is based on one's special characteristics rather than on the similarities shared by others. Thinking becomes more abstract (Hogarth, 1995). Self-reflection is needed to digest all the physical, emotional, and social changes that take place during adolescence.

During adolescence, self-concept is influenced by many things. Relationships with family and peers play an important role in helping to define teens' confidence levels. The development of a sexual identity and the adjustment to a new adult body image must be included in the new concept of self. Adolescence is a time of maturing from the narrowed self-concept of the child to the broader, stronger adult self-concept. The struggle is to define oneself by combining previous roles and new emotions into a reasonably consistent and pleasing sense of self. Without the love, nurturing, and guidance of concerned adults, many teens do not finish the task of developing a comfortable self-concept. They are ill-prepared to assume the many responsibilities of adult life because the struggle to find themselves continues.

Self-Concept in Adulthood

Adults with strong, positive self-concepts can freely explore their environments because they have a background of success and effectiveness. Positive experiences further enhance self-concept, and the cycle of learning, succeeding, and growth repeats itself.

If, however, the concept of oneself is low, weak, or negative, individuals develop views of themselves as inadequate or unable. These people become easily threatened, which in turn increases anxiety levels and forces them to become preoccupied with defending themselves. Soon, this cycle becomes a way of life, and individuals find themselves caught in the trap of looking only at the negative or "down" side of life. The cycle of few successes and much negative reinforcement becomes established, and the adult suffers from a poor self-concept. Most adults function somewhere between these two extremes.

Self-Concept in Older Adulthood

Self-concept is established in childhood, developed in adolescence, strengthened in adulthood, and refined in older adulthood. "In later life there are many occurrences and situations that are threatening to a positive self-concept" (Hogstel, 1994). **Ageism,** the stereotyping of older persons as feeble, dependent, and nonproductive, has contributed to older adults' self-concepts. Threats to the stability of one's lifestyle, such as changes in occupation, social standing, or environment, often lead to changes in self-concept. Nurses can enhance older clients' feelings of self-worth through active listening and demonstrations of caring concern.

Dissociative Disorders

Depersonalization and dissociation lie at the other end of the self-concept spectrum and represent attempts to cope with anxiety or deep-seated emotional distress. Low self-esteem lies somewhere in the middle.

Low self-esteem is a problem for many persons. It is usually expressed through various levels of anxiety and involves feelings of being weak, inadequate, and helpless (see box at right). Low self-esteem is a common component of many mental health problems. It often represents feelings of self-rejection and dislike that are expressed through various behaviors.

The next step in the spectrum of maladaptive self-concept behaviors is **identity diffusion**—the failure to bring various childhood identifications into an effective adult personality. Individuals with identity diffusion are not sure of who they really are because they have been unable to build their "picture" of themselves. They drift through life, like a boat without a rudder, unable to set a course or steer themselves around obstacles.

Not knowing who one is does nothing to foster the development of strong interpersonal relationships. Although these people have feelings of emptiness and anxiety, they often exploit others. Feelings of empathy are often lacking. This leads to problems with intimacy and a lack of caring. Because the self-ideal is confused, moral codes or standards of behavior are often missing (Keltner, Schwecke, and Bostrom, 1995). Frequently, they are so desperate to define themselves that they attempt to bind their self-concepts to another. This type of identity diffusion is called *personality fusing.*

When behaviors at the maladaptive end of the self-concept response continuum interfere with an individual's ability to function, a mental health problem exists. The mental health problems that relate to anxiety and self-concept are called the dissociative disorders.

Characteristics

Dissociation is "the disconnection from full awareness of self, time, and/or external circumstances" (Turkus, 1992). It is a complicated neuropsychological process that "exists along a continuum from normal everyday experiences to disorders that interfere with everyday functioning" (Turkus, 1992). Examples of

BEHAVIORS ASSOCIATED WITH LOW SELF-ESTEEM

CRITICISM OF SELF AND OTHERS
"Doomed to failure" outlook
Negative thinking
Sees normal life stresses as impossible barriers

DECREASED PRODUCTIVITY
Does not complete tasks
Postpones decisions
Works below level of actual abilities

DENIES SELF PLEASURE
Feels need to be punished so refuses things that are pleasurable
Rejects personal strengths and assets

DESTRUCTIVE TOWARD SELF AND OTHERS
May displace self-hate onto others
Becomes accident prone or engages in dangerous activities
Suicide is ultimate act of self-rejection

DISTURBED INTERPERSONAL RELATIONSHIPS
Exploits others
May be demeaning, cruel, withdrawn, or isolated

EXAGGERATED SENSE OF SELF-IMPORTANCE
May boast, brag, or describe special abilities
Makes up for low self-esteem with grandiose thinking
Sets unrealistic goals; has unrealistic dreams

FEELINGS OF GUILT, INADEQUACY, AND WORRY
Uses destructive activities to punish self
Rejects self through nightmares, obsessions, phobias, or reliving of distressing memories
Is irritable and easily angered

NEGATIVE OUTLOOK ABOUT ONE'S BODY, ABILITIES, AND LIFE
Has polarized view of life; everything is either right or wrong, good or bad
Rejects aspects of self that have potential for growth
Refuses to consider real strengths and assets
Has physical complaints and problems

WITHDRAWAL
Becomes socially isolated
May withdraw from reality when anxiety of self-rejection reaches severe levels
May have delusions, hallucinations, dissociation, jealousy, suspicion, paranoia

Modified from Stuart GW, Sundeen SJ: *Principles and practice of psychiatric nursing*, ed 5, St Louis, 1995, Mosby.

normal dissociations are daydreaming or becoming so absorbed in an activity that one loses a sense of time and surroundings.

Children dissociate more easily than adults. When faced with overwhelming abuse or trauma, children psychologically escape or flee their distresses by blocking emotionally damaging information from awareness. Dissociation, when used as a defense in childhood, can grow into a dissociative disorder.

A **dissociative disorder** is a disturbance in the normally interacting functions of consciousness: identity, memory, and perception. With a dissociative disorder, the most anxiety-producing aspects of the self are walled off or split from the remainder of the personality in an attempt to cope with overwhelming anxiety and emotional trauma.

Although they once were considered rare, new evidence (Coons, 1994; Irwin, 1994) reveals that dissociative disorders are becoming more common in the United States, especially in the many individuals who were neglected or abused in childhood. Dissociative

disorders are diagnosed more frequently in women. In other countries, such as Japan, England, and France, the incidence of diagnosed dissociative disorders is low (Kingsbury, 1995). Several interesting culturally defined mental health disorders involving dissociative states are described in Table 24-1.

When the disturbance of a dissociative disorder occurs primarily with memory or consciousness, amnesia or fugue (inability to remember important personal events or travels) results. If the disturbance is with one's identity, parts of the self assume separate personalities, and a dissociative identity (multiple personality) disorder is diagnosed. Posttraumatic stress disorder, although considered an anxiety disorder, is actually a recall of past traumatic events alternating with detachment or dissociation. "All of the disorders are trauma-based, and symptoms result from the habitual dissociation of traumatic memories" (Turkus, 1992). Like the body walls off the infection of an abscess, the mind walls off the extreme distresses of trauma and anxiety. Four types of dissociative dis-

◆ **TABLE 24-1**
Cultural Aspects: Culturally Defined Mental Health Disorders Involving Dissociative States

Disorder	Culture(s)	Description
Amok	Malaysia, Laos, Philippines, Polynesia, Puerto Rico, Navajo	Period of brooding followed by outbursts of aggressive, violent behavior; found only in males
Ataque de nervios	Latinos	Uncontrollable shouting, crying, fainting, and suicidal gestures following stressful event
Falling out	Southern United States, Caribbean groups	Sudden collapse; eyes are open, but individual is unable to see; hears and understands but feels powerless to move
Latah	Japan (imu), Philippines (mali-mali), Thailand	Excessive reactions to sudden fright; trancelike behavior with command obedience, echolalia
Pibloktoq	Arctic and subarctic Eskimos	Extreme excitement and irrational behavior followed by seizures and coma lasting up to 12 hours
Qi-gong psychotic reaction	Chinese	Acute episode of psychotic behaviors following folk practice of qi-gong, the exercise of vital energy
Shin-byung	Korean	Anxiety and somatic complaints that progress to dissociation and possession by ancestral spirits
Spell	African-American, European, Americans from southern United States	Trance in which communication with deceased relatives or spirits takes place
Zar	Egypt, Ethiopia, Iran, Sudan	Spirit possession that interferes with daily activities; may develop long-term relationship with spirit and withdraw from reality

Modified from American Psychiatric Association: *Diagnostic and statistical manual of mental disorders,* ed 4, Washington, DC, 1994, The Association.

orders are classified by the *Diagnostic and Statistical Manual of Mental Disorders* (DSM-IV). They are depersonalization disorder, amnesia, fugue, and identity disorder.

Depersonalization Disorder

During an episode of **depersonalization,** one feels detached or unconnected to the self (Rollant and Deppoliti, 1996). The individual may feel like a robot, working on automatic. There may be a sensation of being an outside observer and of not really being involved.

Depersonalization is a normal response to severe anxiety. It is associated with a blocking of awareness and a fading of reality. One becomes unable to tell the difference between internal and external stimuli because the self-concept becomes disorganized. The body takes on an unreal quality, and the world becomes a dream.

During periods of extreme stress or anxiety, depersonalization serves as a defense mechanism; however, it does nothing to relieve the cause or the distress, so it becomes a maladaptive behavior. In cases in which depersonalization becomes a mental health problem, the individuals react in response to feeling unloved and unwanted. When this response is carried to extreme, people "escape" distress and anxiety by losing their own identities.

Depersonalization is a pattern of maladaptive behavioral responses because it does not deal with the cause of a person's distress. Table 24-2 lists the physical, emotional, intellectual, and behavioral characteristics of this behavioral pattern. Depersonalization is commonly associated with other mental disorders including acute stress disorder, panic disorder, and schizophrenia. These mental health problems can suddenly follow a life-threatening event or develop slowly after years of distress.

In several cultures, dissociative trances and experiences are a part of religious or spiritual practices. Frequently, the devout will enter into altered states in which they communicate or interact with spirits or beings. Nurses who work with clients from different cultural backgrounds must be alert to the customs and practices of the culture (see Table 24-1).

Dissociative Amnesia

Amnesia is a loss of memory. Dissociative amnesia is characterized by an inability to remember personal information that cannot be explained by ordinary forgetfulness. It is an attempt to avoid extreme stress by blocking the memories from consciousness.

Individuals with dissociative amnesia usually have gaps in their ability to recall certain events during their childhood. Most of these lapses in memory are related to extremely stressful events. For example, a rape victim often has no memory of the attack but still experiences the emotional numbness, depression, and distress associated with the trauma. Sights, sounds, odors, and images can trigger emotional distresses long after the event has occurred. Actual memories are too painful to consider, so they stay buried, submerged but not forgotten, walled off but still capable of inflicting pain.

◆ TABLE 24-2
Behaviors Associated With Depersonalization

Areas of Functioning	Description
Affective (emotional)	Feels identity is lost
	Lacks sense of inner togetherness
	Unable to feel pleasure or pride
	Feelings of detachment from self, fear, insecurity, shame, unreality
Behavioral (social)	Affect blunted; emotionally unresponsive and passive; not lively or spontaneous
	Communications odd or difficult to follow
	Loss of drive, decision-making abilities, impulse control
	Social isolation and withdrawal
Cognitive (intellectual)	Confusion; distorted thinking and memory; impaired judgment; disoriented to time
Perceptual (physical)	Dreamlike experiences of world
	Difficulty telling self from others
	Disturbed body image and sexuality
	Auditory and visual hallucinations

Modified from Stuart GW, Sundeen SJ: *Principles and practice of psychiatric nursing,* ed 5, St Louis, 1995, Mosby.

Nurses must remember that these clients require high levels of emotional support. Client safety becomes a primary nursing goal because suicide attempts are common. Although memory may be gone, the emotional distresses still remain. Clients' connections with other human beings are sometimes the only link on the road back to mental health.

Dissociative Fugue

One of the most interesting dissociative disorders is the rare but dramatic amnesiac fugue. The word **fugue** means to escape from reality. The main characteristic of dissociative fugue is sudden, unexpected travel with an inability to recall the past. A fugue occurs in response to an overwhelmingly stressful or traumatic event. It is an extreme expression of the fight-flight mechanism, engaged to protect the individual.

For persons with dissociative fugue, travels may range from a few miles away from home to another continent. Individuals behave quite normally during periods of travel but are confused about their personal identities, which is what frequently brings them to the attention of authorities. Some individuals assume entirely new identities, complete with a new occupation and significant others. The box below describes an interesting case history of fugue.

During an actual fugue, few personality changes are noticeable. Individuals may be more friendly and outgoing, but their behaviors remain appropriate. After the return to the prefugue state, individuals may experience aggressive impulses, conflict, depression, guilt, and suicidal wishes. There may be loss of memory for the events that occurred during the time of the fugue. Recovery is usually rapid, but some amnesia may remain. Here, too, psychosocial nursing care and emotional support are important in the recovery of these people.

Dissociative Trance Disorder

A **trance** is defined as a state resembling sleep in which consciousness remains but voluntary movement is lost. In many cultures, trances are expressions of spiritual or religious beliefs. Cultural trances are entered into voluntarily and cause no distress or harm to the individuals. "Studies show that channelers, psychics, spirit guides, shamans, and the like are rarely mentally impaired" (Kingsbury, 1995).

Cultural influences also have an impact on the type of trance, the associated sensory disturbances, and the behaviors exhibited during the trance. Culturally normative trances involve signs/symptoms and behaviors that are expected by other members of the culture. During these kind of trances, individuals do not lose their identities.

CASE STUDY

Amy was only 3 when she was first abused by her father. By 4, she was hiding when she heard his footsteps coming down the hall; at 6, Amy was slipping out the window to escape.

During those occasions when he could not be avoided, Amy played a game in her mind in which she would fly away to a land where everyone was kind and carried no evil in their hearts. She would wish and dream and hope during those times, ignoring the pain and distress of being violated over and over.

By the time Amy was 13, she had run away from home. Luckily, she found a youth shelter early in her wanderings. There the staff members were understanding and had a genuine interest in seeing Amy survive her adolescence without the pain of her childhood. She stayed at the shelter for about 6 months, learning the skills that were needed for adulthood. Soon Amy became very efficient in coordinating and supervising the daily household events.

Because of her newly learned organizational abilities, Amy was offered a position as a teacher's assistant at the local grade school where she remained for many years. By the time she was 30, Amy had buried the memories of her abuse and forgotten the pain of her childhood. She was married and looking forward to a bright future.

Amy's father became seriously ill the following year. He was alone and in need of care. After having no communication with Amy in 20 years, he wrote to ask if he could come and live with Amy and her family.

The letter arrived and Amy stared, horrified, at the return address. Six months later, she remembers nothing more: not the trip to San Francisco, not the bus ride to Colorado, not even her new fiancé. Today, she can hardly remember who she really is.

Clinical Decisions

1. What happened after Amy read the return address on the letter?
2. If Amy had been admitted to your unit, what psychosocial interventions would you include in the care plan?

Possession trances involve the appearance of one or more distinct identities, which direct the individual to perform sometimes complex behaviors and activities such as culturally appropriate conversations, gestures, or facial expressions. Amnesia following either type of trance state is not uncommon, but it occurs more frequently with possession trances.

A *dissociative trance disorder* exists when trances cause "clinically significant distress or functional impairment" (American Psychiatric Association, 1994). Dissociative trance disorders are listed in the DSM-IV in the category of "diagnoses in need of further study." However, the fact remains that if trances cause a great deal of anxiety and distress in an individual, he/she can likely benefit from psychotherapeutic interventions.

Dissociative Identity Disorder

When stress or trauma is repeated and severe, the personality attempts to protect itself. Abused children use dissociation to escape, distance, and defend themselves from the anxiety, trauma, and helplessness of reality. "Major studies have confirmed the traumatic origins of dissociative identity disorder, which arises before the age of 12 (and often before the age of 5) as a result of severe physical, sexual, and/or emotional abuse" (Turkus, 1992).

A **dissociative identity disorder (DID)** is defined as the presence of two or more identities/personalities that repeatedly take control of the individual's behavior. Dissociative identity disorder develops as a defense against prolonged and inescapable trauma. This syndrome "enables individuals to split off feelings and memories so that they do not become paralyzed by anxiety, fear, rage, or depression" (Riley, 1995).

The diagnosis of DID, which was formerly called multiple personality disorder, occurs more often in the United States than other countries. Some believe that this is a result of better diagnostic tools, whereas others think that DID is overdiagnosed or view it as a culturally related syndrome.

The essential features of DID are associated with the presence of other personalities in one individual. These persons often have a personal history full of time losses, unexplained possessions or changes in relationships, out-of-body experiences, and the awareness of other parts of the self. A history of abuse or trauma is not always identified because emotions are deeply buried.

When different personalities do emerge, each has its own way of thinking about and relating to the world. Each personality is unique and often represents the individual at different developmental stages.

The identities may be helpful, controlling, seductive, or destructive to self or others, but each serves a specific protective purpose. They may differ in age, gender, knowledge, state of health, speech, and behaviors. The primary personality (called the host) may or may not be aware of the presence of the other personalities. Usually, the transition from one personality to the other is sudden and related to stress. At least two identities repeatedly take control of the individual's behavior. Sometimes the identities cooperate with each other, but more often they attempt to take control and refuse to share knowledge with the others (Spanos, 1994). Hostility or open conflict can result among the more powerful personalities.

Individuals with dissociative problems, especially DID, often have symptoms of posttraumatic stress syndrome (nightmares, flashbacks, extreme startle responses). Other mental or physical health problems are frequently present, especially with some of the identities found in DID (Saxe and others, 1994). The goal of treatment for clients is to help the client integrate or combine the personalities into one functional individual, capable of coping with life's stresses in a healthy manner.

Therapeutic Interventions

Treatment for dissociative disorders involves long-term psychodynamic/cognitive therapy in an outpatient setting. Hospitalization is required only in three situations:

1. When anger, aggression, or violence is directed toward self or others and presents a danger
2. When individuals are unable to function because of memory loss, rapid switching between identities, flashbacks, or overwhelming emotions
3. When medications need to be evaluated or adjusted

The stages of treatment for dissociative disorders relate to assessment, stabilization, and reworking past traumas. The most effective results are seen when clients with dissociative disorders are able to work with stable, established multidisciplinary treatment teams.

Treatments and Therapies

Therapy for clients with dissociative disorders begins with *assessment* and *stabilization*. Because the work of coping with deeply seated trauma is difficult and emotionally demanding, an environment in which clients can safely examine their conflicts must first be established. A careful assessment includes the client's history, symptoms, support systems, medical status, relationships and his/her problems, and the presence of substance abuse and sleeping or eating disorders. Family history should include both the family of origin and the current family situation.

During the stabilization phase, the diagnosis is established as the client gradually reveals the complexities of his/her nature. After each treatment team member assesses the client, a plan for stabilization is jointly developed. Therapies are carefully chosen and may include individual psychotherapy, group therapy, family therapy, psychoeducation, and various expressive therapies, such as art, poetry, and dance. Contracts to ensure safety during therapy are established. During this time, clients and care providers develop trust in each other and build client support networks. Although this part of treatment may last for over a year, it is an essential step for the work to come.

The next phase of treatment involves revisiting and *reworking past traumas.* Once the client develops an awareness of other personalities and their purposes, the painful material is slowly and gently analyzed. Each identity is treated equally with respect and is encouraged to communicate with the others. Feelings of shame, guilt, anger, and grief are encountered as each traumatic event is encountered. With time, patience, and hard work, the client eventually begins to integrate or combine the memories (or personalities) into a unique individual who is able to effectively cope with life's stressors, which is the main treatment goal for clients with dissociative disorders.

Pharmacological Therapy

No specific medication exists at this time to treat amnesia, fugues, or other dissociative behaviors. Treatment is often based on symptoms. If high anxiety is apparent, antianxiety agents may be prescribed. When depression is intense, an antidepressant may be ordered. If hallucinations or delusions are commonly present, an antipsychotic medication may be administered. All medications are prescribed for only short periods to encourage the use of inner coping skills.

Nursing Process

As with all other mental health clients, assessments are routinely performed on clients with dissociative disorders. Clients with dissociative disorders can present different pictures to various staff members to manipulate and divide their care providers. They may offer one side of themselves during one minute, and then during the next moment a personality that wants to pick a fight emerges. Assessments should describe the client's behaviors and statements. A much clearer picture is given with descriptions than with psychiatric "buzz words" or jargon.

Nursing diagnoses for clients with dissociative disorders are related to self-concept responses. They may range from impaired adjustment to risk for violence, depending on the identified nursing problems of each client. However, the expected outcome for each nursing diagnosis is a client who is able to obtain his/her maximum level of effective functioning and self-actualization. Primary or main nursing diagnoses include disturbances in personal identity, body image, self-esteem, and role performance.

After clients have established trust with the nursing staff, interventions are directed at helping them examine their situations and related feelings in an environment of safety and support. This process assists the growth of personal insight, the first step toward making behavioral changes. A problem-solving approach helps clients to gradually expand self-awareness, explore and evaluate the self, and eventually plan for actions that result in behavior changes. Clients are emotionally supported and encouraged to actively take part in therapy.

Some clients with dissociative disorders engage in self-destructive behaviors. They may cut, bite, or repeatedly hit themselves or pull out their hair. Because self-destructive behavior is of great concern to care providers, several interventions have been devised to assist clients in achieving control over these behaviors.

First, clients must be routinely assessed for self-destructive thoughts. The easiest way to find out if such thoughts are occurring is to ask the client. Contracts and agreements between client and staff help staff and client to develop trust in the therapeutic relationship and environment. During the admission process, ways of dealing with destructive behaviors should be discussed with the client. If necessary, one-to-one support is provided until the client can achieve self-control.

If the client is willing, a daily journal of thoughts and feelings is kept. This practice has been found to be an "extremely helpful self-control activity" (Riley, 1995). Nurses and other care providers should be limited to a few personnel to provide a stable therapeutic environment. A sample care plan for a client with a dissociative disorder is presented in the box on p. 343.

The care and treatment of individuals with dissociative problems is complex, time-consuming, and challenging. Numerous nursing diagnoses apply to these clients, but the needs of each individual client guide the selection of the most important diagnoses.

Individuals who have been diagnosed with dissociative disorders are suffering from one of the worst human fears: the fear of not knowing and of being out of control over oneself. Although the behaviors may be odd, unusual, or dramatic, each serves a purpose

SAMPLE CLIENT CARE PLAN
MALADAPTIVE SELF-CONCEPT

Assessment

History: Christine is a 35-year-old wife and mother of three children, ages 15, 10, and 7. Although she experienced severe sexual and physical abuse as a child, she has managed to complete college, marry, and raise her family. She is being admitted to the clinic's mental health services for "several episodes of losing myself" that she has experienced in the past 5 months (since her oldest daughter began dating).

Today Christine is distressed because yesterday she was unable to remember to pick up her daughter's dress at the cleaners. Because of this, her daughter refused to attend the school dance and threatened to run away. Lately, Christine has felt like an "outside observer of my own life," "like a robot on automatic." During these episodes she is aware of reality but feels like everything is mechanical. She feels that she may be "going insane" because the "spells" are becoming more and more frequent since her daughter has begun dating.

Nursing Diagnosis

Personal identity disorder related to increased anxiety and past history of abuse

Planning/Expected Outcomes

Christine will decrease the number of depersonalization episodes to fewer than one a week by May 20. Christine will be able to recognize her anxiety and take steps to decrease it before it progresses to a depersonalization episode.

Nursing Interventions

Intervention

1. Establish therapeutic relationship; confirm her identity; support adaptive behaviors; identify strengths.
2. Assist Christine to describe thoughts and feelings.
3. Identify stresses that bring about her "spells."

4. Help to clarify faulty beliefs about self.

5. Encourage Christine to make a plan for decreasing her anxiety during times her daughter is on a date; role play mother-daughter roles.
6. Reinforce strengths, assets, and problem-solving abilities; encourage Christine to focus on her "positives."

Rationale

1. Provides a way of offering emotional support; builds trust; supports adaptive behaviors client already has.
2. Identification is the first step toward focused change.
3. Known stressors can be handled more effectively.
4. Builds confidence; helps focus energies in positive direction.
5. Recalling and using successful strategies helps to decrease anxiety levels, thus preventing depersonalization episodes.

6. Helps to improve coping abilities and ease the pain of feeling powerless.

Evaluation

Christine was able to decrease her episodes of depersonalization to less than one a week by May 29.

and communicates something about the person. Nurses and the other health care providers are challenged with the twin tasks of accepting and understanding the messages sent by dissociated individuals. Treatment of clients with backgrounds of trauma is complex and at times frustrating. At the same time, it can be a rewarding nursing experience.

❖ KEY CONCEPTS

- Self-concept is defined as all the attitudes, notions, beliefs, and convictions that make up an individual's self-knowledge.

- Self-concept develops over time, shaped by one's developmental level and the influences within one's environment.

- Low self-esteem is a common component of many mental health problems and often represents feelings of self-rejection and self-dislike, which are expressed through various behaviors.

- Identity diffusion is the failure to bring various childhood identifications into an effective adult personality.

- Dissociation is a complicated neuropsychological process in which one is disconnected from full awareness of self, time, or external circumstances.

- Dissociative amnesia is characterized by an inability to remember personal information that cannot be explained by ordinary forgetfulness.

- The main characteristic of a dissociative fugue is sudden, unexpected travel, with an inability to recall the past.

- A trance is a state resembling sleep in which consciousness remains but voluntary movement is lost.

- A dissociative identity disorder (DID) is defined as the presence of two or more identities/personalities that repeatedly take control of the individual's behavior.

- Treatment for dissociative disorders involves long-term psychodynamic/cognitive therapy.

- There are no specific psychotherapeutic drugs for the treatment of dissociative disorders.

- Nursing interventions for clients with dissociative disorders focus on safety, trust, communication, and problem solving.

❖ SUGGESTIONS FOR FURTHER READING

This suggestion involves an old movie. *The Three Faces of Eve* is an old but very accurate portrayal of a woman who is suffering from dissociative identity disorder with several interesting and conflicting personalities.

❖ REFERENCES

American Psychiatric Association: *Diagnostic and statistical manual of mental disorders,* ed 4, Washington, DC, 1994, The Association.

Clunn P, editor: *Child psychiatric nursing,* ed 2, St Louis, 1995, Mosby.

Coons PM: Confirmation of childhood abuse in child and adolescent cases of multiple personality disorder and dissociative disorder not otherwise specified, *J Nerv Ment Dis* 182:461, 1994.

Fortinash KM, Holoday-Worret PA: *Psychiatric-mental health nursing,* St Louis, 1996, Mosby.

Hogarth CR: *Adolescent psychiatric nursing,* ed 2, St Louis, 1995, Mosby.

Hogstel MO: *Geropsychiatric nursing,* ed 2, St Louis, 1994.

Irwin HJ: Proneness to dissociation and traumatic childhood events, *J Nerv Ment Dis* 182:456, 1994.

Keltner NL, Schwecke LH, Bostrom CE: *Psychiatric nursing,* ed 2, St Louis, 1995, Mosby.

Kingsbury SJ: What is dissociative trance disorder? *Harvard Ment Health Lett* 11(9):8, 1995.

Riley E: I am what I am: inpatient treatment for people with dissociative identity disorder, *Caps Comm Psychiatr Nurs* 2(2):94, 1995.

Rollant PD, Deppoliti DB: *Mosby's review series: mental health nursing,* St Louis, 1996, Mosby.

Saxe GN and others: Somatization in patients with dissociative disorders, *Am J Psychiatry* 151:1329, 1994.

Spanos NP: Multiple identity enactments and multiple personality disorder: a sociocognitive perspective, *Psychol Bull* 116(1):143, 1994.

Stuart GW, Sundeen SJ: *Principles and practice of psychiatric nursing,* ed 5, St Louis, 1995, Mosby.

Turkus JA: The spectrum of dissociative disorders: an overview of diagnosis and treatment, *Moving Forward* May/June 1992.

Wong DL: *Whaley and Wong's nursing care of infants and children,* ed 5, St Louis, 1995, Mosby.

UNIT 5

CLIENTS WITH PSYCHOSOCIAL PROBLEMS

25

ANGER AND AGGRESSION

LEARNING OBJECTIVES

1. Explain the differences between anger, aggression, and assertiveness.
2. Describe how anger is expressed by children, adolescents, young adults, and older adults.
3. Discuss the impact of anger and aggression on society.
4. List three theories that attempt to explain the causes of aggression.
5. Describe each of the five stages of the assault cycle.
6. State the main characteristics for three mental health disorders that relate to anger or aggression.
7. Describe the process for assessing clients who are angry or aggressive.
8. List four nursing interventions for clients who are experiencing anger or acting aggressively.
9. Describe seven techniques for recognizing and coping with your own anger.

KEY TERMS

acting out
aggression
anger

assault
assertiveness
battery

impulse-control
passive aggression
violence

Anger is a normal emotional response to a perceived threat, frustration, or distressing event. It commonly occurs in reaction to feelings of being threatened or losing control. In a crisis situation, anger is often one of the first coping behaviors used.

Anger can serve several purposes. It can be used as a coping mechanism by some people to meet their needs. According to Maslow's hierarchy (ladder) of human needs, when basic needs are threatened, a person may react with anger. The client who feels powerless at the news of his prolonged recovery may react to the threat of being an invalid by insulting others, or the child who flies into temper tantrums may be attempting to meet the human needs that are required for survival and growth.

Anger can also serve to motivate or encourage a person to act. The college student who as a child felt the anxiety and helplessness of watching her mother being beaten and now studies to become a lawyer and champion of abused people illustrates the use of anger to motivate positive action.

In addition, anger can serve as an opportunity for learning about oneself. When the emotional response is anger, it allows us the opportunity to analyze or look at the reasons behind the anger. Often the cause of anger is unimportant and not worth carrying around.

Anger is an emotion. It is felt, experienced, or suffered. Anger can be expressed in many ways. It can be directed outward as overt or passive aggressive behaviors, or it can be focused inward on oneself. Table 25-1 lists many expressions of anger. Many of the listed emotions and actions, although not pleasant, are appropriate expressions of anger. However, when anger provides the motivation for inappropriate behaviors, it becomes defined as a problem.

◆ TABLE 25-1
Expressions of Anger

Turned Outward		Turned Inward	
Overt Anger	**Passive Aggression**	**Subjective**	**Objective**
Verbalization of anger	Impatience	Feeling upset	Crying
Irritation	Pouting	Tension	Self-destructive behavior
Pacing with agitation	Sulking	Unhappiness	Self-mutilation
Swearing	Frustration	Feeling hurt	Substance abuse
Hostility	Tense facial expressions	Disappointment	Suicide
Contempt	Pessimism	Guilt	
Clenched fists	Annoyance	Feelings of inferiority	
Insulting remarks	Resentment	Low self-esteem	
Intimidation	Jealousy	Sense of failure	
Bragging about violent acts	Bitterness	Humiliation	
Provoking behaviors	Complaining	Somatic symptoms	
Sadistic acts	Deceptive sweetness	Feeling harassed	
Maliciousness	Unreasonableness	Envy	
Verbal abuse	Intolerance	Feeling violated	
Temper tantrums	Resistance	Feeling alienated	
Violation of others' rights	Cynicism	Feeling demoralized	
Screaming	Stubbornness	Feeling depressed	
Deviance	Intentional forgetting	Resignation	
Rage	Noncompliance	Powerlessness	
Argumentativeness	Procrastination	Helplessness	
Overt defiance	Antagonism	Hopelessness	
Threats: words or weapons	Belittling remarks	Desperation	
Damage to property	Sarcasm	Apathy	
Assault	Fault finding		
Rape	Manipulation		
Homicide	Power struggles		
	Unfair teasing		
	Sabotage of others		
	Domination		

From Keltner NL, Schwecke LH, Bostrom CE: *Psychiatric nursing*, ed 2, St Louis, 1995, Mosby.

Anger is associated with anxiety and loss of control. It can include feelings of hopelessness, powerlessness, and regret. Anger can arise intentionally as one "stews" or "gets all worked up" about an event or situation, or it can result from an unplanned outcome of a situation. Some people label anger as justified or unjustified according to their personal values. Anger can also be rational, thought about, and planned, or it can arrive in a blind fury of irrational rage.

Individuals express their anger in a variety of ways. Some individuals will turn it inward and become suicidal or depressed. Others will focus their anger outward through aggressive or violent behaviors and present a danger to others. Some persons live bouncing between aggression and helplessness, whereas others channel their anger into physical complaints and problems.

Aggression relates to behavior. **Aggression** is a forceful attitude or action that is expressed physically, symbolically, or verbally (Campbell and Humphreys, 1993). Aggressive actions (behaviors) are angry feelings and impulses that are converted into action. Aggression is an expression of anger.

Aggression can be expressed in a number of ways. Socially approved aggression is a basic element of many sports, such as football, hockey, and soccer (Stuart and Sundeen, 1995). Aggressive behavior is socially approved for young executives who are climbing the corporate ladder or newspeople who are hot on the trail of some developing story. However, aggressive behaviors become inappropriate when they affect other people or their possessions.

Several other terms describe the actions of an angry person. **Impulse-control** refers to the ability to express one's emotions in appropriate or effective ways. **Violence** is defined as any behavior that threatens or harms another person or his/her property. A *violent act* is a behavior of force that results in injury, abuse, or harm to the recipient. The term **acting out** refers to the use of inappropriate, detrimental, or destructive behaviors to express current or past emotions. In other words, the individual who acts out behaves in inappropriate ways in response to his/her emotions. Children and adolescents often act out in attempts to establish and test the limits of appropriate behavior (Clunn, 1995). Some teens act out to discharge emotional and sexual tension.

Assault is a legal term that describes any behavior that presents an immediate threat to another person. When the assault is carried out, it is called **battery.** The legal concepts of assault and battery were established to define inappropriate aggression and protect people from those who act on their emotions in ways

that are threatening to others. **Passive aggression** involves indirect expressions of anger through subtle, evasive, or manipulative behaviors.

Last is the definition of the term **assertiveness,** the quality for which we strive. Assertiveness is the ability to directly express one's feelings or needs in a way that respects the rights of other people and retains an individual's dignity.

Anger and Aggression in Society

Anger and its expressions have a strong impact on a society. The histories of many cultures are peppered with accounts of uprisings and wars. Children were often sacrificed to the gods of their parents. During medieval times, children were abandoned, abused, and sold. Women and prisoners of war fared little better.

Gender Aggression

"Violence against wives has been tolerated since the beginning of history" (Landers, Jacobs, and Siegel, 1995). Ancient and well-accepted beliefs that men were superior led to values that supported the abuse of women. Beatings and floggings of women were accepted practices throughout ancient Greek and Roman societies. By the fourteenth century, it was legal in France for a man to beat his wife as long as he did not maim or kill her. In 1427, a nobleman encouraged his fellow Italians to treat their wives with as much concern and consideration as they did their livestock and fowl.

In eighteenth-century America, the high incidence of violence against women and children became unacceptable. By 1871, states began to enact statutes that denied the husband's right to physically abuse his wife. Today in the United States, wives can legally sue their husbands for abusing them, but the problems of violence against women and children continue to occur far too often.

Aggression and abuse are still practiced all over the world. Many aggressive acts against women are centered around the concepts of virginity and fidelity. Young women in parts of Africa and the Middle East are forced to undergo circumcision and other mutilating genital surgeries. People of all ages can suffer from the effects of gender violence (Table 25-2).

Aggression Throughout the Life Cycle

The aggressive expression of anger begins in infancy and ends with death. As infants, unmet needs are expressed through diffuse rage reactions with "loud, uncontrollable crying and screaming, profuse perspiration, difficulty in breathing (sometimes turning blue), and flailing of arms and legs" (Keltner, Schwecke, and Bostrom, 1995).

◆ **TABLE 25-2**
Gender Violence Throughout the Life Cycle

Phase	Type of Violence Present
Prebirth	Sex-selective abortion (China, India, Republic of Korea); battering during pregnancy (emotional and physical effects on woman; effects on birth outcome); coerced pregnancy (e.g., mass rape in war).
Infancy	Female infanticide; emotional and physical abuse; differential access to food and medical care for female infants.
Girlhood	Child marriage; genital mutilation; sexual abuse by family members and strangers; differential access to food and medical care; child prostitution.
Adolescence	Dating and courtship violence (e.g., acid throwing in Bangladesh, date rape in the United States); economically coerced sex (African secondary school girls having to take up with "sugar daddies" to afford school fees); sexual abuse in the workplace; rape; sexual harassment; forced prostitution; trafficking in women.
Reproductive age	Abuse of women by intimate male partners; marital rape; dowry abuse and murders; partner homicide; psychological abuse; sexual abuse in the workplace; sexual harassment; rape; abuse of women with disabilities.
Elderly	Abuse of widows; elder abuse (in the United States, the only country where data are now available, elder abuse affects mostly women).

Modified from Heise LL and others: *Violence against women: the hidden health burden,* World Bank Discussion Papers, No 225, 1994, Washington, DC, WDC.

During toddlerhood, individuals engage in temper tantrums, during which they learn to focus their aggression on the person or thing they believe is responsible for their anger (Potter and Perry, 1995). They begin to model or imitate the behaviors of others in their environment and pattern their own actions after them. If shouting, fighting, or other forms of aggression are observed, toddlers understand that aggressive behaviors are acceptable. In some families, a show of aggression is encouraged in children as a way of teaching them to "stand up for their rights." Television is another source of aggression. The results of many studies have shown that violence on television has a direct effect on the children who watch the programs (Wong, 1995).

During the preschool years, children often direct their anger toward other people, especially peers or younger children (Fig. 25-1). Children in the early school-aged years assault or hit each other frequently. By preadolescence, most children stop hitting and learn to channel their aggression into physical activities, such as competitive sports or physical conditioning. Slander, gossip, and practical jokes provide other outlets for aggressive feelings during the school years (Hogarth, 1995).

Fig. 25-1 Preschoolers generally direct their aggression toward peers, especially when their desires are frustrated. (From Wong DL: *Whaley and Wong's nursing care of infants and children,* ed 5, St Louis, 1995, Mosby.)

By adolescence, fighting is organized, controlled, and purposeful. The peer group becomes the greatest source of influence on the individual. If the activities sought by the peer group are illegal or disruptive to others, then the adolescent peer group is known as a "gang."

As an individual's age increases, so does his/her control of emotional reactions and impulses. "Between the ages of 22 and 45 years, most expressions of aggression and fighting occur within the family" (Keltner, Schwecke, and Bostrom, 1995). After age 45, few people engage in fighting until into their 70s, when sensory and cognitive (intellectual) impairments may result in the expression of aggressive or hostile behaviors.

Scope of the Problem Today

Today, aggression and violence are worldwide concerns. Here are a few facts to support this conclusion:

- In the United States, "the Bureau of Justice National Crime Survey states that a woman is beaten in her home every 15 seconds" (Stateman, 1995).
- In Canada, records obtained from physicians, lawyers, police, and social workers indicate that 1 woman out of 10 is abused by her partner (United Nations, 1993).
- In Papua, New Guinea, almost 67% of wives suffer from abuse (Statman, 1995).
- Wife beating is still "common in Bangladesh, Barbados, Chile, Columbia, Costa Rica, Guatemala, India, Kenya, Norway, and Sri Lanka" (United Nations, 1993).
- During one 5-day period in 1992, the King Medical Center in Los Angeles, California, "treated 94 lacerations, 54 gunshot wounds, 87 assaults, and 19 stabbings" (Foster, Siegel, and Landes, 1995).
- In the United States, between 1970 and 1991, unintentional injuries were the second leading cause of death for Native Americans; homicide (murder) was listed as the tenth leading cause of death for all citizens; for black males and 5- to 15-year-old children, murder was the third leading cause of death; and death from suicide ranks as the eighth leading cause of death nationwide for all ages (Landers, Jacob, and Siegel, 1995).

The statistics are impressive, but they cannot tell the stories of how aggression and violence have changed the lives of so many individuals. It is the task of each of us, as nurses, health care providers, and human beings, to help people focus their acts of aggression into more effective (and less violent) ways of functioning in today's complex world.

Theories of Anger and Aggression

Theories about human aggression and violence attempt to explain why certain persons behave the way they do. Many theories about the nature of aggression have been devised through the years, but most fall into one of three basic models: biological, psychosocial, and sociocultural theories.

Biological Theories

Models that credit the causes of aggression and violence to physical or chemical differences are called biological or individual theories. Currently, much research is being focused on the areas of the brain that influence emotional control and aggressive behaviors. The roles of certain neurotransmitters, such as dopamine, serotonin, and gamma aminobutyric acid (GABA), are being investigated as possible factors in the development of violent or aggressive behaviors.

Biological theories explain aggressive behavior as a psychopathology, a deviation or disorder in the biological or physical makeup of a person. Charles Darwin favored his animal model, which stated that aggression strengthened human beings through natural selection. Sigmund Freud believed that the greater the death wish, the greater the need for aggressive behavior. Other biological theories explain aggression as an innate (instinctual) drive. One thing, however, is certain: there are physical problems that cause aggressive behaviors.

Psychosocial Theories

The models based on psychosocial theories "focus on the interaction of individuals with their social environment and locate the source of violence in interpersonal frustrations" (Keltner, Schwecke, and Bostrom, 1995). Psychosocial theories of aggression state that aggressive behaviors are learned responses.

Sociocultural Theories

With the sociocultural theories, aggression is explained from a social and cultural group viewpoint. Cultural theories state that aggressive or violent acts are a product of cultural values, beliefs, norms, and rituals. Many cultures have rules that endorse the use of violence.

The *functional model* states that aggression and violence fill certain functions in a society, serving as catalysts or motivators for action. Behaviors associated with aggression are often used to achieve fame, fortune, and power. For example, athletes must be aggressive if they are to excel.

Conflict theories assume that aggression is a natural part of all human interactions. They state that individuals, groups, and societies seek to further their own causes. This results in disagreements, conflicts, and aggressive actions. Because conflict is a natural part of human associations, conflict theories state that aggression will never be eliminated. It can only be controlled.

The *resource theory's premise* is that aggression is a fundamental part of society. Therefore the person who has the most resources can muster the greatest force or power. With this model, aggression is the result of having many resources and the power that goes with them.

The last theory of aggression is the *general systems model.* Here, the feedback loop is used to demonstrate how aggression and violence perpetuate (feed on) themselves. Violence is viewed as a product of a system that must be stabilized and managed.

As you can see, many attempts have been made to explain the nature of aggression and violence. No matter what the cause, though, society must learn to recognize and cope with the aggressive behaviors of some of its members.

Many factors contribute to the use of aggressive behaviors. Attitudes about work, education, the media, and religion all influence the development of anger, hostility, and aggression. Population problems, such as overcrowding, can influence aggressive behaviors. Available community resources or the lack of them also plays an important role in the occurrence of violent or criminal acts.

The Cycle of Assault

Assaults are aggressive behaviors that violate others' person or properties. Behaviors that are considered assaultive in this society include hitting, biting, pinching, or causing physical pain; certain criminal acts, such as rape, murder, suicide, robbery, theft, assault, and battery; subtle actions of passive aggressive individuals; and many forms of emotional abuse.

Studies have demonstrated that assault and violence occur in a predictable pattern of emotional responses. Each pattern of responses is called a stage or

phase, and there are five stages in the assault cycle. These stages are called trigger, escalation, crisis, recovery, and depression. Fig. 25-2 illustrates the cycle of assault. This section describes each stage a bit more closely.

Trigger Stage

During the trigger phase, a stress-producing event occurs. Stress responses, such as anger, fear, or anxiety then occur. Coping mechanisms—behaviors to deal with the situation—are chosen in an attempt to achieve control. For most individuals, these coping behaviors are appropriate reactions to stress. For persons who are assaultive, however, the choice of coping behaviors becomes automatic. Their abilities to problem solve or choose effective options decrease as aggressive responses increase. Crisis interventions are very successful if begun early in this stage.

Escalation Stage

The escalation stage is the building stage during which each behavioral response moves a step closer to total loss of control. Attempts to use aggressive behaviors to gain control are repeatedly ineffective, resulting in frustration and greater anger. These emotions further flame the fires of aggression. Intervention is crucial at this stage if violence is to be prevented.

Crisis Stage

During this stage, the potential for danger is increased. This phase is a period of emotional or physical blowout during which the actual assaultive behaviors occur. Many individuals act out, physically harm other people and animals, or destroy property, whereas others become verbally abusive or scream and shout. People in this stage of the assault cycle are unable to listen to reason, follow directions, or engage in mental exercises. They are so controlled by their emotional responses they cannot respond to most outside stimuli. The best interventions at this stage are to protect the individual and others in the environment from physical harm.

Fig. 25-2   The assault cycle. (Redrawn from Keltner NL, Schwecke LY, Bostrom CE: *Psychiatric nursing,* ed 2, St Louis, 1995, Mosby.)

Recovery Stage

The recovery stage is the cooling-down period that follows an emotional explosion. The individual slowly calms and returns to normal behavioral responses and actions. Interventions during this stage include assessing for injuries or trauma and providing a safe, quiet environment in which the person can recover.

Depression Stage

The last phase of the assault cycle involves a period of guilt and attempts to reconcile (make up) with others. Aggressors are aware of the assault and genuinely feel bad about it. They may provide loving care for the person they just assaulted or spend extravagant amounts of money on gifts or other offerings of forgiveness. With the passage of time, the assaultive event is slowly placed in the past. Life returns to normal; that is, until the next trigger is cocked, and the cycle repeats itself over, and over, and over again.

Anger Control Disorders

Anger and aggressive responses are components of many mental health disorders. Aggressive behaviors are commonly encountered in clients with substance abuse, mood, anxiety, and depressive disorders. The potential for violence always exists in individuals with schizophrenia and other psychotic disorders. Clients with eating, sleeping, or somatoform disorders seldom behave aggressively toward others, but they are at a great risk for suicide because they focus their anger and aggression inward.

The *Diagnostic and Statistical Manual of Mental Disorders* (DSM-IV) lists three categories of disorders relating to aggressive behaviors. *Conduct disorders* most often occur in childhood. *Impulse-control disorders* usually develop later in life, and *adjustment disorders* can occur at any time. The potential for aggressive actions is present in every client, regardless of diagnosis. Treating each person with respect and concern goes a long way toward removing that potential and helps to establish the groundwork for effective therapeutic interventions.

Aggressive Behavioral Disorders of Childhood

Being a child is like being a stranger in a foreign land, unable to speak the language and unaware of the proper behaviors for that world. Children are like that stranger. They need limits and rules that are lovingly, repeatedly, and consistently applied throughout their childhoods. They need to learn the customs, which behaviors are "right" or appropriate and which behaviors are "wrong," and they require the energies of adults in their environments to help guide them through the foreign lands of childhood and adolescence. Without this attention and guidance, children learn to cope in the best ways they can, even if these ways lead to ineffective or destructive behavioral disorders. Two diagnoses that relate to childhood and adolescent aggression are conduct disorder and oppositional defiant disorder.

Conduct disorder is characterized by a pattern of behavior "in which the basic rights of others or major age-appropriate societal norms or rules are violated" (American Psychiatric Association, 1994). The behaviors associated with this disorder fall into four main groups: aggressive, nonaggressive, deceitfulness, and serious rules violations. Inappropriate behavior patterns occur in a variety of settings: home, school, and community. Individuals with this disorder naturally relate aggressively to others even when the situation is nonthreatening. They seldom have empathy for others, and they lack appropriate guilt feelings. Their inability to tolerate frustration leads to temper outbursts and reckless behaviors.

Conduct disorders are usually diagnosed in late childhood or early adolescence. The majority of persons "outgrow" the problem by adulthood and are able to live effectively. However, a significant number of people go on to develop antisocial personality disorders as adults.

Oppositional defiant disorder is a pattern of negative, aggressive behaviors that is focused on authority figures in the child's life. Children with this problem are constantly involved in a power struggle, always fighting for control and attention. Their behaviors are stubborn, uncooperative, resistant, and hostile. The signs/symptoms of oppositional defiant disorder are often seen by 8 years of age; without intervention, the behaviors often escalate or grow into conduct disorders.

Impulse-Control Disorders

The essential feature of an impulse-control disorder is "the failure to resist an impulse, drive, or temptation to perform an act that is harmful to the person or to others" (American Psychiatric Association, 1994).

The typical individual with an impulse-control disorder begins to feel an increasing tension when presented with the "trigger" stimuli. Emotions continue to build and grow until the individual can no longer resist or control the impulse. He/she engages in the behavior (commits the act) and then experiences gratification, pleasure, and a release of tension. Guilt, remorse, or regret may or may not be felt after the impulse has been fulfilled.

IMPULSE-CONTROL DISORDERS	
Intermittent explosive disorder:	Repeated failures to resist acting on aggressive impulses, resulting in assaultive or destructive behaviors
Kleptomania:	Repeated failure to resist the impulse to steal objects when they are not needed for personal use or survival
Pathological gambling:	Repeated episodes of maladaptive betting, wagering, playing games of chance, or gambling
Pyromania:	Repeated behavioral pattern of starting fires for pleasure, relief of tension, or gratification
Trichotillomania:	Repeated behavioral pattern of pulling out one's hair that results in noticeable loss of hair

Modified from American Psychiatric Association: *Diagnostic and statistical manual of mental disorders,* ed 4, Washington, DC, 1994, The Association.

Impulse-control disorders are named for the impulse that is related to the specific problem. The box above lists six types of impulse-control disorders. Although all types involve some form of aggression, the impulse-control problems encountered by nurses are most often related to clients with intermittent explosive disorder.

Intermittent explosive disorder is characterized by the failure to resist aggressive impulses that result in the destruction of property or assault of another living being. Persons with intermittent explosive disorder have angry outbursts that are out of proportion to the stressor. For example, an individual may strike the teller at the bank for making him wait in line too long, whereas other people would sigh and continue to wait quietly for their turn.

Because these aggressive behaviors place others in the environment at risk for harm, people with these disorders often have difficulty with interpersonal, work, and social relationships. Intermittent explosive disorders more commonly occur in males and may appear during late adolescence through early adulthood.

Adjustment Disorders

The problems associated with coping with a new set of stressors can be overwhelming for any of us. The discomfort of adjusting from one situation to another can lead to certain mental health problems. Adjustment disorders are emotional or behavioral problems that develop in response to an identifiable source.

Persons with adjustment disorders are having difficulty adapting to a new situation. Their distress is so great that it interferes with activities of daily living. The stressor may be a single event, such as leaving a romantic relationship. Stressors may be continuous (like living in a crime-filled neighborhood), or repeated, such as ongoing marital problems. Whatever the cause, the individual has difficulty coping effectively.

Adjustment disorders are also classified on the basis of their most frequent symptoms. The five subtypes follow:

1. Adjustment disorder with depressed mood
2. Adjustment disorder with anxiety
3. Adjustment disorder with mixed anxiety and depressed mood
4. Adjustment disorder with disturbance of conduct
5. Adjustment disorder with disturbed emotions and conduct

By definition, an adjustment disorder lasts no longer than 6 months after the stressor(s) have stopped.

These individuals become overwhelmed with the changes required of them during stressful times. Adjustment disorders are common, with most of us experiencing at least one episode during our lives. Fortunately, human beings are adaptable and most individuals learn to effectively cope with their new situations. However, suicide attempts occur more frequently with persons who are having trouble adjusting to new situations.

Remember, the above diagnoses relate to those mental health problems in which aggression plays an important part. Do not forget that anger, aggression, or hostility can be present in any individual diagnosed with a mental health problem or not.

Guidelines for Intervention

It is important to keep in mind that diagnoses are only labels. You are working with individuals, real people with real problems; your therapeutic interventions must be focused on the person, not the diagnosis.

Assessing Anger and Aggression

The first step in controlling aggressive behaviors is to assess the client's potential for engaging in inappropriate behaviors (Simms, 1995). Obtain a mental status assessment as soon as possible after admission. Use therapeutic communication skills to help clients feel at ease. Try to establish trust and let clients know that they are respected even when angry.

During the mental status assessment, observe the client's general appearance and note the state of dress, cleanliness, and use of cosmetics or jewelry. Be sure to observe the client's activity and behaviors. Many times the clues to violence are being quietly communicated (Kinkle, 1993). Nurses need to be alert enough to receive the message. What about the client's attitude? Are interactions friendly and cooperative or resistive and hostile? Listen for the quality, rate, and amount of verbal communications in the client's speech. Pay particular attention to the individual's mood, affect, perceptions, and thoughts. Have the client describe his/her mood at the time. Listen to the client's conversation for form and content. Does he/she speak logically, with a flow of ideas that are easily followed? What is the problem according to the client? Is the client's judgment or insight clear and easy to follow or does it follow a twisted path of fuzzy explanations for past inappropriate behaviors? Is the client's reliability intact (does he/she give accurate information)?

Next, perform a psychosocial assessment. Find out which internal or external stressors are present in the client's life. Which coping skills are being used to adapt to the stressors? Encourage the client to tell you about his/her important relationships and how they are affecting the situation. Do not forget to pay attention to the cultural, spiritual, and occupational areas of the client's life. Is he/she a member of a specific cultural group, organized religion, or occupation? Is there a value and belief system that the individual feels is valuable, desirable, or worth following? Observe the client's reactions and behaviors during the interview. His/her reactions, behaviors, and attitudes during this time offer many clues to the existence of a potential for aggression or violent behaviors. Remember, the key to effective intervention begins with a thorough and complete assessment. Troubleshooting is always an easier task than controlling a full-blown violent reaction.

Therapeutic Interventions

The nursing interventions for clients with anger and aggression focus on two basic areas: the client and the caregiver.

Interventions for aggressive or potentially aggressive client behaviors can be viewed from three levels. Level 1 interventions focus on the prevention of vio-

lence. The goal of level 1 interventions (the best intervention for aggression) is to establish and maintain a trusting therapeutic relationship with clear and honest communications (Medved, 1995). This is accomplished using a number of simple communication strategies.

Call the client and any family members by name. No one likes to be an anonymous face in the crowd. Explain what is happening, the reason for any delays, why testing is needed. Most important, listen actively, with your whole body, not just the ears. Communicate your concern nonverbally while listening. Maintain good eye contact. Lean forward slightly to communicate your interest. Give the client time to respond. Concentrate on the message he/she is trying to communicate to you. Paraphrase the problem to make sure that you have a good understanding of the client's point of view. Help to identify the emotions associated with the problem and explore appropriate options (see box below).

Level 1 interventions should be practiced routinely as preventive measures. They are also appropriate for clients who are in the "trigger stage" of the assault cycle. Very often, just the caring concern of someone

---

COMMUNICATING WITH ANGRY CLIENTS

First, take a deep breath. Become calm and introduce yourself to the client:

1. *Listen actively.* Use active listening skills to communicate interest in helping the client. Allow client to define the problem that is causing the anger or aggression.
2. *Identify emotions.* Try to understand *what* is causing the problem and *why* the client is reacting with anger. Ask yourself what the client may be feeling and verbalize it. "You must be feeling pretty . . . " or "How do you feel about that?" allows the client to identify and discuss his/her emotions or problems.
3. *Explore options.* Help the client to regain some sense of control by brainstorming possible solutions to his/her problems. You may not be able to solve the problems, but you can assist the client to find his/her own solutions.
4. *Offer positive comments.* Increase self-esteem by finding something the client does well and complimenting him/her. Many clients and their loved ones feel helpless, and the reassuring words of the nurse can provide great comfort.

Modified from Medved R: *Nurs 90* 20(4):67, 1990.

who is willing to really listen is enough to prevent anger from turning into aggression or violence.

Level 2 interventions focus on protecting the client and others from potential harm. These interventions are used when the therapeutic communications and mutual problem-solving interventions of level 1 are ineffective and signs of trouble are beginning to brew. The box below offers a case study. Learn to recognize the verbal and physical signs of impending violence.

Interventions during this stage include measures to maintain a safe environment. Take charge with a calm but firm attitude. Allow the client to act out as long as he/she is limiting behaviors to verbal assaults and harmless physical movements. Assure the client that he/she has a right to express angry feelings but not to impose them on others. Gently but firmly set limits on the client's behaviors by suggesting that he/she take a "time out," a cooling-off period. If it appears that the "time out" is not effective, offer p.r.n. medication. Only after all other measures have been tried, do nurses implement level 3 interventions.

The last level of therapeutic interventions is reserved for those clients who are out of control (escalation stage of the assault cycle). If level 1 and 2 interventions were effective, few clients reach this stage. However, for those who are engaging in violent behaviors, three interventions are available: seclusion, restraints, and intramuscular (IM) medication.

Clients who are out of control fight, bite, kick, scratch, spit, and throw things. They may be verbally abusive or physically aggressive. Without interven-tion, both clients and their care providers are at an increased risk for injury.

A point to remember here is that the use of restraints and seclusion as interventions for the control of assaultive behaviors must be planned ahead. Both strategies involve federal and state laws, institutional policies, and special procedures. Study the procedures for applying restraints and placing clients in seclusion (available in any nursing fundamentals text). Remember to monitor the condition of restrained clients at least every 15 minutes, and use other, less drastic nursing measures as soon as the client has regained behavioral control (Lewis and Blumenreich, 1993). The box on p. 356 presents a sample client care plan that addresses aggressive behavior.

Once the assaultive event has subsided and the client is willing to discuss the problem, begin to enlist his/her help to modify the inappropriate behaviors. Table 25-3 offers an example of an educational plan for controlling impulsive, aggressive behaviors.

Interventions for nurses focus on learning to effectively control your own feelings of anger. Even the most therapeutic care provider experiences anger. Learning to cope with your own feelings of anger or aggression allows you to be more successful in working with the angry emotions of others (Cornelius, 1993) (see box on p. 357). Practice your ability to cope with these feelings and reactions at home and at work. As you improve, you will find yourself becoming more effective when working with the emotional responses of others.

CASE STUDY

Randy, a well-known, hot-tempered 24-year-old man, visits the clinic for weekly dressing changes for his right eye. Today he arrives seething with anger because his girlfriend just broke off her relationship with him.

"That –––––! Just because we had a little fight she can't stand to be with me now. You women are all alike. I could punch you out right now and feel just fine," he snarls through clenched teeth as he glares into your eyes.

"You sound pretty upset. Tell me about it," you calmly reply. As Randy tells you about his relationship with his ex-girlfriend, you can see him becoming angrier by the moment. He begins to pound his fists on the table and stomp around the room. You signal for other staff members who have been keeping an eye on the situation to be prepared to offer help, but so far Randy is just ranting and raving. No damage is being done and no person is in danger of harm.

After a few moments you reply, "Randy, I understand your anger, but stomping around like this is not appropriate. Let's take a couple of minutes to cool off, then maybe together we can think of some way to help the problem." Because you remained calm, quiet, and prepared, Randy responded to your request and took a few minutes to regain his composure.

Clinical Decision

1. How do you think Randy would have reacted if he had encountered three staff members during his "ranting"?

SAMPLE CLIENT CARE PLAN
RISK FOR VIOLENCE

Assessment

History: Bruce, a 15-year-old boy, has been sent to the mental health unit for psychiatric evaluation by the local police. Since age 13, he has been arrested several times for vandalism, drug possession, and menacing. His parents are cooperative but "feel helpless." His older sister is living away from home because she refuses "to be exposed to his violent behaviors."

Current Findings: An unkempt, sullen adolescent boy with tattoos on each knuckle of the right hand. Head is shaved in a pattern. Smoking cigarettes despite the "no smoking" sign posted on the wall.

Nursing Diagnosis

Risk for violence: directed at others

Planning/Expected Outcomes

Bruce will demonstrate absence of aggressive or hostile threats or behaviors by October 10.

Nursing Interventions

Intervention

1. Approach Bruce with respect; avoid judging.

2. Orient to unit routine and policies; give clear, specific rules and the consequences for breaking them.
3. Assess for warning signs of increasing anger.

4. Assess past acts of aggression and determine the potential seriousness of present actions.

5. Demonstrate acceptance of the painful feelings underlying Bruce's behaviors.
6. Use open-ended questions; avoid asking "why."

7. Contract with Bruce for "no violence" while on unit.
8. Teach stress management and problem-solving techniques.

Rationale

1. Adolescents need acceptance from adults as much as they need direction.
2. Assists Bruce until he is able to gain internal control over his aggressive behaviors.

3. Behavioral changes often indicate an aggressive reaction; good assessment skills prevent injury to client and others.
4. Knowledge of previous patterns of violence helps nurse assess Bruce's tolerance for current stresses.
5. Helps to encourage Bruce's self-worth even though his behaviors are unacceptable.
6. "Why" questions call for an explanation or defensive reaction; open-ended questions help explore feelings, thoughts, and reactions.
7. Protects others from injury; encourages Bruce to be responsible for his own actions.
8. Redirects energy created by anxiety and anger into healthier responses.

Evaluation

By September 15, Bruce no longer required daily "time out" sessions. By October 2, Bruce was able to identify one source of his anger.

◆ **TABLE 25-3**
Client Education Plan: Modifying Impulsive Behavior

Content	Instructional Activities	Evaluation
Describe characteristics and consequences of impulsive behavior.	Select a situation in which impulsive behavior occurred. Ask the patient to describe what happened. Provide the patient with paper and a pen. Instruct the patient to keep a diary of impulsive actions, including a description of events before and after the incident.	Patient will identify and describe an impulsive incident. Patient will maintain a diary of impulsive behaviors. Patient will explore the causes and consequences of impulsive behavior.
Describe behaviors characteristic of interpersonal anxiety.	Discuss the diary with the patient.	Patient will connect feelings of interpersonal anxiety with impulsive behavior.
Relate anxiety to impulsive behavior.	Assist the patient to identify interpersonal anxiety related to impulsive behavior.	
Explain stress reduction techniques.	Describe the stress response. Demonstrate relaxation exercises. Assist the patient to return the demonstration.	Patient will perform relaxation exercises when signs of anxiety appear.
Identify alternative responses to anxiety-producing situations.	Using situations from the diary, and knowledge of relaxation exercises, assist the patient to list possible alternative responses.	Patient will identify at least two alternative responses to each anxiety-producing situation.
Practice using alternative responses to anxiety-producing situations.	Role-play each of the identified alternative behaviors. Discuss the feelings associated with impulsive behavior and the alternatives.	Patient will describe the relationship between behavior and feelings. Patient will select and perform anxiety-reducing behaviors.

From Keltner NL, Schwecke LH, Bostrom CE: *Psychiatric nursing,* ed 2, St Louis, 1995, Mosby.

THINK ABOUT

There are several techniques for managing your own anger.

1. *Vent* your feelings. Yell, scream, shout, but do it in a safe place (e.g., in the car with the windows closed).
2. *Change* your focus. Distract yourself for a moment or two by listening to the radio, taking a walk, moving your energies from the anger to another topic. Play with a pet, if possible; it is a great tranquilizer. Even something as simple as counting to 10 can be very effective.
3. *Practice* using your anger constructively. Take the energy that is used to be angry and do something else with it. Clean the house. Organize the junk drawer in the nurse's station. Exercise.
4. *Discuss* your anger with those involved. Talking it out (after you are calm) lets people know what is on your mind and how you feel. Discussion also offers opportunities for personal learning and developing more therapeutic behaviors.
5. *Forgive* those with whom you are angry. If harsh words were exchanged, apologize. Apologies are free; they are not a sign of weakness, and they communicate a willingness to cooperate in the future. Forgiveness is an underused therapeutic tool.
6. *Relax.* Take slow, deep breaths and tell your body to relax and become calm. Remember the effects of our stress neurochemicals? Emotional responses have a strong impact on the physical body. Smile. It requires fewer muscles than a frown and promotes positive reactions in yourself and others.

❖ KEY CONCEPTS

- Anger is a normal emotional response to a perceived threat, frustration, or distressing event.

- Anger can serve as a coping mechanism, a motivator, or an opportunity for learning.

- Aggressive or hostile behaviors are angry feelings and impulses that are converted into action.

- Aggressive behaviors become inappropriate when they affect other people or their possessions.

- Assertiveness is the ability to directly express one's feelings or needs in a way that respects the rights of other people and retains the individual's dignity.

- Gender violence, which is the abuse of members of one sex by members of another, is seen in many cultural and social settings.

- The expression of anger occurs throughout the life cycle.

- Theories about the nature of aggression fall into one of three basic models: biological, psychosocial, and sociocultural theories.

- Assaults are aggressive behaviors that violate others' person or properties.

- Assault and violence occur in a predictable pattern of emotional responses called the assault cycle.

- The DSM-IV lists three categories of disorders relating to aggressive behaviors: conduct disorders, impulse-control disorders, and adjustment disorders.

- The first step in controlling aggression is to assess the client's potential for engaging in inappropriate behaviors.

- Interventions for aggressive or potentially aggressive behaviors are divided into three levels: preventing violence, protecting the client and others, and secluding or restraining the out-of-control client.

- Learning to cope with your own feelings of anger or aggression allows you to be more successful in working with the emotions of others.

❖ SUGGESTIONS FOR FURTHER READING

There are many good articles on this subject in various nursing, mental health, and social work journals. One of the best is "How to unmask the angry patient," by Christine Simms (*American Journal of Nursing*, 95[4]:37, 1995).

❖ REFERENCES

American Psychiatric Association: *Diagnostic and statistical manual of mental disorders,* ed 4, Washington, DC, 1994, The Association.

Campbell J, Humphreys J: *Nursing care for the survivors of family violence,* ed 2, St Louis, 1993, Mosby.

Clunn P: *Child psychiatric nursing,* ed 2, St Louis, 1995, Mosby.

Cornelius GF: Anger management: a key tool for survival, *Correct Today* 55(7):128, 1993.

Foster CD, Siegel MA, Landes A: *Health: a concern for every American,* ed 7, Wylie, TX, 1995, Information Plus.

Hogarth CR: *Adolescent psychiatric nursing,* ed 2, St. Louis, 1995, Mosby.

Keltner NL, Schwecke LH, Bostrom CE: *Psychiatric nursing,* ed 2, St Louis, 1995, Mosby.

Kinkle SL: Violence in the ED: how to stop it before it starts, *Am J Nurs* 93(7):22, 1993.

Landers A, Jacobs NR, Siegel MA: *Violent relationships: battering and abuse among adults,* ed 7, Wylie, TX, 1995, Information Plus.

Lewis S, Blumenreich P: Defusing the violent patient, *RN* 56(12):24, 1993.

Medved R: Strategies for handling angry patients and their families, *Nurs 90* 20(4):67, 1990.

Potter PA, Perry AG: *Basic nursing,* ed 3, St Louis, 1995, Mosby.

Simms C: How to unmask the angry patient, *Am J Nurs* 95(4):37, 1995.

Statman JB: *The battered woman's survival guide: breaking the cycle,* ed 2, Dallas, TX, 1995, Taylor Publishing.

Stuart GW, Sundeen SJ: *Pocket guide to psychiatric nursing,* ed 3, St Louis, 1995, Mosby.

United Nations: *Strategies for confronting domestic violence: a resource manual,* New York, 1993, United Nations.

Wong DL: *Whaley and Wong's nursing care of infants and children,* ed 5, St Louis, 1995, Mosby.

26

VIOLENCE

1. Discuss how violence influences the members of a society.

2. List three groups of theories that attempt to explain the cause of violence.

3. Describe six characteristics of a dysfunctional family.

4. Name three consequences of abuse during pregnancy.

5. List two examples of abuse or neglect for each age group throughout the life cycle.

6. Describe the essential features of posttraumatic stress disorder and rape trauma syndrome.

7. List the special assessments for suspected victims of violence.

8. Describe three interventions for helping clients recover from violence in their lives.

9. Explain how self-awareness can lead to a decrease in violent, abusive, or exploitive behaviors.

KEY TERMS

abuse	incest	rape
battering	machismo	sexual abuse
domestic violence	neglect	shaken baby syndrome
exploitation	pornography	
forensic evidence	prostitution	

Aggressive, violent, and exploitive behaviors occur throughout the animal kingdom. Many animals battle violently for the right to mate and pass on their genes. Starlings exploit other birds by laying their single egg in another's nest. These characteristics are also present in human beings. They are just expressed differently.

When animals engage in aggressive behaviors, there is always a specific goal. The goal may be to procure food, to mate, or to establish dominance in the group. Their use of violence is predictable and useful. Animals seldom risk injuring themselves just to be aggressive.

Human beings, however, are a different story. They engage in aggressive or violent behaviors for a variety of reasons, ranging from boredom to fear. Sometimes motives are clear and understandable. Other times, all we are left with is uneasy questions.

To discuss violence, one must be familiar with its related terms. **Abuse** is the intentional misuse of someone or something that results in harm, injury, or trauma. Abuse can take place in the form of active harm or passive neglect. **Neglect** is harm to another's health or welfare through a failure to provide for basic needs or by placing the individual's health or welfare at unreasonable risk. Neglect often occurs to the more vulnerable members of society, such as children and elders.

Exploitation refers to the use of an individual for selfish purposes, profit, or gain. Children who must labor for long hours with no time for study or play are examples of exploited individuals. Each of these terms describes some type of physical or psychological aggression. The purpose of this chapter is twofold: to help you understand the many ways in which violence is present in society and to provide you with the tools to effectively assess, intervene, reduce, and prevent aggressive incidents.

Social Factors and Violence

No one is certain exactly why violence occurs. We do know, however, that violent acts and their consequences are increasing with alarming frequency. Violence is a major cause of death and disability in most of the industrialized countries. For example, the murder rate in the United States has climbed from 17 murders per 100,000 people in 1970 to an alarming 27 per 100,000 by 1991. Today, the United States has the highest murder rate of all the "civilized countries" in the world, but Finland and Hungary claim the sad distinction of having the highest number of suicides in the industrialized countries (U.S. Bureau of Census, 1994).

These statistics mean that *you will* "come in contact with the victims—as inpatients, outpatients, home-care patients, emergency care patients, parents of patients, friends, and relatives" (Keltner, Schwecke, and Bostrom, 1995). Nurses and other health care providers accept and care for all people, but this philosophy comes with the risk of violence. Therefore it is important to learn as much as possible about the problems and solutions related to the use of violence in society today.

Several cultural and social factors affect violence. Many societies promote the use of aggressive behaviors through beliefs, customs, and rituals. "The American culture of violence is reflected in the history, attitudes, belief systems, and coping styles of the population in dealing with conflicts, frustration, and the quest for wealth and power" (Schacter and Sienfield, 1994). In cultures in which the resources are scarce, violent acts become a way of life (see box below).

Aggressive and violent acts are found in every educational, gender, occupational, racial, and religious group in society, although poverty does play a role in the development of aggressive behaviors. In many societies, productive and financially rewarding work is expected from most adults, especially men. A lack of fulfilling work often leads to poverty, frustration, and in many cases violence. To illustrate, the unemployment rate for young, minority men in the United States is "close to 50%. This group also has the highest rate of violence" (Stanhope and Lancaster, 1996).

Theories of Violence

Several theories attempt to explain the nature of violence. The psychiatric/mental illness model views violence as a mental illness. Both victim and abuser are considered to be mentally disturbed. Recent evidence, however, has found that the incidence of mental illness is no greater in batterers or their victims than the rest of the population.

 CULTURAL ASPECTS

Children in poverty-stricken countries go to work in the rug mills and other manufacturing businesses as young as 4 years old. Many labor for long hours in miserable working conditions for little pay. If a child does not work fast enough or has the courage to complain, he/she is physically punished. Children who are too outspoken about the poor working conditions have been known to "disappear."

The social learning theory states that aggressive and violent behaviors are learned through role modeling others in the environment. Aggression is believed to be a learned behavior based on the values, attitudes, and actions of role models within the individual's environment.

Sociological theories credit environmental and social factors as causes for violence. Environmental factors, such as overcrowding, lack of adequate housing, and poor hygiene, can increase the incidence of aggression. The social factors of unemployment, poverty, crime, drug abuse, and isolation are believed to be related violent acts.

Theories that are based in the study of man's social history (anthropological theories) explain violence and aggression as the result of cultural patterns, social organizations, or sexual differences. Because some cultures encourage the use of aggressive behaviors, their citizens learn to interact and cope aggressively. In other cultures, equality and harmony are stressed. Male and female roles are less defined in cooperative cultures than they are in cultures with hierarchies or degrees of power.

Last is the feminist theories. Here, the concept of machismo is used to explain the occurrence of violence against women. **Machismo** is defined as compulsive masculinity. Feminist theories state that boys are socialized throughout childhood to behave more aggressively and violently. By the time boys have reached adolescence, they have developed "a preoccupation with physical strength and athletic prowess, or attempts to demonstrate daring and valor or behavior that is violent and aggressive" (Whiting, 1965). Men who have a high degree of machismo demonstrate certain social, behavioral, and sexual attitudes.

Machismo is found to be a strong influence on male behavior in many countries (Campbell and Humphreys, 1993). These theories do not imply that every man with a high level of machismo abuses other people. They do, however, remind us that the potential for abuse lies within the machismo belief system (see box at right).

As life in this fast-paced society continues to change, more people are losing the energies that connect them to others. Homes, workplaces, and communities that once offered the protection of a predictable and stable lifestyle now move with the currents of change. Whereas numerous extended family members, relatives, and friends once offered respite from the demands of the current crisis, now an individual is fortunate to have one or two supportive friends.

Today, the computer and its worldwide web of interconnections is changing the ways in which we interact and fill our needs for love and belonging. Researchers (Baumeister and Leary, 1995) have found that social connectedness is more than just an obligation or a desire—it actually fills the basic human need to belong. In these times of public anxiety over so many social forces, people are turning more and more to the Internet, World-Wide-Web, or some other "information highway" in search of supportive relationships.

Dr. Sherry Turkle, a psychologist who studies cyberspace (the world of the computers), believes that computer networks will change the way "people think about themselves and their role in society." Her particular fear is "that young people will succumb to the temptation to leave 'real life' behind for the ever-so-much more controllable realm of cyberspace" (*Technology Review,* 1996). As more people become members of the computer network society, the number of "real," face-to-face interactions decreases. "The lack of supportive relationships has been linked to many negative—even pathological—consequences, including mental illness, crime, and suicide" (Baumeister and Leary, 1995). It appears that social relationships are more important in preventing aggression and violence than was once thought.

CHARACTERISTICS OF MACHISMO

- Attitude of male pride
- Engages in thrill-seeking behaviors
- Competition is his guiding principle
- Is egocentric (self-centered)
- Unable to express emotions except anger and rage
- Dislikes being gentle or vulnerable
- Values sexual virility
- Displays sexist attitudes
    Treats women as objects or commodities
    Sees women as objects of conquest
    Insists on being dominant to girls/women
    Holds to unwritten law that infidelity by a
        woman must be avenged
    Unable to cooperate with women
    Agrees to sexual use/abuse of women
- Glorifies war and violence
    Supports the military
    Enjoys contact sports
- Uses aggression to solve problems
    Solves problems physically

Modified from Campbell J, Humphreys J: *Nursing care of survivors of family violence,* ed 2, St Louis, 1993, Mosby.

Aggression and violence can take many forms. It can occur between individuals, groups, communities, or societies. Violence accompanies illicit drugs, crime, trauma, assault, and ritual abuse. Families that appear to be the "picture of happiness" may hide the fact that home is actually a war zone. Children who once threw rocks now shoot each other. The effects are felt by not only those persons directly involved in the violence but also the rest of society as well.

Abuse, Neglect, and Exploitation Within the Family

For far too long, society has managed to bury the issues of physical and emotional abuse within the family. Traditionally, victims suffer in silence, unable to seek help for fear of being revealed as less than a real person.

Domestic Violence

"Ever since the signing of the Magna Charta, the idea that a 'man's home is his castle' has been inviolate in Western society" (Justice and Justice, 1990). This principle has historically meant that the home is a private place. "What goes on inside one's home is nobody else's business" still remains a popular attitude today.

Battering is a term coined to describe repeated physical abuse of someone, usually a woman, child, or elder. **Domestic violence** is a term that describes abuse and battering within a family. Accurate statistics on the incidence of domestic violence are unavailable because very few victims are willing to share their experiences. However, the statistics that do exist "indicate that one American woman out of every two will be physically abused at some time in her life by the man she loves and lives with . . . . The Bureau of Justice National Crime Survey states that a woman is beaten in her home every 15 seconds" (Statman, 1995). Studies conducted by the March of Dimes indicate that pregnant women (1 out of 12) suffer physical abuse (battering) during pregnancy. These are chilling but true statistics.

A functional family unit is described by what it does and the processes used to achieve its goals. These processes include clear and supportive communications among all family members, conflict resolution, the setting of goals, and the use of resources inside and outside of the family (Potter and Perry, 1995). Families progress through stages as they progress through life.

A dysfunctional family is described by its inability or unwillingness to fulfill its basic functions. The box below lists several characteristics of a dysfunctional family. Not all dysfunctional families have an element of abuse, but the inability of a family to meet the physical or psychological needs of its members greatly increases the opportunity for aggressive or violent behaviors.

"The family is seen as a unit in society entitled to privacy and freedom from intrusion" (Starck and McGovern, 1992). Unfortunately, this doctrine has allowed untold numbers of women and children (and occasionally men) to suffer at the hands of their "loved ones." Violence within the family occurs in several ways. A few of the more common forms include physical, emotional, or sexual abuse and neglect of partners, children, and elderly.

Gender Abuse

Not one woman enters a relationship with the intent of becoming a battered partner, but wife beating is still considered an accepted part of marriage in many groups. Most of us were raised on a rich diet of myth, imagination, and fairy tales. The handsome partner, who was promised to bring true love and continual happiness, often turns out to be less than the Prince Charming one thought he was. The fairy

---

CHARACTERISTICS OF DYSFUNCTIONAL FAMILIES

- Family members are self-centered.
- Authority is inconsistent or lacking; parents feel they cannot control children.
- Roles are not clearly defined; it is unclear who is the parent, who is the child.
- Members are unable to meet own or others' needs; each expects needs to be met, but no one in family is capable of doing this.
- Individualism is not encouraged; autonomy and trust are lacking among family members.
- No common goals can be identified; focus is on the present only; family appears chaotic, disorganized; no one is really aware of what is happening in family.
- Communications are cold and indifferent; family members feel pain and desperation; humor, caring, empathy, intimacy are absent; no clear communications exist.
- Conflict is perceived as negative and is expressed through power struggles, sexual aggression; family may confuse violence with caring.
- Family boundaries are rigid; family feels threatened when outsiders try to enter group; family members are socially isolated; parents usually married young and have few parenting skills.
- Family violence is present.

princess arrives with attitudes, faults, and a personal agenda.

For many years, women believed that the only way they could survive in the world was by pleasing a man. The problem is that most abusive partners cannot be pleased. The notion that "all is fair in love and war" promotes the idea that marriage is a private relationship and the legal system should stay out of the picture—even when the picture includes assault, abuse, or injury.

There is no "psychological profile" of a typical abused woman. Perhaps the trait they have most in common is a trusting nature. Many women were raised to be nonaggressive and traditional, brought up to believe that the man is master of the household, the king of the home (Thorne-Finch, 1993). This point of view is encouraged by numerous social, community, and religious groups.

When abuse occurs, guilt, anger, and terror shatter a woman's self-esteem. She suffers in silence, knowing that the consequences will be severe if she seeks help. Once a woman is battered, a vicious cycle of violence is soon established (Table 26-1). The victims of violence do have some characteristics in common (see box below).

Abuser (perpetrator, batterer) behaviors have several characteristics. The profile of a typical batterer includes poor emotional control, superior attitude toward women, history of chemical abuse, high levels of jealousy and insecurity, and use of threats, punishment, and physical violence to control behavior. It is the picture of a client, a client's partner, a parent, mate, neighbor, friend, or even a loved one. Early recognition of the characteristics of the potential for violence allows for more effective interventions.

THINK ABOUT

Characteristics of victims:
- Feels captive in the system (family, group, community)
- Blames self for problems leading to abuse
- Has low self-esteem; views self as unworthy
- Feels helpless and powerless to change situation
- Is financially, emotionally, or physically dependent on abuser
- Is depressed, unable to see a future without abuse

How many persons do you know who demonstrate these characteristics?

What nursing interventions would you choose for a client who feels like a victim?

Abuse During Pregnancy

Pregnancy should be a time of great joy and anticipation, but for some women, pregnancy only increases their chances of being abused. It is difficult to believe that fathers would intentionally harm the mothers of their children, but trauma "is the leading cause of maternal death during pregnancy . . . . Violence during pregnancy affects more women than hypertension, gestational diabetes, or almost any other serious antepartum complication" (Campbell and Humphreys, 1993).

The statistics on prenatal violence are difficult to gather. One study of public prenatal clinics in two large cities revealed that over 17% of the clients had been physically abused during the pregnancy. It also revealed that 60% of the women being questioned had suffered two or more assaults, indicating that episodes of abuse were recurrent (McFarlane and others, 1992). The frequency and severity of abuse, as well as the potential for homicide, was found to be significantly increased for white women. In addition, abused women of all races were twice as likely to postpone beginning prenatal care until the third trimester of pregnancy, too late to prevent or treat many problems.

The effects of abuse during pregnancy can be devastating. The frequency of low-birth-weight infants and preterm deliveries is almost doubled in women who have a history of abuse during pregnancy (Dickason, Silverman, and Schult, 1994). Because the mother is afraid to seek help, she often delays her entry into the health care system, thus denying both herself and her developing child the benefit of adequate prenatal care.

Child Abuse

Unfortunately, the most vulnerable in society, the children, are often the most abused.

Child abuse occurs in many cultures. To illustrate, a popular saying in the red light (prostitution) district of Bangkok is:

> At 10 you are a woman.
> At 20 you are an old woman.
> And at 30 you are dead.

Child **pornography** (writings, pictures, or other messages pertaining to children that are intended to sexually arouse), child **prostitution** (selling of sexual favors by children), and child sexual abuse exist all over the world. In Brazil alone, it has been estimated that between 250,000 and 500,000 children are involved in the sex trade, but the numbers are even greater in Asia: 800,000 child prostitutes in Thailand, 400,000 child prostitutes in India, and 60,000 child prostitutes in the Philippines (Landes, Quiram, and Jacobs, 1995).

◆ **TABLE 26-1**
Cycle of Violence

Man	Woman

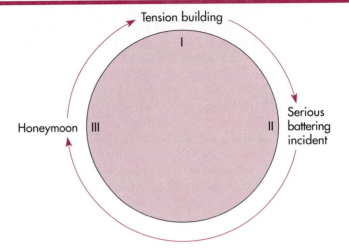

I. Tension building

He has excessively high expectations of her.
He blames her for anything that goes wrong.
He does not try to control his behaviors.
He is aware of his inappropriate behaviors but does not admit it.
Verbal and minor physical abuse increase.
Afraid she will leave, he gets more possessive to keep her captive.
He gets frantic and more controlling.
He misinterprets her withdrawal as rejection.

She is nurturing, compliant, and tries to please him.
She denies the seriousness of their problems.
She feels she can control his behaviors.
She tries to alter his behavior to stay safe.
She tries to prevent his anger.
She blames external factors: alcohol, work.
She takes minor abuse, but does not feel she deserves it.
She gets scared and tries to hide (withdrawal).
She may call for help as the tension becomes unbearable.

II. Serious battering incident

The trigger event is an internal or external event or substance.
The battering usually occurs in private.
He will threaten more harm if she tries to get help (police, medical).
He tries to justify his behaviors but does not understand what happens.
He minimizes the severity of the abuse.
His stress is relieved.

In cases of long-term battering, she may provoke it just to get it over with.
She may call for help if she is afraid of being killed.
Her initial reaction is shock, disbelief, and denial.
Fearing more abuse if police come, she may plead for them not to arrest him.
She is anxious, ashamed, humiliated, sleepless, fatigued, depressed.
She does not seek help for injuries for a day or more and lies about the cause of injuries.

III. Honeymoon

He is loving, charming, begging for forgiveness, making promises.
He truly believes he will never abuse again.
He feels that he taught her a lesson and she will not "act up."
He preys on her guilt to keep her trapped.

She sees his loving behaviors as the real person and tries to make up.
She wants to believe the abuse will never happen again.
She feels that if she stays, he will get help; the thought of leaving makes her feel guilty.
She believes in the permanency of the relationship and gets trapped.

Modified from Walker L: *The battered woman,* New York, 1979, Harper & Row.

Most of them are girls under the age of 16; but in Sri Lanka 20,000 to 30,000 child prostitutes are boys who cater to older men (Landes, Quiram, and Jacobs, 1995). Many children are being sold into prostitution with the belief that they will not be infected with AIDS. Sadly, however, this is not the case. "The Children's Rights Protection Center in Thailand claims the AIDS rate among Thai child prostitutes is approaching 50%" (Landes, Quiram, and Jacobs, 1995).

Children are also bought, sold, and exploited as objects of trade. They are purchased cheaply in one country and sold for a handsome profit in another. "The Japanese mafia imports young girls from the Philippines for prostitution for a business that makes about $1.5 million a day" (Landes, Quiram, and Jacobs, 1995). Many gypsy children are forced into begging, often bringing in hundreds of dollars a day, while under complete control of the abuser.

In some societies, female infants are undesirable. In these cultures, girls commonly receive less food, attention, or education than their brothers. For example, according to the World Bank, the death rate for young girls in India outnumbers the death rate for young boys by over 300,000 deaths per year. After these statistics are reviewed, it is easy to understand why child abuse and neglect is one of the most important issues of our time.

Spanking was, and still is in several countries, a main form of discipline for children. Unfortunately, spanking and other forms of corporal (physical) punishment teach children that power and violence are approved coping mechanisms. Today, the countries of Sweden, Finland, Norway, Austria, and Switzerland, in an effort to curb the growing rates of child abuse, prohibit all forms of physical punishment in schools and homes. Most other industrialized countries "have banned corporal punishment in schools . . . exceptions include the United States, South Africa, and parts of Australia and Canada" (Randall, 1992).

Child abuse went almost unrecognized until the early 1960s. Since then, the number of *reported* incidents has swelled to almost 3 million children (Finkelhor and Dziuba-Leatherman, 1994). One can see why child abuse has been called a national emergency.

The mistreatment of children can take several forms. *Physical abuse* is defined as "inflicted injury to a child that can range from minor bruises and lacerations to severe neurological trauma and death" (Krugman, 1994). *Sexual abuse* is the intentional engaging of children in sexual acts. Sexual abuse can take the form of rape, incest, fondling, intercourse, and other forms of sexual contact. *Emotional abuse* involves rejection, criticism, terrorizing, and isolation. Although the scars of this type of abuse are seldom seen objectively,

they are associated with deep and penetrating wounds for many individuals.

Neglect is the failure to provide the necessities of life. *Physical neglect* is the failure to provide a child's basic needs, such as food, clothing, shelter, and a safe environment. *Emotional neglect* is characterized by a lack of parent-child attachment. *Medical care neglect* is the refusal to seek treatment when it is needed. Delays in treatment are common in abused children. A rare form of child abuse, called Munchausen syndrome by proxy, occurs when caretakers simulate or create the signs/symptoms of illness in the child to receive attention from health care providers.

Abuse or neglect occurs during every stage of childhood. In infancy, shaken baby syndrome should be suspected in every infant with unexplained or vague injuries. **Shaken baby syndrome** is defined as "vigorous manual shaking of an infant who is being held by the extremities or shoulders, leading to whiplash-induced intracranial and intraocular bleeding and no external signs of head trauma" (Coody and others, 1994). This syndrome is difficult to diagnose because of the lack of physical evidence and the parents' refusal to discuss the situation.

Every health care provider must be alert for the possibility of a "shaken baby" whenever there is a history of unexplained lethargy, fussiness, or irritability with an infant. Seizures or bulging fontanel demand immediate investigation. Because the incidence of shaken baby syndrome is increasing, efforts must be made to educate parents and community members about the importance of handling our youngest members of society with gentleness and care.

Children are victimized more often than adults. The types of violent behaviors that abused children must endure include *pandemic aggression* in which the majority of children are assaulted; *acute aggression* in which children are abused, neglected, or exploited; and *extraordinary aggression*, which usually results in death.

Adolescent Abuse

The incidence of abuse in adolescence is greater than once thought. Recent national studies (Council on Scientific Affairs, 1993) have reported that the rate of abuse for older children and adolescents surpasses that of younger children. Abuse of adolescents is often the most overlooked type of family violence. For this reason, teens are less likely to receive needed services and counseling.

Adolescence is a time of emotional development, but not all adolescents have severe mood swings, periods of depression, or suicidal thoughts. Too often, these signs of possible abuse go unnoticed by adults. At other times, the signs of abuse are recognized as natural outcomes of adolescent misbehavior. "He/she had it coming" is still a widely held attitude when it comes to abusing adolescents.

Abused adolescents commonly have significant health risks. High on the list are emotional disorders, resulting from a history of insecurity and self-survival. The incidence of eating disorders, substance abuse problems, delinquent behaviors, and suicidal attempts are increased in adolescents who are suffering from abuse. Premature sexual activity is common and all to often leads to unwanted pregnancies, sexually transmitted diseases, and AIDS. Worse yet, adolescent abuse can result in fatal accidents, murder, and suicide, the three leading causes of death for all adolescents (Roye, 1995).

Girls are more likely to be abused than boys, but boys are more likely to suffer abuse outside the home by peers and others. Sadly, studies have shown that many adults who were physically disciplined as children approve of the use of physical force for controlling another person's behavior (Randall, 1992).

Adolescents are abused by parents, siblings, and persons outside the family. The most common form of violence within the home occurs between siblings. Violence between brothers and sisters is so common that it is often considered to be "normal behavior." "Parents take it for granted that 'kids will be kids,' and tend to ignore sibling violence. Yet it can have long-lasting effects" (Randall, 1992).

Children learn to exploit and victimize each other during the early school years. By the teen years, the use of violence becomes interwoven with the activities of the day. Peer pressure can be great during adolescence, and those who do not fit in or comply suffer the consequences of being different at the hands of their own peers.

Adolescents often receive the most severe abuse, the kind that results in serious disability or death (Council on Scientific Affairs, 1993) (see box below). Often, though, the signs of family maltreatment are vague. A history of abuse is frequently found in teens who are runaways, homeless, or incarcerated (in jail or prison). The blossoming problems of teen violence and abuse can be prevented if nurses are willing to invest their best therapeutic efforts into these "forgotten clients."

Elder Abuse

As the number of older persons grows, the potential for their maltreatment or neglect increases. "Each year approximately 1.5 million elderly persons are victims of abuse or mistreatment, with only one in five cases reported" (Frost and Willette, 1994).

Vulnerable older adults include those with chronic or disabling illnesses, the aged, and those who are poor or have few resources. The "typical victim" of elder abuse is an older woman who is living with a relative and is physically or mentally impaired (All, 1994). She usually has a history of unexplained bruises or injuries, burns in unusual places, sexually transmitted disease, or poor personal hygiene. She may experience extreme mood swings, be depressed, fearful, and overconcerned about the cost of health care. Many times the families of abused elders "health care shop," missing appointments and changing health care providers frequently.

Family members are the most frequent abusers of the elderly. The demands placed on caregivers often

---

CASE STUDY

Pete is a quiet, thoughtful, and charming young man whose intelligence shines through his sarcastic and tough demeanor. Pete is only 17, but he is well-developed and equipped to cope on the streets of Chicago. Pete is also the leader of a street gang and thinks little about using violence.

Pete comes from a family of two older brothers and a younger sister. In his early years, it was a common occurrence to see his mother and father arguing and hitting each other. By the time Pete was 6, his older brother had shot a neighbor and was "doing time." Throughout his childhood, Pete frequently vented his frustrations on his younger sister by hitting, pinching, and spitting on her.

At 8, Pete was initiated into his brother's gang. By

10, his intelligence and creativity had earned him the nickname of "the brain." By 14, he was destined for leadership. Today, at 17, Pete sits in a hospital bed with three .44 caliber bullet holes in his body. His bruised and pregnant girlfriend sits at his side. As soon as he can walk again, he plans to "make a little visit and even the score" with the guys he believes are responsible for his attack.

Clinical Decisions

1. Can you see any learned patterns of behavior in this family?

2. What do you think could have been done to prevent this situation from occurring?

influence the development of abuse (Minaker and Frishman, 1995). Violence most often erupts when caregivers feel stressed, pressured, or frustrated. In addition, many people who abuse their elders are coping with current substance-related or mental health problems themselves.

Neglect and exploitation are also common among the elderly. Neglect can take the form of not providing food, health care, or aids such as dentures, glasses, or hearing aids. Older adults who are unable to walk often suffer from long periods of isolation or abandonment. Neglect also includes deliberate efforts to cause emotional distress, such as threatening harm or withholding important information.

Exploitation of the elderly is often of a financial nature. Many times older adults are forced to sign over their properties, their pensions, or other assets. The elderly may be denied the right to vote or to make their own decisions. On some occasions, they are placed in nursing homes without their consent.

Today, many states have passed laws that require reporting of abusive incidents. Nurses can go a long way toward preventing elder abuse by recognizing the signs/symptoms of abuse, becoming familiar with the laws governing the reporting of abuse, and working to prevent violence in all settings. It is every person's responsibility to protect the aging members of society.

Sexual Abuse

A particularly devastating form of abuse is **sexual abuse,** the unwanted sexual attentions of another. When sexual activities or intercourse occurs between members of the same family (other than between the parents) it is called **incest.** Sexual violence has strong and lasting consequences for the victims. Children who are sexually abused suffer from a wide spectrum of mental health disorders, ranging from chronic headaches to depression, posttraumatic stress disorders, and severe personality disorders (Glod, 1993). Sexual assaults can occur to boys and girls.

Sexually abused adults are most often women. Most sexual assaults are made by women's partners. The most violent form of sexual assault, rape, "seems to occur more frequently in relationships in which other forms of physical aggression are ongoing" (Browne, 1993). Episodes of battering often include sexual and physical attacks. This can be a deadly combination for many maltreated adult women.

Sexual abuse in the elderly, especially women, does occur with all too common frequency. Because sexual mistreatment of the elderly is still a "taboo" subject, it often goes unrecognized by health care providers. Clues to the presence of sexual abuse in the elderly in-

clude complaints of pain, itching, or soreness in genital area; bruises or other evidence of injury around the genital area or elsewhere on the body; difficulty in walking, sitting, or moving; the presence of unexplained venereal disease or genital infections; and stained, torn, or bloody underclothing.

Health care providers, especially nurses, must learn to routinely assess all clients for a history of abuse or victimization and report any suspicious signs/symptoms or behaviors to supervisors and required authorities. An individual's life is worth the effort.

Abuse, Neglect, and Exploitation Within the Community

Aggressive and violent behaviors are fast becoming a common way of coping with problems. Violence against innocent bystanders continues to increase as more people approve of its use or turn a blind eye to its occurrence. No statistic can accurately record the number of violent acts that occur, but in 1993, an estimated 6.6 million violent acts occurred in the United States (Gest, 1996).

Violence, Trauma, and Crime

People use violence against each other in many ways, in both legal and illegal manners. Today, society is confronted with a steady diet of violent behaviors. Although most homicides are committed by family members or friends, a surprising number of them occur at the hands of complete strangers. Robbery has become commonplace in most communities, and an unsettling trend of murder in the workplace is rising. Car theft and drive-by crimes are increasing. Children are being kidnapped, and the incidence of violent crime by and against children and adolescents continues to soar.

Acts of violence are becoming commonly accepted in society. Radio, television, and the "Net" (Internet) surround people with examples of violence, thinly veiled as "adventure stories" or "comedies." Our children are soaked in tales of aggressive actions from the time they are first exposed to cartoons. Studies recently completed by television's cable network group in 1996 revealed that over half the programs on television are violent or aggressive in nature. In most programs, the victims are not hurt, and the aggressor is seldom caught or punished. Is there any wonder children are more willing to solve their problems with violence than critical thinking or problem solving?

Acts of violence on television pale in comparison to those that occur daily in "real life." Daily newspapers and radio and television news programs announce a litany of the day's violent activities. People listen, shake their heads, and then continue with their own lives, unaware that they may be the next victims.

Violence breeds physical and emotional pain for its victims. The basic needs of trust and autonomy (control) are threatened when one is involved with violence.

Victims react with anger, fear, denial, and shame. The well-meaning comments of friends and loved ones may even imply fault. Many victims of violence harbor feelings of unworthiness and contamination. Relationships with family and friends may become disturbed as the victim attempts to put the pieces of his/her life back together.

Crime is a natural vehicle for violence. Many crimes are committed on impulse, whereas others are well planned. Crime may or may not involve physical aggression and violence, but the emotional impact of being victimized by crime leaves deep emotional scars on most individuals.

Group Abuse

Throughout history, people have chosen certain groups of people to define as "being different" from themselves. Individuals within these groups may be kind and gentle, but association with the group labels them as "one of those people." This label somehow justifies the aggressive and violent reactions of persons who insist on viewing the members of the group with hostility. Excellent examples of this convoluted line of thinking can be found throughout history and in the "ethnic cleansings" occurring at this moment in many countries.

Aggression against certain groups is also found in more subtle ways. Admissions to many schools or academic institutions often depend on belonging to the "right group." Job requirements may be structured to attract only a certain "kind" of applicant, and running for a political office can be done only if one "fits in." These forms of aggression against members of certain groups are all quiet, subtle, and usually unspoken, but they still exist, strongly exerting influences over the lives of many good people.

Mental Health Disorders Relating to Violence

Crisis is a part of every violent act. One's usual coping skills are ineffective when dealing with the violation of a violent act. To recover from the effects of violence, new coping behaviors must be found and then applied. The victims of violence suffer through a

number of emotional and behavioral experiences that may take months or even years to resolve. The process of putting one's life back together after a violent act involves many changes that take place over time (Table 26-2).

The process of recovery from violence is influenced by the severity of the trauma, the resources of the victim, and the help and treatment received immediately following the traumatic event.

Aggressive and violent behaviors are a part of numerous mental health disorders; however, the *Diagnostic and Statistical Manual of Mental Disorders* (DSM-IV) defines only one clinical syndrome as directly related to violence: posttraumatic stress disorder. Rape trauma syndrome is a nursing diagnosis that encompasses the essentials of care for the victims of this violent experience.

Posttraumatic Stress Disorder

"The essential feature of posttraumatic stress disorder (PTSD) is the development of characteristic symptoms following exposure to extreme traumatic stressors" (American Psychiatric Association, 1994). PTSD clearly relates to an actual traumatic event that was outside the realm of common human experience. Examples include war and military combat, violent assault, rape, torture, burglary, natural disasters, terrorist activities, fires, bombings, sudden destruction of one's home, and witnessing the assault, injury, or death of a loved one.

Typically, persons with PTSD persistently relive the traumatic event through intrusive thoughts or distressing dreams. Intense fear, horror, and hopelessness are experienced as individuals struggle to rid themselves of their memories. The sudden arrival of these intrusive thoughts (often called flashbacks) motivate individuals with PTSD to avoid any stimuli associated with the traumatic event. Emotional responses in general become blunted except for those related directly to the violent event. This "psychological numbing" effectively shuts out the outside world until the person is exposed to an event, item, or situation that symbolizes some aspect of the traumatic event. For many survivors of the war in Vietnam, just watching television can precipitate flashbacks and stress reactions.

Persons suffering from PTSD often feel removed and detached from other people, even those they love. The ability to feel emotions is reduced, especially those emotions associated with love, intimacy, and sexuality. Often persons with PTSD believe that their lives will be short and wonder why they survived when others did not.

◆ **TABLE 26-2**
Stages of Recovery From Violence

Stage of Recovery	Time Frame	Emotions, Behaviors
Impact: disorganization	Minutes to days	Initial reactions: crying, confusion, denial, disbelief, fear, hysteria, helplessness, shock; may have physical responses, eating or sleeping disturbances; may be calm with others and then react in private
Recoil: struggle to adapt	Weeks to months	Slowly becomes aware of impact of event on his/her life; immediate danger is past but emotional stress remains; may plan for revenge; tries to resume daily routines; needs to discuss details of violent event; may become dependent; needs much emotional support
Reorganization: reconstruction	Months to years	Emotions fade, but event is not forgotten; reviews event with "Why me?" questions; justifies own actions, then gains sense of control over life; grieves over losses; may experience lingering emotions, nightmares; realizes that life will always be different as result of violence; eventually integrates memories and learns to live with reasonable sense of safety and security; may develop mental health problems if reorganization is not successful

Modified from Keltner NL, Schwecke LH, Bostrom CE: *Psychiatric nursing,* ed 2, St Louis, 1995, Mosby.

Rape Trauma Syndrome

Rape is an act of sexual violence by one person against another. Although rape may involve sexual behaviors, it is an act of power that aims to cause pain at the most intimate level of one's being. Forced sexual attentions are a violation of one's personhood whether they occur at the hands of a stranger or a loved one.

A woman may be raped at any age, but the ages of 15 to 24 are associated with the highest risk. Rape is an underreported crime, with estimates of one woman in three being raped at sometime during her life. Although not as common, the incidence of men being raped by other men is rising, but it is rarely reported (Keltner, Schwecke, and Bostrom, 1995).

Many of the victims of rape realize that they have lived through the experience but wish they had died. Bodily injuries may be minor or severe. A threat on the life of the victim or the promise to return may have been made. Some individuals have been tortured or injured during or shortly after the rape episode.

Those who have survived feel severely violated. Feelings of anger, frustration, loss of control, fear, shame, and guilt haunt the victims of this violent act. Following the rape, most individuals feel the need to retreat to a safe place, clean themselves thoroughly, and destroy all reminders of the event. To do this, however, destroys most of the evidence that may be useful in apprehending the offender.

Recovery from being the victim of a rape follows in the same steps as the stages of recovery from violence (see Table 26-2). First, the individual becomes disorganized, then attempts to adjust, and finally integrates the experience into his/her life. The greater the force or brutality, though, the greater psychological harm and recovery time. Many individuals do not report the assault to the police. They carry the burden alone and suffer a silent rape trauma syndrome.

The nurse may very well be the first health care provider with whom a rape victim interacts. Strong support, gentle understanding, and nonjudgmental acceptance has a powerful influence on how well the victim copes with and successfully recovers from this violent assault.

Therapeutic Interventions

Health care providers are concerned with two major goals when working with the victims of violence.

The first and longest reaching goal is to prevent violence from occurring. The second goal revolves around early recognition and treatment for violated individuals.

Working with abused or victimized clients on a regular basis requires special education and training. Many nurses become rape counsellors or advocates for the abused and exploited. However, every nurse can apply special measures to care for the individuals who happen to become the victims of violence.

Special Assessments

Whenever a suspected victim of violence is brought into the health care system, be it the emergency room or clinic, special attention is required. The first priority of care is to ensure the client's safety, but "whenever violence is part of the picture, the preservation of evidence becomes a top priority as well" (Malestic, 1995).

Forensic evidence is information that is gathered for legal purposes. It is the evidence that helps the law find and convict the perpetrator of the violent act. When violence is suspected, nurses' most effective weapons are accurate observations, precise documentation, and notification of the appropriate authorities. By law, health care providers are required to report these incidences. Although the victims of rape are not required by law to report it, all evidence is important and must be gathered carefully.

When assessing a client who has been a victim of violence, document the size, shape, color, and pattern of any wounds, bruises, scars, or other marks. The skin records evidence well. Human bite marks leave a history. Look for them on the ears, nose, nipples, axillae, back, and genitals. Rings, belt buckles, and other items leave telltale marks behind when they are used as weapons. Other physical signs/symptoms that may indicate violence or abuse include odd marks on the skin, hyperactive reflexes, and poor eye contact. Child abuse or neglect is not always easy to spot. Table 26-3 lists numerous signs/symptoms of child abuse and neglect.

Nurses must know how to assess suspicious injuries and describe their findings objectively. The box on p. 373 offers an example of an abuse assessment documentation form. Document objective evidence as accurately as possible. Do not guess or draw conclusions about the cause of any injury. If the client is a rape victim, all specimens should be labeled and saved for analysis. It is wiser to err on the side of gathering too much information rather than not enough.

Treating Victims of Violence

Remember, the first priority of care for *every* victim of violence is to ensure his/her safety and security.

Once a client feels safe, other diagnostic or treatment interventions can be more easily implemented.

Do not leave the client alone. Many victims believe that their abusers may attempt to hurt them again, even when they are seeking help. Explain all procedures simply and ensure cooperation before proceeding. Allow the client to maintain as much control as possible.

The care plan is developed based on each individual client, the type of abuse, and the coping resources available to the client. Nursing diagnoses are chosen according to identified problems. It is important to remember that each nursing diagnosis has many interventions or nursing actions, and the selection depends on each unique client and his/her particular circumstances. However, all clients who have been abused, exploited, or neglected have certain care needs in common. The box on p. 374 offers an example of a basic care plan for a victim of violence.

Preventing Violence in Your Life

Given the statistics, it is likely that each of us will be exposed to violence at some time during our lives. As members of the health care profession, the odds of being involved in a violent act are increasing. Health care providers are less immune to acts of violence than they were in the past. It is important to remain aware that violence can erupt in any client situation.

When interacting with clients, watch for signs of escalating anger or frustration and then intervene quickly to prevent problems from escalating. Trust your own judgment or "gut-level feelings," and seek assistance from other care providers as needed.

Work to prevent violence in your life. Contact the sponsors of violent programs on television; write companies and protest. Support legislative actions that are designed to reduce violence. Volunteer at shelters, crisis hot lines, or support groups. Educate those who will listen about the effects of violence on children. Volunteer to teach a program on problem-solving at local preschools.

Learn to recognize aggression and violence in your personal thoughts, attitudes, and responses. Become aware of how *you* cope with feelings of anger, frustration, and aggression; practice developing more effective methods for working with your emotions.

Howard Zinn, in his book *You Can't Be Neutral on a Moving Train* (1994), titled the epilogue "The Possibility of Hope." In it, he states that "small acts, when multiplied by millions of people, *can transform the world.*" The small acts of nurses and other health care providers help to nourish the human connections that weave us together. Perhaps, just perhaps, we can make a difference in relation to violence—if we are *all* willing to try.

◆ TABLE 26-3
Signs/Symptoms of Child Abuse and Neglect

Category	Child's Appearance	Child's Behavior	Caretaker's Behavior
Physical abuse	Bruises and welts (on face, lips, or mouth; in various stages of healing; on large areas of torso, back, buttocks, or thighs; in unusual patterns, clustered, or reflective of instrument used to inflict them; on several different surface areas)	Wary of physical contact with adults	Has history of abuse as child
	Burns (cigar or cigarette burns; glove or sock-like burns or doughnut-shaped burns on buttocks or genitalia indicative of immersion in hot liquid; rope burns on arms, legs, neck, or torso; patterned burns that show shape of item [iron, grill, etc.] used to inflict them)	Apprehensive when other children cry	Uses harsh discipline inappropriate to child's age, transgression, and condition
		Demonstrates extremes in behavior (e.g., extreme aggressiveness or withdrawal)	Offers illogical, unconvincing, contradictory, or no explanation of child's injury
	Fractures (skull, jaw, or nasal fractures; spiral fractures of long bones [arm and leg]; fractures in various states of healing; multiple fractures; any fracture in child under age of 2)	Seems frightened of parents	Seems unconcerned about child
		Reports injury by parents	Significantly misperceives child (e.g., sees him/her as bad, evil, a monster)
	Lacerations and abrasions (to mouth, lip, gums, or eye; to the external genitalia)		Psychotic or psychopathic
	Human bite marks		Misuses alcohol or other drugs
			Attempts to conceal child's injury or to protect identity of person responsible
Neglect	Consistently dirty, unwashed, hungry, or inappropriately dressed	Is engaging in delinquent acts (e.g., vandalism, drinking, prostitution, drug use)	Misuses alcohol or other drugs
	Without supervision for extended periods of time or when engaged in dangerous activities	Is begging or stealing food	Maintains chaotic home life
	Constantly tired or listless	Rarely attends school	Shows evidence of apathy or futility
	Has unattended physical problems or lacks routine medical care		Is mentally ill or of diminished intelligence
	Is exploited, overworked, or kept from attending school		Has long-term chronic illnesses
	Has been abandoned		Has history of neglect as child
Sexual abuse	Has torn, stained, or bloody underclothing	Appears withdrawn or engages in fantasy or infantile behavior	Extremely protective or jealous of child
	Is experiencing pain or itching in genital area	Has poor peer relationships	Encourages child to engage in prostitution or sexual acts in presence of caretaker
	Has bruises or bleeding in external genitalia, vagina, or anal regions		Has been sexually abused as child

Modified from *Interdisciplinary glossary on child abuse and neglect: legal, medical, social work terms*, DHHS Pub. No. 80-30137, Department of Health and Human Services (WDC, 1980).

Continued

◆ **TABLE 26-3**
Signs/Symptoms of Child Abuse and Neglect—cont'd

Category	Child's Appearance	Child's Behavior	Caretaker's Behavior
Sexual abuse—cont'd	Has venereal disease Has swollen or red cervix, vulva, or perineum Has semen around mouth or genitalia or on clothing Is pregnant	Is unwilling to participate in physical activities Is engaging in delinquent acts or runs away States he/she has been sexually assaulted by parent/caretaker	Is experiencing marital difficulties Misuses alcohol or other drugs Is frequently absent from home
Emotional maltreatment	Emotional maltreatment, often less tangible than other forms of child abuse and neglect, can be indicated by behaviors of child and caretaker	Appears overly compliant, passive, undemanding Is extremely aggressive, demanding, or rageful Shows overly adaptive behaviors, either inappropriately adult (e.g., parents other children) or inappropriately infantile (e.g., rocks constantly, sucks thumb, is enuretic) Lags in physical, emotional, and intellectual development Attempts suicide	Blames or belittles child Is cold and rejecting Withholds love Treats siblings unequally Seems unconcerned about child's problem

ABUSE ASSESSMENT SCREEN

1. Have you ever been emotionally or physically abused by your partner or someone important to you?
   Yes ❑ No ❑
2. Within the last year, have you been hit, slapped, kicked or otherwise physically hurt by someone?
   Yes ❑ No ❑
   If *yes*, by whom _____
   Number of times _____
   Mark the area of injury on body map.
3. Within the last year, has anyone forced you to have sexual activities?
   If *yes*, who _____
   Number of times _____
4. Are you afraid of your partner or anyone you listed above?
   Yes ❑ No ❑
5. If you are pregnant, have you been hit, slapped, kicked, or otherwise physically hurt by someone?
   Yes ❑ No ❑
   If *yes*, by whom _____
   Number of times _____
   Mark the area of injury on body map.

Developed by the Nursing Research Consortium on Violence and Abuse: *1989.*
Readers are encouraged to reproduce and use this assessment tool.

❖ KEY CONCEPTS

- Violence is a major cause of death and disability in most industrialized countries of the world.
- Theories that attempt to explain the nature of violence include the psychiatric/mental illness model, social learning theories, sociological theories, anthropological theories, and feminist theories.
- Battering is a term that describes ongoing physical abuse of someone, usually a woman, child, or elder.
- Trauma is the leading cause of maternal death during pregnancy.
- Since the early 1960s, the number of reported incidents of child abuse or neglect has swelled to almost 3 million children.
- Adolescent abuse is often an overlooked type of violence.
- Each year approximately 1.5 million elderly persons are victims of abuse or mistreatment.
- Throughout history, people have chosen certain groups of people to define as being different and therefore deserving of aggressive behaviors.
- The process of recovery from violence is influenced by the severity of the trauma, the resources of the victim, and the help and treatment received by the victim immediately following the traumatic event.
- The essential feature of posttraumatic stress disorder (PTSD) is the development of characteristic symptoms following exposure to an extreme traumatic stressor.
- Rape is an act of sexual violence by one person against another that involves the use of power.
- Two major health care goals for treating the victims of violence are to prevent violence from occurring and to provide early recognition and treatment for the violated individuals.
- The first priority of care for every victim of violence is to ensure safety and security.
- By law, health care providers are required to report incidences of suspected or actual abuse or neglect.

❖ SUGGESTIONS FOR FURTHER READING

The Battered Woman's Survival Guide, written by Jan Berliner Statman (Taylor Publishing Company, 1995) is a must-read for every health care provider. The true stories contained within will give you a realistic and valuable look into the lives of battered women and their children.

SAMPLE CLIENT CARE PLAN
RAPE TRAUMA SYNDROME

Assessment

History: Sierra is a 19-year-old college student who lives at home. Three weeks ago she met Ben, a road maintenance worker who happened to be visiting a mutual friend. After a short visit, Sierra said she had to get to the health club for her workout. Ben offered to drive her since he was going in the same direction. Sierra accepted, saying that she had to stop at her house first to change clothes.

On arrival, Sierra left the car and walked into the house. She was surprised to see Ben following her. Later that day, Sierra's mother found her beaten and tied to her bed.

Current Findings: A stuporous young woman, lying in the fetal position. Numerous bruises and abrasions are noted on the face, both wrists, legs, and feet. Mother is at the bedside.

Nursing Diagnosis

Rape trauma syndrome related to recent sexual attack and injury

Planning/Expected Outcomes

Sierra will be free of medical or physical complications of rape trauma. Sierra will establish a therapeutic alliance with the primary nurse.

Nursing Interventions

Intervention

1. Allow Sierra's mother to remain with her at all times.
2. Assist with physical assessment and gathering of specimens after consent is obtained.

3. Let Sierra know that she will not be blamed for the rape incident.
4. Convey an accepting, caring, nonjudgmental attitude regardless of the circumstances.
5. Encourage Sierra to acknowledge the pain and anger of the rape experience.
6. Explain the importance of seeking support and counseling for Sierra and her family.
7. Encourage Sierra to report the incident to the police.
8. Make referrals to rape crisis center, family counselors (with permission).

Rationale

1. Mother has historically provided safety and security for Sierra.
2. To assess the extent of her physical injuries, psychological trauma; to gather forensic evidence.
3. Violated persons often feel they will be held responsible for encouraging the assault.
4. Helps to establish therapeutic communications and builds trust.
5. Releasing painful emotions lessens their intensity and power.
6. Provides emotional support during the process of returning to "normal."
7. May help to prevent other occurrences; may help to bring the perpetrator to justice.
8. Long-term emotional support will help Sierra and her family effectively adapt.

Evaluation

Sierra tested negative for sexually transmitted diseases 3 weeks after the incidence. Following 2 weeks of encouragement, Sierra attended her first crisis support group.

❖ REFERENCES

All AC: A literature review: assessment and intervention in elder abuse, *J Gerontol Nurs* 20(7):25, 1994.

American Psychiatric Association: *Diagnostic and statistical manual of mental disorders,* ed 4, Washington, DC, 1994, The Association.

Baumeister RF, Leary MR: The need to belong: desire for interpersonal attachments as a fundamental human motivation, *Psychol Bull* 117(3):497, 1995.

Browne A: Violence against women by male partners, *Am Psychol* 48(10):1077, 1993.

Campbell J, Humphreys J: *Nursing care of survivors of family violence,* St Louis, 1993, Mosby.

Coody D and others: Shaken baby syndrome: identification and prevention for nurse practitioners, *J Pediatr Health Care* 8(2):50, 1994.

Council on Scientific Affairs: Adolescents as victims of family violence, *JAMA* 270:1850, 1993.

Dickason EJ, Silverman BL, Schult MO: *Maternal-infant nursing care,* ed 2, St Louis, 1994, Mosby.

Finkelhor D, Dziuba-Leatherman D: Victimization of children, *Am Psychol* 49(3):173, 1994.

Frost MH, Willette K: Risk for abuse/neglect: documentation of assessment data and diagnosis, *J Gerontol Nurs* 20(8):37, 1994.

Gest T: Violent crime is a serious problem. In Bender D, Leone B, editors: *Violence: opposing viewpoints,* San Diego, CA, 1996, Greenhaven Press.

Glod CA: Long-term consequences of childhood physical and sexual abuse, *Arch Psychiatr Nurs* 7(3):163, 1993.

Justice B, Justice R: *The abusing family,* ed 2, New York, 1990, Plenum Press.

Keltner NL, Schwecke LH, Bostrom CE: *Psychiatric nursing,* ed 2, St Louis, 1995, Mosby.

Krugman RD: Child abuse and neglect. In *Current pediatric diagnosis and treatment,* ed 12, Norwalk, 1994, Appleton & Lange.

Landes A, Quiram D, Jacobs NR: *Child abuse,* ed 5, Wylie, TX, 1995, Information Plus.

Malestic SL: Fight violence with forensic evidence, *RN* 58(1):30, 1995.

McFarlane J and others: Assessing for abuse during pregnancy: severity and frequency of injuries and associated entry into prenatal care, *JAMA* 267(23):3176, 1992.

Minaker KL, Frishman R: Elder abuse: love gone wrong, *Harvard Ment Health Lett* Special supplement, October 1995.

Potter PA, Perry AG: *Basic nursing: theory and practice,* ed 3, St Louis, 1995, Mosby.

Randall T: Adolescents may experience home, school abuse; their future draws researcher's concern, *JAMA* 267(23):3127, 1992.

Roye CF: Breaking through to the adolescent patient, *Am J Nurs* 95(12):19, 1995.

Schacter B, Sienfield J: Personal violence and the culture of violence, *Soc Work* 39(4):347, 1994.

Sessions with a cybershrink: an interview with Sherry Turkle, *Tech Rev* 99(2):41, 1996.

Stanhope M, Lancaster J: *Community health nursing: promoting health of aggregates, families, and individuals,* ed 4, St Louis, 1996, Mosby.

Starck PL, McGovern JP, editors: *The hidden dimension of illness: human suffering,* New York, 1992, National League for Nursing Press.

Statman JB: *The battered woman's survival guide: breaking the cycle,* ed 2, Dallas, TX, 1995, Taylor Publishing.

Thorne-Finch R: *Ending the silence: the origins and treatment of male violence against women,* Toronto, 1993, University of Toronto Press.

US Bureau of Census: *Statistical abstract of the United States: 1993,* ed 113, Washington, DC, 1994.

Whiting B: Sex identity conflict and physical violence: a comparative study, *Am Anthropol* 67:126, 1965.

Zinn H: *You can't be neutral on a moving train: a personal history of our times,* New York, 1994, Beacon Press.

27

SUICIDE

LEARNING OBJECTIVES

1. Describe the range of self-protective behavioral responses.

2. List three myths about suicidal behaviors.

3. Name two cultural or social factors that relate to suicide.

4. Identify four categories of motivation for attempting suicide.

5. Explain how suicide affects family members and friends.

6. State three theories that attempt to explain the causes of suicide.

7. Discuss the occurrence of suicide throughout each life cycle.

8. Describe the process for assessing the suicidal potential of a client.

9. Identify three therapeutic goals and nursing interventions for clients with suicidal behaviors.

KEY TERMS

ambivalence
direct self-destructive behaviors
indirect self-destructive behaviors
parasuicidal behaviors
passive suicide

rational suicide
self-injuries
suicidal attempts
suicidal gestures
suicidal ideation

suicidal threats
suicide
suicidology

Suicide is the action of intentionally taking one's own life. "For most of the last fifteen hundred years, much of Western civilization considered suicide an immoral act committed by the sinful or insane" (Momeyer, 1992). In England, suicide historically was considered an offense against the King. In the 1930s, many people in the United States took their own lives after the stock market crash in 1929 that began the Great Depression. During World War II, Japanese kamikaze pilots intentionally sacrificed their lives for political and religious principles.

Suicide has historically served as a solution to life's great obstacles or disappointments. Today, we grapple with the dilemmas of rational suicide, freedom of choice, and physician-assisted suicide. Discussions about the morality or legality of suicide will grow and fade, but the ending of life by one's own hands will continue to occur as people struggle for control over their particular situations.

Continuum of Behavioral Responses

According to Maslow's hierarchy, safety and security are fundamental requirements for life. Individuals behave in many ways to secure these basic needs. Some people respond with behaviors that promote growth, whereas others begin a journey to self-destruction (Fig. 27-1) (Stuart and Sundeen, 1995). Adaptive behaviors result in a greater understanding and acceptance of oneself, but maladaptive self-protective responses, if not changed, can eventually lead to subtle or overt self-destruction.

Self-destructive behaviors commonly take two forms: direct and indirect. **Direct self-destructive behaviors** relate to any form of active suicidal behavior, such as threats, gestures, or attempts to in-

tentionally end one's life. In this case, the individual is aware of and intends to achieve the desired outcome: death. Although the person may waver between wanting to live and needing to die, the behaviors communicate an active wish to end the suffering of the present.

Many more people, however, engage in indirect self-destructive behaviors, which are the more subtle responses to self-protection. **Indirect self-destructive behaviors** are described as any behaviors or actions that may result in harm or death to the individual's well-being. In this case, people have no actual intention of ending their lives. They may be unaware of the potential for self-harm when engaging in these activities and deny the possibility of danger even when confronted. Examples of indirect self-destructive behaviors include substance abuse, engaging in inappropriate or dangerous activities, and an unwillingness to change negative thoughts and actions. Because many of these behaviors are legal or socially accepted, people do not realize their potential for harm.

As the continuum of self-protective responses moves more toward maladaptive behaviors, indirect self-destructive behaviors progress to active attempts to injure oneself. **Self-injuries** reaffirm to individuals that they are still alive. Pain serves as a reminder of their connection with the body and its physical world.

The last and ultimate maladaptive self-protective response is suicide, the ending of one's own life. Suicide is a complex and emotional issue, but it is one with which most nurses must cope. Although suicidal attempts receive the bulk of attention, those who engage in indirect self-destructive behaviors are at just as high a risk for suicide as those individuals who actually attempt to end their lives.

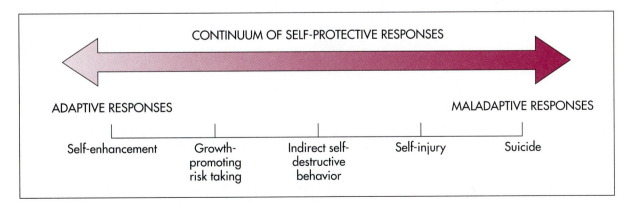

Fig. 27-1   Continuum of self-protective responses. (Redrawn from Stuart GW, Sundeen SJ: *Principles and practice of psychiatric nursing*, ed 5, St Louis, 1995, Mosby.)

Myths About Suicide

Many half-truths and misconceptions about suicide still continue to exist despite educational efforts to promote an accurate understanding of the problem. Although suicide has been around as long as man, little effort was made to understand its nature until the beginning of this century. Today, many false ideas about suicide still exist. Table 27-1 explains several of these myths and offers facts to more accurately reflect the nature of suicide.

Impact of Suicide on Society

Over 1000 suicides occur throughout the world every day. Many suicides are culturally influenced. To illustrate, the number of suicides in 1990 ranged from a low of 7 per 100,000 persons in Italy to a high of 38.2 suicides per 100,000 persons in Hungary (U.S. Bureau of Census, 1993). In the United States, "about 30,000 people complete the act of suicide each year, making it the eighth leading cause of death . . . and the third leading killer of young people" (Stuart and Sundeen, 1995). The true number of persons who end their own lives is unknown because many motor vehicle accidents, murders, and other mishaps are actually intentions to commit suicide. For this reason, it is important for nurses and other health care providers to be well versed in recognizing and intervening with clients who are suicidal.

Cultural Factors

No one knows exactly why a person chooses suicide, but many cultural, social, and individual factors have an influence. The laws, customs, beliefs, values, and norms of a culture usually include a view of suicide. In some cultures, such as ancient Japan, suicide was considered an honorable atonement for transgressions committed during one's life. When the pharaoh kings of Egypt died, it was an expected custom for the widow(s) to commit suicide to join him on his journey across the heavens.

Religious beliefs and customs have an impact on the incidence of suicide. Some Christian faiths, for example, forbid suicide under any circumstances, whereas the taking of one's life may be justified in the beliefs of another religious group.

Customs and rituals may play a role in suicide. The "evil eye" or voodoo practiced by Caribbean islanders

---

◆ **TABLE 27-1**
Myths and Facts About Suicide

Myth	Fact
People who talk about it will not commit suicide. One does not need to take a suicide threat seriously.	Most people communicate their intent, verbally, in writing, through art, with behaviors.
A failed suicide attempt is manipulative behavior.	Manipulation is usually not a factor in suicide.
People who are really serious about suicide give no clues.	Many people communicate warnings of their intent by such things as tidying up their affairs, giving away possessions, and being preoccupied with death.
It is harmful to discuss the subject of suicide with clients.	Most suicidal persons need acceptance and emotional support; discussing the topic demonstrates interest and concern.
Only psychotic or depressed people commit suicide.	Depression is a high risk factor for suicide, but not all suicidal persons are depressed. Mental illness is a risk factor for suicide.
Suicide occurs only in the lower socioeconomic classes, the poor.	Although poverty is a risk factor, suicide occurs in all socioeconomic classes.
Young children never commit suicide.	Suicidal behavior is the leading cause of psychiatric hospitalization for young children. Suicide can occur in children as young as 4.
When people show signs of an improved mood, the threat of suicide is over.	Depressed people often show improved moods, attitude, and behaviors before their deaths because the decision to commit suicide has been made.

Modified from Fortinash KM, Holoday-Worret PA: *Psychiatric-mental health nursing,* St Louis, 1996, Mosby.

is very real for the victim of the curse. Suicide is not a surprising outcome for an individual who has been hexed or cursed in these societies.

Hungary routinely came in first in the World Health Organization's statistics on suicide from the early 1970s until 1993 (Beck, 1995) (see box below). Since 1993, Russia and the Baltic republics have surpassed Hungary in the number of suicides. Providers of health care must remember that people hold strongly to their cultural beliefs and practices. Knowing a cultural group's attitude relating to suicide may someday help prevent it from happening to one of your clients.

Social Factors

There are many influences in society that have an effect on the incidence of suicide. Chief among them is a sense of social isolation felt by members of fast-paced, goal-oriented societies. Family and community support systems have dwindled as mobility, politics, and finances move people away from the only safety and security they have known. The emotional and often physical support of kind neighbors and friends has been replaced by the generic, ready-made support of massive and complicated governmental systems. Crime and other aggressive actions force people to mistrust the intentions of their neighbors and barricade themselves behind locked doors or in secured communities, but the price for security is isolation and its ensuing sense of hopelessness.

The inability to meet basic needs has a strong influence on the occurrence of suicide. Since the emptying of state psychiatric hospitals, the homeless population has swelled. It is now estimated that persons with mental illnesses make up over one third of the homeless population (Torrey, 1992). The risk of suicide for mentally healthy individuals, as well as the mentally troubled, skyrockets when they are unable to meet food, shelter, and clothing needs. Poverty and homelessness lead to depression and hopelessness in the long run. Suicide becomes an acceptable alternative when one is continually hungry, cold, ill, or living in fear.

The availability of weapons, especially firearms, has proven to be a significant factor in relation to the occurrence of suicide. In countries in which the ownership of guns is prohibited, suicide rates are lower. To illustrate, in the United Kingdom, owning a handgun is illegal. According to the U.S. Bureau of Census (1993) the suicide rate for England and Wales was 12.1 people per 100,000. In the United States, where gun ownership is hotly defended and debated, the rate is 20 suicides per 100,000 persons. The availability of firearms is reflected in a country's statistics on suicide and violence (see box below).

One's state of health or illness influences suicidal considerations. Losses associated with old age can lead to depression and feelings of futility. Why struggle when tomorrow is an instant replay of today, and today was not good? Suicide rates climb as age, infirmity, and illness take their toll.

The appearance of HIV/AIDS has had a profound influence on the suicide rates of many countries. In the United States, the "death-with-dignity" philosophy has influenced many AIDS sufferers to choose the time and place of their passing. This form of suicide is called **"rational suicide"** because the choice to end one's life was made from a sound mind, freely, and rationally.

Many other social factors play a role in the number of suicides in a society. The number, availability, and kind of community-based resources for health promotion and treatment have an influence on a society's mental as well as physical health. Without these resources and the support they offer, the stresses of life can overwhelm and consume society's more unfortunate citizens. Be aware of the social changes in this world because hidden among them are clues to caring for clients who are thinking of ending their lives.

Dynamics of Suicide

The act of attempting suicide has a profound impact on the lives of individuals, families, friends, and communities. When enough suicides occur, the soci-

---

🌐 CULTURAL ASPECTS

In some societies, suicide is an accepted, centuries-old tradition. In the country of Hungary, for example, villages dwindle as their residents choose suicide over the uncertainty of living an isolated, lonely life. When people in Hungary "get fed up, they hang themselves, cut their wrists, or swallow pesticides, just like their fathers and grandfathers did," states Dr. Jorge Ulloa, a psychiatrist who runs a suicide clinic near Budapest (Beck, 1995).

◆ THINK ABOUT

Statistics show that gun-related injuries and deaths in the United States increase in households with firearms.

Do you think that gun ownership should be controlled?

If so, how should that be accomplished?

ety becomes affected. Because human beings dynamically function in several realms or dimensions at any given time, it is important to consider suicide from a holistic point of view.

Characteristics of Suicide

Suicide is an act of individual meaning. The actual reasons for choosing such a final course of action will probably never be known to anyone but the individual. However, it is likely that more than one motive drives a person to suicide.

In the physical dimension, thoughts of suicide produce many of the same biochemical changes in the body as depression. Often suicidal persons will not eat, drink, or rest enough to maintain required energy levels. Recent studies have suggested a link between low serum cholesterol levels and suicide attempts in men. The results of one study found that, "among men, those with low cholesterol were about twice as likely to have made medically serious suicide attempts" (Golier and others, 1995). At this time, there appears to be no such correlation for women and cholesterol.

One's method of choice for committing suicide differs by gender. Men prefer to rely on firearms, hanging, or drowning, whereas women prefer to overdose with pills or to inhale carbon monoxide.

The emotional dimension of functioning for the suicidal person is filled with feelings of ambivalence, guilt, anger, aggression, helplessness, and hopelessness. **Ambivalence** is a state in which an individual experiences conflicting feelings, attitudes, or drives. For the suicidal person, the struggle is between self-preservation (life) and self-destruction (death). Often, suicidal individuals threaten or attempt suicide and then seek out treatment, behaviorally acting out their feelings of ambivalence.

Anger and aggression are turned inward in suicidal persons. Fears of being abandoned or rejected add to the dynamics. Many persons who feel trapped in frustrating dependent relationships commonly react with rage that becomes self-directed and harmful.

Guilt can also lead to suicide. Suicidal individuals shoulder the guilt of the world. They feel sinful and carry around the belief that they must have done something very wrong to deserve their misfortunes. Often personal guilt is exaggerated until the only way to make up for one's transgressions is to offer the final sacrifice—the self.

For the suicidal individual, the emotional dimension is marked by overwhelming feelings of helplessness and hopelessness. Nothing the person tries to do works out the way it was expected. The self becomes unable to emotionally function. Life becomes bleak

and hopeless as its meaning and purpose slips from the suicidal person's control. Self-esteem sinks to an all-time low.

In the intellectual dimension, the intense emotional suffering of a suicidal person leads to distorted thinking and self-defeating thoughts. The self becomes devalued, worth little. Everything becomes glum and depressing, which leads individuals to a negative and pessimistic view of the future. One's internal dialogue of self-talk becomes self-defeating, which soon becomes reflected in negative behaviors. Thinking is self-centered rather than oriented toward solving problems. Why continue when the future looks so bleak?

The social dimension of functioning includes the suicidal person's views of others. Many suicidal individuals depend on the feedback of others to frequently reaffirm their self-worth. Self-esteem is very low in suicidal people. Their feelings of inferiority, of being less than others, interfere with social relationships and lead to the isolation and loneliness that often accompanies suicide.

In the last area of functioning, the spiritual dimension, suicidal individuals grapple with the cultural, religious, and ethical dilemmas associated with bringing about one's own demise. Many respond by blaming other people, their society, or their religious practices. Others "make their peace" with the spiritual sides of themselves and experience a spiritual calm and serenity before committing suicide. Some people believe they will be reunited with loved ones in a new life after leaving this reality.

Categories of Motivation

People are motivated or moved to take their own lives for diverse reasons. However, all suicide victims seem to share two major viewpoints. The first is related to a deep, inner, personal disturbance of hopelessness, despair, poor self-esteem, and the feeling of being trapped. The other is described as a logic whereby suicidal individuals consider the act as a way of relieving themselves from the miseries of this life and connecting with a sense of immortality or a life beyond the one they are leaving behind.

There are several categories of motivation for suicide. The first motive for suicidal behavior is called "a cry for help." Most commonly, suicidal persons bounce between the wish to live and the need to die. They feel trapped, enmeshed, and encircled in a situation from which they believe there is no other escape. Killing oneself is seen as an effort to break out and take control and to do something about one's life. These individuals are communicating their need for a particular kind of help, the kind of help that will radically change his/her life and that will bring death to the old way of existence. The box below presents a case study that illustrates this type of motivation.

The second motive for considering suicide is the refusal to accept a diminished quality, style, or pace of life. This motive causes persons to commit "rational suicide." They assess their situation in a clear and rational manner, consider all the options, and then decide to take steps that will end their lives. Decisions and plans are made logically, with little or no emotion. The decision to commit suicide is seen as a logical one. An example would be the 80-year-old man who kills his 78-year-old blind and bedridden wife and then ends his own life after having made all the arrangements for their funerals and property settlements.

The third motivation centers around the need to affirm one's soul. These persons believe that there are values that are more important than life and that suicide is a way of fulfilling one's existence. The 18-year-old who takes his life one summer evening when everything is going well and the future is bright may be searching for that fulfillment.

The fourth motive for suicidal behavior is to relieve the distress related to situations that threaten the intactness of a person. The 70-year-old businessman with prostate cancer who chooses suicide over potentially life-prolonging surgery is an example of this type of motivation.

Last are those individuals "who are preoccupied with suicide almost as their way of life. They derive comfort from the knowledge that they will control the time and circumstances of their death" (Starck and McGovern, 1992). These persons are usually unwilling to accept life on any terms but their own. They set conditions for living and refuse to continue with life unless it is on their terms. Often suicide is the only form of real control they feel they have.

There are numerous motivations for attempting to end one's life. When working with suicidal clients, remember that no matter what the motivation, each individual is experiencing deep discomfort and low, low self-esteem. Compassion and understanding become valuable therapeutic tools when working with suicidal clients.

Theories About Suicide

Because suicide is an end result, it is difficult to understand all the factors that led up to one's decision to end his/her life. The study of the nature of suicide is called **suicidology.** Several theories attempt to explain the causes of suicidal behavior.

The *psychoanalytical theory* states that all humans have the instinct for life and death within them. Suicidal persons experience much ambivalence between wanting to live and wanting to die. Anger turns inward, and when stressful life events activate their death wish, suicide becomes an option.

Sociological theory looks at the relationship between the number of suicides and the social conditions of an area. These theorists believe that suicide rates are affected by group support (or the lack of it), social changes, regulations, religion, legal sanctions or limi-

---

CASE STUDY

Sandy was young, alone, pregnant, and scared. She knew that she was not welcome in the home of her father, who told her when she left for college, "If you get into trouble, don't come crying to me. You'll have to take care of it by yourself."

Her boyfriend, who swore love and devotion, denied that he was the father of her baby and then left town. Even her new friends deserted her on hearing that she was pregnant. Now, the school officials were asking about her plans.

In desperation, Sandy sought to terminate the pregnancy but found that she was "too far along." On hearing the news, she decided that there was only one course of action that could end her troubles. She really did not want to die, but there was no other way out. The thought of facing life alone with a new baby was more than Sandy could tolerate.

As she made her plans, a feeling of calm came over Sandy. She would handle the situation in her own way. At least this way, she rationalized, "I am in control. I am the one who will do something about this."

Later that night, Sandy connected a rubber hose from the exhaust system to the interior of her car, rolled up all the windows, and sat quietly with the motor running. The next morning, when her body was discovered, she held a small note in her hand. It read:

"Daddy, I took care of it myself. Love, Sandy."

Clinical Decisions

1. What do you think motivated Sandy to commit suicide?
2. Do you think this was her only or best course of action?
3. If Sandy had come to you for help, what could you have done?

tations, and philosophical beliefs. In short, the sociological theories consider the impact of social factors on the occurrence of suicide.

Last is the *interpersonal theory*, developed by H.S. Sullivan. Suicide is viewed as the outcome of a failure to work with or resolve interpersonal conflicts (Sullivan, 1968). These three theories formed much of the foundation for further studies into the nature of suicide. However, recent research into the psychobiological nature of the human being is revealing many new facts about suicide and its motivation.

New Biological Evidence

Depression, anxiety, and impulsive behaviors are common in suicidal individuals. As scientists are now able to study the structure and functions of the living human brain, new connections between physical and behavioral activities are being rapidly discovered.

Anxiety and depression are often the forerunners of suicidal thoughts. Researchers have demonstrated that when certain chemicals in the brain (neurotransmitters) are not in balance, people have difficulty regulating their moods. For example, irregularities in a certain neurotransmitter pattern, called the serotonin system, have been found in depressed and suicidal persons. These findings have implications for health care providers. As our understanding of the dynamics of suicide grows, so does our ability to recognize the potential for suicide and effectively intervene.

Effects of Suicide on Others

Suicide, like natural death, has a strong effect on those left behind. "Following the suicide of a loved one, the lives of the survivors can be plagued with anger, sadness, shame, guilt, health problems, and agonizing questions" (Watson and Lee, 1993). The grieving process for the family of a suicide victim is further complicated by social attitudes about taking one's own life.

Because of the emotions attached to a suicidal act, the loss of a loved one through suicide is considered to be a much more stressful event than the grief reaction of a natural death. Guilt is a main response because survivors often think they could have done something to prevent the suicide. Guilt may stem from the unexpressed anger toward the deceased for abandoning family and friends.

Anger may be expressed as "agonized questioning," which helps the survivors cope with their emotional turmoil and disorganization. Some may hide their resentment, anger, and rage, turning it into depression. Children often feel responsible for the suicide. Unless they receive much love, support, and guidance, depression or other behavioral problems may develop.

Socially, the stigma of suicide is soon felt. Forced interactions with health care providers, the police, or the media soon after death can bring home the feelings of rejection that are often experienced by the family members of suicide victims. Friends and relatives, unsure of how to help, withdraw or often do nothing. This reaction limits the social contact and support that is so needed after the suicide of a loved one. The loved ones of a suicide victim may also withdraw from social interactions to protect themselves from the gossip and intrusion of inconsiderate others. Thus begins a cycle of guilt, withdrawal, and blame between the survivors of a suicide and others in their world. With support and understanding, survivors eventually recover and accept that the responsibility for the suicide rests with the individual who did the deed, not with those left behind.

Health care providers are not immune to the effects of suicide. When a client, especially an inpatient, commits suicide, staff members and other clients may experience guilt, anger, helplessness, or despair. Both clients and staff members need to grieve and express the emotions that follow a suicide. Often, other clients on the unit will express anger at the staff, act out, or become self-destructive. Sharing emotions about the suicide allows both staff and clients the opportunity to express themselves and cope with the experience. The survivors of suicide, no matter who they are, must grieve and learn to heal.

Suicide Throughout the Life Cycle

Attempts to end one's life occur in every age group. Although the motivations for suicide may vary with the developmental level, the act remains the same: an effort to die. Understanding how suicide is used at different developmental levels is important. Recognition and treatment of the problems underlying suicidal behaviors are much more effective when begun early.

Suicide and Children

Although depression is usually a component of suicide, with children it may be different. Some experts believe that suicide in children is most often the result of family conflict or disruption (Clunn, 1995). Children commit suicide as a cry for help to change their situations, or they may sincerely have a wish to die. Children with existing mental health problems, such as conduct disorders, attention-deficit hyperactivity disorders, or psychoses, are at a greater risk for committing suicide than other children. Because they are impulsive, many suicides in children are not planned. Often, the loss of a parent triggers suicidal behaviors in children who are not encouraged to grieve. Very young children cannot understand the concept of death as a permanent state. Their wishes to join their lost parent may lead to suicidal behaviors.

The key to recognizing the signs of suicidal intent lies in a change in the child's behavior. Any child whose attitudes or behaviors change dramatically in a short period of time, especially following a stressful event or situation, is a candidate for suicide.

Suicide and Adolescents

The rate of adolescent suicide has risen dramatically in the past 30 years. The suicide rate for 10- to 19-year-olds has almost doubled, from 6.5 per 100,000 people in 1970 to an astounding 12.6 suicides per 100,000 persons in 1990 (U.S. Bureau of Census, 1993). Young men are the most affected by violence and suicide in adolescence. These figures may not accurately reflect the actual number of adolescent suicides because many suicidal deaths are listed as accidental.

During adolescence, any longstanding family or social problems may continue to worsen as the new difficulties of growing up are added. If coping skills or resources are insufficient, adolescents, especially those with low self-esteem, may consider suicide as an option for solving their problems.

Adolescents commit suicide when they feel there is no other way out of their problems. They see their problems as genuinely unsolvable, now or in the future. Death becomes the only way out for these teens.

There appear to be many factors that come into play in adolescent suicide. Depression, poor impulse-control, and emotional isolation are related to suicide in adolescents. Dysfunctional or disrupted family interactions, such as divorce or separation of parents, can devastate many teens (Hogarth, 1995).

Social problems with peers, the use of drugs or alcohol, and a lack of consistent relationships also add to the risk of suicide. When the environment lacks security or presents dangers, many teens feel that their lives will be short and that they will not live until adulthood. The outlook for the future holds little promise with this attitude.

The incidence of suicidal behaviors is also increased in children and adolescents who suffer from chronic disease. A recent study of children and adolescents with insulin-dependent diabetes mellitus concluded that the risk of suicide was higher in this group. Most individuals who actually tried to commit suicide did so by some method relating to their diabetes, such as overdosing on insulin (Goldston and others, 1994). This study reminds nurses to routinely assess *every* client (including those with medical diagnoses or problems) for the presence of suicidal thoughts. Become aware of the risk factors that can play an important role in an adolescent's choice to commit suicide (see box above, at right).

Suicide and Adults

Suicide is a significant problem in adulthood, especially for white men. Women attempt suicide three times more frequently than men, but men are more successful at completing the act. In 15- to 24-year-old men, suicide ranks as the third leading cause of death (Stanhope and Lancaster, 1996) (Fig. 27-2).

RISK FACTORS FOR SUICIDE

- Abuse, neglect, exploitation
- Accident prone
- Academic pressures, school problems
- Chronic illness, disability, HIV/AIDS, terminal illness
- Dysfunctional family relationships
- Family/self history of anxiety, depression, previous suicide attempts or other mental health problems
- Inadequate childrearing practices
- Loss of parent or significant other
- Low socioeconomic status, poverty, homelessness
- Male gender, unmarried, unemployed
- Member of certain religious cults
- Negative outlook for future
- Parental/self history of alcoholism, substance abuse, or previous suicide attempts
- Profession/occupation: policeman, fireman, air traffic controller, physician, psychiatrist, dentist, college student
- Social isolation, lack of social support
- Stressful or unhappy personal relationships, peer pressure

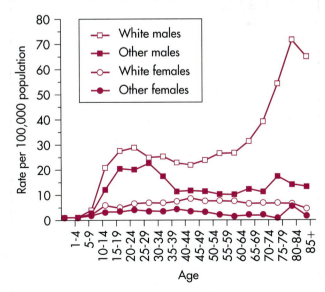

Fig. 27-2 Suicide rate per 100,000 living population, all ages. (Redrawn from Stuart GW, Sundeen SJ: *Principles and practice of psychiatric nursing,* ed 5, St Louis, 1995, Mosby.)

In young adults, suicide occurs when individuals are unable to cope with the pressures of adulthood. Some experience problems associated with interpersonal relationships, such as marital discord, divorce, or loss of a significant other. Some lack personal resources and are poor, hungry, or dissatisfied with their lives.

Loneliness is a factor in adult suicides. The loss of a family or significant relationship, whether through divorce or death, increases the risk of suicide. In addition, certain professions and occupations are associated with higher rates of suicide.

Most adult suicides can be prevented if the clues are uncovered early enough. Do not hesitate to ask clients if they ever think about suicide. The answer to that question may offer an opportunity to help save an individual's life.

Suicide and Older Adults

As age increases, so does the rate of suicide. Many studies "clearly show that the elderly commit suicide more often than other age groups and that the incidence continues to increase with age" (Courage and others, 1993). The actual number of suicides in the elderly is difficult to determine because only active suicides are counted. Many older adults choose to commit a **passive suicide** by refusing to eat, drink, or cooperate with care.

The causes and risk factors of suicide in the elderly are poorly understood. Although 75% of the elderly who commit suicide have had contact with a health care professional within a month before their deaths, their risk was not identified or treated (Courage and others, 1993). Older adults tend not to communicate their intentions unless directly asked, and suicidal attempts in older adults are more successful. One out of every two suicide attempts results in death (Lueckenotte, 1996). These sobering statements must alert every nurse to perform a suicidal risk assessment for all older adult clients.

Most older adults view the timing of death in one of three ways: God controlled, physician and individual controlled, or controlled by the individual alone. Risk factors for suicide in the elderly are advanced age, male gender, low socioeconomic status, chronic pain or illness, and fear of becoming dependent or helpless. The lack of relationships appears to be an important theme. Some studies (Leenaars, 1992) have speculated that a "lack of attachment might be the driving force behind many suicides" in older persons. Other researchers believe that intolerable life circumstances is the main motive for suicides in the elderly.

Social attitudes about suicide in the elderly differ. Some people think that all suicides in the elderly are irrational decisions, based in depression or physical illness. They believe aggressive interventions are always required. Others view elder suicide as the last rational decision, the last act of control over one's life. One theorist (Prado, 1990) describes a preemptive or "rational suicide" in which one consciously and rationally can choose to avoid the "foreseen demeaning decline." Several authors "argue in favor of rational suicide as a sane, honorable choice in old age or, for that matter, in other circumstances as well" (Moore, 1993). The concept of rational suicide in the United States is "at odds with the legal system" (Courage and others, 1993), but in other countries, such as the Netherlands, suicide is an acceptable way to achieve "death with dignity." It may seem that the important questions and issues surrounding the control of one's own death are issues for philosophers and discussions of medical ethics; however, we as nurses will be addressing many of these questions in daily practice.

Therapeutic Interventions

Thoughts about suicide can be described on several levels. **Suicidal ideation** is described as thoughts or fantasies that are expressed but have no definite intent. Ideas may be expressed directly or symbolically. **Suicidal threats** are verbal or written expressions of the intent to take one's life, but they are without actions. As the seriousness increases, **suicidal gestures** may be observed. These are suicidal actions that result in little or no injury but communicate a message of suicidal purpose. **Suicide attempts** are serious self-directed actions that are intended to do harm or end life. **Parasuicidal behaviors** are unsuccessful attempts and gestures associated with a low likelihood of success. The last level is *completed suicide,* the successful attempt to end one's life. Motivation for the successful suicide may be conscious or unconscious (Fortinash and Holoday-Worret, 1996).

Prevention is the most important nursing (health care) action for clients who may be suicidal. Preventing a suicide from occurring means saving a life. Prevention requires a knowledge of the dynamics of suicide and the ability to recognize the potential for suicidal actions in every client. Applying the nursing process is an excellent method for working with clients who may be considering suicide.

Assessment of Suicidal Potential

Because suicide is becoming so prevalent, it is important for nurses to evaluate every client for its potential. To accomplish this, assess the risk factors for the age of the client. Then ask the client directly if he/she has any thoughts relating to suicide. Asking clients will not encourage them to take any suicidal actions. On the contrary, it gives them permission to discuss their feelings and attitudes (Stewart, 1993). The box below offers a list of questions for assessing suicidal intentions.

The most important question to ask is "Do you think you can control your behavior and refrain from acting on your thoughts or impulses?" If the answer is negative, then hospitalization may be required for the client's safety and protection. Not every question may be appropriate for every client, but a series of questions like these will usually bring out expressions of suicidal thoughts if they are present.

Suicidal intentions can exist with any medical or psychiatric diagnosis (Goldacre, Seagroatt, and Hawton, 1993). Clients who are depressed must be carefully monitored for expressions of hopelessness. Table 27-2 lists the basic components of a suicide assessment. When used as part of a nursing history, it will yield valuable information about the client's suicidal intentions (if any) along with numerous clues to help understand the unique individual we call "the client." The box on p. 386, at left, offers an important reminder.

Nursing diagnoses for suicidal persons are based on each client's identified problems and needs. Commonly identified diagnoses include anxiety, impaired adjustment, ineffective coping, denial, body image disturbance, dysfunctional grieving, spiritual distress, risk for self-directed violence, loneliness, and powerlessness.

Nursing Interventions for Suicidal Clients

The first priority for the care of suicidal clients is protection from harm (Bonger and others, 1993). If the client is actively attempting suicide, he/she must be physically prevented from doing so. If the risks are so high that a serious attempt may be made, then *suicide precautions* are implemented. These precautions are standard interventions to prevent a suicide attempt from occurring (McCloskey and Bulechek, 1996) (see box on p. 386, at right).

One of the most important therapeutic interventions (after ensuring safety) with suicidal persons is to establish a connection (rapport). Many suicidal

---

QUESTIONS TO ASK A CLIENT FOR THE POTENTIAL FOR SUICIDE

- What has been the most difficult moment for you in the recent past?
- Have things been so bad that you have thought about escaping? If so, how?
- Are there times when death seems like an attractive option to you?
- Have you thought of harming yourself?
- Have you thought about killing yourself?
- If you were to harm yourself, how would you do so?
- Do you have access to the items you would need to carry out your plan? (This includes a gun, quantities of medication, a rope, an enclosed garage.)
- Have you thought about or attempted to harm yourself in the past?
- What has kept you from harming yourself thus far?
- What might keep you from harming yourself in the future?

From Lueckenotte AG: *Gerontologic nursing,* St Louis, 1996, Mosby.

◆ TABLE 27-2
Suicide Assessment

Assessment	Description
Suicide ideation (thoughts)	Client talks about wanting to be dead, imagines AIDS or other serious illness, seems gloomy, brooding.
History of suicide attempts	Client has tried to end own life before; there may be history of suicide in family.
Present suicide plan	The more detailed a suicide plan, the more likely it will be carried out.
Availability of items to carry out plan	What guns, rifles, knives or other weapons are available? How difficult is it to obtain such items?
Substance use or abuse	Suicide rates are higher in people who abuse alcohol or other chemical substances.
Level of despair	Ask about the future; when despair is high, hope is at a low level.
Ability to control own behavior	Inpatient hospitalization is indicated for individuals who are unable to control their suicidal impulses.

DRUG ALERT

Many medications can cause changes in mood. Much publicity has been given to the drug fluoxetine hydrochloride (Prozac), an antidepressant that has been reported to cause violent and suicidal reactions in some individuals.

The side effects of certain steroids (prednisolone) have been known to cause elation and feelings of well-being in some individuals. The same drug, administered to others, can result in severe depression and suicidal thoughts.

Elderly persons who are taking potent analgesics (pain medications) are at a high risk for feelings of depression.

Obtain a drug and medication history for each and every client. Sometimes something as simple as discontinuing or changing a medication can lift spirits and decrease suicidal thoughts.

NURSING INTERVENTIONS: SUICIDE PRECAUTIONS

DEFINITION
Reducing risk of self-inflicted harm for a patient in crisis or severe depression

ACTIVITIES
Determine whether client has specific suicide plan identified
Encourage the person to make a verbal no-suicide contract
Determine history of suicide attempts
Protect client from harming self
Place client in least restrictive environment that allows for necessary level of observation
Demonstrate concern about client's welfare
Refrain from negatively criticizing
Remove dangerous items from the environment
Place client in room with protective window coverings, as appropriate
Observe closely during suicidal crisis
Instruct client and significant others in signs, symptoms, and basic physiology of depression
Instruct family that suicidal risk increases for severely depressed clients as they begin to feel better
Facilitate discussion of factors or events that precipitated the suicidal thoughts
Escort client during off-ward activities, as appropriate
Provide psychiatric counseling, as appropriate
Facilitate support of client by family and friends
Instruct family on possible warning signs or pleas for help client may use
Refer client to psychiatrist, as needed

Modified from McCloskey JC, Bulechek GM: *Nursing interventions classification (NIC)*, ed 2, St Louis, 1996, Mosby.

people are alone, and most have little self-esteem. The majority of individuals are distressed and experiencing enormous emotional reactions, but they will usually agree to make a *no-self-harm contract* or agreement with their nurses not to engage in self-destructive behaviors.

Establishing a therapeutic relationship with a health care provider is important for clients. The focused communications and concerned actions of nurses encourage suicidal individuals to feel self-worth. With the encouragement and advocacy of their nurses, many suicidal clients are able to develop more effective strategies for living more satisfying lives. The box on p. 387 illustrates an example of a client care plan for an individual who may be suicidal.

Suicide and its associated effects present numerous problems in today's society. Many of us will be or have been personally touched by the suicide of a loved one or friend. As nurses, it is our duty and responsibility to protect our clients, even from themselves, when we must. Hopefully, through all our efforts, the tide of senseless loss of life can be turned, and choices will be made looking toward life instead of away from it.

❖ KEY CONCEPTS

- Suicide is the action of intentionally taking one's own life.
- Many misconceptions about suicide continue to exist despite educational efforts to promote an accurate understanding of the problem.
- Many cultural, social, and individual factors influence the occurrence of suicide.

- The act of attempting suicide has a profound impact on the lives of individuals, families, friends, and communities.
- Thoughts and actions directed at self-destruction affect every dimension of human functioning.
- There are several categories of motivation for suicide, including "a cry for help", the refusal to accept a diminished quality of life, the need to affirm one's soul, an attempt to relieve the distress related to situations that threaten the intactness of a person, and the act of those who are preoccupied with suicide.
- Several theories attempt to explain the causes of suicidal behavior: psychoanalytical theory, sociological theory, and interpersonal theory.
- As scientists are now able to study the structure and functions of the living human brain, new connections

SAMPLE CLIENT CARE PLAN

SELF-DIRECTED VIOLENCE

Assessment

History: Joe, a 19-year-old man, recently lost his best friend in an auto accident. For several weeks, he has been saying that he should have been killed instead of his friend. In the past 2 weeks, Joe has refused to work, eat, or engage in any social activities. Yesterday, he bought a gun.

Current Findings: A depressed-looking young man sitting between two worried parents. Grooming is unkempt; shirt and denims are ragged and dirty. He volunteers no information but states "It's not worth it" to the nurse. After obtaining the past history from parents, Joe was admitted to the unit for assessment and observation.

Nursing Diagnosis

Risk for violence, self-directed related to loss of significant other

Planning/Expected Outcomes

Joe will refrain from making any suicidal gestures or attempts during his hospitalization. Joe will discuss his feelings of loss by August 28.

Nursing Interventions

Intervention

1. Establish contact and rapport with Joe.

2. Establish a no-harm contract as soon as possible.
3. Implement necessary suicide precautions: watch closely.
4. Evaluate and document Joe's suicide potential at least twice daily.
5. Help Joe identify and discuss sources of distress.
6. Offer emotional support and acceptance.

7. Involve Joe and his family in the treatment plan.
8. Explore coping strategies used in the past.

Rationale

1. Open communication and trust must be established before work can begin.
2. Helps prevent Joe from acting impulsively.

3. Protects Joe from self-injury or death.

4. Helps assess for changes in seriousness of client's intent.
5. Increases awareness of feelings; helps to plan effective interventions.
6. Encourages Joe to think more highly of self; helps develop self-worth.
7. Promotes active decision making; provides emotional support and resources.
8. Helps Joe to build on coping mechanisms that have been successful.

Evaluation

During the course of hospitalization, Joe made no attempts at suicide. By August 18, Joe was able to share his sorrow and anger with the unit chaplin.

---

between physical and behavioral activities are being rapidly discovered.

- After the suicide of a loved one, the lives of the survivors can be plagued with anger, sadness, shame, guilt, health problems, and agonizing questions.
- Some experts believe that suicide in children is most often the result of family conflict or disruption.

- Adolescents commit suicide when they feel there is no other way out of their problems.
- Adult women attempt suicide three times more frequently than men, but men are more successful at completing the act.
- Older adults commit suicide more often than other age groups, and the incidence continues to increase with age.

- Prevention is the most important nursing action for clients who may be suicidal.

- Because suicide is becoming so prevalent, it is important for nurses to assess every client for its potential.

- The first priority for the care of clients who may be suicidal is protection from harm.

- With encouragement and the advocacy of their nurses, many suicidal clients are able to develop effective strategies for living more satisfying lives.

❖ SUGGESTIONS FOR FURTHER READING

"Attempted Suicide: How to Assess and Manage an Injured Psychiatric Patient" by Kay Stewart (*Nurs 93* 23[12]:25, 1993) describes the steps to take when a suicidal client is first assessed and treated.

❖ REFERENCES

Beck E: In gloomy Hungary, suicide takes on a life of its own, *The Wall Street Journal* 48(132):A1, May 10, 1995.

Bonger B and others: Inpatient standards of care and the suicidal patient, *Suicide Life Threat Behav* 23(3):245, 1993.

Clunn P, editor: *Child psychiatric nursing,* ed 2, St Louis, 1995, Mosby.

Courage MM and others: Suicide in the elderly: staying in control, *J Psychosoc Nurs* 31(7):27, 1993.

Fortinash KM, Holoday-Worret PA: *Psychiatric-mental health nursing,* St Louis, 1996, Mosby.

Goldacre M, Seagroatt V, Hawton K: Suicide after discharge from psychiatric inpatient care, *Lancet* 342:283, 1993.

Goldston DB and others: Suicidal ideation and suicide attempts among youth with insulin-dependent diabetes mellitus, *J Am Acad Child Adolesc Psychiatry* 33:240, 1994.

Golier, JA and others: Low serum cholesterol level and attempted suicide, *Am J Psychiatry* 152(3):419, 1995.

Hogarth CR: *Adolescent psychiatric nursing,* ed 2, St Louis, 1995, Mosby.

Leenaars AA: Suicide notes of the older adult, *Suicide Life Threat Behav* 22(1):62, 1992.

Lueckenotte AG: *Gerontologic nursing,* St Louis, 1996, Mosby.

McCloskey JC, Bulechek GM, editors: *Nursing interventions classification (NIC),* ed 2, St Louis, 1996, Mosby.

Momeyer RW: Historical perspectives. In Bender DL, Bruno L: *Suicide: opposing viewpoints,* San Diego, 1992, Greenhaven Press.

Moore SL: Rational suicide among older adults: a cause for concern? *Arch Psychiatr Nurs* 7(2):106, 1993.

Prado CG: *The last choice: preemptive suicide in old age,* Westport, CT, 1990, Greenwood Tree Press.

Starck PL, McGovern JP, editors: *The hidden dimension of illness: human suffering,* New York, 1992, National League for Nursing Press.

Stanhope M, Lancaster J: *Community health nursing: promoting health of aggregates, families, and individuals,* ed 4, St Louis, 1996, Mosby.

Stewart KB: Attempted suicide: how to assess and manage an injured psychiatric patient, *Nurs 93* 23(12):25, 1993.

Stuart GW, Sundeen SJ: *Principles and practice of psychiatric nursing,* ed 5, St Louis, 1995, Mosby.

Sullivan HS: *The interpersonal theory of psychiatry,* ed 2, New York, 1968, Norton.

Torrey EF: Avoidable error: the mental-health mess, *National Rev* 44(25):22, 1992.

US Bureau of Census: *Statistical abstract of the United States: 1993,* ed 113, Washington, DC, 1993, US Government Printing Office.

Watson WL, Lee D: Is there life after suicide? The systemic belief approach for "survivors" of suicide, *Arch Psychiatr Nurs* 7(1):37, 1993.

28

SUBSTANCE-RELATED DISORDERS

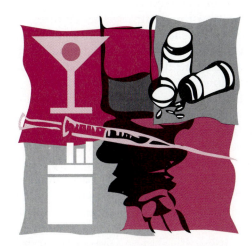

1. Define five terms relating to substance use and treatment.
2. Describe how chemical dependency affects persons from different age groups.
3. List four serious consequences of substance abuse.
4. State four categories of abused substances and give an example from each group.
5. Identify three reasons why inhalants are abused by adolescents and young adults.
6. Describe the three stages or phases of becoming addicted.
7. State three criteria for the diagnosis of a substance-related disorder.
8. Describe what is meant by the term *relapse*.
9. List at least four nursing interventions for clients who are diagnosed with substance-related disorders.

KEY TERMS

addiction
alcohol
amphetamines
disulfiram (Antabuse)
caffeine
cannabis
cocaine
crack

detoxification
habituation
hallucinogens
heroin
inhalants
intoxication
methadone
narcotics

nicotine
phencyclidine (PCP)
relapse
substance
substance (drug) abuse
substance (chemical) dependency
substance use

The practice of using substances to make one feel better is as old as human beings themselves. Even animals have been noted to eat certain plants that appear to change their behaviors or induce drunkenness. Alcohol has played a role in many cultures throughout recorded time, and various drugs, potions, solutions, and formulas that encourage repeated use have been developed as mankind has attempted to cope with the problems of disease and illness. Drugs have also played a role in political history. For example, the Opium Wars of the nineteenth century between China and Britain and the drug movement of the 1970s in the United States changed the course of history. Even today, we are struggling with political and social events that relate to drugs and other illicit substances (see box below).

The world of substance use and abuse is always changing. As health care providers become familiar with the current chemical fad, new and more potent drugs are being introduced. The focus of this chapter is to provide an understanding of substance use, abuse, and addiction; its effects on society; and the current interventions used to treat and educate clients suffering from substance-related problems.

Vocabulary of Terms

To communicate about substance-related disorders, an understanding of terms is necessary. This is not an easy task because various terms are used to describe addictive disorders. We will try to keep it simple here.

A **substance** is defined as a "drug of abuse, a medication, or a toxin" (American Psychiatric Association, 1994). Substances are also called chemicals, drugs, or toxins. **Substance use** is the ingesting (eating, drinking, injecting, or inhaling) of any chemical that affects the body. This includes legal, illegal, and medicinal substances.

Abused substances are those chemicals that alter the individual's perception by affecting the central ner-

vous system (CNS). They are often referred to as *mind-altering substances* because of their ability to enhance or depress moods or emotions.

Substance (drug) abuse is culturally and socially defined. In some cultures, the use of certain drugs is expected to fulfill religious obligations or some other culturally defined duty, whereas in other societies the use of the same substance is considered illegal or immoral. In the United States, Canada, Great Britain, and other industrialized societies, for example, laws define which substances are legal and socially approved. In other cultures, the use of substances that are illegal in these countries is acceptable and even provides economic opportunities. A broad but workable definition of **substance (drug) abuse** is the "excessive use of a substance that differs from societal norms" (Keltner, Schwecke, and Bostrom, 1995). No matter which culture, however, when the use of a substance becomes excessive and falls outside society's definition of approved use, a drug problem exists.

Drug or chemical **habituation** occurs when an individual depends on a substance to provide pleasure or relief from discomfort. **Substance (chemical) dependency** occurs when a user must take his/her usual or an increasing dose of the drug to prevent the onset of withdrawal signs/symptoms. When the dependence on the substance is physical, the term **addiction** is used. Today, the term *substance (chemical) dependency* is preferred when describing a client with an addiction. Abstinence occurs when an addicted individual is not using an addictive substance.

Role of Chemicals in Society

Chemical substances are important in modern societies. Without them, we would be unable to produce food, fight disease and illness, or develop the products that allow us to live as comfortably as we do.

The use of different chemical substances has become an unconscious part of everyday life. The mother who has been rushing around all day takes a drug for her headache. The harried businessman gulps down three martinis at lunch to prepare himself for the afternoon's conference. The teen must have a cup of coffee to wake up in the morning or a cigarette to calm the nerves. Children are unconsciously taught to solve problems by using substances. The doctor prescribes a medicine to help a parent recover from an illness, and the child learns that drugs can be beneficial. Children frequently observe their parents taking pills or drinking beverages that change their behaviors.

We are constantly bombarded with encouragements to ingest chemicals in advertisements on tele-

CULTURAL ASPECTS

Today, in the drug-producing countries of Central and South America, the growing of coca plants is the only means of making a living for many poor farmers. Prices for coca leaves far outstrip the money paid for corn, wheat, and other agricultural products. When officials spray or otherwise destroy their illicit crops, many men, women, and children suffer from hunger and malnutrition as a consequence.

Do you think it is possible to outlaw drugs *and* prevent the starvation of farmers at the same time? How?

visions and radios and even through computers. Commercials are routinely encouraging us to cope with constipation, heartburn, or hemorrhoids by taking drugs, and many of society's athletes and role models freely admit to using body-enhancing chemicals. Is it any wonder that so many people, young and old, are having to cope with the problems of chemical use today?

Substance Use and Age

The use and abuse of chemical substances occurs throughout the life cycle, from the fetus to the elderly. Even the growing life protected within the mother's uterus is not safe from the effects of chemicals. "Each year in the U.S., approximately 375,000 infants are born having been exposed to illicit substances in utero. This estimation does not include maternal use of nicotine and alcohol, which would make the number much larger" (Redding and Selleck, 1994).

There are no safe drugs for pregnant women. Every chemical ingested by a pregnant woman poses a potential danger to her unborn child, especially during the first trimester of pregnancy when the developing fetus is highly sensitive. Chemicals that are ingested during pregnancy can seriously interfere with normal fetal growth and development. They may also alter the placenta itself or interfere with its ability to perform its life-promoting functions.

A sad but common example of the effects of maternal drug use can be seen in infants and children with *fetal alcohol syndrome* (FAS). In countries in which the intake of alcohol is high, the incidence of FAS is greater. FAS results from excessive alcohol use during pregnancy. Children with FAS are smaller at birth, have small heads (microcephaly), and fail to develop normally (Dickason, Silverman, and Schult, 1994). Fig. 28-1 illustrates only the physical effects on the child of a chronically alcoholic mother. The less obvious effects include CNS deficits, various degrees of mental retardation and hyperactivity, irritability, and poor feeding habits. These children also have slow rates of growth, developmental delays, behavioral problems, intellectual impairment, poor judgment, and certain facial characteristics common to the children of alcoholic mothers.

Infants who have been exposed to cocaine in utero have sleeping and eating problems, unusual levels of irritability, and high-pitched cries (Forrest, 1994). Other syndromes and developmental problems result from the use of different drugs, but all drugs have one thing in common: pregnancy and substance use do not mix.

Children who live with substance-abusing parents are at increased risk for injuries and developing drug problems themselves. Research has demonstrated that many children of parents who use both legal and illegal chemicals do poorly in school, have difficulty controlling their emotions, and exhibit low self-esteem. Many of these individuals repeat the cycle of substance use and child abuse when they reach adulthood by choosing alcoholic or drug-abusing spouses and/or abusing substances themselves.

Children abuse substances too, but often the substances are legal and easily available. The 9-year-old who demands cola drinks every day demonstrates the same signs of a caffeine addiction as an adult. The 8-year-old boy who has grown up with beer in the house can become an alcoholic just as quickly as his teenage counterpart. In fact, according to the U.S. Public Health Service (1994), 0.3% of all admissions to substance treatment units were children younger than the age of 12. This startling statistic reminds us that drug abuse problems really do exist among children.

Adolescent substance use, abuse, and dependence is becoming an ever-increasing problem. The National Council on Alcoholism "estimates that as many as 3 million adolescents have serious alcohol problems" (Sullivan, 1995). For people in the 15- to 24-year-old age group, alcohol-related accidents are the leading cause of death.

The developmental levels of teens encourage exploration of the adult world, but their ability to exercise sound judgment is still limited. Adolescents experiment with a variety of attitudes, behaviors, and lifestyles. Substance use becomes a part of that experimentation. By the time students have graduated from high school, over 90% of them have tried alcohol. The younger an individual begins to use substances, the more likely that abuse problems will occur later in life.

Adolescents have various patterns of substance abuse. They may experiment by using drugs on a few occasions. They may use substances (usually alcohol, tobacco, or marijuana) in recreational ways, in social settings for the purpose of relaxation or intoxication. If actual addiction occurs, teens are likely to become involved in illegal activities, such as drug trafficking, prostitution, or criminal behaviors.

In adults, substance abuse is common. "Alcoholics and alcohol abusers represent approximately 10% of the adult population, a proportion that has remained constant for the last two decades" (Siegel, Landes, and Jacobs, 1995). In 1993, over 77 million Americans, aged 12 or older (about 37% of the adult population) had tried some illicit drug at least once. Substance use and abuse occurs most commonly between 18 and 35 years of age, but significant numbers of older adults abuse alcohol and prescription medications.

Older adults are not immune to substance-related problems, but they are often misdiagnosed or treated

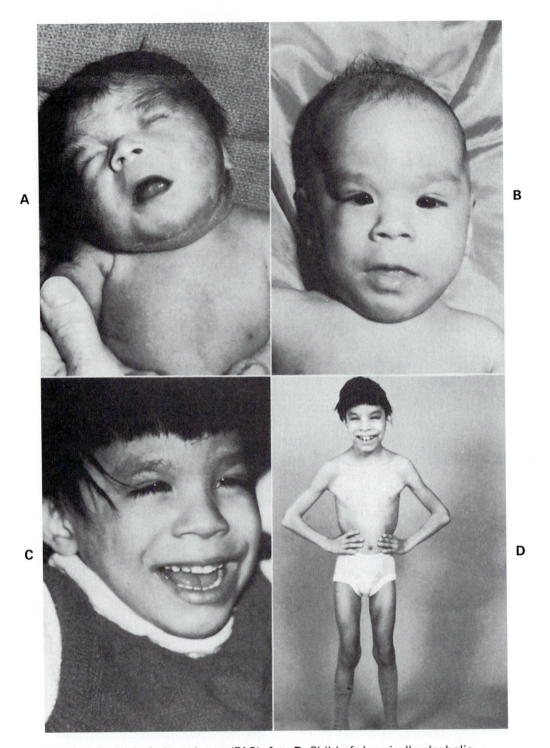

Fig. 28-1 Fetal alcohol syndrome (FAS). **A** to **D,** Child of chronically alcoholic mother, diagnosed at birth with FAS. Although he was raised his entire life in one excellent foster home and participated in various remediation programs, he continues to have an IQ around 45 (more severe retardation than most FAS children), with accompanying hyperactivity and distractibility. (From Streissguth AP: Ciba Foundation Symposium No. 105: Mechanisms of alcohol damage in utero. By permission of AP Streissguth and the Ciba Foundation, Pitman, London.)

inappropriately "since older drinkers and elderly persons who misuse drugs usually are isolated within their social groups or families" (McMahon, 1993). Although the incidence of substance abuse in older adults is unknown, over 40% of all drug reactions occur in persons older than 65 (McMahon, 1993). This fact should alert nurses and health care providers who work with the elderly to be aware of the possibility of substance abuse in every older client.

Substances for abuse vary according to minority group. For example, the use of cocaine is higher among blacks and Hispanics than it is among whites, who appear to prefer alcohol. Drug use also varies with the location. During 1993, current drug use in the United States was highest in the West (7.7%) and lowest in the North Central region (4.6%).

Scope of the Problem Today

The abuse of chemical substances presents many problems for people in today's society. Alcohol and drug abuse have an impact on every citizen not just in financial terms but in terms of human costs. To illustrate, during a 1-month period in Oregon it was found that 5.2% of delivering mothers had used street drugs during pregnancy. This figure was seven times greater than available drug treatment programs could accommodate (Slutsker and others, 1993).

Cocaine- and other drug-exposed infants are filling health and foster care systems as the children of addicted parents are born. According to the Economic Research Service of the U.S. Department of Agriculture, "in 1991, there were 28.6 million children of alcoholics living in the United States—nearly 7 million were under age 18" (Bijur and others, 1992). Children of problem drinkers also have three times the risk of serious injury as children of nondrinking parents (Bijur and others, 1992).

Substance use and dependence cost society dearly. The suicide rate for 15- to 24-year-olds has more than doubled since 1960 (Deykin and Buka, 1994). The use of alcohol and drugs often results in trauma, interpersonal violence, and mental health problems. Alcohol-related motor vehicle accidents are one of the leading causes of death among people younger than age 45. Many of the deaths from falls, drownings, and burns may be related to substance use.

Many of society's homeless and mentally ill people use and abuse chemicals. Homeless persons with alcohol, drug, or mental disorders are one of the most disadvantaged and underserved groups in the United States. The number of people with serious mental illness who also are addicted to or use chemicals is estimated to be as high as 75% (Clement, Williams, and Waters, 1993).

Categories of Abused Substances

Every chemical has the potential for abuse. For example, the current concern over the effectiveness of antibiotic drugs stems from a form of abuse. As people routinely insisted on being treated with antibiotics for illnesses that did not actually require them, the microorganisms the antibiotics were designed to kill grew stronger and became resistant. This practice of overtreating minor illnesses has continued for years; now there are strains of deadly bacteria that are not affected by the administration of antibiotics.

Although nobody "got high" from antibiotic drugs, their repeated abuse has resulted in serious consequences for us all. The lesson here is that not all abused substances are illegal. In this text, however, the discussion of abused substances is limited to those that are currently considered illicit or harmful.

Chemicals of Abuse

The most popular substance for abuse in the United States and most developed countries is alcohol. Other substances increase and decrease in popularity, but the fact that over 10% of the adult population in the United States abuses alcohol has remained constant for over 20 years. The following are the substances of most concern in society today.

Alcohol has been used since the beginning of recorded time. The effects of different alcoholic beverages are caused by the presence of ethanol (ETOH), a chemical that results from the fermentation of yeast and grains, malts, or fruits. "Hard liquor," such as whiskey, brandy, gin, and vodka, is distilled spirits, whereas beer and wine are not.

The process of distillation increases the alcohol content of the beverage. To illustrate, a typical drink of ½ ounce of alcohol is found in one shot of distilled alcohol, one 5-ounce glass of wine, and one 12-ounce can of beer.

Many people think of alcohol as a stimulant because they feel relaxation, stimulation, and pleasure when they drink. The truth is that these feelings are caused by the depressant effects of alcohol on the CNS. Once swallowed, alcohol is rapidly diffused to all the body's organ systems. Because of its high solubility in water, alcohol tends to collect in organs that have a high content of water, namely the brain, heart, liver, and gastrointestinal tract (Wilson, 1994). Alcohol is metabolized in the liver (over a period of time) and excreted by the kidneys and lungs.

Low doses of alcohol cause a rise in blood pressure and pulse, but large doses can affect the pumping action of the heart, resulting in cardiac dysrhythmias. Surface blood vessels dilate, producing flushing of the skin and rapid loss of body heat. Alcohol also causes numbness of the hands and feet, which creates a false sense of warmth. In large doses, alcohol can actually reduce body temperature. The effects of alcohol on the CNS are directly related to the amount (dose) consumed (Table 28-1).

With repeated and continued use, tolerance develops and individuals become dependent on (addicted to) alcohol. If drinking is not stopped, death from multiple organ failure (especially the liver) results, usually after a series of assorted health problems.

Narcotics are central nervous system depressants. They occur naturally, semisynthetically, and synthetically. This means the chemicals found in natural narcotics have been altered to produce new artificially produced (synthetic) drugs. Natural narcotics are opium and its principal ingredient morphine, which is used for medicinal purposes. These substances are often called opioids or opiates and they are obtained by milking a flower called *Papaver somniferum,* or the opium poppy.

The use of opium was documented 4000 years before Hippocrates, and it continues to be a commonly used substance in many countries today. Before the 1900s, opium was readily available in the United States and a common ingredient in many patent medicines. Today, according to the Drug Enforcement Administration (DEA), there is little opium use in the United States as a result of the restrictive laws governing the distribution of the drug (Siegal, Landes, and Jacobs, 1995).

Opium can be found in several forms. The fluid scraped from the base of the poppy flower and rolled into dark brown chunks is called raw opium (Fig. 28-2). Processed opium can appear as a fine white powder.

The semisynthetic narcotics include **heroin,** hydromorphone, and thebaine derivatives. The Bayer Company of Germany first marketed heroin in 1898 as a new pain reliever. In the United States, heroin was legally available to the public until the passage of the Harrison Narcotic Act of 1914.

Pure heroin is a white, bitter-tasting powder, which is usually put into solution and injected. Currently, bumper crops of poppies have resulted in the availability of potent forms of the drug, that are so strong that they need only to be smoked or inhaled to produce the same effect as injecting.

Street heroin is found in colors ranging from white to dark brown depending on the additives (Fig. 28-3). A new form, called "black tar heroin," has become available throughout the western United States. This crudely processed form of heroin is manufactured in Mexico and may contain as much as 80% impurities. It is most commonly diluted and injected. The signs/symptoms of heroin use, overdose, and withdrawal are listed in Table 28-2.

Stimulants are another group of commonly abused substances. They include caffeine, cocaine, and certain prescription drugs, such as amphetamines, appetite suppressants, and methylphenidate (Ritalin).

◆ **TABLE 28-1**
Effects of Alcohol on the Nervous System

Blood Alcohol Content	Approximate Number of Drinks*	Central Nervous System (Behavioral) Responses
0.05%	1 or 2 (½-1 oz of alcohol)	Thought, restraint, judgment slowed; more socially at ease; reaction time slowed; unable to do complicated tasks
0.10%	3 or 4 (1½-2 oz of alcohol)	Voluntary motor actions clumsy; depth perception altered; reaction time to stimuli slowed; eye movement and focus affected; judgment and control continue to decrease; legal limit for driving
0.20%	5 or more (≥2½ oz of alcohol)	Entire motor area of brain depressed; may want to lie down; staggers; loses conscious control of reason; easily angered; may weep, shout, fight
0.30%	6 or more (≥3 oz of alcohol)	Acts confused; may be in a stupor; unresponsive to most external stimuli; losing ability to control involuntary responses; decreased heart rate, blood pressure, respiratory rate
0.40% - 0.50%	7 or more (≥3½ oz of alcohol)	Comatose; medulla severely depressed; death from respiratory failure; death can occur with 0.40% if blood alcohol rises too rapidly; blood alcohol level of 0.50% is fatal without immediate medical attention

Modified from Seigel MA, Landes A, Jacobs NR, editors: *Information plus: illegal drugs and alcohol 1995 edition,* Wylie, TX, 1995, Information Plus.
*Consumed within a 4-hour time period.

Fig. 28-2 Opium. **A,** The milky fluid oozes from the seedpod of the poppy. **B,** An incision is made in the Mexican poppy to release opium. (Courtesy Drug Enforcement Agency.)

Fig. 28-3 Heroin. **A,** Black tar heroin. **B,** Mexican heroin. **C,** Highly refined Southeast Asian heroin. (Courtesy Drug Enforcement Agency.)

◆ **TABLE 28-2**
Signs/Symptoms of Heroin Use, Overdose, and Withdrawal

Heroin Use	Heroin Overdose	Heroin Withdrawal
Constricted pupils	Shallow respirations	Watery eyes
Depression	Clammy skin	Runny nose
Drowsiness	Convulsions	Sweating
Euphoria (feelings of great well-being)	Coma	Muscle cramps
Nausea		Loss of appetite
Respiratory depression		Nausea
		Chills
		Tremors
		Panic

Caffeine is found in every supermarket. It is the main active ingredient in coffee, black teas, most cola drinks, and other bottled beverages. Caffeine stimulates the nervous system, relieving fatigue, increasing alertness, and increasing the body's metabolic rate. In large amounts, it can produce tremors, tachycardia, nervousness, and insomnia. The most prominent withdrawal symptom from caffeine is headache.

Cocaine is a potent natural stimulant. For centuries, the natives of the South American Andes Mountains chewed the weakly psychoactive leaves of the coca plant to relieve fatigue and hunger. Today, coca is grown, processed into cocaine, and shipped to many countries throughout the world.

Cocaine is available "on the street" as a white, crystalline powder that is commonly contaminated with local anesthetics or sugar. It is either injected or "snorted" by inhaling. Cocaine produces an immediate rush of energy, vigor, and feelings of well-being that last less than an hour. The intense pleasurable feelings can lead to a mental dependency that can ultimately destroy one's life as more and more doses are sought and used. Repeated use of cocaine overstimulates the nervous system and can dissolve the nasal septum, resulting in a collapsed nose.

Crack is a type of processed cocaine. Combining cocaine with ammonia or baking soda and heating it removes the hydrochloride molecule. The substance remaining from this process is chips or chunks of highly addicting cocaine, called rocks. These are usually vaporized in a pipe or smoked in combination with other plant material (tobacco, marijuana).

Because of its concentrated form, crack reaches the brain immediately and produces a more intense but shorter lasting high. Tolerance and addiction to the drug develops quickly as users chase the feeling of that first, intense experience.

Amphetamines were originally pharmaceutically manufactured medicines developed to treat depression, narcolepsy, hyperactivity in children, and obesity. Once amphetamines were sold without a prescription in inhalers and diet pills. Today, they are available only by prescription, but many are illegally manufactured.

The last category of abused chemicals, the hallucinogens, is a relatively new one. **Hallucinogens** are natural and synthetic substances that alter one's perception of reality. The active ingredient of the peyote cactus, mescaline, has been used in the religious ceremonies of certain Native Americans for many years (Fig. 28-4).

Lysergic acid diethylamide (LSD), an ergot fungus, was discovered by accident in the 1940s, but the introduction of laboratory-designed hallucinogens in

Fig. 28-4   Peyote cactus. (Courtesy Drug Enforcement Agency.)

the United States did not occur until the early 1970s. Today, such synthetic hallucinogens as LSD (acid), MDA, STP, GHB, and "ice" are easily available in all areas of the country. They are called designer drugs. Most are taken orally or "snorted" (inhaled) and they are frequently contaminated. These hallucinogens vary in onset, duration of action, and potency but all produce a sense of altered reality.

Phencyclidine (PCP) was originally developed for use as an animal tranquilizer. When taken by humans, it produces mild depression with low doses and a schizophrenic-like reaction with higher amounts. PCP is a dangerous drug because it causes people to behave in unpredictable and sometimes violent ways (Table 28-3).

Users of hallucinogens experience everything from profound mind-expanding experiences to "bad trips" in which dangerous behavioral reactions occur. The psychedelic (mind-altering) effects of hallucinogens include a heightened awareness of reality; distortions in time, space, and body image; feelings of depersonalization; and the loss of a sense of reality. Flashbacks, which are a return to the psychedelic experience after the drug has worn off, can occur with the use of hallucinogens. Although they are not considered physically addicting at this time, the repeated use of hallucinogens can lead to various mental health problems.

Cannabis is a term applied to the hemp plant *Cannabis sativa*, which grows wild in many tropical and temperate climates all over the world. The hemp plant has been used for centuries by many cultures in folk remedies and other medicines. Historically, it has been used to treat pain, decreased appetite, muscle

◆ **TABLE 28-3**
Signs/Symptoms of PCP Use

Physical Signs/Symptoms	Psychological Signs/Symptoms
Increased blood pressure	Belligerence (wants to fight)
Increased temperature	Bizarre behaviors
Muscle rigidity, ataxia (uncoordinated, staggering)	Hallucinations
Repeated jerking	Impaired (poor) judgment
Agitated movements	Impulsive behaviors
Vertical and horizontal nystagmus (eye tremors)	Paranoia
	Unpredictable behaviors

Modified from Taylor CM: *Essentials of psychiatric nursing,* ed 14, St Louis, 1994, Mosby.

◆ **THINK ABOUT**

For years, debate about the legalization of marijuana has taken place. Advocates cite numerous commercial and medicinal properties of the substance. They feel that keeping it illegal prevents many medical advances from being made and commercial products (e.g., paper, cloth, and oil) from being developed.

What is your opinion of this statement?

What is your rationale for this position?

---

and gastrointestinal tract spasms, asthma, and depression. It has also been used as an antibiotic and topical anesthetic (see box above).

Cannabis is available in several forms. The dried tops and leaves are called marijuana. Sinsemilla is a potent form of marijuana that contains no seeds. Hashish (hash) is the dried resin that seeps from the top and leaves, and hash oil is the distilled oil of hashish. All are usually smoked, but they may be eaten.

Cannabis produces a sense of well-being and relaxation. It alters time perception and can affect short-term memory and concentration. Motivation, especially for distasteful tasks, may be decreased. Frequently, an increase in hunger leads to the "munchies," a slang term for the desire to eat. Large doses can result in feelings of anxiety and paranoia. There are no proven withdrawal signs/symptoms, but anxious moods, irritability, and sleep disturbances have been reported.

Medications

Many chemicals that were developed to save lives and ease suffering have the potential for being abused. For example, almost all the opium arriving in the United States today is broken down into its most useful alkaloids, morphine and codeine. These substances are then refined into powerful pain-relieving medications (narcotic analgesics). They are available in the United States only with the prescription of a licensed physician, dentist, or nurse practitioner, but they remain a source of abuse.

Morphine is one of the most effective pain killers available. It is marketed as a white powder or in solution for injection. It is administered by injection (intramuscularly, intravenously, or subcutaneously) under the direction of a licensed health care practitioner.

Hydromorphone and the thebaine derivatives are semisynthetic narcotics made from opium. Hydromorphone is commonly called Dilaudid. It is used as an analgesic and is produced in liquid or more potent tablet form. It is shorter acting, more sedating, and up to eight times more powerful than morphine. Although available only by prescription, it is highly sought by addicts. Thebaine derivatives, another opium product, are up to a thousand times more potent than morphine. Because of the danger of overdose, these drugs are used by veterinarians for the care of large animals only.

Commonly abused stimulants include the amphetamines, diet pills, and the appetite suppressants. Methylphenidate (Ritalin), a medication used to treat attention-deficit hyperactivity disorders, is another often abused stimulant. The signs/symptoms of stimulant use include changes in personality, anxiety, tension, anger, restlessness, and rapid speech and movement.

The sedative, hypnotic, and antianxiety drug classes are commonly used in ways other than therapeutic. During the 1950s, many people were unknowingly addicted to the drug diazepam (Valium) and other sedatives. The individual who is unable to sleep without hypnotic medications may be abusing sleeping pills, and many people reach for their "nerve pills" when they feel anxious or upset. Do you see the importance of obtaining a thorough history of clients' medication use?

Inhalants

The breathing in of volatile substances or chemical gasses (**inhalants**) has become popular with adolescents and young adults for several reasons: they are legal, inexpensive and easily available and have a rapid onset of effects. Unfortunately, the practice is also associated with significant complications, such as sudden death caused by cardiac dysrhythmia or respiratory depression. The use of inhalants can also result in hyperactive motor responses, loss of coordination, and seizures.

The most commonly inhaled substances are alcohol solvents, gasoline, glue, paint thinner, hairspray, and spray paints. Less frequently used chemicals used as inhalants include cleaning fluids, typewriter correction liquids, and spray can propellants.

Inhalants are most often used by adolescents in group settings. Several methods are used to inhale the vapors, such as soaking a rag and then holding it to the nose and mouth. The substance may be inhaled directly from the container or placed in a bag or other closed container and then inhaled. Soon after inhaling, the individual feels a "high" that is associated with feelings of great well-being (euphoria), excitement, sexual aggressiveness, a lessened sense of right and wrong, and loss of judgment. Intoxication is marked by delusions, hallucinations, anxiety, and confusion. Although no withdrawal syndrome has been recognized, the repeated use of inhalants can result in profound physical and psychosocial harm.

Nicotine is currently a legal inhalant. It is present in all forms of tobacco (cigarettes, chewing tobacco, snuff, pipe tobacco, cigars, and snuff) and certain medications (nicotine patch and gum). It produces relaxation, increases alertness, and helps to relieve feelings of hunger. Nicotine is frequently used as a method to control body weight.

Although its popularity is declining, tobacco is still a commonly used substance. "In 1994, total U.S. tobacco consumption, including overseas armed forces, was: 485 billion cigarettes, 2.3 billion cigars and cigarillos (small thin cigars), 15 million pounds of pipe and roll-your-own tobacco, and 62 million pounds of snuff" (Siegel, Landes, and Jacobs, 1995).

Tobacco is either smoked or held between the gum and lip and absorbed through the mucous membranes of the mouth. It is never swallowed because of its toxic effects. Tobacco is addictive, and its continued use is associated with many health complications. Recently, in the United States, Canada, and other in-

dustrialized countries, a movement to restrict the sales and use of tobacco products (especially to children and teens) has arisen.

There are many substances that have the potential for abuse. For this reason, it is important to obtain an accurate history of every client's substance use patterns.

Characteristics of Substance Use and Abuse

It is important to remember the differences between substance use and abuse. Some people can use various chemicals to change the way they feel, but the use in no way affects their abilities to perform the activities of daily life. This is substance use. Substance abuse, however, occurs when the use of the chemical becomes more important in the individual's life than his/her activities of daily living.

The causes of substance abuse are unknown, but several theories have attempted to explain why people use mind-altering chemicals (*Harvard Mental Health Letter,* 1995a). Biological theories state that there are variations between ethnic groups that offer genetic and biochemical explanations for substance abuse. Theories relating to psychological factors explore the roles of one's personality and emotional problems; and environmental theories concentrate on the individual, the family, and the sociocultural surroundings in which substance abuse takes place.

Stages of Addiction

Many individuals use alcohol, tobacco, or other chemicals and function very well. Those who move from use to dependency (addiction) follow a fairly predictable course (McCaffery and Ferrell, 1994).

During the early stage, individuals are able to use and enjoy their chosen substance. A desire to repeat the first pleasurable experience leads to a frequent pattern of use in which one may begin to prefer being "high" to other activities.

Soon a habit of excessive use develops as the individual begins to ignore responsibilities and obligations. The person may deny that a problem exists, ignore others' comments, lie to cover up the activity, or conceal the problem by sneaking drinks or doses. During these periods of excessive use, the individual may also become intoxicated.

Intoxication is defined as a state of maladaptive behavioral or psychological changes resulting from exposure to certain chemicals. Intoxicated people are frequently belligerent (looking for a fight or an argument) and have wide emotional swings. They often lack sound judgment, and their ability to think critically is reduced. Commonly, they will stagger or show other signs of impaired motor abilities. The actual picture of an intoxicated individual varies greatly. Psychological effects are based on the person's expectations of what the chemical will do and the setting or environment in which the substance is taken.

During the middle (crucial) stage, the intoxicating episodes increase as the body attempts to compensate for the substance by adapting to the substance. *Tolerance* develops as increased amounts of the chemical are needed to produce the same effects that one dose once produced. Physical tolerance occurs when the body has adjusted to living and functioning with the substance in its system. Psychological tolerance develops when individuals feel that they cannot function without the use of their chosen chemical.

By the time one has progressed to the chronic late stage, tolerance for the chemical is usually quite high. Now the need for the substance leads to a loss of control over one's behavior. Without the chemical, life is miserable. Daily living becomes a nightmare, and every waking effort and energy is focused on obtaining and using the now *required* substance. The box below offers a vivid case study.

Criteria for Diagnosis

For a substance-related disorder to be diagnosed, individuals must meet certain criteria. The pattern of substance use must be disabling and lead to significant impaired functioning and distress. The individual must demonstrate signs of tolerance, withdrawal, and dependence (American Psychiatric Association, 1994).

Clinical Presentation

Unlike the signs/symptoms of a physical illness, there is no classic presentation of a substance abuser. Each person has a unique variety of signs/symptoms, depending on chemical use and individual characteristics. However, because substance abuse affects every body system, there are some common indicators—such as alterations in neurological functioning or appearance—that can help to alert nurses during the assessment and monitoring of clients.

Guidelines for Intervention

"The three types of drugs most commonly abused, separately and in various combinations, are:

1. alcohol and sedative-hypnotic;
2. opiate narcotics, chiefly heroin;
3. stimulants, chiefly cocaine and amphetamines" (*Harvard Mental Health Letter*, 1995b).

The costs and consequences of substance abuse are high. As individuals progress with their drug abuse, their world narrows until chemical use becomes the chosen method for coping with all of life's difficulties. Soon, impaired social and family relationships result, which drives users further into their world of drug

---

CASE STUDY

Ernie's father was 15 years old when Ernie was born. Ernie's mother was 14 and gave custody to the father after the first 6 months of Ernie's life. To keep Ernie quiet during his infant and toddler years, Ernie's father would blow marijuana smoke into Ernie's face. It worked. Ernie would sleep for hours while his father "partied."

By the time Ernie was 5, he was drinking beer. At 8, he graduated to vodka, gin, and tequila. By 10, Ernie was mixing his alcohol with cocaine. School became impossible, so he dropped out at 12; by 14, Ernie was hustling drugs and trying to set himself up to sell the sexual favors of three neighborhood girls.

Where is Ernie today? Fortunately, he overdosed one evening when he was about 17 years old. The nurse in the emergency department, recognizing the potential in this young man, took the time to tell him that his life did not have to be that way and that he had choices.

Ernie listened. His detoxification was painful and his recovery slow and difficult, but he persisted, knowing there was something more than a fog of consciousness.

Today, Ernie has beat the odds. Despite several setbacks, he has been clean for more than 10 years. He is a college graduate, happily married, and the father of two boys. The strongest thing he drinks now is orange juice.

One nurse, one interaction, gave Ernie the opportunity to change. Although the majority of cases do not have results as positive, the lesson is that each of us has worth and deserves an opportunity to succeed. A nurse's offers to help clients change may fall on a hundred deaf ears, but the one who hears is worth all the effort.

Clinical Decision

1. Do you believe that one nurse could really make such an impact on a client's life?

use. As the preoccupation with the substance continues, the individual becomes further and further isolated from occupational and community relationships (see box below).

Absenteeism from work, unpaid bills, and job loss frequently result when chemical use is out of control. Involvement with the legal system can occur with drunken driving or domestic violence charges. Some people completely deplete their financial resources to obtain their substances.

Substance abuse is expensive in terms of both human and financial costs. Accidents, trauma, crime, domestic violence, child abuse, prostitution, suicide, disease, and the loss of safe communities are associated with substance abuse. Therefore it is important for health care providers to be alert to the possibility of substance-related problems in every client.

Assessment

The physical examination, patient history, and emotional assessment should focus on the following aspects.

Central nervous system (CNS).   Assess for orientation, level of consciousness, balance, gait, and ability to follow instructions.

Head and neck.   Examine eyes and check pupils and sclera of the eyes. Note ruddy or pale complexion, distended neck veins, or petechiae (small red dots) on the face. Observe for evidence of injections under the tongue, and inspect the area between the gums and lips.

Chest.   Do not forget to take vital signs. Count pulse and respirations for a full minute. Palpate pedal and radial pulses. Observe for any difficulty in breathing. Auscultate the heart for irregular rates or rhythms.

Listen to the breath sounds, and note any abnormal sounds.

Abdomen.   Inspect the size, shape, and contours of the abdomen. Auscultate all four quadrants and count the bowel sounds. Check for ascites (water in the abdomen), distention, or enlarged organs. Look for bruising, petechiae, and other signs of bleeding. Have the client describe the color and consistency of stool.

Skin.   Observe and document the size, location, and characteristics of any skin lesions or marks. Check for needle marks on the client's arms, fingers, legs, and toes. Note the skin turgor and muscle mass of the arms and legs.

Nutritional status.   Many chemically dependent persons do not eat regularly and therefore run a risk of becoming malnourished. Observe the client's body build and appearance. Ask the client to list everything he/she ate yesterday and tell you how the meals were prepared. Ask if there have been any recent appetite or weight changes. Inspect the client's skin color, hair, and fingernails. If the client lives alone or is homeless, find out how food is obtained on a daily basis.

General appearance.   Is the client tidy or unkempt? Note the client's manner and style of dress, jewelry, makeup, hairstyle, and body marks (e.g., tattoos, symbolic scars).

Behaviors.   Note rate of speech, motor activity, interactions during the interview. Observe for signs of memory loss, difficulty following directions, and problems with communication.

Emotional state.   Watch for any signs of depression, emotional instability (mood swings), suspiciousness, anger, agitation, self-pity, or jealousy. Ask clients if they have ever experienced a hallucination, a blackout (period of time during which the user cannot remember events), any violent impulses, or suicidal ideas.

Social support.   Have clients identify the most important people in their lives. Are these people willing to become involved in treatment with the client? If possible, observe how clients interact with their family and friends. Remember that family members may also need support and treatment.

Motivation.   Obtain a description of the chemicals currently being used: how often, how much, when was last dose? When did use begin? What (if any-

---

💊 DRUG ALERT

Remember, elderly persons are at risk for becoming drug dependent. When an older adult becomes less social and begins to isolate himself/herself, suspect a problem with drugs. The usual culprits in the elderly are pain medications and drug combinations.

Have your elderly clients *bring all their medications to you in a paper bag*. These medications should include all over-the-counter and herbal preparations. In this way, an accurate assessment of their medication use can be obtained. Do not forget to ask about alcohol use.

thing) has been tried to decrease or stop using the chemical? Describe clients' history of treatment for substance-related or emotional problems. Ask what motivated them to seek treatment now. Is the court, the job, or the family insisting on treatment or are the clients seeking relief from the problems associated with the chemical use? The motivation level of clients plays an important part in their recovery.

Diagnostic tests. Diagnostic testing usually includes standard blood and urine examinations. A complete blood count (CBC), urinalysis, and chemistry panel is done to assess for any organ damage. Frequently, tests for hepatitis, HIV, tuberculosis (TB), and other infectious diseases are performed. Clients are also assessed for nutritional or bleeding problems. Other diagnostic tests, such as a computed tomography (CT) scan, magnetic resonance imaging (MRI), electroencephalogram (EEG), or x-ray films, may also be ordered.

Treatments and Therapies

The treatment of substance-related disorders continues to change and grow. A broad range of treatment approaches are available today. Most treatment programs are based on a certain philosophy, although they may offer many different types of therapy.

The *disease model* states that substance abuse is a disease and should be treated as such. Substance abuse has acute and chronic signs/symptoms, a certain pattern of progression, and physical pathological conditions associated with continued use. Two types of treatment programs based on the disease model are 12-step programs and residential treatment programs.

The first 12-step program was a self-help, group-centered program developed by two alcoholics in 1935. The 12-step process involves admitting one's powerlessness to control drug use and then seeking help from a higher power through prayer or meditation, making moral inventories, confessing wrongs, asking for forgiveness, and carrying the message to others. The first 12-step program was Alcoholics Anonymous. Many other 12-step group therapy programs are based on this model, but they have been revised to fit the beliefs of the population they serve. The box at right offers a general listing of self-help groups available in many countries throughout the world. Self-help groups can be very effective when the individual wants them to be.

"The *medical model framework* considers addictions from a public health, chronic disease, and acute infectious disease perspective" (Sullivan, 1995). The *biopsychosocial framework* for treating clients is a medical model that attempts to explain substance abuse. New

understanding of neurotransmitters and other biochemical activities of the brain is leading neuroscientists toward the development of medications that may someday help people cope with their chemical dependencies.

SELF-HELP GROUPS FOR PEOPLE RECOVERING FROM SUBSTANCE ABUSE

ALCOHOLICS ANONYMOUS—for individuals recovering from alcoholism; founded in 1935

AL-ANON—for families of alcoholics

ALATEEN—for teenagers 12 to 20 years of age who have been affected by someone else's drinking problem (usually a parent)

ASSOCIATION OF RECOVERING MOTORCYCLISTS—support group for motorcyclists who are recovering from alcohol or drug addiction

CALIX SOCIETY—Catholic alcoholics who are maintaining sobriety through affiliation with and participation in AA

CHRISTIAN ADDICTION REHABILITATION ASSOCIATION—provides support for individuals with a ministry to addicts

COCAINE ANONYMOUS—for men and women who are recovering from cocaine addiction; a 12-step program

DRUG-ANON FOCUS—for families and friends of persons addicted to mind-altering drugs; a 12-step program

DRUGS ANONYMOUS—for persons addicted to drugs; a 12-step program

DUAL DISORDERS ANONYMOUS—for people with both alcohol or drug addiction and mental or emotional disorders; a 12-step program

FAMILIES ANONYMOUS—for parents, relatives, and friends of drug addicts

GAY AA—provides support for gay and lesbian alcoholics

IMPAIRED PHYSICIAN PROGRAM—provides assistance to physicians and their spouses who have problems with alcohol, drugs, or codependence

INTERNATIONAL NURSES ANONYMOUS—for nurses, nursing students, and former nurses who are involved in a 12-step recovery program

NARANON—provides assistance to drug-dependent individuals and their families

NARCOTICS ANONYMOUS—for individuals recovering from drug abuse; a 12-step program

RATIONAL RECOVERY SYSTEMS—uses rational emotive therapy (vs. a spiritual approach) to assist people in their recovery from substance abuse

From Keltner NL, Schwecke LH, Bostrom CE: *Psychiatric nursing*, ed 2, St Louis, 1995, Mosby.

Psychiatric models view substance abuse as an expression of an underlying emotional conflict or mental disorder. Several therapies are based on this framework.

Sociocultural models state that substance abuse can be treated by changing an individual's environment or teaching people to develop new responses to their current environments. This point of view has led to the establishment of long-term residential treatment programs and therapeutic communities.

Regardless of the type of substance used, the goals of care remain the same. The first step in treatment is for the individual to recognize the need for help. Denial is a strong part of most substance-related disorders. For any treatment to be effective, the client must be truly willing to work toward living without his/her addiction.

Before treatment of the addiction can actually begin, many persons must first go through **detoxification,** the process of withdrawing a substance under medical supervision. Clients who are addicted to opium, narcotics, alcohol, or sedatives are often hospitalized because of potentially fatal complications, such as seizures and respiratory and cardiac problems. Sometimes long-acting medications, such as methadone (drug used to treat heroin addiction), are administered to ease the effects of withdrawing from the chemical.

Once clients are physically free from their addictions (practicing abstinence), the focus turns to uncovering and treating existing emotional or mental health problems. The incidence of psychiatric disorders is very high in substance users. The disorders must also be treated if the individual is to remain drug-free.

The last and perhaps the most difficult goal of treatment is to assist individuals in changing their behaviors. Individual psychotherapy is very effective for clients with certain dependencies (cocaine addictions), but it is expensive and unavailable to many people. Group therapy can offer peer support from individuals "who have been there." It also offers people the opportunity to experiment with and explore their new, drug-free behaviors.

Medications are prescribed with extreme care. Two specific medications used in the care of substance-addicted clients are methadone and disulfiram (Antabuse). **Methadone** is a chemical relative of heroin. Taken orally once a day, it prevents the symptoms of withdrawal and helps to stabilize the lives of these substance abusers. Recently a new form of methadone, called LLAM, has been developed. It requires that a dose be taken only once every 72 hours.

Disulfiram (Antabuse) is a medication taken daily by non-practicing (dry) alcoholics. It causes very un-

pleasant physical reactions when combined with alcohol including intense headache, flushing, nausea, vomiting, hypotension, and blurred vision. It is prescribed as a preventive measure to help to reduce the desire for alcohol. It is very important to thoroughly research each of these medications and routinely monitor your clients for therapeutic and adverse reactions of these chemicals.

Relapse

Long-term recovery is often marked by periods of relapse. **Relapse** is the recurrence of the substance-abusing behaviors after a significant period of abstinence. In other words, the client returns to "using" after he/she has been "dry" for a period of time. Not only do people return to the chemical-abusing behaviors, but they also readopt the psychological and emotional mind-set that brought about the abuse in the first place. Many treatment therapies and programs concentrate on preventing and treating relapses. Remember that clients who have relapsed feel many distressing emotions. True therapeutic care is given when nurses accept and respect these clients even when they are the least accepting and respecting of themselves. Remember, you *are* a therapeutic agent.

Nursing Process

An important nursing intervention for clients with substance-related problems is to act as a therapeutic agent. Practice effective listening skills to gain an understanding of who the client really is. Use your knowledge of the therapeutic relationship to establish trust and cooperation. Learn to act as a role model and teacher, quietly demonstrating problem solving and other effective coping skills; be willing to look beyond the addiction to see the person.

Nursing diagnoses that relate to clients with substance abuse problems are based on identified problems and goals. A sample nursing care plan summary for the diagnosis of ineffective individual coping is seen in the box on p. 403. Although the actual care for each client is individually planned, certain key nursing actions are common to all substance-dependent clients (see box on p. 404).

Caring for clients with substance-related problems is challenging and frustrating. Nurses are in valuable positions to influence their clients' well-being. Nurses' demonstrations of respect, acceptance, and concern can offer many clients the connection that encourages them to work toward freedom from their chemicals. The personalized approaches of nurses allow for discussions about diet, health, problem solving, and other health concerns. Clients are offered opportunities for learning, changing, and developing new and

SAMPLE CLIENT CARE PLAN
INEFFECTIVE COPING

Assessment

History: Mary is a 34-year-old housewife with three children and a husband who works long hours. Two years ago, she complained of feeling jittery and tense to her physician. He prescribed a mild sedative, which Mary took religiously every evening before bed. Lately, she has begun to take her "nerve pill" during the day and uses alcohol to help "stabilize" her. She is being admitted for evaluation and treatment after her husband found her unconscious on the sofa yesterday.

Current Findings: A well-groomed woman with a flattened affect. Mary answers questions when asked but volunteers no information. She stated she does not belong here because she is not really addicted to anything and resents "being treated like a drugger."

Nursing Diagnosis

Ineffective individual coping related to increasing use of sedatives and alcohol

Planning/Expected Outcomes

Mary will abstain from using all mood-altering chemicals. Mary will identify and seek help for her problem.

Nursing Interventions

Intervention

1. Confront Mary with her substance-abusing actions and their consequences and assist her to identify the problem.
2. Encourage Mary to agree to participate in the treatment program.
3. Work with Mary to develop a written contract for behavioral changes.
4. Assist Mary to identify and adopt more effective coping behaviors.
5. Assess the social support systems available for Mary.
6. Educate Mary and her family about chemical abuse and resources for help.
7. Refer Mary to ABC treatment center and provide support until Mary is involved in the program.

Rationale

1. Denial is very common with persons who have a substance-related problem; identification of problems is the first step toward change.
2. Therapeutic interventions are not effective unless the client wants to cooperate.
3. A personal commitment enhances the likelihood of success.
4. Encourages problem solving and the use of more effective behaviors.
5. Supportive significant others are often unavailable for substance abusers.
6. Knowledge helps Mary and her family cope more successfully with problems.
7. Specialized drug treatment programs are likely to be more effective if clients are willing to participate.

Evaluation

During her entire stay, Mary remained chemical free but expressed many discomforts. Mary was able to identify her drug-using behaviors during her stay but refused to participate in ABC's outpatient treatment program.

KEY INTERVENTIONS FOR CLIENTS WITH SUBSTANCE ABUSE AND DEPENDENCE

- Meet the physical needs of clients during detoxification; this intervention is of paramount importance.
- Address the residual physiological alterations resulting from substance dependence in the same manner as these needs would be met in any person.
- Monitor the effects of the somatic therapies that may be prescribed to control the substance use.
- Teach clients about the disease and its progression.
- Focus on clients' strengths and help clients build on them.
- Help clients problem solve functional solutions to dilemmas they fear.
- Encourage clients to focus on the present and the future, not on the past.
- Behave toward clients in a consistent manner, confronting them in a nonjudgmental, nonpunitive manner if they break the rules of the treatment setting.
- Assist clients' families by encouraging them to become involved in group counseling.

From Taylor CM: *Essentials of psychiatric nursing,* ed 14, St Louis, 1994, Mosby.

more effective skills for living. Work to become familiar with the subject of substance abuse. Learn as much as you can because you *will* be caring for clients whose problems are related to the use of chemical substances.

❖ KEY CONCEPTS

- Substance use is the ingesting (eating, drinking, injecting, or inhaling) of any chemical that affects the body.
- Abused substances are those that alter the individual's perception by affecting the CNS; they are often referred to as mind-altering drugs because of their ability to enhance or depress mood and emotions.
- Every chemical ingested by a pregnant woman poses a potential danger to her unborn child.
- The younger an individual begins to use substances, the more likely that abuse problems will occur later in life.
- The most popular substance for abuse in the United States and most developed countries today is alcohol.
- Narcotics are CNS depressants that occur naturally, semisynthetically, and synthetically.

- Stimulants include caffeine, cocaine, and certain prescription medications, such as the amphetamines, appetite suppressants, and methylphenidate (Ritalin).
- Hallucinogens are natural and synthetic substances that alter one's perception of reality.
- *Cannabis* is a term applied to the hemp plant *Cannabis sativa,* which is usually dried or processed and smoked.
- Many medications have the potential for being abused.
- Abused medications include morphine and its derivatives, amphetamines, sedatives, hypnotics, and antianxiety agents.
- The use of inhalants is associated with significant complications, such as cardiac dysrhythmia or respiratory depression.
- Nicotine is currently a legal inhalant present in all forms of tobacco and certain medications.
- Substance abuse occurs when the use of the chemical becomes more important in the individual's life than the activities of daily living.
- Many individuals use alcohol, tobacco, or other chemicals and function well, but the movement from use to dependency (addiction) follows a fairly predictable course.
- For a substance-related disorder to be diagnosed the pattern of substance use must be disabling and lead to significant impaired functioning and distress and the individual must demonstrate the signs of tolerance, withdrawal, and dependence.
- The assessment of clients with substance-related problems should include a thorough nursing history and physical examination.
- Most treatment programs for clients with substance-related disorders are based on a certain philosophy, although many different types of therapy may be offered.
- Detoxification is the process of withdrawing a substance under medical supervision.
- Relapse is the recurrence of the substance-abusing behaviors after a significant period of abstinence.
- The most important nursing intervention for clients with substance-related problems is to act as a therapeutic agent.

❖ SUGGESTIONS FOR FURTHER READING

Two articles to improve understanding of your clients with addictions are "Can you spot the alcoholic patient?" By S. Wilson (*RN* 57[1]:46, 1994) and "Understanding opioids and addiction" by M. McCaffery and B.R. Ferrell (*Nurs 94* 24[8]:56, 1994).

❖ REFERENCES

American Psychiatric Association: *Diagnostic and statistical manual of mental disorders,* ed 4, Washington, DC, 1994, The Association.

Bijur PE and others: Parental alcohol use, problem drinking, and children's injuries, *JAMA* 267(23): 2166, 1992.

Clement JA, Williams EB, Waters C: The client with substance abuse/mental illness: mandate for collaboration, *Arch Psychiatr Nurs* 7(4):189, 1993.

Deykin EY, Buka SL: Suicidal ideation and attempts among chemically dependent adolescents, *Am J Public Health* 84(4):634, 1994.

Dickason EJ, Silverman BL, Schult MO: *Maternal-infant nursing care,* ed 2, St Louis, 1994, Mosby.

Forrest DC: The cocaine exposed infant, part 1: identification and assessment, *J Pediatr Health Care* 8(1):3, 1994.

Keltner NL, Schwecke LH, Bostrom CE: *Psychiatric nursing,* ed 2, St Louis, 1995, Mosby.

McCaffery M, Ferrell BR: Understanding opioids and addiction, *Nurs 94* 24(8):56, 1994.

McMahon AL: Substance abuse among the elderly, *Nurse Pract Forum* 4(4):231, 1993.

Redding BA, Selleck CS: Perinatal substance abuse: assessment and management of the pregnant woman and her children, *Nurse Pract Forum* 4(4):216, 1994.

Siegel MA, Landes A, Jacobs NR, editors: *Information plus: illegal drugs and alcohol 1995 edition,* Wylie, TX, 1995, Information Plus.

Slutsker L and others: Recognizing illicit drug use by pregnant women: reports from Oregon birth attendants, *Am J Public Health* 83(1):61, 1993.

Sullivan EJ: *Nursing care of clients with substance abuse,* St Louis, 1995, Mosby.

Treatment of drug abuse and addiction—part I, *Harvard Ment Health Lett* 12(2):1, 1995a.

Treatment of drug abuse and addiction—part II, *Harvard Ment Health Lett* 12(3):1, 1995b.

US Public Health Service: *State resources and services related to alcohol and other drug problems,* Washington, DC, 1994, US Public Health Service.

Wilson S: Can you spot an alcoholic patient?, *RN* 57(1):46, 1994.

29

SEXUAL DISORDERS

1. Describe the continuum (range) of sexual responses.
2. Explain how nurses' self-awareness affects the care of clients with psychosexual problems.
3. Discuss how sexuality is expressed through each life stage.
4. Describe four modes of sexual expression.
5. List three possible causes of sexual problems.
6. State the difference between a sexual dysfunction and a sexual disorder.
7. Define paraphilia and list three examples of paraphiliac behaviors.
8. Apply the nursing process to the care of a client with a psychosexual problem.
9. Explain the importance of HIV/AIDS counseling for every client with a psychosexual problem.

KEY TERMS

bisexuals
dyspareunia
erotic
exhibitionism
gay
gender identity
heterosexual

homosexuality
lesbian
masochism
paraphilias
prostitution
sadism
sexual disorders

sexual dysfunction
sexual orientation
sexuality
transsexualism
transvestism
vaginismus
voyeurism

ccording to Maslow's hierarchy of needs, sex ranks as a basic physiological need. Humans, like most other creatures, have strong sexual drives; but unlike other creatures, human sexual expression is bound and constrained by the social customs, norms, and laws of society. Human **sexuality** is described as the combination of physical, chemical, psychological, and functional characteristics that are expressed by one's gender identity and sexual behaviors. Sexuality is a difficult term to describe because it is a part of many aspects of our lives. People express their sexuality through a variety of thoughts, attitudes, and behaviors.

Sexuality is important in every area of functioning. The physical dimension of sexuality includes anatomy and physiology, those characteristics that physically define us as men or women. Sexuality in the emotional and intellectual dimensions "encompasses our thoughts, beliefs, and values regarding sexuality, including our sexual feelings" (Denney and Quadagno, 1992). The social dimension of functioning is filled with sexuality. Interactions with others may range from the intimacy of sexual intercourse, to the discussions of sexual attitudes with trusted friends, to passing feelings generated by attractive strangers. Sexuality and its expressions are social in nature.

Cultures have an impact on sexuality. All societies have laws, rules, or customs that regulate sexual behavior. Attitudes, beliefs, and rituals help to define what is appropriate sexually. Religious institutions have a strong impact on an individual's view of what is right or wrong sexual behavior. In some cultures, the sexual act is considered a religious ritual, with taboos and regulations governing the experience. Evidence of the practice of religious **prostitution** (the selling of sexual services in exchange for spiritual gain) has been found dating as far back as 5000 years ago. One thing is certain. Cultural attitudes, beliefs, and behaviors toward sexuality and its expressions have changed throughout the years, and they will continue to change in the future (see box below).

CULTURAL ASPECTS

Margaret Mead, in her book titled *Growing up in Samoa,* describes children with few sexual restraints. Although sexual play and experimentation are accepted methods of expression, the pregnancy rate of the islanders is no greater than other populations.

In Malaysia, children born out of marriage are common. It is the custom for the father to quietly provide for the child's welfare.

Continuum of Sexual Responses

Defining "normal" sexual behavior is difficult to do without making value judgments. Even experts have difficulty agreeing on what is normal. For years, the norm was defined as a married man and woman who engaged in sexual relations for the purpose of procreating (for having children). Today, a wider range of sexual behaviors is considered socially acceptable.

Sexual behaviors can be viewed as occurring along a continuum (Fig. 29-1). At the adaptive end of the spectrum lie satisfying sexual behaviors that respect the rights and wishes of others. As the continuum moves toward maladaptive, sexual behaviors become impaired or dysfunctional. The maladaptive end of the continuum is marked by sexual actions that are harmful to self or others in some manner.

Perhaps a useful definition of adaptive or healthy sexual responses is sexuality that is (1) between two consenting adults, (2) satisfying to both, (3) not forced or coerced, and (4) conducted in privacy (Stuart and Sundeen, 1995). Maladaptive or unhealthy sexual responses are those behaviors that do not meet these criteria. They are, in some way or degree, physically or psychologically harmful for the individual or others. Labeling sexual behaviors must be done with caution because judgments are easy to pass on those who behave differently (see box on p. 408).

Self-Awareness and Sexuality

Because nursing and other forms of health care deal with the human condition, each of us must work to develop an awareness of our thoughts, attitudes, values, and beliefs toward sexuality and its various modes of expression. The nurse's level of self-awareness has a strong influence on discussing sexual issues with clients. Values that may be unconscious to the nurse can be transmitted loudly and clearly to clients. Nonverbal messages of disapproval dampen the effectiveness of the therapeutic relationship and all other interventions. The individual who feels judged is not likely to cooperate with the plan of care.

Developing an awareness of your views about sexuality involves the process of defining and clarifying attitudes and values. Each of us carries a sexual point of view, a way of looking at or considering sexuality. Much of the foundation for this view was established during childhood and adolescence unconsciously as a part of growing up and interacting with others.

Refer to Chapter 3 for the values clarification process. Apply each of the steps to the topic of sexuality, and then think about your values and how they may impact the care of clients with sexual disorders. Choose your positions and prize your choices. Know

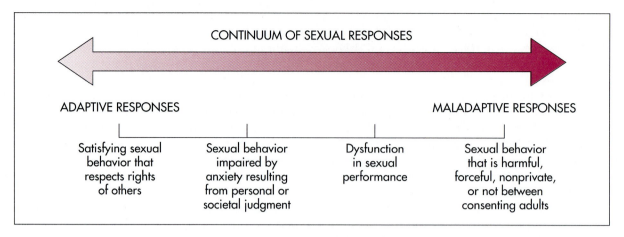

Fig. 29-1   Continuum of sexual responses. (Redrawn from Stuart GW, Sundeen SJ: *Principles and practice of psychiatric nursing,* ed 5, St Louis, 1995, Mosby.)

> ◆ **THINK ABOUT**
> ◆ What is your definition of "normal" sexuality?
> ◆ How does your view compare to the views of a rel-
> ◆ ative, a friend, and a classmate?
> ◆ What is your opinion of those who practice differ-
> ◆ ent means of sexual expression?

that values are not static; they change as one learns and develops. Remember when it comes to working with sexually disordered clients, the nurse's effectiveness is directly related to personal self-awareness and comfort. No client should ever have to suffer from the ignorance of his/her nurse.

Sexuality Throughout the Life Cycle

The expression of one's sexuality begins at birth and ends with death. Sexual differences define roles in society, attitudes about the dynamics of living, relationships with others, and views of who we are. Sex roles develop as new knowledge, attitudes, and behaviors are added to life experiences. A basic knowledge of how sexuality develops throughout the life cycle is important for nurses.

Sexuality in Childhood

"From the moment of birth, children are treated differently by their families based on their biological sex" (Wong, 1995). Female infants are dressed in pink, males in blue. Each is assigned a name, which usually indicates a gender. For example, girls are seldom named Bruce, James, or Joseph, and few boys are addressed by Sarah, Sally, or Marleen.

Families treat boys differently from girls, even in infancy. Female infants are seen as delicate. They are handled and spoken to more tenderly, whereas male infants are stimulated by boisterous voices and play involving motor activity.

Young children are unaware that sex is a permanent attribute. Around the age of 2, children learn to label themselves according to their sex (Clunn, 1991). Most respond to being called "good girls" or "brave boys" by the adults in their environment and soon internalize the label of male or female, boy or girl.

By age 3, the majority of children can accurately label the sex of other persons, but they still believe that their sex can be changed with time if they want it to. By about age 7, they understand that one's sex is permanently assigned and will not naturally change. Between 7 and 9, children learn that one's sex is identified by genital appearance.

Children learn about sex roles in relation to themselves first and then they apply their learning to members of the same sex. Finally, their knowledge is applied to persons of the opposite sex. By about 3 years of age, children can identify the simpler aspects of sex roles. They know, for example, that boys and girls differ in appearance, toy preference, and choice of activities.

By the time they enter school, it is thought that most children identify with the same-sex parent. School is the time to learn about the expected behaviors associated with each sex role. In the past, this identification involved much stereotyping. Girls could not play certain sports, for example, whereas boys were discouraged from taking home economics or engaging in other "sissy" activities. Fortunately, this attitude is fading as individual qualities become more important than playing appropriate sex roles.

Knowledge increases with age; by the middle elementary school years, children are aware of most aspects of their sex-role stereotypes. Future goals, occupational choices, personality traits, and sexual behaviors are influenced by sex roles that were established early in childhood.

Sexuality in Adolescence

During the early teen years, the close relationships with same-sex peers intensify. "Through these relationships children learn about the possibility of intimacy between equals and are exposed to peer standards for appropriate sex-role behavior" (Wong, 1995). As relationships progress, adolescents begin to encounter expectations for mature sex-role behavior from both peers and adults.

Although 12-year-olds are intensely involved with same-sex friends, opportunities for mixed-group activities and dating are increasing. Dating activities in the United States usually begin in the seventh or eighth grade with group social activities, such as dances, picnics, or organized school functions. Group dating moves to double-dating, and by the twelfth grade, most adolescents have been on single-pair dates.

Most teens have difficulty believing that sex can exist without love, so each boy-girl attachment is seen as "true love." Because adolescence is an emotionally stressful time for most individuals, steady dating can offer some relief from insecurity and loneliness and provide a sense of belonging.

In the United States, sexual activity among adolescents has become the norm rather than the exception. Most teens begin experimenting with sexual activity through kissing and petting. As adolescents get older, more adolescents become sexually active. Many adolescents have experienced multiple, serial sexual relationships by the time they are 19. Unfortunately, over "two thirds of adolescent girls use ineffective contraception or none at all" (Hogarth, 1995). Most adolescent boys do not use condoms. Because of this practice, the sexually transmitted disease rate (including HIV/AIDS) and the rate of pregnancy are higher for adolescents than the general population of sexually active adults. Adolescence is a time of intense searching and learning. Much information related to sexuality is gained from peers and other inexperienced or unknowledgeable persons. Nurses should always be alert for the opportunity to assess and correct, if necessary, adolescents' misconceptions about sexuality and its expressions.

Sexuality in Adulthood

"Since the age of first intercourse has decreased and the age at marriage has increased over the years, there are more young adults who are unmarried and sexually active than ever before" (Seidman and Rieder, 1994). Over 90% of young adults are sexually active; but by young adulthood, many are willing to assume responsibility for preventing pregnancy and disease. Between ages 18 and 24, most adults engage in sexual activity with multiple partners and serial relationships. Women tend to be less sexually aggressive than men, who are more likely to seek out and experience sexual relationships with a number of persons.

Among adults 25 to 59 years old, relative monogamy (the practice of having only one partner) appears to be the norm. Sexuality becomes shared with one special person as adults commit to marriage and family relationships. However, as the divorce rate continues to climb, many more adults are involved with multiple sexual partners.

Sexual behaviors during adulthood change to accommodate the situation. After the birth of children, for example, parents are usually less likely to spontaneously engage in acts of sexual expression. The fear of another unplanned pregnancy on a limited income has a strong effect on many adults who are already coping with all they can financially handle.

The sexuality patterns of middle-aged adults have recently changed. More women in their 30s and 40s are bearing children and beginning families. Single parenthood is not uncommon.

Satisfying patterns of sexual functioning are continued throughout the middle years. As children leave home and menopause occurs, many women experience a feeling of sexual freedom. The fear of pregnancy is over. The couple is once again alone and able to spontaneously interact.

Sexuality in Older Adulthood

The typical picture of the older adult is one of an asexual, unintelligent, and uninterested individual. Nothing could be further from the truth. Older adulthood for many people is a time of pursuing one's own interests and desires, including sexuality.

Sexual expression in older adults shifts "from procreation to an emphasis on companionship, sharing, touching, and intimate communication, not just the physical act of coitus" (Edelman and Mandle, 1994). The closeness, intimacy, and sharing of sexuality becomes more important than the physical act for most older adults. Sexuality can also be communicated through touching, stroking, or other means of expression when intercourse is not desirable or possible.

Sexuality persists throughout one's life, and it is important for many older adults (Lueckenotte, 1996). Although sexual activity may decrease in frequency as one ages, established sexual patterns continue. Unfortunately, the sexual expression of older adults meets many cultural and social barriers, attitudes, and expectations. Poor health, medications, disabilities, and the normal aging process may influence one's sexual behaviors, but sexuality is like the need for food or water: it will be with us until the day we die.

Sexuality and Disability

Many permanently disabled persons are able to enjoy rich and satisfying sexual lives with a little adaptation (Cole and Cole, 1978). People with spinal cord injuries, for example, can still be lovers, partners, and parents. Health problems such as diabetes, arthritis, cancer, and cardiovascular disease can affect one's sexuality. In fact, any condition that affects well-being, mobility, or self-esteem has an impact on sexuality and its expressions. However, these conditions only affect the expression of sexuality, not one's sexuality itself.

Men and women who are disabled must learn to adapt to their conditions. Most must also cope with society's negative attitudes toward the disabled. Sexuality that once was natural and comfortable has somehow been replaced by social taboos or disapproval.

People with disabilities have the exact same needs as the rest of the population. Remember, everyone is an individual first; some of us just happen to be different. Improving the quality of life for people with disabilities involves changing social attitudes that limit the disabled.

Modes of Sexual Expression

An individual's sexual attraction to others is referred to as one's **sexual orientation** or sexual preference. In 1948, Kinsey developed a scale of human sexual preference, ranging from exclusively heterosexual to exclusively homosexual (Fig. 29-2). Kinsey stated that most people were not exclusively one or the other because many had experienced both heterosexual and homosexual expressions of sexuality (Kinsey, Pomeroy, and Martin, 1953). There are several modes of sexual expression (Table 29-1).

Heterosexuality

Persons who express their sexuality with members of the opposite sex are known as **heterosexual.** Heterosexual relationships are the foundation for procreation (bearing offspring) and family, although it is not uncommon to encounter families with homosexual or bisexual parents.

Historically, heterosexual relationships have been the norm, the culturally and socially acceptable form of coupling. However, variations of the man-woman relationship have existed throughout history. For example, in ancient Greece it was customary for men to

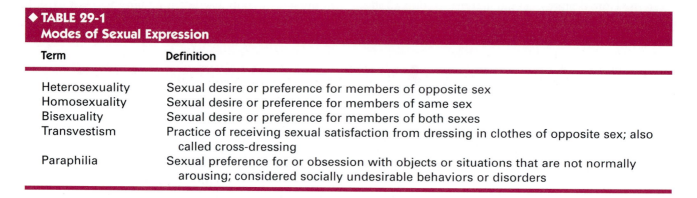

◆ **TABLE 29-1**
Modes of Sexual Expression

Term	Definition
Heterosexuality	Sexual desire or preference for members of opposite sex
Homosexuality	Sexual desire or preference for members of same sex
Bisexuality	Sexual desire or preference for members of both sexes
Transvestism	Practice of receiving sexual satisfaction from dressing in clothes of opposite sex; also called cross-dressing
Paraphilia	Sexual preference for or obsession with objects or situations that are not normally arousing; considered socially undesirable behaviors or disorders

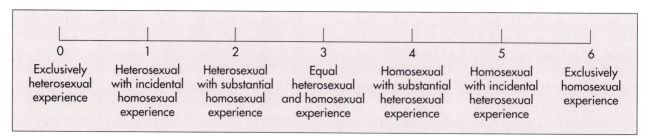

0	1	2	3	4	5	6
Exclusively heterosexual experience	Heterosexual with incidental homosexual experience	Heterosexual with substantial homosexual experience	Equal heterosexual and homosexual experience	Homosexual with substantial heterosexual experience	Homosexual with incidental heterosexual experience	Exclusively homosexual experience

Fig. 29-2   Kinsey's rating scale of sexual preference. (Redrawn from Kinsey AC, Pomeroy WB, Martin EC: *Sexual behavior in the human female,* Philadelphia, 1953, WB Saunders.)

regard the women they married as "useful for little other than having children and taking care of household affairs" (Denney and Quadagno, 1992). The social, emotional, and **erotic** (sexually desiring) needs of husbands often were filled by other men, especially adolescent boys. In this culture, both heterosexuality and homosexuality were considered socially appropriate expressions of sexuality. History is filled with examples of sexual restrictions and permissions that relate to heterosexual relationships, but it appears that this type of relationship is here to stay because biology still requires a male and a female to produce the next generation of human beings.

Homosexuality

The sexual desire or preference for members of one's own sex is known as **homosexuality.** People who prefer homosexuality are often referred to as **gay** (applies to both sexes) or **lesbian** (applies to female homosexuals). Historically, same-sex relationships have been around as long as opposite-sex relationships, but cultural and social attitudes toward them have changed as history has evolved.

One's sexual orientation is established in late childhood and continues to develop through adulthood. For adolescents who are homosexual, adolescence is a particularly difficult time because, in addition to the average development tasks, these individuals are faced with "their own unique issues of identity formation" (Wong, 1995).

The process of establishing an integrated or complete identity as a homosexual is known as *"coming out"* and it occurs in fairly predictable stages (Table 29-2).

Homosexuality has historically been considered a maladaptive mode of sexual expression, but many studies of both sexes have revealed that homosexuals commonly function as well with their love relationships as heterosexual persons. Studies of homosexual couples (Bell and Weinberg, 1978) have found that homosexual relationships or behaviors tend to fall into one of five categories: close-coupled, open-coupled, functional, dysfunctional, and asexual.

Close-coupled relationships are akin to a married couple. Each individual looks to the other for emotional and sexual satisfaction. These couples spend the majority of their evenings at home and do not seek sexual experiences outside the relationship. They are less likely to visit gay bars, and they report few sexual problems. Couples in this type of homosexual relationship are usually well adjusted and more accepting than average individuals.

Open-coupled relationships consist of two persons living together while continuing to have sexual experiences or relationships with others. These couples are less committed to their primary relationship and seek the company of a larger circle of homosexual friends. They visit gay baths and bars and report higher levels of sexual activity than close-coupled homosexuals.

The third type of homosexual relationship is called functional. These persons have no special sexual partner, and they are usually not interested in finding one.

◆ **TABLE 29-2**
Identity Formation Process of Gay Adolescents

Approximate Age/Stage	Steps in Process	Description
Childhood to early adolescence	Identity awareness	Becomes aware of feeling differently about stereotyped gender activities; feels discomfort with gender stereotypes and the expected behaviors that accompany them
Middle to late adolescence (about age 17 in boys, 18 in girls)	Identity recognition	Discomfort with sex-role behaviors increases as attraction to same-sex persons begins to emerge; begins to feel that he/she is probably homosexual; period of identity confusion, isolation, depression, and great discomfort
Early to middle twenties	Identity assumption	Acknowledges homosexual identity; begins to experiment with sexuality; socializes within homosexual community and subculture
Mid-twenties and beyond	Commitment	Individuals assume homosexual lifestyle; state to themselves and world that they are homosexual; give themselves permission to be who they are

Modified from Wong DL: *Whaley and Wong's nursing care of infants and children,* ed 5, St Louis, 1995, Mosby.

Their lives appear to be organized around sexual activity, and they report a greater number of sexual partners than any other group. Many are unconcerned with being homosexual and are openly involved in the gay community.

Dysfunctional homosexuals have a number of worries and problems. They regret their sexual orientation and are often more unhappy, depressed, or paranoid than most people. Although they try, dysfunctional homosexuals have great difficulty in establishing a permanent relationship. Problems can extend to other areas of their lives, as evidenced by the high crime rate for individuals in this group. Many are likely to be involved in long-term counseling or receiving mental health care.

Last is the category called asexual. Individuals in this group feel sexually unattractive, lonely, and unhappy with themselves. They report few sexual partners, little sexual experience, and low levels of sexual activity. They are not likely to visit gay bars or other gathering places, so much of their time is spent alone and withdrawn. Often, mental health problems are present.

It appears that both homosexual and heterosexual behavior styles have much in common. Homosexuality is now receiving acceptance as a mode of sexual expression, but many health care providers still carry attitudes and stereotypes that "may interfere both directly and indirectly with the care provided to gay and lesbian patients" (Smith, 1993). We must all work to develop the self-awareness that will enhance our therapeutic effectiveness, especially with persons of different sexual orientations. The box below offers a case study of this point.

Bisexuality

Persons who are attracted to and engage in sexual activities with members of both sexes are known as **bisexuals.** These individuals identify themselves as bisexual as compared to homosexuals or heterosexuals. Little research has been done on this mode of sexual expression, but estimates put the bisexual population at approximately 20 million people in the United States (Stuart and Sundeen, 1995). Most bisexual individuals appear to be as well adjusted as those who prefer other modes of sexual expression.

Transvestism

Transvestism is commonly referred to as crossdressing. It is defined as sexual excitement from wearing the clothing of the opposite sex. Two types of transvestism are usually practiced. In the first, a man is aroused by a certain article of clothing, such as shoes or undergarments. With the second type, the individual dresses completely in women's clothing (Brown, 1995) (Fig. 29-3). The typical transvestite is a married man with children who is rather secretive about his crossdressing. He is heterosexual, and his behaviors are usually accepted by his wife. Although few reliable statistics are available, many professionals believe transvestism is more common than once thought.

Factors Relating to Psychosexual Variations

Although no one understands exactly why an individual prefers a certain mode of sexual expression, many theories and explanations have been offered.

CASE STUDY

It is evening in a busy medical-surgical unit. You have just received notice that a 42-year-old man, Jim S., is being admitted for injuries suffered in a motor vehicle accident. Because of the severity of his injuries, the physician has ordered that he be visited by immediate family only.

Jim is admitted to the unit and made comfortable in his new surroundings. As you glance around for family members who may have accompanied him from the emergency department, you see only one youngish-looking gentleman, peering anxiously at your client. "I'm sorry, but immediate family only is allowed in here," you say politely, as you usher him out the door.

Later that evening, Jim begins to respond. He keeps calling out for "my love J.J." and asking you

where J.J. is, so loudly that you are sure everyone on the floor can hear. Finally, Jim quiets down only after he extracts a promise from you to find J.J. Exhausted, you agree, hoping she would somehow arrive and help to keep this man quiet.

As you open the door to leave the room, the youngish-looking man from earlier in the evening almost falls through to the floor. With tears in his eyes, he glares intently at you but says nothing. Quietly, you ask if his name could possibly be J.J.

Clinical Decisions

1. What is the lesson to be learned from this case study?

2. How could this experience help you to be a more effective nurse?

Biological theories explain sexual variations as differences in chromosomes, the genetic material that determines hereditary traits. Some studies have "suggested that homosexuality may be inherited from the maternal side of the family through the X chromosome" (Stuart and Sundeen, 1995). Other researchers suggest a correlation between brain structure and sexual orientation (LeVay and Hamer, 1994), whereas others are pursuing the notion that "hormones wire the brain for sexual orientation during the prenatal period" (Byne, 1994).

Psychoanalytical theories as proposed by Freud and his followers consider sexual variations (other than heterosexuality) as behaviors with neurotic or psychopathic motivations (Fortinash and Holoday-Worret, 1996). Problems arise early in life as a result of the child's Oedipus/Electra complex, in which children experience sexual feelings for the opposite-sex parent and resent the same-sex parent. According to this theory, persons with different sexual behaviors also exhibit problems in other areas of their lives. Aspects of the psychoanalytical point of view have been criticized for being male oriented and viewing women as anatomically inferior because they lack a penis. Little scientific evidence has been found to justify Freud's psychoanalytical view of sexual orientation.

Last, the behavioral theories consider the various modes of sexual expression as learned, measurable responses. The learning theory states that individuals are introduced to a certain sexual variation by an accidental experience that is sexually stimulating. When other sexual experiences lead to feelings of inadequacy, the "pleasurable accident" experience encourages continued use of the sexual variation.

Behavioral theorists also believe that the sexual behaviors of adults in the child's environment have a strong influence on the sexual preferences and behaviors of an individual. Several recent studies (Barskey and others, 1994; Hulme and Grove, 1994; Wagner and Linehan, 1994) have demonstrated significant emotional, adjustment, and mental health problems in adults who were sexually abused as children.

Psychosexual Disorders

Because knowledge of human sexuality is still evolving, a broad definition of psychosexual problems is needed. **Sexual disorders** are those problems that cause distress and impaired functioning in an individual or others who are exposed to the sexual behavior. These disorders include problems with sexual functions, gender identity disorders, and methods of sexual expression that are considered socially inappropriate or illegal.

Sexual Dysfunctions

The average human being experiences four stages of sexual excitement and pleasure: appetite, excitement, orgasm, and resolution.

A **sexual dysfunction** is a disturbance anywhere during these 4 stages of the sexual response cycle (American Psychiatric Association, 1994). Its definition also includes any discomfort or pain associated with sexual intercourse such as **dyspareunia** or **vaginismus.** Sexual dysfunctions may be lifelong or acquired after a period of normal functioning. They may be limited by certain situations, partners, or types of stimulation or generalized to every sexual experience. The causes are often related to physical conditions or psychological distresses.

Problems with sexual expression can be caused by medication or illicit drug use and many physical conditions. Arthritis, diabetes, and chronic illness can result in various sexual dysfunctions or alterations in sexual desire. Impaired hormonal functioning and neurological problems can also lead to difficulties with sexual functioning. Table 29-3 describes the most common sexual dysfunctions in men and women.

Paraphilias

The **paraphilias** are a group of sexual variations that depart from society's traditional and acceptable modes of seeking sexual gratification. When the word

Fig. 29-3   Male transvestite. (From Denney NW, Quadagno D: *Human sexuality,* ed 2, St Louis, 1992, Mosby.)

◆ **TABLE 29-3**
DSM-IV Classification of Sexual Dysfunctions

Classification	Disorder	Description
Sexual desire disorders	Hypoactive sexual desire disorder	Absence of sexual fantasies and desire for sexual activity
	Sexual aversion disorder	Active avoidance of sexual contact with partner; reacts to sexual opportunity with anxiety, fear, or disgust
Sexual arousal disorders	Female sexual arousal disorder	Inability to attain or maintain sexual excitement during sexual activity; has little sexual arousal
	Male erectile disorder	Inability to attain or maintain adequate erection during sexual activity
Orgasmic disorders	Female/male orgasmic disorder	Delay in or absence of orgasm following normal excitement
	Premature ejaculation	Ejaculation that occurs with minimal stimulation before person wishes it to occur
Sexual pain disorders	Dyspareunia	Pain associated with sexual intercourse; may occur in both females and males
	Vaginismus	Persistent involuntary contractions of muscles around vagina when penetration is attempted
Sexual dysfunction caused by medical condition	Dependent on medical diagnoses	Significant sexual problems caused by direct effects of medical condition
Substance-induced sexual dysfunction	Dependent on substance used	Significant sexual problems caused by direct physical effects of substance

Modified from American Psychiatric Association, *Diagnostic and statistical manual of mental disorders,* ed 4, Washington, DC, 1994, The Association.

paraphilia is taken apart, the suffix *philia* means "an attraction to." When used to describe a specific behavior, the descriptive term replaces the prefix *para*. For example, pedophilia refers to a person who is sexually attracted (philia) to children (*pedo,* meaning "child"). Several of these behaviors, such as exhibitionism, pedophilia, and voyeurism, are considered illegal in some countries, including the United States. Others are harmless when practiced in private with other consenting adults. The box on p. 415 names and briefly describes the more common paraphilias.

Gender Identity Disorder

One of the first things an individual develops is a **gender identity**, the knowledge that one is a boy or a girl. When there is an inconsistency between the child's biological sex and his/her gender identity, a gender identity disorder is usually diagnosed.

Children with gender identity disorder are unhappy with their own sex. They want to eliminate their sexual characteristics and trade them for those of the opposite sex. Many truly believe they have been born into the wrong body and reject any expectations or behaviors associated with his/her biological sex. Older children often fail to develop same-sex rela-

tionships in school, leading to isolation and loneliness. Adolescents and adults with gender identity disorder commonly find that their desire to be another sex interferes with work and social relationships.

Transsexualism is the persistent desire to become a member of the opposite sex. Transsexuals are discontented with their biological sex and desire to actually become or have the body of an opposite-sex person. Some transsexuals are so uncomfortable that they attempt to change their biological sex to fit their gender identity. This is accomplished by a series of psychological counselings, hormonal treatments, and major surgeries. Because decisions made by the individual are irreversible, the process of changing one's sexual identity is deliberately prolonged and can take as long as 2 years.

Therapeutic Interventions

Treatment of sexual problems depends on the cause, distressing signs/symptoms, and type of disorder. Group or individual therapy may be used to help clients explore their emotions, behaviors, and coping mechanisms. Behavioral therapies, such as positive reinforcement or aversive therapy, focus on changing or

DSM-IV DESCRIPTION OF PARAPHILIAS

EXHIBITIONISM
Exposure of one's genitals to unsuspecting person(s) followed by sexual arousal.

FETISHISM
Utilization of objects (e.g., panties, rubber sheeting) for purposes of sexual arousal.

FROTTEURISM
Rubbing up against nonconsenting person to heighten sexual arousal.

PEDOPHILIA
Fondling and/or other types of sexual activities with prepubescent child (usually under age 13 having not yet developed secondary sex characteristics).

SEXUAL MASOCHISM
Sexual arousal is achieved by being receiver of pain (either physical or emotional), humiliation, or being made to suffer.

SEXUAL SADISM
Sexual arousal is achieved by infliction of pain (either physical or emotional) or humiliation onto another person.

Modified from American Psychiatric Association: *Diagnostic and statistical manual of mental disorders*, ed 4, Washington, DC, 1994, The Association.

TRANSVESTIC FETISHISM
The act of cross-dressing (heterosexual men wearing female clothing) to achieve sexual arousal.

VOYEURISM
Sexual arousal is achieved by observing unsuspecting persons who are naked, in act of disrobing, or engaging in sexual activity ("peeping Tom").

PARAPHILIA NOS (NOT OTHERWISE SPECIFIED)
These disorders do not meet criteria for aforementioned categories:
- Telephone scatologia: obscene phone calling; "900" sex lines
- Necrophilia: sexual activity with corpses
- Partialism: exclusive focus on particular body part for sexual arousal
- Zoophilia: sexual activity involving participation with animals (bestiality)
- Coprophilia: sexual arousal by contact with feces
- Klismaphilia: sexual arousal generated by use of enemas
- Urophilia: sexual arousal by contact with urine
- Ephebophilia: fondling and/or other types of sexual activities with pubescent children who are developing secondary sex characteristics (e.g., pubic hair, breasts); these children are usually between ages 13-18
- Paraphilic coercive disorder: rape; aggressive sexual assault involving act of sexual intercourse against one's will and without consent

managing sexual behaviors in a more acceptable way. Hormonal therapy is sometimes employed to reduce sexual drives (see box at right).

Environmental controls for sexually undesirable behaviors include incarceration (prison or jail). The individual is removed from society and may or may not be accepted into a special program for sexual offenders while in prison.

Most clients with sexual problems are treated on an outpatient basis. However, many medical-surgical nurses work with problems of sexuality in relation to clients and their surgical procedures or medical conditions.

An important point to remember: if you are uncomfortable with any aspect of a client's sexuality, your nursing judgment and behaviors could be affected. Some psychosexual problems are complex and require the skills of specially educated nurses or sex-

DRUG ALERT

Hormones that reduce the sexual drive have many side effects. Make sure you are familiar with each medication and remember to monitor clients routinely for any unusual symptoms.

In addition, remember that many medications prescribed for various medical problems can cause sexual problems.
Examples include the following:
- antihypertensives
- antidepressants and other psychotropic medications
- medications used for problems of the stomach and small intestine, pain-relieving medications

A complete and accurate nursing history should include an assessment of each client's medication (including over-the-counter and street drugs) history, and current use.

ual therapists. Discuss the situation with your supervisor because the goal is still to provide the client with the best possible care. As with other clients, the nursing interventions remain the same: accept, assess, intervene, and educate.

Psychosexual Assessment

Sexuality is a sensitive topic for most persons. For this reason, nurses must be aware of the client's level of comfort when assessing sexual functioning. Hopefully the client will have established enough trust in the therapeutic relationship to honestly share personal information.

Nursing Process

Nursing diagnoses for psychosexual disorders are based on each client's identified problems. The primary nursing diagnoses for problems with sexuality are sexual dysfunction and altered sexuality patterns. Other nursing diagnoses are selected to help to enhance the client's physical, emotional, social, and spiritual functioning.

The quality of nursing care for clients with psychosexual problems is dependent on nurses' abilities to remain nonjudgmental and accepting of their clients. The team treatment approach is usually more effective in treating individuals with sexual problems because it helps to maintain objectivity and prevents any one member from becoming too involved in a client's treatment (Friedman and Downey, 1995). The box on p. 417 describes a client care plan from the nursing viewpoint. In actual practice, each care plan is developed specifically for each client.

Assessment and treatment are only two important functions of client care. Advocacy and education are also important in relation to providing effective nursing care for clients with sexual difficulties. Advocacy allows nurses to provide an atmosphere of acceptance where clients feel safe in discussing sexuality. It also encourages us to discover our prejudices and refine our own professional and personal values about sexuality.

Perhaps most important is the nurse's ability to educate, to share information that could spell the difference between life and death for people. Education about the prevention of HIV/AIDS and other sexually transmitted diseases, appropriate methods of preventing unwanted pregnancies, and various means of sexual expression are within the realm of nursing. If we are to save a population from the ravages of HIV/AIDS, sexual abuse, and mental illness, each health care provider must shoulder the responsibility to teach about sexuality at every opportunity. It is up to us in the helping professions to care for us all.

❖ KEY CONCEPTS

- Human sexuality is the combination of physical, chemical, psychological, and functional characteristics that are expressed by one's gender identity and sexual behaviors.
- Healthy sexual responses are those that occur between two consenting adults, are satisfying to both, are not forced or coerced, and are conducted in privacy.
- The expression of one's sexuality begins at birth and ends with death.
- Many permanently disabled persons are able to enjoy rich and satisfying sexual lives with a little adaptation.
- An individual's sexual attraction to others is referred to as one's sexual orientation or sexual preference.
- Persons who express their sexuality with members of the opposite sex are known as heterosexual.
- The sexual desire or preference for members of one's own sex is known as homosexuality.
- Persons who engage in sexual activities with members of both sexes are known as bisexuals.
- Transvestism, commonly referred to as cross-dressing, is defined as the practice of wearing the clothing of the opposite sex for sexual excitement.
- Theories that attempt to explain why an individual prefers a certain mode of sexual expression include biological, psychoanalytical, and behavioral viewpoints.
- Sexual disorders are those problems that cause distress and impaired functioning in an individual or others who are exposed to the sexual behavior.
- A sexual dysfunction is a disturbance anywhere in the sexual response cycle and includes any discomfort or pain associated with sexual intercourse.
- Problems with sexual expression can be caused by medication or illicit drug use and many physical conditions.
- The paraphilias are a group of sexual behaviors considered to be socially undesirable.
- A gender identity disorder is an inconsistency between a child's biological sex and his/her gender identity.
- Transsexualism is the persistent desire to become a member of the opposite sex.
- Treatment of sexual problems depends on the cause, distressing signs/symptoms, and type of disorder.
- An important point to remember: if a nurse is uncomfortable with any aspect of a client's sexuality, his/her nursing judgment and behaviors may be affected.
- Nurses must be sensitive to the client's level of comfort when assessing sexual functioning.
- The quality of nursing care for clients with psychosexual problems depends on nurses' abilities to remain nonjudgmental and accepting of the client.
- Assessment, treatment, advocacy, and education are important nursing activities in relation to caring for clients with sexual difficulties.

SAMPLE CLIENT CARE PLAN
SEXUAL DYSFUNCTION

Assessment

History: Brian, a 31-year-old man, has been treated for chronic depression for the past 2 years. Since his medications were changed 3 months ago, Brian has been complaining of a lack of sexual interest. He has been married for approximately 10 months, and his wife is "worried."

Current Findings: An anxious-appearing man. General appearance, speech, motor activity, and interactions are appropriate. Brian describes his problem as a "growing lack of interest" and fears that it will interfere with his new marriage.

Nursing Diagnosis

Altered role performance related to treatment for depression

Planning/Expected Outcomes

Brian and therapist will identify the medications he is taking and list their side effects. Brian's anxiety will decrease as he works to solve his problem.

Nursing Interventions

Intervention

1. Assess degree of sexual frustration and dysfunction, beginning with less personal statements.
2. Reassure that symptoms are troubling but not unique.
3. Develop a list of every medication (including over-the-counter drugs) Brian is taking.
4. Consult with physician for possible dosage regulation of Brian's medications.
5. Educate Brian about each medication's effects on sexual functioning.
6. Refer Brian and his wife for sexual counseling.

Rationale

1. Builds trust and rapport; helps to determine extent of problems and plan effective nursing interventions.
2. Provides reassurance that nothing "physical" is wrong.
3. Certain medications, alone or in combination with others, can lead to changes in sexual functioning.
4. Adjustment of dosages may decrease or correct the problem.
5. Learning to recognize side effects early lessens their intensity and offers opportunities for early interventions.
6. Increases knowledge regarding sexuality and its expressions.

Evaluation

Brian listed each medication and demonstrated great interest in learning about side effects. Brian reported a decrease in his level of anxiety as his knowledge of his medications and their effects improved.

• Education about the prevention of HIV/AIDS and other sexually transmitted diseases, appropriate methods of preventing unwanted pregnancies, and various means of sexual expression is an important nursing responsibility.

❖ SUGGESTIONS FOR FURTHER READING

An article by G.B. Smith, "Homophobia and attitudes toward gay men and lesbians by psychiatric nurses" (*Archives of Psychiatric Nursing* 7[6]:377, 1993), offers a thoughtful look into nurses' stigmas and stereotypes about homosexuals.

❖ REFERENCES

American Psychiatric Association: *Diagnostic and statistical manual of mental disorders,* ed 4, Washington, DC, 1994, The Association.

Barskey AJ and others: Histories of childhood trauma in adult hypochondriacal patients, *Am J Psychiatry* 151:397, 1994.

Bell AP, Weinberg MS: *Homosexuality: a study of diversity among men and women,* New York, 1978, Simon & Schuster.

Brown GR: Cross-dressing men often lead double lives, *Menninger Lett* 3(4):4, 1995.

Byne W: The biological evidence challenged, *Sci Am* 270(5): 50, 1994.

Clunn P: *Child psychiatric nursing,* St Louis, 1991, Mosby.

Cole TM, Cole SS: The handicapped and sexual health. In Comfort A, editor: *Sexual consequences of disability,* Philadelphia, 1978, GF Stickley.

Denney NW, Quadagno D: *Human sexuality,* ed 2, St Louis, 1992, Mosby.

Edelman CL, Mandle CL: *Health promotion throughout the lifespan,* ed 3, St Louis, 1994, Mosby.

Fortinash KM, Holoday-Worret PA: *Psychiatric-mental health nursing,* St Louis, 1996, Mosby.

Friedman RC, Downey JI: Psychodynamically oriented therapy for gays and lesbians, *Harvard Ment Health Lett* 12(5):4, 1995.

Hogarth CR: *Adolescent psychiatric nursing,* ed 2, St Louis, 1995, Mosby.

Hulme PA, Grove SK: Symptoms of female survivors of child sexual abuse, *Iss Ment Health Nurs* 15:519, 1994.

Kinsey AC, Pomeroy WB, Martin EC: *Sexual behavior in the human female,* Philadelphia, 1953, WB Saunders.

LeVay S, Hamer DH: Evidence for a biological influence in male homosexuality, *Sci Am* 270(5):43, 1994.

Lueckenotte AG: *Gerontologic nursing,* St Louis, 1996, Mosby.

Seidman SN, Rieder RO: A review of sexual behavior in the United States, *Am J Psychiatry* 151:330, 1994.

Smith GB: Homophobia and attitudes toward gay men and lesbians by psychiatric nurses, *Arch Psychiatr Nurs* 7(6): 377, 1993.

Stuart GW, Sundeen SJ: *Principles and practice of psychiatric nursing,* ed 5, St Louis, 1995, Mosby.

Wagner AW, Linehan MM: Relationship between childhood sexual abuse and topography of parasuicide among women with borderline personality disorder, *J Pers Dis* 8:1, 1994.

Wong DL: *Whaley and Wong's nursing care of infants and children,* ed 5, St Louis, 1995, Mosby.

30

PERSONALITY DISORDERS

LEARNING OBJECTIVES

1. Explain the continuum of social responses.
2. Describe how personality develops throughout the life cycle.
3. Discuss four theories relating to the development of personality disorders.
4. List four characteristics of a personality disorder.
5. Explain the meaning of the term *dual diagnosis.*

6. Identify 10 types of personality disorders and the most significant behaviors associated with each.
7. State the main goal of therapy for clients with personality disorders.
8. Name four classes of drugs used to treat clients with personality disorders.
9. Develop nursing diagnoses and interventions for a client with a personality disorder.

KEY TERMS

antisocial personality disorder
avoidant personality disorder
borderline personality disorder
deceit
dual diagnosis
gregarious
histrionic personality disorder

ideas of reference
impulsivity
manipulation
narcissistic personality disorder
object constancy
paranoia
personality

psychopaths
schizoid personality disorder
schizotypal personality disorder
splitting
temperament

The social dimension (realm) of human functioning is a vital part of being human. People are **gregarious,** sociable, and in need of the company of others. Although some individuals are able to live in isolation as hermits, the vast majority of us need interactions with other people throughout our lives.

During childhood, individuals establish their personalities. One's **personality** is defined as the composite of behavioral traits and attitudes that identify one as an individual. Personality is the unique pattern of thoughts, attitudes, values, and behaviors each individual develops to adapt to a particular environment and its standards. In short, our personalities define who we are.

To find satisfaction in life, people establish relationships with other people. Some relationships assume a special degree of closeness and sharing that becomes important. These relationships develop intimacy, and another person becomes significant in the life of another.

Developing intimate relationships requires a willingness to reveal the private side of oneself: the emotions, beliefs, attitudes, dreams, and anxieties that describe one's personal nature. Most people are able to develop and sustain their social relationships. Families are established, maintained, and transformed. Relationships outside the family grow and fade as individuals interact and life progresses. For many individuals, however, the intimacy of important relationships is not achieved because of lifelong patterns of maladaptive thoughts, social responses, and behaviors.

Continuum of Social Responses

The social responses (interactions with others) of humans range from autonomy and interdependence to the disordered behaviors of manipulation, intimidation, aggression, and hysteria (Fig. 30-1). People who are highly functional move freely along the continuum, recognizing and balancing their needs for intimacy with their needs for solitude. Those with ineffective behaviors cope with feelings of dependence, loneliness, and the need to withdraw from others. Individuals with personality problems struggle to define and meet their social needs.

Personality Throughout the Life Cycle

The human personality is shaped and influenced throughout life. Personalities are unique patterns of being, established early in childhood and molded through experience. Personality expresses the emotional, intellectual, social, and spiritual realms of an individual. A basic understanding of personality and the factors that influence its development helps health care providers assess and plan for more effective and therapeutic care.

Personality in Childhood

Infants do not see themselves as separate beings until about 18 months (Wong, 1995). The majority of infants experience their environments as warm, nurturing, and unconditionally accepting. When each need is immediately met, infants develop a sense of positive self-worth. They develop trust in the persons who are loving and an environment that is nurturing.

As the child matures, trust grows into the capacity for empathy (understanding the feelings of others), an important ingredient for later relationships. Infants who are denied unconditional love and nurturing have difficulties in forming and maintaining signifi-

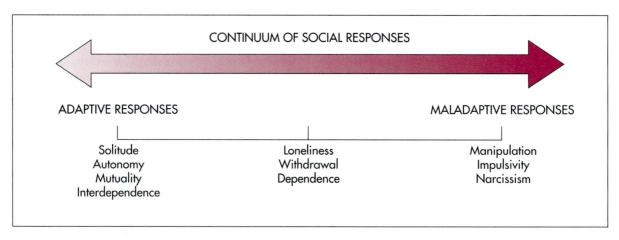

Fig. 30-1   Continuum of social responses. (Redrawn from Stuart GW, Sundeen SJ: *Principles and practice of psychiatric nursing,* ed 5, St Louis, 1995, Mosby.)

cant relationships in adulthood because they have not learned to trust in others.

During the early years of toddlerhood, much of the personality is still fluid, changeable, and undefined. As children age, the personality gradually takes shape and matures. Most researchers believe that, once established, personality traits and temperament are consistent, stable, and generally predictable (Oldham, 1994).

Between 18 months and 3 years of age, toddlers begin to separate from their caregivers to explore the world about them. During this time, they develop a sense of **object constancy,** the knowledge that a loved person or object continues to exist even though it is out of sight or cannot be perceived. Toddlers often seek out their parents for support, encouragement, and approval. If responses to their independent exploratory behaviors are positive, children build a solid sense of self and develop the capacity for interacting successfully with other persons.

Feelings of morality and empathy begin to develop between 6 and 10 years. These years are marked by a preoccupation with self, a strong sense of right and wrong, and interactions with peers. Thinking (intellectual development) moves from concrete to abstract. The focus of their fantasies changes from imagined objects to real ones, and the use of fantasy becomes a primary way of coping with anxiety.

During the early school years, children learn about cooperation, competition, and compromise. Peer relationships begin to assume more importance, and approval from persons outside the family is sought. Conflicts with parents begin to occur in later childhood as the child's search for independence is tempered by the parents' limits on behavior. "During this period a supportive environment that encourages the budding sense of self fosters development of a positive, adaptive self-concept" (Stuart and Sundeen, 1995). Without this support and encouragement, children's needs for guidance and approval go unmet, which sets the stage for numerous problems later in life.

Personality in Adolescence

By the time an individual reaches the teen years, the personality is well established. Relationships with others, especially a "best friend," offer chances for sharing, clarifying values, and learning about the differences in people. "Best friend" relationships become very interdependent and often include active efforts to exclude others (Hogarth, 1991). They are friends, and they support each other in their struggles to assert themselves and cope with the distresses of becoming adults.

As adolescents grow, their relationships expand to include members of the opposite sex. Struggles continue over autonomy within the family. "While young people are involved in these dependent relationships with peers, they are asserting their independence from their parents" (Stuart and Sundeen, 1995).

Today, adolescence is a difficult time for most girls. Mary Pipher, in her book *Reviving Ophelia,* presents the concept of "splitting." She maintains that cultural pressures to be the ideal woman splits young adolescents into a "true self" and a "false" but socially approved self.

Before puberty, children are whole, authentic beings, filled with opinions, a strong sense of right and wrong, and a zest for life. Girls face enormous pressure to split into false selves with the onset of puberty. "The pressure comes from schools, magazines, music, television, advertisements, and movies. It comes from peers. Girls can be true to themselves and risk abandonment by their peers or they can reject their true selves and be socially acceptable. Most girls choose to be socially accepted and split into two selves, one that is authentic and one that is culturally scripted" (Pipher, 1994).

Other girls choose to withdraw, become isolated, and block out the pressures to conform. Some respond to the cultural pressures by blaming themselves and becoming depressed. Those who blame others for their difficulties become angry.

Modern culture is filled with messages to conform to a picture of the ideal woman and man. Because the ideal cannot often be attained, many of our brightest adolescents struggle to define themselves. Perhaps these cultural pressures help to explain the fact that, in women, personality disorders are "diagnosed three times more often than males" (Gabbard, 1995).

Personality in Adulthood

By young adulthood, most persons are making decisions, are self-sufficient, and are involved in give-and-take relationships. Occupational choices are made. Families may be started. Self-awareness grows as individuals learn the balance between personal independence and meeting the needs of others. Sensitivity to and an acceptance of the feelings of other persons is a critical characteristic of mature relationships in adulthood.

By middle adulthood, most persons are comfortable enough with themselves and their personalities to encourage independence in others. Relationships with friends and significant others grow and evolve. Demands on time and resources change as children mature, and many middle adults enjoy new freedoms to pursue their own wishes.

Many experts believe that, once established, the personality remains stable and constant. However, adulthood offers many opportunities for individuals to look within and decide which aspects of their personality they wish to keep and develop and which aspects they would like to change. People are dynamic, always in physical or psychological motion, and change does occur—even with one's "well-established" personality (*Menninger Letter*, 1995).

Personality in Older Adulthood

Older adults must cope with many losses and changes. Old friends are lost. Family members move away. Occupational careers end, and friendships from work fade as time passes.

The personality, however, remains intact as individuals age. Life takes on a deeper meaning as personal accomplishments and contributions to society are reviewed. Older adults with strong, integrated personalities are able to cope with their losses by maintaining what independence they can and accepting their limitations. Their strength of personality carries them through life's rougher times.

An important reminder about older adults: a sudden change in personality is *not* a normal sign of aging. By older adulthood, the personality is deeply entrenched. Patterns of thinking and behaving that make up the personality remain intact until death (Hogstel, 1994). Do not assume that a personality change in an older adult is normal. Changes in emotional control, responses, and levels of interest must be investigated. Many physical and biochemical problems first appear as subtle changes in personality. Alert investigations by health care providers can often spell the difference between functional living and dementia.

Theories Relating to Personality Disorders

Interest in disordered personalities dates back to the time of the ancient Greeks. During the Middle Ages, individuals who behaved or communicated in unusual ways were thought to be possessed by demons or evil spirits. In 1837, the term *moral insanity* was coined to describe a "disorder in which there is gross disturbance in social behavior but no apparent impairment in mental state" (Livesley and others, 1994). The term *psychopath* was introduced in 1891 to describe such disturbed individuals. Today, the differences between normal personality and what constitutes a personality disorder are being hotly debated, but "sharp distinctions are rarely found in nature, and mental disorders are no exception" (Livesley and others, 1994).

It is difficult to tell the exact point at which a blood pressure reading becomes abnormal. It is just as difficult to establish the point at which a normal personality becomes a disordered one. Theories of personality development and disorder have been developed to help understand the complex nature of human be-

ings. Currently, there are four general viewpoints of personality disorders: biological, psychoanalytical, behavioral, and sociocultural.

Biological

As research continues to investigate a possible connection between behavior and body, evidence mounts. Studies of families, twins, and relatives of individuals with personality disorders have demonstrated that behavior and personality are under a strong genetic influence. Researchers have found that one's **temperament,** the biological bases underlying moods, energy levels, and attitudes, is genetically linked (Oldham, 1994). Several studies of twins raised in separate environments have shown remarkable consistency in temperament when tested.

Other biological evidence is beginning to establish "a neurophysiological basis for the characteristic lack of empathy or guilt, shallow emotions, and cold-blooded cruelty" seen in some individuals with personality disorders (Hare, 1995). For example, neurochemical measurements of the spinal fluid of people with schizoid personality disorders are abnormal (Siever, 1992). Brain imaging studies suggest a possible physical basis for a "failure to appreciate the emotional significance of words and images" (Hare, 1995). In other words, the brain mechanism that connects emotions and intellect may be missing or inefficient in persons with personality disorders.

Other research suggests that abnormalities in certain neurotransmitters, such as dopamine and serotonin, are directly linked to maladaptive behaviors (Oldham, 1994). Further studies into the biobehavioral connection are currently being conducted, and new developments will influence the treatment of persons with problem personalities (see box on p. 423, at left).

Psychoanalytical

According to psychoanalytical theories, infants begin to discover the nature of "good/bad" and "love/hate" as the superego grows. If the mother responds to the child in ways that cause frustration, distress, or pain, the child will have difficulty finding the proper fit between aggression and love. Certain patterns of parental responses, ranging from overinvolvement to neglect, prevent the child from developing a strong sense of self (ego) and balance among the three forces of the personality (ego, id, and superego).

Behavioral

Theorists from the behavioral school of thought see personality disorders as the result of conditioned responses caused by previous events. The separation-individuation theory states that the average 1- to 3-year-old is able to achieve object constancy. Person-

THINK ABOUT

The "not guilty due to mental incompetence" defense has been used in many cases of murder and other crimes. Arguments in favor of this type of defense state that many individuals with diagnosed personality disorders did not know what they were doing at the time of the crime and therefore should not be held responsible for their actions. Arguments in favor of abolishing the mental illness defense state that an individual is *always* responsible for his/her actions, no matter what the mental state.

What do you think about the "mental illness" defense?

Should people always be held accountable for their behaviors?

CULTURAL ASPECTS

In some cultures, individuals with personality disorders are considered gifted or connected to spirits. The wife of Russia's last czar, Alexandra, was highly criticized for associating with the monk called Rasputin, a man with a supposed "connection to God." Because of her concern about her hemophiliac son's health, she sought guidance from Rasputin. Rasputin would spend his days in the company of priests, royalty, and generals, but reputedly his nights were saved for drunken sexual parties with prostitutes and other assorted street people.

Rasputin met his demise when poisoned, shot, beaten, and then thrown into a river by a group of noblemen for his unusual behaviors and profound influences on Alexandra while the czar was at the front with the troops. Rasputin may be a compelling historical example of an individual with a personality disorder.

ality disorders occur in persons who are not able to achieve object constancy with their mothers. In other words, they are unable to hold a consistent, stable image of the mother when she is absent. This results in fears that range from abandonment and separation to a complete loss of connection with others. Other behaviorists view personality disorders as the result of unmet needs during critical developmental periods.

Sociocultural

Sociocultural theories find the causes of personality disorders embedded in one's culture and society. They analyze various statistics, such as the fact that the rates of personality disorders are higher for those who have been physically or verbally abused in childhood (Gabbard, 1995), to explain human behaviors. Numerous cultural expectations are seen to influence the use of adaptive or maladaptive behaviors. The box above, at right, offers an interesting historical enigma.

Many social stressors can lead to difficulties with relationships. Family instability, divorce, and mobility often help to isolate people from those they love. Traditions that once bound people together are no longer practiced, adding to the sense of isolation. Rates of violent crime and aggression force persons to seclude themselves from other people for protection. Unemployment, homelessness, and AIDS add to the powerlessness felt by many persons. Sociocultural theorists believe that the foundation for personality disorders is built on society's social and cultural stresses.

Personality Disorders

Personality disorders are defined as longstanding, maladaptive patterns of behaving and relating. Many individuals have maladaptive behaviors but they are not diagnosed as mentally ill because their actions do not deviate from or go beyond society's expectations.

The most important criteria for a personality disorder is that behaviors are "inflexible and maladaptive and cause significant functional impairment or subjective distress" (American Psychiatric Association, 1994). These inflexible, ineffective behavior patterns must occur throughout a broad range of occupational, social, and personal situations. The onset of the maladaptive patterns can be traced back to childhood or adolescence, and no medical or other mental health problem can account for them. The box on p. 424 provides a description of the common characteristics of personality disorders. Study it well because you *will* be caring for clients with these problems.

The DSM-IV has classified 10 separate personality disorders. For the sake of discussion, personality disorders are grouped into three clusters based on similar behaviors: eccentric, erratic, and fearful. Table 30-1 lists the main feature of each disorder. Remember that individuals can exhibit behaviors from different clusters because human beings seldom fit neatly into any category or classification.

Eccentric Cluster

The group of personality disorders called the eccentric cluster is characterized by odd or strange behaviors. Persons with problems in this cluster (group A) find it difficult to relate to others or socialize comfortably. Often they live in isolation and interact only as necessary. Diagnoses in this cluster include paranoid, schizoid, and schizotypal disorders.

Paranoia is a suspicious system of thinking with delusions of persecution and grandeur. Individuals with a paranoid personality disorder have developed

CHARACTERISTICS OF PERSONALITY DISORDERS

COGNITION (INTELLECT, PERCEPTION, VIEWPOINT)

Impaired self-perceptions: has distorted picture of self; tends to hate or idealize self

Impaired thought processes: thinking is concrete, difficulty in abstracting; impaired concentration, memory; poor attention

Impaired reality testing: distorts and confuses inner and outer reality; projects own feelings onto other persons

Impaired judgment: problem-solving abilities impaired; does not understand consequences of behaviors; does not learn from past behaviors

AFFECT (EMOTIONAL RESPONSES, MOOD)

Impaired stimulus barrier: unable to filter out or regulate incoming sensory stimuli; easily excited; responds excessively to noise or light; easily agitated; anger escalates rapidly

CHARACTERISTIC MOODS

Dysphoric feelings, depression; abandonment when significant others are absent; emptiness; fear; guilt; rage

INTERPERSONAL FUNCTIONING (SOCIAL RESPONSES)

Impaired object relations: has rigid and inflexible patterns of relating to others; has difficulty with intimate relationships

Poor impulse control: has uncontrollable pressures to act on internal urges; copes with internal pain by acting out

Examples of acting-out behaviors: verbal and physical aggression, attacks, abuse; psychological abuse; manipulation; inappropriate sexual behaviors, casual sex; suicide attempts

Modified from Rollant PD, Deppoliti DB: *Mosby's review series: mental health nursing,* St Louis, 1996, Mosby.

◆ **TABLE 30-1**
Clusters of Personality Disorders

Cluster/Disorder	Main Characteristic
A: Eccentric	
Paranoid	Distrust and suspiciousness; sees others' motives as malevolent (intend to do harm)
Schizoid	Detachment from social relationships; emotional expression is restricted
Schizotypal	Acute discomfort with close relationships; sensory distortions; odd behaviors, thinking, and speech
B: Erratic	
Antisocial	Disregards/violates rights of others
Borderline	Unstable self-image, affect, and interpersonal relationships
Histrionic	Excessive emotional expression and attention-seeking behaviors
Narcissistic	Grandiose, no empathy, needs to be admired
C: Fearful	
Avoidant	Social distress, feelings of inadequacy, oversensitivity
Dependent	Excessive need to be cared for, resulting in clinging, submissive behaviors
Obsessive-compulsive	Preoccupation with control, orderliness, and perfectionism

Modified from American Psychiatric Association: *Diagnostic and statistical manual of mental disorders,* ed 4, Washington, DC, 1994, The Association; and Rollant PD, Deppoliti DB: *Mosby's review series: mental health nursing,* St Louis, 1996, Mosby.

---

a pattern of behaviors marked by suspiciousness and mistrust. They automatically assume that everyone is out to harm, deceive, or exploit them. The loyalty and trustworthiness of friends is often questioned for hostile intentions. The search for hidden meanings can turn a casual remark into a conflict. Sharing information or becoming close to someone is avoided because it may provide information (ammunition) that may be used against them. Individuals with paranoid personality disorders become constantly alert for harmful intentions from other persons and are quick to counterattack if they feel wronged or slighted. Often a minor event arouses intense hostility and aggression.

These persons are very short-tempered and unwilling to forgive even the slightest error. Feelings of tenderness or respect are nonexistent. Many suffer from pathological (extreme) jealousy and often accuse spouses or partners of secretly having sexual relationships. Problem solving is difficult, and high anxiety levels keep these individuals resistant to change.

Paranoid personality disorders are diagnosed in up to 2.5% of the population. Men are diagnosed more often than women, and substance abuse is common. Between 10% to 30% of all psychiatric inpatients are diagnosed with paranoid personality disorders (Fortinash and Holoday-Worret, 1996).

Schizoid and schizotypal personality disorders are marked by an inability to develop and maintain relationships with other people. Persons with **schizoid personality disorder** lack the desire or willingness to become involved in close relationships. These persons are society's "loners" who prefer solitary activities and their own company. They are emotionally restricted and unable to take pleasure in activities, friendships, or social relationships. Often, individuals communicate emotional detachment, coldness, and a lack of concern for others. Sexual experiences hold little interest. Schizoid personality disorders are slightly more common in men and families with an already diagnosed member.

Persons with **schizotypal personality disorder** have the same interaction pattern of avoiding people as persons with schizoid personality disorders, but the behaviors here are characterized by distortions and eccentricities (odd, strange, or peculiar actions). These individuals often have **ideas of reference,** incorrect perceptions of casual events as having great or significant meaning. They commonly find special, personal messages in everyday events.

Schizotypal people are often superstitious or believe in the paranormal (events outside human understanding). Many think they have special powers to foretell events or read people's minds. Some claim to have magical control over others and are able to make people do their bidding just by wishing or thinking about it. These persons commonly experience perceptual alterations such as sensing that another person is present (when they are not). Speech is often loose and vague, but it can be understood. Often, they will use words in odd combinations or unusual ways.

As with the other disorders in the eccentric cluster, schizotypal personalities are marked by suspiciousness and paranoid ideation, the idea that people are "out to get them," to undermine their efforts or do them harm. Emotional expressions (affect) are usually inappropriate or restricted. Because of unusual mannerisms, style of dress or grooming, and inattention to appropriate social behaviors, these individuals are considered odd or eccentric. They have problems relating to other people and are very anxious in social situations. They have few if any friends because they feel they are different and just do not "fit in."

As many as 50% have signs of major depression. Schizotypal personality disorders are diagnosed more frequently in men.

Erratic Cluster

The main characteristic for the group of disorders called the erratic cluster is dramatic behavior. Each disorder in this cluster (group B) is associated with a dramatic quality in the way in which these individuals live and conduct their lives. The erratic cluster consists of four separate disorders: antisocial, borderline, histrionic, and narcissistic.

One of our most pressing mental health problems today is with people who have antisocial personality disorders. "The central feature of **antisocial personality disorder** is a pervasive pattern of disregard for, and violation of, the rights of others" (American Psychiatric Association, 1994).

These persons are often referred to as psychopaths or sociopaths because they rely on deceit and manipulation to get their way. **Deceit** is lying. It is the act of representing as true something that is known to be false. **Manipulation** is defined as controlling others for one's own purposes by influencing them in unfair or false ways.

The hallmark of **psychopaths** is "a stunning lack of conscience; their game is self-gratification at the other person's expense. Many spend time in prison, but many do not. All take more than they give" (Hare, 1994). Because of these traits, it is important for nurses who care for these individuals to investigate sources other than the client when performing an assessment and to remain alert for these behaviors. The box on p. 426 offers a case study of an antisocial personality.

Antisocial personality disorders are rooted in childhood. Most children develop internal controls for aggression and anger. Some children, however, have trouble controlling their impulses so they become disruptive and antisocial as a way of coping. Many of these maladaptive behaviors are seen as early as 4 years of age (Clunn, 1991).

Most often children with conduct disorders express their distress four ways: they are aggressive to animals and people; they deceive, lie, or thieve; they destroy property; and they break important rules. Many

Rusty was the youngest of two boys born to an older, loving couple. As a child, he was always into some type of trouble. When he was about 7, Rusty broke his femur and was required to wear a body (spica) cast for 6 weeks. Although his mother checked on him frequently, he managed to be mobile. One day Rusty walked out of the house and was seen propelling his casted hips and legs down the street, uninterested in the fact that he could have harmed himself.

By 12 years old, Rusty was self-centered, demanding, and intolerant of his parent's wishes. He often threatened to burn the house down or kill the dog when he did not get his own way. Soon his father was bailing him out of jail for various minor offenses like speeding, skipping school, and stealing. His parents, unable to control him and afraid for their safety, allowed him free run of the house.

At 18, Rusty joined the Army. By 19 he had received a general discharge for not following orders. Much to his parents' dismay, Rusty returned home and announced that he would attend the local college. By this time, however, he was deeply involved with cocaine, alcohol, and a crowd of thrill seekers. His arrest record continued to grow with the passage of time.

One night at a party, Rusty strangled the homeowner's pedigreed cat. The owner became angry and threatened to have him arrested. Rusty coldly looked into the homeowner's eyes, pulled the gun, and fired.

Later, when asked why he did it, he calmly replied, "What else could I do? That guy was in my face and his stupid cat was in my way. I didn't hurt him bad."

Clinical Decisions

1. What are your reactions to Rusty's behaviors?
2. How would you feel if you were assigned to care for him?
3. Do you think anything could have prevented this event? If so, what?

become bullies in school. They are impulsive, quick to anger, and have little regard for the feelings of others. If the child is seen by mental health care providers at this time, a conduct disorder is usually diagnosed.

During adolescence, maladaptive behaviors become well established. Truancy from school, open disregard for rules, and thrill-seeking behaviors often get these teens into trouble with authorities or the law. Fighting and physical and verbal abuse are common in adolescents with antisocial personalities.

By adulthood, psychopaths are usually adept at manipulating and deceiving others. They gain money, power, or influence at the expense of others and feel no guilt. They lie, cheat, con others, and malinger (pretend to be ill) to achieve their goals but are unable to plan ahead and act because they are too impulsive. Decisions are made with no thought to the consequences. Often, they are able to inflict pain and suffering in others and feel no remorse or guilt.

Individuals with antisocial personality disorders (psychopaths) are often full of charm. They are glib, clever conversationalists, complete with compliments and entertaining statements. An inflated view of their own importance places them in the center of attention and in their mind justifies living by different rules.

Psychopaths have a remarkable ability to rationalize their own actions. That, coupled with a lack of guilt and empathy, allows them to shrug off any responsibility for their actions. Their emotions are shallow. Behaviors are impulsive, and the need for excitement often involves breaking rules.

Psychopaths have a "hair trigger" on their emotions; they can fire off with very little cause. However, when they are violent, it is "cold," without the intense emotional arousal that other perpetrators of violence experience. There is little remorse; victims are blamed for being weak, stupid, or in the wrong place (Hare, 1994).

Men are more affected by antisocial personality disorders than women. They may abuse chemicals. Commonly, they fail to become self-supporting and spend years being impoverished, homeless, or institutionalized. Psychopaths constitute a large portion of the populations in prisons and psychiatric institutions.

A **borderline personality disorder** can be summarized as "instability in mood, thinking, behavior, personal relationships, and self-image" (*Harvard Mental Health Letter*, 1994). Intense fears of being abandoned motivate these persons to avoid being alone. Relationships with others are marked by rapid shifts from adoring and idealizing to devaluing and cruel punishment. These same extreme shifts are also seen in the area of self-image. Sudden, dramatic changes in career plans, values, types of friends, and even sexual identities are characteristic of these individuals.

Impulsivity, acting without forethought or regard to the consequences, is a feature of personality disorders. Persons with borderline personality disorders may gamble, abuse food or drugs, engage in unsafe sex with multiple partners, spend money irresponsibly, and engage in self-mutilating or suicidal behaviors. Cutting, burning, pulling out hair, or scratching oneself are very common, and 8% to 10% of these individuals actually commit suicide.

Moods (affect) are unstable. Although people with borderline personality disorders experience chronic feelings of emptiness, they commonly express intense anger and frequent displays of aggression or temper. Emotions range from great joy to deep depression and frequently change within minutes or hours. They express inappropriate anger and have difficulty controlling their aggression. These individuals become easily bored, so they are always busy. During stressful times, individuals with borderline personality disorder may develop paranoid delusions and feelings of depersonalization (loss of contact with the self).

Histrionic and narcissistic personality disorders have the feature of attention-seeking behaviors. Individuals with these disorders are often highly emotional and self-centered. They feel inadequate and unappreciated when not the center of attention.

Histrionic personality disorder is defined as a pattern of excessive emotional expression accompanied by attention-seeking behaviors. Histrionic persons may be flashy or dramatic in style of dress, mannerisms, and speech. A **narcissistic personality disorder** is characterized by a pattern of grandiosity and the need to be admired. These individuals believe they are special, unique, or extra important. Often, they fantasize about unlimited money, power, or love and take advantage of others without guilt or remorse. It is interesting to note that more women are diagnosed with histrionic personality disorder, whereas 50% to 75% of persons diagnosed with narcissistic personality disorder are men (Fortinash and Holoday-Worret, 1996).

Individuals with personality disorders are many of the perpetrators of violence in our culture. Children who were bullies commonly grow up to be partner abusers. Individuals who had problems with anger control and impulsive urges as children find themselves unable to express themselves appropriately as adults. Teens with histories of being "difficult" or "temperamental" often engage in illegal activities. "Even within the criminal population, psychopaths stand out, largely because the antisocial and illegal activities of psychopaths are more varied and frequent than those of other criminals" (Hare, 1994). Psychopaths tend to try every type of crime and then wonder what all the fuss is about when they are caught.

Fearful Cluster

The common characteristic of the fearful cluster (group C) is anxiety. The three personality disorders in the fearful or anxious cluster are avoidant, dependent, and obsessive-compulsive. Each disorder is related to certain expressions of anxiety.

In **avoidant personality disorder,** anxiety is related to a fear of rejection and humiliation. To prevent possible rejection, individuals narrow their interests to a small range of activities. They have a very small if any support system because they are so afraid of the reactions of others. Often, their tension does not allow for new friends who may be critical, so they withdraw into a world of isolation and self-pity. "When all else fails, they retreat into daydreaming and fantasy" (*Harvard Mental Health Letter,* 1996a). Often, individuals with avoidant personality disorders also suffer from general anxiety, depression, or hypochondria.

The anxiety of a *dependent personality disorder* is associated with separation and abandonment. People with this problem carry a deep fear of rejection, which expresses itself as the need to be cared for. To avoid turning people away, they become overcooperative and docile and do not make demands or disagree with others. When alone, they feel helpless; they will go to great lengths to find someone to care for them.

Individuals with dependent personality disorder refuse to take responsibility for their own actions. They are unwilling to begin a task alone, take any independent actions, or assume responsibility for their own activities of daily living. Feelings of worthlessness often motivate them to seek out overprotective, dominating, or abusive relationships.

Dependent personality disorder is one of the most commonly diagnosed personality disorders. Men and women are equally diagnosed, although some studies show a higher incidence in women. Cultural factors must be considered before a diagnosis is made because many societies consider certain dependent roles appropriate.

Persons with obsessive-compulsive personality disorder relate their anxiety to uncertainty about the future. They are extremely orderly and so preoccupied with details that little is actually accomplished. Delegating tasks to others is impossible because no one "can do it as well." Commonly, these individuals are devoted to work, have few leisure activities, and are consumed by the need for perfection. "About two-thirds of compulsive personalities are men" (*Harvard Mental Health Letter,* 1996b).

Dual Diagnosis

Many individuals with personality disorders are also suffering from some other form of mental illness and are categorized as having a **dual diagnosis.** Many times, substance abuse problems are part of the diagnosis as individuals attempt to cope with their problems through the use of alcohol or street drugs. Many dually diagnosed persons are also homeless, unemployed, or involved in legal troubles. Nurses who care for such clients must be aware of the multiple problems involved with dual diagnosis clients. Thorough assessments and careful planning are necessary to address the numerous problems present in this population.

Therapeutic Interventions

The treatment for individuals with personality disorders is complex. Individuals with personality disorders have extremely diverse treatment needs, and no single treatment is appropriate for every client. Unfortunately, many do not seek treatment or refuse to accept it when it is recommended because of their basic mistrust of other people's intentions.

Treatment and Therapy

Treatment decisions are guided by the client's presenting symptoms, complaints, and problems. Persons with personality disorders may have significant impairments in functioning, but they seldom present for treatment because they are usually unable to recognize their problems. When they do cooperate with treatment, a combination of various psychotherapies and medications are used only after any physical causes or links to the disorder are ruled out.

A number of different psychotherapies are selected to treat clients with personality disorders (Nehls and Diamond, 1993). Types of psychotherapy that have been used with success for different personality disorders include psychodynamic, cognitive, behavioral, and group therapy. Cure is not the goal of therapy. Care providers "can hope only to make patients more aware of how their habits affect their lives, modifying their behavior enough so that a personality disorder becomes a more adaptive personality type or style" (*Harvard Mental Health Letter*, 1996b).

Pharmacological Interventions

Medications are used with great caution in the treatment of people with personality disorders. Medications are prescribed to help relieve some of the distressing symptoms associated with these disorders. Most psychotherapeutic medications are prescribed in limited amounts for short periods of time. Table 30-2 lists the target symptoms or behaviors and the medications that are usually chosen to treat them.

Nurses must exercise great care when administering medications to individuals with personality disorders. Compliance must be monitored frequently. Safeguards to prevent or reduce the risk of suicide must be in place. If the client is being seen on an outpatient basis, the amount of any prescribed medication must never equal a large enough single dose for a successful suicide.

Also, be alert to the fact that many clients will "hoard" their medications until they have a lethal dose at hand. Do not hesitate to assess every medicated client for suicidal thoughts or plans. Last, be familiar with each class of drugs and their side effects. The prudent nurse does not wait to research a medication until a client must take one.

Nursing Process

The goals of nursing care for clients with personality disorders are twofold: (1) to help clients identify and then become responsible for their own behaviors and (2) to assist clients in developing satisfactory interpersonal relationships. Short-term goals are based on each individual's assessed problems. They usually focus on the discomforts or ineffective behaviors associated with daily living activities.

The assessment of every client should include a mental status examination, but for the client with a personality disorder, this examination is extremely important. A nursing history will reveal how individuals cope with the many aspects of daily life, including interpersonal relationships.

◆ **TABLE 30-2**
Drug Alert: Medications for Personality Disorders

Target Symptoms	Psychotherapeutic Drug Class
Anxiety	Antianxiety agents: benzodiazepines
Cognitive (intellectual) dysfunctions	Low-dose antipsychotics (neuroleptics), phenothiazines, haloperidol
Perceptual distortions	
Depressive behaviors	Antidepressants: tricyclic antidepressants, MOAIs, SSRIs
To loosen impulse control	
Impulse control or stabilization	Lithium, the anticonvulsant carbamazepine (Tegretol)

Modified from Oldham JM: *JAMA* 272(22):1770, 1994.
MOAIs, Monoamine oxidase inhibitors; *SSRIs,* selective serotonin reuptake inhibitors.

The therapeutic relationship is begun at this time, so it is important for the nurse to remain nonjudgmental. Remember, however, many clients use manipulation, charm, or other subtle behaviors to achieve their purposes. They often use a technique called **splitting**, emotionally dividing the staff by complimenting one group and degrading another.

Consistent limit setting and reinforcement help clients to define their limits, but care providers must keep in mind their own therapeutic boundaries and communicate with each other frequently.

Clients with personality disorders often have several problems at once. The most important ones are identified and linked to the appropriate nursing diagnosis.

 SAMPLE CLIENT CARE PLAN

PERSONALITY DISORDERS

Assessment

History: Sophie was 6 years old when her parents divorced after years of fighting and abuse. She, her mother, and her older brother, Sam, were forced to find shelter in a small hotel room. Shortly after moving in, her mother met a man and began to leave Sophie alone for long periods. Once Sophie set the room on fire. Another time she strangled the neighbor's canary. On one occasion, she was molested by a drunken visitor. By the time Sophie was 13, she had dropped out of school and began living in the streets. Occasionally, she would return home just to see if her mother noticed her absence. She didn't.

Current Findings: Today, 19-year-old Sophie has been admitted to the medical unit for recovery from repeated attempts to "cut herself apart." She is suicidal, angry, and has difficulty in identifying her actions and their consequences.

Nursing Diagnosis

Risk for self-directed violence related to feelings of abandonment, depression, and worthlessness

Planning/Expected Outcomes

Sophie will verbally identify the emotions associated with her self-destructive activities. Sophie will not engage in self-destructive behaviors while hospitalized.

Nursing Interventions

Intervention

1. Inform Sophie that self-harm is not acceptable behavior while she is here.
2. Have Sophie sign a no-harm contract.
3. Institute suicide precautions; monitor continuously if acting out.
4. Assess skin on arms and legs daily for new wounds or signs of trauma.
5. Establish trust and rapport with Sophie.

Rationale

1. Setting limits lets her know which actions are unacceptable.
2. Offers objective data of agreed-on behaviors.
3. To provide for her safety, prevent self-harm, and encourage therapeutic relationships.
4. To monitor for further evidence of self-harm activity.
5. Allows Sophie to identify current behaviors and explore new ones within an atmosphere of safety and trust.

Evaluation

Sophie expressed relief at knowing limits are set on her behaviors 2 days after admission. Sophie was able to identify her emotions following a dispute with another client.

Interventions and evaluations are developed for each diagnosis based on each individual client. The box on p. 429 offers a sample nursing care plan for a client with personality disorder. Caring for these clients can be a challenge, but the process can promote growth in both client and caregiver when willing to work together.

❖ KEY CONCEPTS

- Personality is the composite of behavioral traits and attitudes that identifies one as an individual.
- The social responses of humans can range from autonomy and interdependence to the ineffective, disordered behaviors of manipulation, intimidation, aggression, and hysteria.
- The human personality is shaped and influenced throughout life.
- Currently, there are four general theories of personality: biological, psychoanalytical, behavioral, and sociocultural.
- Personality disorders are defined as longstanding, maladaptive patterns of behaving and relating to others.
- The eccentric cluster (group A) of personality disorders is characterized by odd or strange behaviors and includes the paranoid, schizoid, and schizotypal personality disorders.
- The erratic cluster (group B) of personality disorders is characterized by dramatic behaviors and consists of four personality disorders: antisocial, borderline, histrionic, and narcissistic.
- The fearful cluster (group C) of personality disorders is characterized by anxiety and includes the avoidant, de-

pendent, and obsessive-compulsive personality disorders.

- Many individuals with personality disorders are also suffering from drug abuse or some other form of mental illness and are therefore categorized as having a dual diagnosis.
- People with personality disorders may have significant impairments in functioning, but they seldom present for treatment because they are unable to recognize their problems.
- Types of psychotherapy that have been used with success for different personality disorders include psychodynamic, cognitive, behavioral, and group therapy.
- Medications are used with great caution in the treatment of people with personality disorders and only to help relieve some of the distressing symptoms associated with these disorders.
- The goals of nursing care for clients with personality disorders are (1) to help clients identify and then become responsible for their own behaviors and (2) to assist clients in developing satisfactory interpersonal relationships.

❖ SUGGESTIONS FOR FURTHER READING

A "must-read" for new nurses and other health care providers is "Defusing the violent patient" by S. Lewis and P. Blumenreich (*RN* 56[12]:24, 1993). It offers several important tips for recognizing and managing clients who act out violently, which is not uncommon behavior for people with personality disorders.

❖ REFERENCES

American Psychiatric Association: *Diagnostic and statistical manual of mental disorders,* ed 4, Washington, DC, 1994, The Association.

Borderline personality—part I, *Harvard Ment Health Lett* 10(11):1, 1994.

Can our personality change over time? *Menninger Lett* 3(3):7, 1995.

Clunn P: *Child psychiatric nursing,* St Louis, 1991, Mosby.

Fortinash KM, Holoday-Worret PA: *Psychiatric-mental health nursing,* St Louis, 1996, Mosby.

Gabbard GO: Researchers study causes and treatment of borderline personality disorders, *Menninger Lett* 3(5):1, 1995.

Hare RD: Predators: the disturbing world of the psychopaths among us, *Psychol Today* 27(1):55, 1994.

Hare RD: Psychopaths: new trends in research, *Harvard Ment Health Lett* 12(3):4, 1995.

Hogarth CR: *Adolescent psychiatric nursing,* St Louis, 1991, Mosby.

Hogstel MO: *Geropsychiatric nursing,* ed 2, St Louis, 1994, Mosby.

Livesley WJ and others: Categorical distinctions in the study

of personality disorder: implications for classification, *J Abnorm Psychol* 103(1):6, 1994.

Nehls N, Diamond RJ: Clinical care update: developing a systems approach to caring for persons with borderline personality disorder, *Community Ment Health J* 29(2):161, 1993.

Oldham JM: Personality disorders: current perspectives, *JAMA* 272(22):1770, 1994.

Personality disorders: the anxious cluster—part I, *Harvard Ment Health Lett* 12(8):1, 1996a.

Personality disorders: the anxious cluster—part II, *Harvard Ment Health Lett* 12(9):1, 1996b.

Pipher M: *Reviving Ophelia: saving the selves of adolescent girls,* New York, 1994, Putnam.

Siever LJ: Schizophrenia spectrum personality disorders. In Tasman A, Ruba MB, editors: *American Psychiatric Press review of psychiatry,* vol 2, Washington, DC, 1992, American Psychiatric Press.

Stuart GW, Sundeen SJ: *Principles and practice of psychiatric nursing,* ed 5, St Louis, 1995, Mosby.

Wong DL: *Whaley and Wong's nursing care of infants and children,* ed 5, St Louis, 1995, Mosby.

31

SCHIZOPHRENIA AND OTHER PSYCHOSES

LEARNING OBJECTIVES

1. Explain the differences between a psychosis and other mental health disorders.

2. Describe the continuum of neurobiological responses.

3. Identify the signs/symptoms of psychosis in childhood, adolescence, and adulthood.

4. Discuss three theories relating to the causes of schizophrenia and other psychoses.

5. Name and describe four subtypes of schizophrenia.

6. Describe the signs/symptoms and behaviors exhibited by a person with schizophrenia.

7. Identify the main pharmacological treatments and mental health therapies for persons with schizophrenia.

8. Apply the nursing process to clients suffering from schizophrenia or another psychosis.

9. List three nursing responsibilities related to antipsychotic medications.

KEY TERMS

agnosia
akathisia
akinesia
alexithymia
anhedonia
apathy
bradykinesia
delusions
derealization

dyskinesia
dystonia
extrapyramidal side effects (EPSEs)
hallucinations
illusions
negative symptoms
neuroleptic malignant syndrome (NMS)
oculogyric crisis

perseveration
positive symptoms
poverty of thought
psychosis
schizophrenia
tardive dyskinesia
torticollis

To function effectively in our modern, complex society, individuals must be able "to filter, process, and adapt to countless internal and external stimuli" (Taylor, 1994). Once accomplished, information is tested or validated through interactions with people and the environment. The result is a logical flow of thoughts and actions that allows human beings to function effectively.

Most people who experience mental health problems are able to think and act logically, even when their behaviors are maladaptive. However, for a certain group of people, reality is distorted and disturbed. These individuals suffer from a **psychosis:** the inability to recognize reality, relate to others, or cope with life's demands. The most common psychosis is **schizophrenia,** a group of related disorders characterized by disordered thinking, perceptions, and behaviors.

Although schizophrenia is the most common type of psychosis, other psychotic disorders exist. They include brief psychotic disorder, delusional disorder, and psychoses related to medical conditions or drug use. Brief psychotic disorder and delusional disorders occur less frequently than schizophrenia, but all involve a change in the individual's perception of reality.

Because individuals with psychotic behaviors are often encountered in general medical and nursing settings, the care provider who can recognize and intervene appropriately with these clients is more effective than one who works in ignorance.

Continuum of Neurobiological Responses

Highly adaptable persons are able to integrate all aspects of human functioning into a workable frame-work for coping with the world. In other words, the physical, emotional, intellectual, social, and spiritual realms work in combination, which allows an individual to function effectively.

This ability to function, change, and adapt depends in part on certain physical brain functions, their connections, and their chemical messengers. In psychiatry, these interactions are called neurobiological functions, and they can be viewed as existing along a continuum of behavioral responses ranging from highly adaptive, effective responses to maladaptive, even destructive behaviors (Fig. 31-1).

When everything is functioning in harmony, people are able to successfully adapt to their environments. They use logical thought, have clear perceptions, and are able to socially relate in appropriate ways. This state of functioning represents the adaptive end of the neurobiological continuum.

People who are not as well adapted are placed at the middle of the spectrum. These persons function within reality, but they may have emotional overreactions, distorted thoughts, or odd behaviors. Many will never seek mental health services because their behaviors are not recognized as problems.

Individuals at the maladaptive end of the spectrum are disorganized in their thought, emotions, and social behaviors.

Psychoses Throughout the Life Cycle

As human beings grow and develop they learn to integrate new information to their knowledge stores. Infants begin to unify information at birth, and the process continues throughout life. Because of certain physical, social, or environmental factors, some indi-

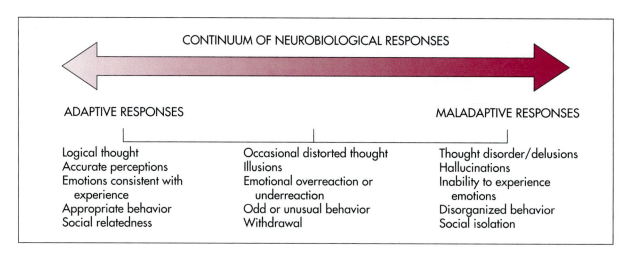

Fig. 31-1   Continuum of neurobiological responses. (Redrawn from Stuart GW, Sundeen SJ: *Principles and practice of psychiatric nursing,* ed 5, St Louis, 1995, Mosby.)

viduals have difficulty in processing, learning from, or relating to new information. Although most cases of psychoses are encountered primarily in late adolescence or adulthood, some do begin in childhood. An awareness of the early signs of possible mental health problems assists both client and care provider in providing early interventions.

Psychoses in Childhood

Children learn about their worlds through observation and experience. During the first 3 months of life, the senses develop and infants become interested in the world around them. By 10 months, children have developed a wide range of complex behaviors and interactions with their caregivers. Around 2 years of age, they begin to integrate emotional and behavioral patterns, and by 4, there is a rich and complex fantasy life.

Also at this time, children are beginning to discover their intellectual side. Basic personalities emerge, and social experiences become important. During the school years, relationships and experiences are combined into the personality as children engage in more complex activities and behaviors.

For some children, however, processing or combining information is a near-impossible task. Infants with *failure to thrive syndromes* have slowed physical growth because of the inability to integrate the physical, emotional, and sensorimotor realms of functioning (Wong, 1995). Most often, this problem is related to off-and-on care or outright neglect from caregivers, environmental problems, or severe family stress. Whatever the cause, children with failure to thrive do not have a consistent opportunity to experience the activities and conditions necessary for normal growth and development.

"Schizophrenia [and other psychotic disorders] can occur in 5- to 8-year-old children" (Clunn, 1991). The actual cause of childhood schizophrenia is unknown but three risk factors have been identified:

1. *Genetic influences.* Studies have found that schizophrenia and other psychoses occur more often in families who have parents, siblings, or other relatives with schizophrenia (McGuffin, Owen, and Farmer, 1995).
2. *Complications during pregnancy or birth.* Exposure to the influenza virus during the second trimester of pregnancy has been linked to some cases of schizophrenia (Bower, 1995).
3. *Winter births.* Persons with schizophrenia "seem to be more likely than others to have been born during the winter or early spring months" (Waddington, 1993).

Signs/symptoms and behaviors of schizophrenic children vary considerably depending on each child's age, developmental stage, quality of previous experiences, and coping mechanisms that each child uses. Basically, there is a core of behaviors that indicates an increasing lack of contact with reality and withdrawal into a world of their own. The results of this change in focus from outward to inward can be seen in the child's behavioral changes relating to *affect* (behavioral display of emotions), impaired interpersonal *relationships,* and language or *communication* disturbances. Because schizophrenia involves every area of functioning, the child has problems with physical motor control, emotional expression and control, perception and understanding, thinking logically, and communicating effectively.

Neuropsychological research is demonstrating that children with child-onset schizophrenia have "an impaired ability to process visual information, regulate attention, and discriminate target stimuli [sort out incoming information]" (McKenna, Gordon, Rapoport, 1994).

Psychoses in Adolescence

The unpredictable, up-and-down behaviors of adolescence are intensified in teens with schizophrenia or other psychotic problems. The difference, however, is that the average teen is in contact with his/her reality, whereas the adolescent with schizophrenia is not. Even before the onset of a full-blown psychosis, family members may notice certain changes in behavior. Poor hygiene and grooming habits are most noticeable. Strange, vague speech and a lack of interest soon lead to social withdrawal. Odd behaviors such as hoarding food or talking to oneself occur. Thoughts and beliefs may be bizarre. Unusual superstitions, the belief that one is able to read other's minds (telepathy), and the idea that one is remotely controlled by others are not uncommon. Self-injury and destructive behaviors often begin in adolescence with these teens. The box on p. 434 describes an adolescent with a psychotic disorder.

Most psychotic adolescents are first treated in the inpatient setting where their behaviors can be assessed, monitored, and controlled. Medical and nursing interventions focus on decreasing acute symptoms and behaviors, improving relationships with significant others through family therapy, and educating client and family about the illness and its management.

Psychoses in Adulthood

The onset of acute symptoms most often occurs in men during the middle 20s, whereas women usually do not present with symptoms until the late 20s. Both

CASE STUDY

Rob was a model child, cooperative, pleasant, and enjoyable—that is, until he turned 17. It all seemed to start when he began a campaign to see every science fiction movie ever made. Soon, he was speaking an "interplanetary space language" that no one but Rob could understand.

About 6 months into his outer space–oriented lifestyle, Rob quit school and began to spend his days "attending intergalactic conferences of great minds." His family became worried when Rob refused to bathe or change his clothes for weeks at a time. Often, they would enter the room to find Rob arguing animatedly with the lamp or listening with interest to the wall. When an outburst of unprovoked anger resulted in injuries to his younger sister, the family sought counseling.

Clinical Decisions

1. What do you think is the family's first priority with Rob?
2. Do you think that Rob needs an inpatient psychiatric setting?

---

want to seek treatment. One study demonstrated that schizophrenic women waited an average 7 months before seeking treatment. Men endured their symptoms for an average 17 months before seeking help (Szmanski and others, 1995). With continued treatment, one third of schizophrenic persons improve; without treatment, one third improve; with or without treatment, one third progress into a chronic downhill course.

The prognosis (long-term outlook) for schizophrenic individuals is improved if adaptive interpersonal relationships, school performance, and work histories were present before the onset of symptoms. The outlook is also better for women. "On the average, men with schizophrenia respond less well to treatment, spend more time in mental hospitals, and have a higher relapse rate than women with the same disorder" (Szmanski and others, 1995).

Families with schizophrenic members face enormous demands. Because the length of institutional stays has sharply decreased, many individuals with schizophrenia return to the home while still psychotic, thus requiring constant observation and support. The demands on family resources can become continual burdens. Social and occupational activities of caretakers are limited by the demands of the illness. The ability to communicate with the schizophrenic family member is limited. Family members, especially parents, struggle with guilt and frustration as they attempt to explain "why" the family member is schizophrenic. Parents suffer the grief of losing a normal child and then must cope with the stigma of having a child who is "mentally ill." Brothers and sisters of schizophrenic people are strongly affected by their sibling's behaviors. On top of all of this are the repeated role changes that occur with each hospitalization and each return home. Most families are ill-equipped to provide psychiatric care.

Psychoses in Older Adulthood

Schizophrenia is seldom diagnosed in the elderly. Most often, older adults with schizophrenia "have had longstanding problems and have been taking antipsychotic medications for years" (Hogstel, 1995). Many suffer from the irreversible side effects of long-term antipsychotic drug use and other chronic medical problems.

Often, the hallucinations and delusions of younger years decrease or disappear. Many older schizophrenics become more withdrawn or paranoid. They may become one of the faceless numbers of homeless. The fortunate elderly with schizophrenia spend the remainder of their days in long-term care facilities.

An important reminder: the acute onset of psychotic behavior in elderly clients *must be investigated.* Older clients who lose contact with reality, experience impaired interpersonal relationships, suddenly have difficulty communicating, or experience great emotional changes are usually not psychotic. Most often, they are suffering from some physical or biochemical change. Changes in electrolyte balances, reactions to medications, drug interactions, and nutritional deficiencies can cause signs/symptoms and behaviors that appear psychotic. In short, the causes of most acute-onset psychoses in older adults are physical problems.

Theories Relating to Psychoses

"Schizophrenia is a condition that exists in all cultures and socioeconomic groups" (Fortinash and Holoday-Worret, 1996). The first theory of psychosis was the notion that individuals who were not in contact with reality were possessed by demons, spirits, or devils. Evidence of this belief has been found in early Chinese, Egyptian, Greek, and Hebrew writings. The box on p. 435 offers an interesting cultural insight.

CULTURAL ASPECTS

In India, a man with schizophrenia is often considered a "wise man" because of his ability to speak with spirits. He is usually honored and sought out for his advice.

In Haiti, psychotic persons are believed to be victims of the "evil eye," called *maldyok,* or to be possessed by supernatural beings.

The "possession theory" existed until the nineteenth century when the work of two psychiatrists began to define the characteristics of schizophrenic behaviors. Emile Kraeplin (1856-1926) described the syndrome of hallucinations and delusions seen in schizophrenics.

The word *schizophrenia* (meaning "to split the mind") was coined in 1911 by a Swiss psychiatrist named Hans Bleuler (1857-1939) to describe the disconnection between the intellectual and emotional aspects of a personality. Today, confusion about the term exists because the general public uses the word to describe someone with multiple personalities.

Once, other psychoses were thought to be the result of faulty parent-child interactions or failure of the ego to combine the drives of the id with reality. Today, scientific evidence points to possible biological (physical) causes for psychotic behaviors. Other theories that attempt to explain schizophrenia relate to psychosocial and sociocultural factors. A brief explanation of each theory group helps nurses to understand clients suffering from psychotic disorders.

Biological Theories

In 1990, the U.S. Congress named the 1990s the "Decade of the Brain." Since then, there has been renewed interest in viewing schizophrenia as a brain disorder. As time passes, the evidence for this point of view is building. For example, the fingerprints of individuals with schizophrenia are different from those of persons without the disorder (Waddington, 1993).

Studies of fetal development have demonstrated a series of cell connections in the brain's prefrontal cortex (which coordinate thinking and motivation) has trouble communicating with other areas of the brain in schizophrenics (Bower, 1996). Research with identical twins found that schizophrenic twins "become permanently different from their co-twins by the age of five" (Torrey and others, 1994). Such data have led to the development of the genetic/heredity model as an explanation of schizophrenia.

The stress/disease/trauma model looks at the effects of stress on the individual, especially during the prenatal period. Immune reactions to viral infections during pregnancy and severe malnutrition during pregnancy have been shown to contribute to the development of schizophrenia in the children, especially the females, of these mothers (Bower, 1996). Complications occurring during birth, such as prolonged labor, difficult birth, or umbilical cord prolapse, have been related to the development of schizophrenia. Cocaine and other drug use during pregnancy has been linked to schizotypal behaviors in the children of users (Scherling, 1994).

Because of the many refinements in brain-imaging technology, scientists have been able to pinpoint certain parts of the brain that are different in schizophrenic people. Scans of the brains of schizophrenics obtained while they are hallucinating have demonstrated that certain structures deep within the brain inappropriately switched on and off. This finding points to the possibility that "at least some of the roots of schizophrenia may lie in a wiring problem deep inside the brain" (Begley, 1995).

Other studies have found that certain chemical messengers (neurotransmitters) are altered in persons with schizophrenia (*Harvard Mental Health Letter,* 1995b). The neurotransmitters serotonin, norepinephrine, and dopamine have been implicated as possible causes of schizophrenia. Theories developed from this type of research are called neuroanatomic or neurochemical models.

Other Theories

Until recently, schizophrenia was thought to result from certain environmental or social factors. Psychological models view schizophrenia as being caused by a basic character flaw combined with poor family relationships. Overprotective, anxious mothers; cold, uncaring fathers; and couples who "stayed together for the sake of the children" were blamed. The child's failure to accomplish a developmental task, such as trust or intimacy, was also thought to be related to schizophrenia.

Sociocultural theories consider the effects of environment on the development of psychoses. Poverty, homelessness, unstable families, and cultural differences have been suggested as factors relating to schizophrenia. Some researchers believe that individuals become psychotic as a way of coping with problems of the modern world. Although environmental and social factors may influence the development of psychoses, evidence for a neurobiological cause of schizophrenia and other psychoses is becoming more and more convincing.

Psychotic Disorders

Schizophrenia

Schizophrenia affects about 1% of the world's population (Andreasen, 1995). Schizophrenia is found equally in men and women. Although it occurs in every socioeconomic class, it is found more commonly in lower socioeconomic levels. Because of the intense discomfort associated with the disorder, 10% of all schizophrenic individuals commit suicide (Andreasen, 1995).

The costs of treating schizophrenia are enormous. In 1980 in the United States, the cost of schizophrenia in terms of lost productivity was estimated at $20 billion, whereas the cost of continued medical care and social maintenance for persons with schizophrenia was an additional $11.1 billion (Wyatt and Clark, 1987). In this day of scarce mental health resources, the costs of treating schizophrenia are even greater. Today, "more than a million people with the disorder account for 75% of all mental health expenditures (*Harvard Mental Health Letter,* 1995a). The costs in terms of distress and suffering of the affected individuals and their families cannot even be estimated.

As stated earlier, schizophrenia is a group of related mental health disorders characterized by disordered thinking, perceptions, and behaviors. It is not a well-defined disease but a group of symptoms and behaviors.

Schizophrenia has an impact on every area of functioning. Physically, schizophrenic persons neglect themselves. Emotionally, they are unable to express themselves. Intellectual functions are impaired because thought processes drift. Social interactions suffer because of an inability to relate to other people appropriately, and spiritual struggles form the core for many of the schizophrenic's delusions. Family members, relatives, and friends also suffer as they work to understand and cope with the effects of this psychosis.

Signs/symptoms and behaviors. The main characteristic of psychotic disorders is loss of contact with reality to the point where it grossly impairs functioning.

Although, each individual with schizophrenia behaves uniquely, many appear to share certain basic symptoms (Table 31-1).

The physical appearance of individuals with schizophrenia is one of an unkempt, disheveled person. Focus on inner matters prevents them from routinely seeking out food or shelter. Often, personal hygiene is poor, and body images are distorted. Motor activity ranges from agitated to immobile.

The signs/symptoms of schizophrenia also affect perception, the way that one views the world. Individuals with schizophrenia suffer from **hallucina-** tions, false sensory input with no external stimulus; **illusions,** false perceptions of real stimuli; and **agnosia,** an inability to recognize familiar environmental objects or people (stimuli). Hallucinations may take the form of smells, sounds, tastes, sight, touch, or feelings of altered internal workings of the body.

In the cognitive (intellectual) area of functioning, schizophrenics suffer from a number of difficulties. They usually have problems with attention, memory, and use of language. Thinking may involve **delusions,** fixed false ideas that are not based in reality; ideas of reference, the idea that people or the media are talking about one; and **derealization,** a loss of ego boundaries, an inability to tell where one's body ends and the environment begins.

Language difficulties involve several incorrect usages. The speech of persons with schizophrenia include a number of unusual characteristics: clang associations, concrete thinking, echolalia, flight of ideas, loose associations, ideas of reference, mutism, neologisms, and word salad. Table 31-2 explains each term and offers an example of each communication difficulty.

Thought processes in schizophrenics vary widely, from contact with reality to fantasy thinking. Negative experiences are remembered more than positive ones. Individuals may demonstrate **perseveration,** the repeating of the same idea in response to different questions, or **poverty of thought,** a lack of ability to produce new thoughts or follow a train of thought. People with chronic schizophrenia have little insight into their problems. Often, their judgment is impaired. Usually there is a general decline in intellectual abilities as the disorder progresses.

In the emotional realm, persons with schizophrenia experience a range of inappropriate emotions. Affect, the outward expressions of one's emotions, is described as blunted, flat, inappropriate, or labile. Other emotional responses include **alexithymia,** a difficulty in identifying and describing emotions; **apathy,** a lack of concern, interest, or feelings; and **anhedonia,** the inability (or decreased ability) to experience pleasure in life.

Behaviorally, schizophrenics display little impulse-control and an inability to manage anger. They may injure themselves and others or act in response to hallucinations commanding them to do something. A lack of energy or motivation (*avolition*) often leads to poor performance at work or school, unemployment, and homelessness. The inability to cope with depression and lack of social supports lead to a high risk for suicide. Many refuse to comply with treatment by not taking their medications or by abusing alcohol and street drugs. These dual-diagnosis individuals present many challenging health care situations. Refer to

◆ TABLE 31-1
Clinical Symptoms of Schizophrenia

Perceptual	Intellectual	Emotional	Behavioral	Social
Hallucinations: 1. Auditory: may be commanding; content matches delusions 2. Visual 3. Tactile: for example, may feel like being surrounded by spider webs 4. Olfactory and gustatory: client may refuse to eat because food seems to smell or taste bad **Illusions:** false perceptions due to misinterpretations of real objects **Altered internal sensations:** 1. Formication: sensation of worms crawling around inside one 2. Chill: feeling of chills in the marrow on one's bones **Agnosia:** perceptual failure to recognize familiar environmental stimuli such as sounds or objects seen or felt; sometimes called "negative hallucinations" **Distortion of body image:** with respect to size, facial expression, activity, amount and nature of detail, exaggeration or diminution of body parts **Negative self-perception:** with respect to ability and competence	**Delusions:** unusual ideas, not reality based: 1. Omnipotence 2. Persecution 3. Controlling or being controlled **Derealization:** loss of ego boundaries; cannot tell where own body ends and environment begins; feeling that the world around one is not real or distorted **Ideas of reference:** notion that other people or the media are talking to or about one **Errors in recall of memory:** due to incorrect categorization **Difficulty sustaining attention:** 1. Unable to complete tasks 2. Errors of omission **Incorrect use of language:** 1. Neologisms (invented words) 2. Incoherence 3. Echolalia, word salad 4. Concrete, restricted vocabulary 5. Comprehension difficulties 6. Looseness of associations **Flight of ideas:** abrupt change of topic in a rapid flow of speech	**Labile affect: range of emotions:** 1. Apathy, dulled response 2. Flattened affect 3. Reduced responsiveness 4. Exaggerated euphoria 5. Rage **Inappropriate affect:** laughing at sad events, crying over joyous ones **Disruption in limbic functioning:** inability to screen out disruptive stimuli and loss of voluntary control of response	**Little impulse-control:** 1. Sudden scream as a protest of frustration 2. Self-mutilation, to substitute physical for emotional pain 3. Injury to a body part believed to be offensive 4. Response to command hallucinations **Inability to cope with depression:** 1. Depressed client has a 50% risk for suicide 2. Frequent exacerbations and remissions in one who has insight 3. Lack of social support to help **Inability to manage anger:** anger and lack of impulse control lead to violence: verbal aggression, destruction of property, injury to others, homicide **Substance abuse as coping:** dulls painful psychological symptoms **Noncompliance with medication:** may feel it is not needed or has too many side effects	**Poor peer relationships:** 1. Few friends, as a child or adolescent 2. Preference for solitude **Low interest in hobbies and activities:** 1. Daydreamer 2. Not functioning well in social or occupational areas 3. Preoccupied and detached 4. Behavioral autism **Loss of interest in appearance:** 1. Careless grooming 2. Introversion **Not competitive in sports or academics:** 1. Poor adjustment to school 2. Withdrawal from activities **May suffer from:** 1. Attention deficit disorder 2. Somatic symptoms

From Fortinash KM, Holoday-Worret PA: *Psychiatric-mental health nursing,* St Louis, 1996, Mosby.

◆ **TABLE 31-2**
Speech Disturbances in Schizophrenia

Speech Problem	Description
Clang associations	Repeating words or phrases that sound alike or substituting a word that sounds like the appropriate word *Example:* "Honey, money, sunny" or "I need some honey to buy the paper"
Concrete thinking	Inability to consider the abstract meaning of a phrase; frequently tested by having clients interpret proverbs *Example:* "A stitch in time saves nine" may mean "sew the holes in your clothes" to a schizophrenic
Echolalia	Repeating words of another after one has stopped talking *Example:* Nurse: "How is your day going?" Client: "Day going, day going, day going."
Flight of ideas	Rapid change in topics with a rapid flow of speech *Example:* "The sky is blue. The dog is dead, and I have two eyes."
Ideas of reference	The belief that some events have special personal meaning *Example:* "The United States is sending satellites into space so that they can spy on me."
Loose associations	Thinking characterized by speech that moves from one unrelated idea to another *Example:* "I'm hungry, but the desert has no rain so it's cold outside."
Mutism	Refusal to speak
Neologisms	Words or expressions invented by the individual *Example:* "The ispy is not happy when the fulgari is green."
Word salad	A random, jumbled set of words that have no connection or relationship to each other *Example:* "Hot happies are spying on me but no men love short feet."

Table 31-1 and review the description of behavioral symptoms in schizophrenia.

Socially, schizophrenics are unable to establish or maintain relationships with others. Social behaviors are often inappropriate. Self-esteem is low, and gender identity confusion may exist. They have few friends and little interest in hobbies or other activities. Many prefer to be alone because of hallucinations or feelings of paranoia. The few family and social relationships that do exist usually follow a rocky course.

The characteristic symptoms of schizophrenia can also be described as falling into two broad categories: positive and negative symptoms. **Positive symptoms** are related to maladaptive thoughts and behaviors. They include hallucinations, speech problems, and bizarre behaviors. **Negative symptoms** are related to the lack of adaptive mechanisms. They include flat affect, poor grooming, withdrawal, and poverty of speech. Physicians and mental health therapists commonly refer to the symptoms of schizophrenia using the terms *positive and negative symptoms.*

Most of the terms used to describe these behaviors are not a part of everyday vocabulary. For this reason, it is important to focus more on accurately describing clients' behaviors, communications, and interactions than finding the best label. If you are not sure of the meaning of the term, *do not use it.* One good behavioral description is worth many psychiatric terms.

Subtypes of schizophrenia. Because schizophrenia is a cluster of related behaviors, it can be classified into different groups or subclasses based on the clinical picture at the time of evaluation. Although many persons have symptoms of more than one cluster, diagnosis is made based on the most prominent symptoms or behaviors. The five subtypes of schizophrenia are catatonic, disorganized, paranoid, undifferentiated, and residual. Table 31-3 explains each schizophrenic subtype and its characteristics.

Phases of becoming disorganized. The course of schizophrenia is marked by episodes of acute psychosis alternating with periods of relatively normal functioning. The symptoms of schizophrenia must occur for at least 1 year before a diagnostic label is assigned.

The slide into schizophrenia commonly occurs through four stages. The *prodromal phase* begins with withdrawal and a lack of energy or motivation. Individuals may appear confused and in a world of their own. They may complain about multiple physical problems or show a new, excessive interest in religion or philosophy. Affect becomes blunted. Ideas and beliefs become odd or unusual. Self-care and personal hygiene are ignored. Some individuals become agitated or angry. Speech may be difficult to follow because the individual is too vague, elaborate, or circumstantial. These symptoms can occur during both

◆ **TABLE 31-3**
Subtypes of Schizophrenia

Subtype	Description
Catatonic	Characterized by marked psychomotor problems: immobility or excessive activity with no purpose; odd movements, rigid posture, stereotyped movements, echopraxia (mimics movements of others); may be extremely negative or mute, echolalia; automatic obedience; may suffer from malnutrition, dehydration, exhaustion; prognosis is fair.
Disorganized	Thinking, speech, and behavior are disordered; affect is flat or inappropriate; primitive, uninhibited behaviors, unusual mannerisms, distorted facial expressions, giggles or cries out unrelated to speech; loosely organized hallucinations, delusions; withdrawn, socially inept; unable to perform activities of daily living; onset is early, prognosis is poor.
Paranoid	Organized delusions of grandeur or persecution, auditory hallucinations; high anxiety levels, guarded, suspicious, aloof, hostile, angry, can be violent or suicidal; onset is late, prognosis is good with treatment.
Undifferentiated	Does not meet criteria for other subtypes; disorganized speech, behavior; hallucinations, delusions, negative symptoms; prognosis is fair.
Residual	Has had at least one acute episode of schizophrenia, is free of psychotic signs/symptoms but still has negative symptoms of withdrawal, emotional changes, disorganized thinking, and odd behaviors; schizophrenia present for many years; time is limited between acute episodes; prognosis is poor.

the prodromal and the residual stages of the disorder (see box at right).

In the *prepsychotic phase,* individuals are usually quiet, passive, and obedient and prefer to be alone. They have few if any friends because of odd, suspicious, or eccentric behaviors. Hallucinations and delusions may be present, but behaviors are not completely disorganized. Family members may report that they can sense the individual "slipping away" in front of their eyes.

Signs/symptoms and behaviors during the *acute phase* vary widely but include disturbances in thought, perception, behavior, and emotion. Frequently, individuals lose contact with reality and become unable to function even in the most basic ways. Refer to Table 31-1 for a list of clinical symptoms that are seen during the acute phase of schizophrenia.

The *residual phase* follows an acute episode. It is marked by a lack of energy, no interest in goal-directed activities, and a negative outlook. Many of the behaviors seen in the prodromal phase are also present during the residual phase.

Following the residual phase is a period of relative *remission.* The ability to manage some basic activities of daily living returns, and the individual experiences some relief from the distresses of psychosis. This is the course of schizophrenia: many acute episodes alternating with periods of decreased symptoms. The outlook for recovery is fair to poor because of the many complex aspects of this disorder.

THINK ABOUT

The prodromal signs/symptoms of schizophrenia often begin in adolescence. As the individual's behavior becomes more bizarre, people grow afraid of the person.

What are your feelings and reactions about people who are unable to share reality?

Do you think it is prudent to be afraid of someone whose behaviors are out of contact with reality?

Other Psychoses

Besides schizophrenia and its related conditions, the *Diagnostic and Statistical Manual of Mental Disorders* (DSM-IV) lists five other psychoses. A *brief psychotic disorder* is a psychotic disturbance that lasts for more than a day but less than a month. A *delusional disorder* is characterized by more than a month of nonbizarre (reality-based) fixed ideas, and a *shared psychotic disorder* is defined as "a disturbance that develops in an individual who is influenced by someone else who has an established delusion with similar content" (American Psychiatric Association, 1994). Psychotic behaviors are also related to the abuse of street drugs and several medical conditions. If the source of the psychosis is reversible, clients usually recover rapidly.

The alert nurse is always observant for changes in behavior or affect in clients. Early detection of behavioral changes, even with general medical-surgical clients, frequently prevents later complications from occurring.

Therapeutic Interventions

Because of their impaired judgment and other problems, many individuals with schizophrenia do not receive treatment. Those who do cooperate with treatment are most often cared for by an interdisciplinary mental health team consisting of psychiatrists, nurses, psychologists, and psychiatric social workers. Individuals are admitted to an inpatient unit during episodes of acute psychoses, when they are a danger to themselves or others, or for stabilization of disorganized or inappropriate behaviors.

The goals of inpatient, short-term care are to stabilize the client, prevent further decline in functioning, and assist the client in coping with his/her disorder. Long-term goals include psychosocial and vocational rehabilitation. When available, family members are included in the care and education of the client.

Treatments and Therapies

Clients with acute psychoses are treated with a combination of therapies and medications. The multidisciplinary treatment team may recommend "personal therapy, social skills training, vocational rehabilitation, and behavioral therapy. In addition, stress reduction, family education, and early intervention are important in the treatment of schizophrenia" (Kane and McGlashan, 1995). Although, psychotherapies may focus on different areas of treatment, each relies on the therapeutic interactions of care providers.

Pharmacological Therapy

Medications used to treat psychoses are called antipsychotic or neuroleptic drugs. High-potency antipsychotics include fluphenazine (Prolixin), haloperidol (Haldol), thiothixene (Navane), and trifluoperazine (Stelazine). The moderate-potency antipsychotics are loxapine (Loxitane), molindone (Moban), and perphenazine (Trilafon). Last are the low-potency antipsychotics: chlorpromazine (Thorazine), mesoridazine (Serentil), and thioridazine (Mellaril).

The desired effects of antipsychotic drugs are to slow the central nervous system (CNS). These effects include an emotional quieting, slowed motor responses, and sedation. Antipsychotics exert their influence on the body by interrupting the dopamine (neurotransmitter) pathways in the brain, thus producing a calming effect throughout the entire nervous system. After an antipsychotic drug is taken, hallucinations and delusions are decreased, thought processes are changed, and hyperactivity subsides. Mental clouding clears and previously withdrawn people begin to socialize.

Antipsychotic drugs interact with many other chemicals. They also have additive effects, that is, the combination of different drugs produces an enhanced effect, thus increasing CNS depression. The side effects and adverse reactions of this group of medications are numerous and troublesome for the client. In fact, as many as half the clients who are prescribed psychotherapeutics do not actually take them or do not take them according to directions because of the side effects. Individuals who abuse alcohol and drugs are more likely to neglect taking their antipsychotic medications (*Harvard Mental Health Letter*, 1995b).

Nursing Process

Caring for clients with psychoses is a team effort. Nurses begin with a thorough physical and mental assessment. Nursing histories include a description of the client's most distressing problems and a complete review of systems if the client is able to communicate appropriately. Interpersonal relationships and support systems are explored.

The mental status examination is performed (see Chapter 13). Safety risks for violence and suicide are assessed, and a past medication history is obtained. After the data are obtained and organized, nursing diagnoses are established for each client problem. Primary nursing diagnoses include altered thought processes, social isolation, impaired communications, and ineffective management of therapeutic regimen. The box below offers several important general prin-

---

PRINCIPLES FOR INTERVENTIONS WITH CLIENTS WITH PSYCHOTIC DISORDERS

- Maintain health and safety.
- Establish a trusting interpersonal relationship.
- Confirm the client's identity.
- Orient the client to reality.
- Assist the client in communication to help the client understand self and others and to be understood.
- Decrease demanding situations and psychosocial stressors.
- Help the client manage anxiety.
- Promote compliance with prescribed therapeutic regimen.
- Assist with activities of daily living.
- Promote social interaction.
- Regulate activity levels (hypoactivity/hyperactivity).
- Encourage/praise socially acceptable behaviors.
- Encourage family involvement and understanding.
- Encourage responsibility for self.
- Teach the client how to identify psychosocial stressors and how to recognize, manage, and prevent symptoms.
- Educate client and family about potential side effects and toxic effects of antipsychotic medications.

Modified from Fortinash KM, Holoday-Worret PA: *Psychiatric nursing care plans*, ed 2, St Louis, 1995, Mosby.

ciples to follow for working with schizophrenic and other psychotic clients.

The basic goals of nursing care are to assist clients in controlling their symptoms and achieving the highest possible level of functioning. For this to happen, clients and their families must be actively involved in the treatment. The expected outcome is for the client to "live, learn, and work at the maximum possible level of success as defined by the individual" (Stuart and Sundeen, 1995). Short-term goals relate to keeping the client safe, restoring adequate nutritional and rest habits, establishing and maintaining contact with reality, and fostering open communications. A sample client care plan for schizophrenia is described in the box below.

 SAMPLE CLIENT CARE PLAN

SCHIZOPHRENIA

Assessment

History: Terry, a 22-year-old man, was found wandering naked in the streets talking to himself. He seems preoccupied and appears to be listening to voices. Further history is unobtainable since Terry is unable to communicate understandably at this time.

Current Findings: A wild-eyed, unkempt young man who seems preoccupied. Clothes are ragged and dirty. Speech unintelligible, carries on animated conversations with self. Since admission, 24 hours ago, Terry has refused to eat, drink, or bathe because "someone is trying to poison" him. He is polite but responds only when addressed. No family or friends can be located.

Nursing Diagnosis

Sensory/perceptual alteration related to social isolation and lack of adequate support systems

Planning/Expected Outcomes

Terry will communicate in a logical manner by September 20. Terry will carry out his activities of daily living independently by September 25.

Nursing Interventions

Intervention

1. Establish therapeutic relationship; be available; listen actively; do not pass judgment.
2. Establish and reinforce a daily routine.

3. Use clear, direct statements when talking; make sure body language is in keeping with the message being sent.
4. Intervene with active hallucinations; move Terry to quiet area, focus on reality, assure client that he will be safe, identify needs filled by the hallucination.
5. Accept and support Terry's feelings and appropriate expressions of emotion.
6. Encourage Terry to take his medications routinely.
7. Carefully monitor Terry's response to his medications.

Rationale

1. Trust must be established if therapy is to be effective.
2. Increases security by knowing what to expect; helps refocus on activities of daily living.
3. Unclear or confusing communications can increase Terry's distorted perceptions.

4. Decreases sensory input; helps divert attention to reality; provides reassurance; helps decrease anxiety.

5. Communicates empathy and understanding; decreases anxiety.
6. Medications help to control psychotic symptoms.
7. Early recognition prevents serious side effects and complications.

Evaluation

On September 13, Terry stated he was in control of his hallucinations. By September 19, Terry was independently eating, drinking, and performing his own activities of daily living but had to be reminded to bathe.

Several special nursing assessments, interventions, and evaluations are required for clients who are receiving powerful antipsychotic medications. Some of the side effects of these drugs are harmless but uncomfortable. Other side effects are life-threatening. The most common undesired side effects of antipsychotic medications are alterations in the CNS and peripheral nervous system functions. CNS alterations include **extrapyramidal side effects (EPSEs),** which can affect up to 75% of all clients who are prescribed psychotherapeutics (Blair, 1990).

EPSEs are best described as "abnormal involuntary movement disorders [that] develop because of a drug-induced imbalance between two major neurotransmitters, dopamine and acetylcholine, in portions of the brain" (Keltner and Folks, 1993). The low-potency antipsychotics, such as chlorpromazine (Thorazine), are more likely to cause anticholinergic side effects than the high-potency drugs, such as haloperidol (Haldol), which tend to be related to the CNS side effects known as EPSEs.

EPSEs include akathisia, akinesia, dyskinesia, dystonia, and drug-induced parkinsonism. The most serious side effects are neuroleptic malignant syndrome and tardive dyskinesia. All these symptoms arise from dopamine depletion in the brain and the subsequent blocking of nerve transmissions.

Akathisia is an inability to sit still. Clients experiencing akathisia report that they feel nervous and jittery or have lots of nervous energy. Assaultive behaviors can result if they are forced to remain in one position for even a short period of time. Akathisic side effects account for many cases of noncompliance. The best treatment for akathisia is to reduce the dose of antipsychotic medication. Nurses must be careful not to assess the signs/symptoms of akathisia as a worsening of the client's psychosis. If a p.r.n. antipsychotic drug is administered at this time, it will cause an increase in the client's symptoms.

Akinesia means the absence of movement, both physically and mentally. Actually, clients who are experiencing this unwanted effect demonstrate **bradykinesia** (slowing of body movements and a diminished mental state). Clients lack spontaneity and do not try to move or speak. They may assume bizarre postures and maintain them for long periods. Here is another case for careful assessment because many of the behaviors associated with EPSEs are very similar to the behaviors for which the clients sought treatment. Astute nurses who routinely observe their clients' behaviors stand a better chance of distinguishing between drug-induced or psychosis-induced behaviors.

Dyskinesia is the inability to execute voluntary movements. It is characterized by involuntary abnormal skeletal muscle movements. They are usually seen as jerking motions and sometimes seriously interfere with the client's ability to walk or perform other voluntary movements.

Dystonia is impaired muscle tone. Dystonic reactions produce rigidity in the muscles that control gait, posture, and eye movements. When dystonia involves the muscles that control eye movements, the eyes involuntarily roll to the back of the head. This is a frightening experience for any person, and it is referred to as **oculogyric crisis.**

Another unsettling dystonic reaction is **torticollis** in which contracted cervical muscles force the neck into a twisted position. But the most serious and potentially life-threatening side effect is laryngeal-pharyngeal dystonia. When the muscles of the throat become rigid, the client begins to gag, choke, and become cyanotic. Respiratory distress and asphyxia result if immediate intervention does not occur. Anticholinergic drugs are used to treat all of these reactions.

Drug-induced parkinsonism is a term used to describe a group of symptoms that mimics Parkinson's disease. Tremors, muscle rigidity, and difficulty with voluntary movements are seen in clients with Parkinson's disease and some individuals undergoing antipsychotic drug therapy. Other unwanted CNS effects of neuroleptic drugs include seizures, which can occur at any time during therapy. The drug clozapine (Clozaril) appears to be associated with a higher incidence of seizures, so clients taking this medication must be carefully monitored for signs of seizure activity.

Undesired effects of antipsychotic drugs also influence the peripheral nervous system. The anticholinergic effects of dry mouth, blurred vision, and photophobia (sensitivity to bright light) are common, especially during the first few days of therapy. Tachycardia is a more serious side effect and can cause sudden death.

Hypotension is another potentially serious anticholinergic side effect. Nurses must protect clients from falls during the first few weeks of therapy because the hypotensive response is greatest when clients stand or change positions suddenly. These hypotensive episodes cause tachycardia as the body attempts to adapt to a lower blood pressure. Antipsychotic drugs are contraindicated in clients who have a history of low blood pressure, cardiac dysrhythmias, or heart failure. Table 31-4 lists the major side effects of antipsychotic medications.

Nurses have three major responsibilities when caring for clients who are receiving antipsychotic drug therapy. The first relates to drug administration.

◆ TABLE 31-4
Side Effects of Antipsychotic Drugs and Nursing Care

Side Effects	Interventions
Peripheral nervous system effects	
Constipation	Encourage high dietary fiber and increased water intake; give laxatives as ordered.
Dry mouth	Advise client to take sips of water frequently; provide sugarless hard candies, sugarless gum, and mouth rinses.
Nasal congestion	Give over-the-counter nasal decongestant if approved by physician.
Blurred vision	Advise client to avoid potentially dangerous tasks. Reassure client that normal vision typically returns in a few weeks when tolerance to this side effect develops. Pilocarpine eyedrops can be used on a short-term basis.
Mydriasis	Advise client to report eye pain immediately.
Photophobia	Advise client to wear sunglasses outdoors.
Hypotension or orthostatic hypotension	Ask client to get out of bed or chair slowly. Client should sit on the side of the bed for 1 full minute while dangling feet, then slowly rise. If hypotension is a problem, measure blood pressure before each dose is given. Observe to see whether a change to another antipsychotic agent is indicated.
Tachycardia	Tachycardia is usually a reflex response to hypotension. When intervention for hypotension (previously described) is effective, reflex tachycardia usually decreases. With clozapine, hold the dose if pulse rate is greater than 140 pulsations per minute.
Urinary retention	Encourage frequent voiding and voiding whenever the urge is present. Catheterize for residual fluids. Ask client to monitor urine output and report output to nurse. Older men with benign prostatic hypertrophy are particularly susceptible to urinary retention.
Urinary hesitation	Provide privacy, run water in the sink, or run warm water over the perineum.
Sedation	Help patient get up early and get the day started.
Weight gain	Help patient order an appropriate diet; diet pills should not be taken.
Agranulocytosis	A high incidence of agranulocytosis (1% to 2%) is associated with clozapine. White blood cell count (WBC) should be performed weekly.
Central nervous system effects	
Akathisia	Be patient and reassure client who is "jittery" that you understand the need to move and that appropriate drug interventions can help differentiate akathisia and agitation. Since akathisia is the chief cause of noncompliance with antipsychotic regimens, switching to a different class of antipsychotic drug may be necessary to achieve compliance.
Dystonias	If a severe reaction such as oculogyric crisis or torticollis occurs, give antiparkinson drug (e.g., benztropine mesylate [Cogentin]) or antihistamine (e.g., diphenhydramine [Benadryl]) immediately, as needed, and offer reassurance. More than likely an order for intramuscular administration will not have been written, so call the physician at once to obtain the order. For less severe dystonias, notify the physician when an order for an antiparkinson drug is warranted.
Drug-induced parkinsonism	Assess for the three major parkinsonism symptoms—tremors, rigidity, and bradykinesia—and report to physician. Antiparkinson drugs will probably be indicated.

Modified from Jaretz N, Flowers E, Millsap L: *Perspect Psychiatr Care* 28:19, 1992.
EEG, Electroencephalogram.

Continued

◆ **TABLE 31-4**
Side Effects of Antipsychotic Drugs and Nursing Care—cont'd

Side Effects	Interventions
Central nervous system effects—cont'd	
Tardive dyskinesia	Assess for signs by using the abnormal inventory movement scale. Drug holidays may help prevent tardive dyskinesia. Since antipsychotic drugs may mask tardive dyskinesia, their use should be reviewed. Anticholinergic agents will worsen tardive dyskinesia, so question their indiscriminate prophylactic use. However, young men taking large doses of high-potency antipsychotic drugs (e.g., haloperidol) are one group in which prophylactic use of antiparkinson drugs may be more prudent than not using them.*
Neuroleptic malignant syndrome	Be alert for this potentially fatal side effect. Routinely take temperatures and encourage adequate water intake among all clients on a regimen of antipsychotic drugs, and routinely assess for rigidity, tremor, and similar symptoms.
Seizures	Seizures occur in approximately 1% of clients receiving antipsychotic drug treatment. Clozapine causes an even higher rate, up to 5% of patients taking 600 to 900 mg/day. If a seizure occurs, it may be necessary to discontinue clozapine.

*American Psychiatric Association Task Force on Tardive Dyskinesia: *Am J Psychiatry* 137:1163, 1980.

CLIENT AND FAMILY EDUCATION: ANTIPSYCHOTIC DRUGS

- Review the anticipated benefits and possible side effects of drug therapy with the patient and family. Review extrapyramidal side effects with the client and family. Since there is no effective treatment for tardive dyskinesia, its appearance should be reported immediately. Fine vermicular (wormlike) movements of the tongue may be the first sign of this side effect. Tell the client and family to report any new signs or symptoms.
- Tell clients that several weeks of therapy may be necessary before full benefit can be seen.
- Instruct clients to swallow extended-release forms whole; do not crush or chew.
- Warn clients to avoid driving or operating hazardous equipment if vision changes or sedation occurs; notify the physician.
- Instruct client to report signs of agranulocytosis including sore throat, fever, and malaise. Tell clients to report signs of liver dysfunction including jaundice, malaise, fever, and right upper quadrant abdominal pain.
- These drugs may interfere with the body's ability to regulate temperature. Warn clients to avoid prolonged exposure to extremes of temperature, allow for frequent cooling off periods when exercising or in hot environments, and dress warmly for exposure to the cold.
- Review possible endocrine side effects with client and family. Assess carefully and tactfully for these side effects. Provide emotional support as appropriate. If side effects are intolerable, consult the physician for possible drug or dosage change.
- Instruct clients to monitor weight (if appropriate to ability and resources). If weight gain is a problem, counsel about low-calorie diets. Refer to a dietitian as needed.
- Caution clients to inform all health-care providers of all drugs being taken. Warn clients to avoid over-the-counter drugs unless first approved by the physician.
- Caution clients to avoid alcoholic beverages while taking antipsychotics.
- Warn diabetic clients that antipsychotics may alter blood glucose levels. Monitor blood glucose levels carefully. Consult the physician about changes in dietary or drug treatment for diabetes.
- Tell clients not to discontinue therapy abruptly or without consultation with the physician. Instruct clients to keep these and all drugs out of the reach of children.
- The drugs may produce false-positive pregnancy results. Women who suspect they are pregnant should consult the physician. Women may desire to use contraceptive measures while taking these drugs; counsel as appropriate. As always, pregnant or lactating women should avoid all drugs unless first approved by the physician.
- If additional drugs are prescribed to treat side effects of antipsychotic agents, review their use and side effects with the client and family.

Modified from Clark JF, Queener SF, Karb VB: *Pharmacological basis of nursing practice*, ed 4, St Louis, 1993, Mosby.

Nurses should review the desired actions, side effects, and incompatibilities for each medication prescribed. If the drugs are administered intramuscularly, choose a large muscle mass, warn the client of a burning sensation on injection, and rotate injection sites. If liquid preparations are ordered, be sure to follow the instructions for dilution. Some neuroleptic drugs cannot be mixed with water, so read the manufacturer's instructions before diluting any liquid medication. Read all labels carefully. Some parenteral drugs are water based, and others are oil based. Oil-based medications are *never given intravenously.* They are intended for intramuscular use only.

The second major nursing responsibility relates to monitoring client responses to each medication. During the first week or two of therapy, assess the client's vital signs every 4 hours, record fluid intake and output, and routinely assess skin condition. Assess frequently for signs/symptoms that may indicate the onset of side effects. The drug class called the phenothiazines has been known to cause contact dermatitis, so avoid getting any of the drug on the skin. Wash your hands after every contact with the drugs and wear gloves if you frequently handle phenothiazines.

The third nursing responsibility, client and family education, has a direct impact on the client's level of functioning. One of the primary tasks of nurses is to assist clients in coping with their daily living activities. When the client and family learn about the client's medications, treatment can be more successful. The box on p. 444 lists the most important points of client and family education.

Keep these general guidelines in mind. Get to know the clients for whom you are caring. The more you know about the person, the better you will be able to tell the difference between behaviors that are related to the effects of medication and those that belong to the client. Antipsychotic drugs are powerful medications. They demand to be treated with respect and require knowledge from those who receive them and those who work with them.

Special Considerations

Because antipsychotic medications affect the body's nervous system, they are potentially harmful chemicals. Nurses must constantly remain vigilant to the occurrence of side effects with each medication prescribed. Thoroughly assess clients before administering any p.r.n. drug because a medication will actually worsen symptoms if the nurse is not able to differentiate a side effect from a behavior. Clients who are receiving antipsychotic drugs are at risk for developing neuroleptic malignant syndrome and tardive dyskinesia. Accurate identification of the signs/symptoms of each may prevent many complications.

Neuroleptic malignant syndrome (NMS) "is a serious and potentially fatal extrapyramidal side effect of antipsychotic or neuroleptic medications" (Blair and Dauner, 1993). The condition is poorly understood and frequently underdiagnosed. Death can occur from respiratory failure, kidney failure, aspiration pneumonia, or pulmonary emboli. Although NMS is usually associated with the high-potency antipsychotics, it can occur with many other dopamine-altering drugs.

NMS occurs more often when two or more psychotherapeutic drugs are combined; when lithium is used concurrently with a psychotherapeutic drug, and with the use of depot (oil-based, long-acting) injections. The development of NMS may occur suddenly after a single dose or after years of drug treatment. It is often associated with other extrapyramidal reactions such as dystonia and akathisia.

The onset of symptoms is heralded by a sudden change in level of consciousness and a rapid onset of rigid muscles (*Harvard Mental Health Letter*, 1994). Often there is an associated respiratory difficulty, tremors, and an inability to speak; however, the cardinal sign of NMS is a high body temperature. Temperatures can reach as high as 108° F but usually range between 101° and 103° F. The temperatures of all clients receiving psychotherapeutic drugs must be frequently and routinely monitored. Without intervention, the client's physical condition declines over a 48- to 72-hour period.

Signs of autonomic nervous system dysfunctions are evident in NMS: tachycardia, rapid changes in blood pressure, increased perspiration (diaphoresis), incontinence, and rapid, labored respirations. CNS alterations include sudden agitation, confusion, delirium, combativeness, and rigid posturing. The severe muscle rigidity leads to tissue breakdown, an increased white blood count, and possible kidney failure.

No specific treatment exists for NMS. Supportive measures, including intensive respiratory care, are instituted, and administration of all medications that may be implicated in the development of NMS is stopped.

Nurses who care for clients who are taking psychotherapeutic medication must be aware of the potential for the development of NMS. A nursing action as simple and routine as obtaining vital signs may save the life of a client. Do not hesitate to notify your supervisor or physician if client develops a sudden fever, changes in blood pressure, sudden changes in alertness, confusion, or altered levels of consciousness.

Subclinical (mild) cases of NMS have been reported (Blair and Dauner, 1993). Nurses should suspect NMS in any client with signs/symptoms of pneumonia or urinary tract infection. Clients who have diaphoresis, tachycardia, an elevated white blood cell count, or any muscle rigidity may be experiencing NMS. Sudden changes in consciousness should always be investigated and reported.

Tardive dyskinesia is a serious, irreversible side effect of long-term treatment. The word *tardive* means "appearing later," and many clients exhibit the signs of tardive dyskinesia after several months of drug treatment. The words *dys* means "difficult," and *kinesis* means "movement" in Greek. So the literal translation, "late difficult movement," explains the condition. Tardive dyskinesia is a drug-induced condition that produces involuntary, repeated movements of the muscles of the face, trunk, arms, and legs.

After a long period of antipsychotic drug use, the body attempts to compensate for the lack of the neurotransmitter dopamine by developing hypersensitive receptors in the brain. When the brain is stimulated by dopamine, it overreacts and produces abnormal muscle movements. The condition usually occurs after months or years of antipsychotic drug usage, but it has been diagnosed sooner in some people. The elderly (especially elderly women) and those who have had a stroke are at the greatest risk for developing tardive dyskinesia, but the symptoms are most severe in young men.

This condition is difficult to treat, and the effects are persistent. At this time tardive dyskinesia is considered irreversible except in the very early stages. Therefore it is most important that nurses carefully monitor all clients receiving psychotherapeutic drug therapy for signs/symptoms that herald the onset of tardive dyskinesia.

The signs/symptoms of tardive dyskinesia usually involve the facial muscles first. The box above, at right, lists the major signs and symptoms.

People who experience the effects of tardive dyskinesia are frightened at their lack of control. In addition, the sight of a person engaged in these unusual movements and behaviors can be unnerving for care providers. Sensitive, caring staff can help to ease the client's distress.

Nursing measures for tardive dyskinesia include routine assessments and measures to prevent injuries. Clients with impaired gag reflexes may require soft foods. Be sure oropharyngeal suction devices are readily available. Every client and family member must be taught how to recognize the signs/symptoms of tardive dyskinesia.

DRUG ALERT

Signs and symptoms of tardive dyskinesia include the following:
- Protrusion of the tongue (fly-catcher sign)
- Puffing of cheeks or tongue in cheek (bonbon sign)
- Grinding of teeth, chewing, lateral jaw movements
- Lip smacking, puckering
- Grimacing, making faces, tics
- Blinking, squinting
- Choreoid (twitching) movements of trunk, legs, and arms
- Shrugging of shoulders
- Thrusting of pelvis
- Toe movements, foot tapping
- Impaired diaphragmatic movements (breathing difficulties)*
- Impaired gag reflex (choking, aspiration)*

*Potentially life threatening.

Most medications are not effective for the treatment of tardive dyskinesia, but some success has been reported with the drugs bromocriptine (Parlodel), reserpine, and clonazepam (Klonopin). Vitamin E was recently found to be effective (Keltner and Folks, 1993). Tardive dyskinesia effects many people on antipsychotic therapy.

Some advances have been made in the treatment of tardive dyskinesia, but the single most important weapon is an astute nurse who is able to recognize the disorder's signs/symptoms early enough to prevent permanent problems. The same can be said for other side effects of these powerful medications.

Caring for persons with psychoses is one of the most challenging areas of mental health. Hospitalization and education are only the beginning steps in a long road toward optimal functioning. Continued treatment and support are needed for family members and clients alike if we are to cope with the devastating effects of schizophrenia and other serious psychotic mental illnesses.

❖ KEY CONCEPTS

- A psychosis is a disorder in which there is an inability to recognize reality, relate to others, or cope with life's demands.
- Neurobiological responses can range from adaptive contact with reality to disorganized thoughts, emotions, and behaviors.

- Although the majority of psychoses are encountered primarily in late adolescence or adulthood, some do present in childhood.
- Today, scientific evidence points to possible biological (physical) causes for psychotic behaviors.
- Schizophrenia is a group of related mental health disorders characterized by disordered perceptions, thinking, and behavior.
- The five subtypes of schizophrenia are catatonic, disorganized, paranoid, residual, and undifferentiated.
- Other psychotic disorders include brief psychotic disorder, delusional disorder, and psychoses related to medical conditions or drug use.
- The treatment goals for inpatient, short-term care are to stabilize the client, prevent further decline in functioning, and assist the client in coping with his/her disorder.
- Long-term goals include psychosocial and vocational rehabilitation as possible.
- Clients with acute psychoses are treated with a combination of therapies and medications. Antipsychotic drugs, which may take weeks to become effective, help to stabilize behaviors.
- Psychosocial therapies include personal therapy, social skills training, vocational rehabilitation, and behavioral therapy, stress reduction, and family education.
- Several special nursing assessments, interventions, and evaluations are required for clients who are receiving powerful antipsychotic medications.

❖ SUGGESTIONS FOR FURTHER READING

An older but still helpful article by M. Lucas is "Understanding schizophrenia" (*RN*, 10:52, 1990).

If you are interested in how people live with schizophrenia, read E. Fuller Torrey's *Surviving Schizophrenia: A Family Manual* (New York, 1983, Harper & Row).

❖ REFERENCES

American Psychiatric Association: *Diagnostic and statistical manual of mental disorders,* ed 4, Washington, DC, 1994, The Association.

Andreasen NC: Signs/symptoms, and diagnosis of schizophrenia, *Lancet* 346(8973):477, 1995.

Begley S: Lights of madness, *Newsweek* 126(21):76, 1995.

Blair DT: Risk management for extrapyramidal symptoms, *Qual Assur Rev Bull* 17:116, 1990.

Blair DT, Dauner A: Neuroleptic syndrome: liability in nursing practice, *J Psychosoc Nurs* 31(2):5, 1993.

Bower B: Schizophrenia: data points to early roots, *Sci News* 148(25):406, 1995.

Bower B: New culprits for schizophrenia, *Sci News* 149(5):68, 1996.

Clunn P: *Child psychiatric nursing,* St Louis, 1991, Mosby.

Fortinash KM, Holoday-Worret PA: *Psychiatric-mental health nursing,* St Louis, 1996, Mosby.

Hogstel MO: *Geropsychiatric nursing,* ed 2, St Louis, 1995, Mosby.

Kane JM, McGlashan TH: Treatment of schizophrenia, *Lancet* 346(8978):820, 1995.

Keltner NL, Folks DG: *Psychotropic drugs,* St Louis, 1993, Mosby.

McGuffin P, Owen MJ, Farmer AE: Genetic basis of schizophrenia, *Lancet* 346(8976):678, 1995.

McKenna K, Gordon CT, Rapoport JL: Childhood-onset schizophrenia: timely neurobiological research, *J Am Acad Child Adolesc Psychiatry* 33:771, 1994.

Scherling D: Prenatal cocaine exposure and childhood psychopathology, *Am J Orthopsychiatry* 64(1):9, 1994.

Schizophrenia update—part I, *Harvard Ment Health Lett* 11(12):1, 1995a.

Schizophrenia update—part II, *Harvard Ment Health Lett* 12(1):1, 1995b.

Stuart GW, Sundeen SJ: *Principles and practice of psychiatric nursing,* ed 5, St Louis, 1995, Mosby.

Szmanski S and others: Gender differences in onset of illness, treatment, response, course, and biological indexes in first-episode schizophrenic patients, *Am J Psychiatry* 152(5):698, 1995.

Taylor CM: *Essentials of psychiatric nursing,* ed 14, St Louis, 1994, Mosby.

Torrey EF and others: Prefrontal origin of schizophrenia in a subgroup of discordant monozygotic twins, *Schizophrenia Bull* 20(3):423, 1994.

Waddington JL: Schizophrenia: developmental neuroscience and pathobiology, *Lancet* 341(8845):531, 1993.

What is neuroleptic malignant syndrome and how is it treated? *Harvard Ment Health Lett* 11(6):8, 1994.

Wong DL:*Whaley and Wong's nursing care of infants and children,* ed 5, St Louis, 1995, Mosby.

Wyatt RJ, Clark KP: Calculating the cost of schizophrenia, *Psychiatr Ann 1987* 17:586, 1987.

32

CHRONIC MENTAL HEALTH DISORDERS

LEARNING OBJECTIVES

1. Describe the experience of mental illness from a client's viewpoint.
2. Explain how deinstitutionalization has affected the delivery of mental health care in the United States.
3. List three psychological and three biological characteristics of chronic mental illness.
4. Discuss how children and adolescents can be affected by chronic mental health problems.
5. Identify the connection between HIV/AIDS and mental illness.
6. Describe the nursing care for clients with multiple mental health problems.
7. List three principles of psychiatric rehabilitation.
8. Apply the nursing process to clients with chronic mental health disorders.
9. List seven basic nursing interventions for clients who are chronically mentally disordered.

KEY TERMS

chemical restraint
chronic mental illness

comorbidity
exacerbations

psychiatric rehabilitation
remissions

The word *chronic* means long-lasting, persistent, or continual. Most chronic mental health problems are characterized by periods of exacerbations and remissions. **Exacerbations** are periods of illness or dysfunction marked by an increase in the signs/symptoms and seriousness of a problem or disorder. **Remissions** are times of partial or complete disappearance of symptoms. The course for chronic mental health problems usually follows this type of up-and-down pattern.

Many mental health problems are acute. They begin abruptly, increase in intensity, then subside after a short period of time. Persons with phobias, anxiety disorders, or depression often respond well to therapeutic interventions and have no further problems for the remainder of their lives. However, for a certain group of individuals, being mentally ill becomes a way of life.

Chronic mental illness is the recurrence of one or more psychiatric disorders that results in significant functional disability (Kessler and others, 1995). Individuals with chronic mental health problems are often referred to as CMI (chronic mentally ill) persons. Many are contributing members of society, struggling to hold onto some degree of mental health. They are also the homeless, the criminal, and the odd neighbor down the street. They are our relatives, friends, and members of our community.

Scope of Mental Illness

Chronic mental disorders are disabling for people in every society and culture. A recent study of 14 countries, covering most major cultures, found that mental illness was associated with disability in every culture (Ormel and others, 1994).

The impact of mental illness can be felt at every level of society in the United States. Each year, millions of individuals seek help for mental health problems. An estimated 27% to 48% of persons seeking treatment from a primary caregiver for physical complaints are actually suffering from a mental disorder (Fifer and others, 1995). One of the most comprehensive studies of the nation's mental health found that about "52 million adults in the United States—more than 1 in 4—experience a mental disorder at some point during a year, but only 28% of those affected seek help" (Foster, Siegel, and Landes, 1995) (see box at right).

The estimated costs of treating persons with mental disorders is about "$20 billion per year, plus $7 billion for nursing home costs, representing 4% of total U.S. direct health care costs" (National Advisory Mental Health Council, 1993). When the social costs of lost

productivity, shortened lives, and implementation of criminal justice are factored in, the total can climb as high as $74 billion (National Advisory Mental Health Council, 1993).

The costs to suffering individuals and their loved ones cannot be estimated. Society encourages people to recover from acute mental disorders and resume normal daily activities, but it tends to ignore the needs of those persons who are (and will always be) unable to cope independently with life. Chronic mental illness has "social stigmas attached to being labeled 'crazy', keeping some sufferers from seeking help" (Foster, Siegel, and Landes, 1995).

Individuals with chronic mental health problems have much higher rates of suicide (Livingston and others, 1994). Because mental health problems affect each area of functioning, each chronically mentally troubled person has a unique life experience with mental illness. Many have attempted to deal with their distressing symptoms by using alcohol, street drugs, or other chemicals. They must cope with an addiction in addition to their illness. Remember, though, that underneath every chronically mentally ill person lies a real person who is attempting to cope and adapt to life.

Experience of Chronic Mental Illness

What is it like to be chronically mentally ill? To face each day knowing the struggle ahead? To wonder if this day will bring acceptance and hope or the slide into "madness"?

Persons who face mental illness must cope with problems that are unknown to the rest of us. Individuals are often lumped into a group labeled CMIs and stripped

---

THINK ABOUT

Did you know that in any given year:
- 52 million adults experience a mental health disorder
- 28% seek mental health treatment
- 9 million Americans develop a mental disorder for the first time
- 8 million individuals suffer a relapse
- 35 million persons have continuing symptoms
- the number of chronically mentally ill persons remains relatively stable at about 28% of the total population

What message does an analysis of these statistics send?

Modified from Foster CD, Siegel MA, Landes A: *Health—a concern for every American,* ed 7, Wylie, TX, 1995, Information Plus.

of their identity, dignity, convictions, and feelings. They lack choice, respect, and control and are expected to co-operate with therapies that make them feel sick. The box below allows us a glimpse into the world of one chronically mentally ill individual. Hopefully, this true account will serve as a reminder that each client is truly a unique individual and should be viewed as such.

Public Policy and Mental Health

Today, chronically mentally ill individuals are cared for in the community. They are expected to provide for their basic needs, protect themselves, and seek help for their problems—all rather complex behaviors. The reality is that most of the chronically mentally ill are unable to meet these expectations.

Effects of Deinstitutionalization

When the first antipsychotic medications became available in the 1960s, chemical restraints replaced physical ones. A **chemical restraint** is a medication that reduces or eliminates psychotic symptoms and quiets behavior. People no longer had to be physically controlled, and the state psychiatric hospitals began to empty, "reducing their overall population from 559,000 in 1955 to just over 100,000 today" (Torrey, 1992). Most people released from the state hospitals could live in the community with the proper support and aftercare. Unfortunately, the aftercare, which was a critical part of the overall plan for providing community psychiatric services, failed to be implemented. Changing political parties and government leaders chose to ignore the chronically mentally ill, thinking

---

CASE STUDY

You spend the whole first night crying because you don't want to be here. There must be some awful mistake. You are very, very naive, only 18. You're not yet a CMI (chronic mentally ill). Next day the "staffing" (as they call it) is very intimidating. The hospital's brass are all there and they just laugh at you when you tell them you do not want to stay. They patronize you: "Oh, we think we will just keep you here for a while." You don't know it yet, but you are on the way to becoming a CMI.

• • •

The first time you experience dystonia from the drugs they've given you, you are extremely frightened. Your tongue is rigid and you can't control its movements. You rush to the nurse's station where they are huddled inside their little cage. No one comes out for fear of contamination. They are puzzled by your presence, but you can't speak because of your tongue's movements. They wait impatiently for you to tell them what is wrong. You wonder what is wrong with them. Can't they see your problem? But, no. It's not that they don't see. They don't feel. Because you don't count. You are on the way to becoming a CMI.

• • •

After your first discharge, you are loaded up on medications, and your follow-up therapist announces that he will not continue with you unless you come in with your family for therapy. But there are 8 of you, scattered all over the state. And they don't want to come, anyway, because they have

_____
Modified from the words of Betty Blaska: *Schizophrenia Bull* 17(1):173, 1991.

been belittled, browbeaten, and laughed at by too many MHPs (mental health professionals) already. So the therapist refuses to see you. And he refuses to refill your prescriptions. So you go through withdrawal. And you end up back on the same psych ward. And then, they say to you, accusingly: "Why did you go off your medicines?" It's then you realize: You're a CMI.

• • •

You've been in and out of hospitals, seen numerous MHPs (some stranger than you), and been off and on loads of psychoactive drugs given in doses you complain are too high. In combinations you complain are too much. And there are the side effects—nausea, diarrhea, dizziness. Vision so bad that you are afraid to cross the street. Drug-induced psychoses so bad you can't leave your bed or look out the window because of the terror you feel. Blood pressure so low that you can't stand for very long, and a voice so weak that you can't be heard across a telephone.

Oh great! Now you're without a job. So they send you to a place called Vocational Rehabilitation where they "help" you get a clerical job. Never mind that you have a degree—or two. You get the clerical job because you are a woman. A woman CMI. But the men CMIs are just as lucky. They get to become janitors! Now you are truly a full-fledged CMI.

Clinical Decisions

1. What "labels" (stereotypes) is this lady coping with?

2. Has reading this case study changed your impressions of the experience of being mentally ill?

that everything would eventually work itself out. To-day, the consequences of our federal mental health policy can be seen in the ever-increasing numbers of homeless persons, prisoners, and county jail inmates.

Meeting Basic Needs

The issues facing mentally troubled individuals are the same as those with which the rest of us must cope: adequate food, shelter, and clothing; gainful employment; and access to health care. People with chronic mental illness must strive to meet their living needs on a daily basis. The majority live with their families. Because their disorders prevent them from planning or logically carrying out an activity, many of the chronically mentally ill are homeless, hungry, and unable to care for themselves. "The seriously mentally ill, who make up one third of the total homeless population, can be seen on street corners chatting amiably with or responding angrily to voices in their heads" (Torrey, 1992).

Many of our society's mentally ill are now housed in county jails and prisons, awaiting available beds in the few state institutions that remain. Another group of mentally ill persons are jailed on "dine-and-dash" charges (eating a restaurant meal they cannot pay for) or as "mercy bookings" just to get them off the streets and provide some basic needs. State prisons are also feeling the increase in mentally ill inmates. It is estimated that 10% to 15% of the 771,000 inmates in state prisons suffer from mental illness (Torrey, 1992).

The chronically mentally ill persons who do man-age to provide for their own basic needs must struggle with the labels and expectations of others. Often, it is difficult for them to remain employed for long periods because of the occasional relapse. As one chronic mental health client put it "I am an effective, loyal worker for over 90% of the time, but the 10% of the time I have troubles are all that's remembered."

Poverty and mental illness go hand in hand. Although many mentally troubled persons receive some financial assistance, most are unable to plan or use the money wisely. Because about half the severely mentally ill population abuse alcohol or drugs, few dollars are spent on life's necessities. Today, more than "250,000 seriously mentally ill—a quarter of a million—are living on the streets, in public shelters, in jails, and in prisons" (Torrey, 1992) (Fig. 32-1).

Access to Health Care

Until the time of community psychiatric care, any person who was suffering from severe or chronic mental health problems was treated (or at least provided with custodial care) through state programs. With ongoing therapy and medications, many people with chronic mental disorders could be returned to their communities and function effectively. However, community support was often not available after hospitalization and many individuals once again fell victim to their psychoses.

Only this time, the tightened admission policies of most institutions did not allow most of the chronically mentally ill back and they were forced to cope with

Fig. 32-1   A "bag lady" with her personal belongings. (Copyright © Cathy Lander-Goldberg, Lander Photographics.)

their disorders the best they could. Other mentally ill persons became involved in the revolving door syndrome, a cycle of repeated short hospital admissions and discharges. This in-and-out of the institution behavior is also called recidivism.

Today, a new generation of chronically mentally ill persons is emerging, known as the young chronically mentally ill. These individuals are young (18 to 35) and severely ill. Most have never sought treatment. Those who do receive treatment commonly refuse to follow therapeutic advice. "They lack internal controls, rarely take psychotropic medications, and exhibit excessive drug and alcohol abuse" (Fortinash and Holoday-Worret, 1996). Many self-medicate to relieve distressing symptoms. Cocaine is often used by persons with mood disorders, whereas alcohol is likely to be used by schizophrenics. Heroin is usually preferred by individuals with conduct disorders. Many of the young mentally ill are polysubstance abusers, that is, they use a variety of different chemical substances, sometimes in combination.

Access to mental health care is limited in the United States today. Currently, over 37.4 million individuals have no health insurance at all (*Harvard Mental Health Letter*, 1994). For many of those who do, mental health services are capped or limited to a certain amount of money per person. Individuals who are suffering from chronic mental problems are often unable to plan for or manage their health care because of their illness, even if they are fortunate to have some sort of insured coverage. Many refuse shelter or treatment because of their paranoia, believing people will harm them.

On the other hand, people who want to receive treatment often find that services are inadequate or unavailable. Even when they are admitted to an institution, their stay may not be long enough to improve their condition. "Furthermore, the supportive outpatient services that are the basis for the mentally ill person's not being hospitalized may either not be available or refused by the individual" (Quiram, Blair, and Jacobs, 1995). Access to comprehensive mental health care remains a problem today. That is why each nurse must be prepared to recognize and assist those individuals whose only crimes are being too mentally disordered to effectively care for themselves.

Characteristics of Chronic Mental Illness

Each person's experiences with mental illness is unique. Diagnoses serve only to group together and label certain behaviors. The real meaning of being "depressed" or "schizophrenic" can be found only within the individual who suffers from the distresses associated with the particular label.

Many mentally troubled persons can be labeled with more than one psychiatric diagnosis. Schizophrenics frequently suffer from severe depression after an acute psychotic episode. Suicidal gestures are higher in depressed persons who are beginning to stabilize from their medications enough to see the hopelessness of their situation. Persons with personality disorders may have disturbing phobias or anxiety. However, the experience and suffering of living with these labels is unique with each individual.

Certain features are common to all persons who must live with mental illness. For the sake of discussion, these characteristics are divided into two categories: psychological characteristics and behavioral characteristics.

Psychological Characteristics

Chronically mentally ill individuals have several intellectual, emotional, social, and spiritual features in common. Intellectually, *altered thought processes* disrupt their abilities to think clearly, solve problems, or make plans. Hallucinations, delusions, and obsessive thoughts are unwelcome intrusions that routinely disrupt the flow of logical, reality-based thinking. Fear, mistrust, and paranoia can complicate the picture by presenting problems with daily living activities.

Chronic *low self-esteem* follows the label of mental illness everywhere. The ability to make logical sense out of life is hampered by the many distresses of being mentally ill. Even when one is strong and adapting effectively, the stigma of being odd, crazy, or eccentric is dragged behind each action. Other people feel uncomfortable and avoid interacting or pry into personal areas, thus reinforcing the differences between "sick" and "well."

Mentally troubled people often see themselves as helpless and ineffective, incapable of change. The experience of a small success will often prevent them from making any further attempts because they "just know" that they will eventually fail. When the self-concept is that low, it is difficult to convince someone that a brighter future can exist.

Depression is a partner of many mental health disorders. It makes a difficult life even more distressing and offers little hope. Depressive episodes can occur when an individual is coping with stress or in association with a psychotic episode. Even when functioning effectively, depression can be a companion for many mentally ill. Prudent nurses assess each client for the presence of depressive symptoms.

Loneliness is the suffering that results when one is isolated from other people. It is commonly known that people need to be with each other and that they suffer when removed from the company of others. People with chronic mental health problems are usually very lonely individuals. Their basic needs for love and belonging go unmet, and they respond by becoming emotionally paralyzed.

Starved for social interactions, some chronically mentally ill persons go to great lengths, such as criminal or violent activity, to gain attention. Others withdraw from society, fearing further rejection, and live a life of mistrust and solitude. Those that do have social interactions often are unable to express themselves, make decisions, or adapt to certain social roles. As the distress of attempting to cope socially increases, many find that retreat into their illness is an easier course to follow than struggling with the complexities of interacting with other people.

Another characteristic of chronic mental illness is *hopelessness,* the catalyst for suicide. The struggle for mental health consumes much energy. Feelings of worthlessness plague self-esteem and lead to depression. Hopelessness brings with it the feeling that there are no solutions to one's problems, that life is destined to remain distressful, and that the only way to relieve the pain is to destroy the sufferer.

Behavioral Characteristics

The nature of one's mental disorder determines the level of disability. Persons with severe chronic mental illnesses are unable to meet even the most basic needs for food, water, elimination, or hygiene. Often, they are unable to function socially or occupationally. Assaultive behaviors or criminal activities may be present.

Persons who suffer from chronic mental illness often have difficulty assuming the behaviors and activities that are required for successful living. Impaired judgment, lack of motivation, or altered realities often lead to an inability to perform even the most basic activities. Individuals may lack a knowledge of personal grooming habits, table manners, or expected social behaviors. They may have difficulty relating to or interacting with others. When added to the difficulties with employment, it becomes easy to understand why the majority of chronically mentally ill are dependent on others for their care. Many times, this involves living with family members or in group homes. For those who try to live independently, it all too often means a life of homeless shelters and nameless streets.

Sexuality and the sexual behaviors of chronically mentally disordered persons pose a concern for health care providers because the sexual practices of this group places them at an increased risk for contracting and transmitting sexually transmitted diseases, such as HIV/AIDS. Research into the sexual behaviors of the chronically mentally ill revealed that more than half of the clients screened were at a high risk for contracting "HIV infection because of one or more of the following factors: IV drug use, sex with an IV drug user, homosexual male sex, street drug use, alcohol use, having a history of STDs (sexually transmitted diseases), or having had a blood transfusion prior to 1985" (Cook and others, 1994). Studies regarding the knowledge of HIV/AIDS and its risk behaviors demonstrated that the chronically mentally ill participants "knew significantly less about AIDS than a comparison sample of public high school students" (Katz, Watts, and Santman, 1994). Clearly, these individuals need education to prevent the increase of HIV infection, and this is one of the greatest challenges for nurses today.

Violence is an unfortunate aspect of many chronically mentally troubled people. The inability to solve problems, make sound judgments, or control emotional behaviors makes some individuals a threat to the safety and well-being of others. Family members, especially children, frequently become the targets for anger and aggression. Life within the community becomes difficult for persons who behave violently; the violent behavior almost always leads to extensive contact with the criminal justice system. Stays in county jails or prisons do little to address the issues underlying violence. Many potentially dangerous individuals are released into the community under the banner of individual rights. Society's response to the problems posed by these individuals reflects the attitude toward people with severe chronic mental illness in general.

Special Populations

Persons with chronic mental illness are a varied mix of ages, sexes, and abilities. Chronic mental health problems can begin at any stage in life, but they are often not noticed until early or middle adulthood. Children, adolescents, adults, and the elderly all suffer from the difficulties of chronic mental illness, but each group poses some unique and special problems that affect their abilities to respond to mental health interventions.

Children and Adolescents With Chronic Mental Illness

The seeds of many adult mental health problems are planted in childhood. However, some children must learn to cope with psychological impairments early in life. Children with *mental retardation* (an IQ below 70 with impairments in functioning) have problems with the intellectual and emotional aspects of life. Also, people who are mildly or moderately retarded "are believed to be more susceptible to mental illness" (Fortinash and Holoday-Worret, 1996). Emotional problems, such as anxiety or depression, often accompany the many challenges faced by retarded individuals. In addition, the conflict between expectations and actual abilities may result in the development of a personality disorder or even a psychosis.

Children with *autism* are in a world of their own. Because they do not develop the ability to respond to and communicate their needs, they remain dependent on others, sometimes throughout their lives. Without the help and care of others, these children could not survive reality.

Childhood *schizophrenia,* although uncommon, does occur and almost always develops into a chronic mental health problem. Other children at risk for developing a chronic mental health problem include those who have been neglected, repeatedly abused, or mistreated and those who have witnessed or experienced violence. Children with conduct disorders, attention-deficit hyperactivity disorders, and depression also have a greater risk of developing a chronic mental health disorder (Clunn, 1991).

During adolescence, many maladaptive behaviors become cemented, and new ones are developed. Because all realms of an individual are related, adolescents with chronic physical health problems, such as arthritis, diabetes, and cystic fibrosis, commonly experience psychological problems as well. For example, teens with diabetes have high rates of depression and suicidal behaviors (Goldston and others, 1994).

Many chronic mental health problems develop during adolescence. Eating disorders, personality disorders, and schizophrenia can begin during the teenage years (Hogarth, 1991). Depression can become a longstanding problem with adolescents who have not learned to cope successfully. The road to chemical dependency most frequently begins in adolescence, and the effects of posttraumatic stress lead teens to maladaptive but stress-reducing behaviors, which over time become chronic patterns of ineffective functioning.

Older Adults With Chronic Mental Illness

The elderly with chronic mental illness fall into two groups: those who have had mental health problems for decades and those who were diagnosed with a mental disorder after age 50. The most common acquired mental health problems in older adulthood are Alzheimer's disease and other dementias. "As many as 20% of elderly persons over the age of 80 suffer from some form of dementia" (Fortinash and Holoday-Worret, 1996). Depression is another frequent chronic mental health problem of older adults, especially if it is accompanied by sensory losses and communication impairments.

The social epidemic of crack cocaine and other drug use has resulted in a whole new group of primary care providers in this country: grandparents who must raise a second family, their grandchildren. Because of the increase in drug abuse, violence, and chronic behavioral problems that leave adult children incapable of raising their children, many older adults have assumed the primary responsibility and care for their grandchildren.

At a time when individuals should be looking forward to personal freedom and decreased responsibilities, the prospect of spending another 15 to 20 years raising more children can be overwhelming (Hatfield and Lefley, 1993). Health care providers, especially nurses, must address the issues of grandparents suffering from the strain of caring for the children of addicts. The mental health of at least two generations depends on timely and supportive health care interventions.

Persons With Multiple Disorders

The word **comorbidity** refers to the presence of two or more mental health disorders. Individuals with a dual diagnosis are suffering from two mental health disorders, one of which is usually substance related. The depressed person who uses cocaine is an example of a dual diagnosis. Substance abuse and mental illness result in an interactive process that can be seen in "physiological, psychological, and behavioral patterns . . . uniquely different from those of persons with only an addiction or serious mental illness" (Clement, Williams, and Waters, 1993).

As many as 75% of individuals with chronic mental illness use or abuse drugs (Clement, Williams, and Waters, 1993). These people present a significant challenge for treatment because of the complexity of their disorders. The multidisciplinary treatment team seems to be the most promising approach for helping clients to cope with their problems in each area of human functioning.

Providing Care for the Chronically Mentally Ill

People with chronic mental health problems are found everywhere in society. Today, the majority of mental health care is provided within the community, outside the world of the institution. For this reason, each interaction between health care providers and clients must address issues or problems relating to mental health.

Inpatient Settings

Persons with chronic mental health problems are hospitalized only when their behaviors pose a threat to themselves or others. Even then, it is often for only a short period of time. Inpatient treatment settings for the chronically mentally ill include the acute care hospital, psychiatric unit of an acute care facility, state psychiatric institution, and private mental health facility.

State psychiatric institutions still provide care for more than 50% of all psychiatric inpatients; however, stays in all inpatient treatment settings are shorter, and readmissions more frequent. The pattern of admission, short stay in the institution, discharge, short stay in the community, and readmission (recidivism) remains a problem for many health care professionals and their chronically mentally ill clients. Frequently, high levels of stress precipitate acute psychotic behaviors. Table 32-1 lists several of the most common stressors that can trigger acute reactions and thus readmissions to inpatient care settings.

Outpatient Settings

Once the acute episode has subsided, many chronically mentally disordered clients are discharged to halfway houses or other group-living environments. Aftercare programs range from partial hospitalization to sheltered living arrangements to home care, depending on the size, economics, and support of the community (see box at right).

The majority of people with chronic mental illness live with their families, who require much support to cope effectively. Foster care programs, in which chronically mentally ill individuals live with therapeutic families, are offered in some communities. Unfortunately, more mental health care is need in settings such as homeless shelters, health clinics for the poor, jails, and prisons.

Psychiatric Rehabilitation

The concept of **psychiatric rehabilitation** focuses on assisting individuals with serious mental illness to effectively cope with their life situations. A multidisciplinary approach uses the special talents of physicians, psychologists, nurses, occupational and physical therapists, and dieticians or other specialists.

Each realm of human functioning is addressed during treatment. Physically, clients are assessed for and

CULTURAL ASPECTS

When chronic mental health clients are cared for in community group housing situations, make sure to perform a complete cultural assessment. Living with people from other cultures requires open communication and a willingness to accept another's point of view—qualities sometimes difficult to achieve, especially when one is mentally troubled.

◆ **TABLE 32-1**
Common Triggers of Acute Psychotic Episodes

Health	Environment	Attitudes/Behaviors
Poor nutrition	Hostile/critical environment	"Poor me" (low self-concept)
Lack of sleep	Housing difficulties (unsatisfactory	"Hopeless" (lack of self-confidence)
Out of balance circadian	housing)	"I'm a failure" (loss of motivation
rhythms	Pressure to perform (loss of independent	to use skills)
Fatigue	living)	"Lack of control" (demoralization)
Infection	Changes in life events, daily patterns of	Feeling overpowered by symptoms
Central nervous system	activity	"No one likes me" (unable to meet
drugs	Stress (lack of survival skills)	spiritual needs)
Impaired reasoning	Interpersonal difficulties	Looks/acts different from others
Impaired information	Disruptions in interpersonal relationships	same age, culture
processing	Loneliness (social isolation, lack of social	Poor social skills
Lack of exercise	support)	Aggressive behavior
Behavioral disorder	Missed environmental cues	Violent behavior
Mood abnormalities	Job pressures (poor occupation skills)	Poor medication management
Moderate to high levels	Poor social skills	Poor symptom management
of anxiety	Poverty	
	Lack of transportation (resources)	

From Stuart GW, Sundeen SJ: *Pocket guide to psychiatric nursing,* ed 3, St Louis, 1995, Mosby.

taught the skills needed to effectively perform the activities of daily living, including proper nutrition, activity, and rest habits. Emotional problems are explored, and clients are taught how to identify their feelings, control their anger, or reach their goals. Intellectually, clients are encouraged to problem solve and set goals. Occupational or vocational training allows individuals the opportunity for employment.

Involvement with psychiatric rehabilitation programs offers many opportunities for people with severe mental illness to meet their often neglected social needs. Many programs offer group therapies and opportunities to learn more socially appropriate behaviors. Some psychiatric rehabilitation programs lend spiritual help in the form of staff members, clergy, or referrals to the religious organizations of the client's choice. Unfortunately, there are far too few psychiatric rehabilitation programs for the many individuals who truly need them.

Therapeutic Interventions

In 1978, the President's Commission on Mental Health recommended that persons with chronic mental disorders be treated in the least restrictive environment, which was defined as a setting that encouraged the "greatest degree of freedom, self-determination, autonomy, dignity, and integrity." However, the concept is not so easily implemented when clients are unable or unwilling to seek out or consent to treatment, and the funding for mental health care remains unstable.

Treatments and Therapies

The basic goals for chronically disordered mental health clients are to achieve stabilization and maintain clients at the highest possible level of daily functioning. Therapies are designed for the individual based on identified problems, available resources, and the client's willingness to cooperate with the therapeutic regimen. Various individual and group therapies along with certain medications are usually recommended by the treatment team after a complete health assessment and consultation with the client.

With support and assistance, many chronically mentally ill individuals are able to function outside the institution. However, a number of problems or situations can disrupt their stability and trigger an acute psychiatric episode. When hospital stays are shorter and acute episodes occur frequently, individuals bounce between living in the community and the institution.

In 1991, the average length of hospitalization for psychiatric problems was 23 days. In 1993, that length

of stay had decreased to just 17.8 days (*Wall Street Journal*, 1994). Today, many hospital stays allow even less time for clients to stabilize and begin treatment.

Pharmacological Therapy

Persons with chronic mental disorders are treated with a variety of medications depending on symptoms and distress levels. Antianxiety agents and antidepressants are often prescribed to improve emotional comfort. Antipsychotic (neuroleptic) drugs are prescribed to help control hallucinations and other symptoms of psychosis. Drug therapy is an important part of treatment; however, the side effects of many of these medications are uncomfortable, and clients often stop taking them as soon as the acute symptoms subside. Nurses must monitor clients routinely to ensure they take their medications.

Nursing Process

The first step in working with severely mentally disordered clients is to obtain the most complete data base possible. Because their disturbances affect every area of functioning, nurses must perform thorough nursing histories and continually assess clients' physical status, perceptions, and behaviors.

After each member of the treatment team completes his/her assessment, client problems are identified, and therapeutic interventions are designed. Nurses focus on helping clients cope with each activity of daily living. Nursing diagnoses are chosen, and basic interventions are agreed on by the treatment team and (when possible) the client. Nursing diagnoses for chronically mentally ill clients are selected according to the client's identified problems.

Nursing interventions are then designed to help the client solve the identified problems. Although each client requires a unique combination of nursing interventions, several fundamental nursing interventions apply to all clients. Table 32-2 lists each intervention and its rationale.

A sample nursing care plan for a chronically mentally ill client is presented in the box on p. 458. Nursing care plans for long-term psychiatric clients are adapted to the particular care setting—be it the home, community day center, clinic, or institution. If the mental health care services are well coordinated, care plans are moved with the client. That is, the care plans established in the institution move to a different care setting when the client does. This method encourages the continuity of care that is so important for coping with severe mental problems.

Once returned into the community, mental health centers provide clients with the ongoing care needed to help them function effectively within their com-

◆ **TABLE 32-2**
Basic Nursing Interventions: Chronic Mental Illness

Nursing Interventions	Rationale
Relating to risk of danger	
Assess risk for harm to self or others.	Ensure safety and prevent violence.
Encourage client to notify staff when feeling angry/when destructive thoughts begin.	Helps prevent violence before it actually occurs.
Frequently orient client to reality in nonthreatening way.	Reduces risk of violence, decreases client anxiety.
Sensory/perceptual alterations	
Assess for delusions and hallucinations.	Helps to determine the level of psychosis.
Ask client to share the meaning of his/her hallucinations, delusions.	To determine client's point of view and intent.
Teach client distraction techniques, such as whistling, clapping hands, telling hallucination to go away when hallucinating.	Offers client strategies for controlling hallucinations.
Activities of daily living	
Establish a schedule for grooming, eating, sleeping.	Increases self-esteem, encourages responsibility, and helps client appear more socially acceptable.
Monitor intake, output, personal hygiene activities.	
Communication	
Use active listening; establish trust; encourage conversation; praise attempts to speak clearly and effectively.	Helps to assess client's communication style and patterns; increases understanding of and respect for client.
Social skills	
Encourage good social skills, such as table manners, personal grooming, appropriate communications, behaviors.	Promotes client's acceptability by other persons; increases self-esteem; helps to teach effective social behaviors.

Modified from Fortinash KM, Holoday-Worret PA: *Psychiatric-mental health nursing,* St Louis, 1996, Mosby.

munities, but many services are unavailable due to unstable sources of funding. Community mental health centers with strong financial bases are able to provide their clients with such services as medical care, medication supervision, individual and family therapy, crisis intervention services, family support services, skills training, and vocational counseling or training in addition to continued emotional support and encouragement. With the long-term support, many individuals with severe mental illness and their families are able to effectively cope with the numerous problems associated with their disorders.

A Look to the Future

As you have read throughout this text, all areas of human functioning are deeply interwoven. Physical illnesses or conditions are always accompanied by some level of emotional, intellectual, social, and spiritual distress and the opposite is also true. Therefore

"psychiatric" or "mental health" nursing is a critical component of *every* nursing situation. Caring for the physical body is not enough. For high levels of wellness and adaptation, the whole individual, every aspect of the dynamic being we call "the client," must be considered with *every* therapeutic action.

The professions of providing health care and nursing care are undergoing change. Clients who were once isolated from the mainstream and treated by specialists are now a part of the general patient population. Because mental distress or illness affects every aspect of a person's life, the care needs of individuals with acute and chronic mental health problems are many.

Although several issues affecting mental health policies in the United States and elsewhere are being explored, too few resources are available for treating the numerous individuals who require therapeutic care. As a result, nurses and other health care providers must consider every interaction with their

Assessment

History: Tom is a 34-year-old man with a history of at least 11 admissions to psychiatric units of various general hospitals. Today, he is being readmitted after he was found wandering the streets arguing with himself and threatening to kill himself or someone else if they "didn't stop calling me names." He was medicated with 1 mg of haloperidol (Haldol) intramuscularly in the emergency room.

Current Findings: An unkempt man with a strong body odor and soiled clothing; speech is slow and disjointed; responds verbally without external stimuli. Emotional state (affect) is flat except for verbal responses to hallucinations. Tom states that he is and has been hallucinating for the past 3 days. The hallucinations are auditory; the voices want Tom to kill himself. He thinks they may be right because during the time he is in the community, he is forced to spy on other people for the FBI and he would rather not be so nosy. When asked what made him take to the streets, Tom replied that he thought he could "outwalk the out talk." He has not taken his prescribed medications since he last saw his therapist about 3 weeks ago.

Nursing Diagnosis

Sensory/perceptual alterations, related to impaired perceptions

Planning/Expected Outcomes

Tom will seek out a staff member when he begins to hallucinate. Tom will not harm himself or others. Tom will report the absence of auditory hallucinations by June 23.

Nursing Interventions

Intervention

1. Orient Tom frequently to place, time, current activity.
2. Speak slowly; use clear, simple messages.
3. Reassure often that he will not be harmed by the voices or other people.
4. Listen to and accept descriptions of his feelings, hallucinations.
5. Set limits on aggressive behaviors; contract with Tom for a no-harm contract.
6. Encourage Tom to take his medications; make copy of the daily medication schedule and encourage Tom to follow it.

Rationale

1. Presents reality; reminds Tom of this reality.
2. Helps to increase Tom's understanding, thus decreasing his anxiety.
3. Helps Tom to trust the safety of his environment; presents reality as safe.
4. Conveys respect and acceptance of the person and encourages communication.
5. Promotes a safe environment for all clients and staff; helps Tom to be responsible for his own behaviors.
6. Medications help to control psychotic symptoms, reduce anxiety, improve functioning; developing a daily medication routine in the hospital helps increase compliance after discharge.

Evaluation

After the fourth day of hospitalization, Tom sought out staff members when he was beginning to hallucinate. With the exception of one acting-out episode on April 30, Tom abided by his no-harm contract. Reports of hallucinations have decreased from "continually" on admission to once or twice a week by June 22.

clients as an opportunity for encouraging high levels of mental health. If we are to make progress with the social problems of crime, violence, abuse, homelessness, and poverty, we must treat each mentally troubled person as our most important client because the mental health of a society depends on the mental health of each of its individual citizens.

❖ KEY CONCEPTS

- Most chronic mental health problems are characterized by periods of exacerbations and remissions.
- Chronic mental disorders are disabling for people in every society and culture.
- Many chronically mentally ill individuals are homeless, hungry, and unable to care for themselves.
- Access to comprehensive mental health care remains a problem in the United States today.
- Each person's experiences with mental illness are unique.
- Chronic mental health problems can begin at any stage in life, but they are often not noticed until early or middle adulthood.
- The social epidemic of violence, crack cocaine, and other drug use has resulted in a new group of primary care providers: grandparents who must raise a second family, their grandchildren.
- Substance abuse and mental illness result in an interactive process that is seen in physical, psychological, and behavioral patterns uniquely different from those of persons with only an addiction or serious mental illness.
- Psychiatric rehabilitation is a multidisciplinary treatment approach that focuses on assisting individuals with serious mental illness to effectively cope with their life situations.
- The basic goals for chronically disordered mental health clients are to achieve stabilization and maintain individuals at their highest level of daily functioning.
- Persons with chronic mental disorders are treated with a variety of medications depending on symptoms and distress levels.
- Nurses focus on helping the chronically mentally ill client cope with each activity of daily living.
- Once returned into the community, the chronically mentally ill require aftercare or rehabilitation services.
- Because all areas of human functioning are deeply interwoven, mental health nursing is a critical component of every nursing situation.
- The mental health of a society depends on the mental health of each of its individual citizens.

❖ SUGGESTIONS FOR FURTHER READING

The popular magazine *USA Today*, March 1994 (122[2586]: 26-30), offers an excellent appraisal of the problems of many chronically mentally ill people in the article titled "Outcasts on Main Street: Homelessness and the Mentally Ill."

❖ REFERENCES

Clement JA, Williams EB, Waters C: The client with substance abuse/mental illness: mandate for collaboration, *Arch Psychiatr Nurs* 7(4):189, 1993.

Clunn P: *Child psychiatric nursing,* St Louis, 1991, Mosby.

Cook JA and others: HIV-risk assessment for psychiatric rehabilitation clientele: implications for community-based services, *Psychosoc Rehabil J* 17(4):105, 1994.

Fifer SK and others: Untreated anxiety among adult primary care patients in a health maintenance organization, *Arch Gen Psychiatry* 51:740, 1995.

Fortinash KM, Holoday-Worret PA: *Psychiatric-mental health nursing,* St Louis, 1996, Mosby.

Foster CD, Siegel MA, Landes A: *Health—a concern for every American,* ed 7, Wylie, TX, 1995, Information Plus.

Goldston DB and others: Suicide ideation and suicide attempts among youth with insulin-dependent diabetes mellitus, *J Am Acad Child Adolesc Psychiatry* 33:240, 1994.

Hatfield AB, Lefley HP: *Surviving mental illness: stress, coping, and adaptation,* New York, 1993, Guilford Press.

Hogarth CR: *Adolescent psychiatric nursing,* St Louis, 1991, Mosby.

Katz RC, Watts C, Santman J: AIDS knowledge and high-risk behaviors in the chronic mentally ill, *Community Ment Health* 30:395, 1994.

Kessler RC and others: Lifetime and 12-month prevalence of DSM-III-R psychiatric disorders in the United States: results from the national comorbidity study, *Arch Gen Psychiatry* 51:8, 1995.

Livingston M and others: Psychiatric status and 9-year mortality data in the New Haven epidemiological catchment area study, *Am J Psychiatry* 151(5):716, 1994.

National Advisory Mental Health Council: Health care reform for Americans with severe mental illness: report of the National Advisory Mental Health Council, *Am J Psychiatry* 150:1447, 1993.

Ormel J and others: Common mental disorders and disability across cultures, *JAMA* 272(22):1741, 1994.

Quiram J, Blair C, Jacobs N: *Homelessness in America: how could it happen here?,* ed 4, Wylie, TX, 1995, Information Plus.

President's Commission on Mental Health: *Report to the president,* Washington, DC, 1978, US Government Printing Office.

Stays shrink at psychiatric hospitals as cost-cutting reshapes the industry, *Wall Street J* 349(44):1, 1994.

The price of paying less, *Harvard Ment Health Lett* 11(6):1, 1994.

Torrey EF: The mental health mess, *Natl Rev* 44(25):22, 1992.

33

CHALLENGES FOR THE FUTURE

1. Discuss three challenges that nurses and other health care providers face in delivering mental health care in the United States.

2. Explain the purpose of the Americans with Disabilities Act of 1990.

3. Describe a typical "old" and "new" homeless person.

4. Explain what is meant by "the right to self-determination."

5. Identify three obligations of the therapeutic partnership for the client and the nurse.

6. List three expanded roles for nurses who care for mentally ill people.

7. Describe two challenges involved with the change process.

8. State two techniques for coping with information overload.

9. Discuss the role of mental health care providers in caring for clients with HIV/AIDS.

KEY TERMS

change
competent
entrepreneur

homelessness
information overload
nurse case managers

psychosocial rehabilitation

The need for mental health applies to us all. Every person experiences periods of emotional turmoil and crises in life, and at some time we all need a little assistance to help us cope. Illness of any kind and its resultant treatments usually produce emotional stresses ranging from indifference to crisis behaviors.

With this thought in mind, every person for whom nurses care becomes a mental health client in some way because an emotional reaction always follows a physical diagnosis, uncomfortable procedure, or day spent in the role of patient. Nurses help to provide the nurturing that *all* clients need (not just those with mental illnesses); but nurses, like other health care professionals, are challenged to provide that care within an ever-changing health care delivery environment.

Changes in Mental Health Care

Health care is undergoing many changes today. Escalating costs in several countries are forcing officials to take a close look at where and how health care funds are spent. In the United States, new patterns of providing health care services are emerging as preferred provider and health maintenance organizations. Social changes such as an aging population, an overburdened welfare system, and a cost-conscious U.S. Congress are exerting their influences on today's health care system.

The influence of many cultures and new technology is changing the way we look at health and illness. Today, clients may not even speak the same language. Technological advances are opening new areas of exploration, and discoveries about the biochemical nature of humans are challenging the very foundations of our thinking.

The treatment and prevention of mental illness (and other health issues) are caught up in the web of change. As a result, nurses and all health care providers will be challenged to deliver effective, cost-accountable care, which will call for creativity and innovation. In this climate, change is a certainty and adaptability is a key.

Change in Settings

Until recently, most psychiatric nursing was limited to the inpatient setting, either a unit at the local community hospital or a long-term care institution. Today, however, most institutions are closed, many inpatient psychiatric units are full, and emergency rooms are becoming havens for those experiencing crisis (Hoff, 1994).

When the large state mental health institutions began to discharge their clients, it was argued that most people "*could* live in the community *if* they continued to receive medication and other aftercare" (Torrey, 1992). Changes in the system that once supported the mentally ill are now moving them into community health care systems, and the "aftercare" that was promised is commonly not provided. Fig. 33-1 illustrates the decrease in mental health clients hospitalized since deinstitutionalization began.

As a result of the unsupported release, many mentally troubled persons became sick again and eventually homeless. The seriously mentally ill now constitute more than one third of the homeless population (Torrey, 1992). Jails and prisons have evolved into holding facilities for people with mental problems. Many of the mentally ill are jailed just to get them off the streets, and many more are found living at the fringes of society, sleeping in abandoned buildings, and depending on the generosity of others for food and clothing.

The treatment settings for people with any type of mental illness have changed to follow the clients from the institution to the street, jail, neighborhood clinic,

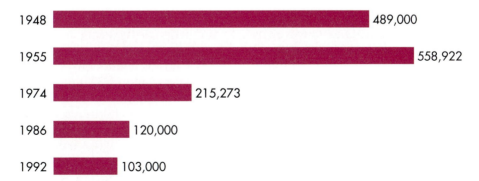

Fig. 33-1 Numbers of mental patients hospitalized between 1948 and 1992. (Redrawn from Keltner NL and others: *Psychiatric nursing,* ed 2, St Louis, 1995, Mosby.)

or local doctor's office. Mental health care is an important component of overall health, and it must be addressed if we are to become capable, adaptable, and functional people. Health care providers must become skilled in assessing and working with clients suffering from mental or emotional disorders, no matter where the setting or what the situation.

Homelessness

Many families function just "one paycheck away from poverty." These families can financially cope for the present; but add one stressor, and the whole situation is threatened. It is not uncommon to hear of the working-class family whose father was laid off his job. If work is not found soon, the family becomes unable to make the mortgage payments and is eventually forced out of their home onto the streets. Sad as it seems, this scenario has become a reality for many families, as well as single people and teenagers.

Homelessness means to be without a permanent residence, a place to live. Homelessness means to have every possession you own stuffed into the back of the car (if you are lucky enough to own a car); homelessness means your children cannot attend school because they have no permanent address, no phone number, and usually no immunization records.

Traditionally, homeless people (1930s through 1970s) were white male adults with an average age of 50. They were usually unmarried, intermittently employed, and without a permanent residence. However, they seldom actually slept in the streets because of the availability of cheap hotels, missions, and flop houses. A study of Chicago's homeless population in the late 1950s revealed that "25% of the homeless people were on Social Security (and trying to live inexpensively), 25% were chronic alcoholics, 20% had a physical disability, 20% had a chronic mental illness, and 10% were maladjusted" (Kiesler, 1991). These men are the "old homeless," the traditionally less fortunate members of society.

During the 1960s and 1970s, the number of homeless people declined in the United States; however, by the early 1980s, a growing number of the "new homeless" began to appear, and that number has rapidly increased ever since. Today's homeless people are young and much poorer than their counterparts of yesterday and have no actual shelter, much less a home. The numbers of women, children, and minorities have swelled the ranks of the homeless to significant numbers (Federal Task Force on Homelessness and Severe Mental Illness, 1994). It is not uncommon now for entire families to be without a home.

Loss of control over the daily events of their own lives leads homeless people toward a loss of self-

worth, learned helplessness, and depression. Children who are homeless for any length of time experience serious threats to their current well-being and their future ability to succeed. Problems affecting homeless children include hunger, poor nutrition, numerous illnesses, developmental delays, poor educational opportunities, anxiety, depression, and behavioral difficulties (Rafferty and Shinn, 1991).

The health status of the homeless, both mental and physical, is poor, and the average age of death for a homeless person in the United States is about 50 (Kiesler, 1991). About one third of today's homeless are mentally ill. Many of these people were relatively adjusted when they were discharged from an institution, but when the medications ran out and the aftercare was not provided, their psychiatric problems returned. Without adequate support, resources, and encouragement, many of the chronically mentally ill find it almost impossible to take steps to improve their lives.

Homelessness has become a national tragedy that in some way affects us all. Most nurses will provide nursing care for many homeless clients because, when people cannot find health care for the smaller problems, they wait until their problems demand immediate attention. This practice brings about a high incidence of severe disorders. The trauma of losing one's home, adjusting to life in a shelter or on the street, and struggling for a way out produces symptoms of psychological and emotional distress. Stress disorders are not uncommon among the homeless, even those with previously high levels of functioning.

The children of this subsociety endure hardships that most of us can only imagine. Low-birth-weight babies and infant illness are common. Studies of homeless women in New York City revealed that infant mortality is "extraordinarily high: 25 deaths per 1000 live births among the homeless women compared with 17 per 1000 for housed poor women and 12 per 1000 for women citywide" (Rafferty and Shinn, 1991).

If the children survive infancy, they can look forward to double the incidence of respiratory infections and skin ailments, as well as the usual childhood diseases. Parasitic infestations, such as lice or crabs, occur in homeless children 35 times more frequently than in the general population (Rafferty and Shinn, 1991).

Few homeless children are immunized, fewer are educated, and many live with chronic malnutrition. Developmental delays including short attention spans; immature motor, speech, and interpersonal skills; and inappropriate social behaviors are frequently encountered with homeless children. Poverty, inadequate shelter, lack of access to day care services, and the stresses of having no home contribute to homeless children's lack of development. Childhood is not the happy time of exploration and learning that it should be for homeless children.

Adolescents are also found in greater numbers among the homeless than two decades ago. "Each year about 1.5 million youth aged 10 to 17 are homeless" (Corsini, 1994). Many of these are the children of dysfunctional families who are frequently neglected, abused, and exploited. Homeless adolescents are at a much greater risk for hepatitis, AIDS, and other sexually transmitted diseases. In addition, life on the streets leads to high rates of depression and frequent suicidal attempts. The future holds little promise for a teen without hopes, aspirations, or emotional support.

Adults with chronic mental illness constitute about one third of the homeless population (Dennis and others, 1991). Because of their illness, the ability to function in daily life is severely limited. Self-care activities, interpersonal relationships, and the ability to work or attend school are compromised for mentally troubled individuals. Usually, financial resources are very limited, and many of the rooming houses that once provided inexpensive shelter have been converted to other uses or destroyed. Publicly financed housing, especially for the mentally ill, is almost unattainable. Add to that a lack of community mental health services, and one can understand why a large number of people with chronic mental illnesses are now wandering the streets of both large and small communities.

When research was conducted to compare the mentally ill homeless with non–mentally ill homeless, people with severe mental illnesses were similar to their counterparts in age, ethnicity, sex, and extent of substance abuse. However, the homeless mentally ill were in poorer health, were homeless for longer periods of time, had to struggle with more barriers to employment, and had less contact with family or friends than the homeless without mental difficulties (Dennis and others, 1991).

The actual number of homeless persons is difficult to determine, but estimates range from less than 1 million to over 7 million. Homelessness is a national health problem that must be solved if we are to save a generation of fellow human beings from the despair of having no future. Health care problems for the homeless are monumental, but they can be addressed. As the providers of health care, we must consider new ways and means of working with this population if we are to protect and encourage the health of all people.

The Americans With Disabilities Act

The Americans With Disabilities Act (ADA) of 1990 is a U.S. federal statute designed to remove the barriers that prevented qualified people with disabilities from having the same employment opportunities that are available to persons without disabilities. The ADA requires employers to make "reasonable accommodation" for disabled individuals, thus allowing them to perform the essential functions of the job.

Under the ADA guidelines, a person is considered disabled when a physical or mental impairment "substantially limits one or more major life activities" (Equal Employment Opportunity Commission, 1992). A mental impairment is defined by the ADA as "any mental or psychological disorder, such as mental retardation, organic brain syndrome, emotional or mental illness, and specified learning abilities." If the condition substantially limits one's functioning, the person is covered by the ADA. Employers can no longer refuse to hire persons solely on the basis of disability and must make reasonable adjustments for the disabled employee (see box below). The implications of this legislation excite and challenge those who work with psychiatric clients.

The intent of the ADA is to tailor the needs of the job with the needs of the disabled individual. However, Congress cannot legislate social change. Only time and successful work experiences with mentally ill employees will remove the stigma of mental illness in the workplace. This is our next challenge: to prepare our clients for gainful employment and, at the same time, convince employers that people with mental disorders can be reliable employees.

Cultural Influences

The world is shrinking. In the past, a person would grow, live, procreate, and die within one community or geographical region. Today, world travelers work in one part of the globe and commute to another area to raise their families. Waves of immigrants move from their homelands in search of a better life, and rapid forms of transportation move thousands of people around the world in a matter of hours instead of days. As more individuals become computer literate and users of the global computer networks, our world

---

THINK ABOUT

You are working as a nurse in a community hospital on the medical-surgical unit. Today, you find that an orderly who has told you that he has a history of mental illness has been assigned to your care team. You have never worked with this person before today.

What is your initial reaction?

How would you go about assigning clients?

Do you think this will affect the activities of the workplace?

will shrink even more. Because of these changes, nurses and other health care providers will be encountering persons from various cultural backgrounds with greater frequency. Learning to interact effectively and respectfully is a challenge that faces all the world's citizens, but for health care workers this is especially important.

The mental disorders or problems of a culture can have a universal quality. There are some behaviors, such as those associated with depression, that all cultures define as mental health disorders. Other mental health problems may be specifically limited to the members of that group. These types of problems are called *culture-bound disorders* because they appear to be related to specific cultures. For the sake of discussion, they are grouped into emotional, paranoid, and disordered consciousness syndromes. For example, the disorder the Hispanics call *susto* is an emotional anxiety that results from "soul loss."

Health, illness, and mental illness are defined differently throughout various cultures. The person who talks to himself may be considered to be "a nut" in one society and revered as a holy man in another. Their behaviors might be exactly the same, but the social context or setting in which they took place differs. Therefore in one society an individual may be in need of treatment, whereas in another he may be the one who performs the treatments. The point is that mental illness is culturally defined to a large extent. To work effectively with clients from other cultures, nurses must discover how *clients* define mental illness.

As displaced individuals adapt to their new cultures, they combine elements of both the home and the host culture into their daily lives. The result is a unique blend of both worlds: "third culture" (Zwerdling, 1994). Bicultural clients require a thorough cultural assessment to discover their individual frames of reference (how they view the world). Only then can therapeutic interventions be planned with the expectation of success. An effective therapy in one culture is not always successful when applied in another culture.

As more and more people emigrate throughout the world, health care providers will encounter many clients whose first language is not English. This presents many challenges, especially when a psychiatric component is involved. Even when the client speaks or understands some English, the stresses of illness (and the complexities of a modern health care system) increase anxiety, and clients often attempt to communicate by reverting back to their native tongue. Many times these communications can be misunderstood and result in poor treatment outcomes. The box above offers an illustration of poor communication. If mental health care providers are to deliver effective care,

CULTURAL ASPECTS

Sam was a white nurse working at a Native American reservation health center. He frequently monitored the physician's chronically ill clients, did his best to educate each of them about their conditions, and provided emotional support to help them cope with their conditions. Why then, he wondered, were all his clients returning with no signs of improvement?

On the suggestion of his physician, a long-term resident on the reservation, Sam began to look at how his behaviors affected his clients. After finding no real answer there, he consulted a tribal elder with his problem. All that he was told was that "the eyes are the window of the soul." This statement perplexed Sam until he realized that he was "staring down" his clients when he was interacting with them. Sam was so intent on putting his client education messages across that he repeatedly missed a nonverbal clue; each of his clients avoided direct eye contact and looked downward when Sam was instructing them. Once he realized that his problem was a culturally based miscommunication, he revised his method of teaching and changed his eye contact behaviors. His clients showed signs of physical improvement and better adaptation to their conditions. Sam had learned a valuable lesson: not all people communicate the same way.

we must be aware of the cultural backgrounds of our clients and develop our plans of care with each client's unique cultural heritage in mind. Caring for culturally diverse clients is another challenge, because our services are only as effective as they are perceived to be by our clients.

Change and Mental Health Clients

Throughout history, mental illnesses have been labeled as being somehow "different" from the physical maladies. People with mental illnesses were obviously not in this reality, so why should they care about how they are treated? This attitude prevailed for many centuries; consequently, persons with mental illnesses were neglected, abused, and confined without hope of improvement.

As new psychiatric theories arose, attitudes toward the mentally ill changed, but individuals were still viewed as culprits or victims who somehow caused their own problems. During this time, the role of the patient was to be a passive recipient of care. Therapies were designed and delivered without regard to appropriateness, whereas patients were expected to quietly cooperate. Relationships between clients and care providers ranged from patronizing to adversarial.

Today, both the providers and consumers of mental health care are striving to change attitudes and practices. Involving clients in treatment means every party must assume an active role. This interaction involves the building of trust, mutual respect, and acceptance.

Changes in Nursing

The profession of nursing has undergone many changes in the past 20 years. The "handmaiden to the physician" model has been replaced by the role of a professional, with all its accompanying rights and obligations. Nurses of today are considered to be experts in the area of assisting people to cope with the impact of health problems on everyday living. Nurses are guided by state nurse practice acts and the profession's standards of care. Appendix A offers a description of psychiatric nursing standards. Nurses participate fully as members of the treatment team. They also provide education for clients and their significant others and coordinate the activities of various support agencies. Nurses' roles are continuing to evolve, and the challenge every nurse must face is to grow with change.

Empowerment of Client

The traditional role of client was passive. Clients were expected to accept the physician's diagnosis, therapies, and comments without question. They were expected to be motivated, cooperative, and passive enough to get well. As a result, people became increasingly detached from the responsibility for their own health care and discontented with the system that delivered that care.

Today, people are becoming more responsible and active consumers of health care, but many health care services remain tied to the old models of the passive client. Individuals entering the health care system are beginning to seek out information about their conditions, weigh the pros and cons of each treatment option, and select the ones that best suit them. Because the consumer's role has moved from a passive to an active one, the term *client* becomes more appropriate than the passively connoted term *patient*. Hopefully, the relationship between care providers and client develops into a dynamic interchange, with therapeutic goals that are mutually acceptable. This therapeutic partnership, however, involves responsibility.

Obligations of Client

To receive the most effective care, clients must fulfill certain obligations. These responsibilities are few, but they are important for success of treatment. First,

clients must be truthful. Many times people are uncomfortable about sharing personal information. They may expect health care providers to pass judgment on their actions or refuse care. Nevertheless, honest, complete data are essential for planning care. Second, clients have an obligation to be responsible for their own behaviors. Even people who periodically lose contact with reality are capable of assuming some responsibility. Third, clients have an obligation to cooperate with treatment; that is, assuming clients *want* to "get well." Consumers of mental health services who are willing to assume the obligations of truthfulness, responsibility, and cooperation can play an active role in successful diagnosis and treatment of their problems.

Obligations of Care Providers

As clients assume certain obligations, so do the mental health care providers who work with them. From the psychiatrist to the technician, each assumes specific responsibilities when working with clients. However, all providers of mental health care have the obligation to perform the following four steps.

First and most important, accept the client "as is." Nurses do not have to like or approve of any behavior, but the *person* must be accepted as a worthy human being, capable of change. Do not pass judgment. We are here to help, not to conjure up emotionally based opinions.

Second, demonstrate respect for clients. Refer to clients by name. Ask permission before entering their space, if necessary. Show approval for gains made in therapy. Express concern for their well-being, and remember to be polite. All these behaviors demonstrate respect for clients much more clearly than words. Even the most ill person responds to respectful care.

Third, empower clients. Much mental illness is associated with feelings of lack of control. Care providers who recognize this can provide small but frequent opportunities for decision making and success. As clients choose among various options, they are exercising some control over their environment. Decisions gradually move from making choices to solving problems. During the process, each success provides encouragement for the next step.

Fourth, mental health professionals, especially nurses and therapists who work closely with clients, have the added obligation to provide educational opportunities—in short, to teach. Unless clients are comatose, they are capable of learning. New knowledge empowers people to change. Empowered clients are more willing to explore and change their behaviors. Table 33-1 summarizes the obligations of the therapeutic partnership.

◆ **TABLE 33-1**
Obligations of the Therapeutic Partnership

Clients	Care Providers
To be truthful	To accept the client as a person capable of change
To be responsible for one's own behaviors	To demonstrate respect and acceptance of the person
To cooperate with treatment	To empower clients

Studies have demonstrated that clients who feel they have some control over their situation report fewer symptoms and less pain. They have speedier recoveries and are able to participate in the activities of daily living earlier than clients who perceive little or no control (Weaver and Wilson, 1994). In short, clients need to be active participants in their own care.

Competency

Are people with mental illness capable of making decisions about proper care and treatment of their problems? Health care providers are often challenged to provide the answers to these complex questions.

To be considered **competent,** an individual must be (1) able to make a choice, (2) understand important information, (3) appreciate one's own situation, and (4) apply reasoning. Results of a study at the University of Massachusetts Medical Center in Worcester revealed that "mental illness often coexists with competent decision making, but many hospitalized patients—up to one half of those suffering from schizophrenia and one quarter of those with major depression—show seriously impaired judgement" (Bower, 1995). Hospitalized clients with severe symptoms, such as paranoia or disorganized thought, scored the lowest for each measure of competency. About one half of schizophrenic clients performed well on all measures, and three fourths of clients with depression were found to be competent. Perhaps those who work with mentally troubled clients could apply the four measures of competence described in the study and develop a tool for assessing a client's decision-making abilities. It may help solve the dilemma of discerning which clients can make reasonable treatment decisions.

The challenge of meeting the human needs of clients without violating their rights is especially true for clients with mental health problems. When people were discharged from institutions into their "least restrictive environments," their rights to freedom, autonomy, and self-determination were protected. However, the concept of the least restrictive setting begins to break down when clients are unable to provide the essentials of daily living for themselves and are in need of treatment.

Individuals are not exercising their rights to freedom when they wander the streets aimlessly, out of touch with reality. They are usually able to determine little for themselves and have virtually no ability to self-direct their lives (Wilk, 1994). In these cases, an institutional setting may prove to be appropriate.

To implement the concept of the least restrictive treatment environment, nurses must be able to assess the available community resources in addition to the unique needs and limitations of each client. The linking of mentally troubled clients with few community resources is, and will remain, a challenge for us all.

Providers of Care

Membership in the health care profession is also changing. Once only doctors, nurses, and family members provided mental health care. Today, assorted technicians, assistants, and aides provide many services that were once exclusively within the realm of psychiatry. As each technician works within a narrow specialty, it becomes the nurse's responsibility to ensure that safe, coordinated health care is being delivered to clients.

The services of nursing assistants are just as important in the mental health setting as they are in the hospital setting. Certified nursing assistants (CNAs) have been employed in psychiatric institutions for many years, helping nurses with client care and treatments. Recently, however, their role has expanded into the community, where they have met with great success.

To illustrate, the Supportive Homemaker Program of Haverhill, Massachusetts (Holland, 1993) employs mental health supportive home care aides (HCAs) to provide emotional and social support for clients in their homes. The program is designed to serve several populations: children who are at risk for abuse or neglect, those people who lack family or social support, the depressed, the severely ill, and the senile elderly.

Potential supportive HCAs are carefully screened because the success of the program depends on their abilities. Those who demonstrate an acceptance of others, compassion, cultural awareness, patience, and a gentle sense of humor are selected. Once a modest training period is completed, each HCA is assigned a caseload and a psychiatric nurse coordinator who provides support and guidance.

Through frequent visits, the HCA establishes a relationship with each client. Because they are nonthreatening, nonjudgmental, and represent no authority or power, supportive HCAs succeed where others have failed. Their energy provides a reliable relationship, which helps to ease the anxiety and apprehension of being alone or unable to cope.

The main function of supportive HCAs is to act as helping individuals. These responsibilities include providing homemaker services, transportation, and instruction. Skills in the daily activities of living, home management, and even self-care are taught and reinforced on subsequent visits. The importance of good nutrition and medical care for children is stressed. If needed, clients are instructed on ways to obtain food, clothing, shelter, and education.

Supportive HCAs encourage clients to use the services of appropriate community resources. They act as advocates by instructing clients about how the service can help, assisting them in making contact with the service, and even providing transportation for appointments. The success of these mental health care providers lies not with their academic or political prowess, but with one fundamental thought: they are there "simply to help, to make things better, and to care" (Holland, 1993).

Other providers of care for mentally troubled people are the psychiatric technicians who are formally trained to provide mental health care in both inpatient and outpatient settings. "Psych techs" were once commonly employed in large state institutions, but as clients were discharged into the community, their numbers became smaller. Today, psychiatric technicians can be found in practice settings ranging from community mental health centers to prisons. As mental health care moves into the community, larger numbers of care providers will be needed.

Expanded Roles for Nurses

As mental health care moves into the community, new roles are opening up for nurses. Hospitals no longer employ the majority of nurses because attempts to control costs have also affected the numbers of nurses per institution. Clients are being discharged from acute care facilities earlier and now require nursing services in their homes and communities. Nurses help people to adjust to and cope with the changes in daily living that result from their illness or condition. Nurses practice in a number of challenging new settings. For example, nurses play a vital role in centers for the homeless. A day treatment center for the homeless chronically mentally ill operates in Manhattan, New York (Foster, 1992). The treatment team of clinicians, social workers, a nurse, and a psychiatrist assesses each client for medical, psychiatric, and social service needs. Clients are referred to the appropriate clinical services for treatment and therapy. The most common psychiatric problems seen in this homeless center are paranoid schizophrenia, manic depressive (bipolar) illness, and chronic substance dependency.

The role of the nurse in this treatment center is "one of facilitator/advocate who assists clients in gaining access to services" (Foster, 1992). The nurse commonly performs unconventional nursing tasks and must be flexible with treatment plans. Collaboration with the multidisciplinary treatment team and numerous community agencies assists the nurse in referring clients to various resources.

The nurse at the Manhattan treatment center is an advocate for clients by making sure that each client is clean and acceptable when requesting services through various agencies. Shower and laundry facilities, as well as personal care items (e.g., combs, razors, soaps, deodorants, toothbrushes), are available at the treatment center. Other tasks performed by the nurse include rescheduling missed appointments, assisting clients in filling out applications for services or employment interviews, clarifying instructions, and monitoring clients' physical and mental changes.

Preventive health care is another main responsibility of the treatment center's nurse. Routine screening for weight, hypertension, and response to medications allows the nurse many opportunities to instruct clients about more healthful living activities. Weekly lectures and discussions about proper nutrition, sexually transmitted diseases, and current health issues are planned and conducted by the nurse. Support groups for various clients are available. Realistic goals are set to encourage clients to commit to meeting their needs, and much support by all members of the staff helps clients to regain their self-esteem (see the box on p. 468 for a case study). With the homeless mentally ill, successful outcomes are few, but the personal rewards and professional satisfactions are many.

Nurses also collaborate with physicians to plan and implement programs for people with serious mental illness. One such program employs only nurses as case managers because nurses "not only value continuity of care, but are also knowledgeable and comfortable with medication management" (Nehls and others, 1992). **Nurse case managers** work with psychiatrists to develop treatment plans tailored to each client's special needs. Clients are encouraged to share their concerns with their nurse case manager, who evaluates the need for psychiatric consultation.

A 30-year-old man presents to the treatment center complaining of overwhelming feelings of agitation and hostility. During the nurse's initial assessment, the client reveals that he has not been taking his psychotherapeutic medications because they make him too drowsy. "So, this is not an uncommon complaint," the nurse thinks; but on further questioning, the nurse discovers that the client becomes vulnerable to street predators when he sleeps after taking his medication. In fact, the client reveals that he has often been mugged and beaten while sleeping in subways.

On the nurse's request, the client's medications were adjusted. The client agreed to come to the center for daily administration and monitoring. After a few months, his behavior changes were so remarkable that he was able to become reunited with his family. He continues to visit the treatment center daily for support and evaluation.

Clinical Decisions

1. What changes did this nurse make in the client's life?
2. How can Maslow's hierarchy of needs be applied to this case?

Nurses and psychiatrists meet weekly for discussions and decisions about each client's medications, therapies, and referrals.

Nurses in this setting provide intake assessments and referral services, initial and ongoing medication services, supportive counseling by telephone or routine visits with clients, individual and group education, and advocacy for clients interacting with family, the legal system, or other parts of the health care system. Because of the nurse case manager's support and guidance, clients with severe mental illnesses are able to function more adequately within their community, and costly and unnecessary psychiatric consultations are reduced. The nurse-physician collaborative practice model may prove to be one solution to the challenge of delivering mental health care to clients within their home environments.

Psychosocial rehabilitation is another area in which nurses are expanding their roles. Evolving as a social model of treatment rather than a medical model, psychosocial rehabilitation is a way of assisting people with mental health problems to readjust and adapt to life in the community. In these settings, nurses are able to use their full range of skills without the focus being placed on illness or disability. Wellness, wholeness, and the abilities of the individual are emphasized. Vocational, educational, residential, social, and personal adjustment services are offered through psychosocial rehabilitation programs. Clients are encouraged to exercise freedom of choice and become consciously self-directed. Individual care plans, called personal service plans, are developed but controlled by clients who identify the goals that are important to them. Resources and support people are chosen by clients with guidance from the treatment team (referred to as a service delivery team).

Self-help is a fundamental concept of psychosocial rehabilitation. Nurses offer social and vocational coaching, but clients must act for themselves. The belief that all people have the inherent capacity for change and the focus on what the client *can* do have resulted in some remarkable successes. Nurses who practice within these settings truly "work with persons in their environment to maximize wellness" (Thompson and Strand, 1994).

As health care moves into the community, the need for mental health clinical nurse specialists will continue to grow. The role of these nurses is to address "the physical and mental health needs of the chronically mentally ill in the community as well as those . . . clients and family dealing with psychosocial crisis" (Mellon, 1993). Mental health home care nurses focus on prevention and wellness care, collaborate with other professionals, and serve as the client's advocate within the mental health delivery system. Clients who are facing the crises of illness are assisted by mental health home care nurses with both their physical and emotional difficulties. Because they are able to intervene during the early stages of dysfunction, the services of mental health home care nurses are proving to be successful as well as cost effective.

One of the most exciting expanded roles for nurses is that of **entrepreneur** or self-employed nurse. Today, nurses are establishing their own nurse-operated clinics, acting as health care consultants, and working to provide a variety of health care services to business and industry. For example, a residential program for mentally troubled clients was created, implemented, and administered by two nurses who were frustrated in their efforts to locate suitable housing for their clients with severe mental illnesses (Dibner and Murphy, 1991). Mental health care nurses are now involved in businesses that provide services for adults, children, employees, organizations, and public and government agencies. Nurses are accepting the challenge to seek out and create innovative models for the delivery of mental health care services to special populations.

Managing Change

The only thing that one can be sure of is change. Because life is a dynamic process, no living thing remains unaffected. Seasons, plants, people, and processes all change. Nurses must keep pace with continual changes in health care, new therapies, theories, medications, and more. Therefore it is important to understand change and how to successfully cope and adapt.

Change is defined as the process of making or becoming different. Change itself is neither inherently good nor bad. It is the reactions of the people involved in the process that tend to label or judge a situation.

People resist change because it implies uncertainty, and uncertainty brings about a disturbance in the status quo. Because human beings exist in a state of dynamic balance, we all resist change to some extent to maintain our equilibrium and keep things "the way they are." People resist change for several reasons. Although major problems may be present in the current situation, they are known and comfortable. Change brings about discomfort when the status quo is disrupted. Individuals may feel that their self-interests are threatened. They may have inaccurate perceptions about the nature or implications of the changes or become so threatened that they begin to use psychological defense mechanisms to defend their viewpoints. Some people offer resistance to change because they truly believe the changes will not be beneficial. Dealing effectively with change requires a period of transition and psychological adaptation. Understanding the change process will help both nurses and clients adapt to the continuing process of change.

Change Process

There are two basic types of change: planned change and unplanned change (Morrison, 1993). *Planned change* is always the ideal but seldom the reality. It is the deliberate effort to make things different within a system. Changes are carefully planned and implemented slowly and deliberately. When done appropriately, planned change meets with minimal hostility and resistance.

"Expect the unexpected" is not a frivolous statement. *Unplanned change* is unexpected, not antici-

pated, and usually not desired. Change happens whether it is planned or unexpected. In health care settings, unplanned changes are daily occurrences.

Mental health care providers must be especially adept at coping with unexpected changes. Whether change is unanticipated or expected, intense reactions are provoked in some people. Although reactions to change are highly individual and can range from simple acceptance to outright hostility, most reactions can be generalized into three categories: anxiety, mistrust, and loss. All these reactions have effects on mental health clients.

When the comfort of a daily routine is lost, people (especially those with mental health problems) become anxious. Planned changes for these clients must be implemented slowly, in small steps, giving time for adjustment. Unexpected change, however, does not allow for this luxury, and anxiety levels increase.

Mistrust develops when people are unclear about what is happening. Once individuals feel threatened, resistance develops, and an "us vs. them" attitude evolves. To keep mistrust at a minimum, maintain open communications with all those involved in the change. Listen to everyone's concerns and provide what information you can.

Any change involves loss and some discomfort. Feelings of loss are encountered when one gives up old, comfortable attitudes or behaviors. Phrases such as "in the old days" or "the way we used to do it" are expressions associated with loss. Replacing loss with hope by focusing on possible benefits helps people to cope with change, especially if it is unexpected (Manion, 1995). Hints for coping with unplanned changes are offered in Table 33-2. Change affects us all, but adaptability, healthy emotional responses, and a willingness to support ourselves and others go a long way toward meeting the challenge of coping successfully with changes in our busy world of today.

Information Overload

No one person can keep up with all the new knowledge constantly being generated. **Information overload** is a state of mind in which so many facts have been absorbed that they all become an unrelated jumble of stored information. Perhaps you have experienced this, say, before an important examination.

It is easy to become overwhelmed with information today. More information has become available to the average citizen of today's world than most great scholars had even 20 years ago. In addition, the megacommunications systems of tomorrow offer opportunities for an even greater availability of information. Clients are becoming more informed, and sometimes their information contains inaccuracies or half-truths.

◆ **TABLE 33-2**
Coping With Unplanned Changes

Nursing Action	Comments
Do not panic	Remain calm no matter what happens.
	Keep your own reactions under control by staying in the "thinking" mode.
	Remember decisions made during high stress are more likely to be ineffective. Stay cool.
Analyze the situation	Define the problems that are occurring as a result of the change.
	Assess why the change is happening now and consider its possible effects.
	Assess resources and limitations.
Reset priorities	Determine what needs to be done.
	List needs in order of importance and then communicate and act.
Match resources with priorities	Match what needs to be done with the best available resource.
	Resources are always limited. Do the best you can with what you have.
Continuously evaluate	This step is even more important when the change is unplanned.
	Monitor individuals and groups as they progress through the change process.
	Monitor the situation's dynamics.
	Be prepared for the possibility of other changes.

Health care providers have the responsibility to be accurately informed and knowledgeable about the health care information each client is receiving.

"But how do I cope with the bombardment of information?" you wonder. Learn something new every day. We cannot be expected to move through our daily activities and spend our remaining hours pondering over the latest facts or theories, but we can commit ourselves to making the effort to discover something we did not know this morning. Strive to learn at least one new piece of information a day. By the end of a year, you will have gained much new knowledge.

Be open to new information. Some things that sound silly in one time period become reality in another. People said in the 1950s that man would never walk on the moon. Now their children take space travel for granted. Do not discard data that does not fit into your way of thinking. Keep it tucked away; sooner or later it will prove itself to be accurate or false.

Learn to think critically. Use logical thinking and the problem-solving process to practice critical thinking skills. Maintain an open mind and a questioning attitude. Realize that knowing how to critically question and relate information is more important than having many facts at hand. This is one of our greatest challenges.

Other Challenges

Life today is filled with a myriad of personal, professional, and social challenges. Personally, we are con-
stantly challenged to move calmly through the struggles of everyday living. Professionally, we are charged with all the obligations and responsibilities of the helping professions, not to mention our duty to the people who become our clients. Socially, we are confronted with many complex and interrelated problems.

Challenges to Society

The social order of many countries is being disrupted by change. Third–world countries must cope with the problems of providing the basic necessities of life (food, clothing, shelter) for their citizens. Health care and education are placed lower on the priority list when a country's people are going hungry or without shelter. Add to this various political disputes, and one can see why so many challenges exist in countries throughout the world.

Modern industrial societies usually manage to feed and clothe the majority of their citizens, but numerous social problems remain. Family structures are changing in many societies; this one factor alone spins off new challenges related to child rearing, financial support, role changes, and group interactions. Homeless families are growing, and with homelessness comes the loss of opportunities for appropriate health care and a solid education. Violence is on the upswing because some persons cannot tolerate the stresses of the modern world.

Social problems affecting health care include challenges to immunize children; control the spread of sophisticated new communicable diseases; provide humane care for the ill, infirm, and aged; and educate

MENTAL SIGNS/SYMPTOMS OF HIV INFECTION

- Slowed thinking
- Decreased memory function
- Tiredness, lethargy
- Apathy
- Poor appetite
- Weight loss
- Sleep disturbances
- Confusion
- Agitation
- Dementia

Modified from Knox MD, Clark CF: *AIDS Patient Care* 4 (6):169, 1993.

the population about healthy living practices. Politically, nurses and all people interested in health are challenged to make health care more accessible, delivering primary care in convenient, familiar community settings.

It is an exciting time to be a nurse. Maintain a positive attitude. Do your best and strive to learn; you will turn most of your challenges into opportunities.

Persons With AIDS

Individuals who are infected with the HIV virus and progress to the next stage of the disease are known as "persons with AIDS," PWAs for short. Because of the long incubation period, the changing nature of the virus, and the attitudes of many people, PWAs pose a special challenge for health care providers.

Knox and Clark (1993) make an impassioned plea for early detection of HIV infections. They believe early detection is especially important for those who work with mental health clients because "many HIV-infected patients show signs of central nervous system damage during the course of the infection which may present as a psychiatric illness" (Knox and Clark, 1993). Many infected individuals demonstrate "mental symptoms" before the better known opportunistic infections develop. Clients may have a single complaint or multiple symptoms (see box above). Many of these complaints can be mistaken for depression, so each must be carefully investigated.

Homeless youth and the chronically mentally ill are at an increased risk for contracting HIV. Lack of judgment, and high-risk sexual and substance abuse behaviors make these groups of people especially vulnerable. The incidence of HIV infection is increasing in the 15- to 25-year-old age group, which seems to be related to the lack of accurate information and the "it can't happen to me" syndrome so common to many individuals of that age. Community mental and physical health care providers, especially nurses, must meet the challenge to develop new comprehensive knowledge and skills to serve an ever-increasing population of HIV-positive clients.

Biology or Psychology

The profession of nursing has historically been referred to as an "art and a science." The science component of nursing is evident. Nurses are expected to have a grasp of the anatomy, physiology, and functions of the human being; use the nursing process to identify and solve clients' problems; and collaborate with other care providers to access the most appropriate health care services for each client.

However, there exists an *art* in nursing that is more subtle. This art is rooted in the concept of caring. People who become nurses are motivated by the desire to relieve human suffering. They care enough about the welfare of others to educate themselves and then devote their professional lives to helping individuals and their families with problems.

People remember the nurses who cared for them, who listened, who held their hand, who supported them when times were rough. These are the interventions of caring, the so-called "soft nursing interventions."

Caring is the essence of nursing and the power of our profession (Dossey, 1991). Do not become so involved in the physical aspects of nursing that you forget to nurture the art of caring for people, because scientific evidence is about to lend new support for the actions that make up the art of nursing.

As discussed in earlier chapters, studies in the field of psychoneuroimmunology (PNI) are demonstrating that connections between the mind and body are actually an intricate network that responds as a whole. Emotions are responses of a whole person, complete with physical and psychological reactions.

Certain nursing actions, such as touch, have been found to reduce anxiety levels and may play a role in actually boosting the immune system by decreasing the immunosuppressive effects of stress (Renz, 1994). Other studies have demonstrated that therapeutic touch can decrease pain and promote wound healing (Mackey, 1995). Currently, the U.S. government is funding research into the effects of therapeutic touch on the immune system's response to stress. Nursing's artful interventions are finally receiving scientific attention. We have known all along that caring is a powerful weapon in the search for health and wholeness.

Health-Oriented Framework

A holistic viewpoint considers a person as an entire being, complete with physical, intellectual, social, spiritual, and emotional aspects. Health is defined by the client's criteria for wellness. Nurses emphasize clients' strengths and their abilities to adapt and to change. By working with clients' personal definition of health, nurses focus on clients' goals and try to understand the unique patterns of interaction between each client and his/her complex and changing environment.

Nurses help clients to adjust to the activities of daily living when clients are confronted by health problems. Because of this, nurses are in the position to shift the focus of health care from one that concentrates on "deficits and deficiencies" to one that considers the possibilities and positive achievements that are within the grasp of each client. This health-oriented point of view allows for successful interventions by concentrating on solutions that draw on clients' strengths and supportive resources.

As you can tell, numerous challenges await us. Perhaps one of the greatest will be to bring the caring that typifies nursing into the community and ensure that health care services will be available to every individual. These are your challenges.

❖ KEY CONCEPTS

- Health care is undergoing many changes relating to escalating costs, social changes, and technological advances.

- Treatment settings for people with mental illness have evolved from the institution to the street, jail, neighborhood clinic, community hospital, and local doctor's office.

- The growing number of homeless people challenges all health care providers to meet the many needs of this population.

- The Americans with Disabilities Act of 1990 states that people with mental health problems have the same opportunity for employment as other people.

- Learning to interact respectfully and effectively with people from different cultures is an important challenge for health care workers.

- The role of client has changed from passive participant to active consumer of health care services.

- To be considered competent, an individual must be able to make a choice, understand important information, appreciate one's own situation, and apply reasoning.

- Today's mental health care providers include certified nursing assistants, home care aides, and psychiatric technicians.

- Expanded roles for nurses include positions in centers for the homeless, collaborating with physicians as case managers, working with psychosocial rehabilitation teams, and meeting the needs of special populations through nurse-owned businesses.

- Change, defined as the process of making or becoming different, is neither inherently good nor bad.

- To cope with information overload, develop your critical thinking skills by using logical thinking and the problem-solving process.

- Early detection of HIV infections is especially important because many HIV-infected clients show signs of central nervous system damage which may present as a psychiatric illness.

- Nursing actions such as therapeutic touch have been found to reduce anxiety levels, decrease pain, and promote wound healing, and it may play a role in actually boosting the immune system by decreasing the immunosuppressive effects of stress.

- Nurses are in the position to shift the focus of health care from one that concentrates on "deficits and deficiencies" to one that considers the possibilities and positive achievements that are within the grasp of each client.

❖ SUGGESTIONS FOR FURTHER READING

In the article "Understanding the seven stages of change" (*American Journal of Nursing* 95[4]:41, 1995), Jo Manion states that understanding the stages of change will help you survive and even grow from the change experience.

❖ REFERENCES

Bower B: Law and disorders: studies exploring legally sensitive judgements in treating mental illness, *Sci News* 147(1):8, 1995.

Corsini RJ, editor: *Encyclopedia of psychology,* ed 2, New York, 1994, John Wiley.

Dennis DL and others: A decade of research and services for the homeless mentally ill: where do we stand? *Am Psychol* 46(11):1129, 1991.

Dibner LA, Murphy JS: Nurse entrepreneurs, *J Psychosoc Nurs* 29(5):30, 1991.

Dossey B: Awakening the inner healer, *Am J Nurs* 91(8):31, 1991.

Equal Employment Opportunity Commission: *A technical assistance manual on the employee provisions (Title 1) of the Americans with Disabilities Act,* January 1992, US Government Printing Office.

Federal Task Force on Homelessness and Severe Mental Illness: Outcasts on main street: homelessness and the mentally ill, *USA Today* 122(2586):26, 1994.

Foster JM: The nurse in a center for the homeless, *Nurs Management* 25(4):38, 1992.

Hoff LA: Health policy and the plight of the mentally ill, *Caps Comm Psychiatr Nurs* 1(1):64, 1994.

Holland L: Mental health supportive home care aides, *Caring* (4):44, 1993.

Kiesler CA: Homelessness and public policy priorities, *Am Psychol* 46(11):1245, 1991.

Knox MD, Clark CF: Early HIV detection: a community mental health role, *AIDS Patient Care* 4(6):169, 1993.

Mackey RB: Discover the healing power of therapeutic touch, *Am J Nurs* 95(4):27, 1995.

Manion J: Understanding the seven stages of change, *Am J Nurs* 95(4):41, 1995.

Mellon SK: Mental health clinical nurse specialist in home care for the 90s, *Iss Ment Health Nurs* (15):229, 1993.

Morrison M: *Professional skills for leadership: foundations of a successful career,* St Louis, 1993, Mosby.

Nehls N and others: A collaborative nurse-physician practice model for helping persons with serious mental illness, *Hosp Community Psychiatry* 43(8):842, 1992.

Rafferty Y, Shinn M: The impact of homelessness on children, *Am Psychol* 46(11):1170, 1991.

Renz MC: Healing touch, *Nurs 94* 24(11):47, 1994.

Thompson J, Strand K: Psychiatric nursing in a psychosocial setting, *J Psychosoc Nurs* 32(2):25, 1994.

Torrey EF: The mental-health mess, *Natl Rev* 44(25):22, 1992.

Weaver SK, Wilson JF: Moving toward patient empowerment, *Nurs Health Care* 15(9):481, 1994.

Wilk RJ: Are the rights of people with mental illness still important? *Social Work* 39(2):167, 1994.

Zwerdling M: Nursing care for the societal client, *Nurs Health Care* 15(8):422, 1994.

GLOSSARY

abstinence: Nonuse of an addictive substance or behaviors.

abuse: Process of causing an individual harm.

acceptance: Act of receiving or taking what is being offered or given.

acting out: Use of inappropriate, detrimental, or destructive behaviors to express current or past emotions.

acupuncture: Insertion of fine needles into the skin at certain specific sites or meridians along the body to treat illness.

adaptation: Change or response to stress of any kind; degree and nature of adaptation shown by a client, regularly evaluated by the nurse; in nursing, the effectiveness of nursing care, the course of the disease, and the ability of the client to cope with stress.

addiction: Physical dependence on a drug that is taken or behavior that is performed despite the physical and psychosocial problems associated with its use.

addictive behaviors: Obsessive-compulsive activities that take the form of certain repetitive behaviors, such as gambling, shopping, working, and engaging in excessive sexual activity.

adolescence: Period of life between 11 and 21 years of age.

adolescent suicide: Act of intentionally taking one's own life by a person between 11 and 21 years of age.

advocacy: Process of providing a client with information, support, and feedback so that the client can make an informed decision.

affect: Outward manifestation of a person's feelings or emotions.

affective: Pertaining to emotion, mood, or feeling.

affective disorder: Ineffective emotional state, ranging from deep depression to excited elation.

affective loss: In dementia, the loss of mood, emotion, and personality.

ageism: Practice of stereotyping older persons as feeble, dependent, and nonproductive.

aggression: Forceful attitude or action that is expressed physically, symbolically, or verbally.

aging: Process of growing older.

agnosia: Inability to recognize familiar environmental objects or people (stimuli).

agoraphobia: Anxiety about possible situations (especially open or public places) in which a panic attack may occur.

AIDS: Acquired immunodeficiency syndrome, a viral infection that prevents the body from warding off infectious diseases.

akathisia: Inability to sit still, commonly caused by antipsychotic drugs.

akinesia: Absence of movement, physically and mentally.

alcohol: Ethanol (ETOH), the results of the fermentation or distillation of yeast and grains, malts, or fruits.

alcoholism: Chronic disease caused by prolonged or excessive alcohol use.

Alzheimer's disease: Progressive, degenerative disorder that impedes the functioning of brain cells and synapses and results in impaired memory, thinking, and behavior.

ambivalence: State in which an individual experiences conflicting feelings, attitudes, or drives.

amnesia: Loss of memory that cannot be explained by normal forgetfulness.

amphetamines: Class of drugs that act as central nervous system stimulants.

anergy: Inability to start an activity.

anger: Normal emotional response to a perceived threat, frustration, or distressing event; occurs in response to an individual's frustration level or feelings of being threatened or losing control.

anhedonia: Loss of interest or pleasure from previously enjoyed activities.

anorexia nervosa: Severe disturbance in eating behavior; can result in a body that is much lower than its ideal weight.

Antabuse: Chemical disulfiram; when taken with alcohol, produces uncomfortable and possibly serious physical reactions.

anticholinergic: Drug used to block the responses to parasympathetic stimulation, which results in dilated pupils, dry eyes and mouth, and rapid heart rate.

anticholinergic reaction: Effect caused by drugs that block acetylcholine receptors and cause such symptoms as dry mouth, blurred vision, constipation, rapid heart beat, and urinary hesitancy.

anticonvulsant: Drug used to treat and prevent seizures.

antipsychotic: Drug used to treat the symptoms of major mental disorders.

antisocial: Pervasive pattern of disregard for and violation of the rights of others.

anxiety: Vague, uneasy feeling experienced by individuals in response to real or imagined stress.

anxiety disorder: Psychic tension that interferes with a person's ability to perform the activities of daily living.

anxiety state: State that occurs when an individual's coping abilities are overwhelmed and emotional control is lost.

anxiety trait: Learned component of the personality in which an individual reacts to relatively nonstressful situations with anxiety.

anxiolytics: Group of drugs designed to reduce anxiety; the antianxiety medications.

apathy: Lack of feelings, emotions, concern, or interests.

aphasia: Disorder in which language function is defective or absent; inability to speak or understand verbal messages.

assault: Any behavior that presents an immediate threat to another person.

assertiveness: Ability to directly express one's feelings or needs in a way that respects the rights of other people and retains the individual's dignity.

assessment: First step of the nursing process, which includes the gathering, clustering, and analysis of data relating to a client.

attention-deficit hyperactivity disorder: Cluster of behaviors associated with inattention and impulsive actions.

autism: Pervasive developmental disorder of the brain. Symptoms appear during the first 3 years of life and include disturbances in physical, social, and language skills; abnormal responses to sensations; and abnormal ways of relating to people, objects, and events.

autonomic nervous system: System responsible for regulating the internal vital functions of the body, such as the cardiac and smooth muscles.

autonomic tone: Ability of tissue to coordinate actions with other tissues. Neurotransmitters of both the sympathetic and the parasympathetic nervous systems affect the function of each organ or tissue, but one branch dominates and sets the tone of that tissue to coordinate with other tissues.

autonomy: Ability to direct and control one's own activities, one's destiny.

battered wife: Repeated physical abuse of someone, usually a woman.

battery: Unlawful use of force on a person.

behavior: Manner of conducting oneself; one's actions.

belief: Conviction that is mentally accepted as true whether or not it is based in fact.

bereavement: Emotional and behavioral state of thoughts, feelings, and activities that follow a loss.

bereavement-related depression: State of bereavement in which the griever feels the loss so intensely that despair, worthlessness, and depression overwhelm everything else in life.

bill of rights: List of client's rights set forth by the American Hospital Association; offers some guidance and protection to clients by stating the responsibilities that a hospital and its staff have toward clients and their families during hospitalization; not a legally binding document.

binge eating: Uncontrolled ingestion (in a certain period of time) of an amount of food that is definitely larger than most individuals would eat in similar circumstances.

bipolar disorder: Behavioral problems caused by sudden, dramatic shifts in emotional extremes.

bisexual: Person who is attracted to and engages in sexual activities with members of both sexes.

block grant: Certain sum of money granted by the federal government to the states for health care.

body dysmorphic disorder: Preoccupation with a physical difference or defect in one's body.

body image: Person's subjective concept of his/her physical appearance.

borderline personality disorder: Instability in mood, thinking, behavior, personal relationships, and self-image.

bradykinesia: Slowing down of body movements and mental state.

bulimia: Uncontrolled ingestion of large amounts of food (called binge eating), followed by inappropriate methods to prevent weight gain (called purging).

caffeine: Active ingredient of coffee, tea, and other beverages that stimulates the central nervous system.

calculation: Ability to perform mathematical problems.

cannabis: Leaves and flowers of the plant *Cannabis sativa;* also called marijuana.

career: One's preparation for and advancements or achievements in a particular vocation.

caring: Concern for the well-being of a person shown in ways such as attentive listening, comforting, honesty, acceptance, and sensitivity.

case management: Assignment of a health care provider to assist a client in assessing health and social service systems and to ensure that all required services are obtained.

cataplexy: Sudden episode of bilateral muscle weakness and loss of muscle tone that lasts for seconds to minutes.

catastrophic reaction: Minor anxieties or frustrations that cascade into severe behavioral reactions in which the person becomes increasingly confused, agitated, and fearful and may wander, become noisy, act compulsively, or behave violently.

catatonia: State or condition characterized by obvious motor disturbances, usually immobility with muscle rigidity, or (less commonly) excessive impulsive activity.

catchment area: Delineated geographical region used for the planning of health care services.

central nervous system (CNS): Brain and spinal cord, which together control all the motor and sensory functions of the body.

change process: Series of steps that result in a difference.

chemical: Substance, drug, or medication.

chemical dependency: Psychophysiological state of being addicted to drugs or alcohol; also called *addiction*.

chemical restraint: Antipsychotic medication; a medication that reduces or eliminates psychotic symptoms and quiets behavior.

child abuse: Mistreatment of children through physical, sexual, or emotional abuse.

chronic mental illness: Recurrence of one or more psychiatric disorders, which results in significant functional disability.

chronicity: Long-term, persistent difficulties; in chronic mental disorders, periods of relative comfort and ease of functioning, alternating with relapses into acute psychiatric states.

clang associations: Use of words that have rhythm.

closed system: Set of interacting, related units with rigid, impermeable boundaries that close out information and energy and eventually shorten survival.

cocaine: Processed extract of the coca plant, which causes central nervous stimulation and intense feelings of well-being.

code of ethics: Statement encompassing the set of rules by which practitioners of a profession are expected to conform.

cognition: Activities of the mind characterized by knowing, learning, judging, reasoning, and memory.

cognitive: Pertaining to the mental processes of comprehension, judgment, memory, and reasoning.

cognitive loss: Decline in cognitive abilities and intellect, including an inability to recall recent events and process new information, agnosia, apraxia, and aphasia.

commitment: Personal bond to some course of action.

communication: Reciprocal exchange of information, ideas, beliefs, feelings, and attitudes between two persons or among a group of persons.

communication disorder: Problems with expressing and receiving messages, pronouncing words, and stuttering that interfere with a child's development.

communication style: Rituals connected with greeting and departure, the lines of conversation, and the directness of communication.

community mental health centers: Outpatient settings in which a comprehensive range of mental health services are made readily available to all members of a community.

community support system: Organized network of caring and trained people committed to assisting the chronically mentally ill to meet their needs within the community.

comorbidity: Two medical or psychiatric disorders present at the same time.

compassion: Symptomatic consciousness of others' distress together with a desire to alleviate it.

competent: State of being able to make a choice, understand important information, appreciate one's own situation, and apply reasoning.

compliance: Act of following prescribed treatments.

complicated grief: Persistent yearning for a deceased person and other related symptoms that often occur without the signs of depression but are associated with impaired psychological functioning and disturbances of mood, sleep, and self-esteem.

compulsion: Distressing recurring behavior that must be performed to reduce anxiety.

compulsive overeating: Pattern of eating to lessen emotional discomfort, anxiety, or distress.

conative loss: Loss of the ability to make and carry out plans.

concrete thinking: Inability to identify or describe feelings, experiences, and behavior abstractly.

conduct disorder: Persistent pattern of unacceptable behaviors, which include defiance of authority, engaging in aggressive actions toward others, refusal to follow society's rules and norms, and violation of the rights of others.

confidence: Belief in the nurse's ability to assist, to help clients cope with the difficulties and implications of their health problems; a trust or belief in one's own abilities.

confidentiality: Sharing of client information only with those persons who are directly involved in the care of the client.

conscience: Knowledge or feeling of what is right and wrong, often accompanied by a strong desire to do the "right thing."

consistency: Behaviors that imply being steady and regular, dependable.

consultation: Process in which the assistance of a specialist is sought to help identify ways in which to cope effectively with client management problems.

context: Setting or environment in which an event occurs.

continuous mental health care team: Group of specialists who assume full responsibility for the care of their clients during all stages of illness, in or out of the hospital.

contract law: Division of private law that focuses on agreements between individuals or institutions.

controlled substance: Certain drug classes manufactured, distributed, and dispensed according to the federal regulations of the 1970 Controlled Substances Act.

conversion disorder: Somatoform disorder in which the individual presents with problems related to the sensory or motor functions.

coping mechanisms: Any thought or action that is aimed at reducing stress.

coping resources: Options, strategies, and methods for dealing with stress.

countertransference: Barrier in the therapeutic relationship based in the nurse's emotional responses to the client.

courage: Response that allows us to face and cope with those aspects of life that are dangerous, difficult, or painful.

covert modeling: Act of mentally rehearsing a difficult performance or event before actually doing the activity.

crack: Type of processed cocaine made by combining cocaine with ammonia or baking soda and heating the mixture to remove the hydrochloride molecule, resulting in chips or chunks of highly addicting cocaine, called *rocks*.

crime: Actions or behaviors that break the laws of a society.

criminal law: Division of public law designed to protect the members of a society.

crisis: Period of severe emotional disorganization resulting from a lack of appropriate coping mechanisms or supports.

crisis intervention: Short-term, active therapy that provides emotional first aid for victims of trauma with the goal of assisting individuals and families to manage the immediate crisis situation and return to precrisis levels of functioning.

crisis stabilization: Goal of crisis intervention; process of assisting clients in coping with crisis situations by placing them in a 1- or 2-day treatment setting where equilibrium (homeostasis) can be reestablished.

culture: Set of learned values, beliefs, customs, and behaviors that is shared by a group of interacting individuals.

culture-bound disorder: Mental problems that appear to be associated to members of a specific culture.

cyberspace: Communications through the use of computers and their networks.

cyclothymic disorder: Pattern of behaviors involving repeated mood swings, alternating between hypomania and depressive symptoms.

data collection: Activities that elicit, retrieve, or discover information about a certain subject.

deceit: Lying; act of representing as true something that is known to be false.

defamation: Any false communication that results in harm.

defense mechanisms: Unconscious, intrapsychic reaction that offers protection to the self from a stressful situation.

deinstitutionalization: At the individual patient level, the transfer to a community setting of a patient who has been hospitalized for an extended period of time; at the mental health care system level, a shift in the focus of mental health care from the large, long-term institution to the community through the discharge of long-term patients and avoidance of unnecessary admissions.

delirium: Change of consciousness that occurs over a short period of time.

delusions: False beliefs that are resistant to reasoning or change.

dementia: Loss of multiple abilities, including short- and long-term memory, language, and the ability to understand (conceptualize).

demonical exorcisms: Religious ceremonies in which the patients were physically punished to drive away the possessing spirit.

denial: Psychological defense mechanism in which one refuses to acknowledge painful facts.

depersonalization: Feeling of unreality and alienation from self with ego and self-concept disorganization.

depression: Emotional state characterized by feelings of sadness, disappointment, and despair.

derealization: Loss of ego boundaries; inability to tell where one's body ends and the environment begins.

development: Increasing ability in skills or functions.

direct self-destructive behavior: Any form of active suicidal behavior, such as threats, gestures, or attempts to intentionally end one's life.

disability: Loss, absence, or impairment of physical or mental fitness.

discharge planning: Process whereby nurses help clients cope with the hurdles of illness or surgery through early identification and intervention of potential problems following discharge from a health care facility.

discrimination: Act of showing favor or disfavor to a person or group of people in a manner unacceptable to society.

disease: Condition in which a physical dysfunction exists.

dissociation: Disconnection from full awareness of self, time, or external circumstances.

dissociative identity disorder: Repeated and persistent episodes in which one feels detached or unconnected to the self.

disturbed communications: Interference in communication related to the sending or receiving of messages, inadequate mastery of the language, insufficient information, or no opportunity for feedback.

domestic violence: Aggressive behaviors directed toward significant others.

drug-induced parkinsonism: Group of symptoms that mimic Parkinson's disease, including tremors, muscle rigidity, and difficulty with voluntary movements.

dual diagnosis: In mental health, the presence of two or more psychiatric disorders, one commonly being substance abuse.

duty to warn: Duty to protect potential victims from possible harm by a psychiatric client.

dying process: Experience of progressing through several psychological stages before the actual death occurs, which allows people to cope with the overwhelming emotional reactions associated with losing loved ones.

dynamics: Interactions among the various forces operating in any system.

dyskinesia: Inability to execute voluntary movements.

dyslexia: Impaired ability to read, sometimes accompanied by a mixing of letters or syllables in a word when speaking.

dyspareunia: Pain associated with sexual intercourse.

dyssomnia: Sleep disorder characterized by abnormalities in the amount, quality, or timing of sleep.

dysthymia: Daily moderate depression that lasts for longer than 2 years.

dystonia: Impaired muscle tone.

eating disorder: Ongoing disturbance in behaviors associated with the ingestion of food.

eccentric: Odd, unconventional, irregular, out of the ordinary.

echolalia: Purposeless imitation of another's speech, repetition of another's statement over and over.

echopraxia: Purposeless imitation of another's movements.

ego: In psychoanalysis, the part of the psyche that experiences and maintains conscious contact with reality; rational part of the personality; seat of such mental processes as perception and memory; develops defense mechanisms to cope with anxiety.

elder abuse: Any action on the part of a caregiver to take advantage of an older adult, his/her emotional well-being, or property.

electroconvulsive therapy (ECT): Artificial induction of a grand mal seizure by passing a controlled electrical current through electrodes applied to one or both temples.

elopement: Announced leaving or running away from an inpatient health care institution.

emotions: Nonintellectual reactions to various stimuli, based on individual's perceptions.

empathy: Ability to recognize and share the emotions and states of mind of another and to understand the meaning and significance of that person's behavior.

empowerment: Active assumption of the rights, benefits, responsibilities, and obligations of a particular role.

encopresis: Fecal incontinence in a child older than 4 years of age with no physical abnormalities; includes the repeated, usually voluntary, passage of feces in inappropriate places.

enuresis: Involuntary urinary incontinence of a child 5 years or older.

environmental control: Ability of an individual to perceive and control his/her environment.

epilepsy: Condition of abnormal electrical activity in the brain, characterized by recurrent episodes of seizure activity, abnormal behaviors, sensory disturbances, loss of or changes in consciousness, or a combination of these events.

equilibrium: Attempt of a system or organism to maintain a steady state or balance within itself and among other systems.

erotic: Inducing sexual feelings.

erratic: Deviating from conventional or customary course; having no fixed purpose or direction.

ethical dilemma: Uncertainty or disagreement about the moral principles that endorse different courses of action.

ethics: Set of rules or values that govern right behavior.

ethnicity: Broad term that refers to the socialization patterns, customs, and cultural habits of a particular group.

evaluation: Process by which one compares data and makes a judgment.

exacerbation: Periods marked by an increase in the signs/symptoms and seriousness of a problem or disorder.

exhibitionism: Exposure of one's genitals to an unsuspecting person followed by sexual arousal.

expectation: Behaviors that one assumes based on what the individual thinks another person expects or desires.

exploitation: Use of another individual for selfish purposes, profit, or gain.

extended family: Household group consisting of parents, children, grandparents, and other family members.

extrapyramidal side effects (EPSEs): Abnormal involuntary movement disorders caused by a drug-induced imbalance between two major neurotransmitters, dopamine and acetylcholine, in portions of the brain.

factitious disorder: Signs/symptoms that are intentionally produced so that one may assume the sick role.

failure: Lack of success; neglect or omission.

false imprisonment: Detention of a competent person against his/her will.

family: Group of people who are biologically or emotionally attached, interact regularly, and share concerns for the growth and development of each member.

fear: Response to an appraisal of a dangerous stressor.

feedback: Responses and intrapersonal communications of each person when messages are being sent and received.

felony: Crime that is punishable by imprisonment or death.

fetishism: Use of objects (e.g., panties, leather, rubber sheeting) for the purpose of sexual arousal.

flashback: Vivid recollections of an event in which the individual relives a frightening, traumatic experience.

flight of ideas: Abrupt change of topic in a rapid flow of speech.

flooding: Method for treating phobias in which the client is rapidly and repeatedly exposed to the feared object or situation until anxiety levels diminish.

forensic evidence: Objective information that is obtained from a victim and used in a court of law to determine guilt or innocence of an alleged perpetrator of violence.

fraud: Act of giving of false information with the knowledge that it will be acted on.

free-floating anxiety: Emotional distress associated with feelings of doom and dread in which the cause cannot be identified.

frotteurism: Practice of rubbing up against a nonconsenting person with the purpose of sexual arousal.

fugue: Escape from reality; dissociative fugue: Sudden, unexpected travel, with an inability to recall the past.

functional assessment: Analysis of each client's abilities to perform the activities of daily living.

gangs: Group of people, generally adolescents, who act, look, and dress alike; share the same values; and follow similar codes of conduct.

gay: Male or female homosexual.

gender abuse: Aggressive, violent, or exploitative behaviors that are directed toward members of one sex, usually female.

gender role: Expected pattern of behaviors based on one's sex.

generalized seizure: Discharge of electrical activity within the brain that generally results in loss of consciousness.

genuineness: Quality of being open, honest, sincere; actively involved.

gerontophobia: Fear of aging and refusal to accept the elderly into the mainstream of society.

gregarious: Sociable, in need of the company of others.

grief: Set of emotional reactions that accompany a loss.

growth: Development from a lower or simpler to a higher or more complex form.

hallucination: False sensory input with no external stimulus, usually in the form of smells, sounds, tastes, sight, or touch.

hallucinogen: Chemical substance that alters one's reality.

health: State of complete well-being, not just the absence of disease or abnormal conditions.

health-illness continuum: Broad spectrum or scale by means of which a person's level of health can be described, ranging from high-level wellness to severe illness.

health maintenance organization: Group of doctors, hospitals, and clinics who deliver health care to enrolled clients who pay a fixed, negotiated fee.

helping boundaries: Professional limitations that define the needs of the nurse as distinctly different from the needs of the patient: what is too helpful and what is not and what fosters independence vs. unhealthy dependence.

heroin: A semisynthetic narcotic of opium.

heterosexual: Person who expresses sexuality with members of the opposite sex.

histrionic: Pattern of excessive emotional expression accompanied by attention-seeking behaviors.

HIV/AIDS: Human immunodeficiency virus; a retrovirus that results in acquired immunodeficiency syndrome and its various resultant disorders.

hoarding: Act of collecting and saving assorted, seemingly useless items.

holistic health care: Philosophical concept designed to consider all aspects of human functioning and help clients achieve harmony within themselves and with others, nature, and the world.

homelessness: Lack of a regular and adequate night-time residence.

homeostasis: Tendency of the body to achieve and maintain a steady internal state.

homosexual: Person who expresses sexual desire or preference for members of one's own sex.

hope: Multidimensional dynamic life force characterized by an anticipated and confident yet uncertain expectation of achieving a future good.

hospice: Philosophy of care for people with terminal illnesses or conditions and their loved ones.

hospitalization: Placing of an ill or injured person into an inpatient health care facility that provides continuous nursing care and an organized medical staff.

human dimensions: Major facets or areas of being human, which include physical, emotional, intellectual, social, and spiritual functions.

humoral theory of disease: Hippocrates' view that illness was the result of an imbalance of the body's humors of blood, phlegm, black bile, and yellow bile.

hypersomnia: Sleep disorder characterized by excessive sleepiness.

hypertensive crisis: Condition in which the blood pressure rises to extreme levels; commonly caused by an interaction between monoamine oxidase inhibitors and other substances.

hypochondriasis: Somatoform disorder in which one has an intense fear or preoccupation of having a serious disease or medical condition based on a misinterpretation of body signs/symptoms.

hypomania: Exaggerated sense of cheerfulness and well-being.

id: In psychoanalysis, the part of the psyche functioning in the unconscious that is the source of instinctive energy, impulses, and drives and is based on the pleasure principle and has strong tendencies toward self-preservation.

ideas of reference: Incorrect perceptions of causal events as having great or significant meaning; finding special, personal messages in everyday events.

identity diffusion: Failure to bring various childhood identifications into an effective adult personality.

illness: State of social, emotional, intellectual, and physical dysfunction.

imagery: Formation of mental concepts, figures, or ideas.

impulse-control: Ability to express one's emotions in appropriate or effective ways.

impulsivity: Pattern of behavior in which actions are taken without forethought or regard to the consequences.

incest: Inappropriate sexual activities with one or more members of one's family.

incongruent communications: Interactions in which the verbal messages being sent do not match one's nonverbal communications.

indirect self-destructive behaviors: Any behaviors that may result in harm to the individual's well-being or death in which people have no actual intention of ending their lives.

inferiority: Feeling of being inadequate or less than others.

information overload: Inability to process data because of their sheer volume.

informed consent: Process of presenting clients with information about the benefits, risks, and side effects of specific treatments, thus enabling clients to make voluntary and competent decisions about their care.

inhalant: Chemical substance that is introduced into the body by breathing in through the nose and mouth.

inpatient psychiatric care: Health care facility that provides 24-hour-a-day care within a structured and protective setting.

insight: Ability to clearly see and understand the inner nature of things.

institutionalization: Result of adapting to an environment to the point at which one is unable or unwilling to live in a different environment.

integrity: State of wholeness, of being complete.

intelligence: Person's general knowledge, including orientation, memory, and ability to calculate and think abstractly.

interpersonal communications: Interactions that occur between two or more persons consisting of the verbal and nonverbal messages that are sent and received during every interaction.

interview: Purposeful, organized conversation with a client.

intoxication: State of being under the influence of a chemical substance or drug.

intrapersonal communications: Messages that are sent and received within oneself.

introspection: Analysis of self, including one's feelings, reactions, attitudes, opinions, values, and behaviors.

invasion of privacy: Violation of a person's space, body, belongings, or personal information.

involuntary commitment: Request for mental health services that is initiated by someone other than the client.

judgment: Ability to evaluate choices and make appropriate decisions.

la belle indifference: Lack of concern or indifference about the nature or the implications of the signs/symptoms of a somatoform disorder.

laws: Controls by which a society governs itself.

learned helplessness: Feeling of no control over self as a result of learning faulty attitudes and behaviors.

learning disorder: Problems with learning to read, write, or calculate.

lesbian: Woman who prefers homosexuality as a mode of sexual expression.

libel: Written communication that results in harm.

libidinal energy: Also called libido; psychic energy or instinctual drive associated with sexual desire, pleasure, or creativity.

life space: Psychological field or space in which one moves, including oneself, other people, and objects.

limit setting: Process of consistently reinforcing the established structure (rules, routine) of the therapeutic setting.

lithium: Naturally occurring salt used to treat mania.

lobotomy: Surgical procedure that disconnects the frontal lobes from the thalamus in the brain and results in a decrease in violent behaviors and mood swings.

locus of control: Power an individual possesses to control his/her environment.

loose associations: Thought disturbance in which the speaker rapidly shifts topics from one unrelated area to another.

loss: Actual or potential state in which a valued object, person, or body part that was formerly present is lost or changed and can no longer be seen, felt, heard, known, or experienced.

lunacy: Medieval term meaning a mental disorder caused by or relating to the moon.

malingering: Somatoform disorder in which one produces symptoms to meet a recognizable, external goal.

malpractice: Failure to exercise an accepted degree of professional skill or learning, resulting in injury, loss, or damage.

mania: Extreme emotional state characterized by excitement, great elation, overtalkativeness, increased motor activity, fleeting grandiose ideas, and agitated behaviors.

manic depression: Older term for a bipolar disorder.

manipulation: Controlling others for one's own purposes by influencing them in unfair or false ways.

masochism: Sexual arousal achieved by being the recipient of pain, humiliation, or suffering.

maturation: Process of attaining complete physical and psychosocial development.

memory: Ability to recall past events, experience, and perceptions.

memory loss: Natural part of the aging process relating to the inability to recall a certain detail or event.

mental health: Relative state of mind in which a person who is healthy is able to cope with and adjust to the recurrent stresses of everyday living in an acceptable way.

mental health care team: Group of professionally trained specialists who develop and implement comprehensive treatment plans for clients with mental/emotional problems.

mental illness: Any disturbance of emotional equilibrium that results in maladaptive behaviors and impaired functioning.

mental retardation: Developmental disorder characterized by significantly below average intellectual level and limited abilities to function.

methadone: Narcotic used to treat long-term heroin addiction.

middle adulthood: Period of life from about 35 to around 65 years of age.

misdemeanor: Crime that is punishable by fines or imprisonment of less than 1 year.

model: Example or pattern that provides a matrix or framework for a theory.

mood: Subjective state of an individual's overall feelings.

mood disorder: Prolonged emotional state that influences one's whole personality and life functioning.

morals: Attitudes, beliefs, and values that define one's basis for right or wrong behavior.

mortality: Condition of being subject to death.

mourning: Process of working through or resolving one's grief.

mutism: Refusal or inability to communicate.

mutuality: Process through which the client assumes an appropriate level of autonomy without blocking the provision of necessary health care services.

narcissism: Pattern of behavior characterized by ideas of grandiosity and the need to be admired; belief that one is special, unique, or extra important.

narcolepsy: Uncommon sleep disorder in which an individual has repeated attacks of sleep.

narcotic: Natural, semisynthetic, or synthetic chemical substance that acts as a central nervous system depressant.

natural selection: Theory that states that only the fittest organisms survive and evolve.

need: Requirement; something that one cannot do without.

negative symptoms: In schizophrenia, behaviors that indicate a lack of adaptive mechanisms, including flat affect, poor grooming, withdrawal, and poverty of speech.

neglect: Lack of meeting a dependent person's (usually a child's) basic needs for food, clothing, shelter, love, and belonging.

negligence: Omission or commission of an act that a reasonable and prudent person would or would not do.

neologism: Invented or made-up word.

neuroleptic malignant syndrome (NMS): Serious and potentially fatal extrapyramidal side effect of antipsychotic or neuroleptic medications.

neuropeptides: Neurotransmitter composed of amino acid strings that interacts with the endocrine, immune, and nervous systems.

neurotransmitters: Chemical found in the nervous system that facilitates the transmission of energy and acts as the body's chemical messenger system.

nicotine: Addictive, active ingredient of tobacco.

noncompliance: Informed decision made by a client not to follow a prescribed treatment program.

nontherapeutic communications: Messages that hinder effective communications.

nonverbal communications: Messages that are sent and received without the use of words, which includes one's intrapersonal communications; the messages created through the body's motions and use of touch, space, and sight; unspoken interpersonal communications; and such behaviors as eye movement, gestures, movement of the body, expressions, posture, and eye contact.

norms: Established rules of conduct that arise from a culture's behavioral standards.

nuclear family: Household unit consisting of two parents and their offspring.

nurse practice acts: State regulations that define the limits and scope of nursing practice.

nursing process: Organizational framework for the practice of nursing that uses the steps of assessment, nursing diagnosis, planning, implementation, and evaluation for the delivery of client care.

nurture: Act or process of promoting the development of persons or things.

obesity: Abnormal increase in body fat; body weight that is more than 20% above one's ideal weight.

object constancy: Awareness that a person or item still exists even though it cannot be perceived (seen, touched) at the time.

obsession: Persistent, recurring, inappropriate, and distressing thoughts.

obstructive sleep apnea: Sleep disruptions caused by abnormalities of ventilation during sleep.

older adulthood: Period of life from around 65 years of age to death.

oliguric crisis: Dystonic reaction in which the eyes involuntarily roll to the back of the head.

open system: Set of interacting, related units with permeable boundaries through which matter, energy, and information pass.

opiates: Opioids; processed products of opium.

outpatient psychiatric care: Health care setting that provides comprehensive services for mentally ill clients within their home environments.

pain disorder: Pain or discomfort that is the major focus of distress when no physical cause of the pain can be identified.

pain management: Series of nursing interventions designed to assist clients in identifying, defining, and controlling pain.

panic attack: Brief period of intense fear or discomfort accompanied by various physical and emotional reactions.

paranoia: Suspicious system of thinking with delusions of persecution and grandeur; pattern of behaviors marked by suspiciousness and mistrust.

paraphilia: Group of sexual variations that depart from society's traditional and acceptable modes of seeking sexual gratification.

parasomnias: Group of sleep disorders that are characterized by abnormal behavioral or physical events during sleep.

parasuicidal actions: Unsuccessful attempts and gestures of suicide associated with a low likelihood of success.

parasympathetic nervous system: Division of the autonomic nervous system that functions to monitor and maintain control over the regulatory processes of the body, which it accomplishes by adapting smooth muscle tone and glandular secretions.

partial seizure: Discharge of electrical activity in the brain that results in a change in consciousness, sensory disturbances, or abnormal behaviors.

passive aggression: Indirect expressions of anger through the use of subtle, evasive, or manipulative behaviors.

passive suicide: Act of taking of one's own life by refusing to eat, drink, or cooperate with care.

paternalism: Attitude in which the care provider becomes the judge of what is best for clients, limiting clients' abilities to make decisions and increasing their dependency on others.

pedophilia: Fondling or other types of sexual activity with a prepubescent child (usually younger than 13 years of age) initiated by an adult.

peer groups: Group of people of similar age, interests, and developmental levels.

perception: Use of the senses to gain information.

peripheral nervous system: Thirty-one spinal nerves that originate in the spinal cord in addition to the 12 spill pairs of cranial nerves; further divided into a motor and an autonomic system.

perpetrator: Person who executes, with or without planning, a crime or act of violence or aggression.

perseveration: Repeating of the same idea in response to different questions or interactions.

personal identity: Composite of behavioral traits and characteristics by which one is recognized as an individual.

personality: Unique pattern of attitudes and behaviors each individual develops to adapt to a particular environment and its standards.

personality disorder: Enduring pattern of inner experience and behavior that deviates markedly from the expectations of the individual's culture, is pervasive and inflexible, has an onset in adolescence or early adulthood, is stable over time, and leads to distress or impairment.

personifications: According to Carl Jung, distorted images of certain relationships that spill over or transfer into other relationships.

pervasive developmental disorder: Problems severe enough to affect several areas of a child's functioning (including difficulty with social interaction skills, communication skills, and learning) and behavior that is different from other children of the same age and developmental level.

phencyclidine (PCP): Drug developed for use as an animal tranquilizer; in humans, produces mild depression with low doses and a schizophrenic-like reaction with higher amounts.

phobia: Unnatural fear of people, animals, objects, situations, or occurrences.

phototherapy: Exposure of clients to full-spectrum light for certain periods during the day for the relief of depressive symptoms that occur during the winter months.

physical properties: In a therapeutic environment, temperature, lighting, sound, cleanliness, and aesthetics.

physiological stress response: Mechanism that protects mammals during times of threat or illness; fight-flight response.

pica: Eating disorder characterized by ingestion of nonfood items, such as hair, string, or dirt.

polysomnogram: Device that monitors the client's electrophysical responses during sleep and includes such measurements as brain wave activity (electroencephalogram [EEG]), muscle movement (electromyogram [EMG]), and extraocular eye movements (electroolfactogram [EOG]).

positive symptoms: In schizophrenia, the signs related to maladaptive thoughts and behaviors, including hallucinations, speech problems, and bizarre behaviors.

postpartum depression: Depressive episodes following the birth of a child.

posttraumatic stress disorder: Problems that develop after a child experiences a psychologically distressing event; characterized by an oversensitivity or overinvolvement with stimuli that recall the traumatic event.

poverty: Inability to secure the basic necessities of life, such as food, shelter, and clothing.

poverty of thought: Lack of ability to produce new thoughts or follow a train of thought.

preferred provider organization: Network of physicians, hospitals, and clinics that agree to provide medical care for the organization's members at a discount.

prejudice: Displacement of unacceptable impulses and behaviors onto a culturally different group.

primary gain: Physical signs/symptoms of an illness used to relieve an individual's anxieties by masking inner emotional turmoil.

principles: Set of standards or code that guides actions.

private law: Rules that define the relationships between individuals.

psyche: Vital or spiritual aspect of the individual as opposed to the body or soma; total components of the id, ego, and superego, including all conscious and unconscious aspects.

psychoanalysis: Branch of psychiatry founded by Sigmund Freud devoted to the study of the psychology of human behavior; also a type of therapy for certain emotional disorders that investigates the workings of the mind.

psychobiology: Study of the biochemical foundations of thought, mood, emotion, affect, and behavior.

psychomotor agitation: Increased motor behaviors, such as pacing, hand wringing, hair pulling, that are associated with emotional problems.

psychomotor depression: Decreased motor activity, such as slowed body movements, stooping posture, and slumping.

psychopath: Person with an antisocial personality disorder and a pervasive pattern of disregard for and violation of the rights of others, often using deceit and manipulation.

psychophysical disorders: Stress-related problems that result in physical signs/symptoms.

psychosis: Inability to recognize reality, relate to others, or cope with life's demands.

psychosocial rehabilitation: Multidisciplinary services that assist people with mental health problems to readjust and adapt to life in the community as actively and independently as possible; includes personal adjustment and social, residential, educational, and vocational services.

psychosomatic illness: Popular term that describes emotionally (*psycho*) related physical (*somatic*) disorders.

psychosurgery: Surgical interruption of certain nerve pathways in the brain, usually performed on epileptic clients with unifocal seizure sites.

psychotherapy: Any of a large number of related methods of treating mental-emotional disorders by psychological techniques rather than by physical means.

psychotherapeutic drugs: Chemicals that affect the mind and treat the symptoms of mental-emotional illness.

puberty: Period in life at which the ability to reproduce is developed, beginning with a 24- to 36-month growth spurt and ending when the reproductive system is mature.

public law: Rules that define the relationship between the government and its citizens.

purging: Recurring inappropriate behaviors to prevent weight gain; usually associated with bulimia.

race: Group of genetically related people who share certain physical characteristics.

rape: Forced sexual assault.

rapport: Dynamic process; an energy exchange between nurse and client that provides the background for all other nursing actions.

rational suicide: Act of purposefully ending one's own life after conscious and rational deliberation.

reasonable and prudent nurse theory: Principle by which the law judges a nurse's actions by comparing what other nurses would do in similar situations with the actions of the nurse in question.

recidivism: Relapse of a symptom, disease, or behavior pattern.

Reformation: Changes brought about by the division of the Catholic Church during the sixteenth century.

rehabilitation: Process of assisting individuals with serious mental illness to effectively cope with their life situations.

religion: Defined, organized, and practiced system of beliefs and practices usually involving a moral code.

religiosity: Delusions of great spirituality; believing one has powers to communicate with God or become a spirit.

remission: In chronic mental illness, times of partial or complete disappearance of symptoms.

resistance: Client's attempts to avoid recognizing or exploring anxiety-provoking material.

resource linkage: Process of matching client's needs with the most appropriate community services.

responding strategies: Therapeutic techniques that relate to the nurse's actions or interventions while communicating.

responsibility: State of being answerable for acts or decisions and able to fulfill obligations.

restraints: Device or drug to aid the immobilization of a client.

rights: Power, privilege, or existence to which one has a just claim.

risk factor: Something that causes a person or group to be particularly vulnerable to an unwanted event.

risk taking: Act of purposefully engaging oneself in unfamiliar activities, then observing one's responses.

role: Expected pattern of behaviors associated with a certain position.

rumination disorder: Uncommon problem of childhood involving regurgitating and rechewing food.

sadism: Sexual arousal achieved by inflicting physical or psychological pain or humiliation on another person.

schizoid: Personalities that lack the desire or willingness to become involved in a close relationship, prefer solitary activities, are emotionally restricted, and communicate emotional detachment, coldness, and a lack of concern for others.

schizophrenia: Condition associated with disturbing thought patterns and a distorted reality.

schizotypal: Interaction pattern of avoiding people with behaviors characterized by distortions and eccentricities (odd, strange, or peculiar actions).

seasonal affective disorder: Levels of mild to moderate depression experienced during long winter days; symptoms begin to lift with the coming of spring.

seclusion: Removal of a client to an area of decreased stimulation; isolation of one person from others.

secondary gain: Situation in which the payoff for remaining ill outweighs the advantages of recovery and clients profit or avoid unpleasant situations by remaining ill.

seizure: Convulsion that is the result of misfired electrical impulses within the brain.

self-actualization: Need to achieve one's full potential.

self-awareness: Consciousness of one's own individuality and personality.

self-concept: All the attitudes, notions, beliefs, and convictions that make up an individual's self-knowledge, including the individual's perceptions of personal characteristics and abilities, interactions with other people and the environment, values associated with experiences and objects, and goals and ideals.

self-esteem: Individual's judgment of his/her own worth.

self-ideal: Personal standards of how one should behave.

self-injury: Attempts to harm or hurt oneself.

self-protective responses: Ways in which individuals behave to meet safety and security needs, ranging from adaptive to self-destructive.

sensorium: Part of the consciousness that perceives, sorts, and integrates information.

sexual abuse: Intentional engaging of children or others in inappropriate or illegal sexual activities.

sexual disorder: Disturbances in sexual desire or functioning that cause marked distress and interpersonal difficulties.

sexual orientation: Individual's sexual attraction to others, also called *sexual preference.*

sexuality: Combination of physical, chemical, psychological, and functional characteristics that are expressed by one's gender identity and sexual behaviors.

shaken baby syndrome: Vigorous manual shaking of an infant who is being held by the extremities or shoulders, leading to whiplash-induced intracranial and intraocular bleeding and no external signs of head trauma.

sick role: Actions and behaviors of a person who is ill and excused from everyday responsibilities.

signal anxiety: Learned anxiety response to an anticipated event.

situational crisis: Event or situation for which one is unprepared, resulting from environmental factors outside the individual.

situational depression: Depressive responses tied to a specific event or situation that can be traced to a recognizable cause.

skill development: Process of learning and applying more effective methods for coping with life and other people.

slander: Verbal communications that result in harm.

sleep disorder: Condition or problem that repeatedly disrupts an individual's pattern of sleep.

social isolation: Removal of or withdrawal from the company and companionship of other people.

social relationship: Relationship between two people based on sharing and enjoyment of each other's company.

soma: The body, as distinguished from the mind or psyche.

somatic therapy: Physical interventions that affect behavioral changes (e.g., electroconvulsive therapy).

somatization: Act of focusing anxieties and emotional conflicts into physical symptoms.

somatoform disorder: Disorder in which a child or adult has the signs/symptoms of illness or disease without a traceable physical cause.

space: Area that surrounds a person.

speech cluttering: Disorder of speech and language processing that results in unorganized, dysthymic, and frequently unintelligible speech.

spinal cord: Long "relay station" of nerve tissue that extends from the base of the brain (foramen magnum) to the first or second lumbar vertebra in the lower back through the spinal canal of the spinal column.

splitting: Emotionally dividing staff members or other people by complimenting one group and degrading another; performed by clients.

standards of care: Written statement describing actions or conditions that direct client care; used to guide practice and evaluate performance; also called *standards of practice.*

stereotype: Oversimplified mental picture of a cultural group.

stress: Any factor that requires a response or change in the functioning of an organism.

substance abuse: Inappropriate use of a drug, medication, or toxin whose use results in dependence, addiction, or withdrawal.

substance use: Act of taking a chemical substance.

suicidal attempt: Serious self-directed action that is intended to do harm to or end one's own life.

suicidal gesture: Suicidal actions that result in little or no injury to oneself but communicate a message.

suicidal ideation: Thoughts or fantasies of suicide that are expressed but have no definite intent.

suicidal intention: Level of seriousness about committing suicide.

suicidal threat: Expressions of the intent to take one's life but without any action.

suicide: Act of intentionally taking one's own life.

suicidology: Study of the nature of suicide.

superego: In psychoanalysis, that part of the psyche, functioning mostly in the unconscious, that develops when the standards of the parents and society are incorporated into the ego.

surgery: Invasive procedure in which the body is entered through an artificially created opening, abnormal tissue or fluid is removed, and the opening is artificially closed.

surveillance: Process of watching over adolescents to determine if they are safe, behaving within acceptable limits, making good decisions, or are in need of adult intervention.

sympathetic nervous system: Division of the autonomic nervous system that prepares the body for immediate adaptation through the "fight-flight" mechanism.

synapse: Small space or gap that separates nerve cells.

tardive dyskinesia: Drug-induced condition that produces involuntary, repeated movements of the muscles of the face, trunk, arms, and legs; usually occurs following a long period of antipsychotic drug use.

temperament: Genetically linked biological bases that underlie moods, energy levels, and attitudes.

terminal illness: Illness or condition likely to result in death.

territoriality: Need to gain control over an area of space and claim it for oneself.

theory: Statement that predicts, explains, or describes a relationship between events, concepts, or ideas.

therapeutic communications: Interactions that focus on the client, foster the therapeutic relationship, and are specifically designed to achieve client outcomes.

therapeutic environment (milieu): Inpatient psychiatric setting that provides safe, stable surroundings that are structured to enhance the client's response to treatment.

therapeutic relationship: Series of interactions initiated by the nurse with the purpose of providing corrective interpersonal experiences.

therapeutic touch: Facilitation of healing by the use of the hands to consciously direct energy.

third-party payments: Payments for medical costs made by someone other than the client, usually through an insurance company or government program such as Medicare or Medicaid.

thought content: What an individual is thinking.

thought processes: How a person thinks, analyzes the world, and connects and organizes information.

tort law: Division of private law that relates to compensation for a legal wrong committed against the person or property of another.

torticollis: Contraction of the cervical muscles that forces the neck into a twisted position.

trance: State resembling sleep in which consciousness remains but voluntary movement is lost, as in hypnosis.

transcultural nursing: Part of nursing practice in which the nurse assesses, plans, and delivers culturally appropriate care.

transference: Client's emotional response to the nurse based on earlier relationships with significant others.

transmission: Conscious and unconscious response of the persons involved in the communication to the message received.

transsexual: Individual who is not comfortable with his/her biological sex and wants to surgically change sexual anatomy and live as a member of the other sex.

transvestism: Practice of dressing in opposite-sex clothing for sexual gratification.

trauma: Physical, emotional, or spiritual injury.

trust: Risk-taking process whereby an individual's situation depends on the future behavior of another person.

unconscious: Part of the mental function in which thoughts, ideas, emotions, or memories are beyond awareness and not subject to ready recall.

unipolar disorder: Classification of mood disorders that includes major depression and dysthymia.

vaginismus: Persistent involuntary contractions of the perineal muscles around the outer third of the vagina whenever vaginal penetration is attempted.

value: Dearly held belief about the worth of an idea, behavior, or item.

values clarification: Method for discovering one's own values by assessing, exploring, and determining what those personal values are and how they affect personal decision making.

verbal communications: Level of communication related to the spoken word, which includes the spoken and written word, use of language and symbols, and arrangement of words or phrases.

victim: Person who has been caused harm through the actions of another.

victimization: Process of causing harm; children suffer more victimizations than do adults, including more conventional crime, more family violence, and some forms unique to children, such as family abduction, neglect, and abuse.

violence: Any behavior that threatens or harms another person or his/her property.

voluntary admission: Request for mental health services that is originated by the client.

voyeurism: Sexual arousal achieved by observing unsuspecting persons who are disrobing, naked, or engaging in sexual activity.

withdrawal: Detoxification; process of allowing an addictive substance to leave the body; usually done under medical supervision.

word salad: In schizophrenia, verbal communications in which a series of words is used that seem to be unrelated.

young adulthood: Period of life that lasts from about 18 to 35 years of age.

American Nurses Association
Standards of Psychiatric–Mental Health
Clinical Nursing Practice*

STANDARD I. Assessment

The Psychiatric–Mental Health Nurse Collects Client Health Data.

STANDARD II. Diagnosis

The Psychiatric–Mental Health Nurse Analyzes the Assessment Data in Determining Diagnoses.

STANDARD III. Outcome Identification

The Psychiatric–Mental Health Nurse Identifies Expected Outcomes Individualized to the Client.

STANDARD IV. Planning

The Psychiatric–Mental Health Nurse Develops a Plan of Care That Prescribes Interventions to Attain Expected Outcomes.

STANDARD V. Implementation

The Psychiatric–Mental Health Nurse Implements the Interventions Identified in the Plan of Care.

STANDARD Va. Counseling

The Psychiatric–Mental Health Nurse Uses Counseling Interventions to Assist Clients in Regaining or Improving Their Previous Coping Abilities, Fostering Mental Health, and Preventing Mental Illness and Disability.

STANDARD Vb. Milieu Therapy

The Psychiatric–Mental Health Nurse Provides, Structures, and Maintains a Therapeutic Environ-ment in Collaboration With the Client and Other Health Care Providers.

STANDARD Vc. Self-Care Activities

The Psychiatric–Mental Health Nurse Structures Interventions Around the Client's Activities of Daily Living to Foster Self-Care and Mental and Physical Well-Being.

STANDARD Vd. Psychobiological Interventions

The Psychiatric–Mental Health Nurse Uses Knowledge of Psychobiological Interventions and Applies Clinical Skills to Restore the Client's Health and Prevent Further Disability.

STANDARD Ve. Health Teaching

The Psychiatric–Mental Health Nurse, Through Health Teaching, Assists Clients in Achieving Satisfying, Productive, and Healthy Patterns of Living.

STANDARD Vf. Case Management

The Psychiatric–Mental Health Nurse Provides Case Management to Coordinate Comprehensive Health Services and Ensure Continuity of Care.

STANDARD Vg. Health Promotion and Health Maintenance

The Psychiatric–Mental Health Nurse Employs Strategies and Interventions to Promote and Maintain Mental Health and Prevent Mental Illness.

STANDARD VI. Evaluation.

The Psychiatric–Mental Health Nurse Evaluates the Client's Progress in Attaining Expected Outcomes.

---

*From Council on Psychiatric and Mental Health Nursing Practice: *Standards of psychiatric–mental health clinical nursing practice,* Kansas City, MO, 1994, American Nurses Association.

A Simple Method to Determine Tardive Dyskinesia Symptoms: AIMS Examination Procedure*

PATIENT IDENTIFICATION   DATE
_____

RATED BY
_____

Either before or after completing the examination procedure, observe the patient unobtrusively at rest (e.g., in waiting room).

The chair to be used in this examination should be a hard, firm one without arms.

After observing the patient, he/she may be rated on a scale of 0 (none), 1 (minimal), 2 (mild), 3 (moderate) and 4 (severe) according to the severity of symptoms.

Ask the patient whether there is anything in his/her mouth (i.e., gum, candy, etc.) and if there is, to remove it.

Ask patient about the *current* condition of his/her teeth. Ask patient if he/she wears dentures. Do teeth or dentures bother patient *now*?

Ask patient whether he/she notices any movements in mouth, face, hands or feet. If yes, ask to describe and to what extent they *currently* bother patient or interfere with his/her activities.

0	1	2	3	4

Have patient sit in chair with hands on knees, legs slightly apart, and feet flat on floor. (Look at entire body for movements while in this position.)

0	1	2	3	4

Ask patient to sit with hands hanging unsupported. If male, between legs, if female and wearing a dress, hanging over knees. (Observe hands and other body areas.)

0	1	2	3	4

Ask patient to open mouth. (Observe tongue at rest within mouth.) Do this twice.

0	1	2	3	4

Ask patient to protrude tongue. (Observe abnormalities of tongue movement.) Do this twice.

0	1	2	3	4

Ask patient to tap thumb, with each finger, as rapidly as possible for 10 to 15 seconds; separately with right hand, then with left hand. (Observe facial and leg movements.)

0	1	2	3	4

Flex and extend patient's left and right arms. (One at a time.)

0	1	2	3	4

Ask patient to stand up. (Observe in profile. Observe all body areas again, hips included.)

0	1	2	3	4

†Ask patient to extend both arms outstretched in front with palms down. (Observe trunk, legs, and mouth.)

0	1	2	3	4

†Have patient walk a few paces, turn, and walk back to chair. (Observe hands and gait.) Do this twice.

_____

AIMS, Abnormal Involuntary Movement Scale.
*From Sandoz Pharmaceuticals, East Hanover, NJ 07936.
†Activated movements.

INDEX

The History of Mental Health Care

Student's Name

REVIEW WORKSHEET

Date

1. Write your definition of mental health and mental illness.

_____

_____

_____

_____

Match the following:

      A. Hippocrates   D. Dorothea Dix
      B. Plato   E. Benjamin Rush
      C. Philippe Pinel   F. Clifford Beers

_____ 2. Surveyed conditions of mental hospitals in United States, Canada, and Scotland

_____ 3. Wrote a book that started the mental hygiene movement

_____ 4. Said life was a dynamic equilibrium maintained by the soul

_____ 5. Wrote the first American textbook on psychiatry

_____ 6. Viewed mental illness as the result of an imbalance of humors

_____ 7. Freed the mentally ill in France from their chains

8. What do you think made witch hunting so popular for 600 years (1200-1700)?

_____

_____

_____

9. Which legislative act called for a neighborhood-based mental health care delivery system?
   a. Mental Health Systems Act of 1977
   b. National Mental Health Act of 1946
   c. Omnibus Budget Reform Act of 1987
   d. Community Mental Health Act of 1963

10. Which legislative act dramatically reduced federal funding for mental health and illness care?
    a. Mental Health Study Act of 1955
    b. Omnibus Budget Reconciliation Act of 1981
    c. Mental Health Systems Act of 1977
    d. Omnibus Budget Reform Act of 1987

CHAPTER 2

Current Mental Health Care Systems

REVIEW WORKSHEET

Student's Name _____

Date _____

Define the following:

1. third-party payment _____

   _____

2. preferred provider organization _____

   _____

3. health maintenance organization _____

   _____

4. diagnosis-related group _____

   _____

5. What factor is considered when admitting a client to an inpatient psychiatric setting? _____

   _____

6. List two outpatient psychiatric care settings.

   a. _____

   b. _____

7. Identify each health care team member to complete the puzzle.

ACROSS
2. Ph.D. who does diagnostic testing
3. M.D. team leader
4. Member who assists clients with specialized needs
5. Member responsible for management of the environment

DOWN
1. Member who evaluates families and their interactions with environment

8. List four components of case management.

   a. _____

   b. _____

   c. _____

   d. _____

9. Define holistic health care. _____

   _____

   _____

10. List two issues that have an impact on care for people with mental dysfunction.

   a. _____

   b. _____

CHAPTER 3

Ethical and Legal Issues

Student's Name

REVIEW WORKSHEET

_____

Date

Match the following terms and their definitions.

A. laws D. nonmaleficence
B. rights E. ethics
C. morals

_____ **1.** Serves as one's personal basis for right or wrong behaviors.

_____ **2.** Power to which one has a just claim.

_____ **3.** To do no harm.

_____ **4.** Shared set of rules that govern right behavior.

_____ **5.** Controls by which a society governs itself.

6. Complete the crossword puzzle.

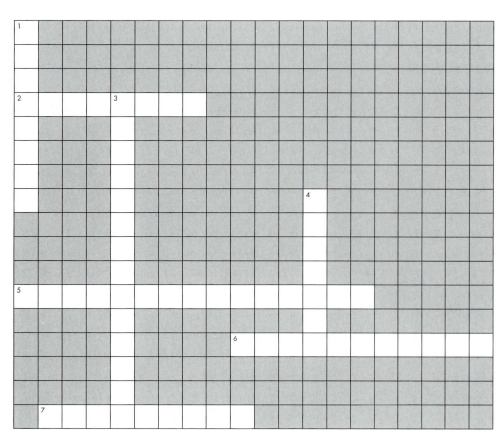

ACROSS
2. Right of people to act for themselves
5. Duty to respect private information
6. Duty to actively promote good
7. Duty to keep promises

DOWN
1. Duty to tell the truth
3. Duty to do no harm
4. Duty to treat all equally

7. Arrange the steps for resolving ethical dilemmas in order.

_____ gather relevant information

_____ take action

_____ assume good will

_____ list and rank values

_____ identify all elements of the situation

8. List three steps of the involuntary commitment process.

a. _____

b. _____

c. _____

Match the following examples with the appropriate tort.
   A. "She's a nasty old lady who bites."
   B. "If you don't cooperate, I'll call the techs and we will lock you up."
   C. Leaving a suicidal client unattended and he harms himself.
   D. Searching a client's belongings without permission.
   E. Charting a medication that was not actually given.

_____ 9. assault

_____ 10. malpractice

_____ 11. fraud

_____ 12. slander

_____ 13. invasion of privacy

CHAPTER 4

Sociocultural Issues

Student's Name

REVIEW WORKSHEET

Date

Fill in the blanks.

1. _____ is a group of people who share distinct physical characteristics.

2. _____ are learned behavior patterns with shared values system.

3. _____ are customs and cultural habits of a group.

4. _____ is an oversimplified mental picture of a cultural group.

5. _____ is an expected pattern of behavior associated with a certain position or rank.

6. List five characteristics of culture.

   a. _____

   b. _____

   c. _____

   d. _____

   e. _____

7. Complete the crossword puzzle.

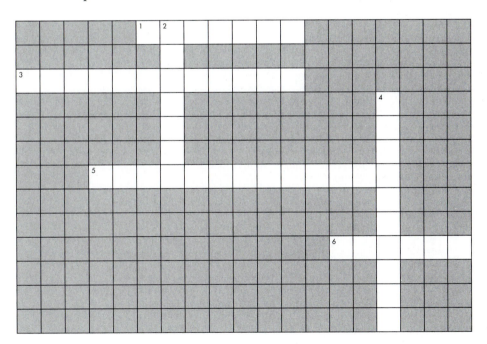

ACROSS
1. Condition in which a physical dysfunction exists
3. Belief that illness is the result of an imbalance of energy forces
5. Belief that illness is the result of punishment
6. Results of living up to norms and role expectations

DOWN
2. A state of physical, social, and emotional dysfunction
4. A belief that is widespread in Haitian culture

8. List which area of the cultural assessment relates to each of the following statements.

a. _____ "I practice Buddhism."

b. _____ "Pleasing the ancestors is more important than today's problems."

c. _____ He speaks Italian and Spanish.

d. _____ She visits an herbalist monthly.

CHAPTER 5

Early Theories and Therapies

REVIEW WORKSHEET

From the list below, match the following people with the appropriate theory.

Hippocrates	Abraham Maslow	Carl Jung
Charles Darwin	Sigmund Freud	Carl Rogers
Jean Piaget	H.S. Sullivan	B.F. Skinner
Erik Erikson		

_____ 1. He introduced the theory that only the fittest survive through the process of natural selection.

_____ 2. He used operant conditioning to change observable behavior through the use of positive and negative reinforcers.

_____ 3. He developed client-centered therapy.

_____ 4. He devised the psychoanalytic theory of human behavior.

_____ 5. He constructed the theory of motivation based on human needs.

_____ 6. His interpersonal psychology focused on the social nature of people and the role of anxiety in personality formation.

_____ 7. He developed the eight stages of psychosocial development.

Fill in the blanks.

8. A _____ is defined as a statement that describes or explains a _____ among ideas, concepts, or events.

9. A _____ is an example or pattern that provides a _____ for a theory.

Match the therapy with the statement that best describes it.

A. actualizing therapy	E. gestalt therapy
B. assertiveness training	F. interpersonal therapy
C. behavior modification	G. logotherapy
D. client-centered therapy	H. psychoanalysis

_____ 10. Based on a person's need to search for meaning and values in life.

_____ 11. Uses dream analysis and free association to uncover unconscious conflicts.

_____ 12. Uses operant conditioning to change specific actions.

_____ 13. Helps clients to uncover how their personifications (distorted images) affect their lives.

_____ 14. The client directs the therapeutic relationship using the therapist as a guide to self-understanding.

_____ 15. Teaches clients to express themselves in constructive, nonaggressive ways.

_____ 16. Goal of therapy is self-actualization, not cure or relief of symptoms.

_____ 17. Clients acted out their conflicts in order to work through their problems.

CHAPTER 6

Contemporary Theories and Therapies

REVIEW WORKSHEET

Briefly describe the following:
1. systems theory _____

_____

2. life space _____

_____

3. homeostasis _____

_____

4. crisis _____

_____

5. psychobiology _____

_____

Fill in the blanks.

6. The concept of equilibrium, devised by Lewin, states that each body system attempts to _____ within itself and among other systems.

7. Thomas Szasz states that mental illness is a _____ and every person is responsible for his/her own _____.

Match the concept or therapy with the most appropriate selection.

    A. covert modeling   D. sociocultural theory
    B. social learning theory   E. individual therapy
    C. behavior modification   F. general adaptation theory

_____ 8. Describes the physical responses of the body to stress and the processes by which they adapt.

_____ 9. People learn by observing the outcomes of various events and then comparing themselves to others.

_____ 10. Used by therapists to define positive behaviors and develop programs with specific reinforcements to change the specified behaviors.

_____ 11. A process described as the act of mentally rehearsing an activity before actually engaging in the activity.

_____ 12. The concept of self is developed through interactions with other people.

CHAPTER 7

Psychotherapeutic Drug Therapy

REVIEW WORKSHEET

1. Circle the correct *parasympathetic* nervous system action.
   a. The pupils of the eye dilate.
   b. Saliva, tears, and respiratory and gastrointestinal secretions decrease.
   c. The smooth muscles of the lungs constrict and restrict airways.
   d. The blood vessels in the heart and skeletal muscles dilate.

2. List the five nursing responsibilities (client care guidelines) for clients on psychotherapeutic drug therapy.

   a. _____

   b. _____

   c. _____

   d. _____

   e. _____

Match the following terms and their definitions.

   A. benzodiazepines   D. hypertensive crisis
   B. anticholinergic reaction   E. tricyclic drugs
   C. EPSEs

_____ 3. Treats depression.

_____ 4. Treats anxiety.

_____ 5. Dry mouth, blurred vision, sweating.

_____ 6. Akathisia, dyskinesia, akinesia.

_____ 7. Stiff neck, throbbing headache, tightness in the chest.

8. What do you suspect is happening to the client who complains of feeling jittery, is unable to sit still, and has problems with eye movements?

   _____

   _____

9. An informed decision made by a client *not* to follow the prescribed treatment program is called

   _____.

Circle the correct answer.

10. Why must salt intake be monitored in clients who are receiving lithium?
    a. Salt and water compete for lithium in the tissues.
    b. Salt and lithium compete for excretion in the kidney.
    c. Salt competes with lithium for detoxification in the liver.
    d. People who take lithium crave large amounts of salt.

CHAPTER 8

Principles of Mental Health Care

Student's Name

_____

Date

REVIEW WORKSHEET

Match the following terms and their definitions.

      A. principle   D. responsibility
      B. empathy   E. consistency
      C. advocacy

_____ **1.** Capability of making and fulfilling obligations.

_____ **2.** Reliability, stability.

_____ **3.** The providing of information to make a decision.

_____ **4.** Code that guides decisions and actions.

_____ **5.** Ability to see the world as another person does.

State which principle of mental health nursing care is being used in the following situations.

6. All clients will be at breakfast by 0800.

Principle:_____

7. Mr. J. is practicing anger control by counting to ten before he speaks out.

Principle:_____

8. Nurse Jane sits with a mute client for 15 minutes every morning.

Principle:_____

9. Nurse Dan is not intimidated by Mr. Jones' rough appearance and salty mannerisms.

Principle:_____

10. Miss Sally is expected to arrive for her appointment at 1300 every other day.

Principle:_____

11. Sam states he is being followed by the FBI, and the nurse responds with "Would you like to talk about it?"

Principle:_____

12. List five concepts (components) of the art of nursing.

    a. _____

    b. _____

    c. _____

    d. _____

    e. _____

CHAPTER 9

The Therapeutic Environment

REVIEW WORKSHEET

1. John S. is a 30-year-old man who has overdosed on methamphetamine. He states that he feels unable to control his behavior. Do you think he should be admitted to an inpatient environment? _____ Explain your answer. _____

2. List three purposes of the inpatient therapeutic environment.

   a. _____

   b. _____

   c. _____

Describe one nursing action (intervention) for each of the following client needs.

3. Nourishment _____

4. Personal hygiene _____

5. Sense of security _____

6. Territory _____

7. Communication _____

8. Social relationships _____

9. Acceptance _____

10. Time _____

Fill in the blanks.

11. One of the greatest roadblocks for people with mental/emotional problems is the _____ attached to mental illness.

12. Repeated admissions to psychiatric inpatient facilities have become a way of life for many people with chronic mental illness. This situation is known as _____.

13. Clients who do not follow their prescribed courses of treatment are called _____.

The Therapeutic Relationship

REVIEW WORKSHEET

Student's Name _____

Date _____

Match the following terms and their definitions.

A. trust   D. caring
B. empathy   E. hope
C. autonomy

_____ **1.** The ability to direct and control one's own activities.

_____ **2.** Confident but uncertain view of the future.

_____ **3.** Process in which one's situation depends on the future behavior of another person.

_____ **4.** Energy that allows nurses to accept and care for each client as a person.

_____ **5.** Ability to share in the client's world.

6. Four steps to develop caring are:

a. _____

b. _____

c. _____

d. _____

7. List four ways in which the nurse instills hope in clients.

a. _____

b. _____

c. _____

d. _____

Identify the phase of the therapeutic relationship.

8. _____ Reviews progress toward meeting goal and prepares client for independence.

9. _____ Gathers data and explores feelings about client.

10. _____ Establishes a working agreement (nurse-client contract) with client.

11. _____ Client and nurse work on meeting the mutually agreed-on goals.

CHAPTER 11

Therapeutic Communication

Student's Name

REVIEW WORKSHEET

Date

1. Complete the crossword puzzle.

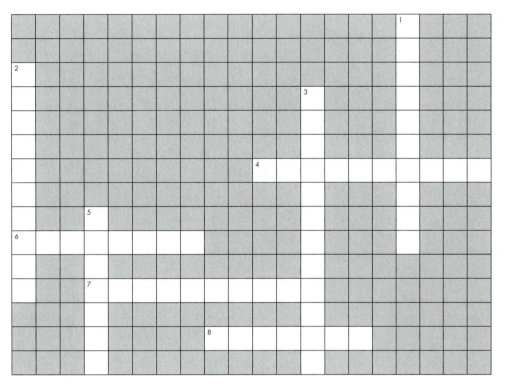

ACROSS
4. All persons have the right to live and have someone care for them
6. Desire to know both positive and negative sides of person
7. Ensures client's safety; anticipates problems and troubles
8. Consistent, open, and frank communications

DOWN
1. Nurse is present, available, and has tangible aid to offer
2. Communicates that it is acceptable to try new ways of thinking and behaving
3. Communications are clear, specific, and to the point
5. Belief in client's ability to solve problems and assume responsibility for his/her own life.

List the communication as therapeutic (T) or nontherapeutic (NT).

_____ **2.** "Would you like to talk about it?"

_____ **3.** "Everything will be alright."

_____ **4.** "I'm glad you decided to do that."

_____ **5.** "You appear tense."

_____ **6.** "Dr. Dee is a very good psychiatrist. You should learn to trust him."

_____ **7.** "How did this make you feel?"

_____ **8.** "I'm not sure I understand."

Fill in the blanks.

9. A speech pattern that is associated with mentally ill clients in which the client shifts rapidly between unre-lated ideas is called _____.

10. A nontherapeutic communication technique in which the nurse responds with cliches or trite expressions is called _____.

The Most Important Skill: Self-Awareness

REVIEW WORKSHEET

Match the following terms and their definitions.

A. caring
E. helping boundaries
B. insight
F. commitment
C. failure
G. nurturing
D. acceptance

_____ **1.** Can provide opportunities for learning.

_____ **2.** The recognition of and attendance to meeting needs.

_____ **3.** Concern for the well-being of another.

_____ **4.** A personal bond to a course of action.

_____ **5.** The ability to understand the nature of things.

_____ **6.** Helps to define the limits of the nurse's therapeutic behaviors.

_____ **7.** The receiving of what is being offered.

8. List three ways to grow from failure.

a. _____

b. _____

c. _____

Fill in the blanks.

9. Peoples' values and belief systems have a strong impact on their _____.

10. A nurse's ability to care for clients depends on how well the nurse _____.

11. Introspection is the process of _____.

12. Professional helping boundaries help nurses to define _____.

13. The nurse's most important commitment is to _____.

CHAPTER 13

Mental Health Assessment Skills

Student's Name _____

REVIEW WORKSHEET

Date _____

Fill in the blanks.

1. The purpose of the assessment step of the nursing process is _____.

2. The holistic nursing assessment focuses on five aspects or dimensions of a person. These dimensions are:

   a. _____

   b. _____

   c. _____

   d. _____

   e. _____

3. The purpose of the mental status examination is _____

   _____.

4. The purpose of a physical assessment (examination) for mental health clients is _____

   _____.

5. List ten areas assessed with the mental status examination.

   a. _____

   b. _____

   c. _____

   d. _____

   e. _____

   f. _____

   g. _____

   h. _____

   i. _____

   j. _____

CHAPTER 14

Problems of Childhood

Student's Name

REVIEW WORKSHEET

Date

Circle the correct answer.

1. Temper tantrums are a common behavior in:
   a. Infants
   b. 1- to 4-year-olds
   c. 5- to 9-year-olds
   d. Children over 10

2. The effects of poverty on children:
   a. Are small and unimportant
   b. Have little impact on their mental health
   c. Can have a strong impact on children's growth and development
   d. Are not considered when making a diagnosis

3. Mental health assistance should be sought for parent-child conflicts when the:
   a. Conflict worsens over a period of time
   b. Parents are tired of dealing with the conflict
   c. Child threatens to run away
   d. Child's behavior is out of control

4. One of the most frequent anxieties of children is a fear of:
   a. Strangers
   b. New people and places
   c. Separation from their parents
   d. Separation from a favorite object

5. Children with depression:
   a. Giggle continually
   b. Often stop talking and stare into space
   c. Strike out at other people
   d. Lose interest in school and friends

Fill in the blanks.

6. A _____ disorder is one in which a child has the signs and symptoms of an illness or disease without a traceable physical cause.

7. _____ usually develops after an extremely traumatic event involving injury or threat to a child.

8. _____ is fecal incontinence in a child 4 years or older with no physical abnormalities.

9. Autism is diagnosed when the child has serious problems with:

   a. _____

   b. _____

   c. _____

10. Three general nursing interventions for children with mental health problems are:

    a. _____

    b. _____

    c. _____

CHAPTER 15

Problems of Adolescence

Student's Name

_____

Date

REVIEW WORKSHEET

Fill in the blanks.

1. Intellectual changes (cognitive development) during adolescence involves learning to use _____

    _____.

2. The most important function of a teen's peer group is _____.

3. A _____ problem exists when an adolescent's difficulties impair performance (school, social, work) or threatens physical well-being.

4. The process of watching over adolescents to determine if they are safe, keeping their rules, making good decisions, or if they need adult intervention is called _____.

Match the following terms and their definitions.

A. behavioral disorder	F. sexual disorder
B. emotional disorder	G. psychotic disorder
C. eating disorder	H. suicidal problems
D. chemical dependency	I. limit setting
E. personality disorder	J. skill development

_____ 5. Becomes preoccupied with ridding self of own characteristics and assuming those of the desired sex.

_____ 6. Anorexia nervosa or bulimia.

_____ 7. Symptoms include fighting, temper tantrums, running away from home, destroying property, and problems with authorities and school.

_____ 8. Thoughts or actions to take one's own life.

_____ 9. Problem solving, social interactions, working cooperatively in a group.

_____ 10. Moods range from depression to hyperactivity, anxiety.

_____ 11. Understanding the rules and consequences of breaking the rules.

_____ 12. Moves from experimenting to burnout.

_____ 13. Characterized by a loss of contact with reality.

_____ 14. A major characteristic is impulsivity, the drive to engage in an act that is harmful to self or others.

CHAPTER 16

Problems of Adulthood

REVIEW WORKSHEET

Student's Name _____

Date _____

1. Describe how a young adult's sense of personal identity affects his/her functioning.

   _____

   _____

2. How would you respond to a 20-year-old who wanted a baby so she would have someone to love her?

   _____

   _____

3. Describe three characteristics of a mentally healthy adult.

   a. _____

   b. _____

   c. _____

Fill in the blanks.

4. When an individual's ability to _____ in effective ways is limited, behavioral and personality problems are much more common.

5. _____ are a frequent source of problems for families with children.

6. Young adults are more vulnerable to contracting HIV/AIDS because they lack the emotional maturity and

   judgment to _____ , and they think that _____.

7. The most important therapeutic tool in the treatment of HIV/AIDS is _____.

8. Beyond the diagnostic labels of mental illness lies _____.

9. Middle adults are faced with accepting their own _____.

10. Joe is a 23-year-old man with AIDS who has had sexual relationships with 12 women and two other men.

    How many women has Joe put at risk for contracting AIDS? _____ How many men? _____

CHAPTER 17

Problems of Late Adulthood

Student's Name

REVIEW WORKSHEET

_____

Date

Identify the following signs or symptoms.

1. Collecting and saving items such as old string, newspapers, medications, and toilet paper is called

    _____.

2. The inability to identify and name once familiar people and objects is called _____.

3. The loss of the ability to perform everyday actions and activities is called _____.

4. The loss of one's ability to use and understand a language is called _____.

5. The loss of the ability to make and carry out plans is called a _____ loss.

6. _____ is the inability to recall a certain detail or event.

7. _____ is a change of consciousness that occurs over a short period of time.

8. The loss of multiple abilities, including short- and long-term memory, language, and the ability to understand or conceptualize, is known as _____.

9. List three general nursing goals for the care of clients with Alzheimer's disease.

    a. _____

    b. _____

    c. _____

10. Explain the concept of respect and its importance to geriatric nursing.

    _____

    _____

    _____

CHAPTER 18

Illness and Hospitalization

REVIEW WORKSHEET

Student's Name _____

Date _____

Circle the correct answer.

1. The experience of being hospitalized is a:
   a. Developmental crisis
   b. Personal crisis
   c. Situational crisis
   d. Maturational crisis

2. An individual's state of health:
   a. Remains stable throughout life
   b. Is constantly changing
   c. Changes through childhood and then stabilizes as an adult
   d. Is in a state of disequilibrium

3. The stage of illness in which a person experiences symptoms is called the:
   a. First stage
   b. Second stage
   c. Third stage
   d. Fourth stage

4. Nurses must always remember that _____ is just as important as good physical care.
   a. Entertainment
   b. Nutritional care
   c. Financial arrangements
   d. Psychosocial care

5. The way a person responds to the stresses of illness or hospitalization is based on:
   a. How the person coped with previous crises
   b. How the person behaves when ill
   c. How the person treats his/her physicians and nurses
   d. His/her insurance coverage

Fill in the blanks.

6. A refusal to acknowledge painful facts is called _____.

7. A feeling of having been mistreated, opposed, or injured is known as _____.

8. An overwhelming emotional state in which the person is unable to process information within the environment is called _____.

9. List the three stages of the hospitalization experience.

   a. _____

   b. _____

   c. _____

10. List three ways in which nurses can support family members and significant others.

   a. _____

   b. _____

   c. _____

CHAPTER 19

Loss and Grief

REVIEW WORKSHEET

Fill in the blanks.

1. The type of losses relating to objects, possessions, the environment, loved ones, and support from others is called _____ losses.

2. Loss of _____ involves some part of an individual: the loss of physical, emotional, sociocultural, or spiritual aspects.

3. _____ is the set of emotional reactions that accompany a loss.

4. _____ is the process of working through or resolving one's grief.

5. _____ is the emotional and behavioral state of thoughts, feelings, and activities that follow a loss.

6. List two types of dysfunctional (unresolved) grief.

   a. _____

   b. _____

7. List the five stages of dying, as defined by Elizabeth Kübler-Ross.

   a. _____

   b. _____

   c. _____

   d. _____

   e. _____

Circle the correct answer.

8. Mary was widowed about 10 months ago. Although she seems to be adjusting well to the loss of her husband, lately she has been refusing invitations to social events. When she is visited by friends, she continually reminisces about her past. During her last visit, she told a friend that she was not really interested in her activities and would prefer to be left alone. Mary is suffering from:
   a. Denial
   b. Normal grief
   c. Complicated grief
   d. Complex grief

9. Nurses should share in the grief experience with the loved ones of a deceased person, but they should remember that their primary goal is:
   a. To work through their own grief
   b. To provide support for the grievers
   c. To provide care for the body
   d. To complete the documentation of the death

10. Mr. Clark is a 26-year-old man who was recently diagnosed with a fatal illness. During one of his visits to the clinic, he tells the nurse that he has decided to refuse further treatment for his condition. Will this decision change the nursing goals of care for this client?
    a. Yes
    b. No

CHAPTER 20

Anxiety Disorders

Student's Name

REVIEW WORKSHEET

_____

Date

Identify the level of anxiety (mild, moderate, severe, panic) for the following behaviors:

_____ 1. After the news of her father's accident, Maria feels "overloaded." She begins to wring her hands, pace, and wander around the room moaning.

_____ 2. Sam is awaiting the results of his examination. He appears to be calm and relaxed.

_____ 3. Rose has just learned that she is being evicted from her home. She reacts by sitting immobilized. When questioned, she is unable to think or speak logically.

_____ 4. Marian is preparing to free-climb a challenging mountain. She feels energized and concentrates on reaching her destination.

5. Describe maladaptive anxiety and list two examples.

   a. _____

   b. _____

6. List three behavioral addictions (compulsions).

   a. _____

   b. _____

   c. _____

7. Identify two useful purposes of anxiety.

   a. _____

   b. _____

Indicate if the following nursing interventions are therapeutic (TI) or nontherapeutic (NI).

_____ 8. Telling the client that everything will be alright as soon as his medication takes effect.

_____ 9. Teaching the client to problem solve.

_____ 10. Assessing every child for the presence of anxiety and stress.

CHAPTER 21

Depression and Other Mood Disorders

Student's Name

REVIEW WORKSHEET

Date

Identify the level of depression and circle the correct answer.

1. Linda is a 22-year-old woman who has recently developed feelings of sadness and loss following a breakup with her boyfriend. She has noticed no appetite or sleep changes.
   a. Mild depression
   b. Moderate depression
   c. Severe depression

2. Harold has become unable to concentrate or follow through with tasks. Lately, even his appearance has begun to suffer. Today, he spent the day staring at a blank television screen.
   a. Mild depression
   b. Moderate depression
   c. Severe depression

3. Rosie has to drag herself from chore to chore throughout the day. She feels helpless and ineffective when she has to care for her children and believes there is no escape from her unhappy situation.
   a. Mild depression
   b. Moderate depression
   c. Severe depression

Fill in the blanks.

4. Food that are high in _____ should not be eaten by clients taking MOAIs.

5. When lithium levels are above _____ mEq/L, toxicity should be suspected.

6. _____ is a term used to describe an exaggerated sense of uninhibited cheerfulness.

7. The main characteristic of _____ is sudden, dramatic shifts in moods.

8. The drug classes most frequently used to treat mood disorders are _____ and _____.

List one nursing intervention for the following complaints.

9. Feelings of wanting to commit suicide: _____

10. Excessive sweating after taking a tricyclic antidepressant: _____

11. Client began antidepressant drug therapy 5 days ago. Today she has suddenly developed confusion and delirium: _____

12. Rex has been taking lithium for about 3 months. Yesterday he urinated more than 4 quarts in less than 24 hours (list two interventions): _____

13. Conchita tells you that she cannot talk to other people because they will find out how stupid she really is: _____

CHAPTER 22

Physical Problems, Psychological Sources

Student's Name

REVIEW WORKSHEET

_____

Date

Match the following terms and their definitions.

    A. primary gain   E. malingering
    B. secondary gain   F. physiological stress response
    C. hypochondriasis   G. body dysmorphic disorder
    D. conversion disorder

_____ 1. Intense fear of having a disease.

_____ 2. They often present as seizure disorders in children under 10 years of age.

_____ 3. Relieves anxiety by masking inner emotional turmoil.

_____ 4. Produces symptoms in order to meet a recognizable goal.

_____ 5. Being relieved of responsibilities; having dependency needs met.

_____ 6. A preoccupation with a physical difference or defect in one's body.

_____ 7. The fight-flight response.

Fill in the blanks.

8. The purpose of the physiological stress response is _____.

9. When the body is under continual or repeated stress, it responds by activating _____, which can result in many of the physical signs and symptoms of an illness, disease, or disability.

10. The _____ theory states that individuals are biochemically patterned to react to stress in childhood.

11. In somatoform disorders, the development of physical symptoms is the result of attempts to _____
_____.

12. Because of the chronic nature of the disorder and the fact that they are "doctor shoppers," clients with _____ are difficult to treat.

13. List three nursing interventions for clients with somatoform disorders.

    a. _____

    b. _____

    c. _____

CHAPTER 23

Eating and Sleeping Disorders

Student's Name

REVIEW WORKSHEET

Date

Match the following terms and their definitions.

A. anorexia nervosa F. narcolepsy
B. bulimia G. parasomnia
C. obesity H. dyssomnia
D. insomnia I. polysomnogram
E. hypersomnia J. sleep apnea

_____ 1. An abnormality in the amount, quality, or timing of sleep.

_____ 2. A disorder of binge eating and the use of inappropriate methods to prevent weight gain.

_____ 3. A disorder of falling or staying asleep.

_____ 4. Monitors the body's electrophysical responses during sleep.

_____ 5. A condition in which an individual refuses to maintain a normal body weight because of an intense fear of becoming fat.

_____ 6. Repeated attacks of sleep.

_____ 7. Excessive sleepiness.

_____ 8. Excessive body weight.

_____ 9. Abnormal behavior or physical events that happen during sleep.

_____ 10. Sleep problems that are caused by abnormal ventilation during sleep.

11. List four nursing diagnoses for clients with eating disorders.

a. _____

b. _____

c. _____

d. _____

CHAPTER 24

Dissociative Disorders

REVIEW WORKSHEET

Student's Name

Date

1. Complete the crossword puzzle.

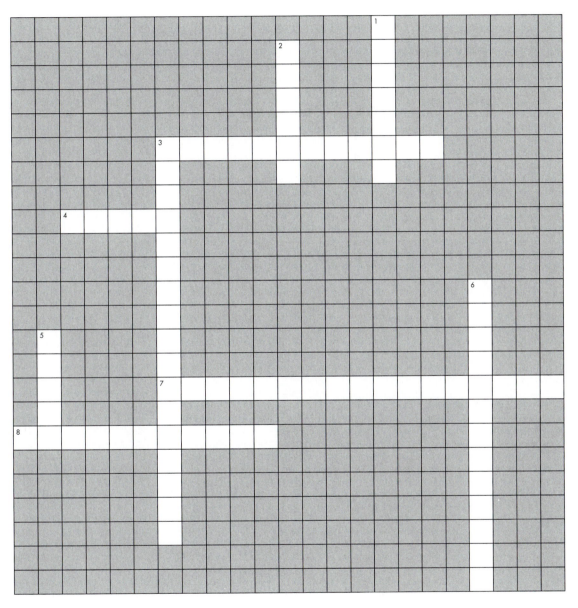

ACROSS
3. Disconnection from full awareness of self, time, and/or external circumstances
4. To escape or run away from reality
7. Failure to bring various childhood identifications into adult personality (two words)
8. Persons are able to struggle with life's problems while feeling good about living if this is healthy

DOWN
1. Loss of memory
2. A state resembling sleep in which consciousness remains but voluntary movement is lost
3. During an episode, one feels detached or unconnected to the self
5. One of the main causes of dissociative disorders
6. Often expressed through various levels of anxiety and involves feelings of being weak, inadequate, and helpless (more than one word)

2. List three nursing interventions for a client with maladaptive self-concept responses.

a. _____

b. _____

c. _____

3. Explain the term *identity diffusion.* _____

_____

4. State the primary treatment goal of care for clients with dissociative disorders.

_____

CHAPTER 25

Anger and Aggression

Student's Name _____

REVIEW WORKSHEET

Date _____

Fill in the blanks.

1. A behavior of force that results in injury, abuse, or harm to another is called _____.

2. Children and adolescents often _____ in an attempt to establish and test the limits of appropriate behavior.

3. _____ is the abuse of members of one sex by members of another.

4. Models of anger and aggression that focus on the interactions of individuals within their social environment and locate the source of violence in interpersonal frustrations are based in the _____ group of theories.

5. List five factors that contribute to the use of aggressive behaviors.

   a. _____

   b. _____

   c. _____

   d. _____

   e. _____

Identify the stage in the assault cycle that most closely matches the listed behaviors.

Stage of the Assault Cycle   Behaviors

_____   **6.** Cries, apologizes, tries to atone (make up) for behaviors.

_____   **7.** Becomes restless, irritable, argues, paces.

_____   **8.** Loses control, fights, kicks, bites, screams.

_____   **9.** Loses ability to reason; becomes flushed or pale.

Indicate if the following statements are true (T) or false (F).

_____ **10.** The most important nursing intervention is to rapidly assess a potentially violent client.

_____ **11.** The use of restraints or seclusion is the last level of intervention for an aggressive client.

_____ **12.** The most therapeutic and experienced nurses and care providers never experience feelings of anger or aggression.

CHAPTER 26

Violence

Student's Name _____

Date _____

Identify the terms that belong in the following blanks.

1. Harm that is caused through a failure to provide for basic needs or by placing an individual's health or welfare at unreasonable risk is called _____.

2. A term used to describe repeated physical abuse of someone, usually a woman, child, or elder, is _____.

3. _____ is the intentional misuse of someone or something that results in harm, injury, or trauma.

4. Information that is gathered for legal purposes and helps the law find and convict the perpetrator of a violent act or crime is called _____.

5. _____ is any behavior that threatens, harms, or injures a person or property.

6. _____ theories state that boys are socialized throughout their childhoods to behave more aggressively and violently than girls.

7. A major nursing care goal for victims of violence is _____.

8. The essential feature of _____ is the development of characteristic symptoms following exposure to extreme traumatic stressors.

9. Every nurse needs to be alert for the possibility of _____ whenever there is a history of unexplained lethargy, fussiness, or irritability with an infant.

10. The most frequent abusers of the elderly are _____.

Bonnie R., a 19-year-old mother of two, arrives in the emergency room with her 18-month-old son, Billy. She gives you a vague history of Billy being pushed off the bed by his older brother about 3 or 4 days ago. Since then, Billy has been irritable and fussy. He refuses to eat and cries "all the time." Whenever Billy tries to walk, his left leg crumples and he falls. Because of his constant fussing, Bonnie admits to having "smacked him" yesterday so he would "stop screaming."

11. Which piece of information in Billy's history provides you with a clue to the possibility of child abuse?

_____

12. What information should your physical assessment include?

_____

13. What is the first priority of care for Billy at this time?

_____

As you assist the physician in placing Billy in traction, you become angry at the thought of Billy having to endure so much unnecessary pain. By the time Billy is finally settled, you are absolutely furious with Billy's mother.

14. How do you cope with these emotions and still remain therapeutic with Billy and his mother? _____

_____

_____

_____

CHAPTER 27

Suicide

Student's Name

_____

Date

Identify the terms that best describe the behaviors characterized in the following statements.

1. Jerry smokes cigarettes, drives his motorcycle too fast, and likes to feel the thrill of being chased by the police:_____

_____

2. Heather repeatedly scratches herself until she bleeds because the pain "lets me know I'm still here": _____

_____

3. Sam states that he will attempt suicide again, but he has not acted so far: _____

4. Mary overdosed with sleeping medications because she "is tired of fighting": _____

5. Yesterday, John gave his cherished car to his best friend. Last night he died from a gunshot wound to the head: _____

Indicate if the following statements are true (T) or false (F).

_____ 6. Suicidal thoughts or intentions can exist in clients with any medical or mental health disorder.

_____ 7. Suicide rates are lower in people who use drugs or alcohol.

_____ 8. All suicidal persons are depressed.

_____ 9. People who talk about suicide will not attempt to do it.

_____ 10. It is harmful to discuss suicide with clients.

Fill in the blanks.

11. The first priority for clients who may be suicidal is _____.

12. Standard nursing interventions that help to prevent a suicidal act from occurring are called _____

_____.

13. Many studies reveal that _____ commit suicide more often than other age groups.

14. A verbal agreement between the client and his/her nurse to refrain from doing anything to injure himself/herself is called a _____.

CHAPTER 28

Substance-Related Disorders

REVIEW WORKSHEET

Fill in the blanks.

1. Physical dependence on a drug that is taken despite the problems associated with its use is called

   _____.

2. _____ occurs when an individual who was previously drug free has returned to substance-abusing behaviors.

3. When a person is not using an addictive substance, he/she is practicing _____.

4. _____ occurs when increasingly larger amounts of a substance are required to produce the desired effect.

5. The incidence of _____ rises when women drink alcohol during pregnancy.

6. Older adults frequently abuse _____.

Identify the type of substance abuse and circle the correct answer.

7. Jerry has "chugged" large amounts of the substance and now is beginning to show signs of respiratory failure.
   a. Antibiotics
   b. Amphetamines
   c. Alcohol
   d. Inhalants

8. The physical assessment of Maria reveals constricted pupils, euphoria, and drowsiness.
   a. PCP
   b. Heroin
   c. Cocaine
   d. Marijuana

9. After injecting or inhaling it, Jamie experiences intense feelings of well-being that last for less than an hour.
   a. Alcohol
   b. Acid
   c. Caffeine
   d. Cocaine

10. Stan had a flashback 2 weeks after taking:
    a. Alcohol
    b. Acid
    c. Caffeine
    d. Cocaine

11. Amber is unable to sit still, her pulse rate is over 120, and she is constantly talking and fidgeting.
    a. Alcohol
    b. Acid
    c. Amphetamines
    d. Alfalfa

12. List four ways that nurses act as therapeutic agents when caring for individuals with substance abuse problems.
    a. _____
    b. _____
    c. _____
    d. _____

CHAPTER 29

Sexual Disorders

Student's Name

Date

REVIEW WORKSHEET

Identify the terms that most closely describe the behaviors characterized in the following statements.

1. Prefers sexual relationships with persons of the opposite sex: _____

2. The practice of seeking sexual excitement from wearing the clothing of the opposite sex: _____

3. An inconsistency between the child's biological sex and his/her identity as a boy or girl: _____

4. A sexual behavior that departs from society's acceptable modes of seeking sexual gratification: _____

5. The process of establishing an integrated or complete identity as a homosexual: _____

6. List four types of homosexual relationships.

   a. _____

   b. _____

   c. _____

   d. _____

7. List three theories that attempt to explain why an individual prefers a certain mode of sexual expression.

   a. _____

   b. _____

   c. _____

8. To effectively care for clients with sexual problems, nurses must first examine their own _____

   and _____.

CHAPTER 30

Personality Disorders

REVIEW WORKSHEET

Student's Name

_____

Date

Match the following terms and their definitions.

A. personality	E. paranoia
B. temperament	F. psychopath
C. dual diagnosis	G. impulsivity
D. manipulation	H. deceit

_____ **1.** A suspicious system of thinking with delusions of persecution and grandeur.

_____ **2.** Controlling others for one's own purposes by influencing them in unfair or false ways.

_____ **3.** Traits and attitudes that identify one as an individual.

_____ **4.** The act of representing as true something that is actually known to be false.

_____ **5.** The biological basis that underlies moods, energy levels, and attitudes.

_____ **6.** Acting without forethought or regard to the consequences.

_____ **7.** Suffering from two or more illnesses or conditions.

_____ **8.** A pattern of disregard for and violation of the rights of others.

9. List three main characteristics of a personality disorder.

a. _____

b. _____

c. _____

10. Why do clients with maladaptive social responses not always benefit from psychotherapy?

_____

_____

11. Identify three classes of medications used to treat clients who have been diagnosed with an antisocial personality disorder.

a. _____

b. _____

c. _____

CHAPTER 31

Schizophrenia and Other Psychoses

Student's Name _____

REVIEW WORKSHEET

Date _____

Identify the terms that most closely describe the behaviors characterized in the following statements.

1. Disorders marked by a loss of contact with reality: _____

2. Lack of energy or motivation: _____

3. Abnormal involuntary movement disorders caused by a drug-induced imbalance between two major neurotransmitters in the brain: _____

4. False sensory inputs with no external stimulus: _____

5. The idea that people or the media are talking about oneself: _____

6. Inability to recognize familiar environmental objects or people: _____

7. False perceptions of real objects or persons: _____

8. Inability to tell where one's body ends and the environment begins: _____

9. Lack of ability to produce new thoughts or follow a train of thought: _____

10. Fixed false ideas or beliefs that are not based in reality: _____

11. Lisa is sitting in the corner with her hand covering her mouth. She is whispering, giggling, and appears to be deeply involved in a conversation, but no one is around. This misperception is called _____ .

12. Jeremy tells you that Jesus is talking to him because he is the only one left who can save the world. This misperception is called _____ .

13. The major responsibilities when caring for clients who are receiving antipsychotic drug therapy are _____ .

CHAPTER 32

Chronic Mental Health Disorders

REVIEW WORKSHEET

Student's Name

_____

Date

Fill in the blanks.

1. Most chronic mental health problems are characterized by periods of _____ and _____.

2. Psychiatric diagnoses serve only to _____ or _____ certain behaviors because each person's experiences with mental illness is unique.

3. Persons with chronic mental illness often have difficulty assuming the behaviors and activities that are required for _____ because of impaired judgment, lack of motivation, or altered realities.

4. Individuals with _____ are suffering from two psychiatric disorders, one of which is usually substance related.

5. List four psychological characteristics of chronic mental illness.

    a. _____

    b. _____

    c. _____

    d. _____

Indicate if the following statements are true (T) or false (F).

_____ 6. People with chronic mental illness are unable to care for themselves.

_____ 7. The sexual practices of chronically mentally troubled persons place them at an increased risk for contracting and transmitting HIV/AIDS.

_____ 8. Psychiatric rehabilitation programs teach severely mentally ill clients about the skills needed to effectively perform the activities of daily living, including proper nutrition, activity, and rest habits.

_____ 9. It is inappropriate to ask a client to describe his/her hallucinations.

_____ 10. Mental health nursing is a critical component of every situation no matter what the diagnosis.

CHAPTER 33

Challenges for the Future

REVIEW WORKSHEET

1. List three outpatient treatment settings for clients with mental health problems.

    a. _____

    b. _____

    c. _____

Fill in the blanks.

2. Children who are _____ experience serious threats to their current and future well-being.

3. The "old homeless" tended to be adult, unmarried _____ with an average age of _____ years old.

4. People with _____ make up about one third of the homeless population.

5. The _____ is a federal law that removes the employment barriers for people with mental or physical disabilities.

6. Mental problems that are limited to a specific cultural group of people are called _____.

Indicate if the following statements are true (T) or false (F).

_____ 7. Nurses can choose to be self-employed and establish their own practices.

_____ 8. Supportive HCAs plan nursing cares for the clients in their caseload.

_____ 9. A basic concept of psychosocial rehabilitation is self-help.

_____ 10. Under certain circumstances, changes can be bad for people or organizations.

_____ 11. Many people with HIV will demonstrate mental signs/symptoms before physical signs/symptoms.

_____ 12. Change involves loss and discomfort.

_____ 13. The first step in coping with unplanned change is to reset priorities.

Mosby
Dedicated to Publishing

A Times Mirror Company

ISBN 0-8151-6964-7

9 780815 169642

90000

27246